Covenant and the Metaphor of Divine Marriage in Biblical Thought

Covenant and the Metaphor of Divine Marriage in Biblical Thought

A Study with Special Reference to the Book of Revelation

SEBASTIAN R. SMOLARZ

WIPF & STOCK · Eugene, Oregon

COVENANT AND THE METAPHOR OF DIVINE MARRIAGE
IN BIBLICAL THOUGHT
A Study with Special Reference to the Book of Revelation

Copyright © 2011 Sebastian R. Smolarz. All rights reserved. Except for brief quotations in critical publications or reviews, no part of this book may be reproduced in any manner without prior written permission from the publisher. Write: Permissions, Wipf and Stock Publishers, 199 W. 8th Ave., Suite 3, Eugene, OR 97401.

Wipf & Stock
An Imprint of Wipf and Stock Publishers
199 W. 8th Ave., Suite 3
Eugene, OR 97401

www.wipfandstock.com

ISBN 13: 978-1-60899-455-7

Manufactured in the U.S.A.

Contents

Preface / vii

List of Abbreviations / ix

1. The Old Testament as the Basis of the Book of Revelation / 1
   Introduction / 1
   Background of New Testament Ideas: New Testament Use of the Old / 2
   The Apocalypse and the Semitic Mind / 14
   The Apocalypse and the New Testament / 32
   Conclusions / 39

2. The Divine Marriage and the Institution of Marriage in Semitic Culture of the Ancient Near East / 40
   Introduction / 40
   Divine Marriage in Ancient Near Eastern Texts / 41
   The Institution of Marriage in the Ancient Near East and Related Issues / 44
   The Institution of Marriage in the OT and Issues Related to It / 51
   Conclusions / 59

3. The Divine Marriage Metaphor in the Old Testament Prophets / 61
   Introduction / 61
   The Divine Marriage in Hosea / 61
   The Divine Marriage Metaphor in the pre-Exilic and Exilic Prophets / 90
   Conclusions / 103

4. The Metaphor of Divine Marriage in Jewish non-Canonical Literature / 106
   Introduction / 106

  The Marriage Metaphor in Jewish non-Canonical Writings / 106
  Topics Closely Related to the Marriage Metaphor in Jewish Literature / 113
  Conclusions / 121

5 The Metaphor of Divine Marriage in the Gospels / 123
  Introduction / 123
  Towards Interpreting Jesus' Parables / 124
  The Synoptic Marriage Parables / 143
  John the Baptist's Testimony to Jesus in the Fourth Gospel / 174
  The Shift in the Divine Marriage Metaphor / 181
  Conclusions / 185

6 The Metaphor of Divine Marriage in the Epistles of Paul / 188
  Introduction / 188
  The Scope of Present Chapter / 188
  2 Corinthians 11:1–6 / 190
  Galatians 4:21—5:1 / 197
  Romans 7:1–6 / 208
  Romans 9:25–29 / 214
  Ephesians 5:21–33 / 219
  Conclusions / 226

7 The Metaphor of Divine Marriage in the Book of Revelation / 228
  Introduction / 228
  Notes Concerning Our Approach / 229
  Explicit Instances of the Use of Divine Marriage Metaphor in Revelation / 250
  Likely Instances of the Use of Divine Marriage Metaphor in Revelation / 271
  Echoes of Divine Marriage Metaphor in Revelation / 308
  Conclusions / 363

Conclusions: Covenant and the Metaphor of Divine Marriage in Biblical Thought / 366

Bibliography / 375

Preface

This book is an adaptation of my PhD dissertation submitted to University of Wales, Lampeter, U.K., in 2005.

The volume examines one of the central metaphors in the OT. It discusses the origins of the divine marriage metaphor in prophetic reflections on the Sinaitic covenant traditions and traces the biblical development of the metaphor. Consideration is given to the shift within the metaphor, from the marriage of Yahweh and Israel in the OT, to that of Christ and his church in the NT. Jesus, viewed as Yahweh's agent, is seen to fulfill the expectations of second temple Judaism regarding the restoration of divine marriage. This happens according to the general framework of the exodus motif, which provides a methodology for approaching the Hebrew Scriptures by NT authors.

The book proposes that the Gospels and some letters in the Pauline corpus consistently focus on the realized aspect of divine marriage restoration. The metaphor in those writings is often associated with other OT motifs, like those of "eschatological feast" and "remnant," and is thus concerned with eschatological salvation. It provides a basis for redefining Israel in the NT.

The metaphor of divine marriage seems to be central in Revelation. Its proper covenantal understanding is indispensable to explaining John's apocalyptic symbolism. The metaphor can inform the thrust of many passages in the Apocalypse and help to explain the historical setting of Revelation in the first century CE. It sheds light on the book's main conflict (caused by unfaithful Jews) and ultimately reveals judgment on this spiritual promiscuity. However, it also points to the joy of messianic salvation established thereafter. The metaphor also informs the ultimate hope of new creation (Rev 21–22).

The book in general attempts to encourage readers of the Christian Bible to consider more carefully the metaphor of divine marriage while discussing biblical covenant, ecclesiology, and eschatology.

• • •

I received enormous help from scholars, many friends and people, while I was doing my research in Wales. It would be impossible to list them all here. I am particularly indebted to Dr. Thomas S. Holland (Wales Evangelical School of Theology) and Prof. D. P. Davies (University of Wales, Lampeter) for providing valuable directions for this work. Special thanks should go to Blythswood Care and John Laski Trust Fund for their financial support of the project. I am also grateful to those who proof-read my dissertation and encouraged pursuing this study: especially Dr. Philip S. Ross, Rev. Alex Collins, Oli and Nicola Roth, and Alastair Roberts.

• • •

I would particularly like to express my gratitude to Dr. Thomas S. Holland, Dr. Kenneth L. Gentry Jr., and Rev. Marek Kmiec for prompting me to have this work published.

Abbreviations

ANE	Ancient Near East
AUSS	*Andrews University Seminary Studies*
BHS	Biblia hebraica stuttgartensia
Bib	*Biblica*
BTB	*Biblical Theology Bulletin*
CBQ	*Catholic Biblical Quarterly*
EvQ	*Evangelical Quarterly*
ExpTim	*Expository Times*
HeyJ	*Heythrop Journal*
HTR	*Harvard Theological Review*
IBS	*Irish Biblical Studies*
JB	Jerusalem Bible
JBL	*Journal of Biblical Literature*
JETS	*Journal of the Evangelical Theological Society*
JNES	*Journal of Near Eastern Studies*
JNSL	*Journal of Northwest Semitic Languages*
JSJ	*Journal for the Study of Judaism in the Persian, Hellenistic and Roman Period*
JSNT	*Journal for the Study of the New Testament*
JSOT	*Journal for the Study of the Old Testament*
JTS	*Journal of Theological Studies*
JVG	Jesus and the Victory of God. N. T. Wright. London: SPCK, 1996.
KUL	Katolicki Uniwersytet Lubelski
LXX	Septuagint Version of the Hebrew Bible
MT	Masoretic Text
NAB	The New American Bible
NASB	New American Standard Bible
NEB	New English Bible
NIV	New International Version

NJB	New Jerusalem Bible
NKJV	New King James Version
NRSV	New Revised Standard Version
N.S.	New Series
NovT	*Novum Testamentum*
NTPG	The New Testament and the People of God. N. T. Wright. London: SPCK, 1997.
NTS	*New Testament Studies*
RB	*Revue biblique*
RBL	*Review of Biblical Literature*
RSG	The Resurrection of the Son of God. N. T. Wright. London: SPCK, 2003.
SBL	Society of Biblical Literature
SJT	*Scottish Journal of Theology*
SNTS	Society for New Testament Studies
Sup	Supplement/Supplement Series
TDNT	Theological Dictionary of the New Testament
TrinJ	*Trinity Journal*
TynBul	*Tyndale Bulletin*
VT	*Vetus Testamentum*
WTJ	*Westminster Theological Journal*
ZAW	*Zeitschrift für die alttestamentliche Wissenschaft*
ZNW	*Zeitschrift für die neutestamentliche Wissenschaft*

1

The Old Testament as the Basis of the Book of Revelation

INTRODUCTION

THE MAIN CONCERN OF this volume is the theme/metaphor of the divine marriage as found in the book of Revelation. In the last three decades there have been several publications dealing with particular themes in Revelation, among which we find, for example, works on the "abomination of desolation," divine warrior, "holy war," or earthquake concept.[1] In recent times, R. Zimmermann has published an article[2] in which he argues that the nuptial imagery in John's Apocalypse[3] is more wide-ranging than was usually acknowledged. However, his publication is quite limited in scope and lacks an in-depth study of the symbolism. It also lacks methodological clarity. Thus the present study is, first of all, an attempt to contribute to the understanding of the theme of divine marriage in the context of John's vision.

The aforementioned studies of particular Johannine themes in Revelation have shown that such themes are in continuity with OT ideas and further develop them.[4] In this chapter we want to propose our approach to the Book of Revelation by arguing for a continuity between

---

1. These are, Ford, *Abomination of Desolation*, esp. 243–314; Longman and Reid, *God Is a Warrior*, esp. 180–92; Bauckham, *Climax of Prophecy*, esp. 210–37; Bauckham, "Earthquake," 224–33.

2. Zimmermann, "Nuptial Imagery," 153–83. He attempted to show that nuptial imagery is present in the seven letters section and the central scene of the 144,000 in Rev 14:4–5.

3. For discussion on authorship see Beale, *Revelation*, 34–36; Beasley-Murray, *Revelation*, 32–36; Hendriksen, *More Than Conquerors*, 10–14; Ford, *Revelation*, 28–37.

4. Cf. Beale, *Revelation*, 88–89.

OT and NT concepts and theologies in general, and a continuity between the Apocalypse and OT material in particular. To achieve this goal we will demonstrate NT theology's dependence upon the OT. Then we will propose that the Apocalypse shares with other NT writings a similar view on the symbolic world of first-century Judaism.

BACKGROUND OF NEW TESTAMENT IDEAS: NEW TESTAMENT USE OF THE OLD

The first century church viewed the OT as Scripture. Rudolf Bultmann noted concerning the early communities' approach to OT writings,

> Yet almost everywhere the Old Testament asserts itself, being accepted as a canonical scripture by all except extreme gnosticizing circles.[5]

Though he questions whether there was a closed collection of Scriptures at the time of the first century CE, Kümmel states that OT writings of all three parts of the later canon were authoritative as Holy Scripture to Jesus and his followers in the early church.[6] A similar statement is made by Lindars who says that, "[The Scriptures, i.e., the OT] have an authority which is unquestioned," for the apostle Paul.[7] Lindars adds,

> Study of the New Testament shows that almost all the books of the Hebrew canon were quarried for supporting texts.... Thus, though the limits are undefined, and a certain degree of fluidity must be presupposed concerning the status of some writings, it would be quite wrong to suggest that the canon shared by primitive Christianity with the contemporary Judaism was anything less than the complete Old Testament.[8]

The Nature of the Problem

INTRODUCTION

A problem, however, arises when scholars try to establish a methodology to account for the use of OT data in the New Testament. When they study the NT use of the Old, their conclusion is often that the herme-

---

5. *Primitive Christianity*, 177.
6. *New Testament*, 476–77.
7. "Place of the Old Testament," 138.
8. Ibid., 138. Cf. Beckwith, *Old Testament Canon*, 235–337.

neutics of the New Testament writers are totally unacceptable in terms of modern exegetical methods. "Those authors used the Old Testament in a haphazard way," is a frequent claim of NT scholars. Some, for example Longenecker, approaching the issue optimistically analyze Jewish hermeneutics of the first century to show that this was the pattern the NT authors followed. This supposedly justifies the apparent unintelligibility of NT methodology.[9] On the other hand, Richard Hays rejects Longenecker's conclusions and claims that Paul's hermeneutic is based on "intuitive readings," and therefore is "unpredictable, ungeneralizable."[10] Despite their disagreements, both accept the OT as a foundation of NT theology. Others, e.g., Grech and Lindars,[11] seeing a lack of logic behind the use of OT quotations in the New, argue against these conclusions.

Still others take another approach to the subject. They suggest that while NT theology was in its formative stage it was under the influence of and started to incorporate the religious ideas of Hellenism. So Bultmann, while recognizing that the NT uses texts from the Old, denies any relevance of "the original meaning and context of the Old Testament sayings" for the NT church.[12] He looks for the background of NT teachings in the Hellenistic culture, which at a very early stage influenced and molded Christian thought.[13]

ABUSE OF THE LITERAL MEANING?

Puzzled by the use of the OT in the New, Morna Hooker describes the dilemma when she says,

> A study of their methods of exegesis must surely make any twentieth-century preacher uncomfortable, for they tear passages out of context, use allegory or typology to give old stories new meanings, contradict the plain meaning of the text, find references to Christ in passages where the original authors certainly never intended any, and adapt or even alter the wording in order to make it yield the meaning they require. Often one is left exclaiming: whatever the passage from the Old Testament originally meant, it certainly was not this![14]

9. His *Biblical Exegesis*.
10. *Echoes of Scripture*, 160.
11. See the following sections.
12. Bultmann, *Primitive Christianity*, 187.
13. Ibid., 175.

14. Hooker, "Paul's Use of Scripture," 279. The problem is also recognized by Longenecker, "New Testament's Use of the Old," 4–8.

Yet however unacceptable their methods are for the modern theologian, they were consistent with the exegetical principles of contemporary Judaism.[15] As Fitzmyer says, "The Jewish roots of the New Testament have always made it *a priori* likely that its use of the Old Testament would resemble that of contemporary Judaism to some extent."[16] Consequently, studies of NT methodology focused on comparing the use of the OT by NT authors to the use of the Scriptures by contemporary Jews, as illustrated in Jewish liturgical forms, the rabbinical writings, the Talmuds, Qumran sect materials, apocalyptic literature and Philo of Alexandria.[17] The study showed that the NT writers were using a hermeneutic characteristic of the Rabbis and Qumran, who often dealt with OT passages in non-literalistic ways so that the meaning they sought, as it appeared, was to be found in the original texts, even though the OT authors never intended it.[18] It was particularly the so-called *midrash pesher* method which allowed them to read out of the OT things that went beyond the intentions of the authors.[19]

Although such an approach to the methodology of the early church partially alleviates the problem of the NT's use of the Old, it still fails to give a satisfactory explanation of why the NT authors drew meanings out of certain OT passages that seem quite foreign to those passages in their immediate and original contexts, and even to OT theology in general. The question is whether the early church was so interested in finding evidence for its beliefs that it could even violate the original meaning of its own Holy Writ. Recognizing the problem many scholars have started to argue that there is no relationship between the theologies of the two Testaments.

15. Hooker, "Paul's Use of Scripture," 279–80. Also Longenecker, "Exegesis of the New Testament," 3–38.

16. Fitzmyer, "Old Testament Quotations," 297. The same assumption characterizes Longenecker, "Exegesis of the New Testament," 16.

17. Longenecker, *Biblical Exegesis*, 6–35. Lindars, "Place of the Old Testament," 139–40. Comparison of the Qumranic and NT methods can be found in Fitzmyer, "Old Testament Quotations," 297–333.

18. Hooker, "Paul's Use of Scripture," 280, observes that "the present tendency in hermeneutics is to emphasize that "meaning" can never be limited to the intentions of an author."

19. The *Midrash-pesher* method interprets OT texts not in their literal sense but from a previously hidden eschatological perspective. The texts are being explained from the perspective of a new setting, new revelation, so that God's word is made relevant to present circumstances. The method, thus, employs both exegesis and eisegesis.

Opinions of Despair—Prosper Grech states that "the NT writers were not interested in the objective, scientific interpretation of scripture."[20] He means by this that they were not interested in the original meaning of the OT texts. For an author of the NT it is not important what the Scriptures said in the past. That which really matters is what they say now in the light of Jesus' resurrection.[21] Grech explains NT methodology in the words,

> ...the NT authors make no attempt to give an objective, detached explanation of the text [of the OT] in question.... In spite of the difference of interpretation between their explanation and the original text they are convinced that the original author would not have objected to their interpretation.[22]

Likewise, Fitzmyer says that the NT use of the Old does not pay much attention to the original meaning of the text but, rather, reads it somehow anew in the light of Christology as formed in primitive Christianity.[23]

Lindars's claim is that the OT citations found in the New were selected and adapted as proof-texts for the Christ-event.[24] They served for resurrection-apologetic purposes in the early church.[25] The "proof-texts," however, were not obtained by means of deliberate studies of Scriptures and therefore their employment does not manifest any coherent logic.[26] In early Christian thought "there is no sign of a direct interest in the Old Testament for its own sake, as at Qumran. The New Testament writers do not take an Old Testament book or passage, and sit down and ask, 'What does this mean?'"[27] They, rather, "employ the Old Testament in an ad hoc way, making recourse to it just when and how they find it helpful

---

20. "Testimonia," 319.
21. Ibid.
22. Ibid., 321.
23. Fitzmyer, "Old Testament Quotations," 331–33.
24. "Place of the Old Testament," 140–41.
25. See Lindars, *New Testament Apologetic*. Professor Lindars argues in his book that the apologetic activity of the early church is the factor which lies behind NT use of OT texts. However, his assumption cannot be defended in the light of evidence for other purposes of the use of the OT in the New. For example, France, *Jesus and the Old Testament*, 223–24, shows that Jesus used the OT to explain his mission.
26. Lindars, "Place of the Old Testament," 141–42.
27. Ibid., 143.

for their purposes."[28] So, according to Lindars, there is no evidence that the OT played any controlling role in the formation of NT theology.[29] In fact the NT, in the light of Christ's revelation, represents the change of the basis of God's religion, from law to grace.

Similar statements concerning this illogical use of the OT by NT writers are made by Klijn[30] and Hooker.[31] According to the latter, the apostle Paul's use of Scripture is accidental and is intended to support his Christian experience. Thus the problem of the NT's dependence on the Old in the formation of its theology remains unsolved for these theologians.

Opinions of Hope—Although rejected by some (e.g., Lindars, Hooker), C. H. Dodd's thesis argues for a different, positive approach to the problem, and proposes a possible solution. Dodd was interested in the process by which theology developed in the early church or, to put it another way, he was interested in the way *kerygma* (the primitive preaching of Christianity about the kingdom of God) developed into theology. He made the point that the development of early church methodology took place "according to the Scriptures."

By examining both explicit and more obscure quotations of OT passages in the NT, he concluded that these passages were not merely isolated proof-texts used without regard for the original meaning by NT writers.[32] Dodd argued that the OT was not a mere apologetic testimony book.[33] He observed that different NT authors used the same stock of textual materials taken from various specific areas of the OT (especially from Isaiah, Jeremiah and the minor prophets, and from the Psalms). Dodd suggested that the materials were gathered into *testimonies*, i.e., collections of Scripture quotations by the early church on different subjects, which served as pointers to the whole context of OT sections which were cited in the NT. He also remarked that other parts of the OT could be attached to those *testimonies* in order to illustrate or elucidate the main concern of the argument. He argued that "the relevant

---

28. Ibid.
29. Cf. ibid., 145.
30. Klijn, "Jewish Christianity," 431.
31. "Paul's Use of Scripture," 290.
32. Dodd, *According to the Scriptures*, 126.
33. Pace Lindars, *New Testament Apologetic*.

scriptures were understood and interpreted upon intelligible and consistent principles, as setting forth 'the determinate counsel of God' which was fulfilled in the gospel facts, and consequently as fixing the meaning of those facts."[34] Thus there was logic behind the influence of the OT on the formation of NT theology. OT contexts were influential in the selection of OT texts for constructing NT theology and the starting point for Paul, the author of the Hebrews, and the Fourth Evangelist. Moreover, Dodd assumes that this hermeneutical phenomenon (the existence of common OT passages that formed the basis of the theology of the NT writers) originated with Christ himself. Dodd says,

> ...it was Jesus Christ Himself who first directed the minds of His followers to certain parts of the scriptures [which later became *testimonies*] as those in which they might find illumination upon the meaning of His mission and destiny.[35]

We have seen earlier that there are some who disagree with Dodd's proposal. Nevertheless, others support his assessment of the NT's consistent respect for the OT context. One such is I. Howard Marshall,[36] who defends Dodd's thesis against its critics claiming that "the hypothesis that the early church turned to specific fields in the OT and used them can still be used as a starting point for investigation."[37]

He also denies that the early church used OT quotations in an unintelligible way,

> ...all that was needed was a recognition that the passage [used by the NT authors] was christological, so that the use of a text from within it was not arbitrary.[38]

Beale[39] also supports and further develops Dodd's thesis. First, he shows that the supposed use of non-contextual methods among rabbis before 70 CE is a proposal that lacks proof and that we are therefore unwarranted to assume that early church authors were influenced by atomistic Jewish hermeneutics.[40] Even if there are cases of non-contextual

---

34. Dodd, *According to the Scriptures*, 126–27.
35. Ibid., 110.
36. "Assessment of Recent Developments," 2–8.
37. Ibid., 7.
38. Ibid., 8.
39. Beale, "Right Doctrine from the Wrong Texts?" 89–96.
40. Ibid., 89.

use of the OT in the New, they are not representative of the overall NT hermeneutical pattern - "they may be exceptional rather than typical."[41] Moreover, these examples can in fact be contextual once a methodology of the use of the OT in the New is established. Then he moves to examining the *a priori* argument that the exegetical methods of the NT resemble those of contemporary Judaism, concluding that they did not have to be identical in every way.[42]

Beale, though accepting Dodd's thesis, does, however, reproach him for failing to show why NT methodology differs from the non-contextual method (assuming it to be so) of Jewish exegesis. His answer is that "Jesus and the apostles had unparalleled redemptive-historical perspective on the OT in relation to their own situation."[43] To this he adds,

> I would argue that this broad redemptive-historical perspective was the dominant framework within which Jesus and the NT writers thought, serving as an ever-present heuristic guide to the OT. In fact, it is this framework which should be seen as the wider literary context within which the NT authors interpreted OT passages. Consideration of the immediate literary context of OT verses, which is what most exegetes affirm as an essential part of the historical-grammatical method, should therefore be supplemented with the canonical literary context.[44]

Beale sees that the problem of many who claim non-contextual use of the OT by the New arises because "the NT applies the OT to new situations, problems and people which were not in the minds of the OT authors."[45] But changes of application do not necessarily imply a disregard for the original OT context. He explains that the

> NT Scripture interprets the OT Scripture by expanding its meaning, seeing new implications in it and giving it new applications. ... This expansion does not contravene the integrity of the earlier texts but rather develops them in a way which is consistent with the OT author's understanding of the way in which God inter-

---

41. Ibid., 90.
42. Ibid.
43. Ibid.
44. Ibid., 91.
45. Ibid.

The Old Testament as the Basis of the Book of Revelation

acts with his people—which is the unifying factor between the Testaments.[46]

Only in the light of the history of redemption can we speak of canon interpreting canon or justify the new meanings of the OT passages cited by the NT. They are, however, not new in the sense that they were illegitimately imposed upon the Jewish Scriptures. LaSor explains this in speaking of *sensus plenior* (full meaning of Scripture of which a particular writer of the OT was unconscious),

> . . . the fullness of meaning can be discovered by attempting to relate [a] situation and [a] prophecy to the on-going redemptive purpose of God. This fuller meaning is the *sensus plenior* of [a] passage. In one sense, it lies outside and beyond the historical situation of the prophet, and therefore it cannot be derived by grammatico-historical exegesis. But in another sense, it is part of the history of redemption, and therefore it can be controlled by the study of Scripture taken in its entirety.[47]

LaSor compares the *sensus plenior* to a seed which contains within itself the future shape of a plant which will develop out of it. Nevertheless, it is impossible to determine what the seed actually contains until it becomes a fully developed plant.[48]

Hays, however, following Hollander's earlier work, presents to us a somewhat different explanation of the new meanings of OT passages in the NT from that of LaSor. Hays says,

> We will have great difficulty understanding Paul, the pious first-century Jew, unless we seek to situate his discourse appropriately within what Hollander calls the "cave of resonant signification" that enveloped him: Scripture.[49]

This "cave of resonant signification" enables one to listen to a text in its context against the background of a new setting. The cave creates a new figuration because it distorts the original voice in order to interpret it. Thus the old voices are heard in new settings. The NT writers used OT contexts as such caves. Although their writings echo OT passages they

---

46. Ibid.
47. LaSor, "Sensus Plenior," 55–56.
48. Ibid., 56.
49. Hays, *Echoes of Scripture*, 21. Hays often refers to Hollander, J. *The Figure of Echo: A Mode of Allusion in Milton and After*. Berkeley: University of California Press 1981.

also encompass aspects which go beyond the OT context because they are amplifying the significance of it. Whether or not we agree with LaSor or Hays, both believe that the OT had a kind of hidden meaning in it.

Dodd's hypothesis also numbers among its supporters Rendall[50] and R. T. France.[51] Both maintain the existence of a fuller meaning in the OT writings which could be opened in a new context.[52] Nevertheless, it is Beale's proposed hermeneutical framework which serves to substantiate Dodd's and his followers' claim of a consistent interpretative method that is followed by the NT authors in their use of the canonical writings of the OT. Beale's proposal also seems to provide an additional aid in solving the problem of some of the examples of uses of the OT in the NT which seem to be inconsistent with or contradictory to the original meaning of the OT. We will particularly bear in mind the proposals of both Dodd and Beale when approaching NT writings. However, their theses will be subject to further verification in the course of our study.

OT or Hellenistic Influence?

HELLENISM IN THE NT

Another problem has also arisen concerning the relationship between the Testaments. As the NT books were written in Greek and had in view the growing Gentile church, the question is raised of the potential influence of Hellenistic culture upon the authors or at least the influence of Greek thought upon the process of adapting the basically Jewish gospel to those communities. The Roman Empire at the birth of Christianity was spreading its influence throughout the Middle-East so that the peoples living there were in constant touch with the culture and religion of the Greco-Roman world, which was mainly of Hellenistic origin. It has been assumed that, situated in such a context, the primitive church was not only exposed to that external mindset, but also that to make its message understandable to non-Jews it started to incorporate ideas of Hellenism. Thus the original message started to develop along the lines

---

50. "Quotation in Scripture," 215–16.

51. *Jesus and the Old Testament*, 225–26. He agrees with Dodd as to the claim that the NT writers learned their use of OT passages from Jesus himself and not from contemporary Jews.

52. Cf. Rendall, "Quotation in Scripture," 221; France, *Jesus and the Old Testament*, 75–80.

of Greek thought, resulting in a reformulation of the originally Jewish gospel. The NT on this interpretation is a syncretistic marriage of Jewish and Greco-Roman thought. Bruce comments,

> Jewish Palestine is not . . . to be excluded from the Hellenistic or Graeco-Roman world, and no sharp dichotomy is to be made between the Palestinian and Hellenistic spheres of Judaism or Christianity in the New Testament period.[53]

He goes on to say,

> Of course there are elements in the New Testament which are essentially Jewish-Palestinian, and others which are equally recognizable as Hellenistic; but there is no hard and fast line of demarcation between the two: in the broad central band of spectrum they merge into each other.[54]

Bruce finds support for his argument in the Gospel of Luke and Acts.[55] Then following Wilamowitz he describes Paul as *einem Klassiker des Hellenismus*, someone who writes and thinks Greek.[56] He continues,

> That Paul is a Hellenist in the ordinary sense of the term—one whose habitat was the Hellenistic world and who made a unique contribution to Hellenistic literature—cannot be doubted.[57]

He finally presents the Hellenistic contribution to primitive Christianity as proof of the genius of the gospel, which lies in its ability to adapt in various cultures.[58]

Another challenge came from Rudolf Bultmann, who also saw the early church with its theology as the outcome of a syncretism of Judaism and the Greco-Roman worldview. He says,

> The Gospel had to be preached in terms intelligible to Hellenistic audiences and their mental outlook, while at the same time the audiences themselves were bound to interpret the gospel message in their own way, in the light of their own spiritual needs.[59]

---

53. "New Testament," 232.
54. Ibid.
55. Ibid., 235–38.
56. Ibid., 238.
57. Ibid.
58. Ibid., 241.
59. *Primitive Christianity*, 176.

For Bultmann Christianity breaks with the original meaning of the OT. On his view "the original meaning and context of the Old Testament sayings are entirely irrelevant."[60] The Old Testament is still God's word only because "it is directly typological and allegorical."[61]

Bultmann focused in particular on arguing that primitive Christianity developed along the lines of Gnosticism. He finds many similarities between Christian beliefs and Gnostic dualism.[62] For Bultmann, Paul's theology resembles to some extent, along with other forms of Greek thought, Stoicism.[63]

Fridrichsen, in his treatment of the apostle John, also represents the approach of those who see the development of NT theology alongside Hellenism. He observes,

> St John represents the climax of the Hellenization of Christianity; he stands on the shoulders of St Paul and continues his work in that he Hellenizes the historical portrait of Jesus also.... St John dogmatizes the man Jesus even before his resurrection, thus bringing about the radical Hellenization of the Gospel.[64]

Counter-arguments/OT Influence

Although studies of the NT in the first few decades of the twentieth century focused on the Hellenistic background of the early church's theology, there have been other scholars who were not satisfied with such conclusions. J. A. Sanders expresses discontent with this view by observing that "a great deal of New Testament scholarship seems to strive to decanonize the New Testament, reading it only in terms of its Hellenistic context."[65]

Others have followed the same line of thought so that interest in the OT basis of NT theology has been systematically increasing. Hubbard, for example, writes,

---

60. Ibid., 187.
61. Ibid.
62. Cf. ibid., 177, 190, 200.
63. Ibid., 185–86.
64. "Jesus, St John and St Paul," 49.
65. "Paul and Theological History," 52.

The Old Testament as the Basis of the Book of Revelation

Not only does Old Testament prophecy lead into the New, but the New Testament appropriates Old Testament promises and reads them as preparation for God's new beginning.[66]

Noack claimed that Paul's gospel was always the same, whether he presented it in Greek or Hebrew.[67] His teaching was also in complete accordance with the Jewish church in Jerusalem. Similarly, John in writing his gospel did not necessarily depend on Greek culture because, ". . . Jewish doctrines may well have played their part in forming the religious setting in which the Johannine group . . . received the Gospel."[68]

Likewise, Wright supports the dependence of NT thought on the OT.[69] He shows that both Jesus and Paul must be understood in the context of Jewish sacred writings.[70] Paul's writings, he says,

> . . . are in fact expressions of the essentially Jewish story now redrawn around Jesus. . . . Paul is telling, again and again, the whole story of God, Israel and the world as now compressed into the story of Jesus. So, too, his repeated use of the Old Testament is designed not as mere proof-texting, but, in part at least, to suggest new ways of reading well-known stories, and to suggest that they find a more natural climax in the Jesus-story than elsewhere.[71]

He stands in the same line as Ellis[72] and Hays. Hays says concerning Paul,

> He saw himself as a prophetic figure, carrying forward the proclamation of God's word as Israel's prophets and sages had always done, in a way that reactivated past revelation under new conditions.[73]

---

66. Hubbard, "Hope in the Old Testament," 55. He refers to Clements, R. E. *Old Testament Theology*, 133. London: Marshall, Morgan & Scott, 1978, who warned against the danger of making a gulf between the Testaments.

67. Noack, "Jewish Gospel," 51.

68. Ibid., 53–54.

69. Throughout his writings. See for example, Wright, *Who Was Jesus?* 47, 54–55. Also Wright, *What Saint Paul Really Said*, 48, 70–71, 80–83; and *NTPG*, 453–54, where he observes that early Christianity was in fact Jewish Christianity, and even so-called Gentile Christianity derived all its beliefs and practices from Jewish Christianity.

70. See the previous footnote.

71. Wright, *NTPG*, 79.

72. Ellis, *Prophecy and Hermeneutic*, e.g., see his conclusion concerning Jesus' dependence on the OT, 253.

73. *Echoes of Scripture*, 14.

In the light of the evidence advanced by the scholars mentioned above the hypothesis that Christianity adopted Hellenistic ideas has to be seriously challenged.[74] Consequently, a student of NT writings should seriously consider the possibility of OT influence upon the formation of NT concepts and theologies, before paying attention to other possibilities.

THE APOCALYPSE AND THE SEMITIC MIND

It is generally agreed that the author of Revelation makes frequent use of material from the OT.[75] Whatever the history of interpretation of the Apocalypse is, the recent trend among scholars has been "to investigate the book in the light of its historical setting, in the light of OT symbolism and apocalyptic writings, and in the atmosphere of NT truth."[76] This is certainly due to recognition of the fact that the author of the book was a Jewish-minded person, someone who identifies himself as a prophet (Rev 1:1–3, 10–19; 4:1–2; 17:1–3; 21:9–10; 22:6–7). Beasley-Murray has observed a scholarly consensus recognizing a Semitic mind behind this writing.[77] He says,

> The Revelation is the product of a mind soaked in the Old Testament—the allusions to the Old Testament text are too numerous to be indicated by the modern method of using heavy type for Old Testament quotations in the Greek text, and the Seer is so much at home in Jewish apocalyptic literature that he finds it natural to express his theological convictions in this mode of writing.[78]

Kümmel similarly concludes that the author of Revelation was a Jewish-Christian prophet.[79]

---

74. Of the same opinion is Marshall, "Assessment of Recent Developments," 5.
75. Trudinger, "Old Testament," 82.
76. H. Hailey, in the Foreword to Jenkins, *Old Testament in Revelation*, 9.
77. *Revelation*, 35.
78. Ibid., 37.
79. *New Testament*, 472.

The Old Testament as the Basis of the Book of Revelation

That John's mind was formed by the OT is recognized by many scholars including Delling,[80] Goulder,[81] Fekkes,[82] Decock,[83] and Beale.[84] In fact, many exegetes have demonstrated that the Apocalypse contains more allusions drawn from the OT writings than any other book in the NT.[85] Since the beginning of the twentieth century scholars have tried to calculate the exact number of OT references in the book, but without reaching agreement. Charles,[86] for example, lists 250, whereas Swete[87] gives 278, *UBSGNT*[88] 634 and Staehlin[89] 700. The problem is that Revelation does not use any introductory formulae and much, if not all, of the OT material is present in the form of allusion.[90] This, however, does not negate the fact that the book draws heavily upon the OT.[91] According to Beale "the OT in general plays such a major role that a proper understanding of its use is necessary for an adequate view of the Apocalypse as a whole."[92]

---

80. Delling, "Johannes-Apokalypse," 136. He states that the author of Revelation was influenced by the OT and thus he passed that influence on to the churches he addressed.

81. Goulder, "Annual Cycle of Prophecies," 342–67.

82. Fekkes, *Prophetic Traditions in Revelation*, 15, 17, 38, 40.

83. Decock, "Book of Revelation," 373–410.

84. *Revelation*, 76.

85. Trudinger, "Old Testament," 82; Beale, *Revelation*, 77. Ford, *Revelation*, 27, states that the visions of Rev 4–22 contain over 400 allusions to the OT.

86. Charles, *Revelation*, I: lxii–lxxxvii.

87. Swete, *Apocalypse of St. John*, cxxxiv–cliii.

88. *United Bible Societies Greek New Testament*, index of quotations. As shown by Fekkes, *Prophetic Traditions in Revelation*, 62.

89. Staehlin, J. *700 Parallelen, die Quellgründe der Apocalypse*. Bern: 1961, as shown by Fekkes, *Prophetic Traditions in Revelation*, 62.

90. Trudinger, "Old Testament," 82. Cf. Moyise, *Old Testament in Revelation*, 13.

91. A possible solution to the problem of identifying allusions in Revelation is given by Fekkes, *Prophetic Traditions in Revelation*, 63–65. Fekkes distinguishes between formal and informal quotations, and allusions, although he sees that the term 'allusion' conveys too little information about an author's use of Scripture, except to indicate that it is not a quotation. He proposes that it is necessary to find authorial motive for each passage studied. He claims that it is essential "to trace the history of each OT text in previous Jewish and Christian interpretation if possible." Beale, *Revelation*, 78–79, recognizes three types of allusions (clear, probable, and possible) and says that the key to identifying the clear and probable allusions is a reasonable explanation of the authorial motive behind the passage referred to.

92. *Revelation*, 77.

Scholars have contended that the book refers to all major sections of the OT. Beale, for example, says,

> The range of OT usage includes the Pentateuch, Judges, 1–2 Samuel, 1–2 Kings, Psalms, Proverbs, Song of Solomon, Job and the major and the minor prophets. Roughly more than half the references are from the Psalms, Isaiah, Ezekiel, and Daniel, and in proportion Daniel yields the most.[93]

Charles, decades ago, also recognized the constant use of the major and minor prophets, by the Seer.[94] He also identified references to such books as Psalms, Proverbs, Canticles, Exodus, Joshua, 1 and 2 Samuel, and 2 Kings.[95] In more recent years, there have been other scholars indicating John's wide-range use of OT material from various parts of Jewish Scriptures.[96] This suggests, at least, that a reader attempting to examine the Apocalypse should allow voices of various OT traditions to be heard in the book. However, in the list of OT references, Ezekiel, Isaiah, and Daniel (probably in this order) are believed to be most influential on the formation of John's visions.[97] Yet, at the same time, the reader must be aware that the author often "fuses" several texts from various strands of the OT.[98]

Although there have been a few scholars advancing the hypothesis that Revelation is a collection of disparate sources,[99] their proposal

---

93. Ibid. See also Beale, "Use of the Old Testament," 258. Beale argues that the greatest number of allusions comes from Daniel 7, although in terms of actual number of allusions Isaiah is first, followed by Ezekiel, Daniel and Psalms. Cf. Swete, *Apocalypse of St. John*, cxlviii.

94. *Revelation*, I: lxv.

95. Ibid.

96. E.g., Paulien, *Revelation's Trumpets*. On a more popular level, see Jenkins, *Old Testament in Revelation*, 25.

97. E.g., Vogelgesang, "Ezekiel in Revelation," and Moyise, *Old Testament in Revelation*, 74, both giving priority to Ezekiel. Fekkes, *Prophetic Traditions in Revelation*, and Kio, "Exodus Symbol," 120–35, both stress the importance of Isaiah in Revelation. Beale, *Use of the Old Testament*, 88–92, argues that Daniel 7 is the strongest influence behind Rev 4–5. Cf. Rowland, *Open Heaven*, 60, who thinks that the apocalyptic material of Daniel and Ezekiel provided inspiration for later apocalypticists, including John.

98. The point initially made by Vanhoye, A. "L'utilisation du livre d'Ezéchiel dans l'Apocalypse." *Bib* 43 (1962) 436–77, esp. 467, and generally accepted ever since. On this, see Mathewson, *New Heaven*, 29.

99. Ford, *Revelation*, 22–28. Cf. Aune, *Revelation*, cx–cxxxiv.

has not been widely approved among NT scholarship.[100] Most exegetes view the book as a literary unit. Goulder affirms this saying that "the Apocalypse is not a random jumble of 'prophecies': it shows clear evidence of ordering."[101] Bauckham adds to the argument,

> The more Revelation is studied in detail, the more clear it becomes that it is not simply a literary unity, but actually one of the most unified works in the New Testament.[102]

He has explained that John consciously integrated various parts of his work into a literary whole.[103] Bauckham justifies his claim by showing that the whole book is a composition, which is directed to its climax in 17:1—19:10 and 21:9—22:9: the destruction of the harlot Babylon and her replacement by the bride of the Lamb, the New Jerusalem.[104]

The unity of the Revelation's material was widely recognized in the past by such scholars as Swete,[105] and more recently by Kümmel,[106] Goulder,[107] Schüssler-Fiorenza,[108] Fekkes,[109] and Beale.[110] Therefore, when investigating the material in Revelation, we will bear this in mind.

John's Use of the Old Testament Material

NT scholars have long debated over the nature of John's use of Jewish Scriptures. The questions posed in the debate touched on the issues of authorial intention, John's exegetical techniques, and the nature of his apocalypse. Although these issues are interrelated, each is important in its own right and therefore will be discussed separately in the consecutive sections below.

---

100. Indeed, Rowland thinks that the attempts at source-criticism have not been successful. Therefore the exegete of Revelation should "attempt an understanding of the text as it stands." *Open Heaven*, 414.

101. "Annual Cycle of Prophecies," 342.

102. *Climax of Prophecy*, 1 n.1.

103. Ibid., 2.

104. Ibid., 4–5.

105. *Apocalypse of St. John*, xliii–l.

106. *New Testament*, 462–66.

107. "Annual Cycle of Prophecies," 342.

108. Schüssler-Fiorenza, *Vision of a Just World*, 33.

109. *Prophetic Traditions in Revelation*, 16, 103. He sees that what unifies the book is its subject matter.

110. *Revelation*, 108–51.

Authorial Intention

On the one side, there have been scholars like Schüssler-Fiorenza who argued that John did not so much interpret OT passages as use their words, images and phrases to achieve his theological goal. The OT material was for him no more than a religious thesaurus or language reservoir, which the author used to compose his work. Schüssler-Fiorenza observes,

> John achieves the rhetorical power of his work by taking traditional symbols and mythological images out of their original context and by placing them like mosaic stones into the new literary composition of his symbolic narrative movement.[111]

And,

> Although John knows how to write proper Greek, he writes the whole book in a Hebraizing idiom that gives its language a hieratic, traditional character. Moreover, he never quotes or exegetes the Hebrew Bible or any of his other sources but uses them as "language" and "models."[112]

In this approach Revelation is a dramatic poem, which should make an emotional impact upon the hearers, and any analysis of sources used by John will not explain the book's images. She concludes that "attempts to express Revelation's images and metaphors in propositional, logical, factual language rob them of their power of persuasion."[113]

Much earlier, Swete expressed a somewhat similar opinion concerning the literary consciousness of John's use of the OT. He claimed an unintentional use of the OT material by John, which was unconsciously organized in the author's visions. He commented,

> ... the Apocalyptist's use of his OT materials is artless and natural; it is the work of a memory which is so charged with Old Testament words and thoughts that they arrange themselves in his visions like the changing patterns of a kaleidoscope, without conscious effort on his part.[114]

---

111. *Vision of a Just World*, 31.
112. Ibid., 29.
113. Ibid., 31.
114. Swete, *Apocalypse of St. John*, cxlix.

The Old Testament as the Basis of the Book of Revelation

On the other side of the debate, however, there have been scholars arguing for John's conscious and deliberate use of OT material. This approach has been represented, for example, by such scholars as Goulder, Fekkes, and Beale.

Goulder argues for John's conscious use and shaping of OT material to reflect the order of the book of Ezekiel and to serve the liturgical purposes of the early church.[115] His liturgical approach shows the purpose behind Revelation's use of the OT.

In his study, Fekkes focused on 150 specific passages where it is certain or virtually certain that a specific OT text or tradition lies behind John's usage. He concludes that "a form-critical analysis of these OT traditions reveals that John's use is in general consciously systematic and purposeful."[116] He adds,

> An overall summary of John's use of OT oracles against the nations reinforces the supposition that he does not randomly select OT passages, but consciously appropriates specific themes and modes germane to the subjects which he wishes to treat.[117]

In his work he develops and argues for the thesis that most of the OT allusions "fall into a limited number of well-defined thematic classifications."[118] John consciously selects OT texts, which fit his topic.[119]

Beale, following Caird[120] to an extent, also argues for the conscious employment of OT material. He observes,

> John's apparent self-identification with the line of OT visionaries implies that he was conscious of developing the ideas of the earlier prophets and, therefore, that the clearer OT references in his work are the result of intentional activity (cf. 1:1–3, 10; 4:1–2; 17:3; 21:10).[121]

In fact, Beale in his works has become an advocate of authorial intention on the part of the author of Revelation. He insists that John deliber-

---

115. "Annual Cycle of Prophecies," 343 ff.
116. Fekkes, *Prophetic Traditions in Revelation*, 70.
117. Ibid., 91.
118. Ibid., 16.
119. Ibid., 16, 103.
120. Caird, *Revelation*, 25–26. Cf. Beale, *Use of the Old Testament*, 64.
121. Beale, *Revelation*, 81 (quoted almost verbatim after his *Use of the Old Testament*, 260).

ately used OT texts but yet looked at them through his new "presuppositional lenses," which he derived from the OT and Christ himself.[122] Thus, although John had respect for the original meaning of the texts, he saw in them new significance corresponding to his historical context.[123] Consequently, Beale criticizes others, including Moyise, for siding with the approaches that support the reader's perspective ("creating new meanings") rather than focusing on the intent of the original author.[124] Beale's critique of Moyise gave rise to an extended debate between the two scholars in their consecutive publications.

Since his early publications, Moyise has set to employ the method of intertextuality to studying Revelation.[125] Dissatisfied with the inadequacy of previous critical methods to describe John's use of the OT, he focused particularly on the way allusions should be interpreted in the Apocalypse. Like Ruiz,[126] Moyise believes that an allusion or relocated text creates a tension in the new context, which invites the reader to engage in discovering how the old and new context interact.[127] He decides,

> Thus the relevant question concerning the presence of Old Testament quotations or allusions in the New Testament is not, "has the author respected the context?," but "in what ways do the two contexts interact?"[128]

---

122. Beale, *Use of the Old Testament*, 45. The "presuppositional lenses" consist of 4 points: (1) Christ is the true Israel; (2) canonical history is unified: its earlier parts correspond and point to its later parts; (3) Christ has inaugurated the age of fulfillment; (4) because of points (2) and (3), the latter parts of biblical history interpret earlier parts (as seen already in later OT tradition). However the centre and interpretive key of biblical history is Christ's own interpretive approach.

123. Ibid, 51–56. Beale sides with Hirsch in the latter's hermeneutical debate with Gadamer.

124. Ibid., esp. 48–51.

125. See his "Intertextuality," 295–98, followed by the publication of the 1995 monograph. Moyise bases his method on earlier literary works of Thomas Greene and John Hollander.

126. Referring to Ruiz, J.~P. *Ezekiel in the Apocalypse: The Transformation of Prophetic Language in Revelation 16:17—19:10*. European University Studies. Frankfurt: Peter Lang, 1989.

127. *Old Testament in Revelation*, 18-19; "Intertextuality," *ad.loc.* The prominent example of intertextual tension being the figure of Lion/Lamb in Rev 5:5-6, which reappears throughout various publications of Moyise.

128. *Old Testament in Revelation*, 19.

In Moyise's approach, the meanings generated in the process of reader's trying to bridge the new and old contexts are more vital to the study of Revelation than John's intended meaning.[129] Thus in its nature, interpreting Revelation is open to the possibility of polyvalent meanings, which are dependent in part on the reader's perspective and level of engagement with the text.[130] And although not denying John's awareness of OT contexts, Moyise contends that the Seer's Christian perspective allowed him "to change, modify and even (on occasions) invert them."[131] In Moyise's opinion, John did not always respect the original meaning of OT texts he used in his work.

It seems that some earlier claims of this type provoked Beale to join in the public debate with Moyise, a debate which focused particularly on the issues of "meaning" and "significance."[132] Starting with the hermeneutics of Hirsch, Beale pressed for an epistemological distinction between the original authorial meaning and later "significance" of the meaning.[133] According to Beale, a NT author's (or John's) placing of an old text in a new context did not involve dissociation from the OT original meaning, but a change of application which Beale classifies under the rubric of "significance." While admitting that NT writers develop "new interpretations" of the OT, Beale denies them the right to develop "new meanings" of it.[134] This is so because meaning is a fixed act, which, however, carries with it a potential for new effects in new contexts.[135] Thus Beale would claim that, whilst John could have seen new significance in the OT text he employed, this new significance was still organically related to the original meaning the Visionary did not (and could not) change.

Moyise argued previously that what Beale calls "significance" most modern scholars would simply call "new meaning."[136] This suggests that

129. Ibid., 142. See also Moyise, "Study of the Old Testament in the New," 15–16.

130. "Study of the Old Testament in the New," 37.

131. Moyise, "A Reply to Greg Beale," 56.

132. See, e.g., Beale, "A Rejoinder to Steve Moyise," 152–80. Moyise, in turn, published an article in *IBS* 23 (Jan 2001) 36–41, in which he commented on Beale's 1998 monograph. The debate was finally moved to *AUSS* 39/1 (2001) 5–22, 23–34, 35–40. This time it also included J. Paulien's article, in which he assumed the role of an arbiter.

133. "Rejoinder to Steve Moyise," 155–56. Referring throughout to Hirsch, E. D. *Validity in Interpretation.* New Haven: Yale, 1967.

134. Ibid., 158–59.

135. Ibid., 160. Following Vanhoozer, *Is there a meaning in this text?*, 255.

136. "A Reply to Greg Beale," 55.

both Beale and Moyise operate with slightly different terminologies and perhaps even different epistemological theories. Now, re-joining the debate, Moyise has argued that John's treatment of temple-material from Ezek 40–48 probably does not give the reader the true meaning of the text.[137] It leaves the modern reader with the impression that John arbitrarily used Ezekiel's motif to suit his purpose and thereby disregarded the author's original intention. Moyise further charges Beale with failure to distinguish between John's and Beale's own intention.[138] And since scholars have simply no access to any fixed "authorial intention," one can only attempt at describing the relationship between old and new context, a process that involves the interpreter's own perspective.[139] Therefore, for Moyise, the reader-oriented approach is a better method for approaching Revelation's complexity.

It seems that the issue between the two scholars has not been successfully solved. Even Paulien's assessment of their variegated approaches remains inconclusive.[140] However, one could agree in substance with Paulien's suggestion that both Beale and Moyise offer their unique emphases: while the former is particularly interested in the influence of the OT on NT writers, the latter shows more concern for the impact the reader brings into the process of intertextual interpretation.[141] And if Paulien is right in his understanding, the difference can be seen to be the difference between a normative, comprehensive, and global approach represented by Beale and a descriptive, immediate, and local approach represented by Moyise.[142]

We are left with the question of whether or not one needs to know John's intention in order to arrive at the meaning of Revelation. It seems that both Moyise and Beale encourage the view that John was unconscious of some correspondences his relocated allusions might generate when read by consecutive generations of readers. However,

---

137. Moyise, "Through a Lens," 40.

138. Moyise, "Authorial Intention," 37.

139. Ibid., 39.

140. Paulien, "Dreading the Whirlwind," 5–22. See also Beale's response to Paulien in which he does not hide his disappointment at Paulien's insufficient consideration of Beale's epistemology and methodology. Beale, "A Response to Jon Paulien," 23–33.

141. Cf. "Dreading the Whirlwind," 11, 19.

142. Ibid., 20. The former seeks to include the divine superintendence of the entire Scripture in authorial intention and the latter limits itself to the human agent.

The Old Testament as the Basis of the Book of Revelation 23

the Apocalypticist could possibly have acknowledged these new correspondences as consistent with his overall purpose.[143] Unfortunately, we can never know this for sure. Therefore the conclusion of Mathewson seems valid,

> Overall, it seems best to speak of Old Testament influence in terms of semantic import and interpretive significance rather than only in terms of authorial consciousness.[144]

Both allusions (which John probably intended) and echoes (which he may not have intended) can carry a potential for interpretive significance.[145] Therefore the reader needs to be allowed to hear echoes beyond the authorial intention. However, hearing them will depend to a large extent on his/her knowledge of the OT and other ancient sources.

John's Exegetical Techniques

Connected to the discussion on authorial intent is the issue of the manner in which John dealt with the OT. In recent years, scholars have made various proposals to address the issue.

J. S. Casey has argued for John's typological reading of the OT and especially the variegated Exodus traditions from the Pentateuch.[146] These traditions characterized by themes of redemption, judgment, and inheritance provided the Seer with a general framework for his use of Exodus typology.[147]

Vogelgesang has proposed that the universalizing of Ezekiel's "restoration material" is John's major technique.[148] The Visionary radically reinterpreted Ezekiel's tradition in order to bend the tradition to his program of universalistic redemption for all humanity.[149] This included an anti-esoteric (i.e., exoteric) way of writing his Apocalypse, which distinguished it from earlier Jewish apocalyptic esotericism.[150]

---

143. Cf. Mathewson, *New Heaven*, 24 n.79.

144. Ibid., 24.

145. Ibid. Cf. Hays, *Echoes of Scripture*, 28. Also Vogelgesang, "Ezekiel in Revelation," xvi.

146. Casey, "Exodus Typology in Revelation," esp. ix–x.

147. Ibid., 135.

148. Vogelgesang clearly follows Vanhoye here. "Ezekiel in Revelation," 9–10.

149. Ibid., 117, 121, 131, 162–63.

150. Ibid., 277, 286–87, 295, 299, 315: Rev 10:4 and 22:10–11 being a negation of earlier apocalyptic esotericism.

Paulien has applied to studies on Revelation Dodd's proposal concerning NT writers' redemptive-historical perspective.[151] He has claimed that the NT authors' fulfillment perspective would also characterize John of Patmos.[152] By alluding to the OT, John wanted his readers to recall the entirety of OT contexts from which his allusions were taken and reinterpreted through the prism of the Christ-event.[153] Thus, as far as allusions go, Paulien talks about authorial intention. However, he was probably the first to apply Hollander's notion of echo to the study on Revelation.[154] For Paulien, a textual echo is not the same as allusion. It does not have to be associated with the authorial intent or point to a wider OT context.[155] An echo merely recalls certain symbols defined in the OT.[156]

J.~P. Ruiz has agreed with Vogelgesang concerning universalization as John's general technique in his approach to Ezekiel, but denies the notion of universal redemption.[157] Further, John's exoteric way of expressing his visionary experience is, for Ruiz, not a reaction to earlier esotericisms of Jewish apocalypses, but a new way of describing development in the redemption-history. Ruiz's major contribution is the idea of re-actualization and re-vitalization of OT metaphors by placing them in the new context of Revelation.[158] By alluding to certain OT liturgical elements in his work, John provided his audience with a liturgy by which they could celebrate the promised victory. He "re-appropriated" the OT tradition for them and directed them to follow his technique of engaging in a dialogue with OT texts, extending their original meanings.[159] This notion stands close to the reader- response approaches. Finally, according to Ruiz, the solecism in John's Greek was intended to give the reader pause and encourage him to interpret.[160]

---

151. *Revelation's Trumpets*, 68–69.

152. Ibid., 161.

153. Ibid., 161–62.

154. Ibid., 171–72.

155. Ibid., 177, 305–6.

156. Ibid., 426.

157. Ruiz has extensively discussed Vogelgesang's work in "Ezekiel in Revelation," 129–80. As described by Beale, *Use of the Old Testament*, 16–19.

158. Ruiz, *Ezekiel in the Apocalypse*, 526–29. As described by Decock, "Book of Revelation," 376–77.

159. Ruiz, *Ezekiel in the Apocalypse*, 225, 520. As described by Beale, *Use of the Old Testament*, 31.

160. Beale, *Use of the Old Testament*, 39.

The Old Testament as the Basis of the Book of Revelation

Bauckham has proposed that the entire book of Revelation reveals the pattern of conscious and deliberate allusion to the OT in order to present the way old prophecies came to fulfillment in the age inaugurated by Christ.[161] Reading the book requires a constant awareness of detailed intertextual relationships with the OT.

Fekkes has argued that John has consistently and purposefully employed a variety of exegetical and literary devices when interpreting the OT.[162] The most prominent of these devices include: combining two or more texts by analogy; uniting two OT passages by means of a third; clarifying one OT text by referring to another parallel OT text; widening the scope of a passage by subtle additions. Fekkes has also contended that Isaianic traditions in the Apocalypse were selected and used thematically, as in previous prophecies.[163]

In his monograph of 1995, Moyise has not focused so much on John's technique of using the OT as on the means by which the reader should discern the tension and interaction between the original and new contexts of a dislocated text. Yet, it is probable that John was choosing from his stock material parts that could become relevant to his churches' situation, when placed in a new context.[164]

Beale has gathered his and others' previous discoveries concerning Revelation in the 1998 monograph. He has dedicated one long chapter to John's techniques in his use of the OT.[165] He has listed eight of these: use of segments of the OT as literary prototypes; thematic use of the OT; analogical use of the OT; universalizing of the OT; informal but direct fulfillment use of the OT; informal and indirect prophetic (typological) fulfillment use of the OT; inverted use of the OT; and stylistic use of the OT. Beale has argued that each category sustains the notion of John's careful exegesis of OT contexts in light of the Christ-event.[166] Even the irregularities in Revelation's Greek (so-called solecisms) were purposefully employed by the author to draw his readers' attention to important OT contexts.[167]

161. *Climax of Prophecy*, x–xi.
162. *Prophetic Traditions in Revelation*, 283.
163. Ibid., 282, 287–88.
164. *Old Testament in Revelation*, 36.
165. *Use of the Old Testament*, 60–128.
166. Ibid., 128.
167. Ibid., 319–45.

Finally, Mathewson's recent monograph is worth-referring to briefly here. Mathewson has presented a slightly different approach to the figure of echo from Paulien. Mathewson has argued that even "the original context of the echo continues to speak through the present text."[168] Thus also echoes can be pointers to OT contexts, which can add to the overall argument intended by the author. Therefore even if John was unaware of echoes he placed in his texts, they are still worth-studying by the reader, who could recognize the subtext and thus see more details of John's symphony.[169]

It was not our intention in this section to critically evaluate every scholarly claim concerning John's technique in using the Scriptures. This sometimes has been done in some of the consecutive publications mentioned above. However, this overview allows us to conclude that some approaches have been inadequate to describe the use of the OT in Revelation. Neither typology nor universalization alone can possibly describe the complexity of allusions and echoes in the Apocalypse. Other techniques need to be borne in mind, including probably all those examined by Beale.

A few scholars have decided that it is important to be aware of the redemptive-historical development and a conscious act by the author when describing John's use of OT material. A few others have implied that focusing on the authorial intent (only?) is inadequate for the study of Revelation. Therefore, while scholarly debate goes on, it seems best to accept the broader and more balanced view of Mathewson, who does not reject completely the notion of authorial intention but also allows the reader to hear various echoes created unintentionally.[170] This approach does not need to assume complete freedom in interpretation because the direction for interpretation is discernible in interaction between the two

168. *New Heaven*, 22.

169. Ibid., 24, 24 n.79, 234. Mathewson was criticized by T. Hieke (in *RBL* 07/2004 review of the monograph by the former) for referring sometimes to the intention of the original author instead of focusing entirely on the input that the reader brings to the text. But it seems that Mathewson's intention was not completely to abandon the notion of authorial intention. He wanted to acknowledge both the authorial intention and the reader's impact.

170. One may wonder if this approach is not itself an echo of earlier hermeneutical claims of Ricoeur, who has claimed that although a text is semantically autonomous, it is not an author-less absolute. The text has a "surplus" of meaning that transcends its original situation. Cf. Ricoeur, *Interpretation Theory*, 30. Polish translation: *Język, tekst, interpretacja*, 102–3. Warsaw: Państwowy Instytut Wydawniczy, 1989.

contexts of relocated texts.[171] One needs to be aware of both continuities and discontinuities in such cases.[172]

The Nature of John's Apocalypse

Lastly in this part, we need to consider the issue of John's use of Jewish Scriptures in relation to his claim of receiving visions directly by revelation. This may shed more light on the above debates. Due to the space limitations of this work, we will briefly describe only a few representative approaches.

In his important work, C. Rowland has set to demonstrate that spontaneity was not a guiding principle for the apocalypticists. He proposes,

> Frequently the visionary experience of the apocalypticist is the result of some kind of preparatory meditation, and it is apparent that the meditation upon Scripture has a large part to play in this process.[173]

To support this proposal, Rowland points to the examples of Daniel's meditation on Jer 25:11–12 prior to his vision of Gabriel in Dan 9. He highlights also the debt that 1 Enoch 14:8ff and Rev 4 owe to Ezek 1 and perhaps Isa 6.[174] Thus, Rowland argues, a starting point for the author of Revelation was probably the vision of God's glory in Ezek 1, followed by a visionary experience transcending the original, and concluding with further reflection on the Scriptures which provided aid in expressing the character of new visions.[175] Consequently, it can be said that the experiential religion of John, although rooted in previous sacred texts, could include innovations of equal importance as earlier prophecies.[176]

Clements has asserted that apocalyptic emerged in the process of scribal activity.[177] This activity involved removing prophecies from their

---

171. This proposal possibly comes close to Moyise's idea of the trajectory of interpretation. See Moyise, "Misappropriate the Scriptures," 20–21.

172. Mathewson, *New Heaven*, 223. Cf. Moyise, *Old Testament in Revelation*, 22.

173. *Open Heaven*, 215.

174. Ibid., 215–23. However, for Vogelgesang, Rev 4 is "a deliberate abridgement, streamlining, and reinterpretation of the whole apocalyptic *merkavah* tradition." "Ezekiel in Revelation," 277.

175. Rowland, *Open Heaven*, 226–38, 361. The prominent example of John later reflection being Rev 17.

176. Ibid., 351, 446.

177. Clements, "Apocalyptic," 19.

original historical contexts and placing them into larger literary contexts, with words and metaphors being able to produce new meanings.[178] According to this approach, John's Apocalypse, although relying heavily on the forms of expression of earlier prophecies, would generate new understanding of God's purpose in its unique context. But Clements has not particularly discussed the relationship between Revelation's written form and John's visionary experience.

Michaels has argued that John was a prophet who received his visions through direct divine revelation, not a scribe interpreting earlier texts.[179] Therefore similarities between Revelation and OT texts are due to the fact that they all come from the same "wellspring of divine inspiration." John relied only on oral prophetic traditions to inform and shape his work, but he created a new oracle.[180] Thus the OT should not serve as framework for interpreting Revelation but only as a base from which John's transformation sprang.

Decock has maintained that John stood in the long tradition of "reworking the existing oral and written texts in order to address the present."[181] His prophetic activity involved adapting and re-writing of earlier prophetic traditions, which were his "pre-understanding" and "horizon of thinking."[182]Thus, believing that the fuller revelation of God's plans was available to him, John trusted that "the old texts would easily bend to the meaning of the new texts."[183] But his starting point was, nevertheless, the old texts.

This brief survey of scholarly proposals concerning the relation between John's visionary experience and his use of the Scriptures suggests, at least, that the prevailing opinion supports his interaction with earlier traditions available, probably both oral and written. The only dissenting voice of Michaels seems outweighed by the examples provided by other scholars, especially Rowland. Thus it seems likely that John imitated earlier forms of prophecy to achieve his "revelatory" goals, yet without simply copying their meaning.[184] Therefore, in line with the former con-

178. Ibid., 20–21.
179. Michaels, "Old Testament in Revelation," 852.
180. Ibid.
181. "Book of Revelation," 395–96.
182. Ibid., 406.
183. Ibid.
184. Cf. Moyise, *Old Testament in Revelation*, 118–38, trying to apply T. Greene's

clusions proposed above, a student of Revelation should be prepared to see interaction between new and old contexts in John's allusions to earlier Jewish writings. He should be prepared to see both continuities and discontinuities in these allusions. He also should be conscious of the impact the reader has on the text when combining together different literary contexts (to extend somewhat freely Clements's proposal). Yet he should be aware of the body of literature which likely constituted John's "horizon of thinking."

Literary Sources of Revelation

It has already been demonstrated that the Apocalypse of John depends heavily on the OT. Two German scholars, A. Schlatter[185] and H. Kraft,[186] have even gone so far as to deny John's dependence on any other source except the OT.

Nevertheless, there is consensus among NT commentators that John alluded to other Jewish writings, and also to some Greco-Roman sources (the two putative examples are the figure of blood flowing as high as a horse's bridle in Rev 14:20, and chains prepared for Satan in Rev 20:3).[187] Vogelgesang is of the opinion that John was influenced "by a large number of extrabiblical traditions and symbols."[188] This view, however, needs to be modified in the light of what has been said by scholars in discussing probable allusions to non-biblical writings.

Bauckham, in dealing with John's suggested dependence on Jewish apocalypses, remarks,

---

forms of imitation (reproductive, eclectic, heuristic and dialectic) to describing John's ways of using the scriptures.

185. *Das Alte Testament in der johanneischen Apokalypse*, 105. BFCT XVI/6. Gütersloh, 1912. Referred to in Fekkes, *Prophetic Traditions in Revelation*, 59.

186. *Die Offenbarung des Johannes*, 16. Tübingen, 1974. Quoted by Fekkes, *Prophetic Traditions in Revelatiion*, 59. Kraft says, "In those passages of Revelation where we have failed to point out the OT source for the apocalyptic prophecy, we have likewise failed to interpret them."

187. Charles, *Revelation*, I: lxv; Swete, *Apocalypse of St. John*, cxxxv–cliii; Bauckham, *Climax of Prophecy*, 1–37; Schüssler-Fiorenza, *Vision of a Just World*, 29; Beale, *Revelation*, 34, 78–79. Cf. Fekkes, *Prophetic Traditions in Revelation*, 38 n.48.

188. "Ezekiel in Revelation," 122.

> Although it is *a priori* quite likely that John had read some of the Jewish apocalypses which we know, it seems to me impossible to prove his specific literary dependence on any such work.[189]

After examining some of the possibilities of such dependence,[190] he concludes,

> Our case studies of apocalyptic traditions in Revelation suggest that the author's use of such traditions is not to be explained by his dependence on Jewish apocalypses known to us.[191]

He proposes that John might have known some other (oral?) traditions, which were used by Jews and Christians in composing their apocalypses.

Beale, more cautiously, suggests that the criteria applied in identifying allusions to the OT should also be used in identifying allusions to other sources, whether Jewish or Greco-Roman.[192] He warns against too much eagerness in looking for Johannine references to non-canonical sources by saying that "one must be circumspect in the search for dependence on such other literary sources and resist the temptation to find parallels where there are none."[193]

Fekkes further remarks that "it must be kept in mind that John's use of previous prophetic and apocalyptic tradition is almost exclusively limited to the Old Testament."[194] And he adds, "the sheer magnitude, variety and consistency of John's use of the OT certainly constitutes this area as a fundamental starting place for the exegete."[195]

It also needs to be remembered that the intention of this work is to examine the metaphor of divine marriage in biblical thought. Therefore it seems right to us to take an approach which would first and primarily pay attention to that which is generally regarded to be the primary source of Revelation's allusions, i.e., the OT. Nevertheless, where there

---

189. *Climax of Prophecy*, 39.

190. Ibid., 40–83.

191. Ibid., 83. See also Beale, *Revelation*, 79 n. 31, referring to Parker, H. M. "The Scripture of the Author of the Revelation of John." *Iliff Review* 37 (1980) 35–51, who argues that John was "saturated with non-canonical apocalyptic Jewish tradition, though direct dependence on this material is small in comparison with direct OT references."

192. Beale, *Revelation*, 78–79.

193. Ibid., 79.

194. *Prophetic Traditions in Revelation*, 38.

195. Ibid., 59.

The Old Testament as the Basis of the Book of Revelation

may be clear or probable references to other traditions due consideration will be given to this.

Still dealing with John's use of OT material, scholars have debated which language version of Scriptures he preferred. The irregularities in his Greek suggested to NT commentators in the past that the Seer worked with Semitic Scriptures.[196] Although at the beginning of last century, scholars sometimes listed references to the LXX,[197] over the last few decades the strong voices of Charles, Vanhoye, Trudinger, and Ozanne have served to form a consensus, always giving priority to Hebrew sources.[198] This prevailing tendency is still observable in the works of, e.g., Vogelgesang, Bauckham, and Fekkes.[199] However, the minority of scholars have acknowledged John's debt to other, including Greek, versions.[200] Recent publications of Beale and Moyise have provided a new challenge to the former consensus. For Beale, solecisms do not necessarily prove John's poor knowledge of Greek, but may point to his use of Greek versions ("Septuagintalisms") of the OT.[201] While not agreeing with all Beale's examples, Moyise contends that the scholarly argument based on similarity/dissimilarity criteria (employed usually to downplay the role of Greek sources) would leave one with no source text.[202] It rather seems (e.g., in Rev 17:16) that John freely used OT material (of, e.g., Ez 23) from various sources to create the intended rhetorical effect.[203] Likewise, Moyise's case study of the use of the Psalms in Revelation, reveals John's knowledge and perhaps use of both Hebrew and Greek versions.[204] Therefore, the previous scholarly consensus remains unproven.

---

196. See Moyise, "The Language of the Old Testament in the Apocalypse," 98. Cf. examples listed in Aune, *Revelation*, cxcix–ccvii.

197. See Swete, *Apocalypse of St. John*, cxxxiv–cliii.

198. Moyise, "The Language of the Old Testament in the Apocalypse," 108. For references to Trudinger and Ozanne's works see ibid., 105 n.18, 108 n.26.

199. See Vogelgesang, "Ezekiel in Revelation," 22; Bauckham, *Climax of Prophecy*, 303; Fekkes, *Prophetic Traditions in Revelation*, 17.

200. E.g., Paulien, *Revelation's Trumpets*, 100; Aune, *Revelation, passim*.

201. *Use of the Old Testament*, 320–21. Examples come from Rev 1:4; 1:5; 2:13; 4:1; 11:5; 12:5; 12:7; 14:7; 14:19; and 20:2. See ibid., 324–45.

202. "The Language of the Old Testament in the Apocalypse," 110–11. Sometimes, there are important divergences from the Hebrew and/or Greek.

203. Ibid., 112.

204. Moyise, "Psalms in the Book of Revelation," esp. 72–81. Moyise also claims that even showing John's dependence on the Hebrew version of Ezekiel does not prove John's dependence on the Hebrew in the case of Exodus, Daniel and the Psalms. Ibid., 71.

In the light of the above discussion, it seems wise to allow for John's use of various scriptural versions in composing his literary work, unless it can be proven otherwise.

THE APOCALYPSE AND THE NEW TESTAMENT

Charles recognized the NT as one of the sources of Johannine composition,[205] and claimed that the author of Revelation used the Gospels of Matthew and Luke, and of the Epistles: 1 Thessalonians, 1 and 2 Corinthians, Colossians, Ephesians, and possibly Galatians, 1 Peter, and James. Goulder also acknowledged some similarities between the Seer's Vision and the Synoptics, especially the "Little Apocalypse" in the Synoptics as a source for the order of the events.[206] Bauckham has also argued for Revelation's dependence on the Synoptic tradition and, in particular, the dependence of the sayings in Rev 3:3, 20 and 16:15 on the Synoptic parables of the Thief and the Watching Servants.[207] Delling found some resemblances, in the participial style of Revelation, with Matthew, Acts, Pauline literature, Hebrews, and 1 Peter, suggesting that this style comes from the Old Testament.[208] Ford again observed similarities with themes in some of the forementioned writings, e.g., 'bridegroom,' in the Apocalypse, and in the Synoptics, John's Gospel and the Epistle to the Ephesians.[209] These examples imply the existence of literary and theological parallels between Revelation and the rest of the NT.

On the other hand, the Apocalypse itself has been the subject of doubt as to its right to be identified as a Christian book. Luther, for example, was concerned that it neither teaches nor makes known Christ.[210] Semler criticized the teaching of Revelation as incompatible with the rest of the NT's doctrine.[211] Indeed, there is a tension between the message of Revelation and that of the rest of the NT (e.g., the call for vengeance in 6:10 which would be irreconcilable with the prayer of Jesus in

---

205. *Revelation*, I: lxv–lxvi.
206. "Annual Cycle of Prophecies," 342.
207. *Climax of Prophecy*, 92.
208. "Johannes-Apokalypse," 123.
209. *Revelation*, 33.
210. See Kümmel, *New Testament*, 473.
211. Ibid.

The Old Testament as the Basis of the Book of Revelation

Luke 23:34 and that of Stephen in Acts 7:60).[212] Does the book then lack harmony with the rest of the NT message?

Kümmel himself is of the opinion that "Revelation can express the full value of its message only within the framework and the limits of the NT."[213] He sees a great need for reconciliation of apparently controversial passages in the Apocalypse and expects that the development in theological understanding of the message of the book will clarify its problematic parts.

A possible solution to Rev 6:10 is given by Beale.[214] He says that the prayer in this verse is not a cry for a personal revenge, which would contradict Luke 23:34 and Acts 7:60, but a prayer of the exalted saints in heaven, an appeal to God to bring wrongdoers who persecute his church to justice. Caird takes a similar line: John used the language not of private revenge but of public justice.[215] John used legal language and applied it to men who, ultimately, would be punished for their wickedness against the saints they put to death. Their retribution would demonstrate before the whole world that the persecutors of the saints were in the wrong.[216] This example shows, at least, that we cannot and should not draw premature conclusions concerning the (dis-) harmony of Revelation with the rest of the NT.

Luther's feelings about the absence of Christology in the book seem to us to be exaggerated. Modern scholars have recognized, for example, that the re-working of Ezekielian themes in Rev 5, which is central to the theology of the book, took place with a view to the Christ-event.[217] It is because of this event that Revelation can display the Christian message of salvation and operate from the perspective of realized eschatology.[218] In accordance with this perspective, Christ's victory on the cross (cf.

---

212. Ibid., 474.
213. Ibid.
214. *Revelation*, 392.
215. *Revelation*, 85.
216. Ibid.; cf. Beale, *Revelation*, 393.
217. Cf. Vogelgesang, "Ezekiel in Revelation," 12, 344. Vogelgesang believes that John's critical hermeneutical perspective was the testimony of Jesus (397). Thus, "Revelation contains a profoundly Christian message" (398).
218. Ibid., 390.

Rev 5) continues in his and his followers' conquering in Rev 12:11 and 19:13–21.[219]

This implies that, in general, NT commentators recognize the Apocalypse's interest in Christology and its significance for the Christian community. Therefore, Paulien could conclude,

> ... although the book has a different style and vocabulary than the rest of the New Testament, we should not expect its theology to be radically different from what we find there. It is filled with the spirit of Jesus and the apostles.[220]

In the light of contemporary studies and the evidence discussed in this chapter it seems right to conclude that we should rather expect to find in Revelation a similar theology to those of the other NT writings, rather than one which is disharmonious. If John used the same traditions as the Synoptics or Paul, it seems very likely that his message would be in agreement with the general message(s) of the NT. It is, however, necessary to find out whether there is a unified NT message. We will suggest a positive answer to this question in the next section.

The Shared Symbolic Universe of NT Authors

It has been noticed by scholars that Revelation resembles other NT writings both in literary style and, more important, in content. It is, therefore, suggested that all the NT writers shared a similar world of symbols which emerged from the OT and which shaped their messages. Is there any evidence of such a shared symbolic world in the early church?

Wright claims that all NT authors had the same theological framework based on OT promises and expectations.[221] According to him the post-exilic community of Jews lived in the hope that Yahweh would come in his power to rule the world in the way he had promised and to vindicate his covenant people, Israel, over her enemies.[222] This expectation was based on the unfulfilled promises of Yahweh. Although after the Babylonian exile had ended many of the Jews returned to their homeland, and the temple was rebuilt, they still believed that the fulfillment of their expectations had not yet come. Evil (i.e., paganism typified by

---

219. Cf. Reddish, "Martyr Christology," 219.
220. *Revelation's Trumpets*, 43.
221. *NTPG*, 456–58.
222. Wright, *JVG*, 203.

The Old Testament as the Basis of the Book of Revelation

Babylon) had not been completely defeated, and Yahweh had not settled in Zion permanently to rule the whole world from the midst of Israel.[223] The "exile"[224] had not finished yet. So they expected that Yahweh would act mightily again as at the time of the Exodus from Egypt, in the future. He would sit on the throne in Zion, defeat all enemies (i.e., paganism) and rule over the whole cosmos. Thus the second temple hope was for the eschatological new exodus "seen as the final return from exile."[225] Wright explains that "the story would reach its climax; the great battle would be fought; Israel would truly 'return' to her land, saved and free; YHWH would return to Zion."[226] This eschatological event would be the climax for covenant history: the coming of the kingdom of God.

Wright makes the point that the early Christians had taken this Jewish set of expectations and redefined it along the lines of the Messiah's event.[227] However, the basic framework of Jewish beliefs remained the same for the early church. Wright argues,

> The god who was thus becoming king had a true people, who would be vindicated when the kingdom finally appeared; for the moment this chosen people would suffer, but their god would win a mighty victory in which they would be vindicated. They would then be established, as Israel had hoped to be, as the vicegerents

---

223. Ibid., 205–6.

224. Wright helpfully explains what he means by this. In his article, "Theology, History and Jesus," 105–12, he explains that the term "exile" is a shorthand to mean, "the time of desolation begun by the Babylonian destruction. 'Exile' in this sense is a *period of history* with certain characteristic features, not a mere geographical reference." See p. 111. In fact, Wright was criticized by Casey for his theory about "exile," in Casey, "Where Wright Is Wrong," 99–100. Casey commented, "The next serious problem is almost a leitmotiv of the whole book: the notion that Jews believed that they were in exile. At the time of Jesus, many Jews lived in Israel. Some lived permanently in Jerusalem. Jews came to Jerusalem from all over Israel and the diaspora for the major feasts. In the Temple, the Tamid was sacrificed twice a day, a special symbol of God's presence with Israel. As Jesus put it, 'And he who swears by the sanctuary swears by it and by Him who lives in it' (Mt 23.21). We would need stunningly strong arguments to convince us that these Jews really believed they were in exile when they were in Israel." Thus Casey's comment challenges Wright's lack of direct evidence that could support the statement that many Jews did view Israel as in a state of exile.

225. *JVG*, 209. Throughout this work, we use "Exodus" to signify the event in Israel's history, but we take "exodus" to refer to another salvific act of God, like the first, or generally to a biblical motif.

226. Ibid.

227. Ibid., 215–20.

of the creator god, ruling over his world. This familiar combination of monotheism and election gave rise, as naturally as did the Jewish expressions of the same beliefs, to eschatology: the creator would act again within history, to bring the kingdom fully to birth. All of this locates early Christian kingdom-language firmly on the first-century Jewish map.[228]

Although the "kingdom of the Messiah" is already established, the "kingdom of God" in its full appearance is yet to come.[229] The kingdom is in a sense present, and yet future. This distinguishes early Christian belief from that of the second temple Judaism. A new phase in God's plan had been inaugurated by the death and resurrection of Jesus of Nazareth. God's people are already partakers of God's kingdom, but full realization of the kingdom still awaits the future.[230] Therefore, Wright argues, "Jewish apocalyptic . . . has been rethought, not abandoned, within early Christianity."[231] He adds,

> The point of the present kingdom is that it is the first-fruits of the future kingdom; and the future kingdom involves the abolition, not of space, time, or the cosmos itself, but rather of that which threatens space, time, and creation, namely, sin and death. The vision of 1 Corinthians 15 thus coheres neatly with that of Romans 8.18–27, and, for that matter, Revelation 21. The creation itself will experience its exodus, its return from exile, consequent upon the resurrection of the Messiah and his people.[232]

Another key area of difference can be seen in the Jewish and Christian understandings of evil. While the Jews expected liberation in the national, racial and geographical sense, the early Christians' hope looked to the exodus of a redeemed humanity and cosmos from the bondage of evil as sin and death. Consequently, the kingdom itself has a different nature from that anticipated by second temple Jews. It is from above and not from this world;[233] it spreads throughout the whole earth;[234] its capital is

---

228. Ibid., 215. See his footnotes 61–63 for references to biblical and extra-biblical material.

229. Ibid., 216.

230. Ibid., 217.

231. Ibid.

232. Ibid., 218.

233. John 18:36–37.

234. Acts 1:6–8.

The Old Testament as the Basis of the Book of Revelation

the heavenly Jerusalem, not the earthly Jewish capital.[235] Nevertheless, the Jewish symbolic universe, albeit redefined by the early church in the light of Christ's revelation, essentially remained the same. Wright concludes,

> The symbolic world of first-century Judaism has been rethought from top to bottom, even while its underlying theology (monotheism, election, and eschatology) has been explicitly retained.[236]

Thus, Wright's proposal is that the NT authors shared the same expectation of the fulfillment of God's promises concerning his kingdom, of the final liberation from evil and of the new exodus, and therefore had comparable eschatologies.[237]

While this view still awaits a reasoned critique from NT scholarship, it gives a possible answer to the question of a shared symbolic universe of the early church, which not only influenced NT authors, but constituted their framework of reference.[238]

A number of scholars have recognized the importance of the new exodus motif in the book of Revelation. J. S. Casey has argued that the Exodus traditions in the Apocalypse are a basis for the book's exodus typology, which can be discerned in the three interrelated themes of

---

235. Rev 21:22; 22:5.

236. *JVG*, 218.

237. Only within the last decade or two have scholars started considering this view. Due attention should be paid to the unpublished PhD dissertation by Holland, "Paschal-New Exodus Motif." Holland develops a whole range of arguments in favor of the "new exodus" motif as a unifying mindset of NT writers. See especially chapter 1 of his thesis. He gives examples of NT scholars who pointed to the importance of the New Exodus expectation as a perspective for understanding the NT. See, e.g., pp. 26–29.

238. Attention should be given to the published evaluation of Wright's theology. See Newman, *Jesus & the Restoration of Israel*. While contributors to this assessment critically evaluate many of Wright's claims, his view of exile and redemption of Israel gains approbation. Evans, "Jesus & the Continuing Exile of Israel," 77–100, on the basis of extra-biblical material, gives the evidence for Wright's notion of second temple Judaism in the state of exile, thus countering Maurice Casey's earlier critique (cf. n.161). Evans (pp. 82–83) shows that there are many Jewish texts which testify that Jews of late ancient times did view their nation as being in exile (e.g., Sirach 36:5, 14, 15–16; 48:10; Tobit 13:3; Baruch 2:7–10; 2 Macc. 1:10—2:18). Likewise there are a number of texts among the Dead Sea Scrolls which refer to second temple Judaism as in a state of exile (e.g., 1 QM 1:3; 1 QpHab 11:4–6; CD 6:4–5; 4 Q504–506). Evans, 83. Similarly, extra-biblical texts express Jewish expectation of redemption from that exile which was still to come (e.g., Tob 13:5, 13; 14:5; Bar 4:36–37; 5:5; 2 Macc. 1:27, 29; 2:17; *Pss. Sol.* 8:28; 11:1–4; 17:4, 21, 26–18; *Targum on Isaiah* 53:8; *Targum on Micah* 5:1–3). See pp. 87–91.

redemption (Rev 1:5–6; 5:9–10), judgment (Rev 8–9; 15–16) and inheritance (Rev 7:1–17; 14:1–5; 15:1–5; 20–22).[239] Relying on traditions of earlier prophets (Jeremiah, Ezekiel, and Deutero-Isaiah), John offered a new exodus theology based on the central (to him) promise of God's reign from Exod 19:5–6.[240] Thus, he 'actualized' Israel's Exodus experience through his understanding of redemption in Christ and its results for the believers.[241]

Paulien has recognized the exodus motif behind the seven trumpet section in which the punitive judgments of the evil ones resemble plagues of Egypt and other Exodus-like judgments found in OT prophets (e.g., in Jer 51).[242] The judgments lead finally to the redemption of God's people, as indicated by the seal-judgments.[243]

According to Bauckham, the new exodus theme in Revelation is best seen in its references to the Passover lamb (Rev 1:5b; 5:6, 9–10; 7:2–14; 12:11, etc).[244] It is through the blood of the Lamb that victory is won and evil overcome. Also, the conversion of the nations is portrayed under the image of new exodus in Rev 15:2–4.[245] This may be in line with Christian expectations concerning the extent of God's kingdom (see Wright's view above). And likewise, the plagues in Rev 15:1, 5—16:21 resemble the plagues of Exodus, leading to Christ's and his people's reign on earth (cf. Rev 20:4–6; 22:3–5).[246]

Mathewson has proposed that the new exodus is a guiding motif behind the removal of the sea in Rev 21:1c, the act of God's deliverance which opens the way towards the redeemed humanity inheritance – the new creation described in Rev 21–22.[247]

The above examples suggest that John may have shared with other NT authors their eschatological perspective built around the new exo-

239. "Exodus Typology in Revelation," ix, 228–34, 238. Cf. Casey, "Exodus Theme in Revelation," 42.

240. "Exodus Typology in Revelation," 236.

241. Ibid., 239.

242. *Revelation's Trumpets*, 321. Second trumpet resembles the description of Babylon's fall in Jer 51. Ibid., 387.

243. Ibid., 335–36.

244. *Climax of Prophecy*, 215–28.

245. Ibid., 296.

246. Bauckham, *Theology of Revelation*, 71–72.

247. The motif is based on Deutero-Isaiah's and Ezekiel's new exodus motifs. See *New Heaven*, 218. Cf. Mathewson, "New Exodus," 243–58.

dus motif. Therefore, in our study we will seek to assess the relevance of the motif for the author of the Apocalypse and its hermeneutical significance for interpreting the message of the book.

CONCLUSIONS

In this chapter we have tried to demonstrate NT dependence on the OT background. We have noted that the first century church viewed the OT as its own Scripture.

The NT authors relied on the Jewish Scriptures, not merely for the sake of giving proof texts, but rather to show continuity in God's redemptive plan throughout the history, both before and after Christ's death. We have discussed various arguments against and in favor of a consistent and intelligible methodology for the use of the OT by those authors. We have found a possible solution to the problem of the apparently haphazard use of OT quotations in the New in the history of redemption approach. We have also questioned the thesis that the NT writers follow the non-contextual methodology of rabbis in the first century CE.

Focusing on Revelation we have acknowledged the scholarly consensus which views the OT as the main source and influence on John's vision. We have also indicated that the Apocalypse is a literary unit that has much in common with the rest of the NT and whose climax is the vindication of God's people in the course of redemptive history.

Therefore it seems to us justified to say that there is a way of doing NT theology, one based on the study of OT concepts, a theology which would view both the Testaments as a continuity and development of certain ideas relating to God's history of salvation.

Thus in studying the concept of divine marriage in the book of Revelation we will attempt to show the origin and development of it in the OT and the use and further development of it in the NT. We will see if it fits into Israel's expectation of an eschatological divine marriage, following the completion of the new exodus.

2

The Divine Marriage and the Institution of Marriage in Semitic Culture of the Ancient Near East

INTRODUCTION

WE HAVE ACKNOWLEDGED THE scholarly consensus concerning the Apocalypse's dependence on the OT. We now need to explore the OT concept of the divine marriage as a basis for exploring the meaning of the divine marriage in the Apocalypse. In this chapter therefore we will investigate the idea of divine marriage in Ancient Near Eastern writings. We will also investigate concepts/practices associated with the theme of marriage among the Semites in general.

There are apparently two possibilities for the origin of the metaphor of divine marriage in the OT. Jewish writers either used their social institution of marriage as a metaphor for their theology to express certain truths about Yahweh or else they borrowed the idea from the Semitic nations surrounding them and transformed it to fit their beliefs. In this and in the following chapter we shall examine which is the more probable.

First in this chapter it is necessary to discuss the institution of marriage in Semitic culture. We shall consider issues such as betrothal, bride-price, dowry, wedding, divorce, adultery and the role of the best man. Babylonian, Assyrian, Canaanite and Hittite texts will be compared with the OT data to determine if there is any dependency of the OT writers on the divine marriage concepts of these ancient societies.

The question of whether the OT borrows its idea of divine marriage from the cultures of Israel's surrounding nations needs now briefly to be considered. The metaphor occurs for the first time in the Jewish writings in the book of Hosea.[1] H. W. Wolff notes in his commentary on Hosea that

---

1. Hall, "Origin of the Marriage Metaphor," 169.

the prophet "adopted the idea of a marriage between a god and his people from Canaanite tradition and used it in his polemic."[2] Then he adds, "In terms of ancient Israel's faith in Yahweh, it is an unprecedented modernism that Hosea so consistently utilizes the Canaanite mythologoumenon of divine marriage."[3] Although we will return to this proposal in the next chapter when we consider the divine marriage according to Hosea, it is worth explaining some points now. Even if we agree with Wolff's thesis then it follows that Hosea not only adopted the myth from Canaan, but also transformed it to fit Israel's theology.[4] In contrast to Canaanite practice the love of Yahweh expressed in Hosea's metaphor has nothing to do with the fertility cult and the sexual act of a god and a goddess as in Canaan. The prophet's imagery points rather to a moral love, the love of Yahweh's covenant expressed in the phrase, "You shall be my people and I shall be your God."[5] The marriage metaphor in Hosea describes the nature of God's covenant relationship with his people and therefore it is profoundly different from the imagery of Canaanite religion.[6] However, fully to appreciate this distinction and to judge Wolff's claim we need first to consider divine marriage in the ANE and then come to Hosea's metaphor, which we will discuss in the next chapter.

DIVINE MARRIAGE IN ANCIENT NEAR EASTERN TEXTS

The earliest known inscriptions concerning divine marriage are of Sumerian origin and are dated at the end of the fourth millennium BCE.[7] They present the wedding of a god and goddess or *hieros gamos*: Dumuzi, the god of the date palm, and Inanna, originally goddess of the

---

2. Wolff, *Hosea*, 16. Similarly, Mays, *Hosea*, 8, claims that Hosea adopts the motifs of the fertility cult of Canaan "to portray the relation of Yahweh and his people." The divine marriage metaphor of Hosea 2 is, according to Mays, a good and a prime example of the prophet's use of Canaan fertility cult themes. Ibid., 9.

3. *Hosea*, 44.

4. Wolff himself states that any sexuality, "so important in Canaanite thinking," with respect to Israel's God cannot be taken into account. Ibid., 16. Likewise Eichrodt sees that Yahweh cannot be viewed as having sexuality so that it would be a mistake to speak of him as having any kind of sexual relationship with his people. See his *Old Testament Theology*, I: 150–51, 223.

5. Hall, "Origin of the Marriage Metaphor," 169–70.

6. Ibid., 170.

7. Hamilton, "Marriage," IV: 561. The story is published among "Sumerian Sacred Marriage Texts" in Pritchard, *ANET*, 637–45.

communal storehouse.[8] Dumuzi comes to his bride in the company of his servants carrying the bridal gifts of fat, milk and beer, and Inanna admits him.[9] Their meeting and sexual act ensures the fertility of nature.[10] "Dumuzi is the personification of the power behind the annual date harvest, and Inanna represents the storehouse in which Dumuzi deposits and stores his yield."[11]

A similar idea of a *hieros gamos* is found in the second-millennium-BCE Canaanite texts from Ugarit.[12] In the poem of Nikkal and the Kathirat[13] the moon-god Yarikh of the West-Semitic (Canaanite) pantheon marries Nikkal-and-Eb, the great goddess of the fruits of the earth, also known as Nikkal: the consort of the moon-god Sin in Mesopotamian mythology.[14] The moon is regarded in mythology as "propitious to childbirth." Again the purpose of the wedding is the fertility of the earth which is symbolized in the child Nikkal-and-Eb bears to Yarikh.[15] The story itself reflects the characteristic customs of ancient Semitic marriage[16] and the poem is probably intended to celebrate the wedding of a mortal woman because as the *hieros gamos* "is annually blessed with the fruits of the earth, so the human marriage may be blessed with the fruit of the woman's womb."[17] We shall return to this story when we deal with bride-price and dowry.

Another second-millennium-BCE Canaanite myth, that of Shachar and Shalim, describes El the father of Baal and the supreme god, who through sexual intercourse becomes the husband of two women: most

---

8. Hamilton, "Marriage," IV: 561.

9. Pritchard, *ANET*, 639. Hamilton, "Marriage," IV: 561.

10. Pritchard, *ANET*, 639. Hamilton, "Marriage," IV: 561; following Jacobson, T. *The Treasures of Darkness: a History of Mesopotamian Religion*, 47. New Haven: Yale University Press, 1976.

11. Hamilton, "Marriage," IV: 561.

12. Published in Driver, *Canaanite Myths*.

13. Ibid., 125–27. According to some scholars this might be a "Hurrian myth in Semitic dress," though this suggestion cannot be well-proved. See ibid., 23 n.8.

14. Ibid., 24; Hamilton, "Marriage," IV: 561.

15. Hamilton, "Marriage," IV: 561.

16. See Driver, *Canaanite Myths*, 24 who refers to C. H. Gordon in *Bulletin of the American Schools of Oriental Research* LXV (Baltimore: 1937) 30–31 and T. H. Gaster in *Journal of the Royal Asiatic Society* LXV (London: 1938) 37–45.

17. Driver, *Canaanite Myths*, 24.

The Divine Marriage and the Institution of Marriage 43

probably Anat and Athirat, the goddesses of fertility.[18] They bear him two divine sons, Shachar (dawn) and Shalim (dusk). The ritual is connected to the Canaanite feast of first-fruits in early summer (June) and so that the *hieros gamos* is set against the background of fertility.[19]

The marriage of Baal, the god of fruitfulness, to Anat, who functions as mistress of love and fertility in Canaanite thought, also serves the purpose of fruitfulness.[20] Their union provides peace or well-being in the land and the company of Anat "is necessary for his [Baal's] dispensation of life in the elements of nature."[21]

The sacred marriages of the Ancient Near East also included those between gods or goddesses and humans. The myth of Inanna speaks of the marriage of the king Iddin-Dagan and the goddess. This relationship is to provide for the well-being of the king and of his people.[22] Another is portrayed in the Akkadian (Assyrian) Gilgamesh Epic (*c.* 2000–1800 BCE) where the goddess Ishtar proposes to mortal Gilgamesh, legendary ruler over ancient city-state of Uruk, though he rejects the offer because of Ishtar's past perversions of love.[23] Another example is that of Marduk, king of all the gods of heaven and earth in Babylon, who married a human woman.[24]

The above examples show that the idea of divine marriage was well-known in the ANE, though apparently none of these examples show similarity to the *hieros gamos* of Israel's God who married the whole nation, not in order to bring fertility upon their land through a sexual act, but to be their God and husband for life.[25]

---

18. Ibid., 123 (Rev. ll 3–20, 21–31), 22, 23, 23 n. 3. Anat is later married to Baal when he is old enough to be her husband.

19. Cf. ibid., 23.

20. Baal V i–iv in Driver, *Canaanite Myths*, 83–89.

21. Habel, *Yahweh versus Baal*, 56–57, 74–75, cf. 103.

22. Pritchard, *ANET*, 640–41.

23. Ibid., 83–84. Hamilton, "Marriage," IV: 561. Dating of the Epic according to Thomas, *Documents*, xv. Gilgamesh was actually two-thirds god and one-third man who had lost his immortality and the human nature "was the ultimate controlling factor of his destiny" (ibid., 17).

24. Thomas, *Documents*, 3; Driver, *Canaanite Myths*, 23.

25. Such a divine marriage is peculiar to the OT. Cf. Kruger, "Israel, the Harlot," 107.

THE INSTITUTION OF MARRIAGE IN THE ANCIENT NEAR EAST AND RELATED ISSUES

On the basis of what is said above it is apparent that the institution of marriage was well established in the Ancient Near East. However, it is worthwhile looking at practices associated with the institution of marriage in the cultures of the nations surrounding Israel.

Relevance of ANE Material

Hamilton has noted that the accounts of marriages from the ANE mostly refer to those of noble men, kings, heroes and gods. It is therefore hard to find any information of the wedding customs of ordinary people of that time.[26] However, it can be argued that the customs of ordinary people reflect those of their rulers. Even today when a royal couple marries there are certain elements of the ceremony which are common to those followed by their subjects, e.g., in Christian culture the ceremony in a church, the oath and wedding rings, are all common elements, although ordinary people will not have a banquet as grand as that for a royal couple. Furthermore, poets who wrote myths and legends concerning ancient heroes, gods and goddesses, described their behavior and customs on the basis of what was common in their culture. Therefore the absence of material relating to the wider population does not prove they were without ceremonies. However, the nature of divine marriage is such that it far eclipsed human experience and therefore the ritual could be expected to reflect its uniqueness. Thus, it is still worth looking at different marriage customs in the ANE, even though our information is limited to those of kings, gods and heroes, because they can uncover the culture common to all Semites of antiquity, regardless of their social status.

Marriages, Contracts, and Marriage Gifts in the ANE

As mentioned above, in the Sumerian sacred marriage the god Dumuzi brought gifts of fat, milk and beer to Inanna. This was in the context of the marriage ceremony.[27] The text itself does not explain the significance of this gift. However, it suggests that it was an essential part of the Sumerian wedding ceremonies. Inanna, after getting permission from her mother to admit Dumuzi, bathed herself, "anointed herself with goodly

---

26. Hamilton, "Marriage," IV: 560.
27. Pritchard, *ANET*, 638.

The Divine Marriage and the Institution of Marriage

oil," clothed herself with the noble garment and "arranged the lapis lazuli about (her) neck," and taking along her dowry and seal opened the door for Dumuzi.[28] After that they embraced and cohabited. The wedding ceremony, which was performed at Inanna's house, finished with Dumuzi taking her to his house.[29] The text points to the fact that they knew each other before the marriage, loved each other, and Dumuzi asked Inanna's mother Ningal for her daughter's hand.[30]

Another example comes from Canaanite mythology. In order to marry Nikkal-and-Eb and take her to his house, Yarikh of Canaan sent word to her father Hiribhi asking him for Nikkal's hand. He promised to pay Hiribhi "a huge sum of silver, gold, and precious stones [lapis lazuli, i.e., stones of sapphire], and to give him fields and vineyards" as the bride-price for Nikkal.[31] Hiribhi, however, advises Yarikh to marry Pidriya (Baal's daughter) instead. But Yarikh refuses to marry any other bride than Nikkal and then sends the gifts already mentioned to Nikkal-and-Eb's house where her family carefully prepares the scales to weight them.[32]

The ancient Babylonian and Assyrian laws dealt in much more detail with matters of matrimony and we will therefore give greater attention to these laws.

The plain and simple laws of Hammurabi's Code (nos. 128–84) dealt with issues like bride-price, dowry, divorce, etc.[33] The marriage contract was absolutely essential for a marriage to be valid (no. 128). It seems that there were at least two ways of bringing about a marriage with a free woman. First, it was the bridegroom's father who contracted with the bride's father and on his agreement gave him gifts (no. 166): the betrothal gift (Bab. *biblum*, which means the provisions for the marriage feast[34])

---

28. Ibid., 639.
29. Ibid., 639.
30. Ibid., 639–40.

31. Gibson, *Myths and Legends*, 31. Driver, *Canaanite Myths*, 125 ("Nikkal and the Kathirat," i 15–23). van Selms, *Marriage and Family*, 22–23. The latter sees Ugaritic *mhr* (Hebr. *mohar*) translated by some as a "bride-price" to mean rather a "compensation gift." See pp. 27–29, 31. We will discuss the issue below.

32. Gibson, *Myths and Legends*, 31; Driver, *Canaanite Myths*, 125–27 (ii 4–9), 24.

33. The text of the Code published in Pritchard, *ANET*, 164 ff. Hammurabi introduced his Code in the second year of his reign, i.e., *c*. 1726 BCE. See ibid., 163, 163 n.1.

34. Driver and Miles, *Babylonian Laws*, I:250.

and the bridal gift (Bab. *tirhatum*).³⁵ Second, the bridegroom could himself approach the bride's father and give him the *biblum* and the *tirhatum* (nos. 159–61). Then the bridegroom and the bride were inchoately married.³⁶ A betrothed woman lived either in her father's house (cf. no. 130) or, in some cases, in her father-in-law's house (cf. nos. 155–56) until the marriage ceremony. The legislation treated her like a married woman, except that the completion of marriage through *copula carnalis* had not yet taken place.³⁷ Van Praag says that in the Code of Hammurabi, the acceptance of the betrothal gift was an agreement to marriage and the consummation was the sexual act itself.³⁸ After giving the gift, the man started to be called son-in-law by the father of his fiancée.³⁹

The principles nos. 137–38, 142, 149 mention the dowry (Bab. *seriktum*), which was kept in her husband's house and which she brought from her father's house. A Babylonian woman could be divorced at her husband's whim, "even though she has committed no fault and has produced him sons" (cf. no. 137).⁴⁰ In order to prevent a man from divorcing his wife without cause the Code of Hammurabi made restrictions. In the case of the divorce of a childless wife, the husband had to give her money to the amount of the *tirhatum*, her marriage-price⁴¹ and to allow the woman to take the dowry with her (no. 138). However, the marriage-price was not compulsory in all cases so the payment was only a mina of silver (cf. no. 139).⁴²

---

35. Ibid., 249. According to the authors the Babylonian word *tirhatum* refers to the Hebrew word *mohar* translated by many as the "bride-price" when referring to marriage by purchase. See discussion below.

36. Because betrothal was something more serious than our engagement Driver and Miles prefer to speak of inchoate marriage. See Mace, *Babylonian Laws*, I: 172.

37. Sexual intercourse was necessary for the completion of marriage. See Driver and Miles, *Babylonian Laws*, 263.

38. van Selms, "Best Man," 67. He refers to van Praag, A. *Droit matrimonial Assyro-Babylonien*, 150. Amsterdam: 1945.

39. See discussion in van Selms, "Best Man," 67. Cf. Neufeld, *Ancient Hebrew Marriage*, 145. Pace Driver and Miles, *Assyrian Laws*, 167–68.

40. Driver and Miles, *Babylonian Laws*, I: 293.

41. The husband had not only to pay the bridal gift to the bride's father at the beginning of marriage but "he is now compelled to pay it second time." Ibid., 296. In fact, this was not only to protect a woman from capricious divorce but also to provide her with a maintenance.

42. In the case of a concubine whose social status was somewhere between the free and the slave woman.

Restrictions were also laid on both parties during the inchoate marriage. The breaking of a betrothal by the prospective father-in-law brought a penalty on him, i.e., he had to pay twice the amount of the *tirhatum* (cf. nos. 159–61). If a man changed his mind about marrying a woman her father could keep the bridal gift (no. 159).[43]

The dowry (money brought by the wife from her father's house) was never the possession of the husband, it always belonged either to the woman or to her children, except in the case when after the death of a childless woman her father did not return the marriage-price to his son-in-law so that the son-in-law was to deduct the full amount of the marriage-price and return the rest of the dowry to the woman's father's house. This implies that the dowry was a greater amount of money than the bride-price (nos. 162–64; cf. 167, 172). However, in texts from Nuzi of the fifteenth century BCE the bride-price is "always greater than the" dowry.[44] There were also cases when a woman had no dowry (no. 167*a*) but if she was associated with the temple as a worker her family had either to provide a dowry for her (in the case her father died) or she could share in the goods of the parental estate (nos. 178–84).

Hammurabi's Code protected the intimacy of marriage and adultery was in many cases a capital offence (e.g., nos. 130–32, 133*a*). However, it was possible for both the husband and the wife to divorce each other merely on the basis of their willingness to divorce (nos. 137–43). The law permits polygamy where the husband has a relationship both with his wife and with maid-servants (e.g., no. 170–71).

The Code does not provide us with information as to the amount paid as a bride-price and the amount of dowry.[45] There has been disagreement among scholars concerning the exact meaning of the *tirhatum*. Writers such as Cook[46] claim that it was purchase-money so a woman was actually bought in Babylon and became the property of her husband, although she was at the same time free to trade and do business or to appeal independently to the law-courts.[47] Similarly Koschaker[48] sees the *tirhatum* as referring to the purchase of a woman although he suggests

43. Cf. Cook, *Moses and the Code of Hammurabi*, 80.
44. Hamilton, "Marriage," IV: 562.
45. But see Driver and Miles, *Babylonian Laws*, I: 297.
46. *Moses and the Code of Hammurabi*, 73.
47. Ibid., 71–72.
48. Referred to in Driver and Miles, *Babylonian Laws*, I: 259–60.

that the word itself meant "earnest-money" which later became money for the purchase, so that the selling of a bride at betrothal was accompanied by payment in advance.[49] There are, however, counter-arguments to this view as pointed out by Driver and Miles:[50]

1. There is no trace of a contract of sale made by giving an earnest in the laws of Hammurabi;
2. The *tirhatum* cannot be both the earnest-money and the purchase-money;
3. The supposed principles of sale in Babylonian marriage did not exist;
4. As the Code of Hammurabi shows (nos. 138–39) the *tirhatum* was not always paid so it cannot be supposed that it was essential to the validity of the marriage. Thus how could the marriage be a sale?
5. The root of the term *tirhatum* connotes sexual relations and has nothing to do with sale;
6. The dowry given by the bride's father to her was greater than the *tirhatum* so such business would be unprofitable to the father.

So they conclude that,

> The Babylonian scribes and lawyers certainly did not regard marriage as a form of marriage by purchase. For a certain number of marriage-contracts are extant and they are in a form quite distinct from that of sale; and, when, in fact, a wife was bought for a man [either slave or concubine], they used a word denoting sale and adopted the form or precedent of sale.[51]

And they propose that "it is therefore far more probable that its [i.e., *tirhatum's*] meaning is a marriage-gift or a gift given to secure marriage . . ."[52]

---

49. Ibid., 260.
50. Ibid., 260–65.
51. Ibid., 263.
52. Ibid., 264.

In the light of the above it would be difficult to agree with the bride-purchase *de facto* in Babylon. We will return to the arguments for and against buying a wife while focusing on Israelite marriage customs.

The Middle Assyrian Laws of the fifteenth to twelfth century BCE also deal with matters of marriage on tablet A.[53] The legislation was, as in the case of Babylonian Law, against adultery and the death sentence was usually the punishment (A. 12–16). Cases of polygamy which did not include the wives of others were considered legal (cf. A. 23).

The law mentions a marriage-gift, ornaments (jewelry or other personal ornaments), which the husband bestowed on his wife at marriage. They became her property (A. 25–26).[54] But he was entitled to take them away if he divorced her (cf. A 38). However, the husband did not have the right to claim any of the possessions of his father-in-law (A. 27). The dowry of a bride was vested in her sons (A. 29). It was the custom that either the father of a prospective groom or the groom himself brought the betrothal-gift to the house of his prospective father-in-law. This consisted of lead, silver, gold and also of edible things, of which the latter were not to be returned if the marriage was not finalized (A. 30–31; cf. 43). The bridal-gift (Ass. *teirhatu*, Bab. *tirhatum*) is mentioned only in A 38 but it is not defined in the Assyrian laws.[55] The only help comes from comparing the *teirhatu* with the Babylonian law where it does not mean anything else than a gift.[56]

The betrothed woman could either stay in her father's house or be taken to her father-in-law's house after the marriage (A. 27, 32). In the case of an aristocrat's daughter,[57] part of the ceremony of betrothal was to pour oil on her head (A. 42–43). This was performed by the father of the prospective husband. In Assyria the betrothed son had to be at least ten years old (A. 43).

The legislation mentions also the marriage contract which was essential to the existence of this institution and which demanded faithfulness on the part of the wife, although if she was a widow a contract for the new marriage was not compulsory (A. 36, 34). In the absence of the

---

53. Text in Pritchard, *ANET*, 180–85. For the dating of the laws see his Introduction, 180.
54. Driver and Miles, *Assyrian Laws*, 193.
55. Ibid., 191.
56. Cf. ibid., 192.
57. Neufeld, *Ancient Hebrew Marriage*, 146.

husband for longer than five years a married woman was free to remarry another man (A. 36). A man could marry his concubine veiling her in the presence of five or six witnesses and claiming, "she is my wife" (A. 41). The Assyrian legislation allowed the husband to divorce his wife at his caprice and to send her out empty-handed (A. 37).

There is no evidence whatsoever of wedding ceremonies among the Babylonians or the Assyrians.[58]

In general both the Babylonian Code and the Middle Assyrian Laws protected wives in the sense of providing for their living. This was the task of their husbands, or sons, in the case of a husband's death. Childless women could be also supported by the state, i.e., a job could be provided for them.

The Laws of Eshnunna (c. 2000 BCE) do not bring much information on matrimonial customs. However, they imply that a man could marry a woman only with the permission of her parents (no. 27) and without their permission the marriage was invalid.[59]

The Institution of Best Man in the ANE

Another important issue in ANE marriages is the role of the best man. As van Selms has shown in his study[60] of the matter, the institution of the best man was known by and mentioned in the Code of Lipit-Ishtar, the Sumerian king, who reigned from 1868 to 1857 BCE in Isin, and whose legislation has many similarities to that of Hammurabi.[61] Of special interest concerning the best man is § 29 which reads, "If a son-in-law has entered the house of his father-in-law and has performed the betrothal gift, and afterwards they have made him go out and have given his wife to his companion—they shall present to him the betrothal gift which he has brought and that wife may not marry

---

58. Ibid., 150.
59. Pritchard, *ANET*, 162.
60. "Best Man," 65–75.
61. Ibid., 65–66. Both kings were Amorites so there is the theory of "Amoritic customary law" upon which both codes were based. The text of the Code published in Steele, F. R. "The Code of Lipit-Ishtar." *American Journal of Archaeology* (1948) 425–50. He thinks that the Code of Hammurabi was directly influenced by the Code of Lipit-Ishtar (abbreviated C.L), 430. Fragments of the C.L. were published even earlier: see Lutz, F. H. *Selected Sumerian and Babylonian Texts*, nos. 100–102. (1919); and de Genouillac, H. *Textes religieux sumeriens du Louvre*, 34. Paris: 1930.

his companion."⁶² By the ceremony of betrothal which consisted of entering and giving a gift, a man was admitted to the intimacy of his future father-in-law's family life.⁶³ Likewise the acceptance of the gift by the father of a girl was a part of the ceremony, i.e., the receiving of it obligated her father to give her in marriage to its donor.⁶⁴ The paragraph, however, deals particularly with a "companion" of the son-in-law. The case of van Selms is that the person mentioned (*kuli*)⁶⁵ is somebody similar to the best man ("the most intimate friend of the bridegroom"), present in the marriage, who could not marry the bride if the marriage was cancelled.⁶⁶ The same principle is reflected in the Code of Hammurabi no. 161. According to both sets of legislation the best man of a rejected bridegroom cannot marry the bride.⁶⁷

THE INSTITUTION OF MARRIAGE IN THE OT AND ISSUES RELATED TO IT

Marriage Ideal

Like other Semitic cultures Israel had its institution of marriage. The story of the first couple in Genesis 2:21–24 points out that the ideal marriage, according to the divine will, was to be monogamous.⁶⁸ Cases of polygamy are, of course, found throughout the OT and such a practice is never condemned by it.⁶⁹ However "the most common form of marriage in Israel was monogamy."⁷⁰

---

62. van Selms, "Best Man," 66.

63. Ibid., 67. van Selms noticed that van Praag, *Droit matrimonial Assyro-Babylonien*, did not believe the gift was actually purchase money.

64. Ibid., 67, following Neufeld, *Ancient Hebrew Marriage*, 146, who says that the betrothal gifts "create[d] a legally binding contract which was discharged by the marriage."

65. The word is singular. van Selms, "Best Man," 68.

66. Ibid., 68. van Selms thinks that behind this prohibition could have stood the expectation of loyalty and solidarity and also of reciprocity among people in the ANE. See ibid., 68–69.

67. Accadian (Babylonian) *ibru* translated in Pritchard, *ANET*, 173, as friend is probably the same as Sumerian *kuli* — companion, the best man. See van Selms, "Best Man."

68. Cf. DeVaux, *Ancient Israel*, 24.

69. Burrows, "Social Institutions of Israel," 135.

70. DeVaux, *Ancient Israel*, 25. See also Paterson, "Marriage," 264; where it reads, "But it might still be open to question whether the practice [i.e., polygamy] was at all general."

Marriage Arrangements and Gifts

Marriages were commonly arranged by the parents of a future couple, although the OT gives some examples where a man chooses a preferred wife for himself, e.g., Gen 26:34–35; 34:4; Judg 14:2.[71] Some have argued that the giving of dowry by the bride's father to be her possession was not a common custom in ancient Israel.[72] They agree that the few instances found in the Old Testament cannot be normative for Israel's overall practice. On the other hand, the same examples show that the giving of dowry was in practice and therefore that the idea was not foreign to a Jewish mind. Mace observes that in patriarchal times it seemed customary for a girl to receive a handmaid as her dowry (cf. Gen 16:1; 24:59, 61; 29:24, 29).[73] Another example is found in the times of Judges when Caleb's daughter requests her father to give her springs of water as her marriage present (Judg 1:14–15). Later in Israel history, Pharaoh's daughter received the city of Gezer as the present at her marriage with Solomon (1 Kgs 9:16).

The Code of Hammurabi recognized the custom of dowry and dealt with it, especially in the context of divorce. But Mosaic legislation did not mention or institute the dowry. Nevertheless, the examples show that the practice was present in ancient Israel, although its extent may be a matter of speculation.

In order to betroth a woman a man had to pay her father a "bride-price," the *mohar*. The meaning of this has been a matter of discussion among the scholars during the past century, similarly like in the case of Babylonian *tirhatum*. The origin of the word is very obscure.[74] The *mohar* was usually a certain (unknown to us ?) amount of money, although in some cases the money was exchanged for some other form of payment: e.g., Jacob worked seven years for Rachel (Gen 29:18.20) and David provided Saul with a hundred Philistine foreskins in order to marry Michal (1 Sam. 18:20–27).[75]

---

71. DeVaux, *Ancient Israel*, 29–31.

72. See Paterson, "Marriage," 271; DeVaux, *Ancient Israel*, 28; Emmerson, "Women in Ancient Israel," 383.

73. *Babylonian Laws*, I: 175–76.

74. Neufeld, *Ancient Hebrew Marriage*, 94 n.1.

75. Some scholars, for example A. Philips, on the basis of Deut 22:29 have concluded that the bride-price had become standardized at fifty shekels. See Philips, "Another Look at Adultery," 9. But DeVaux rightly sees that Deut 22:29 speaks of a penalty for raping a

Neufeld[76] has argued that the idea behind the payment of *mohar* was *de facto* purchase. He supports his view by referring to three OT passages which apparently point to buying a wife: Genesis 31:14–16, Hosea 3:2 and Ruth 4:10. However, his view has been challenged by Driver and Miles who comment on these passages,

> In the first (Gen. xxxi 14–16) Leah and Rachel say of Laban that "he hath sold us" (Hebr. מְכָרָנוּ), but they mean only that he has got rid of them like so many slave-girls, and a protest of indignant women is no evidence of legal custom. In the second (Hos. iii 2) Hosea says of his wife that "I bought her (Hebr. אֶכְּרֶהָ) to me for fifteen pieces of silver" plus other goods; but she seems to have been a faithless concubine as Neufeld admits in a subsequent passage (op. cit. 125 n. 1). In the third (Ru. iv 10) Boaz speaks of Ruth as one "whom I have purchased" (Hebr. קָנִיתִי), but the Hebrew verb here used does not necessarily import purchase but may refer to any mode of acquisition.[77]

With reference to the passage from Ruth others support the view of purchase.[78] Comparing this passage and its use of the verb קנה with Mishnah Kiddushin 1:1 they concluded that it must signify "purchase to be one's wife."[79] Weiss, however, studying both the Mishnah and other non-biblical Jewish writings where the verb is used, claimed that קנה always included all manner of acquisition and was used for stylistic uniformity.[80] He concludes,

> What applies to Mishnaic Hebrew may also be true of biblical usage. The root קנה is ill-suited for normal use in connection with regular marriage because of its predominant connotation of purchase. Hence, the technical term for betrothal in the Bible

---

virgin so that the "ordinary *mohar* must have been less," (*Ancient Israel*,. 26). Other OT passages, such as Exod 21:32; Lev 27:4–5, deal either with a penalty for the death of a female servant or the value paid on the fulfillment of vows so they do not indicate the real price paid for a bride. Rabinowitz is of the opinion that on the basis of comparison of Exod 22:15–16 and Deut 22:29 we can conclude that the biblical *mohar* was fifty shekels of silver, similarly to one Demotic marriage contract which is dated in the year 176 BCE and Mishnah Ketubot 1:2. See his "Marriage Contracts," 93, 93 n.9.

76. *Ancient Hebrew Marriage*, 98 n.2.

77. *Babylonian Laws*, I: 263 n.4.

78. E.g., L. Ginzberg and J. N. Epstein who are referred to in Weiss, "The Use of קנה," 244–48.

79. Ibid., 244.

80. Ibid., 247–48.

is ארש, and for marriage נשא, לקח אשה. However, when marriage (or betrothal) is discussed in conjunction with salable objects (like the belongings of Elimelech, etc., or the field of Naomi), the biblical Hebrew, just as Mishnaic, uses a term which will embrace the latter as well; hence, the term קניתי in Ruth 4:10. The usage is merely stylistic and devoid of any institutional significance.[81]

Because of the above problems with the purchase theory scholars started to explain the *mohar* along other lines. They observed that it did not belong to the father, but was a kind of security for the woman in case her husband died.[82] It was suggested that it was not a price paid for property but the gift which sealed a contract between the families of a bridegroom and a bride so that the wife was not bought or sold like a slave, or concubine.[83] As Grace Emmerson shows, the term *mohar* occurs only three times in the Jewish Testament, in Gen 34:12; Exod 22:17 and in 1 Sam 18:25 which do not prove the case for bride-purchase but, rather, refer to marital gifts.[84] She adds,

> The only instances where the language of buying and selling is used in connection with marriage are the requirement that the seducer should pay money (*šāqāl kesep*) equivalent to the marriage present if he is *not* permitted to marry the girl (Exod. 22.17), the angry words of Leah and Rachel who accuse their father of having sold them and "used up our money" (Gen. 31.15), and Boaz' statement that he has bought (*qānîtî*) Ruth as his wife (Ruth 4.10), although Ruth was clearly no unwilling, passive partner in the arrangement, but had largely taken the initiative. What is in fact purchased is the inheritance on which Ruth has a claim for a potential heir. Thereby the inheritance and the marriage are linked together.[85]

According to Mosaic legislation a father could sell his daughter as a servant (Exod 21:7–11), but it cannot be concluded that giving a girl to become someone's wife would be the same. The complaint of Rachel and

---

81. Ibid., 248.
82. Plummer, "Bride," I: 326. Cf. DeVaux, *Ancient Israel*, 27; Burrows, "Social Institutions of Israel," 135; and Paterson, "Marriage," 270.
83. Burrows, "Social Institutions of Israel," 135. For discussion see DeVaux, *Ancient Israel*, 27. Cf. Emmerson, "Women in Ancient Israel," 382.
84. "Women in Ancient Israel," 382–83.
85. Ibid.

The Divine Marriage and the Institution of Marriage

Leah (Gen 31:15) is thus justified because their father wrongly treated them like objects which could be sold to his own advantage.

It seems also that too much weight has been put on the word בַּעַל (owner: with the following genitive, lord, husband) in order to prove that the Israelite wife was the property of her husband, thus concluding that she was bought like other things.[86] Such a view is supported, for example, by Paterson who referring to Tristram's work[87] claims that an Israelite father, like an Arabic father, regarded his daughters "much as he would his sheep or cattle, selling them for a greater or less price, according to his rank and fortune and their beauty."[88] But Paterson's conclusion seems to be an example of reading back one culture with its customs into another or, to put it in other way, reading Jewish Scriptures through the spectacles of contemporary Arabic culture. Although there may be similarities between many Semitic cultures we need to study them on their own and then try to point out the common customs. Moreover, there is no real evidence within Israel's canonical writings to support bride purchase, except maybe for the case of Laban (cf. Gen 31:15) which was mentioned earlier. Paterson himself accepts that what he said concerning the status of Israelite woman in general does not fit the whole OT data. Thus he needs to make a distinction between the social classes for women of the wealthier strata of society who had greater liberty of action.[89] Then he again needs to relax his bold statement concerning the status of Jewish woman, for the wives of the patriarchs obviously had more value to their husbands than sheep or cattle had for their master![90] Paterson claimed that the bride-price eventually became money which "should be appropriated to ensure the comfort and security of the bride."[91] But Paterson maintains that originally women were sold like any other property which fails to consider that if there was a real business transaction why should the seller give the money back to the property which was just sold. It would be rather difficult to see how these examples sustain

---

86. Part of the argument says that because the Decalogue in Exod 20:17 lists wife among other properties she certainly was the property of the man, therefore it is not unlikely that he purchased or bought her. See, for example, Paterson, "Marriage," 265.

87. *Eastern Customs*, 92. London: 1894.

88. Paterson, "Marriage," 270. The quotation from Tristram following Paterson.

89. Ibid., 265. He gives two examples from 1 Sam 25:18 and 2 Kgs 4:22.

90. Ibid. Cf. Gen 21:10 and 27:13.46. Examples his.

91. Ibid., 270.

Paterson's thesis that a woman in ancient Israel was a mere thing to sell and to buy.

Emmerson observes concerning the word בַּעַל that it would be a mistake to use it in order to prove that a woman was her husband's property since, "it is the word in its context which determines meaning, and the transfer of crude ideas of ownership from one context to another is inadmissible."[92] It is often forgotten that there is another word describing husband, אִישׁ which together with the word אִשָּׁה points to the equality of man and woman or husband and wife (e.g., Gen 2:23).[93] When we look at the Israelite ideal of marriage expressed in the divine marriage metaphors of Hosea 1–3[94] and/or Jeremiah 2:2 "the crude idea of ownership is entirely inappropriate here."[95]

To the above we can add two observations made by Mace:

1. Marriage by purchase is "virtually a contradiction in terms." Truly purchase cannot be marriage.
2. From a sociological point of view, marriage is an older institution than purchase, "and cannot therefore be derived from the latter."[96]

These conclusions are based on the conviction that there was a sharp distinction between wives and slaves, or concubines; that Hosea's use of marriage as a symbol of God's covenant implied a free agreement between the two parties; that a married woman did not lose all connection with her father's family; and finally, that the bride's father gave his daughter a dowry and therefore did not merely exchange value for value.[97]

It seems that the *mohar* in Israel was a present sealing the marriage, although it is not certain that the idea of compensation for loss of a worker stood behind it because, as we have seen earlier, the money belonged to the bride and was her security to ensure her comfort.[98] It

---

92. "Women in Ancient Israel," 382.
93. Bratsiotis, "אִישׁ אִשָּׁה," I: 226–27. Cf. Hamilton, "Marriage," IV: 568.
94. In the case of Hosea 3:2 the woman was bought probably as a faithless concubine.
95. Emmerson, "Women in Ancient Israel," 382.
96. *Babylonian Laws*, I: 171.
97. Ibid., 169.
98. In favor of the compensation view see DeVaux, *Ancient Israel*, 27; and Emmerson, "Women in Ancient Israel," 383, referring to C. Meyers, "The Roots of

seems that the *mohar* was closely associated with the wife's inheritance, which she could claim for a potential heir.

Betrothal among the Jews of old was much more serious than engagement today.[99] A betrothed woman was in many respects treated like a wife and any unfaithfulness on her part before the wedding took place was regarded as adultery and the Mosaic Law prescribed the death penalty for such offences (Deut 22:23, 24; cf. Lev 20:10), although the law was somehow relaxed in practice on behalf of divorce.[100]

Some time after betrothal the wedding followed.[101] There is very little information concerning wedding ceremonies in the OT but some have tried to reconstruct them using various sources of different genres.[102] The wedding was an occasion for gladness and rejoicing (Jer 7:34; 16:9, etc.). The proper marriage began with fetching the bride from her family house to take her to the house of the bridegroom.[103] That took the form of a procession. The bridegroom wearing a diadem (Song 3:11) in the company of his friends marched to his bride's house in order to bring her to his own house. The bride was dressed in a garment decorated with gold and jewels, and veiled, and followed the bridegroom on the way to his house in the company of friends of her youth (Song 4:1, 3; 6:7; Ps 45:14, 15). People participating in the procession sang love songs, danced and shouted, rejoicing on the occasion. After the arrival at the bridegroom's house the marriage feast could last even for seven days. It started when

---

Resurrection: Women in Early Israel," *BA* 41 (1978), 98. Mace, *Babylonian Laws*, I: 170–72. Pace Neufeld, *Ancient Hebrew Marriage*, 98, who argues that the girl sold, by her earlier services, had already repaid the value of her upbringing. See also Burrows, "Social Institutions of Israel," 135, who sees both sides of the argument.

99. Plummer, "Bride," I: 326.

100. Paterson, "Marriage," 273 who quotes an important remark by Lightfoot, "I do not remember that I have anywhere, in the Jewish Pandect, met with an example of a wife punished for adultery with death." Likewise, McKeating, "Sanctions Against Adultery," 59, says, "My conclusion therefore stands that we have no instance of biblical law on adultery actually being put into effect." Cf. Paterson, "Marriage," 271.

101. In general there was no need for an interval of time between betrothal and marriage and once the *mohar* had been paid a man could take a girl to his house. Later, in Talmudic times this interval became obligatory (Kethuboth, 57). See Mace, *Babylonian Laws*, I: 174.

102. Ibid., 178.

103. See Plummer, "Bride," I: 326; DeVaux, *Ancient Israel*, 33; and Paterson, "Marriage," 271.

the wedding supper took place (Gen 29:27; Judg 14:12).[104] The marriage supper after the procession was most probably the marriage ceremony itself.[105] By the end of the supper the bride came to a nuptial chamber where the marriage was consummated on the first night (Gen 29:23; cf. Tob 8:1).

The Institution of Best Man in the OT

The story of Samson's marriage (Judg 14) indicates that one of the bridegroom's friends/companions (Judg 14:11)[106] during the wedding festival was the best-man.[107] After Samson became angry and left the wedding scene which was at the wife's house,[108] she was given to his best-man in spite of the strong tradition which did not allow the best-man to take his friend's bride as wife (Judg 14:20).[109]

The Institution of Divorce in the OT

A man could divorce his wife in OT Israel. This was permissible on the basis of the Mosaic legislation itself (Deut 24:1). A repudiated woman received a bill of divorce and was sent away.[110] As was shown above, the obvious reason for a divorce was unfaithfulness on the part of the wife and this was the only ground according to the renowned sage Shammai of the first century BCE.[111] But Deut 24:1 was a good excuse for a man to

---

104. DeVaux, *Ancient Israel*, 34. Cf. Paterson, "Marriage," 272.

105. Paterson, "Marriage," 272, says, "The view is supported by the fact that at a late period the feast was treated as so essential a part of the proceedings that γάμος stands equally for the marriage and the supper (Mt 22:4)."

106. In normal cases the bridegroom's companions were from his own community. But Samson was given thirty companions from among the Philistines. This was probably because people at the wedding were afraid of Samson as some of the Greek manuscripts suggest. So Moore, *Judges*, 334.

107. van Selms, "Best Man," 71–75.

108. The custom in that time was, however, different. It is an exception that the wedding feast took place at the home of the bride's parents. See Moore, *Judges*, 334. Moore, explaining the wedding customs in the time of Judges, says, "The marriage of Samson is the only instance in the O.T. in which the bride remains in her father's house, and the husband lives with her or visits her there;" although he adds in the same sentence that, "such unions were probably not uncommon in early Israel." See Ibid., 340.

109. van Selms, "Best Man," 71–72, 74.

110. See Paterson, "Marriage," 274. Also DeVaux, *Ancient Israel*, 34–35. Cf. Rabinowitz, "The 'Great Sin,'" 73.

111. Which according to Rabinowitz is the proper interpretation of Deut 24:1.

send his wife away. It allowed divorce if the wife prepared a meal badly or simply because "the husband preferred another woman."[112] This liberal approach to the Mosaic Law was developed by the first-century BCE Mishnaic sage Hillel.

There were several restrictions on the law of divorce. For example, a man could not divorce his wife if he falsely accused her of not being a virgin at the time of the wedding (Deut 22:13–19) or he could not divorce a woman he married after violating her (Deut 22:28–29). Although divorces took place for different reasons, OT wisdom literature and the prophets call husbands to conjugal fidelity (Prov 5:15–19; Eccl 9:9; Mal 2:14–15) and Mal 2:14–15 points out that marriage is a covenant which makes the two one and that God hates divorce (v. 16).[113]

Although the OT does not mention any marriage contract, the fact that it mentions a "bill of divorcement" may suggest "that a written statement was employed at the inception of marriage as well as at the termination."[114] Marriage contracts were probably known to the Jews at Elephantine colony in the fifth century BCE as well as to the post-exilic Israelites living in Palestine, as the book of Tobias suggests (cf. 7:13–14).[115] Yet, it would be difficult to point with certainty to their historical and legal origins.

CONCLUSIONS

In this chapter we have presented examples of *hieros gamos* in Semitic cultures of the ANE. We saw also that there is possibility that Hosea could use Canaanite fertility cult imagery and adapt it to Israel's theology thus introducing the metaphor of marriage of Yahweh and his people. We indicated, however, that even if the prophet used Canaanite mythology he transformed it to fit Jewish beliefs. However, to decide whether there

---

See, "The 'Great Sin,'" 73. He shows that adultery was regarded as a "great sin" both in Egyptian marriage contracts of the 9 century BCE and Jewish law as presented in the Mosaic legislation.

112. DeVaux, *Ancient Israel*, 34.

113. See the discussion in Hugenberger, *Marriage as a Covenant*.

114. Mace, *Babylonian Laws*, I: 174–75. He says that by Talmudic times the marriage contract was certainly the custom in Israel and that it was the bridegroom who made it (cf. Qiddushim 9a). Due consideration of this theory is also found in Neufeld, *Ancient Hebrew Marriage*, 152–61.

115. See, for example, Ginsberg, "Aramaic Papyri from Elephantine," 222–23, 548–49. The book of Tobias was written in the third century BCE.

was real borrowing of ideas from Semitic cultures by Hosea we need to consider his message in the next chapter.

We have also examined the institution of marriage in Ancient Near East and in Israel in particular. Semitic marriages resembled in many respects those of the Israelites. The bride-price was essentially to seal a marriage contract among the Semites. There is, however, no real evidence as to bride-purchase in Israelite culture, i.e., it seems very unlikely that women were actually sold by their fathers and bought by their husbands to-be. The *mohar* in Israel was rather a seal of the wife's inheritance, which also was passed on her offspring.

Betrothed women were treated almost like wives in the ANE and acts of adultery on their part were often capital offences. Marriages were usually arranged by the fathers of a prospective couple and that reflected the father's headship over his family. Betrothal was the first stage of matrimony. It was followed, in some instances at least, by an interval of time during which the bride stayed usually with her parents until she was brought to her husband's house where the completion of the marriage took place. The wedding ceremonies, usually at the bride's parents' house, lasted for a similar period of time (seven days?) and the marriage itself was consummated with the sexual act. Husbands were legally bound to provide for their wives' well-being and if the husband died, the wife was secured with the money he paid to her father at the betrothal.

Having seen the nature of Semitic marriages and issues relating to this institution, and the *hieros gamos* of Semitic literature, we shall focus in the next chapter on the marriage of Israel and God.

3

The Divine Marriage Metaphor in the Old Testament Prophets

INTRODUCTION

IN THE PREVIOUS CHAPTER we looked at *hieros gamos* in Ancient Near Eastern writings. We discovered that the divine marriage of the Semites was strongly associated with the fertility of land. In most of the cases considered the marriage between a god and a goddess was understood to be the basis of agricultural fruitfulness and human fertility. Thus it was the very basis of the nation's survival and prosperity. We have also remarked that, although *hieros gamos* in the Hebrew Bible may be a borrowing from Semitic cultures, an important transformation took place. Therefore in this chapter we will examine the metaphor of divine marriage in the OT prophets and concentrate especially on Hosea, who was the first to use and develop it in the OT.[1] We believe this study will help us to explain differences between Israel's and other Semitic divine marriages.

THE DIVINE MARRIAGE IN HOSEA

OT scholars agree that the eighth century BCE prophet Hosea was the first to use and develop the concept of the marriage of Yahweh and Israel. Introduced by him, it became the means prophets employed to express important truths concerning the history of Israel in the land of Canaan.

---

1. Due to space limitations of this work, we will not be able to discuss other texts in the OT, which allegedly employ the figure of marriage of Yahweh and Israel. Thus, even the instances of Ps 45 and Song of Songs will be excluded from our examination. We have only enough space to consider the explicit uses of the metaphor in Hosea and the Major Prophets.

The metaphor helped them to reflect on some of the great themes of their religious tradition (e.g., guidance out of Egypt, in the wilderness, into Palestine, but especially the life of Israel in the land).[2]

The prophet was born in and ministered to the northern kingdom. Of special interest to us are the first three chapters of Hosea, where he introduces the metaphor of Yahweh as the husband of his people, something which commentators regard as the most important theme of the whole book.[3] Since scholars have struggled with the data in these opening chapters, it is important to review the different approaches that are taken to their subject matter.

Continuity or Discontinuity in Hosea 1–3?

Chapters 1 and 3 of the prophecy are stories from the prophet's life.[4] These symbolize the love Yahweh has for Israel. In chapter 2 Hosea speaks of the relationship between Yahweh and his wife.[5] However, scholars disagree on the relation between the symbolic acts of the prophet in chapters 1 and 3 and their connection to chapter 2.

Part of the problem with chapters 1 and 3 is that they do not show us the complete picture of Hosea's life. The question often asked concerns the women mentioned in these chapters. Are they all references to Hosea's partner?[6] If the answer is positive then another question arises. Are the accounts parallel or consequent? If there are two different women, who is the woman of chapter 3? To these we can add further questions concerning Gomer in chapter 1. Was she promiscuous at the

---

2. Hall, "Origin of the Marriage Metaphor," 169.

3. Wolff, *Hosea*, xxvi. It is worth mentioning that the prophet employs a number of other metaphors throughout the book in order to present to his audience different aspects of Yahweh's dealing with his people. Cf. ibid., xxiv.

4. Modern scholars such as Mays treat these chapters as narratives of Hosea's actual experience, not as his visions (the view found especially among the old commentators). Mays explains, "The very character of prophetic symbolism requires that the divine word be actualized in a representative event." See his *Hosea*, 23. Cf. Davies, *Hosea*, 79.

5. So e.g., Waterman, "Hosea," 100–109. He says that chapter 2 is "devoted entirely to Israel as the faithless spouse." However, Hornsby does not recognize in Hosea 1–3 any reference to Yahweh's wife. She views Israel as an independent prostitute whom Yahweh tries to possess by force. See her article, "Re-reading Gomer," 115–28.

6. I have so far tried to avoid the word "wife" because there are some who reject the claim that Hosea married Gomer in chapter 1. So Davies, *Hosea*, 89–90. According to him Gomer was a mere prostitute with whom Hosea had sex in order to raise children.

time Hosea married her? Did Hosea really marry her? Did she actually become adulterous? These are but a few of the questions asked concerning Gomer. As Rowley has commented,

> The marriage of Hosea has been a perennial subject of discussion amongst scholars, and the problems surrounding it are such that it is improbable that agreement will ever be reached.[7]

The predominant view among scholars is that chapters 1 and 3 relate to different episodes of Hosea's life.[8] Although chapter 3 is of earlier origin, and mostly written by Hosea himself,[9] the events of chapter 1 come first in his life/ministry.[10] The majority of scholars also recognize that Hosea did marry Gomer of chapter 1.[11] Less agreement exists over the identity of the woman in chapter 3. Wolff thinks it could have been Gomer and claims that in the course of time she left Hosea and became the legal wife of another man.[12] Mays, Rowley, Andersen and Freedman, Kaiser, and Waterman, also think that Gomer is probably the woman in chapter 3.[13] However Batten, Tushingham, and McDonald, reject this interpretation.[14]

---

7. Rowley, "Marriage of Hosea," 66.

8. So Davies, *Hosea*, 79–80. But see Rowley, "Marriage of Hosea," 71 n.1, who mentions a few scholars who have argued for parallelism between chapters 1 and 3.

9. For consideration of the textual unity of chapter 3 and the question of redactionism see Emmerson, *Hosea*, 13–14, 101. Cf. Wolff, *Hosea*, xxiii, xxix; Andersen and Freedman, *Hosea*, 118. Also Waterman, "Hosea," 101. But Batten, "Message and Marriage," 257–73, argues that chapter 3 is not Hosean; see esp. 270–73. So Haupt, "Erring Spouse," 41–53, arguing for the post-Exilic authorship of chapter 3. See also pp. 47–48. Cf. North, "Hosea's Marital Problems," 128–29.

10. So Wolff, *Hosea*, xxix, 9–13. Mays, *Hosea*, e.g., 2–3, 54–55. Rowley, "Marriage of Hosea," 70–72, 88. Davies, *Hosea*, 88. The last claims that chapter 1 refers to the events which happened c. 750 BCE onwards, whereas chapter 3 relates the period c. 730–720 BCE. Further, Andersen and Freedman, *Hosea*, 116, 119.

11. Wolff, *Hosea*, xxii, 12–14; Mays, *Hosea*, 23–25; Rowley, "Marriage of Hosea," 90–94; McDonald, "Marriage of Hosea," 153–54; North, "Hosea's Marital Problems," 129; MacIntosh, *Hosea*, 9; Waterman, "Hosea," 101; Kaiser, *Hard Sayings*, 216; Tushingham, "A Reconsideration of Hosea," 157. Against this view, in recent years, see Davies, *Hosea*, 88–91 and Hornsby, "Re-reading Gomer," 118–25. Both argue that the women of chapters 1 and 3 are mere prostitutes whom Hosea never married but with whom he had sex.

12. *Hosea*, xxii, 59–60.

13. Mays, *Hosea*, 55; Rowley, "Marriage of Hosea," 90–95; Andersen and Freedman, *Hosea*, 292–301; Kaiser, *Hard Sayings*, 219; Waterman, "Hosea," 101.

14. Batten, "Message and Marriage," 272; Tushingham, "A Reconsideration of Hosea," 156; McDonald, "Marriage of Hosea," 155.

While both parties are able to provide good arguments to support their conclusions, it must not be forgotten what the book is about. Emmerson states that a successful reconstruction of Hosea's life does not bring one automatically to the heart of Hosea's message. She says,

> ...the narrative is not concerned primarily with the prophet's life and circumstances, but is the account of symbolic actions (four in ch. 1 and one in ch. 3) performed by Hosea as the means of proclaiming Yahweh's word to the nation.[15]

She continues,

> Whatever the relationship of chs. 1 and 3 to each other, they are not the means by which the prophet came to know of Yahweh's judgment or his love. They are the proclamation of that judgment and that love in dramatic fashion to the nation. Had the narratives been concerned with the means of revelation to the prophet, greater attention must have been paid to details of the prophet's experience.[16]

Emmerson thus sees in the material of chapters 1 and 3 prophetic proclamation, not biography. Similarly, Mays regards both chapters as stories of symbolic acts which are not concerned with Hosea's biography. They are prophetic messages from Yahweh.[17] He says,

> Modern questions formed out of legitimate curiosity about just what happened are frustrated and will never be answered with final certainty because the data are missing.[18]

Therefore, any reconstruction of the prophet's life is doomed to fail because of the lack of evidence. Nevertheless, we can assume that the chapters under consideration are consequent stories of Hosea's life.

While there has been much debate concerning the relationship of chapters 1 and 3, scholars have paid growing attention to the thematic unity of chapter 2 with the preceding and the following passages. Thus, for example, Wolff sees the relationship between chapter 2 and the content of chapter 1 and claims that the sayings of chapter 2 were referring

---

15. *Hosea*, 17.
16. Ibid., 18.
17. *Hosea*, 3, cf. 23.
18. Ibid., 24.

to the time in which chapter 1 was set, i.e., c. 750 BCE.[19] Then, he also explains that chapter 3 should be understood in terms of chapter 2 and not 1 because chapter 3 is "the immediate continuation of chapter 2, since it corresponds completely with its theme."[20] Waterman states that the content of the first part of chapter 2 (vv. 2–13; MT 4–15) fits Hosea's family life in chapter 1 and chapter 3 follows that.[21] Andersen and Freedman argue that chapter 2 develops the thought of chapter 1 and that chapter 3 explains what actually happened after the scene of chapter 2.[22] Although Davies does not agree with this common approach, he highlights the one guiding feature, which characterizes scholarly approach as to the relationship between chapter 2 and chapters 1 and 3. He says,

> Chapter 2 portrays the whole relationship between Yahweh and Israel as a marriage broken and restored, and the narratives which flank it have been assumed to combine to make a similar story. It may seem that ch. 2 only makes sense if Hosea's marriage, separation and reconciliation were there in the background to suggest the pattern.[23]

This widely accepted view seems the most reasonable to us as well.

In fact, there is no end to the discussion on Hosea's marriage, as we have already noticed. Likewise, the whole issue of the transition of particular verses in chapter 2 is yet unresolved.[24] Because of this it seems right to us to follow Andersen and Freedman in their assumption that,

---

19. *Hosea*, 33.

20. Ibid., 59. But Chavasse, *Bride of Christ*, 28 n.2, claims Hos 3 should come between chapters 1 and 2.

21. "Hosea," 102, 104. Cf. Batten, "Message and Marriage," 256. He says that 1:1–9 must be connected to 2:2–13 and chapter 3 to 2:14–23.

22. *Hosea*, 116–18. They believe chapter 2 refers both to Hosea's own situation and his action towards his wife as well as to Yahweh and his dealings with Israel. Thus Hosea's family experience is interwoven with the experience of Yahweh and his people. See pp. 218, 220. So, the story of Hosea's life is interlaced with an oracle of Yahweh. But Batten argues against the view that 2:2–13 refers to Gomer as well as to Israel. See, "Message and Marriage," 269. Similarly, Waterman, "Hosea," 102, says that chapter 2 is entirely devoted to Israel, the faithless spouse, and Gomer nowhere appears. See also Rowley, "Marriage of Hosea," 70, who says that in chapter 2 Hosea does not have in mind his wife and children but Israel.

23. *Hosea*, 91. Cf. 91 n. 30.

24. See e.g., Wolff, *Hosea*, 35. But pace Emmerson, *Hosea*, 23. Cf. Clines, "Structure and Interpretation," I: 83–103.

> In dealing with cc. 1–3 in their present form we proceed on the assumption that it has been arranged deliberately and should make sense when rendered and treated in consecutive fashion.²⁵

Therefore we shall turn to analyzing chapter 2 on the assumption that its meaning can be interpreted on the basis of its present form. Where necessary, text critical notes will be made.

The Nature of Yahweh's Marriage

SITZ IM LEBEN

We have noticed that chapter 2 refers to the events following 750 BCE and that therefore it stands in close relation to the narrative of chapter 1. At that time Jeroboam II was the king over the northern kingdom of Israel (Hos 1:1).²⁶ This was a time of prosperity in the land as chapter 2 itself indicates (abundant prosperity: vv. 5, 8, 9, and a prosperous cult: vv. 11, 13).²⁷ However, the people of the land turned their backs on Yahweh to worship Baals. They had not forsaken Israel's religion as such, but rather, in their practices, they mixed Yahwism with Baalism. The long process of religious syncretism in the northern kingdom had reached its climax.²⁸ People worshipped the Baals as deities of the land (Hos 2:13, 17;²⁹ 9:10; 13:1), whom they regarded as responsible for its fertility (2:5, 8, 12; 7:14). They involved themselves in sexual rites associated with the fertility cult similar to those of Canaan (4:11–14), which were forbidden according to the Deuteronomic law (Deut 23:17). They sacrificed to Baals in order to secure their blessings for themselves (Hos 4:13; cf. 8:11, 13; 10:1).³⁰ Therefore Yahweh says, "My people are bent on backsliding from me. Though they call to the Most High, none at all exalt him"

---

25. *Hosea*, 119.

26. Mays thinks that the speech of chapter 2 must have been delivered during the final years of Jeroboam II. See *Hosea*, 36.

27. Cf. Emmerson, *Hosea*, 19. Mays, *Hosea*, 36.

28. Mays, *Hosea*, 11. Emmerson, *Hosea*, 26, explains that it is clear from 8:2 that the nature of Israel's apostasy was not an open disregard of Yahweh in favor of Baal, but the confusion of two different views of the deity. See also Fensham, "Marriage Metaphor in Hosea," 73.

29. Throughout the chapter we will follow the English Bible in numerating the verses in Hos 2.

30. Mays, *Hosea*, 11.

(11:7 NKJV). He is about to bring judgment (1:4, 6, 9), but he still struggles for the soul of Israel (chapter 2). Mays says,

> All the terrible suffering which he brings on Israel is not so much judicial and legal punishment as the assault of his love as husband and father of the people upon their unfaithfulness.[31]

Hosea's actions are to symbolize Yahweh's dealings with his promiscuous people.[32] For the prophet there is but one God, who revealed himself in the Exodus from Egypt. He alone is to be revered (12:9–14). In this context of religious unfaithfulness Hosea employs the metaphor of divine marriage.

STRUCTURE

Most commentators divide chapter 2 (vv. 2–23) into two main sections. The first unit, vv. 2–15, is a series of Yahweh's speeches where he is pictured as the husband (2, 7b, 13, 15) of his unfaithful wife Israel (2, 5, 7, 12–13, 14).[33] The second unit is a "loosely knit series of sayings and fragments of sayings."[34] It is further divided into three minor sections by the phrase "on that day" (vv. 16–17, 18–20, 21–23). There is also a thematic change in the second part of the chapter. While the unfaithful wife is the subject throughout vv. 2–15, vv. 16–23 refer subsequently to Baal (16–17), covenant of peace (18), covenant of marriage (19–20), answer (21–22), and divine covenant (23).[35] Nevertheless, as shown by Clines,[36] the whole chapter resembles the same conceptual pattern of *belonging*

---

31. Ibid., 14. Pace Fensham, "Marriage Metaphor in Hosea," 71–78, who believes that the picture is one of legal judgment and punishment as well as that of abrogation and termination of the Sinaitic covenant. But why then is God still interested in winning Israel back (2:6, 9–13)? Cf. Kruger, "Israel, the Harlot," 111.

32. Wolff, *Hosea*, 10–11.

33. Ibid., 32. Cf. Clines, "Structure and Interpretation," 83, who recognizes the claims of the "kerygmatic" unity of these verses. But Brueggemann, *Theology*, 546–47, divides chapter 2 into two thematic units. Vv. 2–13 deal with Israel "under curse" and vv. 14–23 deal with Israel "under blessing." He explains, "In the first part Yahweh had given to Israel the abundance of creation (v. 8). But now, in rage, Yahweh will withdraw the blessings of creation, so that Israel's life is no longer viable (vv. 9, 12)." "In the second part of the poem Yahweh is moved by passion to allure Israel back to a relationship. Along the acts of allurement is a covenant with the elements of creation, the one lost in 2:3 (2:18)."

34. Wolff, *Hosea*, 47.

35. This is according to Wolff, ibid., 47.

36. "Structure and Interpretation," 88ff.

and *not belonging* which is expressed in the language of marriage. Clines explains,

> *Belonging* is the crucial datum of the poem: Israel belongs to Yahweh, Yahweh belongs to Israel. But the poem begins at a point where the relationship of belonging has been negated: Israel has behaved as if she were no wife to Yahweh (היא לא אשתי, v. 2a),[37] and Yahweh is consequently unable to act as husband to Israel (ואנכי לא אישה, v. 2a). To be more exact, he can still exercise husbandly functions of authority over her, to the extent of stripping her of her gifts (vv. 3a, 9), or invoking legal processes against her. But this is not what Yahweh expects of marriage: he intends by marriage a 'speaking to the heart' of Israel (על לבה ודברתי, v. 14), and a loving response (ענה, v. 15b) from her, an intimate address with the term 'my husband' (אישי) rather than a respectful address with the term 'my lord' (בעלי, v. 16), and a permanent 'espousal' (cf. NAB) (וארשתיך, vv. 19 *bis*, 20) in which he will guarantee as bride-price integrity (JB) or salvation (Wolff), justice, unfailing devotion (NEB), love, and fidelity (NEB). Israel (or its offspring) is intended to belong to Yahweh as 'sown by God' (Jezreel), the beloved one (reversal of Lo-ruhamah), and 'my people, my kin' (עמי) (vv. 22–23).[38]

Thus we can assume that the whole chapter reflects the concept of Yahweh's marriage with Israel. Although commentators debate the proper order of the verses in chapter 2, there is no clear consensus. Because of this we will proceed to interpret the passage as it stands.

Analysis of the Metaphor

While there is a symbolism of Israel's apostasy from the religion of Yahweh in Hos 1:2 pictured by a woman's adultery[39] it is not until 2:2 that the metaphor of the marriage between Yahweh and Israel is introduced. However, the metaphor is used in a negative way to speak of a broken relationship, of a people who have gone astray from the covenant rela-

---

37. For convenience we change Hebrew numeration of the verses to English throughout the entire chapter. This also applies to the changes in the quotations therein.

38. Clines, "Structure and Interpretation," 89. Although we do not agree with every element of this interpretation, the approach shows the unity of thought in the chapter. This shows that marriage can be a unifying concept of the entire chapter.

39. North, "Hosea's Marital Problems," 129, says that Hosea's harlotrous wife symbolizes the land of Israel, just as the prostitute mother does in chapter 2.

tionship with their God.[40] As we have seen in chapter 2 above, marital unfaithfulness on the wife's part was a capital offence (cf. Lev 20:10), not only in Israel but in Semitic cultures in general. Despite this, the death sentence in Israel was most likely commuted to divorce (cf. Deut 24:1–4). This highlights the seriousness of the relationship in which a couple is involved. Religious apostasy destroys the intimacy of Yahweh's relationship with Israel, just as unfaithfulness destroys the intimacy of marriage. The nature of the covenant relationship thus becomes analogous to that of a marriage, or rather the ideal of marriage in the OT.[41]

Hosea used a number of different metaphors throughout the book. He speaks of Yahweh as a father watching over the first steps of his son Israel (Hos 11:1–2), as a physician (14:4; 7:1; 11:3), a shepherd (13:5), or as a hunter in his judgment (7:12), etc. But the metaphors are not merely decorative. They are an important revelation of Yahweh through Hosea. In Hosea's thought, the divine marriage becomes the story of Yahweh's experience with Israel in the land of Canaan, in the context of the covenant relationship.[42] The covenant at Sinai was in the prophet's mind a wedding between Yahweh and Israel, when he proposed to her and she agreed, "If you keep my covenant, you shall be my treasured possession among all the peoples. . . . You shall be to me a kingdom of priests and a holy nation. . . . all the people *responded* as one . . ." (Exod 19:5–6, 8).[43] Thus the prophet saw the covenantal mutual relationship as a marriage.

The metaphor is one of the most important in the book. Some scholars even believe it can be the central metaphor of the entire OT.[44] It explains the nature of the covenant and Yahweh's expectations concerning Israel. He "wants not only obedience or even the loyalty of His 'wife,' but her *loving* obedience and loyalty."[45] But, so far, Yahweh has to struggle for this kind of relationship since his wife turns to others. His people are

---

40. Yet, on the same metaphorical level, the abundance of Yahweh's marital love for his wife is also revealed as a positive aspect of the *hieros gamos*. See below.

41. Cf. Stienstra, *YHWH Is the Husband*, 95.

42. Cf. Mays, *Hosea*, 9.

43. Friedman, "Israel's Response," 202. Italics and translation his. Friedman here follows Ginzberg, *Legends of the Jews*, 6.36 n.200. Brewer, "Three Weddings," 15, also recognizes the event at Sinai as Yahweh's marriage. Brueggemann, *Theology*, 414–15, points to the Exodus-Sinai narrative as the origin of Yahweh's/husband's initial love for Israel. It was based on *hesed* of the Exodus rescue.

44. Wolff, *Hosea*, xxvi; Stienstra, *YHWH Is the Husband*, 97.

45. Stienstra, *YHWH Is the Husband*, 97.

promiscuous, like Hosea's wife (1:2),[46] and they have given themselves to "whoredom." Israel has become unfaithful to Yahweh. "The metaphor of 'the first husband' (2:7, 16) thus has the purpose of elucidating the accusation that Israel is guilty of whoredom and adultery."[47] Israel's adultery in Hos 2 has a religious character; it is committed with Baals (vv. 7, 10, 12, 13; cf. 4:12; 5:3, 7; 9:1).[48]

The metaphor employs different characters: a husband, his unfaithful wife, their children, and lovers of the wife and the mother. The husband is Yahweh (2:2, 7b, 13, 15); the unfaithful wife stands for the corporate people of Israel, although at times she is referred to as the land (2:3; cf. 1:2); the children are individual Israelites over against the corporate nation (2:2), but are also identified with the national guilt (2:4), and the lovers are the Baals (2:5, 7, 10, 12, 13), the gods of Canaan.[49]

The series of Yahweh's speeches (2:2–15) begins with the husband who calls upon the children to rebuke (NIV) their mother (2:2). The Hebrew verb רִיב[50] in verse 2 has led some exegetes to conclude that the scene takes place in a courtroom where Yahweh appears first as the plaintiff, who summons the accusing party for the beginning of the legal dispute.[51] Because the words, "For she is not my wife and I am not her husband," in this verse correspond to 1:9,[52] the statement is regarded as

46. אֵשֶׁת זְנוּנִים the plural abstract form refers to the personal quality of a woman, not to her activity. Such an understanding of the abstract plural derives from Hebrew grammar rules. See Kautzsch, *Hebrew Grammar*, 417. Cf. Kaiser, *Hard Sayings*, 218. Pace Hornsby, "Re-reading Gomer," 119–20, and Davies, *Hosea*, 89. Whether Gomer committed adultery is a question of exegesis which depends on the approach to chapters 2 and 3. However, Andersen and Freedman explain that "It would be a mistake in analyzing the word *znwnym* to separate the idea from the action, since these are organically related in biblical thought. Anyone described as 'a promiscuous wife' is engaged in activity consistent with her character, which is expressed by the word *znwnym*." See, *Hosea*, 157. They claim that the phrase points to a wife which is promiscuous (ibid., 162).

47. Wolff, *Hosea*, xxvi.

48. Thompson, "Israel's Lovers," 477 n.5. In Ezek 16, 23 the adultery is of a political nature. See p. 476. Cf. Batten, "Message and Marriage," 260.

49. Mays, *Hosea*, 35–36. Wolff, *Hosea*, 31. Examples of Canaanite gods are given in chapter 2 above.

50. The word רִיב can have legal connotations. Thus it could be translated "accuse" or "bring charges."

51. Wolff, *Hosea*, 33; Mays, *Hosea*, 36. Cf. Stienstra, *YHWH Is the Husband*, 86–87.

52. It is argued that this verse points to the end of the covenant. It is the reverse of a covenant formula (cf. Exod 6:7) which says that the covenant in no longer in force, that Yahweh divorces Israel (2:2). Wolff, *Hosea*, 21. Mays, *Hosea*, 29. Ehrlich, "Hosea 1:9,"

The Divine Marriage Metaphor in the Old Testament Prophets   71

a divorce formula.[53] As a result of this divorce Israel suffers famine and nakedness (2:3–13).[54] Judah is still married to God (cf. 1:4–8). Yet, on "the day of Jezreel" Israel and Judah will be united and reconciled to God (1:11; 2:14–23), and then they will again together call God 'my husband.'[55] This also finds support in other parts of the book of Hosea (e.g., 9:15).

Mays, however, while acknowledging the character of a legal proceeding, rejects the idea of divorce in 2:2.[56] The point of chapter 2, he says, is not divorce, but reconciliation. The legal style "is used as clothing for indictments of guilt and announcements of punishment in the more usual prophetic fashion."[57] There is no strong evidence for an oral divorce formula in OT times in Israel.[58] It is true that Israel has broken the covenant (1:9), which is represented by the figure of marriage. But Mays explains,

---

15, also says there is a negation of covenant formula, "You are my people and I am your God," in this verse.

53. Wolff, *Hosea*, 33. Brewer, "Three Weddings," 4, says that God eventually divorced Israel using the Ancient Near Eastern divorce formula, "You are not my wife and I am not your husband." Ortlund, *Whoredom*, 54–56, 56 n. 23, states that divorce takes place but only for the people of Hosea's generation. Thus Yahweh is the ex-husband of this generation of Israelites. Fensham, "Marriage Metaphor in Hosea," 71–79, favors complete separation on the basis of Lo-Ammi in 1:9.

54. Some scholars have also suggested that uncovering could have been symbolic of divorce (Hos 2:10). Cf. Kruger, "Garment in Marriage," 82. But Kruger remarks also that Hos 2:3 in its contexts refers more to disgrace and humiliation than to divorce. See p. 82 n.19.

55. Brewer, "Three Weddings," 4. According to Deut 24:1–4 remarriage of a former spouse is prohibited. Brewer argues, however, that Judah has never been divorced and God's remarriage of Israel united with Judah does not violate the Deuteronomic law. See, pp. 4–5, 13–16. To the problem of Judah having two marriage covenants Brewer finds a solution in Paul. Because Christ's disciples died with him, the old marriage covenant ended with death (Rom 7:1–4). See pp. 22–23. However, Brueggemann, *Theology*, 223, claims concerning Deut 24:1–4 in connection with Hos 2:14, 19–20 that Yahweh "will override the old prohibition of Mosaic command against remarriage." He sees this as possible on the ground of an "extraordinary dialectic of freedom and passion in the character of Yahweh." See pp. 410–11.

56. *Hosea*, 36–38.

57. Ibid., 36.

58. Ibid., 37. The only piece of evidence consists perhaps of a "bill of divorcement" mentioned in Isa 50:1. Some scholars have signaled that cutting of the garment's hem or uncovering of the wife could symbolize divorce in the ANE. See Kruger, "Garment in Marriage," 79–86. However, the evidence in this case is not very strong either.

> The use of marriage as an analogy for the covenant provides a concentrated emphasis on the personal dimension, on the relation itself, which transcends the cultic and legal. This husband is not preoccupied with his legal rights to separation or the punishment of his guilty wife. He wants her back.[59]

Similarly, Andersen and Freedman reject the idea of divorce in 2:2. They argue against a setting in the courtroom because "there is no summons to witness, no invitation to defend the charge, no appeal to a vindicator."[60] It is, rather, the husband who takes the law into his own hands. They explain,

> 'She is not my wife and I am not her husband' ... is not a divorce formula. It means, 'We are no longer living together as husband and wife.' Thus the children must take up the matter with their mother.[61]

Furthermore, they do not view Hos 1:9 as formal dissolution of the covenant because Yahweh's covenant "nowhere makes provision for such an eventuality. Covenant-breaking on the part of Israel (unilateral withdrawal) calls for severe punishment."[62] This punishment maintains the covenant. Hosea's threats of punishment (1:4–5, 6, 9; cf. 2:3) point rather to the fact that reconciliation, not divorce, is in Yahweh's mind. If the real divorce took place the husband could no longer claim any rights over the divorced wife, nor could he remarry her (Deut 24:1–4).[63] But Yahweh

---

59. Ibid., 38. Andersen and Freedman claim that the correspondence between marriage metaphor and the covenant of Yahweh is not perfect in every detail. See *Hosea*, 220. But Brewer argues that the treaty covenant from Sinai is a parallel to a marriage covenant in the OT and therefore regarded as a legal reality. See "Three Weddings," 1–3. The divine marriage is not a mere metaphor but covenant reality. Therefore he would not agree with the claim that there is a lack of correspondence between marriage and covenant.

60. *Hosea*, 218. MacIntosh, *Hosea*, 41, also argues in favor of a family quarrel rather than a law court scene. He does not believe that the passage deals with divorce. For him the statement, "She is not my wife ... " is a gloss or editorial explanation.

61. Andersen and Freedman, *Hosea*, 220. They further explain that apart from the verb *rîb* "which can bear a technical meaning, the ensuing discourse does not reflect courtroom language. This word alone is not enough to shape the rest of the speech," (ibid., 221).

62. Ibid., 221. Pace Fensham, "Marriage Metaphor in Hosea," 74–78.

63. However, as we shall see below, the metaphor of divine marriage allows divorce on the metaphorical level. Then, it stands for separation as a result of exile. But even then it does not equal covenant dissolution. It rather symbolizes and stands for the negative aspect of God's covenant.

The Divine Marriage Metaphor in the Old Testament Prophets 73

wants to restore the broken relationship through discipline (2:14–20) and miraculously transform it into a first marriage (2:15).[64] The formula "she is not my wife and I am not her husband" expresses the estrangement of husband and wife and the motivation for Yahweh's action.[65] In Emmerson's view, "It stands as the remainder of a relationship which is still *de jure* but no longer *de facto*, for were the former no longer true there would be no basis for Yahweh's concern and for his action. The statement therefore describes not the finality of divorce but a broken relationship which needs to be restored."[66]

Thus Hos 2:2 introduces a reader to a broken covenant, a broken marriage. The guilty party is Israel. Yahweh wants his wife to repent of her harlotry. Her guilt is evident (cf. 2:5) but Yahweh's admonition through Hosea is to spare the punishment for her sins (2:2b; cf. Amos 3:7).[67] It is the children (individual Israelites) who are to do something concerning their mother's (national) guilt. They should expose their mother's error so that she may stop continuing in her whoredom and return to the marriage bond.[68] She should put away all the marks which make her a harlot.[69] If she refuses to do this, Yahweh as the wronged husband will severely punish her (2:3). He will "strip her naked and expose her, as in the day she was born."[70]

In the Israel of Old Testament times, clothing the wife was the obligation of the husband (Exod 21:10). As shown in Hos 2:9, it was Yahweh who provided clothing for his wife Israel (wool and flax). Nakedness as

---

64. Andersen and Freedman, *Hosea*, 222. Cf. Kruger, "Israel, the Harlot," 111. Clines, "Structure and Interpretation," 86, explains that Hos 2:14–15 speaks of Yahweh who "will love Israel out of her unfaithfulness, and in response to her harlotry will woo her to himself and renew his gifts to her." It seems to us that if he had divorced her these verses would not make much sense. See also Ringgren, "Marriage Motif," 425.

65. Emmerson, *Hosea*, 15.

66. Ibid., 15.

67. Cf. Wolff, *Hosea*, 33.

68. MacIntosh, *Hosea*, 40.

69. It is possible that some marks on the face manifested a woman's prostitution (cf. Jer 4:30; Ezek 23:40). In reality, the marks refer to Israel's malpractices in the Baal cult (cf. 2:13). See Kruger, "Israel, the Harlot," 109–10.

70. Although Wolff, *Hosea*, 34, sees in this undressing a divorce ceremonial there is no evidence for his conclusion. Andersen and Freedman counter-argue that in similar passages in Ezek 16 and 23 there is a great deal of stripping naked, but no question whatsoever of divorce appears (*Hosea*, 225).

such signified shame.⁷¹ Yahweh will expose Israel to shame if she does not stop her harlotries with Baal.⁷² But this stripping is a symbol of a literal drought of the land (the wife stands for the land in this verse), which will make it infertile, bare, dead (the wilderness is a land of death).⁷³ This shows who really has the power over fertility in the land. Yahweh has always been responsible for the land's/nation's fruitfulness and for the rain bringing this fertility: this was his blessing for covenant faithfulness on the part of Israel (e.g., Deut 28:4, 5, 8, 11, 12; cf. Hos 2:8). Israel's covenant-breaking brought the withdrawal of blessing (e.g., Deut 28:17, 18, 21–23, 24; cf. Hos 2:9). It is worth observing that the drought in Hos 2:3 links the metaphor of marriage with covenant curses (cf. Deut 28:24) and not the sanctions for marital unfaithfulness, which were death or divorce (Gen 38:24; Lev 20:10; Deut 22:23; 24:1–4). Later, verses 9, 12 show the devastation of 2:3b brought about by Yahweh.

The mother/land will die of drought if unrepentant, if she does not remove from the land the sanctuaries of Baal which are marks of her harlotry (2:2b).⁷⁴ In fact, the children themselves (individual Israelites) have to repent because they are guilty of the same sin as their mother (2:4). They are involved in the nation's religious apostasy and are children of her union with Baal.⁷⁵ Their very existence testifies against the nation's guilt, for they are called בְּנֵי זְנוּנִים.⁷⁶ They are also so closely tied

---

71. Kruger, "Israel, the Harlot," 111. Mays, *Hosea*, 38, notices that 'nakedness' may refer to the punishment of covenant breaking in the ANE.

72. Passages like this are of concern for the feminist theology movement. They view them as pictures of male violent authority over female, as biblical examples of pornographic propaganda against the dignity of woman, who is always in the wrong. See, for example, Brenner, "Pornoprophetics Revisited," 63–86. Stienstra, however, argues that this is "inevitable in the case of a metaphor in which the relationship between God and man is pictured as a marriage. If God were to be female, it would be the husband who was always in the wrong." See *Yahweh is the Husband*, 97. We need to remember that the metaphor of Israel as unfaithful wife includes both the men and the women of Israel. Therefore, all the shame falls on the men as well as on the women. Finally, Brueggemann, *Theology*, 362, argues that the idea of potential or implicit abusive violence present in the husband imagery is not "propaganda" focused.

73. Tushingham, "A Reconsideration of Hosea," 156 n.42, points out that the wilderness is a symbol of destruction. Thus, although Hos 2:3 does not speak of killing the unfaithful wife, the imagery comes close to the punishment for adultery: death.

74. Wolff, *Hosea*, 34.

75. Yahweh does not say here that they are his own. They are the offspring of their immoral mother. Cf. Ortlund, *Whoredom*, 57.

76. Clines, "Structure and Interpretation," 91, explains that they never protest against

to their mother that both the national and individualistic transgressions are practically the same.⁷⁷ For this reason they do not accuse their mother because they would immediately see their own sin.

Verse 5 finally states the guilt of the nation. She has turned her back on Yahweh seeking her prosperity in the cult of Canaan. The people "played the harlot" and disgraced themselves chasing their lovers. This involved idolatrous worship.⁷⁸ The wife's sin finds its evidence in her very words, "I will go after my lovers, who give me my bread and my water, my wool and my linen, my oil and my drink" (NKJV). She forgot that, according to Yahweh's covenant, it was He who provided for her well-being. He sent the rain so that the land was fertile.⁷⁹ She started believing that she is indebted to Baals for the rich prosperity of the times. She ascribed to Baals the things which the husband was obliged to give her (Exod 21:10; cf. Hos 2:8–9).⁸⁰ This points to the degree of Israel's wrongdoing against her loving husband. The verse emphasizes the fact that Israel has wantonly, consciously, and deliberately forsaken her husband Yahweh.

Verse 6 introduces a new section (vv. 6–15) which describes three movements in Yahweh's treatment of Israel.⁸¹ Each starts with לָכֵן ("therefore").⁸² Clines's structure of the section is convincing,

---

their mother. In fact, they have nothing to say. Their existence is a protest itself. This is why they disappear in the later part of the chapter.

77. Ibid. Cf. Andersen and Freedman, *Hosea*, 227–28. Vv. 4–5 is a unit dealing with the children and the mother together.

78. Cf. Waterman, "Hosea," 102.

79. Cf. comments above on 2:3. Also Andersen and Freedman, *Hosea*, 232. Yahweh will demonstrate that it is he who gives water to the land, not Baal.

80. Food and water are basic nourishments; wool and linen are materials for clothing, and oil and drink are the luxuries of prosperous life. See Mays, *Hosea*, 39. Exod 21:10 points to food, clothing and love which a husband had to provide for his wife.

81. Clines, "Structure and Interpretation," 85.

82. Verses 6–7 have often been transferred to follow v. 13. However, Wolff argues that the MT order is a satisfactory one. He shows that v. 7b is an antithesis to 5b. See *Hosea*, 35. Emmerson shows that commentators often linked verse 7b with v. 14 because of the woman's admission that life with her husband was preferable to her present state, and her expressed intention to return. But v. 7b does not speak of repentance (see below).

1. [Because she has played the harlot]

Therefore (לכן) I will bear [her] way   6a

   (viz., I will prevent her harlotry happening again)   6–7

But she (והיא) does not acknowledge . . .   8a

   [viz., that *I* am the giver of her gifts]

2. [Because she does not recognize me as the giver]

Therefore (לכן) I will take back [my gifts]   9a

   (viz., I will prevent her from enjoying what she has been   9–13
enjoying)

But me (ואתי) she has forgotten.   13b

3. [Because she has forgotten me (in the enjoyment of my gifts)]

Therefore (לכן) I will persuade her . . . woo her   14

   [viz., I will cause her to remember me, and (by implica-   14–15
tion) to abandon her harlotry][83]

The three acts of Yahweh are to prevent the harlotry occurring again by putting obstacles in the way of Israel (v. 6), to bring Israel to recognition of her dependence on Yahweh (v. 9), to resume Yahweh's exclusive relationship with Israel (v. 15).[84] Thus Israel is first "deprived of access to what she believes to be her source of her well-being; . . . second, she is deprived of the well-being itself; . . . third (remarkably) she has her well-being restored by the one who is its true source."[85] Whereas the two first "therefore" tell of disciplinary/corrective measures Yahweh will take to stop his wife's promiscuity, the third one points to a reversal of punishment.

Because of Israel's waywardness Yahweh is going to intervene immediately (הנני) (v. 6). Although "therefore" often introduces prophetic judgment speech, here it expresses a direct response to the wife's attitude.[86] The husband, out of his desire to preserve the marriage, will

---

83. "Structure and Interpretation," 85. This pattern attests the Massoretic reading.

84. Ibid., 85–86.

85. Ibid., 86.

86. "In the older prophets, לכן almost always marks the transition from the proof of guilt to the threat of punishment. But vv. 6 and 14f are an exception, since the threat has been replaced by Yahweh's corrective measures." Wolff, *Hosea*, 35–36. Pace Clines, "Structure and Interpretation," 86.

block the ways to Israel's lovers (cf. 2:5b), viz., the pilgrim's roads to sanctuaries.[87] People will not find it easy to worship the Baals (2:7). They will be unable to commit religious adultery.[88] They will still desire to visit the shrines,[89] but they will not reach their goal.[90] Frustrated and desperate they will reconsider their well-being, and remember the happier past in the wilderness, at the time when they worshipped Yahweh alone.[91] They will be made to reconsider the blessings of the covenant (grain, new wine, oil, resembles the language of Deut 7:13; 11:14; 12:17, 23; 18:4; 28:51), blessings which they had attributed to the Baals during their apostasy (v. 8).[92] They used the gifts of their husband to pursue adulterous love. They must learn through discipline (v. 9) that Yahweh is the giver of the land and its produce (cf. Deut 26:1, 2, 3, 9, 10, 11). Until now (v. 8a)[93] Israelites still do not recognize the source of their well-being. Therefore (second 'therefore' in the series) Yahweh will proceed to discipline her (v. 9). He will take away the gifts, which he has given to his wife: grain and new wine (cf. v. 8), wool and flax (cf. v. 5). These were given by Yahweh to the land in due seasons "comparable to the regularity of the rain which was tied to its seasons" (Deut 11:14; 28:12; Lev 26:4).[94] Jer 5:24 explains further the idea, "They do not say in their heart, 'Let us now fear the Lord our God, who gives rain, both

---

87. MacIntosh, *Hosea*, 51, explains that "wall" and "thorns" in the verse refer to the frustration of human traffic.

88. The whole picture refers to an adulteress who goes after her lovers, not to a prostitute being sought by clients. See Andersen and Freedman, *Hosea*, 238. Pace Hornsby, "Re-reading Gomer," 115–28.

89. "To seek" is a technical term for religious gatherings in search of some token of divine favor (cf. 5:6, 15). See Mays, *Hosea*, 40.

90. van Dijk-Hemmes, "Two Biblical Love Songs," 75–88, shows, following van Selms, that the theme of "seeking but not finding" in Hos 2:7 resembles the story of the Song of Songs 3:1–4. While the woman in the Song of Songs seeks but cannot find her beloved, the woman in Hos 2:7 is prevented by her husband from finding her lovers.

91. The last part of verse 7 does not refer to a genuine repentance (cf. Mays, *Hosea*, 40; Wolff, *Hosea*, 36), but a selfish desire for well-being.

92. Silver and gold were another mark of prosperity at the time of Jeroboam II. To the prophet, they were the lavish gift of the husband/Yahweh.

93. The perfect of the stative verb ידע in the context points to the present tense. Israel still does not know that it is Yahweh who provides for her. See MacIntosh, *Hosea*, 54–55.

94. MacIntosh, *Hosea*, 57. The grain harvest began in April and May. The vintage lasted from August to early October. See ibid, 57 n.27. Cf. Andersen and Freedman, *Hosea*, 245–46. It is again evident that a polemic against the fertility cult is implied. Cf. Kruger, "Israel, the Harlot," 116.

the former and the latter, in its season. He reserves for us the appointed weeks of the harvest'" (NKJV). Wolff sees the punitive measures of this verse as parallel to the Semitic marriage laws of the Code of Hammurabi (§ 141): the wife humiliating her husband is cast out with no means of support.[95] This again refers to the husband's duties established in Exod 21:10. The husband will stop providing for his wife so as to prove her failure in attributing to her lovers what came in fact from her husband's. Yahweh will withdraw his blessings so that Israel will realize who really is the giver of the land's fertility. Without clothing and with her genitals uncovered she will be exposed to public shame and complete disgrace (v. 10). Her lovers will be powerless to help her. This will demonstrate that the power of nature does not belong to the Baals but to Yahweh alone. Without the necessities for living, Israel's festivals will cease (v. 11). The fertility of the land will be removed so that the feasts connected to the agricultural year come to an end (cf. Exod 23:14–17; 34:18–23).[96] As a result the whole pattern of Israel's life, connected so closely to the cultic calendar, will be cancelled. It was during these festivals that Israel committed adultery by worshipping the Baals.[97] She treated them as the feast days of the Baals (cf. v. 13). Mays comments that the pronoun "her" points to the fact that these festivals now belonged to Israel and no longer to Yahweh.[98] By withdrawal of the agricultural products Yahweh was going to terminate Israel's festivals. But he will also destroy the vine and the fig trees, the very symbols of Israel as Yahweh's plantation which recalled the idyllic wilderness period (2:12; cf. 9:10; 10:1).[99] They were also symbols of peace, independence and affluence.[100] Israel treated them as wages[101] from her lovers, the Baals. "What Yahweh gave as his blessing under covenant, expecting only thanksgiving and confession in return,

95. *Hosea*, 37.

96. Mays, *Hosea*, 42.

97. This was most likely linked with a sex fertility cult (cf. Hos 4:14). Wolff, *Hosea*, 38, suggests that the New Moon festival may have included *hieros gamos* sexual rituals.

98. *Hosea*, 42. Amos 5:21–23 pictures a similar situation.

99. So Andersen and Freedman, *Hosea*, 251. However Fox, "Desert Ideal," 441–50, does not regard the wilderness period as an idyllic one, but the opposite.

100. MacIntosh, *Hosea*, 64.

101. אֶתְנָה means "gift, wages of prostitution," thus the payment a woman received for the sexual pleasure she provided to men. See Davidson, *Hebrew and Chaldee Lexicon*, 765. This, however, does not imply that Israel was a professional prostitute. For a discussion on the connotations of this *hapax legomenon* form see MacIntosh, *Hosea*, 63–64.

Israel thought it necessary to purchase through a ritual of sympathetic magic."[102] The rituals of Baal worship which were performed by Israel were compared with sexual acts by Hosea. She believed she owed her prosperity in the land to those base religious acts.

The destruction of Israel's vineyards and the fig trees brought the situation close to the devastation announced in 2:3b. It also demonstrates more clearly the identity of the true provider. He will punish her for her allegiance with the Baals to whom she sacrificed (2:13; cf. 4:13). She put her trust in Baals as the providers of her fertility and put much effort into pleasing them.[103] Israel forgot her true god and husband (cf. 11:1, 3–4). "It is in the seductive smell of sacrificial worship . . . , in its excitement, unrestrained glamour and immediacy that faithfulness to Yahweh and his demands is dismissed from the minds of his people."[104]

Israel was unable to repent. She had forgotten her husband (2:13). Yet this did not exclude the future hope of restoration. The third "therefore" speech points to another action Yahweh will take in order to win back his unfaithful spouse (2:14). "The soliloquy continues but the mood changes abruptly from punishment and coercion to coercion through love."[105] "[Because she has forgotten me (in the enjoyment of my gifts) *therefore* (לכן) I will persuade her . . . woo her [viz., I will cause her to remember me, and (by implication) to abandon her harlotry."[106] Yahweh himself will take responsibility for the reconciliation with his faithless wife.[107] He will do all that is necessary to restore the original relationship. Verses 14–15 show that deprivation of Yahweh's blessings (2:9, 11, 12) has a saving purpose. Emmerson explains,

---

102. Mays, *Hosea*, 43.

103. "Adorning" herself with earrings and jewelry, and going after the lovers is viewed by some commentators as a reference to participation in a cult procession. So Mays, Hosea, 43; Wolff, *Hosea*, 40. But Andersen and Freedman oppose this interpretation (*Hosea*, 259). Also MacIntosh, *Hosea*, 66. The main counter-argument to Mays and Wolff is that "going after her lovers" points to the mental attitude of Israel (cf. 2:5b: "I will go after my lovers"). We need to remember that Israel's worship is not Baal cult *per se* but rather a mixture of Yahwism and Baalism. The shape of the religion was still connected to Yahwism (cf. 2:11), but Yahweh himself was exchanged for Baal, or He was thought of as Baal.

104. MacIntosh, *Hosea*, 66–67. "Forgetting" in a covenant context means "treachery." See Andersen and Freedman, *Hosea*, 262.

105. MacIntosh, *Hosea*, 69.

106. Clines, "Structure and Interpretation," 85.

107. Mays, *Hosea*, 44.

The nation's response is not the prerequisite of Yahweh's saving action, but issues from it, the result of his gracious act on her behalf. This initiative in the renewal of the broken relationship lies not with Israel's repentance but with Yahweh's persistent love. The prophet's hope rests not on the nation's efforts at reform but solely on Yahweh's grace.[108]

Yahweh will allure[109] Israel. This verse is striking because Yahweh is described here as a seducer, the one who will cajole his wife from following others, so that she ceases to be the wife that enjoys her adulteries. It seems that Yahweh is involved in a competition with many other suitors in trying to allure a young woman.[110] But in the context of the preceding verses and Israel's "forgetfulness" this is to bring her back to her senses, to her repentance, to change her attitude of mind.[111] Yahweh will take Israel into the wilderness.[112] The wilderness refers to the place as well as to the time and situation when Israel was close to Yahweh and had experienced his kind care (cf. 13:4–5).[113] This is a clear reference to the Exodus from Egypt.[114] "The story begins here with the escape from Egypt; how the latter-day Israel got back there is not explained although

---

108. *Hosea*, 23.

109. The Piel form of פָּתָה means "to persuade, entice" and "to deceive, seduce." Davidson, *Hebrew and Chaldee Lexicon*, 636. "The verb is used of deceit (1 Kgs 22.20ff; Jer 20.7; Ezek 14.9) and, between the sexes, of seduction and enticement (Exod 22.16; Judg 14.15; 16.5)." MacIntosh, *Hosea*, 69 n.c. Cf. Wolff, *Hosea*, 41; and Mays, *Hosea*, 44.

110. Cf. Wolff, *Hosea*, 41. But Andersen and Freedman, *Hosea*, 271–72, say that in the context of tenderness in 2:14b this should have the connotation of "the artful wooing of a simple girl."

111. MacIntosh, *Hosea*, 70.

112. Most commentators regard the wilderness period as the "honeymoon" of Yahweh and Israel after he married her at Sinai. Thus the desert is regarded as the ideal time of Israel's obedience. But Fox, "Desert Ideal," 449, argues for the opposite. He says Hosea himself does not view that period as one of obedience on the part of Israel (see 9:10; 13:5–6).

113. Ortlund, *Whoredom*, 68. Cf. Mays, *Hosea*, 44. The historical setting is uncertain. The question whether taking Israel to the wilderness refers either to her return to a nomadic life or to exile cannot be answered with certainty. Wolff, *Hosea*, 41. Wolff sees the former option as more likely since the verse speaks of Yahweh being alone with Israel and the next one gives the promise of the vineyards "from there." However, Stuart, *Hosea-Jonah*, 53, believes that the focus of the action is eschatological and that v. 14 refers to the exile period. The breaking of the covenant implied exile from the land (Lev 26:33; Deut 28:64, 6, taking back to Egypt, however, by sea).

114. Andersen and Freedman, *Hosea*, 272.

later passages in Hosea clearly contemplate such a return (7:16; 8:13; 9:3, 6; 11:5)."[115] The desert is the place where Yahweh will be alone with her, with no Baals. The whole action, therefore, refers to a new beginning. The husband will speak there to the wife's heart[116] to comfort her, to reassure a confused woman.[117] As Emmerson puts it, "Yahweh's answer to Israel's ignoring him will be to turn the clock back and let her begin her history with him all over again."[118]

Thus Israel will be restored. She will receive the land again together with its vineyards which were earlier destroyed in the disciplinary action of Yahweh (2:15). The vineyards as the sign of well-being will now be recognized as the gift from Yahweh.[119] There is a new beginning and a new hope for the promiscuous wife. "As though he were a bridegroom bringing his bride to her new home, Yahweh will make 'Emek Achor'[120] a door of hope, an entry into a life of promise, a future unlimited by the painful past."[121] From the desert Israel will repossess the land which Yahweh will again make fruitful. She will respond[122] to Yahweh's court-

---

115. Ibid.

116. Brueggemann, *Theology*, 361, explains this to mean "to speak tenderly." Wolff, *Hosea*, 41, says this reflects the language of courtship and has the connotation of love and awareness of belonging together. van Dijk-Hemmes, "Two Biblical Love Songs," 84, views this as the beginning of the husband's love song (2:14–23) who starts to sing it after the speeches filled with much sexual violence. For van Dijk-Hemmes "speaking tenderly" can well mean "saying sweet nothing" in order to seduce the female-lover and establish the authority of the man over the independent, powerful woman who as a result becomes his totally passive bride (pp. 85–86).

117. MacIntosh, *Hosea*, 70. Cf. Wolff, *Hosea*, 42.

118. *Hosea*, 24.

119. Therefore, we agree with Ringgren, "Marriage Motif," 425–26, that Hosea's polemic with the fertility religion of Baals pointed right from the beginning to the fact that it is Yahweh who is the true God, even in fertility. Cf. below on vv. 21–22.

120. According to Josh 7:24–26 "'Achor' is reminiscent of 'Achan' upon whom Yahweh's wrath 'brought misfortune' after he had 'brought misfortune' upon Israel." Wolff, *Hosea*, 43. This Valley of Misfortune Yahweh changes to the Door of Hope.

121. Mays, *Hosea*, 45. MacIntosh, *Hosea*, 73, believes that the vineyards may denote a bridal gift.

122. The verb עָנָה means simply "to answer." It can sometimes mean "to sing" (so NKJV). But this rendering is unjustified by the context. See the next note. However, Fox opts for the meaning "to sing." He indicates that the singing of Israel is her response to salvation (cf. Jer 31:4–5). In punishments, Yahweh took away all her festivals (2:11), but now her joyous festal singing is restored. After the once-broken relationship is restored Israel sings joyfully as she did after the deliverance from Egypt. See Fox, "Desert Ideal," 449.

ship in v. 14 accepting "the hand of her Benefactor" and following him.[123] She will act willingly as in the days of her youth when Yahweh brought her out of Egypt (11:1). Jer 2:2 lists Israel's characteristics from the time of her youth: loyal devotion (חֶסֶד), love (אַהֲבָה), and discipleship (אַחֲרֵי לֶכֶת).[124]

Yahweh's disciplinary acts (2:6–13) together with his courtship and comfort (2:14–15) will cause Israel to come back to her senses. In the time of renewal[125] she will no longer confuse Yahweh with Baal (2:16). She will answer to Yahweh (2:15) recognizing him as her husband who provides and cares for her. She will repent from the syncretistic religion of Hosea's days where Yahweh was assimilated with the Baals of other nations.[126] She will return to the marriage bond of the covenant.

בַּעַל had earlier been used to signify Yahweh in the nation's history. The term is never to be used again in Israel's religious vocabulary so that her husband will not be ever again confused with other deities bearing this title. The husband will take away the names of Baal from his wife's mouth for good (2:17).

Yahweh will take every action to reconcile Israel with himself. There is an eschatological promise for his people. In the future, Yahweh will create "an environment of peace, the manifestation of his blessing" (2:18).[127] Yahweh will reverse the hostility of animals (indicated in v. 12), which will signify the restoration of covenantal peace (cf. Lev 26:6). Consequently, Israel will not be harmed by the hostile nations but will experience times of quietness under the restored covenant. These blessings are solely a sign of Israel's restoration by Yahweh's grace.[128]

---

123. Wolff, *Hosea*, 43. Friedman, "Israel's Response," 200, sees v. 14 as the allusion to God's proposal of remarriage and v. 15b as Israel's response, which is connected to v. 16. The support for this interpretation of v. 15 can be found, according to him, in v. 23.

124. Wolff, *Hosea*, 43. Pace Fox, "Desert Ideal," 441–46.

125. 2:16–23 forms a new section with three units (vv. 16–17; 18–20; 21–23) divided by the phrase "in that day." This phrase refers to a promise of good things to come in the time of salvation, after the judgment. The section is linked thematically with the preceding (v. 16 interprets "she will respond" in v. 15b). See Wolff, *Hosea*, 47. Clines, "Structure and Interpretation," 96, having examined the conceptual pattern of the whole chapter concludes that Hos 2:2–23 is an integrated work.

126. Cf. Andersen and Freedman, *Hosea*, 278. There may have been a mingling of attributes between Yahweh and the storm god of Syria. However, to what extent Yahweh was called Baal is not clear.

127. Mays, *Hosea*, 49.

128. Mays, *Hosea*, 50. Cf. Kaiser, *Old Testament Theology*, 199, explains that although

The new intimate relationship of Yahweh with Israel is compared to betrothal, i.e., Yahweh is making a permanent commitment (2:19–20).[129] The initial marriage was violated by Israel. Yahweh has changed the wife's attitude by his dealings with her so that this future relationship is like a remarriage. However, because we have observed earlier that Hos 2 does not speak of divorce, it must be concluded that the meaning of Yahweh taking Israel again is *de facto* covenant renewal. Yahweh no longer looks at Israel as at an adulterous woman (2:2–13), but treats her anew like a partner in marriage. Her virginity (i.e., "innocence") is restored by his grace.[130]

However, some scholars still argue along the lines of divorce and remarriage. They say that the list of Yahweh's attributes: righteousness (צֶדֶק), justice (מִשְׁפָּט), loving-kindness (חֶסֶד), compassion (רַחֲמִים), and faithfulness (אֱמוּנָה), signifies the bride-price Yahweh pays at the establishment of the new marriage.[131] Mays, however, recognizes that there is no father to receive the payment so the analogy breaks down.[132] This observation favors the claim that the imagery is marriage renewal. Since there is no analogy to the practice of the bride-price in Hos 2 (cf. chapter 2 on the bride-price) and the argument is constructed only on the similar occurrence of the verb אָרַשׂ in 2 Sam 3:14 we find this common interpretation unconvincing. Andersen and Freedman opposing the conclusion of others explain,

> Righteousness, justice, loyalty, and love are four of the greatest of Yahweh's attributes. In the marriage to come, the bride will receive the fruits of these qualities, and will share in them eternally. They

---

Israel failed to fulfill her covenant obligation of the "loyal love" (*ḥesed*) towards her God (Hos 4:1; 6:4, 6; 10:12; 12:6), Yahweh's "loyal love" endures forever.

129. The verb אָרַשׂ (Pi. 'to betroth') used here in a figurative sense has no parallel elsewhere in the OT. Emmerson, *Hosea*, 27. When the verb is followed by nouns with the prefix בְּ it points to the price paid for a girl. Davidson, *Hebrew and Chaldee Lexicon*, 48.

130. Stienstra, *YHWH Is the Husband*, 121.

131. So e.g., MacIntosh, *Hosea*, 83–84; and Clines, "Structure and Interpretation," 89. This conclusion is certainly based on the grammar of the verb אָרַשׂ followed by the prefix בְּ *per analogiam* to 2 Sam 3:14, which is quite unlikely. See Andersen and Freedman, *Hosea*, 283.

132. *Hosea*, 51. Cf. Wolff, *Hosea*, 52 and Clines, "Structure and Interpretation," 94. The latter two also recognize the breakdown in the analogy. If, however, our conclusion from chapter 2 is correct, the *mohar* could be regarded as a gift which the bride receives from her husband, and not as payment to her father.

constitute at once what the groom contributes to and expects from the relationship. *The attributes are promises for marriage, and not once-for-all payments at the time of engagement.*[133]

This whole renewal is to bring Israel back to the state similar to that of her youth (cf. 2:15). Yahweh will himself maintain this renewed relationship on the basis of his attributes.[134] Clines also believes that these qualities will be internalized by Israel and will then characterize her behavior.[135] Thus Israel will fulfill the expectations of Yahweh (cf. 4:1) and will become his faithful wife again. She will fully acknowledge Yahweh and will be no more forgetful (2:20b; reversal of 2:13b). She will know[136] him in a personal intimate way within the covenant/marriage.

In the time of salvation Yahweh will make the land fertile again (2:21–22). He is the true God, who manifests himself even through the land's fertility.[137] The produce of the land is a means of knowing Yahweh (2:20b; reversal of 2:8).[138] The husband will cause a chain reaction to make the land fruitful. This chain reaction runs through all the stages in the fertility cycle: deity—heavens (rain)—land (soil)—grain, wine, oil (inclusive of crops, cf. 2:8)—people. The unit shows the route of human nutrition from Yahweh down to the land.[139] This shows further reversal of the calamity brought earlier by Yahweh's discipline (2:3, 9). The Canaanite fertility religion with its rain gods is no longer remembered; only Yahweh is in the heart of Israel, his wife. It is Yahweh who again sends rain upon the once dried ground which in turn will give fruit. Grain, new wine, and oil are the blessings of the restored covenant. In

---

133. *Hosea*, 283. Italics ours.

134. Both Wolff (*Hosea*, 53) and Mays (*Hosea*, 52) see Hos 2:19–20 as a forerunner of Jeremiah's new covenant in 31:31–34. Mays also suggests that Hos 2:19–20 is a proclamation of the eschatological bride of Christ (Eph 5:23–30). Wolff, *Hosea*, 55 sees the culmination of Hosea's metaphor in the NT's metaphor of Christ as the bridegroom of his bride, the church.

135. "Structure and Interpretation," 94.

136. The verb יָדַע has sexual connotations and in a theological sense points to the intimacy of a relationship. Furthermore, it also has covenant connotations. Andersen and Freedman, *Hosea*, 284, explain that the betrothal is a covenant. To live in the covenant is to know Yahweh.

137. Ringgren, "Marriage Motif," 425–26. Fertility is again in focus in Hos 14:5–6.

138. Mays, *Hosea*, 52.

139. Wolff, *Hosea*, 53. Jezreel refers here either to "the starving people of Israel" or "the Valley of Jezreel" which was a fertile plain which was the source of food for people living there. See ibid., 54.

fact, Yahweh will reverse all that was associated with his punishment. Jezreel, first symbolizing judgment (1:4), becomes a sign of grace and renewal of the covenant (2:23a). Jezreel, meaning "God sows,"[140] points to the re-planting of Israel which is the result of the restoration brought by her husband. She finds again mercy (reversal of 1:6) and is called "my people" (reversal of 1:9). This mercy upon God's covenant people calls forth a renewed confession: "You are my Elohim" (cf. 2:16).[141] Thus the mutual relationship of *hieros gamos* between a God and his people is restored and renewed.[142]

Israel has been brought back from her wayward life, her unilateral relationship with the gods of other nations. She continually gave to the Baals, but she received nothing back. She wrongly thought that the gifts of her husband had come from them. Yahweh's covenant faithfulness, mercy and love, has brought her back to her senses through a process of discipline. She has been restored to a reciprocal relationship with her loving husband. She has acknowledged again that she owes all her well-being to her caring spouse who keeps his covenant.

The marriage metaphor expresses Yahweh's strong passionate love towards his erring covenant people. As her husband, Yahweh did not give up, but prompted by his loving-kindness he strove to win her back. Yahweh was angry with his unfaithful wife. He had every reason to punish her, but discipline is not the last word for him; love is. Yahweh struggles within himself because his wife deserves punishment and yet he has committed himself to her in love. And it is this commitment which does not allow him to abandon her completely. Hos 11:8–9 is the best expression of God's love for his wife, "How can I give you up, Ephraim? How can I hand you over, Israel? . . . My heart churns within me; my sympathy is stirred. I will not execute the fierceness of my anger; I will not destroy Ephraim. For I am God, and not a man, the Holy One in your midst; and I will not come with terror."

---

140. In 1:4 Jezreel could have referred to negative "sowing" of malediction and destruction. Cf. Fensham, "Marriage Metaphor in Hosea," 74. Now the "sowing" is reversed and refers to re-establishment of Israel in her land amidst God's blessings.

141. Wolff, *Hosea*, 54.

142. Levenson, *Sinai and Zion*, 79, explains that redemption in this context is God's "gracious offer to Israel to reenter the legal/erotic relationship and the renewed willingness of Israel to do so."

Origin of the Metaphor

Having examined the first occurrence of the divine marriage metaphor in the Hebrew Bible we can now consider the question of the metaphor's source raised at the beginning of chapter 2.

Because of Hosea's polemic against the Baal fertility cult, many scholars conclude that the cult itself provided the prophet with the imagery of the marriage metaphor in which Yahweh is the husband of his wife Israel. Wolff says,

> Here Hosea's theology develops openly in dialogue with the *mythology* of his day in a remarkable process of adaptation of and polemic against this mythology.
>
> Hosea's use of the *mythologumenon* of Yahweh as Israel's husband has its roots in the prophet's recognition of Israel's specific guilt: the people have given themselves to "whoredom." By her cultic practices and her dependence upon Canaanite mythology and thought, Israel has become unfaithful to Yahweh.[143]

Mays explains the shift from the *hieros gamos* of Canaanite religion to Yahwism saying,

> In Hosea's hand the myth of the divine marriage became an allegory of Yahweh's experience with Israel in Canaan; and the context in which the relation was understood was removed from the magical and cultic world of Canaan to the moral structure of the covenant.[144]

This adaptation of the fertility myth as expressed in marriage and the sexual act of a god and a goddess had one main purpose, namely showing that the whole realm of fruitfulness in the land belongs to Yahweh alone. It was also intended to show that the focus of Yahweh is the obedience of his worshippers within the mutual relationship of covenant, and not fertility of crops *per se*. So the whole Canaanite mythology needed to be changed and replaced.[145] Yahweh's partner is not some goddess, but historical Israel.

---

143. *Hosea*, xxvi.

144. *Hosea*, 9.

145. Wolff, *Hosea*, xxvi.

The different claims of scholars such as Emmerson,[146] Oesterley and Robinson,[147] Batten,[148] Ortlund[149] and Ringgren[150] suggest that they also favor this view. Stienstra, however, believes that the Baal myth was only a catalyst for Hosea to develop the metaphor. She argues that fertility of the land is not the main focus of the prophet. She says,

> . . . the marriage metaphor is very different from the mythical marriage between a god and a goddess, even if this is supposed to be directly related to the wellbeing of man. In the marriage metaphor, it is man who has to respond positively to the divine Bridegroom, and it is this aspect of the metaphor which Hosea emphasizes.[151]

Although she does not deny the influence of the Canaanite religion upon Hosea's thought, Stienstra is less enthusiastic towards the statement that the metaphor has its origin in the polemic against Baal fertility cult.

Chavasse argued along similar lines,

> The plain fact is that the Marriage of Yahweh and Israel is no spiritualized form of the union of a vegetation-god and a mother-goddess. Throughout the prophets the whole emphasis is placed on the infidelity of the human bride, Israel, and on the unfailing love, tender and yet stern, of her divine Husband. In the fertility cult the constant note is the pursuing, passionate, unthinking devotion of the mother-goddess for the fertility god. The two are very different. The one is Agape, the other is Eros.[152]

Thus both Stienstra and Chavasse challenge the view that the Old Testament metaphor is saying the same as the myths of the fertility cult religions.

Thompson[153] develops his argument along the lines of Israel's covenant history. For him the metaphor could well have been developed

---

146. *Hosea*, 25. She explains that the metaphor arose from Hosea's creative use of motifs associated with the fertility cult of Canaan against which the prophet's polemic is directed.
147. Oesterley and Robinson, *Hebrew Religion*, 237.
148. "Message and Marriage," 261.
149. *Whoredom*, 61 n. 41.
150. "Marriage Motif," 425.
151. *YHWH Is the Husband*, 100.
152. *Bride of Christ*, 245.
153. "Israel's Lovers," 475–76.

on the basis of close connections between the treaty covenant and the institution of marriage. In covenant terms Israel was to love Yahweh just as a vassal should love his suzerain. She was to be loyal in that friendship. Other allegiances than that to the suzerain meant unfaithfulness and therefore harlotry.

Friedman claims that Hosea might have read Exod 19:5–6, 8 allegorically, interpreting the Sinai event as the initial proposal of marriage by Yahweh and the people's response.[154] The passage referred to reads, "If you keep my covenant, you shall be my treasured possession among all the peoples. . . . You shall be to me a kingdom of priests and a holy nation . . . all the people *responded* as one." Friedman believes that God's declaration together with the people's response were regarded by Hosea as a marriage formula. Therefore the prophet introduced the metaphor on the basis of the re-reading of the already existing covenant tradition.

Brewer[155] says that there was a shift in the later prophets regarding ways of expressing the covenant relationship between Yahweh and his people. He observes that,

> . . . the theme of God's covenant with Israel continues to be important, but it takes on a different aspect. Now, instead of being a treaty covenant, it is often expressed as a marriage covenant. (. . .) The reason why the prophets treated this concept of God's marriage so seriously was probably because they regarded God as the origin of the concept. As far as the prophets were concerned, God himself had declared this marriage to be real in his revelation to Hosea where he revealed that he was married to both Judah and Israel.[156]

Thus Brewer's claim is that the origin of the metaphor came directly through God's revelation to Hosea. The prophet used marriage on God's authoritative revelation not as a metaphor, but as a counterpart to the covenant. Hosea's own experience with his unfaithful wife helped him to understand Yahweh being a victim of an adulterous wife.

It seems to us, however, that Hos 1–3 does not establish the question of the metaphor's origin. In chapter 2, Hosea does polemicize against Canaanite religion as well as developing the covenant tradition. The latter helps him to bring new meaning to the metaphor, along the lines of

---

154. "Israel's Response," 202.
155. "Three Weddings," 3.
156. Ibid.

Yahwism. The background for Hosea's understanding is Israel's apostasy to the Baal religion. He was certainly someone who could with a high degree of freedom express theology by the use of metaphors.[157] His use of various metaphors throughout the book does not allow us to exclude his creativity and a wide theological knowledge. God's command to marry a promiscuous woman enabled him to connect the experience of his relationship with the contemporary situation of his nation. Therefore we conclude that the origin of the marriage metaphor emerged out of Hosea's contemporary context, his knowledge of the covenant tradition as well as his experience caused by divine command.[158] But at the same time we need to conclude that the *hieros gamos* of Yahweh was totally different from the marriage of a god and a goddess in fertility religion. The former implied a mutual relationship of love within the context of covenant, the latter was based on an unthinking devotion of a goddess for a god as expressed in the sexual act. Both Baal and Yahweh were owners of the land, according to their cults, but there were also important differences between the two gods. In the case of the former, it was Baal's sexual activity that created the land's fertility. The land symbolized by a goddess was a passive element in the sexual life of Baal. The intercourse of Baal and a goddess was regarded as a prototype of everything that happened on earth.[159] This was expressed in the cult itself: a priest symbolizing the god having sex with a female temple prostitute signifying the land/goddess. Magic rites were performed to secure the fertility of the land and that of people's wives. Yahwism, however, was different. It was removed from the magical and cultic world of Canaan. It offered a totally different view of god. Yahweh was a different god from the Baals of Canaan or Phoenicia. He was not restricted to nature or to the cycle of fertility in nature and in woman (cf. Exod 20:2).[160] The land belonged to Yahweh and its fertility depended on his gracious, elective loving-kindness, and the people's covenant obedience. Thus Israel's fertility could not be forced by magic rites of temple workers. It was because Israel had a totally new god, the free and sovereign one, independent of human actions, that marriage in Israel was dissociated from these pagan fertility

---

157. Cf. Mays, *Hosea*, 8–10.
158. Cf. Hall, "Origin of the Marriage Metaphor," 170.
159. Cf. Schillebeeckx, *Marriage*, 13.
160. Ibid., 14.

rites.¹⁶¹ For her own part, Israel, Yahweh's spouse, was not like a goddess of Canaan a passive element in cultus, but she was expected to respond with her love to the love she received from her husband.

THE DIVINE MARRIAGE METAPHOR IN THE PRE-EXILIC AND EXILIC PROPHETS

Other prophets, following Hosea, also used the metaphor of divine marriage to describe the relationship of Yahweh and his people applying it to their own contexts. The clearest examples of this use occur in the prophecies of Jeremiah, Second Isaiah¹⁶² and Ezekiel. We shall, therefore, briefly examine those occurrences; however, due to the length limitations of this volume, not in same detail as in considering Hosea. For the same reason we will also leave aside questions of textual criticism and base our discussion on the Masoretic Text.

Divine Marriage in Jeremiah

The first part of the book of Jeremiah (2—25:14) speaks about the guilt and iniquities of Judah, and warns of the destruction of Jerusalem in 587 BCE.¹⁶³ Jeremiah employs the metaphor of divine marriage on several occasions, mainly in chapters 2 and 3. It is thought that he depends heavily upon Hosea in using the metaphor.¹⁶⁴ For him Jerusalem, as representative of the people of Judah, is Yahweh's wife, and never representative of the land as in Hosea.¹⁶⁵ He introduces the metaphor in 2:2 and uses it to describe the infidelity of God's people. The happy bridal days of Israel's youth during the wilderness period (vv. 2–3), Jeremiah contrasts

---

161. Ibid.

162. And perhaps the Third Isaiah. We will, however, not discuss the authorship of the Book of Isaiah because the scope of this volume does not allow us to do so. Instead, we attribute chapters 40–66 to Second Isaiah in order to distinguish them from chapters 1–39 which come from the hand of First Isaiah, the pre-exilic prophet. First Isaiah refers to Jerusalem as a woman (see 1:21; 3:26), but he does not introduce the marriage metaphor as such. See Stienstra, *YHWH Is the Husband*, 162.

163. Carroll, *Jeremiah*, 113.

164. See e.g., Thompson, *Jeremiah*, 81–85. Carroll, *Jeremiah*, 119.

165. Stienstra, *YHWH Is the Husband*, 162. An individual case of regarding Israel as husband and Yahweh as wife in 2:13 has been proposed by DeRoche, "Two Evils," 369–72. We would, however, suggest that this view is unlikely in the context and that it would need further evaluation by OT experts.

with her recent behavior (vv. 4–13).[166] They are the basis for the charge brought against her by the prophet. Verses 4–13 indicate that Israel's unfaithfulness to Yahweh is her idolatry. Verse 20 further supports this.[167] Jerusalem is a whore who takes any opportunity to engage in idolatry with Baals and in the fertility cult.[168] Nothing will wash off her iniquity (2:22). Despite all her experiences with Yahweh, Judah loves strangers more than Yahweh (v. 25b).[169] Verses 20–22 show the unchangeable state of the nation. She is rebellious, degenerate and polluted by her immorality.

Jer 3:1–3 is another explicit instance of the marriage metaphor. Yahweh's wife has defiled herself by committing adultery with many lovers. She has forgotten her husband and worshipped the idols (cf. 2:6, 11). By being promiscuous, Judah has created an impossible situation. Redemption is no longer possible as, according to Deut 24:1–4, a man may not remarry a divorced wife because that would pollute the land (3:1). But in fact it is the wife's adultery (=idolatry; Lev 18:20, 21) which pollutes the land (3:2). As a result of her bad behavior the land will experience drought (3:3). Lev 18:24–30 says that the punishment for polluting the land is drought (cf. also Hos 2:3).[170]

Although the legislation of Lev 18:18 prohibits marrying two sisters, the political situation of Palestine in Jeremiah's times induced the prophet to "split" Yahweh's wife into two women, the Northern and Southern

---

166. Fox, "Desert Ideal," 441–47, does not regard the wilderness period as one of happiness and of Israel's obedience. He refers to Jer 7:25; 11:7–8; 32:30, in order to show that Israel was stubborn and rebellious from the time of Exodus. But the opposite interpretation finds support among such scholars as Thompson, *Jeremiah*, 162, 165; Zipor, "Scenes from a Marriage," 86; and Ortlund, *Whoredom*, 83. One can wonder if the statement in Jer 2:2 must be as absolute as to disregard the other accounts of Israel's early rebellion. Could "love of the espousals" refer to the period before the "Golden Calf" incident? If marriage proper took place at Sinai (Exod 19:5–6, 8), perhaps the "love of the espousals" could refer to the period of Israel's wanderings before that. The instances of disobedience, thus, would not be ignored.

167. However, some argue that this verse is a mere reference to cultic prostitution. See Stienstra, *YHWH Is the Husband*, 163.

168. Thompson, *Jeremiah*, 177; Carroll, *Jeremiah*, 130.

169. Strangers can here be foreign nations, as in Ezekiel: Egypt, Assyria, and Chaldea. Cf. Stienstra, *YHWH Is the Husband*, 164. Carroll, *Jeremiah*, 139.

170. We have already noticed that drought in Hos 2:3 kills the land: the picture can be close to the death penalty for a wife's adultery.

Kingdoms (3:6–11).[171] Thus his marriage appears to be polygamous and contrary to the law (Lev 18:18). But it is rather Jeremiah's context which allows him to use the metaphor in this way. He is not concerned with the legal side of matrimony so much as with the breaking of the close and intimate relationship of marriage. Jeremiah explains that Yahweh has divorced the Northern Kingdom for her adultery after he called her to repentance (v. 8). She went into Assyrian exile: the Northern Kingdom ceased to exist and its population has been deported. Therefore exile is divorce, a concept which did not occur in Hosea.[172] But her sister Judah did not learn from that. Although the Southern Kingdom witnessed religious reforms in the days of king Josiah, the people remained unrepentant. Their repentance was not sincere (v. 10).[173] Judah has ignored the dire warning of Israel's exile and multiplied her harlotries. In fact, her sins make her sister Israel appear less guilty (v. 11). Therefore Yahweh begins to relent towards Israel (vv. 12–13). Although he gave her the writ of divorce he can hardly go on rejecting Israel. She must, of course, acknowledge her guilt of rebellion against her husband (v. 13). But Yahweh still regards himself as Israel's husband despite the fact she has been divorced by him and sent into exile (v. 14). Thus the marriage imagery breaks at this point. There is a possibility of Israel returning from divorce/exile to be Yahweh's wife again (against Deut 24:1–4).

Verses 20–27 of chapter 13 employ many metaphors. Jerusalem is a violated woman who experiences shame for her iniquities (vv. 22, 26). She will suffer at the hands of her lovers, the nations with whom she made alliances thus playing the harlot. Carroll explains,

> The images used are graphic and violent. They are metaphors of the city's humiliation and defeat, but they are drawn from the real world of horrendous aggression directed against women in time of war and invasion. In such brutal times the women are led off to the invaders (38.23), stripped naked and savagely raped—their genitals suffer violence and their shameful humiliation is made a public spectacle. Metaphors and reality combine to portray a sickening picture of battered sexuality and torn flesh, an image of a culture invaded, raped and devastated.[174]

---

171. Cf. Stienstra, *YHWH Is the Husband*, 167.
172. Ibid.
173. Cf. Ortlund, *Whoredom*, 94. Thompson, *Jeremiah*, 196.
174. *Jeremiah*, 304.

All this happens to her for the greatness of her iniquity and the lewdness of her harlotry (vv. 22, 27).

But Jeremiah offers also eschatological hope of salvation and the restoration of Judah in terms of the marriage metaphor (31:3–5). Yahweh will not only forgive her iniquities, but totally rehabilitate her so that she will again be like a virgin (cf. Hos 2).[175]

Divine Marriage in Second Isaiah

Chapters 40–66 of Isaiah describe the situation of Israel during and after the exile. Isa 50:1 introduces a few characters who play their particular roles in the divine marriage drama: the mother is Zion, representative of the corporate people of Judah, her children are individual Judeans, and her husband is Yahweh, the father of the children.[176] In this passage Yahweh disputes with his children about the charge made by Zion in 49:14.[177] Jerusalem must have charged Yahweh that he has somehow arbitrarily abandoned his people. They regarded their captivity as Yahweh's fault. In response Yahweh, the husband, proves to his children that Jerusalem's own transgression caused the exile.[178] Two rhetorical questions are asked by Yahweh to prove that he did not divorce his wife arbitrarily (although a husband in that patriarchal society could perhaps do that; cf. Deut 24:1–4 and chapter 2 above), nor did he arbitrarily sell his children. Zion has been divorced and her children sold only because of the people's sin. They are in exile only because of their own fault and transgressions.

Another instance of the marriage metaphor is found in 54:1–10. The passage concerns the childless wife: Zion, restored by God's kindness, and the future hope of salvation. The text moves from alienation towards restoration.[179] Once disgraced by her barrenness (as every barren woman in Israel lived in shame; cf., e.g., 1 Sam 2:1–10), the misery of the exile, which emptied the land of its population, the woman will have very many children (vv. 1–3). Scholars are not sure if the barrenness

---

175. See Stienstra, *YHWH Is the Husband*, 170.
176. Cf. North, *Isaiah 40-55*, 115. Also Westermann, *Isaiah 40–66*, 224.
177. Oswalt, *Isaiah: Chapters 40–66*, 317.
178. Brueggemann, *Isaiah 40–66*, 120. Cf. Stienstra, *YHWH Is the Husband*, 170–71.
179. See Brueggemann, *Isaiah 40–66*, 150.

echoes the story of, barren first and then fertile, Sarah (cf. Isa 51:1–3),[180] or refers in a special way to the song of Hannah in 1 Sam 2:1–10, "with its references to the shame of childlessness (vv. 3–5), and to the children of the barren and the forlornness of the fertile (v. 5)."[181] There is also disagreement among exegetes concerning the referent of the married woman. Brueggemann has proposed that she is Babylon,[182] although the context could hardly point in this direction. If the comparison with Sarah was developed further, the question could be raised if the fertile woman does not echo Hagar. Yet the text itself does not suggest such a conclusion. Therefore the whole comparison with the Sarah-story has its limits and remains a debatable point. Others have suggested that the barren and fertile women refer successively to the pre-exilic and exilic Israel.[183] In favor of this reading would be the parallel text in Isa 62:1–5 with its similar terminology. There, once desolate Zion becomes a "Beulah" land (like the married woman in 54:1), fruitful and productive (see below). The point is that Zion's shame of childlessness and widowhood (which was also a state of misery for a woman in Israel)[184] will be taken away in the time of Yahweh's redemption (vv. 4–5). Although repudiated by Yahweh in his anger, she will be taken back by him "with everlasting kindness" (vv. 6–8). Having been abandoned by her husband for a moment, she will once again become the object of his mercy. The huge assurance of compassion "completely overrides the 'moment' of abandonment."[185] He promises his wife that he will never repudiate her again, nor will he be angry with her any more (vv. 9–10). This promise

---

180. So Delitzsch, *Isaiah*, II: 342. Cf. Motyer, *Isaiah*, 445; and Brueggemann, *Isaiah 40–66*, 151.

181. Oswalt, *Isaiah: Chapters 40–66*, 416.

182. *Isaiah 40–66*, 151.

183. Delitzsch, *Isaiah*, II: 342–43. Motyer, *Isaiah*, 445, strongly objects to this view pointing to the fact that the barren woman never had children. However, he seems to introduce an unnecessary contrast between Israel and the church at this point. Isaiah seems to be concerned with Israel in exile and its restoration by God's miraculous intervention.

184. The widowhood here does not refer so much to the real state of the divine marriage (for her husband has not died) as to the misfortune and misery of her situation. Stienstra, *YHWH Is the Husband*, 173–74. The widowhood, thus, points to the Babylonian exile. See Oswalt, *Isaiah: Chapters 40–66*, 418.

185. Brueggemann, *Isaiah 40–66*, 154.

is as sure as the covenant Yahweh made with Noah and all creation after the Flood (see Gen 9:8–10).[186]

North explains that vv. 6–8

> . . . almost convey the suggestion that Yahweh regrets that he had to treat his people so severely (cf. Jer. 21.20). This thought is continued in vv. 9f. if we read them, as we must, in the light of Gen. 8.21f.; 9:14ff. Before the Flood Yahweh "repented" (Gen. 8.6) that he had made man; after it his feelings were tinged with regret. . . . God, in the Bible, is never heartless or unfeeling, as a pure transcendental monotheism could so easily represent him.[187]

Although the prophet abandons the metaphor by verse 10, verses 11–12 point to the glory of Zion/Jerusalem in the final days.

A number of scholars have pointed out that Isa 61:10 is another example of the marital imagery describing Yahweh as the bridegroom of his bride Israel.[188] Here, Zion joyfully praises her God for what he has done to her through his servant, clothing her with salvation and righteousness as a husband adorns his bride (cf. 52:1). The second part of the verse can support this interpretation because it refers to a wedding imagery.[189] Moreover, it seems that the wedding is guaranteed at the time of Yahweh's salvation (v. 11).[190]

Verses 3–5 of chapter 62 also employ the divine marriage metaphor. They speak of the restoration of Jerusalem after the exile. Ashes of destruction caused by Yahweh's anger now give way to beauty.[191] The marriage theme of 61:10 is continued. By his salvation Zion becomes the crown of beauty and a royal diadem of Yahweh (v. 3). Once forsaken by her husband (cf. 54:7), Jerusalem becomes his restored wife

---

186. Stienstra, *YHWH Is the Husband*, 175, sees here the reference to the marriage covenant.

187. *Isaiah 40–55*, 143.

188. Oswalt, *Isaiah: Chapters 40–66*, 575; Motyer, *Isaiah*, 505. See also Fekkes, "Isaian Nuptial Imagery," 269–87. The bridegroom appears as one wearing a priestly turban (?) or an ornamental headdress (of a bridegroom?). This is signified by יְכַהֵן פְּאֵר. Cf. Watts, *Isaiah 34–66*, 301. At Isa 61:3 the Servant of the Lord provides Zion with such headdress in place of ashes. See Oswalt, *Isaiah: Chapters 40–66*, 575. This perhaps can be referring to the restoration of priesthood in Isa 61:6.

189. Oswalt, *Isaiah: Chapters 40–66*, 575.

190. Hanson, *Isaiah 40–66*, 226.

191. Cf. Oswalt, *Isaiah 40–66*, 580.

(v. 4). The desolate land becomes productive.[192] The city representing the nation is married again by her God.[193] The repudiated wife is reloved and remarried (vv. 4–5). Yahweh rejoices over his bride. The situation is like a completely new relationship between a young man and his bride. It is like restoration of virginity to Israel and return to the happy days of youth.

Divine Marriage in Ezekiel

Ezekiel's prophetic activity took place in the time of the Babylonian exile (c. 594–570 BCE).[194] Babylon had laid siege to Jerusalem for the second time (587 BCE) and that was followed by the deportation of almost all of Judah's inhabitants. Ezekiel's message is a message of doom which can be summarized in the words, "Whatever happens to you is YHWH's punishment for your sins, your faithlessness, your disregard for His laws and His covenant, and serves you right."[195]

Ezekiel, unlike Jeremiah and Second Isaiah, has two long passages elaborating the marriage metaphor. Chapters 16 and 23 employ the metaphor in order to make evident to Jerusalem her abominations (16:2).

Ezek 16 introduces Jerusalem as a child of a pagan origin who is neglected by her parents and left to die (vv. 3–5). Yahweh's intervention is her salvation (v. 6). Being saved from her misery she grows up and matures (v. 7). Then, Yahweh passing by a second time notices her nubil-

---

192. Verse 4 says that the land is now called "Beulah" which means "married." Brueggemann, *Isaiah 40–66*, 221, explains that the term "married" is from the same root as Baal, the god of fertility. The land that is "married" is a land "baaled" (i.e., "Buelah land"). The same word was used in Isaiah 54:1 concerning the fertile woman. Thus nuptial imagery expresses the agricultural condition of Israel's land. The "married" land is opposite of a desolate and barren country. Cf. Ringgren, "Marriage Motif," 426–27. We have seen above that the barren land could signify death. Perhaps, the land becoming fertile again could signify returning to life, i.e., resurrection.

193. The MT speaks of Zion's sons (בָּנָיִךְ) marrying her. But such a rendering of בניך does not make much sense in the context. BHS in its critical apparatus suggests reading בֹּנֵךְ or בֹּנַיִךְ ("your builder" or "your builders"). Stienstra has argued that the word should preferably be rendered as "builder" and therefore refer to Yahweh who is the builder of Jerusalem (cf. 54:11–12; also 54:5 where God the husband is Zion's Maker). Such a reading fits better the marriage metaphor. See, *YHWH Is the Husband*, 176. In English translation, NRSV has followed this rendering whereas NJB has 'rebuilder'. The LXX, however, follows the MT.

194. Eichrodt, *Ezekiel*, 1. Stienstra, *YHWH Is the Husband*, 127.

195. Stienstra, *YHWH Is the Husband*, 128–29.

ity and the marriage metaphor is overtly introduced (v. 8).[196] He marries her (covering a woman with a garment expresses acquiring her; cf. Ruth 3:9) and enters into a covenant with her (v. 8a).[197]

But scholars do not agree on Ezekiel's marriage–metaphor as applied to Jerusalem. Some, such as Eichrodt[198] and Zimmerli,[199] argue that the story of a "foundling child" describes the city's origin. In this view Ezekiel is saying that Jerusalem, once a pagan town, has been chosen by Yahweh to be the centre of Israel's religious life. The city was of Aramean and Hittite origin, i.e., the people of these nations laid down her foundations but she was despised by them. However, the view that Jerusalem stands as representative of the people of Judah seems more likely. Yahweh never entered into a covenant with a city, but he did with the nation of Israel at Mount Sinai.[200] It is, therefore, assumed that the story of a "foundling child" refers to Israel's history.[201] The origin of the nation is indeed from the uncircumcised. When the people sacrificed their first-fruits to Yahweh they were to memorize their Aramean origin and their time in Egypt (Deut 26:5; cf. Ezek 16:3). Thus the time interval between Yahweh's first and second passing by is Egyptian bondage.[202] The growing up of the child describes the nation's increase in number and strength. Yahweh's second intervention, on this view, is the time of redemption from Egypt and the marriage refers to making the covenant on Mount Sinai. Therefore, the story of verses 6–8 can be treated as Yahweh's two acts which were to preserve and increase the nation as well as to glorify it by taking it as his own possession.[203] Whereas in Hosea the land represents the people of Israel, in Ezekiel the capital city stands for the people of Judah.

---

196. Cf. ibid., 131. "Love" (דדים) in v. 8a has some erotic overtones. It is noteworthy that in v. 8 covenant and marriage become closely linked concepts. Cf. Ringgren, "Marriage Motif," 426.

197. Entering the covenant may refer either to the marriage covenant (cf. Mal 2:14 and Pro 2:17) or to the covenant from Mount Sinai. The latter is more likely in the context of chapter 16 describing Israel's history. See below.

198. *Ezekiel*, 203.

199. Zimmerli, *Ezekiel*, 337–38.

200. Cf. Keil, *Ezekiel*, I: 201. Stienstra, *YHWH Is the Husband*, 132, 136.

201. McKeating, *Ezekiel*, 78, who views chapters 16 and 23 as a figurative form of interpretation of Israel's history as it is found in Ezek 20.

202. Stienstra, *YHWH Is the Husband*, 133–35.

203. Keil, *Ezekiel*, 199.

Israel is indebted to Yahweh for everything he has done for her. He did not allow her to die and cared for her. He saved her and married her. He has dignified her in the eyes of other nations (v. 14).[204] He washed her,[205] clothed her with precious clothes (cf. Ex 21:10 and Hos 2:5, 9), and gave her jewels worthy of a queen (vv. 9–13a).[206] He also gave her the finest food so that by his marital care she became "exceedingly beautiful, and succeeded to royalty" (vv. 13–14).[207] But the bride does not recognize the one who cares for her. She does not recognize her divine husband to whom she owes her life, livelihood and beauty (v. 15a). Instead, she trusts in her own beauty (not its giver) and abuses Yahweh's gifts whoring with every passer-by (v. 15b).

The rest of chapter 16 is the long list of accusations the husband brings up against his wife. As in the account of Hosea, she involves her-

---

204. Cf. Ortlund, *Whoredom*, 102.

205. See, e.g., Eichrodt, *Ezekiel*, 206. The meaning of the purifying washing is a matter of dispute among scholars. Zimmerli, *Ezekiel*, 340, thinks that washing and anointing refers to the helplessness of a child although he considers also that on the basis of Ruth 3:3 (cf. Sus 17: the bath does not seem prenuptial though) prenuptial ceremonies could be involved. The problem with the latter view is that in the nuptial bath the wife-to-be washed herself. Block, *Ezekiel Chapters 1–24*, 484, on the other hand, thinks that the blood in v. 9 refers to virginal bleeding in consequence of the first intercourse (cf. Deut 22:13–21). This symbolizes the innocent status of the virgin Israel. The bathing could refer to washing the virginal blood after Yahweh has deflowered the naked maid Israel. So Pope, "Ezekiel 16," 393–94. However, we would suggest that on such a rendering it is more difficult to see the connection with the blood in v. 6. Moreover, although such an interpretation is able to explain the divine marriage on the metaphorical level, it does not help much in clarifying its referents in reality. It is also worth noticing that spreading the garment's hem/wing can refer merely to the establishment of a new relationship and husband's oath to provide for the wife's sustenance. See Kruger, "Garment in Marriage," 79–86. Therefore, we would incline to follow a more likely interpretation proposed, e.g., by Allen, *Ezekiel 1–19*, 238. He has suggested that Israel is cleansed from her ritual and natural impurity, which reverses her depraved state of v. 4. As a result, she enters a newborn state. We would also like to suggest that since the marriage of Yahweh depicted the Mosaic covenant itself, one could argue that the bath referred to covenant purification (cf. Exod 24:8).

206. All these might refer as well to a Jewish wedding associated with ceremonies of fetching the bride. Cf. chapter 2 above. But why does the bridegroom wash the bride and adorn her? We have seen that the bride bathed and clothed herself before the wedding ceremonies took place.

207. One can wonder if verse 13b echoes Exod 19:6 with its promise of royalty to Israel. She was to be a kingdom of priests. It is interesting that the punishment bestowed on the harlot Israel in Ezek 16:41, i.e., burning, was the sentence for the harlotries of a priestly daughter (Lev 21:9). See below.

self in idolatry thus misusing her husband's gifts (vv. 16–19). She even offers her husband's children (i.e., individual Israelites) to Moloch (vv. 20–21). She forgets her origins, her miserable condition without Yahweh (v. 22). By making political alliances with the Egyptians (v. 26), the Assyrians (v. 28) and the Chaldeans (v. 29) she commits adultery.[208] She seeks protection in them instead of in her husband, thus denying his sufficiency.[209] "She sinks to being a common prostitute who serves the demands of the whole public"[210] (vv. 22, 25). She has been warned by Yahweh's punishment in the past (v. 27),[211] but she has been unrepentant. She is worse than a mere prostitute (vv. 31, 33–34). She is a nymphomaniac who seeks and hires men to satisfy her sexual desires. Constantly she turns to others, but her lust remains unsatisfied. She whores for the sake of whoring.

Such behavior demands punishment (see vv. 35–43). She will be exposed to shame in the front of her lovers. Foreign nations will strip her off her clothes leaving her naked (vv. 37, 39). She will be robbed of all the gifts she received from her husband at the wedding. She will receive the punishment for adultery and murder (v. 38). She will be stoned to death and her body will be cut to pieces (v. 40; cf. Deut 22:21–24).[212] The houses of Judah shall be burnt with fire so that she will stop her harlotries (v. 41).[213] Stienstra explains the series of punishments,

> The total impression is that of a furious husband who inflicts all punishments imaginable on his wife, in spite of the fact that

---

208. Thompson, *Lovers*, 476.

209. Stienstra, *YHWH Is the Husband*, 145. Also Ortlund, *Whoredom*, 108.

210. Eichrodt, *Ezekiel*, 207.

211. Both Eichrodt (*Ezekiel*, 208) and Zimmerli (*Ezekiel*, 345) see in v. 27 possible reference to the event of 701 BCE when the Assyrian king Sannacherib reduced Judah's territory joining some of its districts to the Philistines after Judah made an alliance with Egypt.

212. Although stoning is mentioned as the penalty for adultery in Jewish law, cutting a body to pieces does not find a parallel in the OT. However, the Code of Hammurabi refers to such cutting in the case of adultery (see nos. 129; 142–143). Since the punishment is to be carried out by lovers we may suppose that Yahweh exposed his wife not to the penalties provided by the OT law but to the sentences of other Semitic laws, which were often more cruel than those of Israel.

213. According to Lev 21:9 burning with fire was the sentence for an immoral daughter of a priest. This may suggest the priestly character of Judah.

one might be tempted to say that capital punishment is final and will do.²¹⁴

And yet there is an end to his fury caused by his wife's unfaithfulness. After the well-deserved punishment, Yahweh's anger will cease and he will become quiet again (vv. 42–43). Before that happens, however, the wife needs to realize the horror of her behavior. The metaphor, thus, presents Yahweh as a "very human" betrayed husband who acts in a fury and then calms down.

In addition to the main metaphor of the chapter, Ezekiel introduces a somewhat different picture whose purpose is to make the wife feel ashamed (vv. 44–58). The prophet introduces two new characters, the sisters of Jerusalem: Samaria and Sodom, although he builds his plot upon v. 3.²¹⁵ Judah is no better than her mother, a Hittite "loathing her husband and children" (vv. 44–45).²¹⁶ But the main emphasis of the passage lies in the comparison of Jerusalem and the two sisters. It becomes clear that the behavior and sin of the former were much worse than those of the latter (vv. 46–48, 52). The comparison was probably to shock the recipients of the message because both Samaria and Sodom were regarded as places cursed by God,²¹⁷ even more so because of the illusion of Judah's attitude of self-righteous (v. 52). Jerusalem must experience the depths of her degradation in order to understand her heavy load of guilt (vv. 52, 52, 58).²¹⁸ But there is a hint of restoration to God's favor in the passage, which refers to the return from exile after the price for her 'lewdness and abominations' has been paid (v. 55). There will be also deliverance for Samaria and Sodom (v. 53).²¹⁹

---

214. *YHWH Is the Husband*, 149. However, killing the unfaithful wife was the proper punishment for adultery (Lev 20:10).

215. Cf. Eichrodt, *Ezekiel*, 214.

216. The story does not state clearly who were the husbands of Samaria and Sodom whom they "loathed." It seems, however, in the context that Yahweh could be the husband of the three sisters (?). Nevertheless, this lack of clarity does not affect the main point of the passage.

217. For Sodom as a symbol of God's punishment see, e.g., Isa 13:19; Lam 4:6; Jer 49:18; 50:40.

218. This may refer to the events following 587 BCE.

219. Yet, Sodom may be used figuratively to signify that which was previously under God's judgment.

The Divine Marriage Metaphor in the Old Testament Prophets   101

Ezekiel closes the chapter saying that Yahweh will deal with his wife according to her breaking of the covenant (v. 59).[220] But he will not forsake the covenant from Mount Sinai and on the basis of this he will establish an everlasting covenant with Jerusalem (vv. 60, 62).[221] The wife, however, will always remember her past offences against the background of Yahweh's gracious redemption (vv. 61, 63). In the context of such unfathomable mercy, Yahweh's wife is left without a word to say.

Ezek 23 resembles to a certain extent chapter 16.[222] However, it has stronger political overtones. The marriage metaphor introduces two sisters: Oholah (Samaria) and Oholibah (Jerusalem), representing respectively the Northern and Southern Kingdoms. Yahweh's marriage is polygamous here, as in Jer 3:6–10. It would be wrong to seek in the story one-for-one correspondence between textual detail and historical reality.[223] The story of the sisters' youth is presented very briefly without going into much vivid detail (vv. 2–4).[224] They have been harlotrous right from the beginning in Egypt and lost their virginity there. In the context of Ezekiel's time this emphasizes Judah's strong dependence upon Egypt.[225] This shows that Israel's love towards this foreign paramour has a long history. Nevertheless, these two sisters bore sons and daughters, i.e., individual Israelites, to Yahweh (v. 4).

The metaphor jumps straight to the misbehavior of the older sister, Oholah (vv. 5–8). While married to Yahweh Oholah committed adultery with the Assyrians, as a young naive girl struck by the beauty of a group of young officers.[226] The Northern Kingdom made alliances with Assyria and worshipped their idols (v. 7; cf. 2 Kgs 15:19).[227] She turned also to the

---

220. Cf. Zimmerli, *Ezekiel*, 352–53.

221. Cf. Eichrodt, *Ezekiel*, 216. He further explains that God's faithfulness to his first covenant with the chosen people pushed him to give eternal validity to the relationship set up on Sinai, in spite of unfaithfulness on the human part. See also Pope, "Ezekiel 16," 395, who has also argued that the restoration of the original marriage is in view.

222. Zimmerli, *Ezekiel*, 480. But Stienstra, *YHWH Is the Husband*, 155, disagrees.

223. See Ortlund, *Whoredom*, 118. It has already been explained in discussing Jer 3:6–10 that the Jewish law did not allow marrying two sisters (cf. Lev 18:18). The metaphor seems to work above the law.

224. Cf. Eichrodt, *Ezekiel*, 320.

225. See Zimmerli, *Ezekiel*, 483.

226. Ortlund, *Whoredom*, 121.

227. This verse indicates that becoming a vassal of another country meant very often adopting the deities of that country. Cf. Thompson, *Jeremiah*, 163. Eichrodt, *Ezekiel*, 324.

Egyptians seeking help in that alliance (v. 8; 2 Kgs 17:4). She committed adultery with "political" lovers. This resulted in her husband's punishment, the exile executed by the one who was her very lover, Assyria (vv. 9–10).

But her younger sister did not learn from that lesson and became an even greater harlot than her sister (v. 11). Her whoredom was "a self-willed and treacherous political policy."[228] Acting from similar motives to those of her older sister, Judah committed adultery with the Assyrians (vv. 11–12). Then attracted by their power, she became the vassal of the Babylonians (vv. 14–17a).[229] Feeling the yoke of her dependence on her new lover, Judah alienated herself from the Babylonians (v. 17b).[230] But her husband alienated himself from her just as he had turned from her sister (v. 18). She turned still more to her lovers in political alliances (vv. 19–21). Her lust was unsatisfied and she was exactly the same nymphomaniac as Jerusalem in chapter 16. As a result she must suffer Yahweh's punishment (vv. 22–35). The allied lovers whom she had rejected will come to fight against Judah and will judge her according to their own law (vv. 22–24). They will be executors of the divine wrath of her husband (v. 25). They will cut off her nose and ears,[231] kill her inhabitants by sword and fire, expose her to shame, stripping her naked and taking away her precious possessions (v. 26). In this way Yahweh will stop once and for all his wife's adulteries (v. 27). His judgment upon his wife is determined and sure. Her lovers will deal harshly with her because she went after them despising her matrimony like her sister before her (vv. 28–31). She will be punished because of her political alliances with the gentiles and for adopting their idols. She will have to drink the cup of Yahweh's wrath and experience ruin and desolation as a result of her harlotry (vv. 32–35).

The rest of the chapter lists the sins of the two sisters (vv. 36–44) and gives a condensed version of the punishment to be inflicted upon

---

228. Eichrodt, *Ezekiel*, 324.

229. Reference to the years following 625 BCE and the raising of the new imperial power: Babylon. Ibid., 325. After the battle of Carchemish (605) Jehoiakim started paying tribute to Nebuchadnezzar. See Zimmerli, *Ezekiel*, 487.

230. In 601 BCE the Egyptian army defeated Nebuchadnezzar and Jehoiakim withdrew his loyalty from the Babylonian king (see 2 Kgs 24:1). Zimmerli, *Ezekiel*, 487.

231. Punishment for adultery known in Mesopotamia. Cf. Stienstra, *YHWH Is the Husband*, 160; and Eichrodt, *Ezekiel*, 329.

them and executed by their lovers (vv. 45–49; cf. 16:37–41). The chapter does not leave the addressee with any hope of salvation.

It is worth noticing that Ezekiel has a somewhat different perspective of Israel's past from his predecessors in using the divine marriage metaphor. McKeating[232] points out that the prophet's view of the nation's overall history is as negative as in chapter 20 (see vv. 6–8, 10–13, 18–21, 27–31). Israel is totally unworthy and unresponsive to her husband from the very beginning (16:4–5; cf. Deut 7:6–8). She is promiscuous even from the time of her youth, while still in Egypt (Ezek 23:2–4).[233] And she continues in that after the settlement in the land of Canaan (16:15–29; 23:5–21). Hosea and Jeremiah state that Israel's adultery began after the settlement in Canaan, but Ezekiel puts the origin of this sin back to the time of the nation's beginnings in the land of Egypt.

Although Ezek 23 does not contain any eschatological hope of restoration, chapter 16:53–55 speaks of the return of the punished wife of Yahweh from the exile. Compared with Ezek 20:33–44 this is pictured as a second exodus, which "unlike the former exodus, will lead to a successful outcome."[234] The reason for this deliverance is not to preserve the marriage. 20:44 says that Yahweh will restore Israel only "for the sake of his name."

CONCLUSIONS

Having examined the divine marriage among the OT prophets we may conclude that its nature is completely different from the *hieros gamos* of other Semitic nations. While the latter was concerned with marriages of deities in which the primary feature was the sexual act which was thought to bring fertility to the land, the marriage of Yahweh and his people was strongly connected to the ideas associated with the covenant of Sinai. The relationship was based on God's election, salvation and care, resulting from his love, mercy, righteousness, loving-kindness and faithfulness. We may put this in another way, while the *hieros gamos* of Semitic nations of the ANE was focused on a sexual act between deities, the marriage of Yahweh to his nation was based on love in the sense of

---

232. *Ezekiel*, 78–81.

233. The Pentateuch narratives mention only that Israel has been rebellious from the time of the Exodus from Egypt (Deut 9:7), during the years of wandering in the wilderness (cf. Deut 8:2–6).

234. McKeating, *Ezekiel*, 81.

hesed. Such love expects loyalty and loving response on the part of the wife, similar to human marriages in ancient Israel.

The purpose of the divine marriage for such nations as Canaan was to bring fruitfulness to the land. This was secured by the rituals of sacred prostitution performed by priests and sacred prostitutes at the temple and did not presume an intelligent relationship between man and gods. On the other hand, Israel repaid the fertility of her land to Yahweh himself, by being loyal to his covenant, by loving and intelligent response to her caring husband. In fact, she was indebted to him for everything she owned. Her well-being depended totally on her relationship with her husband as in the case of human marriages in Israel. The sexual act *per se* was excluded from the marriage of Yahweh and his people with regard to the nature of this relationship. This, however, did not exclude Yahweh from loving his wife with passion and showing his fury over her unfaithfulness. Despite her sin, God graciously continued to love her, for his name's sake.

The divine marriage, as understood by the prophets, was a mutual relationship of love within the context of covenant and not unthinking devotion of a goddess for a god, as in the religions of the nations surrounding Israel.

The divine marriage metaphor of the OT adds another dimension to our understanding of the covenant. Introduced in the context of constant unfaithfulness on the part of Yahweh's wife, it presents to us God as a husband engaged so deeply in the relationship, both emotionally and actively, that we may see the real closeness and intimacy of Yahweh's relationship with his people. From a biblical point of view such closeness and intimacy is only possible within wedlock. Even the metaphor of a father and his son does not carry the same experience of intimacy.

And yet the divine marriage metaphor in the OT is mainly about the disappointed love of a husband, about the broken intimacy of the closest relationship possible on the part of his wife. According to the marital laws he had every right and reason to divorce her, totally abandon her, or even punish her with capital punishment, of which there are some hints within the metaphor (the land dies). But he acts differently. In his freedom, he fights to win Israel back, to restore the original condition of the marriage. And even more, he wants to give a new quality to the marriage.

Before restoration comes to the marriage he punishes his wife even to the point of abandoning her 'for a moment' in order to bring her back to her senses so that she may realize the horror of and be ashamed of her sin. Although she is now regarded as divorced or dead, she will be restored. Before that happens, the husband needs to give vent to his rightful wrath. But then Yahweh offers his wife total forgiveness, receiving her back as though she had never offended: the thing which only God is able to do. This hope applies not only to the immediate future after return from the exile, but extends far into the dimension of eschatological event.

We have also suggested that the metaphor originated from a complex of several sources. The dialogue with the Canaanite cult of Baal enabled Hosea to develop the metaphor. But in order to do that and remain faithful to Yahwism, he needed knowledge of the covenant tradition and the insight gained from marrying a promiscuous wife which enabled him to comprehend and connect all the factors together.

In the next chapter we will examine the way in which the Jewish community of late second temple period viewed the divine marriage. We will seek to establish if there were expectations in this community for further fulfillment of the eschatological hope associated with the marriage of God and his people. We will also look for any shifts within the understanding of the metaphor among the Jews which could be of significance to the understanding of the NT.

4

The Metaphor of Divine Marriage in Jewish non-Canonical Literature

INTRODUCTION

As indicated at the end of the last chapter, in this chapter we shall focus on examining the Jewish non-canonical writings in order to trace developments in understanding the metaphor of divine marriage in post-OT literature. In the OT Yahweh is the husband of his people Israel. In the NT it is Jesus of Nazareth who is presented as the bridegroom and his bride is the church. We will examine the literature to see if anything has changed to accommodate this transition. Of special interest to us will be the works written before the writing of the NT literature because these could have influenced Christian thinking on the divine marriage. We will deal first with the marriage metaphor itself and then turn to the themes related to it.

THE MARRIAGE METAPHOR IN JEWISH NON-CANONICAL WRITINGS

The metaphorical use of the sacred marriage theme is not developed either in the OT Pseudepigrapha[1] or in the documents known to us as the Dead Sea Scrolls (abbreviated DSS hereafter). While it would be difficult

---

1. Jeremias, "νύμφη νυμφίος," IV: 1102, stated that 4 Ezra 7:26 in its Syriac version cannot be taken as an example that first century CE Judaism spoke of Jerusalem as the Messiah's bride. The word 'bride' is a textual corruption. For the text of 4 Ezra 7:26 see Charlesworth, *Pseudepigrapha*, I: 537, 537 n.7d. Jeremias claims also that the Christian-Gnostic novel "Joseph and Asenath" does not support the figure of Joseph as a prototype of the Messiah. "νύμφη νυμφίος," IV: 1102. Jeremias's argument that 4 Ezra 5:24, 26 supports the claim that in the first century CE Israel was understood as the bride of God (I: 1102 n.28) is doubtful. The text does not state this explicitly because it reads,

The Metaphor of Divine Marriage in Jewish non-Canonical Literature

to look for any particular reason for not mentioning the metaphor in the Pseudepigrapha, a few things need to be noted concerning the Qumran community. The *hieros gamos* of Israel's God is a theme which occurs on several occasions in the Midrash. Therefore, after looking at the DSS we will turn to these rabbinical works.

Qumran Literature

The DSS have been of great value to biblical studies since their publication in the second half of the last century. Their content has shed much light upon the conceptual Jewish world of second temple Judaism and the ways in which the OT was interpreted. The DSS have, furthermore, contributed to translations of various OT texts in the past years. They have also helped in establishing the *Sitz im Leben* of NT books. However, the documents known to us do not explain much regarding the marriage metaphor. Why is this so?

We need to realize that we are not in possession of all the documents of Qumran and many of those that we do have are incomplete due to damage over the centuries. For instance, we only have a small portion of the Qumran commentary on Hosea (4Q166–67) together with biblical quotations that have been discovered. The surviving portion deals only with a few verses of the prophet, i.e., 2:6, 7, 8, 9–10, 11; 5:13b, 14a, 15; and 6:7.[2] Whereas the full commentary on Hos 2 might have contributed to our understanding of the metaphor, the few surviving verses do not help much. The commentary never calls God the husband of Israel, but rather offers a historical explanation of the Hosean verses. Thus 2:6 which according to the commentary reads,

> ["So now I am going to block her passage] with thorns, her paths [she cannot find"][3]

O sovereign Lord, from every forest of the earth and from all its trees you have chosen one vine, and from all the lands of the world you have chosen for yourself one lily, and from all the depths of the sea you have filled for yourself one river, and from all the cities that have been built you have consecrated Zion for yourself, and from all the birds that have been created you have named for yourself one dove, and from all the flocks that have been fashioned you have provided for yourself one sheep, and from all the multitude of people you have gotten for yourself one people; and to this people, whom you have loved, you have given the Law which is approved by all. (4 Ezra 5:23–27)

2. See Wise et al., *Dead Sea Scrolls*, 214–15.

3. Ibid., 214.

is explained thus:

> [This refers to . . . in madness] and blindness and confusion [. . .] and the time they turned traitor and did not [. . .] they are the generation [God] punished [first . . .] [. . . to be] gathered in the times of wrath, for [. . .][4]

Although fragmentary, this note on Hos 2:6 shows that the Qumran community understood God's actions as judgment on the generation to whom the prophet addressed his message.

The commentary explains that part of Hos 2:7, "["So she said, I'm going back to my first hus]band, because [I was better off then than now"],"[5] refers to the return of Israel from captivity.

Hos 2:8–11 as quoted and interpreted at Qumran is worth citing in full,

> ["She was not aware that] it was I who had given her the grain, [the wine,] [the oil, and the silver that] I multiplied, and the gold they made [into Baal"] (2:8).
>
> [This meaning is] that [they ate] and were satisfied and forgot God who [gives them the blessings, because] they left behind His commandments that He had sent them [through] His servants, the prophets. Instead they listened to those who deceived them. They honored them and revered them in their blindness as if they were gods.
>
> "So I will again take away my grain in its time, my wine [in its season]. I will withdraw my wool and my flax from covering [her nakedness]. Now I am uncovering her infamy in front of her [lovers. No one can] rescue her from my power" (2:9–10).
>
> The passage means that He assailed them with famine and nakedness, so that they became a disgr[ace] and a scandal in front of the Gentiles on whom they had relied, but who could not save them from their punishment.
>
> "I will put an end to all of her joy: her pil[grimages, new] moons, Sabbaths, and all her sacred days" (2:11).
>
> This means that [all the sacred] days they will take away in exchange for Gentile sacred days, so that [all] [her joy] will be turned into mourning.[6]

---

4. Ibid.
5. Ibid.
6. Ibid., 214–15.

The Metaphor of Divine Marriage in Jewish non-Canonical Literature 109

This passage brings a somewhat different interpretation to the meaning of Israel's lovers. While we have acknowledged in the previous chapter that the lovers were Baals, idols of Canaan, the commentator at Qumran characterized them as Gentiles, a political power (see on Hos 2:9–10), whom they followed (cf. 4Q167 Frag. 7 on Hos 6:7). The commentary as preserved lacks any interest in the marriage metaphor. It interprets Hosean verses by the characteristic Qumran method, "this means that," to refer texts only to a particular historical context, Israel before the Exile in this case.

Fragments of five Qumran commentaries on Isaiah (4Q161–65) likewise do not deal with the titular metaphor of this volume.[7] We do not have a commentary on Jeremiah and available references to Ezekiel do not deal with the divine marriage theme. Similarly, fragments on Exodus do not contribute to understanding the covenant at Sinai as the marriage between Yahweh and Israel. Thus we are left with no mention of the *hieros gamos* in the Qumran literature. We may assume either that there were texts dealing with the matter which have not survived or have not been discovered yet, or that the community was not interested in the subject at all.

A collection of messianic proof texts (4QTestimonia or 4Q175) points to the coming of a prophet like Moses, a royal descendant of David, and a proper high priest.[8] But divinity is not attributed to the Messiah and the Qumran texts never call him bridegroom or husband of his people.

Midrashim

The Jewish literature known as Midrash is of later origin than the DSS and dates from various centuries of the first millennium of our era.[9] It is associated with the rabbinic movement which originates from before the time of the destruction of Jerusalem's temple in the year 70 CE.

The Midrash[10] mentions Yahweh's betrothal to Israel at Sinai. For instance, Midrash Debarim Rabbah III.12 (on Deut 10:1) says,

---

7. See ibid., 209–14.
8. Ibid., 229–31.
9. Cf. Stemberger, *Talmud and Midrash*, 1–2.
10. The meaning of midrash can be defined only by description. Thus it is "a type of literature, oral or written, which stands in direct relationship to a fixed, canonical text, considered to be the authoritative and the revealed word of God by the midrashist

12. AT THAT TIME THE LORD SAID UNTO ME: HEW THEE (X, 1). *Halachah*: When a Jew betroths a woman, who has to pay for the writing of the document of betrothal? Our Rabbis have learnt thus: Documents of betrothal and marriage are written only with the consent of the two parties, and the bridegroom pays the fee. And this we learn from God from His betrothal of Israel at Sinai, as it is written, *And the Lord said unto Moses: Go unto the people and betroth them to-day and to-morrow* (Ex. XIX, 10) ...[11]

The Midrash takes וקדשתם of Exod 19:10 in the MT ("sanctify them") as קידושין which refers to writing the betrothal document.[12]

Another instance comes from Midrash Shemoth Rabbah XLI.6 (on Exod 31:18),

6. Another explanation of AND HE GAVE UNTO MOSES. R. Abbahu said: All the forty days Moses was on high, he kept on forgetting the Torah he learnt. He then said: 'Lord of the Universe, I have spent forty days, yet I know nothing.' What did God do? At the end of the forty days, He gave him the Torah as a gift, for it says, AND HE GAVE UNTO MOSES. Could then Moses have learnt the whole Torah? Of the Torah it says: *The measure thereof is longer than the earth, and broader than the sea* (Job XI, 9); could then Moses have learnt it all in forty days? No; but it was only the principles thereof which God taught Moses – hence KEKALOTHO OF SPEAKING WITH HIM. THE TWO TABLETS OF THE TESTIMONY. Why *two* tablets? To correspond with heaven and earth, with a bride and bridegroom, with the two groomsmen, and also with this world and the World to Come ...[13]

---

and his audience, and in which the canonical text is explicitly cited or clearly alluded to." See ibid., 235. Stemberger quotes here the definition given by G. Porton. He further explains that midrash is not just allusion to a biblical text but to a biblical event as well. "However, the hearers' or readers' attitude to the expounded canonical text (or biblical event) does *not* properly belong to the definition of midrash (*pace* Porton), since that would almost always remain unverifiable." Italics his.

11. Freedman and Simon, *Deuteronomy*, 81. Cf. *Aggadat Bereshit* 41, 126 as referred to in Ginzberg, *Legends of the Jews*, 36 n. 200. According to Ginzberg, *Aggadat Bereshit* 41, 126 supports the view that rabbinic literature regarded God as the bridegroom of Israel. The text can be found in Buber, S. *Aggadat Bereshit*. Cracow: 1903; reprinted 1973.

12. Freedman and Simon, *Deuteronomy*, 81 n. 3.

13. Freedman and Simon, *Exodus*, 475.

The Metaphor of Divine Marriage in Jewish non-Canonical Literature   111

The editors of the text explain in the footnote that the last sentence of our quotation refers to the Torah and the Tablets as groomsmen because they helped towards the marriage between God and Israel.[14]

Jeremias[15] observes that Midrash Exodus XV.30 on Exod 15:2 suggests that the verse can also be translated: "In this world they (the Israelites) were betrothed . . . , in the days of Messiah they will be married." But the marriage still refers to one between Yahweh and Israel, and not Messiah and Israel. Furthermore, Jeremias cannot prove that Midrash Exodus XV.30 comes from the first century CE. But he still looks for evidence for his claim that the use of the divine marriage metaphor by the Rabbis was as early as the first century. The only support he offers comes from Mekhilta Exodus on 19:1.[16] He links that text with Rabbi Jochanan b. Zakkai (c. 40–80 CE). However, significant doubts about the date of the work as well as problems concerning its authorship seriously weaken Jeremias's argument.[17]

Midrash Shir ha-Shirim offers an allegorical interpretation of the Song of Songs. It describes the mutual love of God and Israel. Simon explains,

> On God's side this is shown chiefly by the giving of the Law and the redemption from Egypt; on Israel's side it is shown chiefly by the acceptance of the Law and by readiness to undergo martyrdom for the sake of God.[18]

These are few examples of the *hieros gamos* in late rabbinic literature. But *Midrashim*, like the Talmud, never refer to the Messiah as the bridegroom.

There is, however, no possibility that the Midrash could have influenced NT writers. All the instances cited above come from writings of much later origin than the NT. Midrash Deuteronomy was prob-

---

14. Ibid., 475 n.7.

15. "νύμφη νυμφίος," IV: 1102 n. 32. The author of this book checking Jeremias's ref-erence has not found in Midrash Exodus XV.30 any mention of Exod 15:2.

16. Ibid., IV: 1102 n. 28.

17. Stemberger, *Talmud and Midrash*, 247–75. See also pp. 2, 4, 7, 10, 54, 60, 66, 68, 272, 285 on R. Yohanan b. Zakkai for a discussion of difficulties arising with the dating of his activities and attributing to him certain works.

18. Freedman and Simon, *Esther and Song of Songs*. From the introduction to Song of Songs by M. Simon, vii.

ably composed sometime between 450 and 800 CE,[19] Midrash Exodus before the tenth century CE at the earliest,[20] and Midrash Song of Songs must be dated to the middle of the sixth century CE.[21] Aggadath Bereshit referred to by Ginzberg probably comes from the tenth century of our era.[22]

Although it can be argued that parts of these writings come from an oral tradition going back centuries before the rise of Christianity, there is not sufficient independent evidence to confirm that they do. Stemberger notes the methodological problem of many contemporary scholars in referring to the rabbinic literature when he says,

> It is particularly the widespread theory that the rabbinc tradition was handed down orally through the centuries with absolute faithfulness which has led to an utterly uncritical use of rabbinic material. This is true both for the historian who often accepts the rabbinic texts without examination as factual reports, merely eliminating, for example, numerical exaggerations and obviously legendary traits; and for the scholar dealing in rabbinic theology, who often does not pay (sufficient) attention to the different periods of origin of the various writings, nor to the specific intention of a literary genre, and thus arrives at a rather undifferentiated image of "the" rabbinic theology. Because of its simplicity and homogeneity, this image is readily adopted in the comparative history of religion and especially in New Testament exegesis ...[23]

This situation is evident when one looks, for example, at articles in Bible dictionaries.[24] They often refer to H. L. Strack & P. Billerbeck's *Kommentar*

---

19. Stemberger, *Talmud and Midrash*, 307–8. See also Freedman and Simon, *Deuteronomy*, Introduction by J. Rabbinowitz, vii, who refers to Zunz's late dating at c. 900 CE.

20. Stemberger, *Talmud and Midrash*, 309.

21. Ibid., 315. Although it contains some older material as well. Jeremias, "νύμφη νυμφίος," IV: 1102 n. 28, claims that the allegorical interpretation of the Song of Songs was known as early as the first century CE and thus the book was included in the Jewish canon. This interpretation was later developed by R. Aquiba, who according to Jeremias, died c. 135 CE. But see Stemberger, *Talmud and Midrash*, 72, who says that "various 'biographical accounts' (e.g., that he only turned to study at the age of 40, or even accounts of his imprisonment and execution), are relatively useless for a description of the historical Aquiba." Stemberger also discusses problems connected with the study of rabbinic biographies (56).

22. Stemberger, *Talmud and Midrash*, 311–12.

23. *Talmud and Midrash*, 45.

24. See, for example, Günter, "γαμέω," II: 575–77. Also Jeremias, "νύμφη νυμφίος," IV: 1099–1106 and Stauffer, "γαμέω γάμος," I: 648–57.

zum Neuen Testament aus Talmud und Midrash[25] as a source of useful quotations from rabbinic material without regard for a proper historical dating.[26] One is given the impression that the Talmud or/and Midrash constitute a real support or basis for NT exegesis.

Neusner[27] criticizes the way scholars use the rabbinic literature in NT studies. According to him, NT commentators often treat it gullibly and their references to it lack a critical approach. He argues that Midrash Rabbah and the Talmud can only offer views which were expressed by the compilers of these works centuries after Jesus Christ and that therefore they are irrelevant to Jesus' situation. He has expressed his disapproval of such a method when he said,

> Ordinarily critical scholars abandon all pretense of criticism when they open rabbinic literature, ignoring its traits and history of documentary fabrication and imputing to it traits of historicity and facticity that literature does not exhibit or pretend to value.[28]

Therefore, in the light of the above discussion we doubt the relevance of *Midrashim* to the *hieros gamos* theme of the NT. Even if they help us to grasp something of Jewish thinking on certain Scripture passages they can hardly constitute a foundation for our NT study of the titular metaphor of this volume.

TOPICS CLOSELY RELATED TO THE MARRIAGE METAPHOR IN JEWISH LITERATURE

Leaving aside later Jewish writings, we will turn to those which could have influenced NT writers.

Messianic Banquet

Muirhead,[29] while discussing the parable of the Wedding Feast in Matt 22:1–14 where Jesus identifies himself with the bridegroom, mentions

---

25. München: Beck, 1922–1961.

26. Cf. Stemberger, *Talmud and Midrash*, 46.

27. Neusner, *Rabbinic Literature*. The whole book deals with methodological problems in approaching rabbinic writings. However, for critique of NT scholars' misuse of the literature, see esp. pp. 2, 7,14, 27, 85–86, 92, 94, 177 n.5, 182. For further examples of the misuse of rabbinic material by NT scholars see Silberman, "Use of Rabbinic Material," 153–55.

28. *Rabbinic Literature*, 85.

29. Muirhead, "Bride of Christ," 182.

that it refers to the messianic banquet theme widely used not only in the OT (e.g., Isa 25:6) but also in Jewish sources. He identifies references to the banquet in 1 Enoch 62:14 and 3 Enoch 48:10.

1 Enoch 62:13–14 reads,

> The righteous and elect ones shall be saved on that day; and from henceforth they shall never see the faces of the sinners and the oppressors. The Lord of the Spirits will abide over them; they shall eat and rest and rise with that Son of Man forever and ever.[30]

The passage comes from the part of 1 Enoch called the Book of the Similitudes (chapters 37–71) which is dated from the first century CE.[31] The Similitudes present a figure of a messiah in the context of the eschatological last judgment, the destruction of the wicked, and the triumph of the righteous people.[32] Chapter 62 refers to that judgment of the wicked and the glorified state of God's elect ones. Black[33] in his commentary on 1 Enoch 62:14 says that the phrase "they shall eat and rest" (or "they shall eat and lie down") has its counterpart in Zephaniah 3:13 (יִרְעוּ וְרָבְצוּ, "they shall feed and lie down")[34] where it is used to describe the security of the remnant on their return from dispersion. According to Black, 1 Enoch 62:14 has a similar meaning, i.e., it refers to the security of the righteous ones. Even if we render the phrase as constant eating with that Son of Man, it still does not explain much of the messianic banquet. Indeed, it does not even mention a banquet or feast as in Isa 25:6.

However, what Black says of the following verses is interesting. 1 Enoch 62:15 speaks of "garments of glory" which the righteous and elect ones will wear. These are the same as in 62:16 "garments of life" and, according to Black, refer to "garments of immortality," therefore they should be rendered as garments of eternal life.[35] They have their parallel in Isaiah's "garments of salvation" in 61:10, the passage we have studied in the previous chapter concerning OT use of the marriage metaphor.

---

30. Isaac, "1 Enoch," I: 44.

31. Ibid., 7.

32. Ibid., 9.

33. Black, *I Enoch*, 236.

34. Against the reading of NKJV, "they shall feed *their* flocks and lie down." יִרְעוּ is Kal future of third person masculine plural of רָעָה "to feed, to pasture" (a flock) but also "to feed down, to consume." See Davidson, *Hebrew and Chaldee Lexicon*, 686. Therefore "to eat" in NIV, "they will eat and lie down."

35. *I Enoch*, 237.

The Metaphor of Divine Marriage in Jewish non-Canonical Literature   115

There Yahweh clothes Zion, his restored bride, with "garments of salvation." These garments are worn by the saved ones in Revelation (cf. 3:4, 5, 18; 4:4; 6:11, 7:9, 13, 14).

3 Enoch 48:10 reads,

> Moreover, the kingdom of Israel, gathered from the four quarters of the world, shall eat with the Messiah, and the gentiles shall eat with them ... [36]

Alexander[37] explains that this verse refers to the messianic banquet. The idea is, however, not developed in the passage, although it is connected to the eschatological salvation. The verse in its context does not say anything beyond the content of 1 Enoch 62:14.

The text of 3 Enoch 48 cannot be as early as the first century CE and probably was not composed before the latter half of the third century.[38] Therefore it can hardly be of direct relevance to NT exegesis.

Heavenly Jerusalem

The theme of the heavenly Jerusalem is connected to that of Christ's bride in Rev 21:2 and possibly to the heavenly city in Gal 4:26. Therefore it is worthwhile examining the topic in Jewish writings.

There are a few references in the Pseudepigrapha that point to a city recognized by some as the heavenly Jerusalem.

The story of Joseph and Aseneth is said to contain such references. Certain fragments of the work might be pre-Christian (the end of the first century BCE).[39] According to the story, an Egyptian virgin Aseneth, the daughter of the priest of Heliopolis who is Pharaoh's chief counselor, is later married to Joseph the son of Jacob the patriarch (cf. Gen 41:45). Before this happens she repents from idolatry (chapters 10–13) and is visited by the chief of the angels who gives her the name "City of Refuge" (15:7; 16:16; 17:6; 19:5) for she is to be such an eternal city for all who will repent like her. The latter passages are worth quoting here because

---

36. Alexander, "3 Enoch," I: 302.
37. Ibid., 302 n. x.
38. See ibid., 225–29.
39. Burchard, "Joseph and Aseneth," II: 187–88. However, Jeremias argues that this story is a Christian-Gnostic novel whose author was one of the Valentinians (second century CE onwards). See "νύμφη νυμφίος," IV: 1102, 1102 n. 36.

this will help us to examine the argument of Aseneth being like the heavenly Jerusalem. In 15:7 the angel says to Aseneth,

> And your name shall no longer be Aseneth, but your name shall be City of Refuge, because in you many nations will take refuge with the Lord, the Most High, and under your wings many people trusting in the Lord God will be sheltered, and behind your walls will be guarded those who attach themselves to the Most High God in the name of Repentance. For Repentance is in the heavens, an exceedingly beautiful and good daughter of the Most High. And she herself entreats the Most High for you at all times and for all who repent in the name of the Most High God, because he is (the) father of Repentance. And she herself is guardian of all virgins, and loves you very much, and is beseeching the Most High for you at all times and for all who repent she prepared a place of rest in the heavens. And she will renew all who repent, and wait on them herself for ever (and) ever.[40]

After Aseneth invited the angel to eat at her table, he gave her to eat a portion of a honeycomb, saying (16:16),

> Behold, you have eaten bread of life, and drunk a cup of immortality, and been anointed with ointment of incorruptibility. Behold, from today your flesh (will) flourish like flowers of life from the ground[41] of the Most High, and your bones will grow strong like the cedars of the paradise of delight of God, and untiring powers will embrace you, and your youth will not see old age, and your beauty will not fail forever. And you shall be like a walled mother-city of all who take refuge with the name of the Lord God, the king of the ages.[42]

Aseneth had seven virgin maidservants so she wanted the angel to bless them as he had blessed her. The angel blessed them with the words (17:6),

> May the Lord God the Most High bless you. And you shall be seven pillars of the City of Refuge, and all the fellow inhabitants of the chosen of that city will rest upon you for ever (and) ever.[43]

---

40. Burchard, *Joseph and Aseneth*, II: 226–27.
41. Or "garden." See ibid., II: 229 n.s.
42. Ibid., II: 229.
43. Ibid., II: 231.

The Metaphor of Divine Marriage in Jewish non-Canonical Literature   117

It is noteworthy that the phrase "fellow inhabitants" signifies "women immigrants."[44] This may refer to women proselytes who will inherit the city.

After Joseph returned home, Aseneth explained to him what had happened after her conversion and what the angel had said to her. In 19:5 she reports,

> And he said to me, "Your name will no longer be called Aseneth, but your name will be called City of Refuge and the Lord God will reign as king over many nations for ever, because in you many nations will take refuge with the Lord God, the Most High."[45]

Joseph, in response to her words, says (19:8–9),

> Blessed are you by the Most High God, and blessed (is) your name for ever, because the Lord has founded your walls in the highest, and your walls (are) adamantine walls of life, because the sons of the living God will dwell in your City of Refuge, and the Lord will reign over them for ever and ever.[46]

Then by three kisses Joseph subsequently gave her the spirit of life, of wisdom and of truth (19:10–11). This is loosely linked to the blessed bread, cup and ointment which also provide life (cf. 8:5). The kisses may refer either to an erotic motif in a spiritualized form or to imparting a spirit to Aseneth that Joseph himself possesses. Burchard explains,

> That life, soul, spirit, or the like can be transferred or exchanged (or taken away, for that matter) by a kiss is a very old idea underlying many kinds of human behavior and ritual, and expressed in a host of texts, both religious and profane (e.g., Gen 2:7; Jn 20:22; OdesSol 28:6f.; Xenophon of Ephesus 1.9.6) . . . Maybe we are to understand that life is first mediated by intimate contact with a Jew and then sustained by other things. But perhaps the author in 19:11 just makes use of a different tradition to express the same general idea that adherence to Judaism means life.[47]

The passages above cited are used to support parallelism between Aseneth, the City of Refuge, and the heavenly Jerusalem as found in

---

44. Ibid., II: 231 n.f.
45. Ibid., II: 233.
46. Ibid.
47. Ibid., II: 233 n.m.

Jewish and Christian canonical writings. Burchard[48] sees in Aseneth a continuation of the tradition of Zion, the City of God. All who seek shelter in her will find protection. These are those who repent like her, the proselytes. Burchard, however, explains,

> To be "in" Aseneth, however, is not similar to being "in" Christ. Both concepts are comparable in that salvation depends on association with an historical person, but association means different things in each case. Aseneth did not continue to be present as a person. She does not continue to live "in" proselytes similar to the way "Christ lives in me" (Gal 2:20). Only the promises and qualities with which she was endowed remain available, like the physical and material heritage that is inherited by a particular family.[49]

Aseneth therefore is a prototype of those who follow her steps by becoming proselytes.

In order to fully understand the passages we need to grasp some of the story's theology.[50] According to the book only the Jews recognize God and it is they alone whom he favors, assuring them of their welfare and all the privileges that come with divine adoption. Others are godless idol worshippers. They remain in darkness and error, and are like the dead. The thing that distinguishes the two societies is their way of life as expressed in certain practices, for example, the use of food and ointment (8:5; cf. 8:9; 15:5; 16:16; 19:5; 21:13–14, 21). Salvation in the story is a necessity for the non-Jews, but does not require a redeemer. It is rather associated with the idea of conversion from polytheism to the Jewish way of life.

The Jews experience fullness of life. They enjoy supernatural beauty, wisdom, comfortable living and divine protection, almost an angelic state, simply because of their adherence to God. The situation of those in darkness may be changed by earnest repentance and acceptance of the Jewish way of life. The proselyte receives all the privileges of the Jews and by repentance comes to the "angelic status naturally possessed by the Jews."

The eschatology of the story is all about the individual life of the elect in heaven, a place of rest (8:9; 15:7–8; 22:13). The Jew arrives at that

---

48. Ibid., II: 189–90.
49. Ibid.
50. See ibid., II: 190ff.

rest immediately after death. However, we are not given much information of the after-life state.

In the process of her conversion Aseneth is mourning with ashes on her head, confessing and praying. The chief angel appears to her and wants her to take courage (14:11; 15:2). He assures her that her prayers have been heard in heaven and that from now on she will be "renewed and make alive again" (15:5). This means she will experience the blessings of divine childhood, she will be placed in that almost-angelic state belonging to the Jews. She will become a new person of a new quality.

In 15:7 Aseneth the proselyte receives the name City of Refuge, but the passage does not suggest that she has become a heavenly city which will be inhabited by the righteous. There is rather a place of rest in heaven prepared by God and Repentance (8:9; 15:7). The phrase, "because in you many nations will take refuge with the Lord God, the Most High, and under your wings many peoples trusting in the Lord God will be sheltered, and behind your walls will be guarded those who attach themselves to the Most High God in the name of Repentance," makes sense only if we understand, following Burchard,[51] "being in Aseneth" as repenting like her, becoming a proselyte like her. Those "in her" will gain the same promises and qualities as Aseneth. The passage, furthermore, seems to emphasize the glory and greatness of Aseneth's act of repentance as well as the courage that is brought through naming her by the angel.

16:16, "And you shall be like a walled mother-city of all who take refuge with the name of the Lord . . . ," only supports this interpretation. It seems that Aseneth is a prototype for all who will convert to Judaism after her. She has found security in God and proselytes "in her" will also find the same refuge in the Lord.

17:5 explains that the seven maidservants of Aseneth became the pillars supporting the City of Refuge. But the meaning of belonging *in* that city has already been explained.

The words of 19:5 resemble those of 15:7a. However, the response of Joseph may cause some misunderstanding. He says in 19:8, ". . . and blessed (is) your name for ever, because the Lord God founded your walls in the highest, and your walls (are) adamantine walls of life, because the sons of the living God will dwell in your City of Refuge, and the Lord God will reign as king over them for ever and ever." These words

51. Ibid., II: 189–90.

are in the context of Joseph rejoicing over Aseneth's conversion. He was told by the chief angel what had happened to Aseneth and therefore he expresses joy at his return home. But again the verse does not suggest that City of Refuge is a heavenly city. It rather expresses the greatness of the state Aseneth arrived at by her conversion. She has found her refuge with God in heaven (her walls are founded in heaven) and her position remains unshaken ("your walls (are) adamantine walls of life"). Moreover, the verse suggests that Aseneth knows or has access to the City of Refuge ("the sons of the living God will dwell in *your* City of Refuge") rather than constitutes this city. Interpreted along the lines of the meaning of previous verses and the lines of the story's theology, this verse sets Aseneth as a prototype of all proselytes who will gain similar refuge with God.

The content of the story of Joseph and Aseneth, therefore, makes it very unlikely that any parallel to the heavenly Jerusalem occurs within the poem. However, another issue related to our study needs to be discussed here.

The view that Aseneth represents the heavenly city rests on a figurative interpretation of Joseph in the tale. Stauffer claims that,

> The Jewish legend of Joseph and Asenath, which deals with the marriage of Joseph to a daughter of the Egyptian king, is obviously interpreted and allegorically exploited in Judaism with reference to the marriage of the Messiah to a city of God ...[52]

This claim, however, lacks any convincing evidence. Stauffer argues that in 19:11 Joseph imparted the Spirit of God to Aseneth in a kiss. This is a very unlikely interpretation in the context of the story as well as in the context of that which was said earlier concerning the *three* kisses of Joseph. Likewise the epithet "son of God" (see 6:3, 5; 13:13) accorded to Joseph does not support the claim that he represents the figure of the Messiah. The epithet is used in the book to describe a Jew, the one who knows God and therefore has life, wisdom and prosperity, and is almost like an angel, in general (16:14; 19:8). Moreover, Jeremias[53] doubts Joseph was ever a prototype of the Messiah in pre-Christian Judaism.

To sum up, it seems very unlikely that the legend of Joseph and Aseneth contributes to our understanding of the heavenly Jerusalem

---

52. "γαμέω γάμος," I: 657.
53. "νύμφη νυμφίος," IV: 1102.

as found in the NT. Similarly, other passages in the Pseudepigrapha are either not clear references to a new Jerusalem (1 Enoch 90:28–29)[54] or are of later origin than the NT (4 Ezra 7:26; 10:25–28; 41–49; 2 Enoch 55:2; 2 Baruch 4:2–7; 3 Enoch 48A:3–4)[55] and therefore could not have influenced ideas found therein.

The idea of a new city is found in a few texts from Qumran (1Q32; 2Q24; 4Q554–55; 5Q15; 11Q18). They mainly describe rather in the manner of Ezekiel's vision (chapters 40–48), but differing in many details, the enormous size of, dimensions of and the material used to build a new city, supposedly Jerusalem.[56] The description of the temple is lacking in the texts, though the temple is mentioned several times. There is, however, no information suggesting that the city is heavenly or descending from above as in Rev 21. It could well have been an earthly city built (by divine intervention because of its enormous size?)[57] according to angelic plans.[58] The texts, therefore, do not contribute much to our understanding of ideas associated with the titular metaphor of this book. However, they reveal something of Jewish longings and expectations in the pre-Christian era. Although the Temple in Jerusalem and the city itself had been rebuilt after the Babylonian exile, there was some expectation of another, greater temple (cf. Ezek 40–48; Ezra 3:12) placed in a greater, far more glorious city (cf. e.g., Isa 54:11–12).[59] The Jews still looked forward to the fulfillment of that which was promised by God through the prophets.

CONCLUSIONS

Having examined various Jewish writings we have discovered that they do not contribute much to our understanding of the divine marriage theme as found in the NT. They do not help us to understand the shift within the metaphor from Yahweh being the husband of Israel in the OT to Christ being the bridegroom of the church in the NT. We have

---

54. See in Charlesworth, *Pseudepigrapha*, I: 71. This can refer to a temple being replaced by a new one.

55. Ibid., successively, I: 520, 537, 547–48; I: 94–95, 182; I: 616–17, 622; I: 225–29, 300–301.

56. See Wise et al., *Dead Sea Scrolls*, 180–84.

57. Cf. ibid., 180.

58. Cf. Vermes, *Dead Sea Scrolls*, 55.

59. Cf. Wise et al., *Dead Sea Scrolls*, 180.

also observed that Jewish literature is of little help concerning the ideas linked to the metaphor of the divine marriage in the NT.

Nevertheless, we have recognized a serious methodological problem for NT scholars. They sometimes use later rabbinic literature in a somewhat arbitrary manner, as if it was directly influential on the NT. The literature, according to Stemberger and Neusner, was composed relatively late and with too little interest in "factual reports" to be regarded as such.

We have also acknowledged that pre-Christian Judaism had great expectations concerning Jerusalem and its temple which had not yet been fulfilled. The Jews looked forward to a new, glorious city of heavenly origin.

Finally, our study suggests that only by turning to the NT literature will we trace the development of the divine marriage metaphor to introduce the Messiah as the bridegroom. Therefore in the next chapters we will focus on passages in the gospels and the Pauline literature, which contain references to the *hieros gamos*.

5

The Metaphor of Divine Marriage in the Gospels

INTRODUCTION

IT MAY SEEM SOMEWHAT strange to start tracing the development of the divine marriage metaphor in the NT by focusing first on the gospels. The reason for this is that the vast majority of scholars believe that the gospels are later than Pauline writings.[1] And therefore, one would be expected to turn first to the letters of Paul in looking for the first documentary use of the metaphor of divine marriage in the NT.[2] One might also argue that if some NT writings influenced the others regarding the metaphor it must have been Paul's letters having an impact on the gospels, not the other way around.

Our intention is not to deny the priority of the Pauline literature in regard to dating, but we believe that a case can be made[3] that the gospels' references to Christ's marriage imagery could have been of earlier origin than the Pauline ones. These references include Jesus' parables[4] in the Synoptic gospels and John the Baptist's testimony about Jesus in the fourth gospel. Therefore, our aim in this chapter will be to study these passages.

---

1. E.g., Hays, *Echoes of Scripture*, x; Schnelle, *New Testament Writings*, 13, where he says that Pauline letters are indisputably the oldest writings in the NT. Cf. Sanders, *Jesus and Judaism*, 16.

2. As does Batey, *Nuptial Imagery*, 12. There he claims that "in the New Testament the first extant documentary use of bridal imagery is II Corinthians 11:2, 3."

3. See below, contra, e.g., Batey. Part of our task will be to show that the parables employing the marriage metaphor are dominical.

4. Here the phrase "Jesus' parables" is used in the broadest sense to describe all forms of comparative language which the evangelists ascribed to Jesus.

Acknowledging the complexity of parable studies in the last century, however, we will first attempt to work out our attitude toward Jesus' parables. Following this will come our discussion of Mark 2:18–22 (and pars.), Matthew 22:1–14 (cf. Luke 14:15–23), Matthew 25:1–13, and John 3:22–30 in the context of John 2–4. Questions of the origin of these passages together with their *Sitz im Leben* will be included in the discussion. These discussions will go alongside considering the relationship between the passages, and especially the relationship of material in the fourth gospel to that of the Synoptics. In turn, we will discuss the shift in the metaphor of divine marriage from the OT picture of Yahweh being the husband of Israel to the Messiah being the bridegroom of his bride, since the intertestamental literature did not prove to be helpful in this respect.

TOWARDS INTERPRETING JESUS' PARABLES

There have been a number of publications in recent years describing the twentieth-century trends in interpreting the parables of Jesus.[5] Our task here is not to repeat the whole history of interpreting the parables. However, we want to pay attention to the main arguments in the debate in order to develop our approach to the parables.

"One-point-of-comparison" Historical Method

Dissatisfied with the allegorical method of earlier centuries, Adolf Jülicher[6], applying the categories of Greek rhetoric, initiated a new trend in interpreting the parables of Jesus as expanded similes rather than as expanded metaphors (i.e., allegories).[7] He proposed that a parable has only one point of comparison or one central thought as distinguished from an allegory which uses many images to describe various aspects of the idea or experience being delineated.[8] He felt that the allegorical interpretation cannot be controlled or determined by the original context and meaning and therefore it opens a way to imposing the already held

---

5. A good summary of the approaches to the parables until 1970s can be found in Bailey, *Poet & Peasant*, 16–26. For more recent publication on the subject see Snodgrass, "Parables of Jesus," 3–29.

6. In his famous work *Die Gleichnisreden Jesu*.

7. Cf. Snodgrass, "Parables of Jesus," 6.

8. Via, *The Parables*, 2.

beliefs of the interpreter upon the details of the parable.[9] Thus in practice the allegorical method permits an infinite variety of arbitrary interpretations. Jülicher believed that the historical method would prevent this. He therefore focused on extracting one central point of the parable that requires the most general possible application.[10] The parable, for him, functions as a means of presenting general religious maxims.[11]

The Jülicherian approach became widely known to the English-speaking world only when it found an adherent in C. H. Dodd. He paid attention to the fact that the gospels themselves encourage the allegorical method of interpretation.[12] He remarked, however, that those allegorical parts were later interpolations of the evangelists based on misunderstanding of the original stories of Jesus. Thus he examined the parables at two levels: that of the original story of Jesus and that of the story as understood by the early church. He noticed that the crucial passage is Mark 4:11–20, which claims that some people do not understand the parables because their meaning is veiled for them. They were not predestined to salvation so they could not understand the revelation in Jesus. And thus the passage, according to Dodd, points to the primitive church's solution to the problem of why the disciples of Jesus failed to win the Jews after the death of their master.[13] Therefore he concludes,

> But that He [i.e., Jesus] desired not to be understood by the people in general, and therefore clothed His teaching in unintelligible forms, cannot be made credible on any reasonable reading of the Gospels.[14]

Beside this, Dodd argues that the parables were a common form of illustrating ideas among the Jews and they could be allegorically mystified only in the Hellenistic world.[15] As for being understandable to the recipient, the parables are presenting truths in concrete pictures. Expressing the same in the form of a general definition,

---

9. Cf. Donahue, *Gospel in Parable*, 11.

10. This "widest possible generality" of the teaching of the parables proved to be Jülicher's error. This fact is recognized by J. Jeremias, *Parables of Jesus*, 19.

11. Snodgrass, "Parables of Jesus," 8.

12. Dodd, *Parables of the Kingdom*, 13.

13. Ibid., 14–15.

14. Ibid., 15.

15. Ibid. Dodd claims that Jesus' parables are similar in form to rabbinic parables.

> ... the parable is a metaphor or a simile drawn from nature or common life, arresting the hearer by its vividness or strangeness, and leaving the mind in sufficient doubt about its precise application to tease it into active thought.[16]

Dodd sees also three distinguishable kinds of parables, although sometimes the classification is not that arbitrary.[17] The basic parable is a simple metaphor or a figurative saying (e.g., "a town set on a mountain cannot be hidden"). A simple metaphor can be developed into a picture and then it becomes a similitude (e.g., Mark 2:21). But it can be also elaborated into a shorter (e.g., "The Lost Sheep") or longer (e.g., "The Two Houses") story or a full-length tale (e.g., "The Prodigal Son") and then it constitutes a parable proper. But, again, interpretation must be determined by a single point of comparison in which case the details do not have an independent meaning.[18]

Dodd's method of studying the parables is to reconstruct their original setting in the life of Jesus as opposed to the setting given by the evangelists which was not the original setting.[19] He proposed two steps to be taken towards this reconstruction. They are worth quoting in full here:

> (i) The clue must be found, not in ideas which developed only with the experience of the early Church, but in such ideas as may be supposed to have been in the minds of the hearers of Jesus during his ministry. Our best guide to such ideas will often be the Old Testament, with which they may be presumed to have been familiar. Thus the images of a vineyard, a fig-tree, harvest, a feast, and others, had associations which could escape no one brought up on the Old Testament. (ii) The meaning which we attribute to the parable must be congruous with the interpretation of His own ministry offered by Jesus in explicit and unambiguous sayings, so far as such sayings are known to us; and in any case it must be such as to fit the general view of His teaching to which a study of the non-parabolic sayings leads. A preliminary task,

---

16. Ibid., 16.
17. Ibid., 16–18. This, to some extent, resembles Bultmann's classification.
18. Ibid., 18–19.
19. See ibid., 26–27. The point was earlier made by Cadoux, A. T. *The Parables of Jesus: Their Art and Use*. London: James Clarke and Co., 1931, but it only received wider attention following the publication of Dodd's work. Jeremias later valued highly Dodd's work as the first really successful attempt to place the parables in Jesus' *Sitz im Leben* (*Parables of Jesus*, 21).

therefore, will be to define, so far as we can, the general orientation of the teaching of Jesus.[20]

Dodd argues that this general orientation is the (long-expected by the Jews) kingdom of God (understood as God's rule over the whole world) being realized in the ministry of Jesus.[21]

Dodd's work was continued by Joachim Jeremias. For Jeremias, the parables as a particularly "trustworthy tradition" are entirely free of allegorization.[22] Mark 4:12 does not relate to the possibility of understanding the parables by disclosing some secret meaning hidden from outsiders, but rather speaks of Jesus' preaching in general.[23] To those who are not his disciples Jesus' words remain obscure because they do not acknowledge him unless they repent (cf. Isa 6:9–7). The parables as such are understandable pictures reflecting the character of Jesus' preaching. The only difficulty in understanding them is for subsequent generations after Jesus who need to recover their original setting and therefore their original meaning. Partially, the problem appeared when the parables had to be translated into Greek from Jesus' mother-tongue, Galilean Aramaic.[24] The translation itself already introduced some Hellenistic elements to the teaching of Jesus thus distancing it from its original form. The early church took that already modified material and applied it to its own situation "characterized by the delay of the *Parousia* and the Gentile mission."[25] Somewhat helpful in the task of recovering the original utterances of Jesus is the *Gospel of Thomas* which contains its own version of eleven of the synoptic parables.[26] The OT still remains

---

20. Dodd, *Parables of the Kingdom*, 32.

21. Ibid., 35–55.

22. Jeremias, *Parables of Jesus*, 11–12, 18.

23. Ibid., 17–18.

24. Ibid., 25–27. The so-called "Aramaic hypothesis" is based on the logical and historical inference that Greek, although being the *lingua franca* of the Greco-Roman world, never fully replaced Aramaic and that Jesus is recorded in a few instances in the gospels as using Aramaic. See, however, Porter, "Jesus," 200–201, 201 n. 7. Porter challenges this widely held view arguing that the gospels themselves notice the misunderstanding of those standing by at Jesus' crucifixion, possibly suggesting that they did not understand Aramaic (cf. Mark 15:34). He claims that there is strong epigraphic and literary evidence for the widespread knowledge of Greek throughout Palestine including Galilee (p. 213).

25. Jeremias, *Parables of Jesus*, 66

26. Ibid., 24. According to the subsequent logions, they are as follows: (9) The Sower, (20) The Mustard Seed, (21b and 103) The Burglar, (57) The Tares among the Wheat,

important, although the main focus is on reconstructing Jesus' setting from the parables themselves and ideas developed by the early church.[27]

Jeremias recognized the problem which Jülicher created by imposing on the parables the categories of Greek rhetoric. He preferred to view them in the sense of Hebrew *mašal* (=Aramaic *mathla*) which embraced all forms of figurative speech.[28] He was, however, dissatisfied with Dodd's limited view of eschatology which governed his interpretation, the one-sided nature of his conception of the Kingdom as already having broken through in Jesus' ministry. Jeremias rather prefers to emphasize the conflict aspect of the parables because they are for him "weapons of controversy," not, as Jülicher claimed, general maxims teaching morals.[29] They challenge the listeners to realize that the day of salvation has already come, that God is merciful to sinners and that he will deliver them from the imminent catastrophe, the coming tribulation. They must repent and make a decision for him now, before it is too late.[30] Jeremias's eschatology seems, therefore, to be progressive, i.e., in the process of realization.[31]

The one-point-of-comparison historical method was used to reconstruct the original *Sitz im Leben* of Jesus' parables, assuming that the parables as we have them today in the canonical gospels were reworked and reshaped by the early church in order to support its beliefs and expectations. Scholars differentiated only as to the goal the parables were to achieve. For Jülicher the parables were to teach general ethics; Dodd saw them as teaching in concrete pictures the general truth proclaimed by Jesus, i.e., that the Kingdom of God has come; Jeremias acknowledged

---

(63) The Rich Fool, (64) The Great Supper, (65) The Wicked Husbandmen, (76) The Pearl, (96) The Leaven, (107) The Lost Sheep, (109) The Treasure.

27. Here, it seems, the focal point is somewhat different from that of Dodd who emphasized the importance of focusing first on the OT in order to grasp the mindsets of Jesus and his hearers.

28. Jeremias, *Parables of Jesus*, 20. He claims that *mašal* can stand for any of the following: parable, similitude, allegory, fable, proverb, apocalyptic revelation, riddle, symbol, pseudonym, fictitious person, example, theme, argument, apology, refutation, jest. He derives these meanings mainly from the rabbinic literature. But in terms of the OT, the word refers rather to whatever is proverblike. Cf. Scott, *Parable*, 13.

29. Jeremias, *Parables of Jesus*, 21. He bases his claim on the earlier observation by Smith, C. W. F. *The Jesus of the Parables*, 17. Philadelphia, 1948.

30. Cf. Donahue, *Gospel in Parable*, 3.

31. This Jeremias admits himself. See *Parables of Jesus*, 230.

them as weapons of controversy that justify, defend, attack and challenge at particular moments of Jesus' life.[32]

Linnemann also supported the one-point-of-comparison historical method of interpreting the parables. She divided the parables into similitudes, parables proper, illustrations and allegories.[33] Yet she recognized that there is one, though only one, obvious example of the parable as allegory in the gospels and this is in Matt 22:1–14.[34] The parables, for her, are intended to win the opponents' agreement by reaching the depths of the conflict existing between Jesus and those opposing him.[35] The parable's task is to touch the depths of existence compelling the listeners to make a decision that can change their understanding of themselves and thus create a new life.[36] Jesus' parables are language events bringing in a new situation and demanding a decision of faith or unbelief. Jesus proclaims the time for repentance and believing in the gospel concerning the kingdom of God. The hope of late Judaism expecting the coming of the kingdom is incorporated, in Jesus, in faith.[37] The *now* of decision influences the whole of existence: whether it is based on the things perceivable in this world or on belief which is made possible through the heard word. But the existence based on belief is a life full of faith in God's future judgment and salvation.[38]

Although Linnemann's starting point was the methodological achievement of earlier historical critical scholarship, she used it to

---

32. Cf. ibid., 21.

33. Following Bultmann in this. See Linnemann, *Parables of Jesus*, 3ff. In her view, similitude is an image taken from real life; parables proper are freely composed stories about one particular, even extraordinary, case; illustrations produce examples to prove a point; and allegories are similar to the parables proper except that they are a series of pictures "which hint at reality and yet veil it."

34. Ibid., 8. Matt 25:1–13, according to Linnemann, was wrongly identified as an allegory.

35. Ibid., 19, 22.

36. Ibid., 31–32.

37. Ibid., 36–38.

38. For Jesus, like his contemporaries, God's judgment and salvation are still something future (ibid., 38). Linnemann constructs an argument that Jesus did not expect the nearness of the kingdom. She explains that Jesus did not understand the idea of the kingdom of God as did contemporary Jews, including John the Baptist. They saw the kingdom as a frontier of time, the frontier between two radically different ages (39). The kingdom of God for Jesus is rather the "Time to . . ." And Jesus believed that now was the time to repent and believe in the joyful message (39).

promote the views of existential philosophy common to Bultmann's school.

The more recent adherents of the method starting with Jülicher and moving through Dodd and Jeremias are the participants of the Jesus Seminar. With the conviction that the parables bring one closely to the authentic voice of Jesus,[39] the Jesus Seminar scholars attempt critically to determine the original sayings of Jesus by moving backwards through the layers of primarily oral tradition, from the beliefs of the primitive church back to Jesus' original utterances.[40] The scholars work on the assumption that both the Synoptics and the Gospel of Thomas are the sources to be used in this task.[41] They assume that the original parable did not contain a conclusion, but teased the hearer with its possible application.[42] It had a plot structure which involved a reversal of roles and never used more words than necessary.[43] The plots themselves were uncomplicated and employed sets of not more than two or three characters.[44]

The Jesus Seminar classified as parables thirty-three of the sayings ascribed to Jesus, some of them occurring exclusively in the Gospel of Thomas.[45] However, they voted only five of the thirty-three to be, very likely, Jesus' original utterances.[46] It would seem that the Jesus Seminar

39. Following Jeremias in this. Funk et al., *Parables of Jesus*, 14.

40. Ibid. 5–6. The layers of the tradition are as follows: (1) Jesus talking about the kingdom of God; (2) Disciples talking about Jesus talking about the kingdom of God; (3) Community talking about Disciples talking about Jesus talking about the kingdom of God; (4) Community talking about itself talking about Disciples talking about Jesus talking about the kingdom of God (see p. 5).

41. Only the original versions of Q and the Gospel of Thomas, which went through the editorial process at least once, can be more reliable than the Synoptics themselves because these two are believed to be of earlier origin (50–60 CE) than Mark (shortly after 70 CE), Matthew and Luke (both composed between 70–90 CE, most probably c. 85 CE). See ibid., 12–13. Q and *Gosp. Thom.* did not contain narrative material which points to less editorial activity than in the case of the canonical gospels. See ibid., 10.

42. Ibid., 17–18.

43. Ibid., 17.

44. Ibid.

45. See ibid., 21.

46. These are: "The Leaven" (Matt 13:13b; Luke 13:20b–21; Thom. 96:1); "The Good Samaritan" (Luke 10:30b–35; Luke 10:36–37); "The Dishonest Steward" (Luke 16:1–8a; Luke 16:8b–9); "The Vineyard Labourers" (Matt 20:1–15); and "The Mustard Seed" (Matt 13:31b–32; Mark 4:31–32; Luke 13:19; Thom 20:2). See ibid., 26.

They used four colors during the voting: red, pink, grey, and black. They signified in turn: red, "Jesus undoubtedly said this or something like this"; pink, "Jesus probably said

conclusions are the logical conclusion of the form critical approach to the parables of Jesus.

Modifications to the One-point-of-comparison Historical Approach

The line was drawn between the parables as wholly figurative speech and as wholly literal to the advantage of the latter. But the widely accepted one-point-of-comparison historical method has been questioned as to its validity. Other theories of figurative speech have started making their way into modern scholarship. Some NT exegetes have tried to modify or even to set aside the claims of the developed Jülicherian approach.

Early Dominic Crossan has pointed to the already existing dissatisfaction with the one-point approach saying that,

> The possibility that allegory, with its many points, and parable, with its single point, were but ends of a sliding scale within which one had to talk of parabolic allegories or allegorical parables began to be discussed by the second half of [the twentieth] century.[47]

Crossan believes, contrary to Jülicher, that Jesus' parables are extensions of metaphors, not similes.[48] Speaking of the figurative language he observes that it serves two functions,

> One is to illustrate information so that information precedes participation. The other is to create participation so that participation precedes information. The former function produces allegories and examples . . . The latter produces *metaphor* on the verbal level and *symbol* on the nonverbal level.[49]

---

something like this"; grey, "Jesus did not say this, but the ideas contained in it are close to his own"; black, "Jesus did not say this: this represents the perspective or content of a later or different tradition". See ibid., 21.

47. Crossan, *In Parables*, 9.

48. Here it seems one can recognize Crossan's debt to Funk. Cf. Funk, R. W. *Language, Hermeneutic, and Word of God.*, 133–222. New York: Harper & Row, 1966. The latter work as cited by Thiselton, *New Horizons*, 116 n.184. Thiselton have also suggested Crossan's dependence on Funk; see pp., 115–16. Although, more recently, it has been proposed that the parables are expansions of comparisons so that the view turns somehow back to Jülicher's claim. See Westermann, *Parables of Jesus*, 3, 6, 152. However, Westermann agrees that the parables are not mere illustrations but narratives (ibid., 159–60).

49. Crossan, *In Parables*, 15.

As to its function, metaphor can be either parable or myth. And the parable is a realistic or even factual story.[50] But the metaphor functions in itself, i.e., it creates its own world which can be interpreted only by someone who "lived" through it.[51] The truth expressed in a metaphor is not so much conceptual as experiential.[52] Jesus' parables are poetic metaphors characterized by their normalcy as opposed to myths which relate metanormalcy.[53] By definition, they are not allegories which create a possibility of participation only after information is given. As such the parables are also not linked to any specific biblical texts which need interpretation.[54] Their function is proclaiming the kingdom/dominion of God in the light of permanent eschatology, i.e., the permanent presence of God who shakes man's world and introduces his rule over and against it.[55] The parables are neither timeless truths nor are they to be "located *in* Jesus' own historical experience as visual aids to defend a proclamation delivered before them and without them."[56] They are not the "weapons of warfare," but the cause of the war. They constitute an advent within man which subverts their worlds. Therefore, in their nature, they contain polyvalent meaning dependent on the recipient. Thus the whole emphasis is on the call of God demanding the recipient's response which creates the historicity of the recipient. Crossan firmly rejects both Jülicher's view of the parables as timeless moral truths and Jeremias's view of the parables as supporting and defending the proclamation of Jesus.[57]

Donahue's approach is similar to Crossan's. The major modification, however, seems to be his emphasis on the aesthetic of the parable. He is not interested any longer in looking for different traditions in the parables. He focuses on them in their contexts as reflecting the major

---

50. Ibid.

51. Ibid., 13. One needs to get to know the imagined (or implied) world of the text in order to grasp the metaphor. A helpful discussion linked to the subject of referential world can be traced in Walhout, "Narrative Hermeneutics," 71–79.

52. Crossan, *In Parables*, 18.

53. Ibid. 21.

54. Ibid., 20.

55. Ibid., 23, 26–27. Crossan rejects apocalyptic eschatology (a better world elsewhere after the end of this world) in favor of prophetic eschatology (an ending of the world; no world after this one). He bases his claim upon his understanding of Luke 17:20–24 (ibid., 25).

56. Ibid., 32–33.

57. See ibid., 32.

themes in particular gospels.⁵⁸ Although the parables may have an unlimited number of applications, there is only a limited number of overtones from their biblical heritage, i.e., the OT.⁵⁹ There is no such thing as absolute meaning to a parable; it has multiple meanings.⁶⁰ Donahue prefers also to speak of one central focus of the parable rather than a single point of application.⁶¹ In his view, even the secondary characters in some parables have important roles for the general reception of these metaphors. As ever creating the point of contact between God and man, the parables create the language event which always challenges human existence.⁶²

The structural approach to the parables has found support in B. B. Scott.⁶³ He admits that Mark's theory of hardening (Mark 4:11–12) fits the meaning of *mašal* since the term also denotes a riddle and mystery.⁶⁴ But the parables in the Synoptics are mere reperformances by the evangelists which do not transmit Jesus' words but only structures.⁶⁵ Thus in conclusion, the parables are liberated from one particular *Sitz im Leben*.⁶⁶ As narrative fictions they have one distinctive characteristic: their literal level always leads to the nonliteral.⁶⁷ As metaphors, they cannot be reduced to specific points at all.

The challenge of the structuralist approach to the parables came from the language theorists themselves. The main argument against

---

58. *Gospel in Parable*, 4.

59. Ibid., 12. Here he observes that "the 'unpacking' of possible OT allusions or references does not constitute allegorizing."

60. Ibid., 25, 17.

61. Ibid., 12.

62. Here the existential overtones of Linnemann's earlier work are more obvious than in Crossan's case. Cf. ibid., 14.

63. *Parable*, 18. The structure of the parable (*ipsissima structura*) is more important than the original words (*ipsissima verba*), contra Jeremias. Cf. ibid., 40. The structures of the parables go back to Jesus (oral cultures remembered the structures), but their content was reshaped in the tradition. All we can do is to reconstruct the implied author of the corpus of parables (ibid., 63–65).

64. Ibid., 24. Interpretation of this connotative language always assumes the risk of misunderstanding.

65. Ibid., 63. It is not possible to have an original parable. The parables were oral so they could not be remembered regarding their content, but only their structure (40).

66. Ibid., 42. But the text still belongs to the phenomenological world of first-century Palestine (76).

67. Ibid., 44–48.

Crossan and his followers rests on the conviction that putting too much emphasis on the structure of a text harms the meanings and beliefs expressed in a story. This leads, in turn, to the dismissal of the authorial agency and intention as well as a lack of concern for historical meaning.[68] Thiselton remarks,

> But the parables . . . perform more functions than advocates of deconstructionism or radical indeterminacy usually recognize. They are also part of the *kerygma* of Jesus. This necessitates issues of agency and authorial discourse that radical reader-response theories tend to bracket out as irrelevant.[69]

One may ask to what extent is this reader-response mark of *post*modern hermeneutics a counter-reaction to the historical approach that seemed to deprive the parables of their universal and timeless applications. Surely, Linnemann with her existential philosophy, and/or D. O. Via, with his emphasis on the aesthetic,[70] tried to make the parables objects speaking live to the contemporary recipients cross-culturally. Their influences are recognizable in the works of Crossan, Donahue and Scott. Although some of them still acknowledge an element of historicity, they are forced by their methods to forsake the fact that the content and function of metaphor depends on a particular situation described in the narrative

---

68. Thiselton, *New Horizons*, 116. Here he relies on the earlier work of Poland, L. M. *Literary Criticism and Biblical Hermeneutics: A Critique of Formalist Approaches*, Ill. A. A. R. Academy Series 48. Chicago: Scholars Press, 1985. Cf. Snodgrass, "Parables of Jesus," 15. Cf. Blomberg, *Parables*, 137, who notes that "the new hermeneutic describes what the parables do rather than what they mean."

69. "Communicative Action," 163.

70. Bailey, *Poet & Peasant*, 21, classifies Via's approach as existential-aesthetic. The limitations of this work do not allow us to focus on Via's work. The same can be said of the precursor of the aesthetic approach, G. V. Jones (his work distinguished itself by focusing on the art forms of the parables). But, briefly, as for Via's approach it can be said that he rejected the 'one-point' approach simply because it did not work: it is impossible to escape allegorizing the parables because the parable itself contains allegorical elements. See Via, *The Parables*, 3. He observed that there is a difference between making an allegory and giving an allegorical interpretation (p. 4). The parables are often illustrating the things one already knows and they have many points of comparison, although there is usually one central thought in them (p. 13). Reconstruction of their *Sitz im Leben* at times is impossible because the gospels are not biographies (p. 21). But knowing Jesus' general orientation on eschaton we can translate the parables, the works of art not conditioned by time, into our historically conditioned language so that they can create the language event (pp. 25–32).

and recognized by the audience.⁷¹ Nevertheless, there were also strong points brought in by the postmodern critics. Donahue, for instance, in his literary approach pointed out that reconstructing different traditions in the parables is a somewhat unsuccessful task and therefore a more secure approach is to concentrate on the text itself within its context. In general, the existential-aesthetic and, later, structuralist approaches pointed to some weaknesses of the "one-point" approach and challenged students of the parables to reconsider their methodologies, or rather the *status quo* of the one-point-of-comparison historical method.

Some, therefore, have tried to find other solutions by combining the best of both historical and literary approaches. Bailey⁷² proposed linking historical with aesthetic. For him, the historical must be re-examined from the cultural milieu of the parables and the aesthetic must be viewed in the light of Oriental literary forms.⁷³ The first he sets out to achieve by a careful study of isolated peasant cultures of Southern Egypt, Lebanon, Syria and Iraq. He assumes that they have flawlessly preserved their antiquity and at the same time that their culture(s) are similar to that of ancient Israel.⁷⁴ On the basis of his study of the oral traditions in the still archaic communities of the Middle East he concludes that there is no reason to doubt "the basic authenticity of the parables as parables of Jesus of Nazareth."⁷⁵ Thus he challenges the widely held view of layers of tradition between which the original Jesus' *Sitz im Leben* has been lost. He stresses, at the same time, that the settings given by the evangelists may well have been faithfully preserved and transmitted in the tradition together with the parables.⁷⁶ Therefore to interpret the parables one needs to approach them as they are in the gospels, paying attention to

71. So Lynn Poland referred to in Thiselton, *New Horizons*, 116.

72. *Poet & Peasant*, 24. He recognized that it is impossible to have access to the raw material for "a precise delineation of the culture that informs the text" (contra Dodd and Jeremias). And, from an aesthetic standpoint, it is more natural to look at the parables as integral units. Even existentialism with its attempts to translate the parables into modern terms so that they can create language events, according to Bailey, fell short of its goal (p. 25). It ends up, like others, in parting with the historical (p. 29).

73. Ibid., 26.

74. Ibid., 30–36. Bailey observes that not only the customs but even the oral traditions of those communities have been preserved changeless by their constant controlling by the so-called "preservers of the customs" (p. 31). The belief of those primitive tribes is that "only in the static [is] there meaning."

75. Bailey, *Peasant Eyes*, x.

76. Ibid., xiii.

their context (of the theological debate between Jesus and his audience) and their function. Moving thus towards the aesthetic, Bailey states three points about the parables:

1. They have one or more points of contact[77] with reality (often pointed out as "referents"[78]) which he calls "symbols";
2. They contain the response that the original listener is pressed to make;
3. They contain a combination of theological motifs that pressed the original listener to make a response which Bailey calls "theological cluster." Reconstruction of this cluster helps in applying the parables to the non-original receivers.[79]

The parable as such is not an illustration but "a mode of theological speech used to evoke a response."[80] It is "a play within a play" where the play is taking place between Jesus and his audience.[81] Rhetorical criticism helps to establish both the points of contact as well as the theological cluster of a parable.[82]

Blomberg, on the other hand, has attempted to reconcile the historical with the literary approach giving allegory, as he understands it, its proper recognition as a literary genre.[83] According to Blomberg the major problem of interpreting the parables prior to Jülicher was an in-

---

77. He means that a parable "usually has a number of symbols which contribute to a single argument." See *Poet & Peasant*, 39. He combines the point of comparison as understood by Cadoux and Linnemann.

78. In the light of more recent discussion by Walhout, it would be better to describe the relationship between the elements of the parable and their references in the real world in terms of *mimesis*. See, "Narrative Hermeneutics," 71.

79. *Poet & Peasant*, 37–38. *Peasant Eyes*, xxi–xxiii. This requires the following eight steps: (1) determining the audience; (2) examining the setting and interpretation provided by the evangelist or his source; (3) identifying the play within a play; (4) discerning cultural presuppositions of the story; (5) checking if the parable speaks down into a series of scenes which resemble a thematic pattern; (6) asking what symbols could the original audience identify; (7) establishing the single decision/response required from the original listeners; (8) discerning the cluster of theological motifs.

80. *Poet & Peasant*, 43.

81. *Peasant Eyes*, xiii.

82. Ibid., xvii.

83. *Parables*, 20. Cf. ibid., 42 where he states that "any narrative with both a literal and metaphorical meaning is in essence allegorical."

The Metaphor of Divine Marriage in the Gospels 137

ability to set limits for allegorizing.[84] Arriving at the conclusion that certain details in the parables are in fact allegories does not have to lead to allegorizing all the details. But this presumes, contrary to Crossan, that the parables are illustrations rather than metaphors. And for Blomberg, they are illustrations of the inbreaking kingdom of God which subvert Jewish tradition.[85] Setting the details for reading the parables as containing allegories, Blomberg argues that the majority of the parables make usually two or three main points marked out by the narrative's main characters.[86] They make many allusions to the Hebrew Scriptures, but after a somewhat midrashic fashion.[87] This is why many people could not understand fully all the elements of Jesus' parables (Mark 4:1–34).[88]

Blomberg argues also for a more positive approach to the Synoptic problem. He proposes that similarities between different versions of the parables in the Synoptics outweigh the differences which, after all, can be harmonized.[89] He also rejects the idea that some of the parables, and even the canonical gospels in general, were retrospective and as such referred to some political conquest.[90] He sees that many parables refer to the final judgment at the eschaton which, for Blomberg, is future.

It seems that the proposals of the last two scholars are steps forward towards a more positive approach to the parables. However, one may recognize some difficulties in them. In the case of Bailey, the problem is in the assumption that contemporary peasant cultures of the Middle

---

84. Ibid., 20. On p. 166 he says, "To avoid the errors of past allegorizers, modern interpreters must also assign meanings to the details of parables which Jesus' original audiences could have been expected to discern."

85. Ibid., 67.

86. Ibid., 21, 68, 163. On an allegorical level the meaning of these main characters was expected to have been grasped by the original audiences in their historical setting. Often the main points can be combined into one central thought. Because we cannot be sure about the mindset of Jesus' original audiences we have to turn to allegorical meaning (p. 166). Thus it seems that in Blomberg's case the literary again takes over the historical.

87. Ibid., 78. However, we have already indicated in chapter 1 that reading NT allusions to the OT as midrash creates the problem of unintelligibility of the NT writers' methods.

88. Ibid., 112. Jesus wanted only his most intimate followers to understand the full import of specific details, "hence the allegorical explanations."

89. Ibid., 118.

90. Ibid., 120.

East are the same as the Jewish culture of Jesus' day.[91] He simply cannot just prove his claim. Beside this, we have already indicated in chapter 2 that equating contemporary oriental cultures with the culture of ancient Israel does not always do justice to both historical and biblical evidence. Therefore Bailey's assumption seems somewhat dubious.

Blomberg's approach also raises some problems. It should be illegitimate to take allegory as a literary genre rather than as a literary mode.[92] Also, previous study of the parables has suggested that they are not mere illustrative additions to the *kerygma* of Jesus: they are part of its core. It is also apparent that Blomberg's approach is governed by his wholly futuristic eschatology which often places the historical in the remote future. The *Sitz im Leben* of the parables further loses its significance as he believes that they quote arbitrarily from the OT after the manner of midrash.

Thus all proposals of parable scholarship have proven weak at some point, even if sometimes strong at others. In the next section we will attempt to use these observations as guides in formulating an approach that will do justice both to scholarly research already done on the parables as well as to the proposal of this work that NT ideas are a continuation and development of OT ones.

Proposed Approach

We have certainly discovered that studying the parables involves many different issues of both a literary and a theological nature. Also, different emphases in parable study result from different overall views and methodologies used to interpret the gospels. Our suggestion is that we proceed in a similar manner, taking into account the considerations from chapter 1.

We have noticed earlier that the issue of the historical context of parables cannot be dismissed. If we accept that authorial intention is still relevant to the original meaning of a text[93] we need to ask questions

---

91. Cf. Snodgrass, "Parables of Jesus," 17. However, see Wright, *JVG*, 135, who supports Bailey in his observation that early Christianity was able to preserve and retell its tradition in a similar manner to contemporary peasant cultures (cf. 1 Cor 11:2, 23; 15:1–3).

92. Snodgrass, "Parables of Jesus," 16, 20.

93. The importance of authorial intention is often stressed by Caird, *Language and Imagery*, 165.

about the historical context in studying the parables. Dodd's point that the OT is the guide in searching for this context can be valid in this case.[94] Thus we would argue that the OT was an influential source upon Jesus' composition of the parables.[95] Many scholars who have studied the genre of the parables would agree with C. A. Evans that "Jesus derived the parable form of teaching, whether directly or indirectly, from the Scriptures of Israel."[96] We suggest, however, that the influence was more direct because of similarities between Jesus' parables and parabolic stories in the OT.[97] These OT stories reached a particularly high point in the apocalyptic visions of the prophetic tradition.[98] Therefore, with N. T. Wright, we propose that Jesus, standing in the prophetic tradition of the OT, told the parables as prophetic and sometimes even apocalyptic stories.[99] This fits Evans's observation that many parables are juridical, just like the prophetic utterances themselves, and are addressed to Jewish leaders.[100] It seems that this approach does justice to the language of the parables. As with prophecy and apocalyptic, they contain a metaphor-system that gives historical events a theological significance.[101] They inform and at the same time they affect the recipient.[102] Some parables of the kingdom

---

94. Cf. also Drury, *Parables*, 7. Here Drury observes that, "The historical study of the New Testament has to work with very fragmentary evidence. The subject is a jigsaw with important pieces missing." But the study is by no means impossible because "there is one major piece of the jigsaw, or major group of pieces, which we do possess. It is the Old Testament."

95. Stein, "Genre of the Parables," 39, adds to the argument of some adherents of the historical method, although he claims also that Jesus' understanding of the parables came also from early rabbinic *mashalim*. But we cannot talk about a rabbinic movement with its parables until after 70 CE. It is therefore difficult to see with certainty, even recognizing the oral tradition stage, how Jesus could have been influenced by the movement. Cf. Evans, "Parables in Early Judaism," 58.

96. "Parables in Early Judaism," 52.

97. Following Wright, *NTPG*, 433. Wright's proposal has been assessed positively by Snodgrass, "Overreading the Parables," 64.

98. Wright, *NTPG*, 433.

99. Ibid. See also Wright, *JVG*, 97. Cf. Shillington, "Engaging with the Parables," 2.

100. They require the hearer to pass judgment on himself. Evans, "Parables in Early Judaism," 65–66.

101. Wright, *JVG*, 96. Thus the "imaginative parable" has its particular place within history and explains theologically this history. Cf. Drury, *Parables*, 17, 19.

102. Cf. Stein, "Genre of the Parables," 48.

(e.g., The Pearl, The Seed Growing Secretly, etc.) are, of course, merely didactic.[103] But this does not diminish the overall picture.

As the evidence of recent scholarly research has shown, the one-point-of-comparison approach to the parables does not pass the test of literary criticism.[104] On the other hand, opening the text to polyvalent meaning makes it difficult to consider the issue of authorial intention.[105] It is therefore proposed in this work that a parable of Jesus can have a number of correspondences with reality. It can make more than one point. Such an approach does not lead, we would like to imply, to allegory as an exegetical method (deriving from a text meanings which the author did not intend). Rather the parable can present explicit/literal (simile) and implicit/non-literal (metaphor) comparisons.[106] Caird explains that,

> . . . it does not follow that one is clear and the other mysterious. The understanding of both figures depends on our correctly identifying the point of comparison, and this may be as hard with simile as with a metaphor.[107]

Taken in this sense, the parable can be an allegory (literary form rather than genre) as an extension of one metaphor or a compilation of a few metaphors.[108] The task remaining is the identification of comparisons in the parable. We suggest that the OT is again an indispensable guide in doing this, considering the fact that it has already established the meanings of many symbols, which reoccur in the parables.[109]

We would also accept in part the view of Blomberg that the main characters of the story mark out its main points. We would, however, modify this view in the light of the valid claim that these points usually serve one main focus of the parable, as Donahue has remarked. Also, as Drury has observed, the relationship between persons, things and places

---

103. Caird, *Language and Imagery*, 164. Snodgrass, "Overreading the Parables," 65.

104. Cf. also Caird, *Language and Imagery*, 160–67.

105. Cf. ibid., 165.

106. Cf. ibid., 144.

107. Ibid., 162.

108. Ibid., 164. Bearing in mind that metaphor is an implicit comparison. In fact, fable, parable, allegory and typology are elaborations of simile or metaphor. Cf. ibid., 144–45.

109. Wright, *NTPG*, 433. See also Wright, *Challenge*, 22–23.

in the story can symbolize similar concatenations in reality.[110] We have already seen this in studying the metaphor of divine marriage in the OT prophets, in chapter 3 of this volume. In Hosea, covenant history becomes a drama which employs different characters: a husband (=Yahweh), his unfaithful wife (=Israel), their children (=individual Israelites), and lovers of the wife and the mother (=Baals, gods of Canaan). The wife can also be a land (Hos 2:3). But such symbolic surrealism should not surprise us, either in the case of prophetic stories in the OT or in the parables in the gospels.[111] The promiscuity of the wife could be either religious (Hosea) or religious and political (Ezekiel) unfaithfulness. The places can symbolize historical events (Jezreel in Hos 1:4 probably signifies the bloodshed of Jehu at this place). We therefore suggest that we can find similar symbolism in the parables of Jesus. If this is found to be so, it should not surprise us that they function as challenges to the hearers to change their views and behavior, just as OT prophecies did.

Furthermore, we suggest that viewing the parables as an apocalyptic revelation offers a possible solution to the so-called hardening theory in Mark's gospel relating to 4:11–12.[112] Verse 12 points to "an epistemology integral to apocalyptic" in which the knowledge has an element of secrecy that can only be unveiled by a "supernatural agency of explanation."[113] Mark 4:33–34 further supports this view. Drury explains,

> The implication of the scene-setting is clear: parables are spoken in public, their meaning is got only within the inner circle of discipleship. Jesus stands to the disciples as the angel stood to Ezra in 2 Esdras.[114]

110. *Parables*, 5.

111. Cf. Drury, *Parables*, 12, 28, 58.

112. Wright, *NTPG*, 433. These words are used by the evangelist in the context of the Parable of the Sower (4:3–8). Drury (*Parables*, 51–52) observes that the parable has its historical fulfillment in the lives of Jesus' generation. Mark himself indicates this. 1) The birds are Satan who takes away the word (4:15). In 8:32 Peter tries to remove Jesus' prophecy of doom so Jesus says, "Get behind me, Satan!" (8:33). 2) The shallow rocky ground represents those who fall away in the face of persecution (4:17). In 14:50, when Jesus is arrested, the eleven desert him and flee away. 3) The seed sown among thorns represents those who delight in worldly possessions (4:18–19). In 10:17 Jesus confronts a rich man who goes away with sorrow because he cannot give up his wealth. 4) The seed on the good ground points to the post-resurrection church in the hope of those who will bring good fruit in the future.

113. Drury, *Parables*, 60.

114. Ibid., 42. In a similar way, in 2 Esdras, a later work than Esdras, the angel Uriel is the interpreter of parables (see p. 24).

Here Mark stands, in fact, in the same tradition as Moses speaking to Pharaoh in Egypt, and as Isaiah or Ezekiel speaking to their audiences. In each case the receivers of these messages could not heed the words because their hearts were hardened.[115]

These would all lead also to a different type of implication. The approach presented here does not need to presume that the parables of Jesus were originally just simple one-dimensional stories which developed later into more complex forms, taking upon themselves apocalyptic or other allegorical characteristics.[116] There are some parables which seem to fit more the situation of the early church than to reflect the context of Jesus' ministry (e.g., The Tares among the Wheat at Matt 13:36–43). Moule makes an important observation in this context,

> But criticism ceases to be scientific if, on the basis merely of such more or less clear examples as [this], it jumps to the conclusion that no allegory can have been dominical, that all the attack and reproof in the original parabolic teaching of Jesus was directed to his opponents, and that Jesus never told parables having the ultimate "end of age" or directed to his own disciples' condition. The fact is that a far greater bulk of parabolic teaching, as it stands in the Gospels now, can be fitted quite naturally into a setting within the ministry of Jesus, than critical (but perhaps too *little* critical) scholarship sometimes allows; and that we must not too lightly assume the marks of "edificatory adaptation" everywhere.[117]

Such a reflection could, assuming it gives a possible alternative to the traditional form-critical method, challenge the claims of those who give priority to the simple parables of the Gospel of Thomas, or the claims of those who argue for simple parables in Q, as not founded in solid evidence.[118]

"We have literally no language and no parables of Jesus except and insofar as such can be retrieved and reconstructed from within the lan-

---

115. Cf. ibid., 41–42. Drury observes that even Jeremias himself, who denied any relevance to Mark 4:11, cannot escape the notion of secrecy in Jesus' proclamation of the kingdom of God and that he refers exactly to Mark 4:11 in his conclusions, thus showing his inconsistency (pp. 42–43). Cf. Jeremias, *Parables of Jesus*, 230.

116. So Wright, *NTPG*, 433–35.

117. Moule, *Birth*, 113.

118. Cf. also Wright, *NTPG*, 437–43. A very important question is raised in the context of Wright's discussion about the Q hypothesis, i.e., if first-century editors were allowed to add material, could they not also omit some?

guage of their earliest interpreters."[119] This statement of Crossan reminds us of the problem that modern criticism faces on its own assumption. It is unable to present to us an univocal conclusion on the original parables of Jesus. But our approach may point to the legitimacy of the view that the parables, or at least some of them, as we find them in the Synoptics, can be a reflection of Jesus' original utterances retained in their original *Sitz im Leben*. Therefore we propose to proceed by taking the parables, as they are accessible to us, in the gospels' contexts.[120] It seems that only in this way can we reconstruct their probable setting in the life of Jesus. And, of course, our proposal remains open to further verification as we progress in our interpretation.

THE SYNOPTIC MARRIAGE PARABLES

Markan Pericope about Fasting

We begin our investigation in Mark since most exegetes take this gospel to have been written prior to and been an influence on the other Synoptics. We want to focus particularly on 2:18–20 (cf. pars., Matt 9:14–17; Luke 5:33–35), where Jesus compares the present time to the time of joy during wedding festivities rather than a time of fasting.[121] The claim of scholars has often been that, whereas verses 18–19a refer to the original situation of Jesus, verses 19b–20 were composed by the post-Easter church in order to justify its later practice of fasting.[122] Scholars have also doubted whether at this early point Jesus could have referred to his own death. Further doubt was cast on the verses because the idea of Messiah being a bridegroom is foreign to both the OT and late Jewish literature.[123] Therefore the view of vv. 19b–20 being a later addition has been more favored. But at the same time scholars admit that at least part of the pericope at Mark 2:18–22 was pre-Marcan and belonged to

---

119. Crossan, *In Parables*, xiii.

120. Similarly to Drury, *Parables*, 4.

121. Cf. Martin, *Mark*, 184. But the question demanding an answer is whether this passage indicates a meaning on a metaphorical level.

122. So, e.g., Bultmann, *Synoptic Tradition*, 19, 92, 151. He argues also that v. 18a could be a later addition fashioned on v. 18b (p. 19). Similarly, Jeremias, *Parables of Jesus*, 52 n. 13. Also Langkammer, 117. Cf. Martin, *Mark*, 185.

123. Cf. Jeremias, *Parables of Jesus*, 52. Also his article "νύμφη νυμφίος," IV: 1101, 1103. Cf. Discussion in chapter 4 above.

a collection of the controversy narratives.¹²⁴ They have, however, noted that it is difficult to find any connection between 2:15–17 and 2:18–22.¹²⁵ Nevertheless, virtually all commentators view the passage under consideration as reflecting a conflict between Jesus and different groups in Judaism concerning fasting.¹²⁶

As one of the adherents of the form-critical school, Jeremias has concluded, taking Mark 2:19b–20 as a later addition, that 2:19a does not present the Messiah as a bridegroom.¹²⁷ It seems that, for him, Jesus' answer at 2:19a is a mere simile without any further metaphorical meaning. The only point made by the passage is that it is improper for Jesus' disciples to fast in exactly the same way as it is improper to fast during a wedding. Jeremias supports his argument partly by noticing that the clause ἐν ᾧ ὁ νυμφίος μετ' αὐτῶν ἐστιν means simply "during the wedding."¹²⁸ Nevertheless, he cannot escape the symbolic note in 2:19a. He sees in the wedding a symbol of the day of salvation, which implies realized eschatology.¹²⁹ Lacking consistency at this point, Jeremias has opened the way to another view of the passage.

Cranfield¹³⁰ is of a different opinion from Jeremias. He argues,

> The words ἐν ᾧ ὁ νυμφίος μετ' αὐτῶν ἐστιν are odd in connection with an ordinary wedding, for they seem to imply that the celebrations are ended by the bridegroom's departure, whereas actually it was the guests who left the bridegroom; but they are appropriate, if the presence of allegory is admitted.¹³¹

Thus it seems that the construction of v. 19a itself points to parabolic language which, as we have acknowledged earlier in this chapter, contains some unrealistic pictures. On such a view, verses 19b and 20 seem

---

124. Cf. Guelich, *Mark 1—8:26*, 108.

125. Bultmann, *Synoptic Tradition*, 62. Langkammer, *Marka*, 115.

126. In Mark 2:18 the people raising questions about fasting are not defined. In Matt 9:14 John the Baptist's disciples challenge Jesus on this issue whereas the context of Luke 5:33 points to the Pharisees and the scribes as the group asking Jesus about his attitude to fasting.

127. *Parables of Jesus*, 52 n. 13.

128. Ibid.

129. Ibid., 117. It is noteworthy that Jeremias's whole evidence comes from Rev 19:7, 9; 21:2, 9; 22:17. He interprets the pre-Marcan statement through the post-Marcan book of Revelation.

130. Cranfield, *Mark*, 107.

131. Ibid., 109. (The phrase ἐν ᾧ means "as long as," "while"). See also p. 111.

no longer strange additions because they only elaborate the content of v. 19a.[132]

Others, such as Cullmann[133] and Martin,[134] also treat Mark 2:19–20 as a unit. Cullmann argues that the early church could have hardly invented v. 20 because it was conscious of living in the time of salvation rather than of mourning.[135] Martin argued similarly to Cranfield. He says,

> Even on more strictly form-critical grounds there is much to be said for keeping the verses together as an independent and self-contained unit, since the entire *logion* is a good example of semitic antithetic parallelism, which would be destroyed if verses 19b–20 were excised as a later addition. The argument that the idea of the removal of the bridegroom in verse 20 is already implied in verse 19a requires that all the references to the term should be taken as Jesus' self-identification; and this is perhaps the chief contextual reason why doubt is cast on the verses as authentic.[136]

If the unity of the logion can be sustained then other questions need to be answered. Could Jesus use the symbol of bridegroom to describe the Messiah? What did he mean by speaking of the bridegroom being taken away? All scholars recognize that there is no precedent in the OT and late Judaism of the Messiah being called bridegroom. They say also that at this point in his ministry Jesus could not have revealed his true identity. In fact, the characters in Mark's narrative are puzzled by Jesus' identity because they did not have the gospel's prologue.[137] Nevertheless, this lack of precedent does not have to lead to negative conclusions. Martin explains,

> But the case for regarding verses 19b–20 as additions on the ground that Jesus could not have used "bridegroom" as a self-designation is not foolproof. The most that can be alleged is that there is no precedent for this title as a messianic description and

---

132. Earlier even Dodd did not regard v. 20 as necessarily a later addition. See *Parables of the Kingdom*, 116 n. 2. That the allegory is already established in v. 19a is also supported by Dewey, "Mark 2:1—3:6," 150 n. 14. Although Matthew and Luke drop the restatement of v. 19b, they keep the allegory (Matt 9:15; Luke 5:34–35).

133. Cullmann, *Christology*, 61–62.

134. *Mark*, 185.

135. *Christology*, 62.

136. *Mark*, 185.

137. Matera, "Key to Mark's Gospel," 296.

that Jesus would not have publicly confessed his Messiahship prior to the climax of his ministry (so Jeremias apparently contends). But this overlooks the possibility that he was using the term as an indirect way of expressing himself, comparable with his use of "Son of man."[138]

If the Messiah had been viewed in second temple Judaism as God's agent bringing Israel's eschatological hopes to fulfillment,[139] a suggestion could be made that God also brings, through him, the fulfillment of his promise of a new eternal betrothal from Hos 2:19–20. We have already noticed in chapter 3 that this promise has an eschatological dimension. This eternal betrothal is viewed as covenant renewal with the once wayward wife Israel.[140] But such a claim needs to be set aside awaiting further evidence. Nevertheless, there exists a possibility that Jesus could have reworked the metaphor of divine marriage of the OT prophets alongside the eschatological expectations of second temple Judaism.

Scholars have tried to give a more positive answer to the problem of Jesus' prediction of his own death in Mark 2:19–20 from that presented in traditional form-criticism. Dodd has proposed that the problem of Jesus' alleged prediction of death can be solved by viewing verse 20 not as symbolical of a particular event, but rather as a mere antithetical parallel to the joy of festivities.[141] In other words, there is no specification of any time of fasting but this antithesis stresses more the joy of the wedding. Dodd's proposal supports the view that v. 20 could go back to Jesus rather than being an invention of the early church. As Cullmann has noticed,[142] the early church was focused on living in the time of salvation and joy rather than on mourning. Therefore it is improbable that the church itself invented v. 20. But Dodd is unable to give a satisfac-

138. *Mark*, 186. In favor of the view that Jesus applied the symbol of bridegroom to himself see Muirhead, "Bride of Christ," 181.

139. See Sanders, *Jesus and Judaism*, esp. 79–87 (cf. Isa 49:5–6; Ezek 34, 37). Wright, *Challenge*, e.g., 76–81 (see Ezek 1; Dan 7; 2 Sam 7:11–14). Cf. Caird and Hurst, *Theology*, 365–66.

140. See chapter 3 above. It is worth noticing that Jesus, similarly to OT prophets, calls his contemporary generation of Israelites an "adulterous generation." See, e.g., Mark 8:38 (cf. Matt 12:39; 16:4).

141. *Parables of the Kingdom*, 116 n. 2. Also Lane, *Mark*, 111. Lane, however, says that the verse could have been understood metaphorically from the perspective of the post-Easter church on the basis of its link to Isa 53:8LXX. See ibid., 111 n. 70.

142. *Christology*, 62. Cranfield is of the opinion that we do not have definite evidence of any custom of regular fasting before post-apostolic times. Cranfield, *Mark*, 111.

tory explanation of the fact that removal of the bridegroom from the wedding scene is a surprise. A possible solution comes from Cranfield,[143] Martin[144] and Guelich.[145] All three think that the phrase ἀπαρθῇ ἀπ' αὐτῶν ὁ νυμφίος in verse 20 echoes Isa 53:8LXX with its phrase αἴρεται ἀπὸ τῆς γῆς ἡ ζωὴ αὐτοῦ. Isa 53 is another instance of the Song of the Lord's Servant, which ends on a note of the servant's violent death for the sins of God's people. One could expect that the author of the gospel, and perhaps Jesus himself, had in view this wider context when speaking of the bridegroom's removal (cf. chapter 1 of this work on the question of contextuality of *testimonies*). The note on fasting after the removal could possibly echo the ending of the Song of the Servant in Isa 53. Although, there is no explicit mention of the death of Jesus in Mark 2:19–20, the verses refer to the mourning accompanying the loss of the bridegroom.[146] It has been also recognized that these verses fit well the whole structure of Mark's gospel. Dewey comments,

> The controversy section fits naturally into the structure of Mark's Gospel. Mark, after he showed the enthusiastic response of the crowds to Jesus in chapter 1, then demonstrates the hostility that these actions of Jesus aroused, which eventually resulted in his death. The conclusion in Mark 3:6 . . . serves not only as a conclusion to the story of the withered hand, but also to the entire controversy section. To *this* result Jesus' actions lead.[147]

---

143. *Mark*, 110–11.

144. *Mark*, 186–87.

145. *Mark 1—8:26*, 112–15. Cf. also Best, *Mark*, 20. He thinks 2:19–20 is indeed an early reference to Jesus' death.

146. Guelich, *Mark 1—8:26*, 113. Another question in the debate would be concerning the time of fasting that Jesus referred to. Was it a particular day (ἐκείνῃ τῇ ἡμέρᾳ: Mark 2:20)? Or was it rather a period of time, the days in the future, the time of apostolic church (ἡμέραι ὅταν: Matt 9:15; ἐκείναις ταῖς ἡμέραις: Luke 5:35)? Were they annual fast days? See ibid., 112, for a summary of different opinions. It seems, in the context of our discussion, that the day may refer to the reaction of disciples at the removal of the bridegroom and their grievance after the loss of their master, just as in the case of John the Baptist's disciples (cf. Cranfield, *Mark*, 109). Marshall, *Luke*, 226. Marshall believes that the fasting of the church is a companion of prayer and has nothing to do with mourning for the absence of Jesus. However, in the context of the metaphor of bridegroom one might ask if grieving (which was often expressed by fasting in ancient Israel) is not a proper expression of a shock caused by a sudden and violent (Isa 53) removal of the bridegroom during the wedding festivities.

147. "Mark 2:1—3:6," 148. Dewey's argument is supported by the structure of controversy narratives in Mark 2:1—3:6. She proposes that the whole passage has a chiastic structure which is as follows (pp. 141–42):

This additionally dispels doubt that Jesus could refer to his own death at this early stage of his ministry. Both contextual evidence and the OT background of Mark 2:19–20 make a point that Jesus could have been conscious of his approaching death, although his companions did not see this clearly.

It is also noteworthy that the immediate context of Isa 53 is Isa 54:1–10 with its use of the divine marriage metaphor. There, a once miserable wife sent into exile receives an eschatological hope of glory when Zion is restored by her husband Yahweh (cf. chapter 3 on this). The one who was barren rejoices in having many children (Isa 54:2–3). She returns from exile (v. 6) back to the marital union with her compassionate husband and God (v. 7). Therefore, if Isa 53 was really in the mind of the author of Mark 2:19–20 one should not be surprised by the fact that he could easily combine the themes of the joy of bridegroom's companions and the sorrow caused by the bridegroom being taken away. Then also, the lack of any reference to the bride in Mark 2:19–20 does not create unnecessary suspicion. Having in mind the wider context of deutero-Isaianic prophecy, the bride is the restored Zion/Jerusalem (Isa 54:1–10). And it seems that because of the lack of mention of any bride, Jesus, according to the Markan account, can still remain unrecognized by many. In fact, our entire argument does not necessarily imply that people had recognized Jesus' identity at the point he called himself the bridegroom. The question of their ability to associate Jesus' words with Isaiah's prophecy remains a matter of supposition because of the lack of explicit evidence.[148] Nevertheless, Isaiah's context gives a possible

---

A (2:1–12) The healing of the paralytic (healing of the resurrection type).
 B (2:13–17) The eating with tax-collectors and sinners (concerns eating).
  C (2:18–22) The question concerning fasting.
 B' (2:23–28) The plucking of grain on the Sabbath (again concerns eating).
A' (3:1–6) The healing of the man with a withered hand (another resurrection type healing).

All the sections are thematically linked with each other (ibid., 142–47). Dewey recognizes also that the author of this literary structure may have used earlier collections of traditions to construct the whole section. Although some disagree with Dewey's proposal of literary structure, they still see the connection between 2:18–22 with the preceding and following on the basis of thematic unity, i.e., the issue of eating. See, e.g., Guelich, *Mark 1—8:26*, 83–84. But almost all agree that Matt 2:18–20 and 2:21–22 are based on pre-Markan tradition. See p. 108.

148. Sanders, *Jesus and Judaism*, 129, remarks that Jesus was enigmatic but it would be very unlikely that his disciples completely misunderstood him. Jesus' ideas corresponded with first-century Judaism.

solution to the question of the appropriateness of the reference to fasting after the bridegroom is taken away. It is also noteworthy that Isaiah uses the marriage metaphor again at 62:3–5. Although it is not in the immediate context of chapter 53, it continues the thought of preceding chapters. In this passage, Yahweh reloves and remarries the once repudiated wife Zion/Jerusalem at the time of his salvation. It is interesting that the marriage is like Yahweh marrying a virgin (παρθένῳ Isa 62:5aLXX). He himself is presented as bridegroom (νυμφίος 62:5bLXX) rejoicing over his bride (νύμφῃ 62:5bLXX). Thus for Israel, marriage became a metaphor of the time of salvation (62:5; cf. 61:10).[149] This could also suggest that the author of Mark 2:19–20 had in mind a wider context of Isaiah combined with messianic hopes of late Judaism. He could have employed Isaiah's symbolism of the bridegroom in order to point to the time of fulfillment of the promises announced by the prophet. If he could use different traditions as freely as the OT prophets before him, he could have easily made them fit his historical context. We have indicated in chapter 3 that Isaiah borrowed the metaphor of divine marriage from Hosea and reworked it for his own purposes. Isaiah's mention of a new marriage of a bridegroom and his bride is reminiscent of Hosea's remark about future eternal betrothal. Thus it seems that Mark 2:19–20 could indirectly echo Hos 2, through the prophecy of Isaiah.[150] If this is true, the only possible attitude of those who recognize the background of Jesus' words is joy, although the extent of their understanding remains a matter of speculation. And, at this point, the narrative itself indicates that these are Jesus' disciples who are also the υἱοὶ τοῦ νυμφῶνος.[151]

---

149. Langkammer, *Marka*, 117.

150. Cf. Ortlund, *Whoredom*, 137–39. Also cf. Martin, *Mark*, 186.

151. Lit. "sons of the bridechamber." But the meaning and significance of the phrase have been much debated among scholars. Edersheim, *Jesus the Messiah*, I: 662, believes the phrase refers to all invited guests. Others support the view that the expression refers to groomsmen. Cf. Guelich, *Mark 1—8:26*, 110. Also Mounce, *Analytical Lexicon*, 331. But some suggest that the phrase refers to the closest attendants of the bridegroom who played an essential part in the wedding ceremony. See Arndt and Gingrich, *Greek-English Lexicon*, 547. van Selms, "Best Man," esp. 74, has pointed out that οἱ υἱοὶ τοῦ νυμφῶνος are similar to the thirty companions of Samson in Jdg 14:11 among whom there was one man who took lead as the best man (71). This may point to the special role of Jesus' disciples in his wedding. The sons of the bride chamber accompanied the bridegroom to his house where the wedding was held and the marriage was consummated. Cf. Chavasse, *Bride of Christ*, 54–55. Can this mean that Jesus' disciples accompany Jesus towards eschatological wedding? Thus the scene would indicate that Jesus is

The closest companions of Jesus are those who are going to witness the long-promised remarriage, the new covenant.

Turning back to the main theme of the Markan controversy at 2:18–20, i.e., fasting, one can find still different echoes of the OT. But the arguments of scholars have often been that in this place Jesus opposes the patterns of Jewish religion. The emphasis is often on the Pharisees fasting out of their piety[152] and John the Baptist's disciples fasting possibly to express repentance,[153] but then on Jesus, in a prophet-like manner, opposing the old forms of religion.[154] As new wine cannot be poured into old wineskins, so it is inappropriate to keep the old patterns of religion alongside the new teaching (2:21–22). The Pharisees were interested in the externals, but Jesus was interested in the heart.[155] But a number of scholars have proposed a different solution, one that fits more the overall picture of Jesus' attitude to Judaism with its practices. Their argument is that Jesus did not so much oppose Jewish forms of religion as point to the arrival of the eschatological times marked by the renewal of the covenant of Yahweh and Israel. N. T. Wright has remarked that fasting at the time of Jesus' ministry was associated strongly with the hope of second temple Judaism that God would restore the fortunes of his people.[156] Thus fasting was not simply an ascetic discipline. It expressed the expectation of God's eschatological deliverance. As Zechariah had promised, the regular fasts of Israel would be turned into the joy of festivities in the time of fulfillment (cf. 8:19). If Jesus is Yahweh's agent acting to bring to fulfillment the eschatological promises of Hebrew Scriptures then the fasting is inappropriate. The eschaton has been brought in by the Messiah and through him, Yahweh brings in salvation for his people. He

---

the bridegroom, Zion to whom comes restoration is his bride (the corporate people of Israel) and Jesus' disciples as individuals are his close companions in the wedding.

152. E.g., Lane, *Mark*, 109; Langkammer, *Marka*, 116. They notice that the Pharisees regularly fasted on Mondays and Thursdays.

153. So Lane, *Mark*, 109. Langkammer, *Marka*, 116, thinks that we simply do not know what the reason of John's disciples' fasting was. Guelich goes along with Lane (*Mark 1—8:26*, 109). He adds that John's fasting was also to express penitence and humility in the face of the coming of the Kingdom of God. Cranfield, *Mark*, 109, proposes that the motive of the disciples' fasting could have been their masters' death. But he himself sees the impossibility of giving the final answer.

154. So Gould, *Mark*, 46–47. Cf. Edersheim, *Jesus the Messiah*, I: 663.

155. Cf. Batey, *Nuptial Imagery*, 41.

156. *Challenge*, 49; *JVG*, 433. See also Guelich, *Mark 1—8:26*, 110–11, 115.

The Metaphor of Divine Marriage in the Gospels 151

restores the fortunes of Israel. The time is fulfilled and the exile is over; the bridegroom is at hand.[157] Mark 2:21–22 fits well in this context because it speaks metaphorically of the eschatological time of salvation.[158]

Another thing worth noticing here is that our interpretation of Mark 2:19–20 fits in the broader context of Mark's narrative. He begins his gospel by combining quotations from Exodus, Malachi and the passage in deutero-Isaiah that begins the announcement about God redeeming Israel from exile by a new exodus (Mark 1:2–3; cf. Exod 23:30 and Mal 3:1; Isa 40:3).[159] This may suggest that Mark has put the content of his narrative into the framework of second exodus motif. On this view John the Baptist is the messenger who prepares the way for the Lord's coming to deliver his oppressed people as during the Exodus from Egypt. And although most characters throughout the gospels are puzzled by Jesus' identity (maybe except the demons, cf. 1:24; 3:11; 5:7), the possible echoes of the OT may well indicate who Jesus really is. If somebody properly interprets Jesus' words and actions, it is assumed, he can recognize in him an agent of God's salvation.[160] Furthermore, if the second exodus is the framework in which Jesus' actions need to be interpreted, then we would suggest there is a connection between our passage and Mark 2:15–17. The idea of feasting instead of fasting in Mark 2:19–20 may actually recall the common theme of messianic banquet in second temple Judaism.[161] And the preceding passage describes Jesus dining at Levi's house, which may symbolize the messianic banquet.[162] In fact, the synoptic gospels present a number of instances of Jesus having meals with people which can be regarded as a foretaste of the messianic ban-

---

157. Wright, *JVG*, 434.

158. Cf. Jeremias, *Parables of Jesus*, 118–19. Jeremias notices that the old age is compared to an old garment so that the "New Age" cannot be patched to the old. And wine is a symbol of salvation which begins through judgment the "New Age" (e.g., Joel 3:13). See also Guelich, *Mark 1—8:26*, 115, 107–8.

159. Matera, "Key to Mark's Gospel," 293. Cf. Watts, *New Exodus in Mark*, 56–91. Watts believes that Mark picks up the idea of new exodus already present in Isa 40–55. Israel had failed to obey God's promises of deliverance from exile through Cyrus and therefore a new eschatological exodus was needed at the eschaton. See Watts, "Consolation or Confrontation," 31–59.

160. Ibid., 296–97.

161. Wright, *JVG*, 532. Cf. Marshall, *Luke*, 222.

162. So, e.g., Lane, *Mark*, 106–7, 113.

quet (e.g., Luke 14:1–23).¹⁶³ Thus it is possible that the aim of the author of the controversy narratives in Mark was to connect the themes of messianic banquet at 2:15–17 and divine marriage at 2:19–20 linking in this way two OT motifs loaded with eschatological significance.¹⁶⁴ And as we have already indicated, the narratives could have been gathered together in this way in the collections of early testimonies, though they originate with Jesus himself.

In conclusion, we want to suggest that there exists a way of viewing Mark 2:18–20 as an early instance of marriage metaphor in the NT with the view that it was reshaped according to the framework of second temple Judaism's eschatological expectation. In this case, Jesus acting on God's behalf as his agent takes upon himself the role of the bridegroom of Isaiah's prophecy and indicates that the promised restoration for the repudiated Zion has come. She can finally return from exile. The bridegroom's companions should rejoice in the time of his presence with him which will, however, be interrupted by his violent removal. Thus the picture seems to be that the wedding is in progress, but the element of strangeness has marked the image. There will be a moment of mourning for the loss of the bridegroom.

Matthean Parable of the Wedding Banquet

The parable in Matt 22:1–14 has been the subject of discussion no less than the Markan pericope examined above. Because of the space-limits of this volume, we will discuss only the main points in the debate in the following sections as well as in the footnotes.

Part of the problem, it seems, emerges from comparing Matt 22:1–14 with a similar parable in Luke 14:16–24. A story with a similar theme occurs also in the Gospel of Thomas logion 64. All three parables are alike with regard to the refusal of the invitation to a banquet by the invited guests and their replacement by the next best.¹⁶⁵ However, because of different interpolations in the Matthean version which make it somewhat unnatural, scholars usually conclude that the Lukan account is closer to the original words of Jesus.¹⁶⁶ Nevertheless, it can be argued that parts of

---

163. Keesmaat, "Strange Neighbours," 274. Cf. Bailey, *Peasant Eyes*, 88.

164. Pace Bultmann, *Synoptic Tradition*, 62. Cf. Lane, *Mark*, 113.

165. Cf. Jeremias, *Parables of Jesus*, 63. Also Manson, *Teaching of Jesus*, 84.

166. Linnemann, *Parables of Jesus*, 7–8, 93, 94 n.k. She believes Matt 22:1–14 is a reshaping of the Great Supper parable as found in Luke 14:15–24. This becomes obvious

Matthew's parable come from the early source Q.[167] Matthew, it has been claimed, allegorized an earlier parable of a banquet in order to answer the question of why Israel rejected the preaching of the apostles, while the Gentiles received it.[168] Thus the Parable of Wedding Banquet was made to meet the situation of the post-70 CE church.

It also seems fair to take the Matthean parable as independent of Luke's (or the one Luke used to construct his own). Although there are some similarities between the two, there is a possibility that the wedding banquet story of Matthew was told by Jesus on a different occasion.[169] In fact, at a number of points Matthew's version reveals even more similarities to his previous parable of the Wicked Tenants in the Vineyard (21:33–41; cf. 22:2,4 and 21:36; 22:6 and 21:35–36) and the evangelist's teaching in general (e.g., 22:1 cf. 18:23; 22:13 cf. 8:12), than to the Lukan account.[170] Matt 22:1–14, with its main focus on the judgment on Jewish leaders, continues the theme of judgment in Matthew's two previous parables (21:28–31; 21:33–41).[171] Although Luke's parable reveals also a note of judgment on the Jewish leaders,[172] it has its own focal points

---

when verses 6–7 and 10–14 are removed from the Matthean passage. Manson, *Teaching of Jesus*, 84, even went as far as to state that the Matthean intrusions make nonsense of the parable (e.g., the feast was ready in v. 4 and it is still ready in v. 8 after the servants have been murdered and an army has been mobilized and sent against the murderers of the king's servants). The Jesus Seminar scholars gave Luke 14:16b–23 color code pink (although 14:24 is black), whereas Matt 22:2–13 was classified as grey. See Funk et al., *Parables of Jesus*, 42–43, 74–75.

167. Martens, "Parables of Judgment," 155, 162–63.

168. Linnemann, *Parables of Jesus*, 93–96. Cf. Bultmann, *Synoptic Tradition*, 175, 195. Also Jeremias, *Parables of Jesus*, 69. Luke 14:15–24 could also well be concerned with similar matter.

169. Blomberg, *Parables*, 237. France, *Matthew*, 311–12. Cf. Wenham, *Synoptic Problem*, 73. Wenham observes that there are not enough similar words in the accounts of Matthew and Luke to assume the same source behind the parables. Pace Fitzmyer, *Luke X–XXIV*, 1052.

170. Cf. Hagner, *Matthew 14–28*, 627–28. Cf. also Drury, *Parables*, 97. Drury claims that "without having read the *vineyard* parable the *marriage feast* is not intelligible." Jones, *Matthean Parables*, 403. Also Manson, *Teaching of Jesus*, 86, who says that Jesus liked to duplicate sayings. So "it would not be at all surprising that the parable of the Vineyard should have a companion piece, conveying the same lesson in a different form."

171. Cf. Martens, "Parables of Judgment," 152. Martens observes that Matthew's three parables of judgment in 21:28—22:14 immediately follow three narratives that speak of judgment on the temple and Jewish leaders and nation in 21:12–27.

172. The original guests, by their own choice, shut themselves off from fellowship

on the acceptance of religious and social outcasts (Luke 14:21, 23).[173] The Gospel of Thomas 64 seems to have more in common with Luke 14:15–24, although its ending (sending a servant to the streets) is closer to Matthew.[174] However, the conclusion of logion 64 points more to the author's concern with the material in a negative sense (here it is 'buyers and merchants' who "will not enter the places of [Jesus'] Father"[175]). Therefore, it seems better to take Matthew's parable on its own terms and within its own context. Regardless of its similarities to other versions, it makes and emphasizes its own points, and because only Matthew's version speaks of a wedding, it seems appropriate to leave other versions aside and to deal only with the account of this evangelist. Besides, even if Matthew's parable seems to be unrealistic at times (esp. v. 7), we have already learnt that surrealism is one of the characteristics of Jesus' parables. Therefore the apparent distraction of thought flow in verse 7 cannot stand as an argument against the authenticity of the parable.

If we allow Matthew's story to be independent of Luke's version in all its parabolic strangeness, verses 11–14 do not seem to create an additional problem.[176] They rather naturally extend verses 1–10 explaining that even the admittance of both 'good and bad' to the feast (v. 10) needs to have a further qualification.[177] We shall discuss this further in one of

---

with the host. See Bailey, *Peasant Eyes*, e.g., 112. Cf. Marshall, *Luke*, 586. Cf. Sanders, *Jesus and Judaism*, 227.

173. Bailey, *Peasant Eyes*, 100, and France, *Matthew*, 311. However, Sanders, *Jesus and Judaism*, 118, observes that the "highways and hedges" in Luke 14:23 and the "streets" in Matt 22:9–10 could possibly refer to Gentile lands.

174. Fitzmyer, *Luke X–XXIV*, 1051. Moule, *Birth*, 112, remarks that logion 64 "invites guesses as to its different setting and purpose and theological outlook."

175. See the whole of logion 64 in Elliott, *Apocryphal Christian Literature*, 143. France, *Matthew*, 312, suggests that the Gospel of Thomas 64 could have preserved at this point Jesus' original teaching that it is impossible to serve both God and mammon (cf. Matt 6:24).

176. Contra Bultmann, *Synoptic Tradition*, 175; and Jeremias, *Parables of Jesus*, 65. See Manson, *Teaching of Jesus*, 35. It does not matter that someone taken from a street cannot wear a wedding garment. A parable should surprise. Pace Linnemann, *Parables of Jesus*, 94 n.k. Cf. Via, *The Parables*, 129. It is often believed that vv. 11–13 make a completely different point from the preceding verses. V. 14 is often taken as another addition that fits neither the Wedding Feast nor the Wedding Garment parables. See Hagner, *Matthew 14–28*, 628.

177. Hultgren, *Parables*, 346–47. On this view also v. 14 is a conclusion to both vv. 1–10 and 11–13. See also Wright, *JVG*, 287 n. 168.

The Metaphor of Divine Marriage in the Gospels

the following sections. Therefore we propose to focus on Matt 22:1–14 as a coherent unit that resembles the words of Jesus.[178]

The majority of scholars agree on the basic meaning of the successive characters and events occurring in the parable of the Wedding Feast, which addresses Jewish leaders (cf. Matt 21:23; 45).[179] The king stands for God, the son is Jesus, the king's servants are God's messengers,[180] the original invitees are Israelites.[181] The readiness of the wedding banquet

---

178. Most commentators agree here that at least the main core of the parable comes from Jesus. Cf. Hultgren, *Parables*, 348 n.41. Via argues, contrary to the Jesus Seminar adherents, that both Matt 22:1–10 and Matt 22:11–13 come from earlier tradition (129). He also argues strongly that Matt 22:11–13 is consistent with Jesus' teaching. A similar point about the pre-Matthean origin of 22:1–14 is made by Jones, *Matthean Parables*, 400–410. In the light of our earlier discussion on the parables' nature in general, we see no good reason for dismissing parts of the parable as not being Jesus' original words.

179. Martens, "Parables of Judgment," 153–54, explains that Matthew introduces the chief priests and elders in 21:23 as being leaders 'of the people.' They are representative of the whole nation; therefore the whole nation is under the judgment. Cf. also Swartley, "Banquet People," 181–82.

180. Jeremias, *Parables of Jesus*, 68–69, believes that the first group of servants (v. 3) signifies the prophets, the second (v. 4) refers to the apostles and missionaries sent to Israel, and the third group (v. 8–10) refers to the Gentile mission. However, Martens ("Parables of Judgment," 163) takes the first two groups of servants as referring to the NT apostles and Christian missionaries sent to invite Israel to the royal messianic banquet. Their mission ended with the destruction of Jerusalem in 70 CE. The third group of servants refers to the post-destruction apostles and Christian missionaries who go this time to the Gentiles (διεξόδους τῶν ὁδῶν, v. 9). See ibid., 165. It seems, however, that Martens's conclusion is based more on comparing Matthew to Luke's version and his focus on the Gentile mission than on the Matthean context. Comparing Matt 22:1–14 with Matt 21:33–41, it could be concluded that the first two groups of servants refer to OT prophets, whereas the third group stands for the mission of the early church to all nations straight after Jesus' resurrection. So Gundry, *Matthew*, 434, 437. Two groups of servants sent with the king's invitation can be confusing, but it is likely that in the ancient Semitic culture there were two invitations to a banquet: one at the beginning expressing the host's intention of preparing a feast and the second, at the hour of the banquet, announcing that everything was ready. In this case there could be a longer interval of time between the two invitations. Cf. Bailey, *Peasant Eyes*, 94–95. Yet the fact is that in the Matthean parable the invitees refuse the invitation even at the first call. May it not be that the king's servants refers simply to God's messengers of any kind, whether prophets or apostles regardless of the time when they actually addressed Israelites with God's invitation? After all, it seems that the messengers are not as important in the story as the characteristics and the acts of those who have been invited and the king's response to those acts. See also Hultgren, *Parables*, 344. Blomberg, *Matthew*, 327, suggests also that at Matt 13:39 the messengers are the angels so that we cannot be sure who the messengers are. But can Matt 23:34 be of any relevance to this discussion?

181. Blomberg, *Matthew*, 326–27, and Drury, *Parables*, 98. But Swartley, "Banquet People," 179 n. 1, believes that 'the guests' refers to God's covenant people in general.

resembles the Kingdom of God having drawn near.[182] Rejecting God's invitation and killing his servants results in a punitive expedition against the murderers, and destruction of their city (Matt 22:6-7). Although the destruction is viewed by some commentators as referring to the historical event of destruction of Jerusalem by the Roman army in 70 CE,[183] it could be merely a note about the judgment coming on the Jewish leaders.[184] The important factor supporting the latter approach is that it was just the temple and not the whole city of Jerusalem that was destroyed by the Roman army in 70 CE.[185] The significant thing for us, however, is that Matthew's banquet is γάμος, a wedding banquet. Those who link Matt 22:1-10 (11-14) with Luke 14:15-24 immediately conclude that the banquet in both instances refers to the OT idea of the eschatological messianic banquet as found, for example, in Isa 25:6-7.[186] But whereas the 'great banquet' of Luke 15:16 may be echoing the OT motif of eschatological banquet, it is more difficult to see the same in the case of the Matthean wedding banquet. The OT itself does not seem to anticipate a future wedding banquet at the eschaton when Yahweh would fulfill his promises. Thus Matt 22:1-14 taken on its own terms seems to create additional difficulty in terms of the significance of the γάμος.

We would like to suggest, however, that as in Mark 2:18-20, the author of Matthew's Parable of Wedding Feast combines two OT motifs: that of the eschatological banquet with the divine marriage metaphor.

---

182. Dodd, *Parables of the Kingdom*, 121; Hultgren, *Parables*, 344. Cf. Blomberg, *Matthew*, 327.

183. E.g., Linnemann, *Parables of Jesus*, 95-96, 164 n. 17, and Martens, "Parables of Judgment," 154, 163-64. On this view, it is easy to see why exegetes prefer a post-70 CE construction of Matt 22:1-14. Then, they can claim that verse 7 looks to the destruction of the city *ex eventu*.

184. Gundry, *Matthew*, 436-37, believes that destroying the city echoes Isa 5:24-25, just as Isa 5:1-7 undergirds the Parable of the Tenants in Vineyard. Therefore it is not necessary to view the destruction as Matthew's retrospection on Jerusalem in 70 CE. Matt 22:7 is rather a dramatic figure of judgment "drawn from Isaiah's prediction of a past destruction of Jerusalem, a judgment consisting in God's rejection of the Jewish leaders resident in that city," (437). Although, it is still possible that after 70 CE the parable in Matt 22:1-14 was viewed as allusion to the historical event of Jerusalem's destruction, the destruction of the city may simply mean that God is judging not only Jewish leaders, but their whole nation for their faults. Cf. Schrenk, "ἐκλεκτός" IV: 186.

185. Blomberg, *Matthew*, 327-28, 328 n. 88. Cf. France, *Matthew*, 312. This interpretation then remains consistent with Jesus' prediction of destruction of the Temple in Matt 24:2, not of the whole city.

186. Swartley, "Banquet People," 187, and Hultgren, *Parables*, 344.

As such, this is not unique in the gospel of Matthew. The two concepts have previously been linked at 9:14–15,[187] granted our explanation of the Controversy over Fasting is relevant. It is a fact often overlooked by NT scholars that deutero-Isaiah also develops the motif of an eschatological banquet at 55:1–2 and 65:11ff.[188] We have already observed in discussing Mark 2:18–20 that subsequent chapters of deutero-Isaianic prophecy could be the source of early testimonies and also a part of the broad redemptive-historical perspective on which both Jesus and the NT writers operated.[189] In this case it does not seem strange that the wedding feast could stand side by side with the idea of an eschatological banquet. This would resemble two different plots of the same Isaianic utterance of chapters 54 (which employs the divine marriage metaphor in vv. 1–10) and 55 (which refers to the banquet in vv. 1–2). We cannot be sure that these chapters were certainly in the background of the material in Matt 22:1–14, but this proposal fits the wider Matthean context and appears to be consistent with our methodology.

The point of Matthew's parable would therefore be that Israelites who were initially invited to the wedding feast, i.e., God's kingdom in the eschatological age of salvation (cf. Matt 8:11),[190] are met by the king's anger instead (cf. 21:41). This followed their refusal to accept his invitation and their murder of his messengers. It is worth noting that this idea of rejection was not foreign to deutero-Isaianic prophecy. Chapter 65, for instance, speaks of Yahweh revealing himself to those who "did not seek him" (v. 1) and punishing those who were his but forsook him (vv. 11–12). Then, only the faithful servants of Yahweh would eat his meal (v. 13–16). Although we cannot press this point too far, it suggests at least that for somebody steeped in OT prophecy, a note on God judging his people and their leaders would be by no means strange. Jewish leaders will not partake of God's meal, because they have ignored the invitation to his eschatological meal which is ready (Matt 22:4–6), so they have proved themselves unworthy (v. 8; cf. 3:8; 10:10–11, 13, 37–38).[191]

---

187. Cf. also Hagner, *Matthew 14–28*, 629.

188. But see Swartley, "Banquet People," 187.

189. Cf. chapter 1. We have indicated there that, according to Dodd, the testimonies came especially from Isaiah, besides Jeremiah and the minor prophets as well as the Psalms.

190. Cf., e.g., Hultgren, *Parables*, 344.

191. Cf. Swartley, "Banquet People," 181. Cf. also Jones, *Matthean Parables*, 404–5. Hagner, *Matthew 14–28*, 630, observes that vv. 4, 8–9 give a hint of realized eschatology.

Nevertheless, it must still be recognized that some Israelites were favorably disposed towards Jesus (cf. 21:46). As a result, the invitation will be extended to others, those who were originally not invited (22:9-10). It seems that the logical conclusion would be that if those originally invited were the Jewish leaders and other Israelites who then rejected the message of Jesus,[192] the new invitees are somebody else, probably the Gentiles (cf. 21:41, 43).[193] But Matt 22:9-10, and similarly Matt 21:43, does not mention the Gentiles. The entire context of the parable is concerned with the Jews and especially with their leaders. Even the parable itself seems to address the Jewish leaders. So the sudden mention of the Gentiles may seem somewhat strange here. Nevertheless, it is sufficient for our purpose to state that the original people invited to the wedding banquet will be replaced by those who were not. And this seems to be the main emphasis in the parable. The wedding feast itself is important only insofar as it makes the point that those who had expected a share in God's eschatological salvation (cf. 8:11) would meet only with God's judgment because of their disobedience and fruitlessness (cf. 8:12; 21:34, 43).[194] In other words, the wedding feast itself is not as important as what had happened in connection with it. This could partly explain the total lack of interest in the bride or even in any further note about the son, the bridegroom.

It is also worth observing that chapter 23 contains seven woes uttered by Jesus against the Jewish leaders which continue the theme of judgment on the Jewish leaders.

192. See, e.g., Wright, *JVG*, 234, 328; France, *Matthew*, 313.

193. Cf. Jeremias, *Parables*, 69. It is worth pointing out that Matthew is specially interested in the mission to the "lost sheep of the house of Israel" (10:5-6, 23; 15:24, 26), but there are also a few instances which may refer to the Gentiles and a mission to them (8:11-12; 10:18; 24:14; 28:16-20). See Hultgren, *Parables*, 345, and Sanders, *Jesus and Judaism*, 218-21. However, here as in the case of the Vineyard Parable it is merely an assumption that the other groups of people refer exclusively to the Gentiles. It seems clear that Jesus' message was primarily directed to the Jews, although it is assumed to be referring to the later Gentile mission. But one needs to remember that the early church was still a Jewish-Gentile church and not merely a Gentile one. Therefore it would be hard to read of the vineyard being given to another people in Matt 21:43 as a reference to the Gentiles only. Cf. France, *Matthew*, 310; Gundry, *Matthew*, 429-30; Hultgren, *Parables*, 372-73. It is as if the definition of the vineyard has changed. It belongs to the nation that produces its fruit.

194. Jones, *Matthean Parables*, 408-10. Pace Homerski, *Mateusza*, 295. Homerski is of the opinion that the emphasis is on the king's goodness and his magnanimity rather than on his judgment.

God's eschatological salvation becomes available to those who had not been expecting it (Matt 22:9; cf. Isa 65:1–16).[195] They become the invitees who appear at the wedding banquet the king has prepared for his son.[196] Thus it seems as if they are participating already in the Kingdom of Heaven (Matt 22:10).[197] However, the description of the invitees as both 'bad and good' necessitates an explanation that follows in verses 11–14.[198]

Verses 11–13 describe the king's inspection during the wedding feast and a man being found without a wedding garment.[199] The man could stand corporately for the bad people of verse 10[200] and symbolize, similarly to verses 3–6, some Jewish leaders.[201] The king's decision to throw the man out into outer darkness is usually taken as a reference to the last judgment.[202] But we suggest that this is not the only possible

---

195. If the destruction of the city does not have to signify the destruction of Jerusalem in 70 CE, the third invitation does not have to refer to the post-destruction apostles and Christian missionaries. So Gundry, *Matthew*, 437. Contra Martens, "Parables of Judgment," 165.

196. The question could be raised as to whether a new invitation should not also involve two steps, as in Bailey's theory. However, one could argue that the tendency in Jesus' parables is to use shortcuts as the story advances.

197. Whether entering it by the means of baptism or not (cf. Jeremias, *Parables of Jesus*, 69) cannot be answered here with certainty.

198. France, *Matthew*, 313, and Hultgren, *Parables*, 346–47. The emphasis falls on the "bad." The phrase, πονηρούς τε καὶ ἀγαθούς, occurs in Matt 5:45. Cf. Hagner, *Matthew 14–28*, 630.

199. Probably clean clothes are meant rather than any special attire. Gundry, *Matthew*, 439. Via, *The Parables*, 130. Homerski, *Mateusza*, 296, proposes that the garment symbolizes the kind of righteousness Jesus spoke about in Matt 5:20; 6:33. But in general, they can symbolize works of righteousness (cf. Rev 19:8). See also Hagner, *Matthew 14–28*, 631. However, Rev 19:8 is dependent on Isa 61:10. See Fekkes, "Isaian Nuptial Imagery," 270, 273. Both in Rev 19:8 and Isa 61:10 the clothing is a gift from God and symbolizes righteousness as a spiritual quality. Therefore Matthew does not have to be absorbed with the question of how the people taken from the streets could have found clean garments. However, Hagner, *Matthew 14–28*, 631, disputes the validity of the custom of host providing the proper garment for the wedding feast in antiquity. But the suggestion can be made that if Matthew operates here on the metaphorical level, then the providing of the clothes by the host does not create a problem, especially if the reference to Isa 61:10 could be sustained (cf. 2 Kgs 25:29; Esth 6:8–9).

200. Hultgren, *Parables*, 347.

201. So Hagner, *Matthew 14–28*, 631, following Sim, "Wedding Garment," 165–78, although they claim this on the assumption that verses 11–13 were originally an independent parable.

202. Blomberg, *Matthew*, 329; Drury, *Parables*, 99; France, *Matthew*, 313; Gundry, *Matthew*, 439.

conclusion. If destroying the city refers not to Jerusalem in 70 CE, but to God's judgment on the Jewish leaders in general, then verses 11–13 may also refer to this general judgment on Jewish leaders who do not produce good fruit, and do not possess the works of righteousness (cf. Matt 3:7–10, some of them try to enter the kingdom for fear of the coming judgment; Matt 21:34, 43; 25:26). It could be said that, like the Pharisees and Sadducees in chapter 3, the "bad" Jews come to the wedding feast, entering the kingdom (through baptism?), because they are threatened by the coming judgment. They want to enter it, however, on their own terms (Matt 11:12 cf. Luke 16:16), and there is lack of righteousness in their lives. Throwing them into "outer darkness" does not have to symbolize the final judgment in the future but can refer generally to exclusion from the Kingdom of Heaven (cf. 8:12).[203] Then, like the destruction of the city, it could find its historical counterpart and asseveration in the events of 70 CE.

The parable finishes with a general remark in v. 14, "many are invited, but few are chosen," that fits both verses 1–10 and 11–13.[204] The sentence can simply mean that a large number of people have been invited to the feast (both the "bad and good"), but not all of them will qualify at God's judgment.[205] However, the phrase ὀλίγοι δὲ ἐκλεκτοί has long troubled exegetes, who have made different proposals concerning its meaning.[206] But we believe that the following suggestion can contribute to the understanding of this puzzling statement. If the author of the parable did have in mind both the metaphor of divine marriage and the texts relating to the eschatological banquet in deutero-Isaiah, another

---

203. On this approach Jeremias's note of the parable being an outline of the plan of redemption fails (cf. *Parables of Jesus*, 69).

204. E.g., France, *Matthew*, 313–14, Hagner, *Matthew 14–28*, 632, and Hultgren, *Parables*, 348. But, negatively, Via, *The Parables*, 129.

205. This is to say that within the church there are people who in the end will not qualify at the last judgment. But this view can be challenged. See below.

206. France, *Matthew*, 314, remarks that the word "chosen" by itself points to the fact that somebody's fate does depend on somebody else. Hultgren, *Parables*, 348, points out that the word "chosen" implies that "one's status can never be taken for granted." Only those who remain after the final judgment can be called the "chosen." Blomberg, *Matthew*, 329–30, Gundry, *Matthew*, 440–41, and Hagner, *Matthew 14–28*, 632, all seem to struggle with giving an exact meaning to the phrase. Instead each of them attempts to explain his own view of God's election. Hagner mentions also that in 24:22, 24, 31 the word ἐκλεκτοί becomes shorthand for Christ's disciples (see p. 632). But again this conclusion does not bear a direct significance to the understanding of 22:14.

possibility for the meaning of the phrase appears. In the LXX version of Isa 65, which we have commented on earlier, the author uses the word ἐκλεκτοί. In verses 8–9, Yahweh says that, although he will punish the people and their leaders for their iniquities and disobedience, he will not punish all his servants: he will save some, the remnant,[207] who are chosen (ἐκλεκτοί, v. 9; cf. also for the same word v. 23). The chosen are those who seek the Lord (v. 10) and it is they who will participate in the Lord's joyful feast (v. 13f) when Jerusalem/Zion, and even the whole cosmos, are transformed at the eschaton (vv. 17–18).[208] Although Yahweh dealt with the whole nation in the past, now, because of the people's unworthiness (they forsook their God; v. 11–12), he will spare only the remnant at the time of his judgment: ὀλίγοι ἐκλεκτοί, one might say. So in Matthew, the Messiah came to save his people (cf. Matt 1:21; 15:24), many in the sense of all, but those invited to rejoice in this salvation were not worthy (= did not produce the good fruit, 22:8), therefore they will meet God's judgment. Yet the remnant, the faithful ones, will enjoy God's banquet as they have been chosen by himself to constitute the people of the new Zion.

To summarize, the overall plot of the story would be that the Jewish leaders who have been initially invited to God's eschatological wedding banquet are punished because of their unworthiness. Still other unfaithful leaders and people who get to the banquet not being clothed by God in a proper attire are excluded from the salvation feast. But the remnant, God's chosen, enjoy his feast of salvation as they constitute the eschatological nucleus of the new Zion.

This approach, while not itself without weaknesses,[209] could to some extent solve different problems that appeared in the study of Matt

---

207. Cf. Webb, "Zion in Transformation," 72–73. Webb observes that "the key to the transformation of Zion is purifying judgment . . . The result is the production of a purified remnant which becomes the nucleus of the new Zion of the eschaton." See p. 72. The remnant appears in deutero-Isaiah 46:3 and the concept is still present in the last chapters of the book where God makes a distinction between his "servants" (65:13–14; 66:14; cf. 65:8–10) and the "rebels" (66:24; cf. 65:2–15). Cf. ibid. 73. Although Webb does not explicitly mention the verses under consideration in this article, one can refer to his commentary, *Message of Isaiah*, 244. Here he identifies God's servants in vv. 8–10 as God's faithful remnant. Cf. also Oswalt, *Isaiah: Chapters 40–66*, 645–46.

208. Webb, "Zion in Transformation," 68–69. Webb explains that "the eschaton towards which the book as a whole moves is a new cosmos centred on a new Jerusalem/Zion (cf. 2.1–4)." See ibid. 69.

209. One of which would be to explain why the other people, who were brought to the wedding after the destruction of the city, were not mentioned as those who also had

22:1–14. But as such it does justice to the wider context of Matthean parable and also explains the sources behind it, i.e., mainly Isaiah, while at the same time supporting unity of the whole passage. The approach also proposes that there is a way of looking at the Parable of the Wedding Banquet as resembling Jesus' earlier teaching.

Thus, as far as the marriage metaphor is concerned, the eschatological marriage feast seems to have begun, but a number of Jews do not enter it and fall under God's judgment because of their disobedience. Others, who try to enter the wedding unqualified, perhaps by their own methods, are excluded. But the faithful remnant of the King enjoys his long-promised salvation expressed in the wedding banquet symbolism.

Matthean Parable of the Ten Maidens

Matt 25:1–13 is another instance of a parable employing the wedding motif. The parable is unparalleled in the other Synoptics, although many scholars recognize that its first part resembles Luke 12:35–38 and that verses 10–12 have similarities with Luke 13:25–27.[210] In Mark a theme related to this parable of Matthew occurs in 13:33–37. Regardless of the similarities of the two passages, "Matthew appears to be dependent on his own special source for the parable."[211] Therefore, one of our aims in this part of our study will be to suggest a possible background for this parable. Besides this, our main focus will be not on the interrelationship between different synoptic parables, but on the plot in Matt 25:1–13.[212]

---

an invitation (on the assumption that they are also the Jews). However, a proposal can be made that at the beginning the parable refers to those who were strongly convinced of their right to participate in the Kingdom of God. They thought they would be saved, while at the same time rejecting God's way (=invitation). They were convinced of this being at the same time unworthy in God's eyes. The other group, 'the bad,' had a sense of God's coming judgment so they tried to join the community of the invited celebrating the eschatological salvation in their own ways. But they were not faithful and therefore not chosen; their clothes were improper.

210. Bultmann, *Synoptic Tradition*, 118, stresses that the material gathered in Luke 12:35–38 is secondary and came late after the primitive church started to recognize the delay of the parousia. Therefore Matt 25:1–13 is also late. Cf. Linnemann, *Parables of Jesus*, 126–27, and Jones, *Matthean Parables*, 443.

211. Hagner, *Matthew 14–28*, 727.

212. Marshall, *Luke*, 536, denies Luke 12:35–36 has any reference to the messianic banquet because this account follows the parousia. But for an opposite opinion see Green, *Luke*, 501. See below on the issue of reading such passages in the context of Jesus' alleged teaching on his own parousia.

We shall therefore proceed by focusing on the passage in its own context.[213] But before we do this we shall discuss in brief the present state of the study of Matt 25:1–13.

The debate on the Parable of the Ten Maidens seems to be focused on either comparing its details to Jewish wedding customs in the first century CE or on the parable's eschatological teaching on the parousia of Jesus.[214] The issues of debate in the first approach have been, for example, whether an ancient Palestinian wedding could have been held during the night[215] or what was the role of the maidens in the wedding procession, and whether they were the bridegroom's or the bride's attendants.[216] But it seems that not all the details of the parable are essential to interpreting it.[217] We do not have to expect one-to-one correspondences with reality in the case of any parable. The story can be surrealistic. Nevertheless, the discussion has still been concerned with supposed allegorical elements in the parable, with some scholars concluding that originally it was not an allegory.[218] On the other hand, there have been exegetes who have proposed a totally allegorical approach to the Ten Maidens Parable,[219]

---

213. A similar starting point has been proposed by Donfried, "Ten Virgins," 415–28. Although we believe that contextual study of Matthew is fully justified, we shall modify Donfried's approach according to our methodology which seeks to trace the connections between the idea of divine marriage in both the Old and New Testaments. Donfried's methodology appears limited in this respect.

214. Cf. Donahue, *Gospel in Parable*, 101. Via, *The Parables*, 124, noted that "the exact relationship of the parable to the wedding customs of Jesus' day remains unresolved." We suggest that this relationship does not matter in the case of the parable.

215. But it does not matter to Matthew. So Drury, *Parables*, 103.

216. To this kind of debate there seems to be no end. See, e.g., Burkitt, "Ten Virgins," 267–70. But against his conclusion that the maidens are little girls of the neighborhood see, Manson, *Sayings of Jesus*, 244. Jeremias, *Parables of Jesus*, 171, deals with wedding customs. So does Linnemann, *Parables of Jesus*, 124–25. Hultgren, *Parables*, 170, discusses, for example, the exact kind of λαμπάδας used by the maidens and the method of refilling them. Cf. Gundry, *Matthew*, 498.

217. Donfried, "Ten Virgins," 417 n.11, and France, "Being Ready," 181.

218. So Jeremias, *Parables of Jesus*, 171. The parable as it now stands in Matthew's gospel has very little in common with Jesus' teaching according to the Jesus Seminar adherents. It has been qualified as color grey. Although, as the authors of the report admit, some of the Jesus' Seminar scholars voted for the parable as authentic "because they thought its content matched Jesus' expectation of the kingdom's future coming." See Funk et al., *Parables of Jesus*, notes to p. 67 and p. 75.

219. Special attention should be paid to the work of Ford, "Foolish Scholars," 107–23. Ford argues that the parable is told by Jesus against the hypocrisy of Jewish teachers who "monopolised the nuptial imagery of the covenant on Sinai and tended to exclude

but seemingly everyone accepts a moderate treatment of the parable as an allegory as it now stands in Matthew's gospel. Our argument is that its symbolism does not necessarily have to assume later composition by the early church and that it could well have resembled Jesus' original teaching.[220]

Once the allegorical character of Matt 25:1–13 is recognized, the majority of scholars, taking the passage in the context of Matt 24, conclude that it must refer to the delayed parousia of Christ.[221] Thus, verses 10–12 refer to the final judgment at the end of the space-time universe. The wise virgins are often taken as referring to true believers/Christians, and the foolish ones to false disciples who are judged to remain outside the kingdom of heaven.[222] Others, however, have recognized that some elements in the parable point rather to an imminent eschatological crisis,[223] though they have needed to deconstruct the parable, in relation to the view of later changes made by the early church, in order to show

the less learned from an intimate relationship to God." See p. 113. But the whole study is based on comparing the details of the parable with symbols of late Judaism as presented mainly in Midrashim, so that the lamps symbolize the Torah, the night is the proper time for studying it, midnight is the hour of special revelation, the oil is a symbol of good deeds; the leading into the nuptial chamber signifies gaining instruction. Ford recognizes that the rabbinic material used to support these conclusions is most probably of later origin than the NT, but continues to propagate this approach (cf. pp. 110 n. 2, 118). Hagner, *Matthew 14–28*, 728, opposes Ford's views. We need to add that in the face of the arguments presented in chapter 4 above, it is difficult to give any legitimacy to Ford's treatment of the rabbinic material as the basis for interpreting the NT.

220. Donfried, "Ten Virgins," 425 n. 46, observes that if the allegory was composed by the early church it would have made a reference to the bride as a picture of itself since the symbol of church being the bride of Christ was already known from Pauline literature. Blomberg, *Parables*, 195, supports this claim. Some late uncials mention both the bridegroom and the bride at Matt 25:1. But this supports the argument that the original parable did not mention the bride and therefore was pre-Pauline.

221. E.g., Donfried, "Ten Virgins," 426, France, "Being Ready," 181, and more recently, Keener, *Matthew*, 597, 599. However, Jones, *Matthean Parables*, 444, suggests that the parable in its pre-Matthean form could point to the role of good works in the 'afterlife.' But then again the unity of the parable cannot be sustained, with vv. 9–11 being seen as editorial additions (ibid., 452).

222. Taking the maidens to be Jesus' disciples may be due to reading Mark 2:19–20// Matt 9:15 into the parable. But it is possible that the metaphor in Matt 25 had been adjusted to the new context.

223. So Jeremias, *Parables of Jesus*, 53. In this he follows Dodd, *Parables of the Kingdom*, 172–74. The crisis is linked with Jesus' first coming because it is a time to judge oneself whether one is wise or foolish, faithful or unfaithful. This crisis anticipates the second and final world-crisis at the end of the time-space universe.

this.²²⁴ We intend to present an approach that will do justice to the unity of the parable within the context of Matt 24, to its allegorical character, as well as to the note of the imminence of the coming crisis. Therefore we propose to focus briefly on the teaching of Matt 24 and the issue of Jesus' parousia.

Matt 24 (Mark 13//Luke 21) opens with Jesus' prediction of the destruction of the temple (vv. 1–2). In turn, his disciples ask him about the time in which this will happen (v. 3). Then, most scholars conclude that Jesus answers them out-of-connection bringing in the issue of the end of the world understood as the end of the space-time universe.²²⁵ Only a few exegetes view Matt 24 as referring both to the destruction of Jerusalem in 70 CE and to the end of the space-time universe.²²⁶ We, however, want to suggest that these two approaches are the outcome of a misunderstanding of the apocalyptic language in the Bible as well as of a misuse of the word "parousia."²²⁷ Jesus, as his words are reflected by Matthew in chapter 24, in a Daniel-like manner (cf. Dan 7) was predicting the imminent crisis which would come within the generation of his contemporaries (Matt 24:34, 42, 44) upon impenitent Israel (cf. Matt 23). The judgment which in OT thought was to come upon the pagan nations was coming now on those who refused to follow the way Yahweh had appointed through his Messiah. However, he would vindicate his elect "who cried to him day and night."²²⁸ Israel would be rescued from "destruction by holding firm to the end; but now the Israel that holds firm,

---

224. This is necessary for Jeremias because he views Matt 24 as speaking of Christ's parousia and 25:1 as linked to this theme by the word τότε. See, *Parables of Jesus*, 51–52.

225. Cf. Caird and Hurst, *Theology*, 255. The text in Matt 24:3 speaks of Jesus 'parousia' (τῆς σῆς παρυσίας) and the end (close) of the (this) age (συντελείας τοῦ αἰῶνος).

226. See particularly France, *Jesus and the Old Testament*, the whole of Appendix A, pp. 227–39. Cf. also France's list of other adherents of this view on p. 231. France believes that Matt 24:1–35 deals with the destruction of Jerusalem (although verse 27 refers to both 70 CE and the parousia), and vv. 36–51 refer to the final judgment at the parousia of Christ at the end of space-time universe.

227. Here following Wright, *JVG*, 320–68. In the past some German scholars claimed that the parousia occurred with Christ resurrection, according to the accounts of Mark and Matthew. But Luke corrected this and shifted it to some future event. See Bartsch, "Christian Eschatology," 387–97. We suggest, however, that our view does more justice to the similarity of Synoptic teachings.

228. Wright, *JVG*, 324, 336.

and so is rescued, consists of his [Jesus'] own disciples."²²⁹ The language used in Matt 24 should be read as metaphorical. It describes catastrophic judgment coming on Jerusalem which was at that time the main obstacle to advancing the kingdom of God.²³⁰ Similarly, the word 'parousia' does not mean 'the second coming'; neither does it refer to the literal coming of Jesus on literal clouds at the close of the space-time universe. Wright explains,

> But why should we think—except for reasons of ecclesiastical and scholarly tradition—that *parousia* means "the second coming," and/or the downward travel on a cloud of Jesus and/or the "son of man"? *Parousia* means 'presence' as opposed to *apousia*, "absence"; hence it denotes the "arrival" of someone not at the moment present; and it is especially used in relation to the visit "of a royal or official personage."²³¹

Thus the question of the disciples in Matt 24:3 asks about the time Jesus is going to be installed and vindicated as the rightful king of Israel.²³² This time will be marked by the destruction of Jerusalem's Temple. "The close of the age," therefore, pointed to the end of the present evil age and to the introduction of the age to come which would end "Israel's period of mourning and exile" and begin the time of "her freedom and vindication."²³³ Its historical asseveration took place in 70 CE at the time the Roman troops destroyed the temple thus confirming Jesus' words about the imminence of the disaster (i.e., within 'this generation').²³⁴

---

229. Ibid., 348. This means that God's people are being redefined.

230. Ibid., 340. Cf. Gould, *Mark*, 241, 252, who himself believes that all of Matt 24 refers to the destruction of Jerusalem.

231. *JVG*, 341. Cf. Oepke, "παρουσία, πάρειμι," V: 858–71. Oepke recognizes that the basic meaning of the word "parousia" is "presence" or "arrival." While the OT LXX does not help much in establishing its technical meaning in the NT, Hellenism used it in the context of "the visit of a Ruler," "the visit of the Gods," "the presence of the gods at sacrifices," and Josephus used the word as referring to "God's presence to help," or the presence in the sense of Shekinah. But then Oepke seems to impose his theology on the meaning of "parousia" in the NT.

232. Wright, *JVG*, 342, 346.

233. Ibid., 345–46. Wright points out that the age to come is "still very much this-worldly." See p. 346.

234. Gould, *Mark*, 252, remarks that comparing Matt 24 with 26:64 teaches that a visible coming is not applied and also that the coming is not a single event, but rather "repeated interferences in crises of the world's history, of which this destruction of Jerusalem was the first." For Gould "sitting on the right hand of Power" and the coming

All the disciples had to do was to watch the signs of the time (24:42, 44) and flee at the proper moment of Jerusalem's doom (vv. 15–20).

Although scholarship has recently attempted to challenge this view critically,[235] it seems this has not so far been successful.[236] Therefore the approach presented here, while awaiting further evaluation by scholars, agrees with the evidence advanced as well as challenging traditional eschatological views.[237] The approach can also

---

"are connected in such a way as to mean that [Jesus] is to assume power in heaven and exercise it here in the world" (252). That assumption of power was to take place at Jesus' departure from the world (perhaps after his resurrection). Caird, *Language and Imagery*, 268, arrived at a similar conclusion that "the coming of the Son of Man on the clouds of heaven would be seen not merely at the end of time but continuously or repeatedly from the moment of Jesus' death." Moreover, Caird applying Bultmann's existentialism to his corporate view of eschatology (i.e., historical eschatology) concluded that Matthew stresses the final judgment not because of his "preoccupation with the end of the world," but because of "a recognition that the final judgment is for ever pressing upon the present with both offer and demand" (268). In this sense the end is 'bifocal': on the one hand it points to the destruction of Jerusalem, and on the other to the End." See Caird and Hurst, *Theology*, 256. May not Caird have taken his particular view on Matthew's eschatology because he also was not sure what to do about the parousia and its immediacy in, e.g., Matt 24:29? See ibid., 263 n. 40. Nevertheless, it must be stressed that from Jesus' perspective the end referred to the imminent coming of Jerusalem's doom which took place in 70 CE. See Wright, "In Grateful Dialogue," 270–72, cf. 318 n. 32. It is also worth noticing that our view of Jesus' eschatology does not contradict Christian theology of the future as found in Rom 8, 1 Cor 15 and Rev 21–22. Cf. Wright, ibid., 265.

235. The main counter-arguments came from Allison, "Victory of Apocalyptic," 126–41. Allison tries to challenge Wright mainly on two points: (a) his metaphorical reading of Mark 13 and parallels, and (b) the unsolved problem of theodicy. Another disagreement comes from Snodgrass, "Overreading the Parables," 72–73, but he only expresses his dissatisfaction with Wright's conclusions. The dissatisfaction is most probably affected by his essentially futuristic view of Jesus' eschatology.

236. Wright himself has responded to Allison's objections. See Wright, "In Grateful Dialogue," 261. Allison's attempt to read Mark 13 or Matt 24 literally seems to fail in the face of Wright's evidence for metaphorical reading of these passages. Likewise, Allison's challenge on the issue of theodicy seems unjustified facing Wright's explanation about the difference between Jesus' achievement and not implementing it perfectly by the church in this world. See ibid., 272. We would like to remark that Allison's stress on the literal reading of Matt 24 does not help him much in referring to the remote future end because of the marks of imminence in the prediction as well as the meaning of the word "parousia."

237. However, one cannot deny that a number of people in the past have held a similar view of Matt 24 having its fulfillment in the first-century. Beside Gould referred to above, cf., e.g., Russell, *Parousia*, 549. And closer to our times, Feuillet, A. "Le Sens du Mot Parousie dans l'Évangile de Matthieu." In *The Background of the New Testament*

give a possible solution to the problem of interpreting Matt 25:1–13 in its context, as indicated earlier.

We have already noted that scholars have interpreted Matt 25:1–13 in the context of chapter 24. While agreeing on the approach, we must set aside the conclusions because of our different view of Jesus' eschatology. It also seems right not to dismiss the content of chapter 23 while interpreting our passage. We take the point of Jeremias[238] that τότε in verse 1 of the Parable of the Ten Virgins refers back to 24:44 and 24:50 with their mention of the parousia of the son of man. Likewise, verse 13 of the parable repeats the command to be watchful while waiting for the imminent parousia.[239]

The kingdom of heaven in the parable is compared to the situation of ten young women,[240] who awaited the arrival of the bridegroom.[241] The number ten does not have any further significance, since it is just "a favourite round number to describe a fair-sized group of people."[242] The identification of the maidens themselves, however, seems more complicated.[243] Although almost all commentators have had no difficulty in viewing them as disciples of Jesus on the basis of the Matthean context (cf. 9:15; 24), it seems that the background for their identity goes beyond Matthew to the OT. Chavasse[244] has claimed that the virgins (παρθένοι) echo Ps 44:14LXX (=45:15 Eng. tr.), which speaks of girls (παρθένοι)

---

and Its Eschatology, edited by W. D. Davies and D. Daube, 261–80. Cambridge: 1956; and Gaston, L. *No Stone on Another*, 483–87. Leiden: 1970. References given by France, *Jesus and the Old Testament*, 229–30.

238. *Parables of Jesus*, 51.

239. Cf. ibid. But pace Jeremias on the point that v. 13 misses the original meaning of the parable.

240. The basic meaning of παρθένος is "young woman who just reached maturity," therefore "virgin." But there is no special emphasis on virginity per se. See Delling, "παρθένος," V: 826–37.

241. Cf. Hagner, *Matthew 14–28*, 728. The kingdom is compared to a wedding, not the virgins, and what they did in this context. Cf. Jeremias, *Parables of Jesus*, 174

242. Linnemann, *Parables of Jesus*, 124. She adds that "the precise proportion of one to one is not important to the story: the numbers are brought in only to express graphically the division into two groups" (125). Pace Ford, "Foolish Scholars," 115–16, who thinks that 10 refers to the circles of study as at Qumran.

243. Unless one automatically reads υἱοὶ τοῦ νυμφῶνος of Mark 2:19//Matt 9:15 into παρθένοι of Matt 25:1. Of course, some scholars have still denied any allegorical significance regarding the maidens. Cf. Delling, "παρθένος," V: 834.

244. *Bride of Christ*, 56.

attending the bride. It is possible that Ps 45 has messianic overtones and that the bride is the Messiah's bride,[245] but this still does not solve the problem of the identification of the maidens. Certainly, the emphasis in the Psalm is on the king and later on the princess, but by no means on her companions. On the other hand, the word παρθένος with its cognates was used in the LXX on a number of occasions to designate Israel (e.g., Isa 37:22; Jer 18:13; 31:4=38:4LXX; 31:21=38:21LXX; Lam 2:13). The nation was addressed and known as virgin Israel. It is also interesting that Isa 62:5a uses the word in a simile of Yahweh marrying the virgin Zion: "As a young man marries a virgin (παρθένος), so shall your builder[246] marry you." We have already noted that Isa 62 and other parts of Isaiah and Jeremiah could have been included in early testimonies originating with Jesus and used by the writers of the NT (cf. chapter 1 above). In addition, it is worthwhile observing that the word παρθένος was earlier used by Matt at 1:23, while quoting Isa 7:14. This for exegetes puzzling verse in Isaiah uses the word παρθένος in the LXX to describe a maiden giving birth to Immanuel, which signifies Yahweh's salvation. Although usually central to the debate on the virgin-birth of Jesus, Isa 7:14 can alternatively be read metaphorically, in which case παρθένος can be viewed corporately as the daughter Zion (cf. 1:8; 10:32; 16:1; 22:4).[247] The examples of the corporate use of παρθένος to describe the people of Israel have been discussed above. Therefore, the case is not peculiar unless other readings are preferred *à priori*. Simultaneously, Immanuel is also a corporate figure referring to the remnant, Isaiah and his followers in the nearest context (8:11–18).[248] Thus the meaning of Matt 1:23 is also

---

245. E.g., Craigie, *Psalms 1–50*, 340–41. Cf. Delitzsch, *Psalms*, II: 72–90. The strong argument is that this Psalm could not have been included in the canon unless it had been understood messianically. Later, the letter to the Heb 1:8 transfers Ps 45:6–7 into the Christ hymn linking it with the Messiah-figure. See Kraus, *Psalms 1–59*, 457. Chavasse, *Bride of Christ*, 57, insists that the parable comes after Jesus has ridden into Jerusalem as the King of Ps 45, to claim his bride. But then he must distinguish between the bride and her attendants concluding, with no support, that they refer to the Gentiles.

246. On the rendering of the word בֹּנָיִךְ see chapter 3 on Isa 62:5a.

247. All the linguistic tensions in the verse as well as in its context point to a metaphorical rendering. So Webb, "Zion in Transformation," 82. See also Rice, "Immanuel Prophecy," 222–25. See also p. 226 n. 6 & 7 for further references.

248. Rice, "Immanuel Prophecy," 222. Rice explains that "In the default of the king [Ahaz] and the nation at large Isaiah and his followers become the remnant. Whereas YHWH is no longer with Ahaz and Judah or 'this people,' it is precisely the point of the sign given to Ahaz that he is with Isaiah and those who have said 'Amen' to his ministry.

corporate: the virgin is Israel and the child is the new faithful remnant, a movement within Israel started by Jesus.[249] Thus Matthew himself could have created a good basis for understanding the significance of παρθένος in his Gospel. And, having in mind the metaphor of divine marriage in the OT, one need not be surprised that a metaphorical figure can refer to a nation as a collection of all its individuals. Also, if Isaiah and Jeremiah were behind the sources of testimonies originating with Jesus and used by the authors compiling the stories about him, then it is possible that the word παρθένος already had strong connotations for a Jewish mind and immediately recalled to it Israel as a maiden. Therefore, it is likely that Jesus himself employed this widely recognized title for Israel in his teaching, and that the author of Matthew later mirrored this teaching with its characteristic symbolism. Taking all this into account, we suggest that the ten maidens in Matt 25:1–13 refer neither to the bridegroom's nor to the bride's attendants, but stand together as the παρθένος, people of Israel. After all, it is the bride who is important to the bridegroom and vice versa. However, for the parable's authorial purpose the maidens had been divided in two groups: the foolish ones and the wise ones, making her plural παρθένοι.[250] This immediately solves the problem of who the bride is in the parable: she is Israel, but this Israel needs to have a further qualification, because there are two different groups within God's

---

They are the only ones in Israel on this occasion who can say, 'God is with us.' Ahaz and Judah have even forfeited their right to the land of Judah; it has become Immanuel's land (8:8b). Isaiah and his disciples live amidst, but apart from their fellowmen as a visible and tangible reminder to the king and the nation of their failure and as a witness to the power that comes through repentance and faith (8:16–18). The 'disciples' in 8:16 and the 'children' in 8:18 are synonymous; collectively they are Immanuel." I have changed slightly the format of Rice's Scripture reference and quotation marks. Cf. Webb, "Zion in Transformation," 82.

249. Rice, "Immanuel Prophecy," 226.

250. Manson, *Sayings of Jesus*, 243, suggested earlier that the place of the bride was taken by the maidens, but he came to this conclusion only after reading the rest of the NT into the parable. He explains further (244) that the bride, who is only conjectured, stands for Israel, whereas the ten virgins stand for the Gentile converts. The wise are those who conform to the Jewish-Christian standard of Law (lamps and oil stand for the Law). But this seems to undermine his earlier conclusion. And then one is left with the impression that the Gentile converts are not coming in as a part of the new Israel, but as attendants only. How then do the attendants become the bride later in the early church's thought? Moreover, we cannot see why the issue of Gentiles should at this point replace the focus on Israel. Nevertheless, Manson's case shows that our proposal may be a step forward in solving a few exegetical difficulties, as well as those pointed out by Jeremias, *Parables of Jesus*, 174–75.

people.²⁵¹ Nevertheless, all of them expect the arrival of the bridegroom, which is why all of them take their lamps to meet him as he comes. One is already familiar with Jesus depicted as the bridegroom from Matt 9:15 and 22:1–14. Moreover, the context of chapter 24 further supports this conclusion. But again this inference can be accepted only on the assumption that Jesus is Yahweh's agent who brings his promises to fulfillment. In general, the parable is about Israel who expects the coming of her bridegroom.²⁵²

It was suggested above that the moral of the parable is to be watchful as the coming of the Son of man is delayed, according to verses 1 and 13.²⁵³ In this sense, our parable resembles the previous one in which the master of a household's return is delayed (24:45ff.). However, a problem emerges from the fact that in Matt 25:1–13 all the maidens fall asleep (v. 5) and therefore are by no means watchful, and yet only the wise who took more oil enter the wedding banquet (v. 10).²⁵⁴ On the other hand, if the sleep signifies a long period of waiting for the coming of the bridegroom,²⁵⁵ as the context of chapter 24 suggests, then not all the details are crucial to understanding the parable.²⁵⁶ The thing that mat-

---

251. The problem of the lack of explicit mention of a bride is an old one. Some late manuscripts already tried to add the bride together with the bridegroom in verse 1, but this rendering is unnecessary on our explanation. Donfried, "Ten Virgins," 425–26, recognizes that Matthew could understand παρθένος to be a term for Jesus' bride in the same way as Paul did. This is a bride awaiting the parousia. But, of course, his conclusions are different since he believes that the bride is the Christian church and the parousia will take place in the remote future.

252. It has been indicated elsewhere that at this time in Israel's history the hopes of fulfillment of God's promises had been increasing. Cf. chapter 1 of this volume.

253. Similarly, Muirhead, "Bride of Christ," 183.

254. Cf. Donahue, *Gospel in Parable*, 101. One of the popular approaches was to treat the sleep as the death of God's people. Then the crying out at midnight is to wake all the dead for the final judgment. Donfried, "Ten Virgins," 421. More recently, Jones, *Matthean Parables*, 444–45. But then the going of the foolish to get more oil, after their death, seems inconsistent with the story as a whole. The context of Matt 24 also does not suggest the "afterlife."

255. Cf. Scott, *Parable*, 71.

256. Blomberg, *Parables*, 196, explains that "probably the incident with the oil simply supports the main theme of preparedness . . ." Pace, e.g., Jones, *Matthean Parables*, 452, who sees in oil a symbol of good deeds. So does Donfried, "Ten Virgins," 243, and Drury, *Parables*, 499, on the basis of Matt 5:14–15. Also the apparently 'scandalous' way in which the wise treat the foolish should rather be denied any further significance. Cf. Scott, *Parable*, 71. Everybody is responsible for his own readiness. See France, "Being Ready," 182.

ters in the parable is being prepared in advance,[257] choosing the way of wisdom rather than of folly. Wright explains,

> What matters is this. Jesus is urging his followers to grasp, or perhaps to be grasped by, the true wisdom, since only those who did so would be ready for the great day which was coming, the day of judgment and vindication.[258]

Thus, we could say, having in mind all that has also been mentioned concerning Matt 24, that the wise part of Israel (φρόνιμοι παρθένοι) are those who heed Jesus' words; they are his disciples.[259] They will meet their bridegroom in order to be in the kingdom of heaven, enjoying the messianic wedding banquet with him. They will enjoy the advantages of covenant renewal. On the other hand, those who reject the warning of the coming judgment are the foolish part of Israel (μωραὶ παρθένοι); they are those who disregard Jesus' prophetic utterances, the leaders of Israel from Matt 23, who therefore remain unprepared for the coming crisis: the day of the Son of man. They will be left outside the wedding banquet (cf. Matt 22:1-14)[260] with no other chance to be prepared (although they still tried to obtain more oil, 25:9-10). So they also will be excluded from the new covenant. They will be completely surprised by the judgment directed against Jerusalem with those who support its political system, i.e., themselves. Thus the overall picture seems to be that not all who formally constitute the bride, virgin Israel, are going to enjoy the wedding. Some appear to be excluded as the not-bride because of their unpreparedness. Therefore, the eschatological wedding is

---

257. Cf. France, "Being Ready," 181. Cf. Hagner, *Matthew 14–28*, 729. With both we agree in principle but not in detail. See also Dodd, *Parables of the Kingdom*, 172–74. Blomberg, *Parables*, 195, explains that "watchfulness" in v. 13—γρηγορέω ("to keep watch")—does not necessarily mean "to stay awake" but merely "to be prepared."

258. *JVG*, 315. Jesus, similarly to other Jewish wisdom teachers, confronted "his contemporaries with a choice between wisdom and folly *seen in terms of* the choice between following the prophetic call to covenant renewal and following the merely human way, the way of the world, which would lead to ruin". Ibid., 314. Cf. also Matt 7:24–27. But pace Bertram, "μωρός κτλ.," IV: 842, who believes that the wisdom refers to the "common sense" prudence that one can gain from a life-situation.

259. I.e., they are those whose righteousness must exceed "that of the scribes and Pharisees." Matt 5:20. Israel is being redefined. God establishes his kingdom in a way, which leaves many of Israel's leaders outside to be exposed to his judgment. Cf. Wright, *JVG*, 327.

260. Although they might have believed that their participation in the wedding is guaranteed. Cf. Via, *The Parables*, 126.

linked with eschatological judgment. Moreover, it should be noted that our explanation of the parable is consistent with Jesus' overall teaching on the kingdom of God.[261] Hence, it is possible that Jesus himself spoke a parable like this in Matt 25:1–13.[262] Consequently, our approach can reconcile most of the tensions between the different claims of scholars about the notes of imminence in the context of the parable, as well as sustaining the unity of its teaching.

An interesting remark of Drury is worth considering here. He suggests that the "cry at midnight" in verse 6 of the parable may echo Exod 12:29–30 which describes another "cry at midnight" as an outcome of Yahweh judging those who did not heed his voice in Egypt.[263] In Matt 25:1–13 the judgment of the bridegroom comes on those who did not listen to his voice. Therefore it is suggested that the part of Israel who is not faithful to God's voice through Jesus the prophet[264] will suffer in the same way as the great enemy of Israel in OT times. The judgment which came upon the pagan nation is now going to strike the unfaithful within the bride of Yahweh. Nevertheless, the Exodus-like judgment will lead to the vindication of the true Israel, the faithful bride. Thus it is possible that the Parable of the Ten Maidens contains an exodus motif, but this idea needs further evaluation in a different place.[265]

Compared to the Markan note on the sudden withdrawal of the bridegroom from among his companions, Matt 25:1–13 presents a waiting bride Israel who is being redefined. This is to constitute the true bride who enters the messianic wedding banquet at the Messiah king's vindication. The unfaithful part of the bride is going to be judged on the imminent day of the Son of man. Therefore, one can sense some similarities with Matt 24:1–14. There it also appeared that not all who expect the wedding banquet are worthy to enter it. Those who are unqualified for the wedding cannot enjoy it either. But the faithful remnant, like the

---

261. See above. Cf. Wright, *JVG*, 326–36.

262. This is no different from the conclusion of some of the members of the Jesus Seminar. See Funk et al., *Parables of Jesus*, notes on p. 67.

263. *Parables*, 103.

264. Jesus can stand here in the same relationship to the unfaithful part of Israel as Moses did to Egypt.

265. But Ford, "Foolish Scholars," 118, claims that the exodus motif in the parable consists of similarities between Jesus' coming to his bride in order to enter with her into the new covenant and Yahweh coming on Mount Sinai to marry Israel in the covenant of Moses. While this is a possible echo of the OT, again it needs further evaluation.

wise maidens, experience God's salvation, the blessings of his renewed covenant. Although introduced earlier by Jesus' ministry, this salvation is established amidst the events of 70 CE when the main obstacle in the way of God's kingdom had been destroyed.

JOHN THE BAPTIST'S TESTIMONY TO JESUS IN THE FOURTH GOSPEL

John 3:27-30 records the final testimony to Jesus by John the Baptizer. The immediate context concerns the issue raised by John's disciples about Jesus' baptizing apparently as John's rival.[266] In part, the issue dealt with the fact that Jesus was drawing greater crowds than John (v. 26).[267] This might have caused jealousy among the disciples of John.[268] The Baptizer's response to them is once again to set Jesus' superiority over against his own position (vv. 29-30; cf. 1:26-27). As he himself expressed it, Jesus "must become greater," and he "must become less" (3:30).[269] He had already testified in a similar way to the Pharisees that he is not the Messiah (1:25; cf. 1:28), but someone far inferior to him (1:27). Here, in the passage under consideration, he compares himself to the φίλος τοῦ νυμφίου, a special friend of the bridegroom. Most of the commentators

---

266. Although the gospel right from the beginning (1:6-8) intends to show that John is Jesus' witness, not a rival. Cf. Moody Smith, *Gospel of John*, 23.

267. Cf. Schnackenburg, *John*, I: 414.

268. They seem not to have understood earlier. However, their exact motives are not clear. See ibid. Cf. Smalley, *John*, 99.

269. But see Lee, *Fourth Gospel*, 58-60. She claims that vv. 29-30 are not concerned with John's personal humility. They rather focus on the superiority of the new religion represented by Jesus (which is symbolized by his Spirit baptism) over the old one, represented by John (symbolized by his water baptism). This approach enables her to explain why John 3:22-30 was placed directly after the Nicodemus episode: John the Baptist is ready to make the transition from the old to the new and therefore is opposed to Nicodemus who is not able to do so. Thus verses 28-30 imply also the proper answer expected from Nicodemus. But it should not be forgotten that John the Baptist as a historical person is the forerunner of Jesus announcing the coming of God's kingdom. Thus the two characters are not opposed to each other as representatives of two religions, but rather working towards the same end, introducing the kingdom of God. In this view, John is the forerunner of Jesus, the one sent ahead of the Messiah (cf. 1:23). Therefore it would be difficult to see John with his baptism as symbolizing "the ending of the old era" rather than beginning a new one, as Jesus' older colleague. Nevertheless Jesus' baptism, which is linked with the one in the Holy Spirit, expresses the idea of its superiority over John the Baptist's one. Cf. Dodd, *Fourth Gospel*, 310-11; and Fredriksen, *Jesus of Nazareth*, 197. In the narrative sequence there is a change of scene in 3:22.

The Metaphor of Divine Marriage in the Gospels 175

agree that John compares himself to the best man in relation to Jesus, the bridegroom. As such, he can by no means lay any claim to the bride so, in fact, John is saying he is the last who could compete with the bridegroom (cf. chapter 2 on best-man).[270] Thus the majority of exegetes have recognized in John 3:29 a short parable.[271] However, some have denied any allegory about Jesus and his bride in the verse.[272] This immediately helps them to solve the problem of identifying the bride in the sentence, ὁ ἔχων τὴν νύμφην νυμφίος ἐστίν (3:29a). But others have suggested that the metaphor of Jesus being the bridegroom of his bride, the messianic community, was intended on the lips of John the Baptist.[273] Then, some conclude, this may be the first historical instance of the use of the metaphor of Jesus being the bridegroom of his community, the bride.[274] Such a remark, however, raises the question of the relation of the fourth gospel to the Synoptics as well as of the gospel's use of early traditions. We shall mention the issues very briefly as the space-limits of this work do not allow us to discuss them more comprehensively.

In general, NT scholarship has long agreed that the fourth is the latest of the canonical gospels. Although it shows certain similarities to the Synoptics, it also shows differences from them.[275] There have been attempts to make John the evangelist dependent on at least one of them,[276] but with no great support among contemporary NT critics. It is rather proposed that John had access to a tradition similar and/or parallel to that behind the Synoptics.[277] Thus the tendency has been to view the fourth gospel as a development of tradition-material similar to that used by the Synoptists.[278] It is believed that the gospel at many points shows

---

270. Cf. van Selms, "Best Man," 74; also Carson, *John*, 212.

271. E.g., Barrett, *John*, 185; Schnackenburg, *John*, I: 416, who strongly rejects any claim that it could be similar to the ἱερὸς γάμος of "pagan Hellenism." See ibid., I: 417.

272. So, e.g., Beasley-Murray, *John*, 53; Schnackenburg, *John*, 416.

273. So Barrett, *John*, 184, Carson, *John*, 211, Carmichael, "Marriage and the Samaritan Woman," 333.

274. So Batey, *Nuptial Imagery*, 48 n.2, 50, arguing that it is very likely that John 3:22–30 preserves a pre-canonical tradition.

275. See Fredriksen, *Jesus of Nazareth*, 23–33, for a fairly detailed list of problems concerning the inter-gospels relationship. Cf. Lindars, *John*, 9; Smalley, *John*, 13–40.

276. Barrett, *John*, 108, claims that John certainly knew Mark. Also Robinson, *Redating*, 254.

277. Lindars, *John*, 13–14, and Smalley, *John*, 38, 40.

278. See Dunn, "John and the Synoptics," 304–5. See also Lindars, *John*, 28.

the marks of later theological reflection, some of which emerged from issues significant for the contemporary church. Therefore the tradition has been shaped to fit that particular *Sitz im Leben*. Some have even proposed that the gospel was composed in three different stages by different authors and that this helps in classifying different parts with their theological ideas.[279] However, this remains largely a matter of speculation.

Parallel to the discussion on John's relation to the Synoptics, there have been a growing number of arguments for John's dependence on Jewish rather than on Hellenistic thought.[280] This shift in emphasis was partly due to comparative study of the gospel and the documents discovered at Qumran.[281] Thus in recent years practically nobody denies John's dependence on the OT, if not directly, then through the sources accessible to him.

As a result of the two debates mentioned above, the fourth gospel has been recognized as another, supplementary, source of reconstructing the history of the gospel as well as of Jesus' life.[282] But, more recently, there has been a tendency to disregard earlier attempts to reconstruct the historical events in the gospel.[283] Consequently literary critics focus instead on the stylistic unity of the gospel interpreting it on its own terms. However, even among them there has been an honest recognition of the limitations of their methodology, apart from form criticism, and therefore also of the history of traditions.[284] Hence, one cannot easily dismiss questions of the historical in studying the gospels.

The problem for our study lies in the fact that, whereas the parables in the Synoptics have gained a general consensus of scholars concerning their resemblance to Jesus' original utterances, John's material raises more doubts about the date and origin of its particular traditions. So, although Batey claims that we probably have the earliest instance of the use of nuptial imagery in the NT at John 3:29, one still wonders if this is not a later reflection on the Baptist's testimony in the face of the later situation of the church and its already developed understanding of the Jesus event (vv. 31–36 suggest this conclusion). One could conclude that

279. Smalley, *John*, 119–20.
280. Davies, "Jewish Background," 43–64. Dunn, "John and the Synoptics," 304.
281. Fredriksen, *Jesus of Nazareth*, 5.
282. Cf. Moody Smith, *Gospel of John*, 20.
283. Cf., e.g., Hengel, "Wine Miracle at Cana," 90–93.
284. See esp. Stibbe, *John*, 11.

the statement, "The one who has the bride is the bridegroom," presupposes previous knowledge of the identities of the two.[285] Whatever later additions and interpretations of history there may be in the Synoptics, their parables present to us Jesus only subtly suggesting that he as the Messiah fulfils also the promises of Yahweh concerning his new eschatological marriage. His disciples do not appear to fully grasp this at that time. It seems that the Synoptics carry the reader over to the past when not all was so clear. But John the Baptizer's testimony in John 3:29 seems bold, as though he and others exactly know the identity of the bride and from this knowledge he proceeds to identify the bridegroom.

The other problem emerges from the difficulty of establishing a chronology in the fourth gospel. Because the exact sequence of the events cannot be established in the evangelist's account, one has difficulty in fitting the testimony into the Synoptics' chronology. One cannot be sure if it came, for instance, before or after Jesus' response to the fasting controversy. One cannot then assume that the Baptist's words about Jesus being the bridegroom are indeed the earliest use of the nuptial imagery in regard to Jesus. Still another difficulty, maybe less important, comes from the fourth evangelist's reference to the bride as νύμφη. Whenever Paul or the Synoptics mention the bride in nuptial metaphor, they use the word παρθένος. But the word νύμφη and its cognates are used metaphorically in the NT only in John 3:29 and three times in the Apocalypse (21:2, 9; 22:17). One can but ask if this supports the late origin of John 3:29?

On the other hand, the case for the pre-canonical origin of the tradition behind the Baptist's testimony can also be supported by powerful arguments. The common reason for this view is that the Baptizer's humility in John's gospel may indicate the most primitive tradition. Once the riddle of his identity was resolved in later Christian thought, John the Baptist started to be highly estimated: he was Elijah (Matt 11:14; 17:10–13; Luke 1:17).[286] Thus the fourth gospel reports an early stage when the Baptist denied that he was an Elijah. However, one could still remark that since the Baptist had to reject being compared with Elijah, there was a tendency among people to recognize in him the promised prophet (1:21, 25). So the argument can be pushed in a different direction. Since

---

285. Or the metaphor of Jesus being the bridegroom of his bride in general. Barrett, *John*, 186, remarks that John 3:29 may well be dependent on the synoptic tradition as found in Mark 2:19–20 and parallels.

286. Smalley, *John*, 26.

people did recognize in the Baptist somebody of Elijah's stamp, while he is presented as somebody who avoids this sort of conclusion, one could ask whether this does not point to a late reworking of the tradition. An editor at any stage of the gospel's redaction may simply have changed the emphasis in order to set the identity of Jesus against that of the Baptist, possibly in the face of difficulties that arose concerning the exact relationship between the two, later in the first century.[287]

Another point worth considering here is that scholars support the claim that John the Baptist knew the Hebrew Scriptures.[288] Therefore he had at hand the material to develop the OT marriage metaphor alongside the messianic expectations of second temple Judaism. It could be argued that the Baptizer did recognize Jesus' identity as Messiah and therefore applied to him OT passages among which there were also those referring to the eschatological marriage. Even the use of the word νύμφη instead of παρθένος does not create particular problems, since the former also occurs in the Septuagint in connection with divine marriage (cf. Isa 61:10; 62:5; Jer 2:32). In fact, Isa 62:5LXX links the two terms in referring to the bride Israel. Thus, it is possible that the two words could have been used interchangeably to refer to Israel as Yahweh's bride. And as such they could have been available to John the Baptist.[289] While this argument cannot be taken on its own, with no regard to what was said above, going back to the OT background could solve the problem of the bride's identity in John 3:29. However, this does not help us in determining whether the Baptist's identification of Jesus as the bridegroom comes from pre-Easter sources. Therefore one cannot be really sure if this use of the nuptial imagery for Jesus as the bridegroom is the earliest one. We cannot also simultaneously state that the testimony of John the Baptist has any influence on our understanding of the marriage metaphor in the

---

287. Cf. the remark of Dunn, "John and the Synoptics," 305, who believes that, "for some reason John has developed the Baptist tradition to reduce the Baptist's role to that of witness to Christ, while enlarging that role itself." See also Beasley-Murray, *John*, lxxxix, who suggests that such an emphasis might have emerged primarily out of the conflict between disciples of John the Baptist and Christians (cf. Acts 19:1–7) and later perhaps out of Jewish polemic against Christians.

288. E.g., Barrett, *John*, 185–86. However, more evident is the use of the LXX in the fourth gospel in its completed form. Ibid., 22.

289. We have already noticed that deutero-Isaiah could have been a source of early testimonies for NT writers. But this does not imply that they were as early as to be available to John the Baptist. However, if John knew the Hebrew Scriptures, second-Isaiah's imagery could have been available to him.

Synoptics. We cannot say that it helps in any other way towards explaining the transition in the use of the metaphor within the NT either. All it could do in this respect is support the conclusions of our study of the parables earlier in this chapter.

Attempts have also been made to determine the bride's identity from the context of the Baptist's testimony itself. Some commentators have tried to find hidden allusions to the bride either in the previous account of the so-called Cana miracle (2:1–11)[290] or in the following story of Jesus meeting a Samaritan woman at Jacob's well (4:4–26).[291] But such approaches assume the later compilation of different traditions by the final editor of the gospel and his conscious imposing of a deeper (here in the sense of allegorical) theological meaning on the gospel's accounts.[292] Implicit links between the accounts would also have to be assumed as having some allegorical meaning. This, however, shifts John the Baptist's testimony from being a possible early piece of tradition to being a fairly late redactional reworking of earlier traditions. Obviously, this explanation of the bride's identity does not prove helpful in establishing the basis of the transition in the marriage metaphor from its OT form to its NT counterpart.

The last thing which needs a brief mention here is the nature of the joy expressed by the best man in John 3:29. The Baptist rejoices at hearing the bridegroom's voice. Those who hesitate to allow the passage an allegorical meaning usually explain the joy as that which the best man

---

290. In the past Chavasse (*Bride of Christ*, 59) proposed that Mary be looked at in a corporate sense as representing Womankind, "the type of the Bride." More recently, Hengel, "Wine Miracle at Cana," 102, has pointed to the possibility of viewing Jesus' mother as a figure embodying Israel. Cf. Stibbe, *John*, 46, 60–61, who does not accept the claim of Mary being the symbol of Jesus' bride but rather argues that the wedding feast at Cana is a symbol in itself: the symbol of eschatological wedding linked with the messianic banquet (cf. Isa 25:6).

291. On the literary level the story resembles OT examples of courtship at a well. Therefore the Samaritan woman becomes the figure symbolizing Jesus' bride. See Carmichael, "Marriage and the Samaritan Woman," 336. Here, the author links the story with an OT background: by cleansing the temple (John 2:12ff.; cf. 2 Chr 29:3, 17; 30) Jesus announces the Passover during which there will be reunification of all Israel, including the Samaritans (2 Chr 30:1–9). Thus the bride of Yahweh is the whole Israel. Cf. Stibbe, *John*, 68, who points out that the marital imagery occurs especially in John 4:16–18. The Samaritan woman is a symbol of the eschatological bride for Stibbe, because she is not Jewish. Eslinger, "Wooing of the Woman," 165–82, emphasizes that the whole episode is full of sexual language.

292. Cf. Hengel, "Wine Miracle at Cana," 96.

expresses after hearing the triumphant shout of the bridegroom from the nuptial chamber after being united sexually to the bride.[293] This, then, is joy at the consummation of the marriage by *copula carnalis*. But such an approach does not necessarily explain the parable in the best way. Instead, others have proposed that the joy alludes to Isa 66:10 and the hope of restored Zion/Jerusalem again bearing children.[294] So the Baptist's joy is at the prospect of birth resulting from the new marriage union. It is complete, as though the Baptist's role as the best man was fulfilled (John 3:29c). We presume therefore that the remnant that inhabits the transformed Zion is in view.[295] Although a sexual act between Jesus and his bride *per se* is not implied, the metaphor allows one to anticipate some offspring coming from the union. The relation of John 3:29 to Isa 66:10 remains, of course, a matter that needs further evaluation. Nevertheless, this link can provide a background for understanding the words of John the Baptist. Even it is not accepted, John 3:29 itself has some notes of fulfillment,[296] since the best man knows that the bridegroom has come and therefore his role is fulfilled. Thus, in more general terms, the Baptist's joy can be simply at the fulfillment of the OT promises concerning the eschatological restoration of Israel, as also expressed in the divine marriage metaphor. In this sense, the joy is similar to that implied in Mark 2:19–20//Matt 9:15//Luke 5:34–35. In Jesus, Yahweh's promises come to fulfillment and in him the eschaton is introduced. The

---

293. So, e.g., Beasley-Murray, *John*, 53. But, as Schnackenburg, *John*, 417, observes, this can be only understood within the parable because the Baptist could not have heard the bridegroom at that time, so ἀκούειν is with genitive.

294. So Carmichael, "Marriage and the Samaritan Woman," 333–34.

295. And thus according to Carmichael, ibid., 342, the united Israel is in view. But this view, of course, presumes the allegorical interpretation of John 4:4–26. See also Webb, "Zion in Transformation," 81. It is worth observing that in Isa 66 the birth spoken of is a supernatural one, because the woman Zion gives birth to her children even before the pains of labor come upon her. Such birth would have to be the total reversal of the curse from Gen 3:16. Therefore one expects that such painless delivery is possible only through God's act, an intervention from above. Cannot this find its fulfillment in Jesus who was appointed from above to fulfill the promises and in this sense be referring to God's intervention from above? Cf. John 3:27.

296. Hengel, "Wine Miracle at Cana," 101–2, shows that Jesus the bridegroom brings in the reversal of God's words to the prophet Jeremiah found in Jer 16:8–9. They are a part of Yahweh's judgment upon his people: the voice of bridegroom and the bride will cease from among his people. But with Jesus sorrow comes to an end and joy is brought in. Although John 3:29 might point to the end of the sorrow of the exile, it is difficult to see its direct dependence on Jer 16:8–9.

covenant of Sinai is being renewed. This suggests realized eschatology which Jesus brings to fulfillment as the agent of Yahweh, the Messiah.[297]

To sum up, we can conclude that although probably not dependent on the historical account of the Synoptics, John 3:22–30 reveals similar ideas to those found in them. It speaks also of Jesus as the bridegroom of his bride, at the same time redefining her identity (since the reunited Israel may be in view). It also gives hints of realized eschatology, as fulfilled by Jesus. Finally, it may also suggest that deutero-Isaiah was a source of early testimonies for NT authors. On the other hand, the proposal that John the Baptist's last testimony about Jesus in John 3:27–30 is the earliest historical use of the nuptial imagery in connection with Jesus, cannot be sustained in the face of the difficulties pointed out above. If the parables of Jesus are assumed to reflect Jesus' original words, John's gospel as such seems a later theological reflection on the traditions about Jesus. Nevertheless, whichever opinion on the dating of John the Baptist's testimony gains more favor among NT scholars, John 3:29 does not add to or change the primary conclusions derived from the use of the marriage metaphor in the canonical gospels. It is more probable that it was Jesus himself who first pointed out that he is the bridegroom.

THE SHIFT IN THE DIVINE MARRIAGE METAPHOR

Before closing this chapter, we would like to discuss the problem raised already at the end of chapter 3, i.e., of the transition in the metaphor from Yahweh being the husband of Israel in the OT to Jesus being the bridegroom of his bride in the NT. Our study of Jewish literature from the intertestamental period did not help us in tracing such a development in the metaphor of divine marriage (see chapter 4 above). We have seen that the Messiah was never depicted as the bridegroom of a people prior to the NT. Therefore this issue needs further discussion now, in the light of our study of the gospels.

It has been a few decades since Batey[298] advanced his view on the shift in the metaphor. He believed that under the impact of apocalyptic thought in first century Judaism the prophetic marriage symbolism be-

---

297. Cf. Stibbe, *John*, e.g., 46, 61, who sees the gospel of John as emphasizing realized eschatology.

298. *Nuptial Imagery*, 10.

came somewhat unpopular. Jews started to reject the idea that they had been married to Yahweh at Sinai. Batey explains,

> Disillusionment and pessimism regarding earthly existence prompted the apocalyptists to look longingly into the future for some decisive divine deliverance. This anticipation of a future age of messianic bliss made it difficult to take seriously the idea that Israel was married to "the Holy One, Blessed be He" in her immediate historical condition. The prophetic metaphor was consequently modified with the Bride figure rather than the wife figure becoming increasingly emphasized. Israel was chosen, to be sure, but the full inheritance was not yet hers. Israel must wait until the messianic days when that which she possessed through promise would become hers in reality at the messianic marriage. It is this development of the nuptial imagery which exemplifies the strongest affinity to the New Testament figure of the church as the Bride of Christ...[299]

Thus, it seems, Batey distinguishes between the apocalyptic and the prophetic in first century Judaism. Only later, after the failure of the Bar Cochba revolt c. 132 CE, did apocalyptic eschatology fade and the prophetic perspective on divine marriage become favored again.[300] As for the first-century church, it inherited the modified image of the bride of Yahweh, rather than of the wife, from contemporary Jewish apocalyptic.[301] Thus it also adopted the view that the marriage was to occur in the future at the "parousia" of Christ.[302] The time between Jesus' first and second coming is consequently the period of betrothal.[303]

We want now to make a judgment on Batey's arguments, employing all the observations made in this work so far. First, we need to note that Batey's view is a hypothesis resulting probably from his overall theology. Thus none of his claims concerning the transition of the metaphor finds support in the literature that could have had a direct influence on the NT (cf. chapter 4). Secondly, in the light of recent developments in the study of Jewish apocalyptic, it is difficult to agree with Batey on the distinc-

---

299. Ibid.

300. See ibid., 10–11.

301. Cf. ibid., 15.

302. Ibid., 14. Here Batey apparently views the parousia as an event in the remote future, at the *Endzeit*.

303. Thus Batey's opinion is similar to that found in an earlier work by Muirhead, "Bride of Christ," 181.

tion between apocalyptic and prophetic in first-century Judaism. It has been shown that Jewish apocalyptic is in line with OT prophecy, that the former depends to a great extent on the latter, that both use similar imagery, that both deal with expectations for the future, so that they are not separated, but co-exist in second temple Judaism.[304] The apocalyptic is distinguished from the prophetic only to the extent that it envisions and describes the "state of affairs" otherwise anticipated in prophecy.[305] Thirdly, since we have noticed that the marriage metaphor in the OT expresses the covenant from Sinai and that it provides a way in which to express the covenant, it is again not easy to agree with Batey. Does he want to undermine the validity of the covenant of Sinai by saying that the Jews in the first century did not believe that their marriage to their God had yet taken place? If anything can be said with any degree of certainty about second temple Judaism, it is that it held firm to the worldview which can be called "creational and covenantal monotheism."[306] In other words, this belief was what marked Israel out from all other nations. It included a strong conviction concerning the God who created the whole cosmos, who was always present, always acting in it, and who had chosen Israel out of all the nations of the earth in order to be for her her God that she might be for him his people.[307] He entered into a unique covenant relationship with her. He was always faithful to his covenant, but she broke their marital union. As a result, the nation was divorced, i.e., sent into exile, and, as we have observed in chapter 1 of this volume, they believed that they remained still in exile during the second temple Judaism period. But they had been given promises of future restoration, of an Exodus-like event in the future when Yahweh would marry them anew, forgive their sins, treat them as though they were a virgin who had not had any extra- or pre- marital affairs. This all pointed to the renewal of Yahweh's covenant with them (see chapter 3 above). They believed in the age to come, as also expressed in Jewish apocalyptic, during which the promises that were grounded in OT prophecy and constituted part of the Jewish beliefs in the first century CE would be fulfilled. Therefore,

---

304. Cf. Wright, *NTPG*, esp. 286–89. It is worth recalling that on our view Jesus' parables belong within apocalyptic.

305. Cf. ibid., 280–99. Thus apocalyptic with its special form of communication deals to a great extent with historical events.

306. Ibid., 283.

307. Cf. ibid., 298, 268–72.

fourthly, we cannot agree with Batey's suggestion that the bride figure in late apocalyptic suddenly made an impact on and shaped that Jewish worldview to the extent that they believed that their past was only a betrothal, not a marriage proper. As we have noticed on a number of occasions in this chapter, the bride imagery was already at hand in OT prophets. But, turning back to chapter 3, this did not mean that the marriage/covenant was non-existent or at least not yet enforced. It testified to the fact that Israel sinned so greatly that Yahweh divorced her. The only hope was their renewal at God's intervention (cf. Hos 2:19–20) as they are reloved and remarried (Isa 62:3–5), which is sometimes expressed in the language of betrothal, i.e., Yahweh renewing a permanent commitment to his forgiven bride which will bring her outstanding advantages. This kind of expectation was associated with the hope of a second exodus. So, fifthly, neither can we agree with Batey's view of Jewish first-century (apocalyptic, according to him) eschatology. The Jews at that time would have expected an eschatological marriage after a period of betrothal and not the other way round. This appears evident from the OT, the only reliable evidence we possess on the subject. Jewish hopes had been awaiting their fulfillment. Furthermore, since later apocalyptic writings[308] are the continuation of, rather than being a diversion from basic OT prophetic thought, this only reinforces our proposal. Sixthly, Batey has discussed Jewish expectations of the coming Messiah. Here our disagreement with him, as we have indicated in discussing this figure in this chapter,[309] is that as Yahweh's agent the Messiah was expected to bring OT promise to fulfillment and not to take Yahweh's place in the on-going betrothal simply to point to some still future fulfillment expressed by the consummation of this betrothal in marriage. On Batey's view, all that Jesus did during his first coming was to introduce the betrothal (to the church?),[310] which, by the way, was already in force (in Israel) before his coming. Also, we cannot follow Batey's conclusion concerning eschatology because of

---

308. It must still be said that it is apparently impossible to determine which apocalyptic writings and how many of them were available to the first century Jew. Cf. ibid., 289.

309. Unfortunately, space-limits of this volume do not allow us to discuss the messianic hopes of second temple Judaism. But the reader may refer to a fairly detailed analysis of the subject in Wright's *NTPG*, 307–20.

310. Cf. Batey, *Nuptial Imagery*, e.g., 27–28, where he interprets Jesus' death as a betrothal gift. "The acceptance of this gift by the church is the response in faith which completes her betrothal (Eph. 2:8,9)." Ibid., 28.

our different views of Jesus' parousia, as indicated earlier in the chapter. And, finally, we suggest that Batey's proposal concerning the shift first from "prophetic eschatology" to an "apocalyptic one" in first century CE and then in the reverse order, from the latter to the former in the second century, seems somewhat unnatural. It looks as if this shift was posited to fit Batey's view of the Jesus-event as well as of his eschatology. In summary, while apparently fitting-the-Jewish-worldview his proposal evidently dissociates itself from the content of this worldview. We rather suggest that the transition in the marriage metaphor occurred according to the basic beliefs of second temple Judaism. It was Jesus himself, the self-attested agent of Yahweh, who associated the OT divine marriage metaphor with the messianic office he claimed to have taken upon himself, as we learn from the parables studied in this chapter.[311] It is he who for Yahweh fulfils the OT promise of betrothal, the covenant-renewal.

CONCLUSIONS

Studying Jesus' response to the controversy over fasting as well as those of his parables which employ nuptial imagery, we have observed that marriage became for the Jews a metaphor of the time of salvation (cf. Isa 62:5; 61:10). Together with the promise of an eschatological banquet, it symbolized future divine intervention which would introduce a new covenant when Yahweh would finally remarry (or permanently betroth) his people. In second temple Judaism, the anticipated end of exile, defeat of Israel's enemies, and fulfillment of God's promises could have been linked to the metaphor of divine marriage, which probably served as another element undergirding its beliefs.

On the other hand, Judaism of that time, or at least a part of it, had strong messianic expectations. It awaited the coming of a special figure who would act as Yahweh's appointed agent, bringing all his promises to fulfillment. Thus Jesus testifying about his own identity referred to the basic structure of Jewish first-century beliefs. He claimed, although at times only implicitly, that he was the expected anointed Messiah acting on Yahweh's behalf. At the same time he redefined the Jewish symbolic universe around his own person. Thus he gave new meaning to the OT

---

311. To the extent that it was Jesus himself who brought this shift about, we agree with Muirhead, "Bride of Christ," 181–83 and Chavasse, *Bride of Christ*, 52–53. Cf. also Schillebeeckx, *Marriage*, 107.

prophetic material, explaining it alongside messianic hopes as fulfilled in him.

Jesus used the marriage metaphor to claim implicitly that through him the long-awaited eschatological time of salvation had come. As God's agent he fulfilled for Yahweh the role of the bridegroom of Isaiah's prophecy. He brought in the covenant renewal together with its blessings. Israel is married to him, although during the wedding there is a time when the bridegroom is taken violently away from his bride, probably by his death. Therefore the companions of the bridegroom, the disciples of Jesus, have to bear witness to the fulfillment of the long-awaited marriage, the covenant renewal.

We have already mentioned that Jesus reshaped the basic worldview of second temple Judaism, although still doing so within its general framework. Consequently, he also redefined the figure of virgin Israel, though not in a completely arbitrary way. He stated that those who remain faithful to Yahweh and heed the words of his prophet and Messiah are included in the eschatological feast of salvation. Regardless of their national origin they constitute the wise bride of Israel. So, eschatological salvation is open to Jews and Gentiles alike. On the other hand, those who reject God's word through the prophet are left outside the joyous festivities. Some leaders of Israel, although claiming their right to participate in the eschatological wedding, bring God's judgment upon themselves because of their unbelief. They do not bear good fruit that pleases God; they reject his way. Thus historical Israel experiences her restoration in the Jesus-event, but it appears that not all who belong to the nation really constitute the saved, remarried virgin Zion. Only the remnant is the bride. As the Messiah enjoys the wedding with his prudent bride, the unfaithful are judged in their city which together with its corrupted political system constitute the main obstacle in the way of the Kingdom of God. But in judgment the king, Messiah, bridegroom is vindicated and his kingdom/salvation firmly established.

Therefore, in the light of the evidence available to us, we conclude that it was Jesus himself who first used and applied the metaphor of divine marriage in the NT, but that he did so in terms of his contemporary Jewish beliefs based on the OT. The metaphor helped him to claim that it is he, the personified act of Yahweh, who brings restoration and covenant renewal. The bride is forgiven so that she can return from exile to union with her husband. Thus the "theology of fulfillment" has been initiated by Jesus. We have remarked in chapter 1 that it was Jesus himself who first directed his followers to certain parts of the OT which later became testimonies.[312] Therefore one would expect some of the developments in this theology of fulfillment to come from Jesus' followers. This is the point that leads us into the next chapter. There, we want to focus on a few examples of the use of divine marriage imagery in the Pauline letters in order to trace the growing interest in the meaning of Jesus' mission and destiny. This will also prepare us for the main focus of this book, which is the divine marriage in John's Revelation.

---

312. Following Dodd, *According to the Scriptures*, 110.

6

The Metaphor of Divine Marriage in the Epistles of Paul

INTRODUCTION

IN THE PREVIOUS CHAPTER we explored the material of the four canonical gospels tracing developments in the titular metaphor of the present work. We have suggested that it was Jesus, Yahweh's anointed agent, who transformed the OT traditions of *hieros gamos* to elucidate his messianic eschatological mission. Jesus' refocusing of the traditions onto himself provided his followers, including NT authors, with a hermeneutical pattern for approaching the Hebrew Scriptures. He deliberately utilized the theology of eschatological fulfillment in the OT to interpret his ministry. As a result, his disciples looked at the sacred writings of Israel from the perspective given by their master and this no doubt included the divine marriage metaphor. Thus one could anticipate the same kind of approach in the Pauline letters.

We have acknowledged in chapter 1 the tendency among biblical scholars to juxtapose the themes of John's Revelation with those of the Synoptics and Paul. We have already explored the gospel material. The only remaining task, before turning to the main focus of this volume, is to examine the Pauline use of the divine marriage traditions. We want to examine a number of his texts in order eventually to assess the extent to which Paul's use of the metaphor informs its use in the book of Revelation. This is the task of the present chapter.

THE SCOPE OF PRESENT CHAPTER

Our special focus on the letters of Paul in this chapter should by no means imply that there are no other biblical authors, outside the gospels

The Metaphor of Divine Marriage in the Epistles of Paul

and Apocalypse, who employ the marriage metaphor. Quite the contrary, passages such as 1 Pet 2:4–10 (implicitly) and 2 John 1, 13 (more explicitly) are often regarded as instances of the metaphor's use.[1] Again, Jam 4:4 requires a further examination in relation to the marriage metaphor.[2] However, we shall ignore these texts, as the space limits of this book do not allow us to explore them further.

An apprentice in theology would quickly realize that studying the Pauline literature, with the multitude of books and articles written on it, is a life-long commission.[3] We doubt that even at the end of this journey one will be able to claim that he has exhausted the vast amount of scholarly data concerning the apostle's teaching. Thus, on the one hand, the apprentice could be discouraged and even give up, facing the somewhat impossible task of researching all that has been written on Paul. On the other hand, however, he could well conclude that, although limited in many ways, his involvement in the ongoing debate can perhaps identify some problems and offer possible solutions to them. Thus our examination of a number of Pauline texts and their relation to his overall opinion on a particular subject can by no means be exhaustive (especially as one of Paul's themes often knits together with a number of others). This is not the goal of this chapter. Instead, we aim to discuss the major points made in a variety of works by those who have studied the Pauline literature.

In choosing the passages for our examination, we have employed two major criteria: 1) whether the text explicitly refers to the divine marriage metaphor (as in the case of 2 Cor 11:2–3 and Eph[4] 5:25b–27); or 2) whether the text has been a frequent subject of scholarly debate concerning the metaphor even if no consensus has been reached (as in

---

1. Cf. Chavasse, *Bride of Christ*, 86–88.

2. Ortlund, *Whoredom*, 140–43. He shows that James 4:4 is a warning to Christians who associate themselves with "the world." This association is compared to adultery. Here each individual who wishes to persist in such an alliance can be charged with adultery (μοιχαλίδες is noun feminine vocative plural) and makes himself God's enemy. It seems that James' words recall Israel's alliances with foreign nations, which were condemned time and again in OT prophetic utterances. The LXX at Ezekiel 16 and 23 uses the cognates of μοιχαλίς referring to the religious/political adultery of Israel and Judah. Yet, James' emphasis seems to be more on the individualistic than corporate (national) level.

3. This probably applies as much to any other area in theology as to Paul, although in the case of Paul this is particularly evident.

4. There is, of course, no agreement among scholars regarding the authorship of Ephesians. We will return to the issue while dealing with the passage.

the case of Rom 7:1–4; 9:25–26; and Gal 4:26–27). In this way we have selected five passages that need to be re-examined in their contexts.

The sequence of our study will not follow the succession of letters in the Greek New Testament. Instead, we will accept majority scholarly opinion on the chronology of Paul's writings.[5] Thus we will discuss in turn: 2 Cor 11:1–6; Gal 4:21—5:1; Rom 7:1–6 and 9:25–29; leaving the Pastoral Eph 5:21–33 (of debatable authorship) until last. Where possible, questions of the interrelatedness of these texts will be considered.

2 CORINTHIANS 11:1–6

Present State of Study of 2 Corinthians 11:1–6

2 Cor 11:2–3 refers explicitly to the marriage metaphor. Paul says in verse 2 that he has given the Corinthian church in marriage (ἡρμοσάμεν) to Christ. And his intention has been to present her to him as a pure bride (παρθένος ἁγνός). However, the Corinthians are now in danger of being led astray from their husband (v. 3).

Thus scholars have rightly concluded that 2 Cor 11:2–3 may be the earliest documentary use of the marriage metaphor in the NT.[6] They have, however, struggled with issues such as the dis-/unity of the letter and the vital question of the identity of Paul's opponents, especially in chapters 10–13. However, we will not discuss these debates in detail, as the space-limits of this work do not allow us to do so. We will, instead, signal the issues in dealing with the text itself.

---

5. See, e.g., Kümmel, *New Testament*, 247–387. It does not matter very much whether the chronology accepted by us is entirely correct. This is not essential to our studies. We only utilize such a succession as useful scaffolding for our work, since it can sometimes help in tracing the development of an author's thinking.

6. Cf. Batey, *Nuptial Imagery*, 12. Although Jesus was most probably the first to use the imagery concerning himself. See chapter 5 above. There have also been attempts to show that Paul used the divine marriage imagery in 1 Cor 6:12–20. The most prominent case has been made by Rosner, *1 Corinthians 5–7*, entire chapter 5. The argument supporting his thesis rests mainly on Paul's use of the κολλάω terminology as well as him quoting from Gen 2:24LXX in 1 Cor 6:16–17 (cf. pp. 130–34) He explains that the terminology used is associated with marriage. Even if one accepted 1 Cor 6:17 to be a variation on the marriage theme, it would still be difficult to see how this would inform the development of divine marriage metaphor of the OT. The text does not seem to go beyond the point that the believer has a unique ("spiritual") relationship with his Lord who does not tolerate sexual immorality.

The Structure of 2 Corinthians 11:1–6

The train of thought in this passage is straightforward. Paul is here comparing himself to his opponents and the whole section is his justification for this.[7] Yet at the same time the unit serves as an introduction to the whole argument that follows in vv. 7–15.[8] In verse 1, he pleads with the Corinthians that they should bear with his foolishness as he is going to speak to them. This, in fact, reveals an irony, which serves as a rhetorical device to gain the Corinthians' attention (cf. 11:16).[9] Verses 2–3 explain the reason for Paul's entering into the argument against his opponents. He does that because of his God-like jealousy,[10] because it was he who brought them to Christ. The γὰρ of v. 4 seems to refer back to v. 1 rather than directly to v. 3.[11] The repetition of ἀνέχεσθε points in that direction. Therefore the issue in v. 4 is rather hypothetical.[12] In general, Paul wants to say that the Corinthians should pay some attention to him since he brought them to Christ, and even more so because they are eager to listen to anybody else who comes to them with a different gospel, although such people have not shared in bringing them to Christ. How much more attention they should pay to their founder. They should listen to him because he is by no means inferior to those people. So verses 5–6 stand close to ἀνέχεσθε in v. 1.[13] Thus our passage may be divided into three sub-units. Verse 1 expresses the main concern. Verses 2–3 explain it, with the γὰρ of v. 2 referring back to v. 1 and δέ of v. 3 linking it to v. 2. The γὰρ in v. 4 refers back to v. 1; likewise the γὰρ of v. 5. Thus both relate directly to the issue of v. 1 and develop it. The δέ of v. 6 links the verse to v. 5.

Marriage Metaphor in 2 Corinthians 11:1–6

The structure of the passage shows that Paul's use of the marriage theme is secondary. He is concerned above all with his position *vis à vis* rival

---

7. Plummer, *Second Corinthians*, 291.
8. Thrall, *II Corinthians*, II: 657.
9. Cf. Witherington, *1 and 2 Corinthians*, 444–45.
10. Martin, *2 Corinthians*, 332. The jealousy reflects the character of Yahweh as husband of Israel.
11. Cf. Thrall, *II Corinthians*, II: 664.
12. Cf. Munck, *Salvation of Mankind*, 178.
13. Ibid., 177; Thrall, *II Corinthians*, II: 664.

missionaries. As we have noticed, their identification has caused scholars much trouble. Whole volumes have been written on this particular subject.[14] Yet no final agreement has been reached on the issue. Nevertheless, it does not seem necessary for us to know their exact identity to deal with the marriage metaphor in the passage. However, a few points may be noted.

It is possible that the missionaries were Judaizers connected to the Jerusalem church.[15] They may have summoned the Corinthians to Torah observance (cf. 11:15).[16] But another possibility emerges that they could have been Hellenistic Jewish missionaries of the diaspora, as the conflict was not one concerning Jewish nomism.[17] The issue was not so much "another Jesus" deprived of earthly humility,[18] as the character of apostolic ministry.[19] The whole issue is, of course, connected to the debate about the letter's unity.[20] Being unable to decide between these two general options in this place, we will focus mainly on the first three verses of 2 Corinthians 11, while still bearing in mind that the issue at stake is an alternative to Paul's conduct. As he himself puts it, the issue is the Corinthians' sincerity and devotion to Christ (11:3). The problem appears to be that they are only concerned about the manner and credentials of preachers, not paying enough attention to the content of the message, which they hear.[21]

Scholars focusing on the marriage metaphor in 2 Cor have usually tried to establish its referents in reality. First, they have been interested in showing how it relates to the overall view of salvation history.

---

14. E.g., Georgi, *Opponents of Paul*.

15. Barrett, "Paul's Opponents," 233–54, and Barrett, *Essays on Paul*, 80, 102–3. Cf. Hays, *Echoes of Scripture*, 125–26.

16. Thrall, *II Corinthians*, II: 698.

17. Georgi, *Opponents of Paul*, 60, 248; Munck, *Salvation of Mankind*, 168.

18. See Murphy-O'Connor, "Another Jesus (2 Cor 11:4)," 238. Cf. Fee, "Another Gospel," 111–33. The situation in v. 4 is rather hypothetical and therefore does not reveal the actual state of affairs in Corinth. See Munck, *Salvation of Mankind*, 177–78.

19. Thielman, *Paul and the Law*, 85. Cf. Wright, *Climax of the Covenant*, 176.

20. See different approaches to the subject as proposed by Barrett, *Essays on Paul*, 2, Georgi, *Opponents of Paul*, 18, Munck, *Salvation of Mankind*, 169, and Kümmel, *New Testament*, 287–93. See also more general discussions on unity in Martin, *2 Corinthians*, xl–lii, and Thrall, *II Corinthians*, I: 3–49.

21. Barrett, "Paul's Opponents," 242.

The Metaphor of Divine Marriage in the Epistles of Paul 193

The question of Paul's role regarding marriage has followed. Thus we will now discuss the two points in turn.

The majority of NT scholars have concluded that since the meaning of the verb ἁρμόζω in the middle refers to betrothal or giving in marriage, then the marriage proper and its consummation will take place at some point in the future, the *Endzeit*, the parousia.[22] The present relation of the church to Christ is one of betrothal, which, however, remains more serious that its counterpart in contemporary Western cultures. Thus realization of the marriage is moved forward to another coming of Jesus at the end of the space-time universe. However, this conclusion can be supported neither from the passage itself, nor even from the rest of the letter. One does wonder if the influence of other passages from the NT (e.g., Rev 19:7) has been at work here. At the same time such scholars are unanimous in their conviction that Paul borrowed the metaphor from the OT. They have also noticed that Paul had in mind the prophets employing the divine marriage metaphor in v. 2 and Genesis 3 in v. 3.[23] Still another question demanding a response concerns Paul's relation to the OT. Was he simply borrowing pictures from the Hebrew Scriptures in order to depict his own missionary situation? Was he, at all, concerned with the continuation and fulfillment of those Scriptures in the messianic age? Before answering the questions raised in this section, we will briefly discuss Paul's role in the "betrothal." We believe that this together with the previous matter can contribute to our final proposal.

NT exegetes have attempted to identify Paul's role in the metaphor of 2 Cor 11:2–3. Their conclusions have normally been divided between adherents of the best-man view[24] and that of the bride's father.[25] We do not know much, in fact, about the institution of the best man in ancient Jewish culture. Nevertheless, we have acknowledged in chapter 2 that he was a close friend of the bridegroom who participated in negotiating the marriage settlement. He was prohibited from marrying the woman if the betrothal was broken. It seems that if 2 Cor 11:2 were taken on

---

22. So, e.g., Fee, "Another Gospel," 119, Hanson, *Pastoral Epistles*, 71, Martin, *2 Corinthians*, 333, Thrall, *II Corinthians*, II: 660, and Witherington, *1 and 2 Corinthians*, 445.

23. Barrett, "Paul's Opponents," 239; Thrall, *II Corinthians*, II: 661.

24. So Batey, *Nuptial Imagery*, 12, although he has referred to the man as a father's agent, i.e., the bridegroom's father's agent. Martin, *2 Corinthians*, 332, and Witherington, *1 and 2 Corinthians*, 445, explicitly.

25. Plummer, *Second Corinthians*, 294, Thrall, *II Corinthians*, II: 661.

its own one could conclude that Paul is playing the role of best man in this settlement. But Paul seems to be more concerned with his closeness to the bride than to the bridegroom. When we look at v. 3, it becomes evident that Paul is concerned with the chastity of the Corinthian bride. But the role of guardian of the virgin's purity belonged to the girl's father, according to the OT (Deut 22:13–21). Thrall explains concerning Paul,

> First, in 12.14, as also in 1 Cor 4.15, he regards himself as the parent of the Corinthian church. Secondly, in everyday life it would usually be the parents who arranged a betrothal. Thirdly . . . in Jewish society it would be the father who would be responsible for safeguarding his daughter's chastity.[26]

Thus, textual evidence seems to favor the bride's father theory. The picture would therefore be of a father who has given his daughter in marriage in the hope that she would remain a pure virgin. But is there any significance in the fact that Paul referred to OT sources? Or does he merely use OT material as a helpful source of illustrations?

In the light of what we have said so far in this volume (see chapters 1 and 5), we would incline to the view that Paul used OT imagery in order to present a theological truth, and not simply to help his rhetoric. He believed that the age of fulfillment had dawned with Jesus the Messiah. He would, therefore, most likely look for ways of showing this from the OT. There are some good reasons for this view as regards 2 Cor 11, and we seek to present them now.

Some scholars have concluded that there is no biblical warrant for calling a group of people collectively παρθένος.[27] We have, however, acknowledged that in the OT Israel was called παρθένος in the LXX on a number of occasions (e.g., Isa 37:22; Jer 18:13; 31:4=38:4LXX; 31:21=38:21LXX; Lam 2:13). The nation was known as virgin Israel (cf. chapter 5 on Matt 25:1–13). She would receive the fruits of God's attributes of righteousness, justice, loving-kindness, compassion and faithfulness, at the time of her restoration, at the covenant renewal (Hos 2:19–20). Moreover the restoration of virginity to God's people was an important eschatological expectation in the OT prophets. God's Israel

---

26. *II Corinthians*, II: 661. See also Roberts Gaventa, "Apostle and Church," 195.

27. Esp. Horsley, *Early Christianity*, 71, although, at the same time, it would be a mistake to look for a counterpart to παρθένος ἁγνή in Hellenistic ἱερα παρθένος. Martin, *2 Corinthians*, 333, has followed this view remarking that this is not an OT ecclesiological title.

was to be made pure. A once wayward nation would be eternally betrothed to her God as a pure virgin (Hos 2:19; Jer 31:4; Isa 62:3–5; cf. chapter 3 above). Furthermore, we have already examined Matt 25:1–13 where Jesus regarded the faithful remnant of Israel as a virgin who participates in the eschatological wedding banquet (cf. chapter 5 above). The virgin/remnant was to be joined by faithful pagans in the times of eschatological fulfillment. The mission of the post-Easter church could therefore be regarded as realization of this part of Jewish tradition. One could also assume that Paul had heard of Jesus' tradition concerning the divine marriage fulfilled in him. The oral *testimonia* could have been there to point Paul to particular places in Hosea, Isaiah, Jeremiah and perhaps Ezekiel. Thus it would be possible for Paul to use the word παρθένος to recall those traditions. Furthermore, because scholars have insisted that Paul used the OT as a source for his marriage metaphor, we suggest that he used it deliberately to make a theological point.[28] One could also follow Barrett's[29] observation that chapter 11 of 2 Corinthians speaks about the right understanding of the fulfillment of Judaism in Christianity. In fact, Paul seems to juxtapose Judaism and Christianity throughout the letter.[30] So on this approach, our suggestion seems to be in line with the overall purpose of 2 Cor 10–13. The picture may thus be as follows: Paul, as the church's founder and therefore father (1 Cor 4:15; 2 Cor 12:14; cf. Acts 18:1–11), has brought the Corinthian believers to a relationship with Jesus the Messiah, her husband, in order for her to be faithful to him (2 Cor 11:2).[31] The Corinthians became part of the eschatological παρθένος,[32] who by the union with Christ becomes pure and devoted to him. The two aorists of v. 2 could, in such a case,

---

28. Some scholars have suggested that 2 Corinthians is theology in the making. Cf. Hay, "Theology in 2 Corinthians," 136. This, however, does not diminish the point that Paul was dealing with missionary situations having a certain theological understanding of both the OT and his times (cf. p. 152).

29. *Essays on Paul*, 65.

30. Cf. Wright, *Climax of the Covenant*, 176–86.

31. Sampley, *Ephesians 5:21–33*, 83, has noted that the verb παρίστημι should be rendered almost as 'make,' or 'render.' Thus Paul betrothed the Corinthians to Christ "in order to make or render them a pure bride to their husband."

32. One should not deduce from this passage that the Corinthians are exclusively Christ's body. They are only partakers of a reality belonging to Christ's entire church expressed in the metaphor. Cf. Chavasse, *Bride of Christ*, 83, 88, and Caird and Hurst, *New Testament Theology*, 214. The use of the metaphor in the OT has already revealed something of the universal expressed in particular.

point to an ongoing marriage-like relationship between Christ and the Corinthians, which began at Paul's establishment of the church. While the Corinthians should live according to their status in Christ, there is a threat that they may abandon their devotion to the husband. However, in this context, the passage could hardly refer to a remote future experience of marriage. It is rather a theological reminder to the Corinthians about their relationship with Paul and Christ, as the former is their father and the latter their husband. This can, however, operate only on a limited metaphorical level, as in other places God is regarded as the father of believers (1 Cor 8:6; cf. Rom 8:15). Nevertheless, the metaphor well suits Paul's purpose in his argument.

If we follow this train of thought, we will soon realize that the logic of our metaphor follows in 2 Cor 11:3. This verse is widely recognized as alluding to the story of Eve's deception in Gen 3. In fact, no scholar known to us disputes that Paul could have freely juxtaposed two marital traditions: metaphorical with literal.[33] By doing this, he can achieve his goal: to regain his authority among those whom he dedicated to Christ. So, in v. 3 he uses a picture from another well-known marriage, which was exposed to disturbance by an intruder, the serpent. Thus he is able to illustrate the danger for the Corinthians' relationship, as expressed in the marriage metaphor. He draws a parallel between the two marriages. He indicates that some intruders can disturb their marital union with Christ in a similar way (cf. 11:13–14). Paul is again not interested in future events, but contemporary dangers. The comparison of v. 2 with v. 3 implies some sort of an ongoing marriage-like union, not a betrothal with a prospect for future marriage.

It has been especially by linking v. 3 with vv. 13–14 that NT interpreters have been made to look for traditions speaking about Satan deceiving Eve as the angel of light (ἄγγελος φωτός). They often point

---

33. Barrett, *Essays on Paul*, 67, has been cautious not to press the divine marriage metaphor too far as it is mixed with Gen 3. Thus he has suggested that Paul did not begin with the OT but the contemporary situation and then looked for a means of illustrating the problem. Although one cannot object that Paul started with his missionary situation, we want to suggest that there is another way of looking at the matter. Paul might have used the divine marriage as his main metaphor and then described the danger for the people with an illustration from another story. This solution would also solve the problem raised by Best, *One Body in Christ*, 171, viz., whether the church in general can be spoken of as a second Eve. On our reading, such a conclusion is not necessary. Paul uses Gen 3 as a mere illustration.

to the *Life of Adam and Eve* 9:1[34] and *Apocalypse of Moses* 17:1.[35] While the former refers to Satan transforming himself into the brightness of angels, the latter speaks simply of him appearing in the form of an angel. In both instances Satan tries to seduce Eve: either for the second time (after the expulsion from Eden) or during the original temptation at Eden. However, the question of dependency needs to be raised here. The surviving manuscripts of both books are very late and the composition of the texts took place possibly any time between 100–400 CE.[36] Thus it is unwise to claim Paul's dependence on those texts. We simply cannot be sure whether the texts reveal earlier Jewish traditions or if they are later (i.e., post-70 CE) reflections on the biblical material.[37] The best we can do is admit Paul's own invention in this context.[38] Furthermore, v. 3 does not need any other background than that of Gen 3, as the main issue is one of deceitfulness by an intruder. Other matters like the nature of Eve's seduction (e.g., physical), although maybe interesting in themselves, do not have to be raised in this place either.[39] As far as v. 3 is concerned, the deception of the Corinthians implies their cognizance.

Thus we may propose that Paul uses the OT divine marriage metaphor in 2 Cor 11:2, after it has been reshaped in the context of the Christ event, to make a theological point in his argument with the Corinthians against his opponents. V. 3 is an illustration, from a well-known marriage story, of the main marriage theme of v. 2.

GALATIANS 4:21—5:1

Introduction

Gal 4:21—5:1 is another passage, which has created some difficulties for NT scholars. The main reason for this is Paul's use of OT material in an allegedly arbitrary manner. Although he himself remarks that his words

---

34. Cf. the text in Johnson, "Life of Adam and Eve," 260.

35. Ibid., 277–78.

36. Ibid., 252. *Apocalypse of Moses* is preserved in Greek manuscripts from twelfth-seventeenth centuries and *Life of Adam and Eve* in Latin dated between ninth-fifteenth centuries. Cf. Neusner and Green, *Dictionary of Judaism*, 12.

37. On methodological difficulties regarding the use of Jewish writings see chapter 4 of this volume.

38. So Martin, *2 Corinthians*, 352. Cf. Thrall, *II Corinthians*, II: 662.

39. But see Thrall, *II Corinthians*, II: 662; and Hanson, *Pastoral Epistles*, 65–77.

need to be read allegorically (v. 24), exegetes are not unanimous as to what exactly he meant by this. However, because of his use of the quotation from Isa 54:1, some have suggested that the metaphor of divine marriage was in the background of his argument.[40] Therefore we will focus in turn on the meaning of allegory in Gal 4:24, the wider context of the passage, and the significance of the citation from Isa 54:1.

Paul's "Allegory" in the Passage

Paul's use of OT material has created some difficulties for many NT exegetes. However, in the case of Gal 4:22–30 the peculiar problem is his use of the OT story of Abraham and Sarah in support of his argument against the need for Torah observance by Gentile Christians (cf. Gal 3:13–14; 24–25). If the matter of dissent in Galatia was the circumcision of Gentiles (5:2–12) then Gen 21:1–10, on its historical reading, could have better supported the Judaizers' claims.[41] In the story of Abraham's family, both Ishmael and Isaac were circumcised (Gen 17:23, 25; 21:4). Furthermore, the Jews were descendants of Abraham (17:10–14).[42] How, then, can Paul use the story to make his point against the circumcision of the Gentile Christians, as a part of the new Israel?

The answer to that question lies in Paul's explanation, viz., that he treats Scripture in an allegorical way (Gal 4:24). Some exegetes have claimed that the apostle uses the word allegory to signify Philonic-like allegorical interpretation.[43] They have argued that Paul was not interested in historical interpretation of OT material, but simply in contemporizing it. In such a case, the apostle was not interested in the characters of the OT story itself, but only in new referents, to which the story points. However, this opinion has not satisfied the majority of NT scholars. They have observed that there is more to the language of the passage than mere allegory. It is, they say, tempered by typology.[44] Paul is interested,

---

40. E.g., Best, *One Body in Christ*, 171; Chavasse, *Bride of Christ*, 66 67.

41. Cf. Jobes, "Jerusalem, Our Mother," 300.

42. However, some believe that Galatians is not concerned with physical descent at all; it is rather interested in Abraham as the exclusive way of salvation for both Jews and Gentiles. Cf. Brinsmead, *Galatians*, 109.

43. Witherington, *Grace in Galatia*, 323, 326–29. Also Perriman, "Galatians 4:21—5:1," 34–39.

44. Martyn, *Galatians*, 436, Betz, *Galatians*, 239, Hanson, *Paul's Technique and Theology*, 94, Lincoln, *Paradise Now and Not Yet*, 14. See also Cosgrove, "No Children," 221 n.12. He claims that Paul's interpretation of the Abraham story in vv. 24–27 is typological, as a salvation-historical frame informs it.

The Metaphor of Divine Marriage in the Epistles of Paul 199

after all, in the original meaning of the story, although he reinterprets it from his own perspective. Bruce explains,

> [Paul] is not thinking of allegory in the Philonic sense ...; he has in mind that form of allegory which is commonly called typology: a narrative from OT history is interpreted in terms of the new covenant, or (to put it the other way round) an aspect of the new covenant is presented in terms of an OT narrative.[45]

Thus Paul's language in our passage resembles a technique well known to the OT prophets, which pictures subsequent stages in God's salvation history with already established patterns.[46] We have observed in chapter 1 that Paul is interested in the meaning of the Hebrew Scriptures, as they relate to the new situation inaugurated by Jesus the Messiah. The revelation in Jesus has brought to light previously latent meanings. Thus Paul, following the method of Jesus himself, is able to show how the story of Abraham and Sarah has now arrived at its climax.[47] He has entirely rethought Judaism. As a result, the OT could have been on his side.[48] By thinking in categories of promise and fulfillment, Paul engages various techniques to show historical continuity.[49] Only from the Jesus-event perspective is he able to show how the story in Gal 4:22–30 relates to the incorporation of the Gentiles into God's covenant, as Abraham's descendants. Therefore, we should also look at the story as explaining something of the fulfillment in Christ. Although Paul's hermeneutic is ecclesiocentric, as recent studies have shown,[50] it is nevertheless based on his Christology.[51] Thus the question of the legitimacy of Paul's use of the OT material in a different-from-original way should be looked at in the way just indicated. Paul claims that he applies allegory. But this does not say much more than that the things he talks about should not be

---

45. Bruce, *Galatians*, 217.
46. Cf. ibid. E.g., return from the exile was understood as another exodus.
47. Here following Wright who argues for a sense of real historical continuation between Paul and the OT. See *Climax of the Covenant*, 264–65.
48. Pace Räisänen, *Paul and the Law*, 269, who has completely denied this.
49. Moody Smith, "The Pauline Literature," 279.
50. Hays, *Echoes of Scripture*, 86
51. Ibid., 120–21. See also Hays, "Response to Critiques," 77–78, where he further explains the relationship between ecclesiology and Christology. Cf. Wright, *Climax of the Covenant*, 55.

taken at their face value.[52] They are to be looked at from the perspective revealed through Christ. Bearing this in mind we will turn to the context of our passage in order briefly to discuss some issues concerning Paul's "ecclesiological Christology."

The Context of Galatians 4:21—5:1

The letter to the Galatians focuses mainly on the entry of the Gentiles into the people of God.[53] A problem had arisen concerning their right to be God's people without submitting to the Torah requirements.[54] The Judaizers wanted them to be circumcised and keep the Law. In Gal 3–4, the apostle employs the theme of Abraham and his covenant (cf. Gen 15 and 17)[55] in order to argue for the equal standing of Gentile Christians alongside their Jewish brothers. He does not want them to submit to the Law because all the Torah could do was to bring God's people into exile, another bondage (cf. 2:4; 3:22; 4:3–5).[56] The central figure of chapter 3 is Jesus the Messiah who, by his death and resurrection, brought Israel's exile to an end[57] and opened the way to Abraham's inheritance through faith, for both Jews and Gentiles (v. 11–14).[58] He brought God's people

---

52. Hays, *Echoes of Scripture*, 116. He has explained that it means that, "they are to be read neither merely as history nor as a self-enclosed fictional narrative . . ."

53. Sanders, *Jewish People*, 31.

54. Hays, *Echoes of Scripture*, 105, 212 n.53. Cf. Davies, "Paul and the Law, 7, Wilckens, "Paul's View of the Law," 21, and Hooker, "Covenantal Nomism," 48. See further Sanders, *Paul*, 50; and Munck, *Salvation of Mankind*, 87–90.

55. This he did quite likely because his opponents, the Judaizers, did that in the first place. Cf. Lincoln, *Paradise Now and Not Yet*, 12, and Brinsmead, *Galatians*, 107. They might have claimed, similarly to the Jews from the gospels, that their father was Abraham (Matt 3:9//Luke 3:8; John 8:39), unlike the Gentiles'.

56. Cf. Betz, *Galatians*, 242.

57. Wright, *Climax of the Covenant*, 146–49. The exile was caused by Israel's failure to keep the Torah perfectly (cf. Deut 27–30). She was a transgressor and therefore needed God's redemptive mercy to reverse her fortunes. She needed a new exodus, which has happened in Christ. Cf. Thielman, *Paul and the Law*, 136. Dan 9:24–27 gives the reason why the exile was extended: the chastisement was being exacted sevenfold (cf. Lev 26:18, 21, 24, 28). This is following Scott, "Galatians 3.10," 200–201. Israel had to wait until the curse was atoned for (cf. Gal 3:10, 13; 4:4–5). The Messiah took on himself the curse of Israel and exhausted it. So Wright, *Climax of the Covenant*, 151. Sanders, *Palestinian Judaism*, 513, however, denies all links between the establishing of a new covenant and a new exodus theme.

58. It appears that the inheritance was linked to the promise that in Abraham all the nations would be blessed, which probably referred to the restoration of their relationship with God and ultimately to a renewal of his creation in Abraham's family.

freedom from the bondage caused by their disobedience to the Law (v. 13). In the same way, he brought to its climax the covenant with Abraham allowing, at the same time, the Gentiles to enter it. He became a light to the nations, the very thing Israel failed to fulfill.[59] 3:14 says that through faith both Christian Jews and Christian Gentiles become members of the renewed Abrahamic covenant.[60] All baptized into Christ constitute one Abrahamic family and inherit all his promises (vv. 26–29). This is exactly what the Abrahamic covenant was intended for: to create one family that inherits the promises given to the patriarch (vv. 15–18).[61]

It is noteworthy that when Paul uses 'we' or 'us' in 3:10–14, he refers to the situation of the Jews before and after the Christ event.[62] They were under the Law in order to be brought to Christ (3:22–25). But the Gentiles have never been subject to the Torah.[63] They belong now to Abraham's seed only if they belong to Christ. They are heirs of his promises. Thus Paul himself indicates that he sometimes speaks about the Jews and sometimes about the Gentiles, and often to both of them.

Paul continues the theme of 3:15–29 at the beginning of chapter 4.[64] He is still concerned with the covenant promises given to Abraham. He is still concerned with two groups within the Galatian church: Christian Jews and Christians Gentiles. 4:1–10 indicates that there were some who were subject to the Law, i.e., Jews (v. 5), but on the other hand there were also those who did not know God and therefore served other gods (v. 8): a statement, which would not suit Jews at all. Thus, in the first part of chapter 4, Paul further qualifies the situation of Israel under the Law and in Christ (4:1–5) as well as of the Gentiles first outside and then inside God's covenant (vv. 6–8).[65] As scholars have recognized, the beginning

---

59. Wright, *Climax of the Covenant*, 154.

60. Ibid. Wright has shown, moreover, that the Spirit is one of the blessings of the renewed covenant (cf. Gal 3:1–5). Thus the Spirit is not a mere allusion to a new dimension of religious experience. The experience can rather be compared to Abraham's experience of God. Cf. Jobes, "Jerusalem, Our Mother," 299. Hays, *Echoes of Scripture*, 110–11, has also argued that the Spirit is granted by God to the Gentiles as a sign of Abraham's true promised children.

61. Wright, *Climax of the Covenant*, 163. Cf. Sanders, *Paul*, 59.

62. Cf. Wright, *Climax of the Covenant*, 143.

63. Ibid.; contra Betz, *Galatians*, 242.

64. Hafemann, "Exile of Israel," 332.

65. Contra Sanders, *Jewish People*, 66; who has claimed that up to v. 7 the issue is the Law's custody.

of Gal 4 speaks of an exodus.[66] They have paid attention to the Jewish background of this idea here. However, because Paul himself has in mind two different groups of people, this exodus could have slightly different significance for the two. To the Jews, it was a second exodus redeeming them from the Law, i.e., from its curse that their disobedience brought about (v. 5). To the Gentiles, it was an exodus bringing freedom from slavery to false gods (v. 8). Both groups were in slavery but of a diverse nature. The Gentiles joined Israel's second exodus, which became their own exodus from bondage to idols. However, the problem is that the Gentile group, having been freed of their bondage to the gods, wants to come under exactly the same bondage from which Christ had to free the Jews (vv. 9–10; τὰ ἀσθενῆ καὶ πτωχὰ στοιχεῖα could perhaps be juxtaposed to τὰ στοιχεῖα τοῦ κόσμου in v. 3). Paul addresses the rest of the chapter mainly to them. Later in 5:3, Paul says that the circumcised one has to keep the whole Law. But Israel's story has shown that this is impossible: the Law can only bring exile and bondage. Nevertheless, the tendency among Gentile converts is to succumb to the Judaizers' endeavors and undergo circumcision in order to become zealous for the Jewish way (4:17). Therefore, in 4:11–20, Paul wants the Galatians to take heed of his reasoning, as he is the one who brought them to Christ (vv. 13, 20). The argument presented in 4:21—5:1, partly in an allegorical way, has the task of showing the Gentile Christians that, by choosing the Judaizing way, they put themselves under slavery to the Law. It is Paul's way of arguing about the heirs of Abraham.[67] Therefore the issue at stake seems to be freedom in Christ as opposed to the bondage of the previous state. With this in mind, we can now approach our passage.

Theological Issues in Galatians 4:21—5:1

Before we concentrate on the quotation from Isa 54:1 and its significance in the passage, we want briefly to discuss the drift of Paul's argument in the verses under consideration.

Paul's argument addresses, primarily, the Gentile Christians who want to come under the Law (4:21). The issue at stake is their freedom in Christ. The majority of scholars have claimed that there is a shift in 4:21 from the concrete requirements of the Torah in 21a to the Pentateuch

---

66. Hafemann, "Exile of Israel," 334. Also Thielman, *Paul and the Law*, 136.
67. Barrett, *Essays on Paul*, 157.

in general in 21b.⁶⁸ Some have also suggested that the law in v. 21b means the summary of Gen 16:15; 21:2–3, 9.⁶⁹ But there is nothing in the passage or in the previous sections to suggest such a change. Paul is still concerned with the same issue as in chapter 3: he has in mind the Torah, the Mosaic stipulations as presented throughout the Pentateuch.⁷⁰ What follows v. 21 is not a quotation from the Law, but an explanation of the end, to which the Law leads, and indeed had led Israel. It is simply shorthand in Paul's thinking. The law in 4:21 has the same meaning as Scripture in 3:22.⁷¹

The apostle returns to the theme of Abraham in 4:22, which could previously have been a weapon in the hands of Judaizers.⁷² He introduces two groups of opposites: a group represented by a son born to Abraham from a slave woman and a group represented by a son born to Abraham from a free woman. It is this slave/free polarity that Paul emphasizes here, rather than the circumcised or uncircumcised state.⁷³ The former son was born according to the flesh, whereas the latter according to the promise (v. 23). Paul makes here a theological distinction between two spheres of life: flesh, which is connected with the Law, and promise, which is linked with the Spirit, a distinction he had already made in 3:1–5.⁷⁴ This is in anticipation of verses 28 and 29, which clearly state the position of Gentiles who are in Christ. They are, like Isaac, the children of promise and therefore the children of Abraham (v. 28). They are free, as both the context and the beginning of the section show. They inherit the promises of their father and they experience the Spirit of the covenant renewal (vv. 29–30). However, those who keep the Law persecute them (v. 29; cf. 1:13, 23; 5:11; 6:12–13).⁷⁵ They are born according to the flesh

---

68. See, e.g., Bruce, *Galatians*, 215, and Lincoln, *Paradise Now and Not Yet*, 11. Cf. Witherington, *Grace in Galatia*, 328.

69. Cf. Betz, *Galatians*, 241.

70. Possibly Barrett, *Essays on Paul*, 161. Cf. Thielman, *Paul and the Law*, 123–24.

71. Thielman, *Paul and the Law*, 124.

72. We cannot be sure if Paul's opponents in Galatia referred to the Sarah-Hagar story.

73. Hays, *Echoes of Scripture*, 113.

74. Brinsmead, *Galatians*, 83

75. Cf. Hays, *Echoes of Scripture*, 117. The meaning is that the advocates of the Torah persecuted the non-Torah-observant Christians. We cannot be sure what sort of tradition Paul had in mind while speaking of Ishmael persecuting Isaac. Gen 21:9 LXX speaks about Ishmael playing with Isaac. See also Barrett, *Essays on Paul*, 164.

and so are in bondage, exile, because of the Law. Verse 30, then, does not seem to be speaking about literal casting out of the Law with its observants.[76] The context indicates that the focus is on inheritance: those who follow the Law do not inherit Abraham's promises, because the Torah only led them into exile.[77] For this reason, the Galatians should reject submitting to the Law and its advocates.[78] They are free as God's new creation in Christ and they are the restored Israel of God (cf. 6:15-16).

Paul wants to say that in Christ both Jews and Gentiles are free, no longer in slavery either to the Law or false gods. None of the Galatians should be willing to return into slavery (5:1). They experience the eschatological freedom of the new exodus.[79]

Paul is also interested in the contrasting women of our passage. He compares the two sons to those who are under the Law and those who are free in Christ, but at the same time he explains that the two women relate to two covenants (v. 24). The Hagar correspondence is obvious since it is clearly stated in v. 24. She stands for the covenant from Sinai and particularly the Torah as its main characteristic.[80] However, the free woman's correspondence is a matter of dispute among NT exponents. Dunn, for instance, has argued that the two covenants refer to two different aspects of the Abrahamic covenant, one embodied in the Torah.[81] However, this view has gained few supporters as it is difficult to show that Paul thought of the Mosaic covenant as an extension of

---

But Witherington, *Grace in Galatia*, 338, has denied that there is any hint in the letter suggesting that the Galatians were persecuted. Nevertheless, 5:11 and 6:12 could point to the fact that the pressure from the Law observant group is so enormous that Paul regards it as persecution.

76. It seems that Paul identified the bondwoman with the Sinaitic covenant (v. 24) and more precisely with its stipulations. Therefore we cannot agree with Martyn, *Galatians*, 446, that the bondwoman represents the teachers of the Law and her son the Galatians attracted by their teaching.

77. Cf. Dunn, *Galatians*, 258. Also Longenecker, *Galatians*, 217.

78. This seems, in context, more likely than Barrett's proposal that it is God's command to his angelic agents, expressing the fate of the opposite parties in Galatia. See his *Essays on Paul*, 165. Perriman, "Galatians 4:21—5:1," 41, claims that Paul speaks of rejecting just the Sinaitic covenant but this does not explain the referents in the allegory.

79. Cf. Thielman, *Paul and the Law*, 138.

80. Cf. Cosgrove, "No Children," 224-25. Thus Sinai is a synecdoche for the Torah (cf. p. 229). Hanson, *Paul's Technique and Theology*, 95, has also remarked that Hagar was an Egyptian and in Rev 11:8 Egypt symbolizes Jerusalem.

81. *Galatians*, 249-50.

The Metaphor of Divine Marriage in the Epistles of Paul

the Abrahamic.[82] Longenecker, on the other hand, has proposed that the two covenants relate to the old covenant, focused upon the Torah, and the new covenant, centered upon Christ.[83] However, in the context (3:15–18) the more obvious antithesis is between Abraham and Moses.[84] Therefore scholars have concluded that the second covenant, the Sarah correspondence, relates to the Abrahamic covenant, which finds its true meaning in Christ.[85] This is in agreement with Fung's observation that the unnamed covenant is the covenant of faith from Gal 3:17.[86] Yet the contrast between the two women gains a further dimension when Paul says that Hagar is also Mount Sinai in Arabia. Although this may seem to be a geographical reference at face value,[87] scholars have suggested that the information brings to mind the exilic context.[88] Arabia is outside the Promised Land and in this sense in exile. Paul wants to say that all the present Jerusalem stands for, together with those who support its system, is in bondage, in exile. The Sinai covenant brought an exile. But Paul sets the Jerusalem above against that system. It is noteworthy that the apostle does not speak of it as future, in opposition to the present in v. 25. However, because scholars have usually interpreted v. 26 in connection with v. 27, we will discuss the significance of this quotation in its context. This will also bring us closer to the source of the claim that Gal 4:21—5:1 alludes to the metaphor of divine marriage.

---

82. Cf. Witherington, *Grace in Galatia*, 330.

83. *Galatians*, 221. Cf. Hanson, *Paul's Technique and Theology*, 94.

84. Hays, *Echoes of Scripture*, 114.

85. Ibid.. Also Thielman, *Paul and the Law*, 137, and Hafeman, "Exile of Israel," 363. Pace Witherington, *Grace in Galatia*, 325. He has concluded that Sarah, the free woman, must stand for Paul since it was the apostle himself who bore the Galatians in freedom (4:19–20). Similarly, the women in vv. 27 and 30 relate also to Paul (pp. 329, 336). Thus Paul would be exhorting himself in the verses. However, Witherington is unable to answer the question of how Paul can be at the same time both the free woman and her child (cf. v. 31). Furthermore, as Betz, *Galatians*, 248, has demonstrated, Paul has in mind two diverse concepts when he speaks of himself as a mother in 4:19 and 'our mother' in v. 26.

86. Fung, *Galatians*, 207.

87. E.g., Martyn, *Galatians*, 438, favors the mere geographical reading. Cf. Betz, *Galatians*, 244. Cosgrove, "No Children," 228, has suggested that Arabia is the land where Hagar and Ishmael were driven to (Gen 21:14–21).

88. E.g., Brinsmead, *Galatians*, 108, and Fung, *Galatians*, 207. But this does not imply that the church in Jerusalem is particularly in view. Pace Bruce, *Galatians*, 220.

Function and Theological Significance of Isa 54:1 in Gal 4:27

Gal 4:26 with its use of the personal pronoun "our," indicates that Paul has both Christian Jews and Gentiles in view. They are not linked to the system characteristic of the earthly geographical Jerusalem. They are rather associated with the restored Zion of Isaianic prophecy (Isa 54:1).[89] We have already suggested in chapter 1 that when NT authors quote from the OT they have in view the wider redemptive-history context, in which a given passage occurs. Thus we should read Isa 54:1 in its wider context.[90] We have seen in chapter 3 that the barrenness of Zion was another metaphor illustrating the misery and shame of exile.[91] It pointed to the emptying of God's land of its population (cf. 64:10). Israel's exile was expressed also by the metaphor of widowhood in Isa 54:4. That was, however, followed by a great prospect of Yahweh restoring his wife's fortunes at the end of exile and renewing his covenant with her (54:5–10). Thus, in using Isa 54:1, Paul does not so much complete "the implied parallels between Hagar and Sarah,"[92] but between the present and restored Jerusalem/Zion. The renewed Zion was to be full of inhabitants to possess the nations (54:2–3). She was supposed to give birth to her offspring miraculously (66:7–11). This has happened, according to some commentators, through the resurrection of Jesus.[93] This has been fulfilled in Jews and Gentiles being freed by Christ (cf. Gal 4:28). The Jewish-Gentile church is free from the bondage that the Law led to.[94] This is because she is God's restored wife in the renewed covenant. She is the wife who regained her freedom because of her husband's mercy (cf. 5:1). She is the wife who bore and is bearing many children, even more than before the exile. Her offspring will receive the nations as their

---

89. In this sense, therefore, one should take belonging to the heavenly Jerusalem as being under its influence and acting as her agents on earth. Cf. Wright, *Christian Hope*, 8.

90. Hays, *Echoes of Scripture*, 119–20, has proposed that the verse should be read in the context of starting at least at Isa 51:1 and going through the rest of the book.

91. Cf. ibid., 119.

92. Pace Jobes, "Jerusalem, Our Mother," 303. She recognizes that the barrenness of Sarah and later her miraculous childbearing were the basis for the Isaianic metaphors (pp. 308, 316). While this observation seems possible, the emphasis in Gal 4:26–27 is on the systems represented by the earthly and heavenly Jerusalems.

93. See ibid., 316.

94. Cf. Hanson, *Paul's Technique and Theology*, 97.

inheritance (Isa 54:3).[95] Consequently, the Jerusalem above is virtually identical with the new system introduced by Christ, in which he himself is the law (cf. 6:2).[96] It is not an earthly restored city, as many ancient Jews would have expected (cf. chapter 4 above). Neither is it future.[97] At the same time, however, it is not identical with the church on earth, but refers to a spiritual realm, which encompasses Abraham's promised offspring, and which brings freedom.[98] The restored Zion belongs to the same realm as the new earth and heaven (cf. Isa 65:17–25).[99] By implication, when quoting from Isa 54:1, Paul says that the spiritual Jerusalem has more children than the earthy Jerusalem had before the exile robbed her of her children.[100]

Thus it seems quite likely that Paul had in mind a wider tradition of divine marriage when referring to Isa 54:1 at Gal 4:27. It provided him with imagery, which could explain the situation brought about by Christ. It set the condition of God's wife from before the exile over against the state of the restored wife in the new covenant. The exile turned into joy and the abundant fertility of Yahweh's wife. The Gentiles are now also the children of Jerusalem and the children of God. They receive the inheritance of their mother. Only this kind of fruitfulness is able to fulfill the promise to Abraham from Gen 17:4–5. As a consequence, the "old" wife must be ashamed in comparison to the fertility of the restored Zion (1 Sam 2:5; cf. also Gen 30:1–13 and chapter 3 on Isa 54:1–10). She was never this fruitful before. She has become "Beulah" indeed (Isa 54:1; cf. 62:4). Therefore, God through exile brought his people into a far more glorious state. He freed them through his Messiah and realized for them the promises of old. It seems that this discussion about Christian freedom in relation to the condition caused by the Law functions within the Jewish framework of exodus motif, as Paul opposes bondage with redemption leading to freedom. We have already seen that the marriage metaphor is closely linked to the concept of new exodus, return from

---

95. Possibly the mother's *mohar* closely linked with her inheritance (cf. chapter 2 of this volume).

96. Betz, *Galatians*, 247. Concerning Christ as the Law see Seifrid, *Christ, Our Righteousness*, 97.

97. Pace Hanson, *Paul's Technique and Theology*, 96. See Fung, *Galatians*, 210.

98. Cf. Lincoln, *Paradise Now and Not Yet*, 25–27.

99. Ibid., 18.

100. See Fung, *Galatians*, 211, and Dunn, *Galatians*, 255.

exile. Therefore, we can conclude that, although not very clear at face value, the metaphor of divine marriage does inform Paul's argument in Gal 4:21—5:1.

ROMANS 7:1-6

Introductory Remarks

Because Paul employs in Rom 7:2-3 what many have recognized as a marriage analogy, scholars have often concluded that the present passage is another instance of the apostle's use of the divine marriage metaphor.[101] Nevertheless, other scholars have concluded that no real analogy or allegory is involved here but merely an illustration.[102] This latter group has claimed that all that Paul wanted to convey in the illustration was what he had already said in v. 1, viz., that death ends the force of the Law. This more negative approach has emerged from the general difficulty in finding consistent referents on the more allegorical reading. J. A. Little has expressed this scholarly disappointment in saying,

> No matter how one distributes the roles, there is no way to get around the fact that these roles cannot be consistently applied throughout the first four verses. The analogical approach cannot get around the switch Paul makes in the subject of freedom from the man in v. 1 to the wife in v. 3. The allegorical approach cannot get around the splitting of the role of the man in v. 1 into two roles of husband and wife in v. 2.[103]

Thus the lack of consensus among NT exegetes has been caused by a difference of opinion concerning the referents of the law, the first husband, and the wife, throughout the passage as well as of the person (ἄνθρωπος) in v. 1. We wish to suggest, however, that a solution to these problems

---

101. Chavasse, *Bride of Christ*, 79, Earnshaw, "Marriage Analogy," 68–88, Wright, "Messiah and the People of God," 148, Wright, *Climax of the Covenant*, 196, Dunn, *Romans 1-8*, 362. Also Stuhlmacher, *Romans*, 103, although for him the metaphor is only in the background to Paul's thought. He believes that the main concern is "the change from the reign of the Law to the reign of Christ."

102. Batey, *Nuptial Imagery*, 18–19, Nygren, *Romans*, 270–72, Cranfield, *Romans*, I: 335, and Moo, *Romans 1-8*, 437. Cf. Käsemann, *Romans*, 187, who differs from the others in that he has not taken the law in v. 1 as referring to the Torah but just to Roman civil law.

103. Little, "Analysis of Romans 7:1-6," 86. Cf. Best, *One Body in Christ*, 52. For Räisänen, *Paul and the Law*, 46, Paul's allegory is "lost in internal contradictions."

can be found by focusing first on the wider context of Rom 7 and then, in turn, looking at Paul's analogy or illustration in the context of the whole unit of Rom 7:1–6. We believe that this will help us to establish whether the apostle used the OT divine marriage metaphor in his present argument.

The Context of Romans 7

The majority of scholars, Käsemann excepted,[104] agree that chapter 7 of the epistle to the Romans is a continuation of what was said earlier in chapters 5–6. While the scope of the present work does not allow us to join the debate concerning the plot of the letter, we can, nevertheless, mention several points that more recent scholars have made.

In Rom 5 and 6, Paul draws a contrast between two spheres of life: flesh[105] and Spirit and between letter and Spirit.[106] This has the wider purpose of contrasting the situation under the old and new covenants. In chapter 6, the apostle focuses particularly on the Christian's death to sin.[107] Because Christ died, all who are in him died to sin as he did (6:10). But in more general terms, Paul argues in Rom 5–8 that those who belong to the Messiah constitute God's renewed creation and inherit all the promises and responsibilities of God's people.[108] In the background of Paul's argument is the issue of God's faithfulness to his promises regarding Israel with its God given Torah.[109] Thus the Law and covenant are central categories in Rom 5–8.[110] This becomes even more evident when one turns to chapter 7. The discussion concerning the Law probably looks back to the statement made in 5:20, viz., that the Torah "exacerbated" the fleshly nature of Israel's existence.[111] By their association with Adamic humanity, they were slaves of sin (6:17–18) and this

---

104. *Romans*, 187.

105. "Flesh" in Rom 5–8 does not refer to the physical body but bears its *hamartiological* meaning.

106. Stuhlmacher, *Romans*, 102–3.

107. Little, *Romans*, 82. Cf. Nygren, *Romans*, 266; Earnshaw, "Marriage Analogy," 72.

108. Wright, "Messiah and the People of God," 142–43, and his *Climax of the Covenant*, 194–95.

109. Wright, *Climax of the Covenant*, 194. Cf. Hays, *Echoes of Scripture*, 53.

110. Wright, *Climax of the Covenant*, 195.

111. Ibid.

became evident through the Law.¹¹² As a result, Paul treats the Law as an enslaving power. As with Paul's thought in Gal 3–4, the Torah also causes bondage here, although it remains itself good (7:12). This time, however, the bondage Paul speaks about is bondage to sin. Thus the beginning of chapter 7 is an announcement of freedom from the bondage of sin caused by the Torah.

Paul's Marriage Theme in Romans 7:1–6

The beginning of the section indicates that Paul is addressing the Christian Jews, those who know the Law (v. 1a).¹¹³ Consequently, the law here, most likely, refers to the Torah (7:4; cf. 6:14), which is a peculiar possession of Israel according to the flesh.¹¹⁴ Thus, the ἄνθρωπος may have in view Rom 6:6 with its "old man," who is in Adam, especially as regards Israel. The main point of Paul's argument is that the Law rules over this man as long as he lives (cf. 6:7).

Difficulties appear, however, when one approaches verses 2–3 and tries to link them with verse 4. Commentators have earlier suggested that the first husband in vv. 2–3 was the Law.¹¹⁵ This, however, complicates the link with verse 4 because it speaks of the death of those who died through Christ, not the death of the Torah.¹¹⁶ The Law does not cease to exist but it does not rule over the Christian anymore. Therefore the most convincing suggestion is that it is the νόμος in vv. 2–3 that refers to the Torah. The law of the husband in this case could resemble that part of the Mosaic legislation, which regulated the matter of marital faithfulness (cf., e.g., Num 5:12–31). But it could also simply refer to the authority the

---

112. Cf. Wright, "New Exodus, New Inheritance," 29–35.

113. Although others have claimed that they were not necessarily Jews, but Gentiles associated with the synagogues and Jewish worship. This is why they knew the Law. Cf. Stuhlmacher, *Romans*, 103. Wright, *Climax of the Covenant*, 195, has observed that the church in Rome consisted mainly of ex-proselytes. Thus, in general, the text deals with those who were historically under the Law.

114. Wright, "Messiah and the People of God," 143. Also Wright, "Theology of Paul," 50. Moreover, see Wright, *Romans*, 558, where the author argues that the conjunction "or" in 7:1 connects the paragraph with 6:14. On reference to the Torah in the passage see also Räisänen, *Paul and the Law*, 58. Pace Käsemann, *Romans*, 187. Because of the space limits of the present volume, we will not enter the discussion on Pauline theology of the Law in his letters generally.

115. E.g., Best, *One Body in Christ*, 52.

116. Cf. Moule, *New Testament Interpretation*, 154, and Nygren, *Romans*, 272.

Law has given the husband over his wife. In other words, it was the Law that defined the act of the woman. Who then is the husband and wife? Some have proposed that the woman refers to Israel.[117] This would, however, imply that the divine marriage metaphor of the OT has suddenly taken on a new turn: either it would need to say that the husband, i.e., God, was to die, or that Israel's husband was not God at all. Either possibility would seem somewhat inconsistent with other occurrences of the metaphor. Furthermore, putting Israel in the place of the woman would imply in v. 4 that she corporately died to the Law. Although this could be true in itself, the problem is that vv. 2–3 speak of a death of the husband, not the wife. Thus the analogy breaks down, which suggests that taking Israel to represent the wife does not seem a particularly good solution.

Earnshaw has brought another peculiar opinion to the fore. He has argued that while the νόμος τοῦ ἀνδρός refers to the Mosaic Law, both the first and the other husbands stand for Christ.[118] The believer participates with Christ both in his death and resurrection. This is why Christ can signify the two husbands. He explains,

> . . . we can state the thesis that Paul's marriage analogy is properly understood only when *the wife's first marriage is viewed as illustrating the believer's union with Christ in his death and her second marriage is viewed as illustrating the believer's union with Christ in his resurrection.*[119]

The wife, then, refers to the believer who was married to Christ in his death. Later, the believer lives joined to another, i.e., this time to Christ in his resurrection. Christ's death involved both his physical dying and his and the believer's dying to the law.[120] Therefore the ἄνθρωπος in v. 1 stands for both the ἀνήρ and γυνή in vv. 2–3.[121] Although this view solves

---

117. Chavasse, *Bride of Christ*, 79. He has argued that the husband of the "Jewish church" was the Law. But we have seen that it is very unlikely that it was the Law that died. Wright, "Messiah and the People of God," 148, has argued that the woman is Israel indeed, although there is no continuity with the OT metaphor. The true husband of Israel was not God as the Jews supposed but Adam, the "old man" of v. 6.6. But Wright himself seems to have differently emphasized this interpretation in his later works. In *Climax of the Covenant*, 196, he has argued that both the husband and wife constitute the self of man.

118. "Marriage Analogy," 72–73.

119. Ibid., 72. Italics his.

120. Ibid., 84.

121. Ibid., 81.

to some extent tensions between vv. 2–3 and v.4, it does not seem fully justified. The main problem with Earnshaw's proposal seems to be his assumption that two marriage unions between Christ and the believer are involved. The ἕτερος in v. 4 does not seem to signify the contrast between Christ's earthly and glorified mode of existence.[122] It rather refers to a sharper qualitative contrast, in a similar way to 7:23 (the Law of God vs. the law of sin). The death of Christ in v. 4 was a means by which the Christian Jew could, joined to another husband of different qualities, bear fruit for God instead of for death (v. 5). Thus, it would seem that the previous husband was someone or something that influenced the man to bear fruit for death. This could not have been, then, Christ in his death, as the death had another purpose. Given the argument of chapter 6, the husband could rather be expected to be something that put the Jews into bondage. The Law empowered sin to bring Israel into slavery, as we have noticed. The problem was, it seems, Israel's old sphere of life, namely its fleshly nature. In the face of these observations, Earnshaw's argument does not exactly match the content of our passage.

We would like to suggest that it is possible to solve the puzzle of Paul's illustration in vv. 2–3 by taking Rom 7:5–6 together with vv. 1–4. Verse 5 suggests that it was the flesh that created problems for those under the Law. Since "flesh" occurs here in its *hamartiological* sense, the real problem was sin that enslaved the παλαιὸς ἄνθρωπος, humanity joined to Adam in 6:6.[123] The sin used the Torah against Israel. Yet God provided a solution. The Christian's σάρξ has died through the σῶμα of Christ.[124] Thus the first husband could be the old "fleshly"/ the "in Adam"-self and the wife could be the self that is married to (or simply joined to) Christ in v. 4.[125] The contrast is between the Jewish self in the flesh (v. 5) and the Jewish self in Christ (vv. 4, 6).[126] Thus the illustration

---

122. Ibid., 87.

123. Cf. Wright, *Climax of the Covenant*, 196.

124. Σῶμα refers here to Christ's earthly body, not in the corporate sense of the church. Cf. Cranfield, *Romans*, I: 336.

125. Cf. Wright, *Climax of the Covenant*, 196. This is a slightly different explanation from that of Thielman, *Paul and the Law*, 197, who has proposed that the believer is like the husband in his death to the law and like the wife free to marry another. See also Thielman, "Theology of Romans 5–8," 190. Γίνομαι + dative is used for the act of marrying, e.g., in Deut 24:2 and Ruth 1:12–13. Cf. Earnshaw, "Marriage Analogy," 71 n.13.

126. Cf. Robinson, *Wrestling with Romans*, 78. The personal pronoun "we" in vv. 5, 6 suggests that Paul has the Christian Jews in view.

in Rom 7:1–4 supports Paul's argument about two spheres of life, which continues through chapters 5 and 6. The ἄνθρωπος of v. 1 could then encompass both the husband and wife of vv. 2–3, i.e., the "self." Those who were enslaved to sin under the Torah have died through Christ to their old self, to the realm of humanity in Adam, and have been joined to the realm of Christ. As a result, they can live in the "newness of the Spirit" serving God (vv. 5–6), bearing fruit for him.[127]

Thus the idea, which Paul presents in our unit, is not so much focused on the marriage of the believer to Christ as on the resulting freedom of the Jewish Christian made dead to the Law through joining to Christ. The point is simply that the believer is free from the bondage to which the Law has led him, the bondage of death (cf. 7:9–10).[128] It would be rather difficult to find in this analogy a development of the OT divine marriage metaphor, although 7:4 can to some extent suggest a variation on the marriage theme itself. The lack of a pointer to the OT *testimonia* puts in doubt Paul's consistent use of the OT divine marriage metaphor here.[129] If pressed further along the lines of the OT metaphor, his analogy would break down. Israel does not appear here as God's re-loved and restored wife. God could not be the husband in vv. 2–3. Israel, it seems, is here put to death to her old self (as presented in the role of husband), her rebellion in Adam, through her union in Christ's death. She can live fruitfully/obediently to God now. She has been freed from the Law, which, though being good, led her into bondage. Paul shows that the problem was the human sinful nature of Israel, exacerbated by the Law, from which the man had to be freed by Christ's death.

---

127. There is probably no reference to childbearing in the metaphor of fruit bearing in v. 4. Cf. Dunn, *Romans 1–8*, 363. Also Cranfield, *Romans*, I: 337. The contrast seems to be between bondage of sin and freedom in serving God. One can also wonder if bearing fruit for God is not reminiscent of Jesus' words in, e.g., Matt 21:33–43.

128. I am in agreement with Thielman, "Theology of Romans 5–8," 181; that death signifies destruction and exile (cf. Deut 28:15—29:29). Similarly, life signifies the blessings of the covenant, esp. the length of life in the promised land (see Deut 30:15, 20; cf. 4:1; 32:47).

129. Although the editors of The Greek New Testament UBS third edition (p. 908) propose that Rom 6:21 alludes to Ezek 16:61, 63, one still cannot show how Rom 7:1–6 could be consistently developing the OT divine marriage metaphor.

ROMANS 9:25–29

The Nature of the Passage

The verses under consideration form a mosaic of quotations from Hosea and Isaiah. It is evident that verses 25–26 refer subsequently to Hos 2:23LXX (2:25MT) and 1:10LXX (2:1MT). The case of vv. 27–28 is more complex. Although Paul claims that he refers to Isaiah, he seems to be relying on both Hos 1:10LXX and Isa 10:22–23LXX.[130] He uses υἱῶν Ἰσραήλ of Hos 1:10LXX instead of λαός Ἰσραήλ from Isa 10:22LXX probably because he wants vv. 27–28 to be read as complementary to the quotations in vv. 25–26.[131] Then, in v. 29 the apostle quotes verbatim Isa 1:9LXX. We shall briefly discuss the purpose of Paul's quotations as revealed throughout their context.

In chapter 9 of the epistle to the Romans, Paul sets out to settle the issue that is characteristic of other parts of the letter as well, viz., God's faithfulness regarding his promises made to Abraham as they relate to Israel.[132] The question he poses is about the place of ethnic Israel in God's eschatological salvation. As had happened during his ministry, most of the Jews have rejected Paul's gospel, the salvation of God through Christ. But to them belonged God's covenantal promises. What, then, went wrong? Has God's word failed? Has he not fulfilled what he promised his people? Thus Paul is defending God's faithfulness in Rom 9:6–29. In fact, the whole section seems to be a defense of the proposition in v. 6a: "but it is not that the word of God has failed."[133] However, the second part of v. 6 is equally important as it explains the former statement, "for they are not all Israel who are *descended* from Israel" (NASB). We would suggest that failing to take the meaning of the whole verse into account led scholars to accuse Paul of being inconsistent throughout Rom 9–11.[134]

---

130. Cf. Dunn, *Romans 9–16*, 573–74.

131. Aageson, "Romans 9–11," 273.

132. Cf. Moo, "Theology of Romans 9–11," 242. Wright, *Climax of the Covenant*, 234.

133. Moo, "Theology of Romans 9–11," 242. At the same time, v. 6a picks up the problem suggested in vv. 1–5. It can be at the same time a heading to the whole section. Then, it is possible that v. 7 together with v. 29 form an inclusion. Cf. Stegner, "Romans 9.6–29," 49.

134. See, e.g., Räisänen, *Paul and the Law*, 264. The problem is apparently that Paul first argues for Israel's hardening in Rom 9 and notorious disobedience in Rom 10 and then, in Rom 11, that Israel's obduracy is but temporal until all Gentiles come in.

Paul appears to imply that Israel has been redefined: not all Jews belong truly to God's Israel. It is worth remembering in this place that Jesus has already introduced the idea of redefining Israel, for instance, in his parable of the Ten Maidens (cf. chapter 5 above). There, the true Israel consists of the people who heed Jesus' words, his disciples. Others, who reject God's word in Jesus, are left outside of God's salvation. Only the faithful enjoy salvation in God's kingdom. Thus Paul is not very original when he says that not all descending from Israel are God's Israel. The belonging rests rather on God's promise (9:7–8), as the stories of the patriarchs show (vv. 7, 9, 10, 12, 13). Even more, this belonging rests on God's election (v. 11), God's righteousness in showing mercy to whom he pleases (vv. 14–15; as he revealed it through Moses in Exod 33:19), and his will (v. 18).[135] At the same time, nobody can argue with God about his will (vv. 19–21). Being a sovereign potter, he can keep some vessels to reveal his power and wrath (v. 22, cf. 17) and some to reveal the riches of his glory (v. 23). Thus, according to his will, he has chosen from among both Jews and Gentiles a people who experience his glory, and to whom he reveals himself (cf. Exod 33:19, as he did to Moses). He makes himself a people from different ethnic groups (v. 24). He remains faithful to Israel according to his will.

As we noted in chapter 1, NT quotations from the OT can be pointers to bigger redemptive-history contexts. Thus Paul's literature can be regarded as generally using OT material in an intelligible way. We therefore cannot agree with Käsemann[136] that Paul does not have any interest in the original context of the LXX of Hos 2 or the wider context of Isaiah. Our study has argued so far that in referring to OT prophecies the NT authors often pointed to their fulfillment in Jesus Christ and that their meaning was fixed in the context of his work. Consequently, we

---

135. Wright, *Climax of the Covenant*, 239, has rejected any notion of God's arbitrary choice of individuals. Instead, he has spoken of God choosing a nation to condemn evil in it. Why this and not another nation? Whatever way one approaches the question of God's will, the point remains that God's choice is sovereign and in this sense arbitrary. Salvation comes as result of God's sovereign love. Cf. Moo, "Theology of Romans 9–11," 243 and Munck, *Salvation of Mankind*, 42. It is noteworthy that Israel as God's people is now redefined. It experiences God's deliverance, a second exodus, although not all physical Israelites are included in it: only the remnant (cf. Rom 9:27). Others remain in bondage. Paul seems to be implying that Israel (as God's people) remains the same, although its content changes now.

136. *Romans*, 274.

would like to submit that, by quoting the OT in Rom 9:25–29, Paul is consistent with this general approach of the NT writers.[137]

His first reference to Hos 2:23LXX echoes God's promise of restoration of the unfaithful wife Israel. She has been rejected, become as if she were not his wife, not his people, because of her idolatry (cf. chapter 3 above). But she was to be re-planted on the earth, re-loved by God (2:25MT speaks of God showing mercy), and called "my people" (as a reversal of 1:9; cf. chapter 3 above). Aageson[138] has observed that Paul changes ἐρῶ ('I shall say') to καλέσω ("I shall call"), which is not found in Hos 2:23LXX. But we have already argued in chapter 3 that Hos 2:23 is a reversal of 1:9, where God calls his people not his people. For Hos 1:9 LXX, in fact, uses the verb καλέω, which can suggest that Paul read Hos 2:23 exactly as such a reversal. Moreover, he has already used the verb referring to God's calling people whom he chose in Rom 8:28, 30 (they are those who 'love God' in v. 28, i.e., Christians). Paul seems to be saying that God's restored people in the renewed covenant, the children of the Abrahamic promise (cf. καλέω in 9:7; cf. Gen 21:12), are those whom God called from both Jews and Gentiles (9:24). They are God's restored wife, who comes to a renewed relationship with her husband through a wilderness experience, through Emek Achor, the door of hope. They come to a new intimate relationship with Israel's God.[139] In the context, it seems that the Gentiles join part of Israel according to God's plan and election. 9:26 with its reference to Hos 1:10 establishes further the idea of fulfillment. This seems particularly striking in the context of Rom 8, which evidently speaks about 'sons of God' (vv. 14–17).[140] In the redefined Israel, it is both Jews and Gentiles that are betrothed anew to God, i.e., experiencing the blessings of his covenant renewal. In this sense, Paul

---

137. However, we believe that more than a mere typology is involved. Paul seems to be concerned with historical continuity, not just with the Northern Kingdom being a type of rejected pagans. Pace Cranfield, *Romans*, II: 500, and Dunn, *Romans 9–16*, 572.

138. "Romans 9–11," 272.

139. Which was to be characterized by Yahweh's bestowing on his restored people gifts of his righteousness, justice, loyalty and love (see chapter 3 above). We suppose that another work would be required to examine whether the letter to the Romans speaks of the renewed people actually receiving these gifts.

140. Rom 8 appears to speak of Christians and their adoption to God's family, as first-fruits of new creation. The creation still awaits the completion of its exodus from the bondage of sin and death. Cf. Wright, *JVG*, 218. It seems also that Rom 8 gives hints on Christian inheritance, which appears to be the renewed and restored creation. Cf. Wright, "New Exodus, New Inheritance," 30.

could have in mind the OT marriage metaphor in order to explain the outcome of Christ's work as applicable to his mission, which included both Jews and Gentiles.

It seems also that Hos 1:10 creates a good link between this prophecy and that of Isaiah. The concept of the multitude of the sons of Israel (especially sand of the sea) links to Isaiah's theme of the remnant returning from exile in 10:22–23.[141] This helps Paul to explain, it appears, his redefinition of Israel and the fact that only part of the Jews experience God's deliverance.[142] God chose to save Israel through its remnant.[143] Thus part of ethnic Israel become vessels of God's mercy and another part vessels of wrath. It is also worth noticing that the development of the remnant concept in deutero-Isaiah (esp. chapters 56–66) assumes the opening of the restored community to outsiders, i.e., pagans.[144] The double climax in Isa 65:17–25 and 66:22–23 testifies to this expansion in the remnant idea. Webb explains,

> In the end the remnant is not defined in national or ethnic terms, but in confessional and behavioural terms. Being Israelite does not guarantee inclusion in the remnant, and being foreign does not entail exclusion from it. But the final verse of the book stands as a grim reminder that while the remnant may be inclusive it is not universal. The remnant is a remnant still. It is not everyone. Salvation and judgment are both final realities and not merely temporal ones.[145]

---

141. The relationship between this theme and the promise to Abraham in Gen 22:17 (which assures him of a multitude of his descendants comparing it to the sand of a seashore) could be examined at a different occasion. In Rom 9, Paul is more concerned with division within Israel than the fulfillment of this particular promise.

142. Cf. Dunn, *Romans 9–16*, 574.

143. In Isaiah's prophecy the key to the transformation of Zion is a purifying judgment, which produces a purified remnant that becomes a nucleus of the new Zion at the eschaton. See Webb, "Zion in Transformation," 72–73. He has explained that the remnant in Isa 1–12 is a few survivors, who repent after the devastation of Zion (cf. 1:27), and who lean on Yahweh and no longer on Assyria (10:10–21). They will be redeemed. However, those who do not repent are destroyed. This can explain, we suggest, why Paul refers to part of Israel's nation as "vessels of wrath."

144. See ibid., 79. Cf. Isa 56:6–7; 60:6–7, 10; 66:18–23. Therefore we cannot agree with Hays, *Echoes of Scripture*, 68, who has suggested that the quotation from Hosea shows that God calls Gentiles, and the one from Isaiah that he calls Jews. We have demonstrated that Paul's use of quotations has more nuances.

145. "Zion in Transformation," 79–80. Webb has indicated (p. 80 n.1) that one should contrast "all the flesh" in v. 23 with v. 16, and finally compare with v. 24.

Although Paul does not refer directly to those later parts of Isaiah here (but he does soon after in Rom 10:20: to Isa 65:1–2), we could expect him to have been familiar with the remnant concept throughout the book. His quotations serve most likely as pointers to bigger OT sections describing God's redemptive history. Moreover, it appears that in Paul the redefinition of Israel is a more developed concept than in Jesus' parables. Compared to the Wedding Banquet parable, as examined by us in chapter 5, Paul's argument brings to the fore the issue of Gentiles alongside the remnant of Jews. Although the issue has been already present in Isaiah, it was Paul who used it more explicitly in the context of his Gentile-focused mission. Nevertheless, it appears that both Jesus and the apostle have seen in this particular Isaianic tradition a basis for their theological thinking on Israel at the eschaton.

Verse 28 is dependent on Isa 10:23LXX. The original verse in Isaiah is an announcement of God going to realize fully his will because his judgment is irrevocably decided.[146] He will judge Israel, saving a remnant. In the context of our passage, this can mean that what happens to Israel in Paul's ministry is the realization of God's purposes regarding his people, viz., saving them through the remnant. Then, verse 29 quoting Isa 1:9LXX states positively that this remnant prevents Israel from becoming completely desolate.[147] God continues with his people through the remnant. His word has not failed since a remnant of Israel has been elected.[148] They experience God's mercy, his deliverance, an exodus.

In Rom 9:30—10:21, Paul continues explaining God's righteousness regarding his word (cf. 9:6), especially in relation to Israel.[149] The point is that God revealed his righteousness in Christ (10:4), so that the part

---

146. Cf. Childs, *Isaiah*, 95, and Delitzsch, *Isaiah*, I: 273.

147. Cf. Dunn, *Romans 9–16*, 574. Sodom and Gomorrah are symbols of desolation followed by God's judgment. Cf. Gen 19:24; Deut 29:23; Isa 13:19; Jer 50:40; Amos 4:11; and Zeph 2:9. It is worth noting that the word used here for the remnant is σπέρμα. It is quite possible that, through Rom 9:7–8 and 4:18, this can refer to the promise to Abraham in Gen 15:5 of him becoming a father of many nations. See also Cranfield, *Romans*, II: 503.

148. Stegner, "Romans 9.6–29," 49.

149. God's righteousness is his covenant faithfulness. Following here Wright, *Climax of the Covenant*, 239–41. Although Wright has concluded that it is Rom 9:30—10:21 that speaks of the transformation of "an ethnic people into a worldwide family," we have already proposed that chapter 9 did this to a certain extent.

of Israel, which looks for it in the Torah, fails.[150] The point is that God, according to his covenant plan, has established his own righteousness in Christ, the goal of the Torah,[151] which Israel was not able to fulfill. Their attempts to find righteousness their own way fail.[152] In the context, as explained above, it is only the remnant that chooses God's way of righteousness and they indeed obtain it through Christ (cf. 10:9–10, 12–13, 16).[153] Nevertheless, we have argued that Paul has used OT divine marriage traditions combined with the remnant theme in order to explain the eschatological salvation of Gentiles alongside the remnant of ethnic Israel. The remnant of Israel, together with people of different nations, enters God's new betrothal, the renewed covenant of his righteousness. In this way, those who were once regarded as not-God's-people, despite their ethnic origin, become his beloved wife.

EPHESIANS 5:21–33

Introduction

The last passage we will examine in this chapter is Eph 5:21–33 with its mention of the marriage between Christ and his church in verses 25b–27. The authorship of the epistle to the Ephesians has been a matter of dispute in critical scholarship over the past century or more.[154] However,

---

150. Cf. Sanders, *Jewish People*, 37, although not agreeing with his corollaries. See also Hays, *Echoes of Scripture*, 75–76, and Wright, "Theology of Paul," 56.

151. Τέλος points rather to the climax of the Law, in the sense of its fulfillment. As the Torah was a characteristic and boundary of God's covenant so now Christ is, encompassing the Law in himself. See Wright, *Climax of the Covenant*, 241–44. Cf. Hays, *Echoes of Scripture*, 76. Thus τέλος cannot mean the end in the sense of abolition or termination. Pace Räisänen, "Difficulties with the Law," 306. Also Sanders, *Jewish People*, 37.

152. Cf. Munck, *Salvation of Mankind*, 42.

153. It is worth mentioning here that our explanation of Israel's re-definition may possibly help in solving the exegetical problem of the salvation of all Israel in Rom 11:26. It seems that 'all Israel' refers to the re-defined Israel, whereas in v. 25 it refers to the ethnic nation. God in time saves his Israel, of both Jews and Gentiles. And although only the remnant of the ethnic Israel is saved, in fact all Israel is saved, as it consists both of the Jewish remnant and of Gentiles. But believing Gentiles should not vaunt over Jews in their status. They are implanted into God's people and not the other way round. Cf. Wright, *Climax of the Covenant*, 249–51.

154. The traditional Pauline authorship has been challenged for several reasons. We will mention only those directly touching on our passage. (1) The letter has been recognized as focusing more on ecclesiology than on Christology, which is uncharacteristic

it seems that the letter can be taken, at least, as a continuation of Pauline thought.[155] Furthermore, there is still a considerable group of exegetes who do not see enough evidence for the rejection of Pauline authorship.[156] Therefore it seems justifiable to include the passage in this chapter. We propose to focus on its main points as regards the marriage metaphor.[157]

---

of Paul. It has therefore been concluded that Paul could not be the author of the epistle. But more recent scholarship has demonstrated that the widely recognized letters in the Pauline corpus are also ecclesiocentric (cf., above discussions esp. on Galatians and Romans). Furthermore, ecclesiology depends on Christology. Cf. Barth, *Ephesians*, 668. (2) The use of alleged traditions in Ephesians has also contributed to the questioning of Pauline authorship. As regards our passage, scholars have claimed that since the letter refers to the Haustafeln forms (cf. Col. 3:18—4:1), it cannot be Pauline. Paul would not have used such forms, since he was more realistically informed about the situation in the churches. Cf. Best, *Essays on Ephesians*, 193. However, some NT interpreters have seriously challenged the whole issue of the presence of a household table in the letter. It could well have been that the author of Ephesians was addressing a particular problem that churches in the Ephesus district were struggling with. Cf. Witherington, *Women in the Earliest Churches*, 43. (3) Another problem raised by scholars to the disadvantage of Pauline authorship is the letter's use of OT material. Perhaps one issue directly connected with our passage will suffice here. Some exegetes have concluded that the use of Gen 2:24 in Eph 5:31 cannot be Pauline, because it is inconsistent with other instances of its use by Paul (e.g., in 1 Cor 6:16). It is alleged that the author of Ephesians applies Gen 2:24 to Christ's spiritual union with the church. Cf. Lincoln, "OT in Ephesians," 48. But such a conclusion has already been challenged. It has been demonstrated that the use of Gen 2:24 in Eph 5:31 is concerned, more than anything else, with mutual love between husband and wife as in God's purpose of creation. See Farla, "New Testament Marriage Texts," 72–75. (4) Another reason sometimes given by scholars for dismissing Pauline authorship is the different view on marriage in the Pauline corpus from that in Ephesians. It has been claimed that Paul was in favor of the unmarried state, which could have led to the dissolving of marriages in his churches. The author of Ephesians tried to stabilize that situation. See Merz, "Wedded Wife," 131–47. However, such a claim regarding Paul lacks biblical support. It has been previously demonstrated by some scholars that Paul, on occasions (e.g., 1 Cor 7), defended the value of marriage. Cf. Farla, "New Testament Marriage Texts," 75–82.

155. Cf. Sanders, *Palestinian Judaism*, 431–32, and Whiteley, "Christology," 51, 55. It is rather doubtful that a form of Jewish Gnosticism could have influenced the letter. Thus pace Batey, "Jewish Gnosticism," 122. See Best, *One Body in Christ*, 172 n. 1.

156. See esp. Barth, *Ephesians 1–3*, 10–31. Cf. Beale, "Eschatological Conception," 36, Sanders, "Pauline Authorship," 9–20, Kostenberger, "Mystery of Christ and the Church," 80 n.2, Ortlund, *Whoredom*, 152 n. 38, and Witherington, *Women in the Earliest Churches*, 55. However, Martin, "in Search of a Life-Setting," 296–301, has proposed Luke as the author of the letter. But various parallels with the Pauline corpus seem more evident.

157. It is an impossible task to discuss the entire text in its depth within the limits of several hundred words. Others have written whole monographs on this particular passage, e.g., Sampley, *Ephesians 5:21–33*.

Ephesians 5:25b-27 in Its Context

The reference to the marriage of Christ and his church comes in the middle of a section (vv. 21–33), where the author admonishes husbands and wives to live in their relationship according to Christian standards. This is part of a larger paraenetic section of the letter starting at 4:1.[158] The recipients of Ephesians are summoned to live according to their new position (4:24), imitating God (5:1), which is walking in love (5:2): the theme developed thereafter.[159] The commands to wives and husbands are therefore a practical application of living in love in a Christian marriage.

Eph 5:22–33 follows the general admonition to Christians to submit to one another in the fear (reverence) of Christ in v. 21.[160] However, later in our passage it is only the wives that are called to submit to their husbands (v. 22), after the example of the church being subject to Christ (v. 24).[161] The husbands, on the other hand, are urged to love their spouses in a way that resembles the self-sacrificial love of Christ towards the church (v. 25). The submission of wives has its basis in the order of creation, as woman derives her origin from man. The husband is the head of his wife, her beginning, and therefore, as Christ (her beginning) is over the church, he has authority over his wife.[162] Κεφαλή refers also to the position of leadership and representation.[163] Thus wives, in the wider context of Eph 5, express their Christian love towards their husbands by submitting to them as their leaders. The husbands have their own task:

---

158. Sampley, *Ephesians 5:21–33*, 9.

159. Ibid., 10.

160. Suski, "Pieśń o miłości Chrystusa," 8, has suggested that vv. 21 and 33 form an inclusion by their use of φόβος. However, this seems insufficient to justify such a conclusion. It is more likely that v. 21 is a heading for the whole section of 5:22—6:9. See Sampley, *Ephesians 5:21–33*, 10.

161. So we agree with Sampley, *Ephesians 5:21–33*, 116–17, that the admonition in v. 21 is directed to wives, children and the slaves within the Haustafel. Husbands are never exhorted to submit to their spouses. Ἀλλήλοις can thus function as a challenge to those who misuse their authority. There is no place for an absolute predominance of one class over another in the Christian household.

162. Bedale, "κεφαλή in the Pauline Epistles," 211–15. Thus the passage does not speak of an "over-lordship." Also Bedale, "The Theology of the Church," 69–72. Cf. Fennema, "Unity in Marriage," 63, who has also denied a notion of 'over-lordship' here. See also Cothenet, *Exégèse et Liturgie*, 241.

163. Culliton, "Body of Christ," 52; Best, *One Body in Christ*, 172.

Marriage of Christ and the Church in Ephesians 5:25b–27

NT exegetes have generally recognized Eph 5:25b–27 as an instance of a developed divine marriage imagery in the NT.[164] They have also suggested that the closest OT parallel to the picture presented here is the first part of Ezek 16.[165] There, Yahweh washed his future wife and bestowed on her royal attire and jewels (vv. 4–13). But it can hardly be concluded that the washing was a prenuptial bath. It was rather cleansing her from the birth blood, which probably symbolized purification from ritual and natural depravation (cf. chapter 3 above). In this sense, the bath took place at the establishment of the covenant between Yahweh and Israel. It resulted in Israel becoming a kingdom of priests (cf. Exod 19:6). In Eph 5:26, the cleansing can refer to purification at the covenant renewal.[166] Therefore we would suggest that the "washing of water" refers more probably to the cleansing act of the Spirit applied to the church,[167] rather than to the rite of baptism.[168] Consequently, ἐν ῥήματι does not

---

164. E.g., Muirhead, "Bride of Christ," 180. Cf. Best, *One Body in Christ*, 172, and Sampley, *Ephesians 5:21–33*, 16. Some have also argued that the verses resemble an early Christian liturgical hymn. Cf. Suski, "Pieśń o miłości Chrystusa," 3–4, and Barth, *Ephesians 4–6*, 622. It is worth noting here that Christ is not explicitly called husband or bridegroom in the passage. Neither is the church called wife or bride. The use of the marriage metaphor is based on the comparison with human husbands and wives.

165. Sampley, *Ephesians 5:21–33*, 131, and Cothenet, *Exégèse et Liturgie*, 245, although not agreeing on his links to the Greek milieu.

166. Promised by God in, e.g., Ezek 36:25 ("I will sprinkle clean water on you... I will cleanse you from all your filthiness and from all your idols" NASB). Cf. Barth, *Ephesians 4–6*, 671, although not agreeing on his entirely futuristic view of Rev 19. See also Brewer, "Three Weddings," 20. Murihead, "Bride of Christ," 181, has objected to the view that a restoration of marriage/covenant is in view.

167. See Sampley, *Ephesians 5:21–33*, 131, 131 n3. The other occurrence of the word λουτρόν in Tit 3:5 points to a bath of regeneration. See also Barth, *Ephesians 4–6*, 689–94. Both, however, have remarked that a further reference to the rite of baptism can be implied. See also Merz, "Wedded Wife," 144–45. She seems to prefer a fully corporate view of the church's baptism.

168. See Batey, *Nuptial Imagery*, 28. He believes that the sum total of individual baptisms is the single cleansing act for the whole church. The sacramental view is supported by, e.g., Schillebeeckx, *Marriage*, 113. Cf. Suski, "Pieśń o miłości Chrystusa," 24.

refer so much to a baptism formula[169] as perhaps to the pronouncement of covenant by Christ over the church (cf. Ezek 16:8).[170]

Nevertheless, the main act of Christ regarding his marriage is giving himself up for the church (Eph 5:25b).[171] By his death, Gentiles could have been included in the "covenants of promise" (cf. 2:11–22). Christ's death was a sacrifice to God, which completely purified his people (5:2; cf. vv. 3–5).[172] As a result, Christians of both Jewish and Gentile origin are the same people of God (2:19), Christ's beloved spouse (5:25).[173] There has been a suggestion that this sacrificial death of Christ is a betrothal gift.[174] On the contrary, it could have been merely an expression of his love for his people[175] and also a remedy to their situation prior to his death. We would like to suggest that the picture could echo the *mohar* payment as far as it was understood in the sense of a gift guaranteeing the wife an inheritance (see chapter 2 above). In fact, Eph 5:5 explains that the inheritance of Christians is the kingdom of Christ and God (cf. 1:11). Moreover, the Holy Spirit has been given as a guarantee of the inheritance (1:14). Yet, scholars have tried to refer to the betrothal and its gift in order to solve problems emerging when a completely new relationship is assumed here: a completely new marriage.[176] But it appears

169. Pace Suski, "Pieśń o miłości Chrystusa," 28.

170. Cf. Barth, *Ephesians 4–6*, 690–91. This can be reminiscent of the covenant formula: "I will be your God and you will be my people" (cf. Exod 6:7).

171. This is a rather evident reference to Christ's crucifixion. Cf. Best, *Essays on Ephesians*, 545.

172. The sacrifice (θυσία) that causes a sweet aroma (εὐωδία) seems to be reminiscent of the burnt offering in the context of atonement. Exod 29:41LXX uses both Greek words in the context of atoning for the altar (cf. v. 37). It is interesting that the altar was to be cleansed by the atonement sacrifices and sanctified by anointment (v. 26). Can this have some link to cleansing and sanctifying the church in Eph 5:26? It is also worth noting that similar terminology to that in Eph 5:2 can also be found concerning sacrifices in connection with atonement for people (cf. Lev 1:4; 2:1–2), peace (salvation/deliverance in the LXX) offering (Lev 3:6–11; 17:3–9), firstfruits offering (Lev 23:13, 18) linked also with atonement (Num 28:26–31), atonement for unintentional sin (Num 15:22–26), and regular daily and monthly offerings (Num 28:3–6; 11–13).

173. We agree with Best, *Essays on Ephesians*, 545, that the marriage (or rather remarriage in the OT context) has taken place at the crucifixion.

174. But Batey, *Nuptial Imagery*, 30, has eagerly stated so.

175. Cf. Sampley, *Ephesians 5:21–33*, 36, 128.

176. So, e.g., Brewer, "Three Weddings," 21–22; also previously Muirhead, "Bride of Christ," 181, who has denied any notion of a marriage restored linked to an everlasting covenant.

that a continuation of God's covenant is in view throughout Ephesians (cf. 2:11–22).[177] Thus the marriage metaphor in chapter 5 should be expected to work within the already established covenant framework. In turn, all the consequences mentioned in vv. 26–27 seem to follow the sacrificial death of Christ. In this sense, they refer to the already accomplished work and not to some future fulfillment assumed to be the marriage proper, which follows a long period of betrothal.[178] The death of Christ has already sanctified, purified and made the church blameless. The subjunctive aorists in vv. 26–27 seem to point to this. The whole emphasis is on the act of Christ on behalf of his people. The beauty of the bride in all her glory probably echoes Ezek 16:10–14 with its mention of Yahweh adorning his wife.[179] However, unpacking the metaphor, it seems that v. 27 is still concerned with purity in a ceremonial and ethical sense (cf. Lev 21:17–23; cf. Eph 1:4).[180] Christ has already presented his church to himself as a result of his death. It is, however, doubtful that he acted in this case as his own best man.[181] Similarly to 2 Cor 11:2, παρίστημι refers to making or rendering.[182] Thus, Christ by his death made the church ceremonially clean, a prerequisite necessary for the organism constituting his body. He provided her with everything she needed as his wife, like Yahweh in Ezek 16.[183] However, at the same time, he nourishes her

---

177. This is so even if one takes Ezek 16 and 36 to be a background to Eph 5:25–27. Both chapters speak rather clearly about a covenant renewal (cf. 16:60–63; 36:8–38). However, Suski, "Pieśń o miłości Chrystusa," 20–21, has argued that Eph 2:11–22 points to the complete discontinuity between the church and OT Israel. Why, then, does Paul refer to the previous exclusion of the Gentiles from God's people in vv. 12, 19?

178. Even regardless of the fact that, as such, the church in history is still not completely free from the sphere of sin. The same was true of Israel in Ezek 16, after her being washed. The language seems to point to some sort of qualification that makes possible the church's relationship with God. Cf. Suski, "Pieśń o miłości Chrystusa," 12. Also Merz, "Wedded Wife," 144–45.

179. Best, *Essays on Ephesians*, 546.

180. See Sampley, *Ephesians 5:21–33*, 70–72, 75. Also Lincoln, *Ephesians*, 377.

181. Pace Cothenet, *Exégèse et Liturgie*, 247.

182. See Sampley, *Ephesians 5:21–33*, 136. It is also noteworthy that this lack of spot or blemish brings to mind the requirement for sacrifices in the OT.

183. Brewer, "Three Weddings," 21, has stated that this one-sidedness in giving marks the difference between the old and new covenants. We cannot agree with this opinion in the context of our discussion on Ezek 16 in chapter 3. However, it is true that Yahweh himself declared that the new covenant would rest completely on his attributes (cf. chapter 3 on Hos 2:19–20). It is also possible that the passage alludes also to Deut 24:1: Christ makes sure that his wife has no indecency. See Sampley, *Ephesians 5:21–33*, 70.

on a daily basis, as a husband should care for his wife (v. 29; cf. Exod 21:10).[184] This sort of care is, in fact, assumed in the marriage covenant union as first mentioned in Gen 2:24 (quoted at v. 31). Becoming "one flesh" symbolizes the constitution of a new familial "bond-ness" together with its responsibilities of caring and obligations of loyalty.[185] In this sense, therefore, the "one flesh" union can refer to Christ and the church, the covenant that exists between them (v. 32).[186]

As indicated earlier, there has been a disagreement among scholars as to the stage of Christ's marriage in our passage: is it just a betrothal or a marriage proper, or perhaps a mixture of the two? As with 2 Cor 11:2–3, they seem to have imposed the categories of human marriage upon the metaphor. They assume that Christ's marriage must have, according to the ancient customs, at least two stages: betrothal and the marriage proper (cf. chapter 2 above). But such an approach completely dismisses the OT context of our titular metaphor. Even as the knowledge of the social institution of marriage was useful in examining the beginnings and development of the metaphor, one needs to pay particular attention to the covenant context in which it functions. It cannot be assumed that every subsequent occurrence of the metaphor in the NT is valid on its own terms, regardless of historical continuity with the OT. In this case, one will quickly notice some inconsistencies. Scholars have often been puzzled over the NT references to the church sometimes as wife and at other times as bride.[187] They have tried to explain this on the basis of the significance of ancient betrothal, which was legally as binding as

---

184. It is more probable that some sort of spiritual nourishment is in view here, rather than a sacramental reference to the Eucharist. Thus pace Cothenet, *Exégèse et Liturgie*, 248.

185. Cf. Hugenberger, *Marriage as a Covenant*, 162–63.

186. Thus the Gnostic idea of the restoration of human wholeness is not implied here. Pace Batey, "Union of Christ and the Church," 270–81, and Batey, "Jewish Gnosticism," 121–27. In our view, Paul's use of Gen 2:24 in Eph 5:31 does not need to be inconsistent with other places in his letters (e.g., 1 Cor 1:16), once the 'one flesh' as a marriage covenant is taken into view. Cf. Schillebeeckx, *Marriage*, 109. There is no substantial difference in Christ having spiritual union with his people in 1 Cor 6 and Eph 5. It does not suddenly change into mere fleshly marital union in Eph 5. Pace Lincoln, "OT in Ephesians," 36, 48. The covenant union is what matters in both contexts. Gen 2:24 in Eph 5:31 is not, therefore, an elaboration on the organic metaphor of the body. Pace Rodgers, "Genesis 2:23 at Ephesians 5:30," 92–94. Gen 2:24 enhances the covenant aspect of both human and divine marital union in the context of the husband's responsibility.

187. Cf. Best, *Essays on Ephesians*, 531.

marriage.[188] But such an explanation ceases to be necessary when one recognizes that in the prophets both the metaphor of betrothal and that of remarriage referred to the covenant renewal at the eschaton. We suggest that this is why the NT can use the imagery of betrothal and marriage interchangeably. The prophecies talked about a time when Yahweh would reveal his salvation through an event similar to the Exodus from Egypt. We believe that, on the basis of the evidence provided so far in this work, the NT authors regarded the event of Jesus the Messiah as the fulfillment of such expectations, even as regards our metaphor. It seems also that those who prefer speaking of the present stage of the church as betrothal (on the basis of vv. 26–27) are influenced by their futuristic approach to Rev 19:7–9.[189] Otherwise, there is nothing in the letter to the Ephesians itself suggesting a future marriage of Christ, presumably at the parousia understood as the end of the space-time universe.

CONCLUSIONS

In this chapter we have examined five alleged instances of Paul's use of the divine marriage metaphor. We have concluded that one of them, namely Rom 7:1–6, does not actually develop the OT metaphor. In fact, to insist otherwise puts one in serious exegetical difficulties.

On the other hand, we have recognized that the remaining four texts, 2 Cor 11:1–6, Gal 4:22—5:1, Rom 9:25–29, and Eph 5:21–33, elaborate on the OT marriage metaphor in a consistent way. We have suggested that Paul believed that the fulfillment of the OT promises and prophecies came in Jesus the Messiah. It was this fulfillment-perspective that allowed the apostle to look at the OT divine marriage traditions as realized in Christ for the church. This is why he, sometimes by allusion (2 Cor 11, Eph 5) and sometimes by direct reference to OT traditions (Gal 4:27, Rom 9:25), could address various issues in familiar congregations by putting them on the map of a wider theological theme of God's covenant/marital love for his people.

We have also noted that the tensions within Paul's view of continuity regarding God's dealing with the ethnic Israel have been solved by the apostle's reflection on the Isaianic remnant idea. The same motif

---

188. Lincoln, *Paradise Now and Not Yet*, 164.

189. Best, *One Body in Christ*, 175 n. 3, in fact, has indicated that Matt 22:1–14; 25:1–13 as well as Rev 19:7–7 and 21:9–11 point to the fact that the marriage belongs to the future. But in his opinion, the marriage in Ephesians 5 already exists.

The Metaphor of Divine Marriage in the Epistles of Paul

also allowed him to explain the Gentiles' inclusion in God's covenant. Following Jesus' example, he pointed to a redefinition of God's chosen people. He has developed and applied the Israel-Gentile theme that was only hinted at in the Gospels.

We have also observed on a number of occasions that the developed marriage metaphor in Paul fits into the wider framework of the exodus motif, which the NT authors used concerning the Christ-event. Therefore we cannot agree with the conclusion of M. D. Hooker, who has suggested that Paul's preoccupation with the Abrahamic covenant made him less interested in the Mosaic covenant and therefore also the exodus theme.[190] On the contrary, the exodus motif created an opportunity for Paul to link various OT traditions into one eschatological picture centered on Christ's accomplished task. However, we should also notice that this motif was still only part of a bigger scheme, viz., God's covenant. Nevertheless, it was exactly the Exodus that pointed to the eschatological salvation ending Israel's exile, the covenant's negative aspect.

Taking into account all the above, it seems that Paul's use of the divine marriage material from OT *testimonies* was in line with the model introduced first by Jesus himself. The apostle has evidently succeeded in presenting its relation to the early Jewish-Gentile church.

The remaining part of this volume will focus on the book of Revelation. We will examine the significance of the divine marriage metaphor for the plot of the book. We will also try to establish the book's dependence or lack of dependence on the data studied so far. This will perhaps allow us to define the stage of development of the divine marriage motif within NT thought.

---

190. See her "Covenantal Nomism," 51–52.

7

The Metaphor of Divine Marriage in the Book of Revelation

INTRODUCTION

HAVING EXAMINED THE MAJORITY of the explicit instances of the divine marriage metaphor in biblical thought, we are finally ready to approach our main focus, i.e., the book of Revelation. This chapter will suggest that the scope of the metaphor in the book is far more wide-ranging than has usually been acknowledged by NT scholars. In treating the metaphor, they have almost exclusively focused upon chapters 19 and 21.[1] However, we will propose that the theme of divine marriage is more central to the book. We will suggest that it is explicit in the last chapters, alluded to in a few chapters in various parts of the book, and possibly echoed throughout the book of Revelation as a whole. We shall discuss also, when necessary, the way in which the motif of new exodus helps us to understand the use of our metaphor in John's prophecy.[2] Finally, we will investigate the relationship between the divine marriage metaphor and the conflict(s) envisioned by the Seer. Thus we will attempt to explain the purpose of the metaphor in John's thought.

---

1. An exception being the recent article by Zimmermann, "Nuptial Imagery," 153–83, in which he suggests that the metaphor can be also traced in Rev 2, 3, and 14.

2. As indicated in chapter 1, the motif of new exodus is present in Revelation. One can consult also Ulfgard, *Feast and Future*, esp. 36–37. Ulfgard argues that the three exodus-linked themes of redemption, judgment and inheritance are intertwined in Revelation. We believe that our two previous chapters have indicated the importance of the exodus motif in the Gospels and in Paul. This implies that the motif provides a common framework for NT writers.

NOTES CONCERNING OUR APPROACH

Prior to engaging with the text of Revelation, we need to discuss some general points about our approach.

We have already acknowledged Revelation's dependence on the Jewish Scriptures in chapter 1. In fact, following the opinion of distinguished scholars, we have observed that OT material is the single most important source of John's ideas. We have indicated that possible extra-biblical sources will be considered when necessary. Moreover, learning from the scholars, we have suggested that although John may have deliberately evoked many OT texts, the study of Revelation's echoing of the Jewish Scriptures need not be constrained by his authorial intention. The study depends, to a large extent, on the reader's knowledge of OT material as well as his abilities to describe the role that OT texts play in their new context. Nevertheless, an awareness of the techniques that John may have used when composing his work can aid in determining the manner in which we should interpret his visions. Likewise, an appreciation of the nature of his visions (relying on "old texts," yet with a prophetic creativity) serves as a reminder that the author did not always strive for unanimity with OT material, but generated certain innovations, which show development in the prophetic thought.

Yet, approaching the Apocalypse, we should bear in mind the way in which Jesus influenced NT authors regarding their hermeneutical techniques. He provided them with a new perspective on OT traditions, which were now being shaped according to his eschatological messianic mission. If we recognize John as a Christian seer (as proposed by a number of scholars referred to in chapter 1 above), we should expect his approach to be in line with this general approach.

Other issues that are important to our understanding of Revelation need to be discussed in the following sections. These include: the genre and form of the book, its *Sitz im Leben*, and its structure, which is linked to the sequence of the events described in it.

Genre and Form

In this section we want to focus on the literary genre of Revelation. It is important to clarify this issue as the book has been exposed to multiple forms of reading by modern scholars. Whilst everybody recognizes that the work contains various symbols, not everybody applies the same method or tools to determine their meaning. This, we suggest, may, in some instances, be the outcome of scholarly confusion regarding the purpose of the genre and form of Revelation. While we do not attempt to provide here a comprehensive definition of Revelation's genre, we shall discuss the issues that seem most important to our understanding of the work.

Some interpreters have proposed an over-simplistic model for understanding the form of Revelation. For them, the book's style resembles that of a Greek drama.[3] However, such a proposal cannot offer much help beyond the suggestion that the Apocalypse uses two groups of characters opposed to each other. We need a more precise working tool.

One author has put forward a somewhat eccentric view, viz., that Revelation should be read in terms of astronomy or even astrology.[4] For him, John was only a Jewish/Christian astral prophet reading the "skyscape" in order to discover divine purposes for the Resurrected Jesus movement.[5] Scholars have rejected Malina's view as doing justice neither to Revelation's descriptions of astrological phenomena nor to the proper genre of the apocalyptic contained in the book.[6] It seems that Malina has not paid proper attention to the meaning of symbolic language in the Apocalypse. Scholarly consent rather assumes historical correspondence for the symbols used by John. Caird may be seen as representative of this approach,

> The writers [of apocalypses] believed that every earthly person, institution, and event had a heavenly equivalent, so that a seer, transported to heaven in an ecstatic rapture, could see enacted in the symbols of heavenly drama the counterpart of earthly events, past, present, and future.[7]

Thus,

> . . . in order to explain an apocalypse, we must first identify the earthly realities to which the heavenly symbols correspond, and

---

3. Chavasse, *Bride of Christ*, 90.
4. Malina, "Wedding of the Lamb," 75–76.
5. Ibid., 76. Also Malina, *Genre and Message of Revelation*, xv.
6. See, e.g., Aune, *Revelation 1–5*, lxxxix.
7. Caird, *Revelation*, 9.

then see how by the use of this symbolism the author has tried to interpret earthly history.[8]

This comment of Caird restrains us from adopting Malina's views. Furthermore, recognizing the importance of analyzing the book of Revelation's symbolism in its ancient context, we cannot engage in the pictorial reading of the book characteristic of the feminist approach, represented by such scholars as Tina Pippin.[9] Such an approach seems overly concerned with imposing modern ideologies on ancient texts.

Other exegetes, however, have paid due attention to the three different literary forms present in John's work: apocalyptic (1:1), prophetic (1:3), and epistolary (1:4–6; 22:6–7, 18–19). Hence, Bauckham concludes that "Revelation seems to be an apocalyptic prophecy in the form of a circular letter to seven churches in the Roman province of Asia."[10]

The least problematic element in this statement is the epistolary element. There has not been a scholar, it seems, who does not recognize the prologue, epilogue, and addresses to the churches in Revelation as epistolary. The major difficulty in reading the book emerges from understanding the apocalyptic in Revelation. Some scholars have assumed that the genre is primarily concerned with eschatological events predicting a Christian future beyond the sphere of history.[11] However this notion has been challenged in a thorough study of the apocalyptic by Rowland. He has argued that the apocalyptic was concerned with revealing divine plans for contemporary history and thus relating it both to the past and the future.[12] Literature of this kind cannot be identified with a form of eschatology understood to be describing future hope alone.[13]

Helpful as it is, Rowland's work does not discuss important differences between John's apocalypse and other earlier and contemporary Jewish apocalypses. The tendency to impose meanings from those

8. Ibid., 10.

9. For samples of Pippin's pictorial reading see, e.g., Pippin, "Eros and the End," 193–210; or her "The Heroine and the Whore," 67–82. For a critique of this approach see Paul, "Image, Symbol, and Metaphor," 134.

10. Bauckham, *Theology of Revelation*, 2.

11. This approach was popular among a group of commentators associated with Dallas Theological Seminary in the latter part of twentieth century, commonly called dispensational premillennialists. However, a more moderate approach of this sort can be discerned in Mounce, *Revelation*. Cf. Beale, *Revelation*, 46–48.

12. Rowland, *Open Heaven*, esp. 14, 189, cf. 9–10, 38.

13. Ibid., 2.

apocalypses onto John's visions can be observed in various commentaries.[14] However, some scholars have argued that John's Apocalypse has a particular character that distinguishes it from the standard Jewish apocalypses. Vogelgesang has claimed that its Christology, ecclesiology, particular approach to *merkavah* traditions, anti-esotericism, epistolary form, and its claim to be a prophecy make Revelation quite distinct from other apocalypses of that time.[15] In addition, Bauckham has argued that John's knowledge of non-canonical Jewish apocalypses is a dubious thesis.[16] Since others also recognize John to be a Christian author,[17] we would maintain that the Christian character of his Apocalypse needs to be appropriately acknowledged when interpreting his visions. One simply cannot assume that John's interests were the same as those in contemporary Jewish apocalypses.[18]

Finally, we need to discuss the relation of the Apocalypse to OT prophecy. We have indicated in chapter 1 that John imitated earlier prophetic traditions. A number of scholars, however, have tried to identify distinctions between the two genres. Beasley-Murray has written,

> As in prophecy, the great theme of apocalyptic writings was the coming of the day of the Lord and the kingdom of God. But the doctrine became more systematized, even more transcendent, and reflection on the relation of that day to the process of history led to the formulation of a kind of philosophy of history, of which the all important factor was God's sovereign purpose working towards its triumphant end despite the resistance of evil powers. Unlike prophecy, apocalyptic was literary rather than oral, composed in longer prose episodes rather than in short poetic oracles.[19]

---

14. This is evident when identifying Babylon with Rome. E.g., Beale, *Revelation*, 18–19.

15. Vogelgesang, "Ezekiel in Revelation," 2, 12, 297–308, 393.

16. Bauckham, *Climax of Prophecy*, xi.

17. Cf. Schüssler-Fiorenza, *Vision of a Just World*, 49, and Yarbro Collins, *Crisis and Catharsis*, 31, who acknowledge the Christian character of the book. Indeed, John the Seer understood himself as a Christian prophet. See Schüssler-Fiorenza, "Structure of Revelation," 355.

18. It is possible that Christians and Jews went different ways soon after the destruction of Jerusalem temple in 70 CE. Cf. Gentry, *Before Jerusalem Fell*, 229–31. See also the list of scholars supporting this view in Gentry's footnotes on the indicated pages. Also, Robinson, *Redating the New Testament*, 227.

19. Beasley-Murray, *Revelation*, 14. Cf. Bauckham, *Theology of Revelation*, 6, who believes that the apocalyptic is a vehicle of prophecy in Revelation.

Thus his major distinction focuses on the literary as opposed to the oral, character of apocalyptic. This is somewhat unfortunate given the instances of written prophecy (see esp. Jer 36:2, 10, 32; in fact, all biblical prophecy available to us has come to us in a literary form). Beale has offered a more helpful distinction,

> Too much distinction has typically been drawn between the apocalyptic and prophetic genres. Indeed, some OT books combine the two to one degree or another. Apocalyptic should not be seen as too different from prophecy, though it contains a heightening and more intense clustering of literary and thematic traits found in prophecy.[20]

This certainly represents a kind of moderate approach to Revelation's genre, though there have been other researchers who have viewed the book exclusively as prophecy.[21] Their voices are undoubtedly of great importance to the exegete who needs to be reminded that NT apocalyptic does form a sort of continuity with OT prophetic thought.[22] In fact, John understands himself as a prophet, not an apocalypticist.[23] Thus, according to Fekkes, his use of the Greek word ἀποκάλυψις in 1:1 points more to a general description of all that follows as divine revelation rather than being a technical term signifying the genre of the book.[24] In general, this approach is a heavy counter-balance to the arguments of scholars classifying Revelation as reflecting the genre of other non-canonical "apocalyptic" and even political writings.

And yet, whatever closeness there exists between the prophecy of John and other canonical prophetic books, it seems that a simple distinction between them can be drawn regarding their focus and purpose. It appears that the book of Revelation displays a distinctive reliance upon metaphors to describe the heavenly significance of the earthly reality together with the events of history.[25] This is not very different from the

---

20. Beale, *Revelation*, 37. He suggests (pp. 37, 50) that the word *apocalypse* in Rev 1:1 resembles Dan 2:28–30, 45, where the idea of apocalypse is linked to that of a prophetic revelation. Cf. Newman, "Fallacy of the Domitian Hypothesis," 133.

21. Chilton, *Days of Vengeance*, 27. See also Hill, *New Testament Prophecy*, 70–93.

22. Fekkes, *Prophetic Traditions in Revelation*, 81. This continuity concerns mainly the new exodus motif associated in NT prophecy with the Christ event.

23. Ibid., 48.

24. Ibid.

25. See Wright, *Millennium Myth*, 30, 35–36. Cf. Wright, *NTPG*, 282, 290.

prophetic. It, rather, intensifies the prophetic imagery, especially with regard to visions of heaven. Therefore the prophetic can be a natural context, in which the meaning of apocalyptic metaphors can be established. It also can be helpful in determining the time references of John's Apocalypse. Thus the terminology of the 'end' does not automatically have to be applied in a literal cosmic sense to the closure of the space-time universe, as if in contradistinction to its prophetic antecedents.[26] It can rather point to events associated with divine visitation at a significant point in history.[27] Moreover, if prophecy is taken as the context for the Apocalypse, one can expect to find references to God's covenant within it.[28] We have already pointed to the significance of the exodus motif in the NT as a major theme linked with God's covenant. But, Revelation's covenantal interest will be discussed below in the two sections relating to its *Sitz im Leben* and structure. The following case study should verify the observations.

Sitz im Leben

The vast majority of scholars have dated the composition of the book of Revelation towards the end of Domitian's reign (95–96 CE). They have usually argued that the major conflict presented in the book was Rome's hostility towards Christians and the latter's hope for a reversal of their fate by divine intervention. However, there exists no agreement among these academics as to the details of this reconstruction. We shall consider the validity of their proposals now.

Scholars have generally agreed that the Neronic persecution of Christians was confined to Rome and was not strictly religious in its nature. It commenced because Caesar wanted to find someone to blame for the great fire in the Empire's capital.[29] Christians just happened to be the least popular group amongst the populace of Rome. Yet, other scholars have argued that a widespread persecution of the church happened under Domitian[30] and that Christians suffered because of their refusal

---

26. Cf. Wright, *NTPG*, 298.

27. See also Caird, *Language and Imagery*, 243–71.

28. Chapter 3 of this book in particular has acknowledged OT prophets' interests in the covenant.

29. Beale, *Revelation*, 5.

30. Cothenet, *Exégèse et Liturgie*, 252.

to participate in the worship of the emperor.[31] These notions, together with statements by Irenaeus, are believed to establish the case.[32] But yet, scholars opting for the late date have not found enough historical evidence for a persecution of Christians under Domitian.[33] Consequently, some of them have abandoned the persecution theory and turned to other arguments to accommodate the late dating.

Yarbro Collins has advanced a thesis that John dealt only with a perceived crisis, which many of his fellow Christians did not see.[34] According to her, John "hoped to reinforce whatever hostility to Rome his readers might already have had and to awaken an anti-Roman attitude in those who were neutral or even open to Roman culture."[35] The Seer wanted to intensify his readers' emotions and give them hope for public vindication and thus compensation for their relatively disadvantaged situation.[36] Bauckham has followed a somewhat similar line of reasoning. He believes that Revelation perceives the Roman Empire as an oppressive system. For him, the oppression is characterized mainly by political idolatry and economic exploitation.[37] Hence, Revelation becomes a political and economic critique of the imperial system.[38]

Others have advanced alternative solutions to the implied crisis in John's Apocalypse. Slater has argued for local Asian harassment and discrimination against Christians. He explains,

---

31. Metzger, *Breaking the Code*, 16. He claims that no earlier emperor demanded this kind of worship. Beale, *Revelation*, sees internal evidence for the imperial cult in Rev 13:4–8; 15–16; 14:9–11; 15:2; 16:2; 19:20; 20:4. Bauckham, *Theology of Revelation*, 38, views Revelation as "the most powerful piece of political resistance literature from the period of the early Empire." But the persecution of Christians was still to come.

32. The late second century CE statement of Irenaeus is regarded as referring to the date of Revelation's composition. Irenaeus, *Against Heresies* 5:30:3; also Eusebius, *Ecclesiastical History* 3:18:3

33. Yarbro Collins, *Crisis and Catharsis*, 77; Wengst, *Pax Romana*, 119. Also Moberly, "When Was Revelation Conceived?," 377, who does not support the late date view.

34. *Crisis and Catharsis*, 77.

35. Ibid., 111.

36. Ibid., 143, 154, 165.

37. *Climax of Prophecy*, xiii. Cf. Kraybill, *Commerce in John's Apocalypse*, 147–49.

38. Bauckham, "Economic Critique of Rome," 47–90, which became chapter 10 in *Climax of Prophecy*, 338–83.

> While Domitian might not have demanded worship, or even expected it, Asian pagans themselves promoted the imperial cult and would have been adamant concerning its observance.[39]

Slater assumes that certain Asian pagans turned against Christians in their zeal for the imperial cult.

It seems, then, that the majority of scholars have regarded the main crisis in Revelation to be the result of Rome's imperial policy.[40] We want to argue, however, that this opinion does not take into account other issues involved in the crisis described by John.

First of all, some scholars have acknowledged that this popular view regarding Revelation's *Sitz im Leben* relies mainly on Irenaeus's testimony.[41] Yet, the testimony does not prove to be historically reliable because its author is not consistent.[42] Even if Irenaeus' statement in *Against Heresies* 5:30:3, that John's Revelation appeared at the end of Domitian's reign, were accepted as historical evidence, the statement could still have referred only to a re-disclosure or re-issue of the book.[43] Recognizing the difficulties created by the external evidence, some scholars urged their colleagues to concentrate more on internal evidence for establishing Revelation's *Sitz im Leben*.[44]

Nevertheless, the difficulties are not solved by simply taking this last reflection into account. It is still argued that the context of the Apocalypse is Rome's attitude towards Christianity. Beale has even gone so far as to claim that the use of the name "Babylon" for Rome is the strongest piece of internal evidence for a post-70 CE date of the com-

---

39. Slater, "Social Setting of Revelation," 238.

40. It is noteworthy that Moberly, "When Was Revelation Conceived?," although opting for the earlier date for Revelation, completely rejected any conflict between Jews and Christians in the main vision of Revelation (chapters 4–20).

41. Marshall, *Parables of War*, 88–89, 95.

42. Gentry, *Before Jerusalem Fell*, 45–67, who dedicates a whole chapter to showing Irenaeus's historical unreliability. Also Newman, "Fallacy of the Domitian Hypothesis," 138–39. Newman (136) explains that Irenaeus's approach to Revelation is *continuous-historical* or *allegorical* rather than *contemporary-historical*. Irenaeus's goal was to use Revelation in order to demonstrate the fate of apostates in all generations and in particular in the context of Christians being attracted to gnosticism.

43. Smith, *Redating the Revelation*, 57. See also Aune, *Revelation 1–5*, lviii, who suggests that the final edition of Revelation was completed toward the end of Domitian's reign but that the first edition was composed in the 60s.

44. E.g., Wilson, "Problem of the Domitianic Date," 598.

position.⁴⁵ However, the name's meaning is established mainly on the basis of non-canonical post-70 CE apocalyptic literature (4 Ezra 3:1–2; 28–31; 2 Baruch 10:1–3; 11:1; 67:7; Sibylline Oracles 5.143, 159–60).⁴⁶ We have already indicated that such a method of studying Revelation overlooks important dissimilarities between it and the apocalypses. But commentators have still maintained that such verses as Rev 17:18 can be understood appropriately only when applied to the first-century Rome.⁴⁷ This argument, of course, is used to support the late date of the book. However, we would suggest that there exists evidence to challenge this common notion.

If one agrees that the letters to the seven churches "set the terms in which the whole Apocalypse must be read,"⁴⁸ he is struck by the realization that the epistles do not refer to a Roman persecution.⁴⁹ They do mention the Roman Empire once at 3:10 (οἰκουμένη),⁵⁰ but apparently the main opposition comes from some non-messianic Jews (2:8–10; 3:7, 9).⁵¹ We think this evidence weakens the common argument concerning the conflict with Rome in Revelation. Moreover, Beagley's observation regarding the name 'Babylon' exposes this belief to further doubt,

> Later Christian writers do apply the name "Babylon" to Rome, but this may be a later development: they may have taken the term over from the Jews . . . or they may have been applying Revelation 17–18 to Rome, even though that was not its primary intention—just as modern writers and preachers sometimes designate present-day nations as "Babylon."⁵²

45. *Revelation*, 25. See also Friesen, *Imperial Cultus and the Apocalypse*, 138.
46. Beale, *Revelation*, 18.
47. Boxall, "Many Faces of Babylon," 54.
48. Knight, "Christ of Revelation 5:6," 44. Cf. Beale, *Revelation*, 132–33, who follows the earlier conviction of Farrer, *Revelation*, 83–86.
49. So Beagley, *Church's Enemies*, 34.
50. Cf. Bell, "Date of John's Apocalypse," 102. He shows that the Empire was shaken during the turbulent year of 69 CE, when the Empire experienced great political instability. Cf. Gentry, *Before Jerusalem Fell*, 142–43, who remarks that the contemporary civilized world, i.e., the Roman Empire, was the οἰκουμένη.
51. See Gentry, *Before Jerusalem Fell*, 222. Also Yarbro Collins, "Revelation," I: 392. She argues that the mention of 'synagogue of Satan' at Rev 2:9 points to the local Jewish community, which rejects Jesus as the Messiah. This resembles the Qumran community's polemic against other Jews who did not join their new covenant society.
52. Beagley, *Church's Enemies*, 101. He follows Hunzinger, C.~H. "Babylon als Deckname für Rom und die Datierung des I Petrusbriefes." In *Gottes Wort und*

Furthermore, it is an often overlooked fact that the statement of 18:20, 24 concerning Babylon would better suit Jerusalem, in line with early Christian witnesses concerning the place of prophetic martyrdom (e.g., Matt 23:37; Luke 13:33–34; cf. 11:49–51).[53] If John is allowed to be a Christian prophet, somebody who drew from Jesus' tradition, this is demonstrated to be a plausible claim. Even if we follow those who take the "harlot-woman" of chapters 17–18 to be the same city as Sodom and Egypt in 11:8, the ultimate conclusion would be that Jerusalem is the city referred to.[54] These considerations seem to imply that scholars have tended to assume much in their claims concerning "Babylon." Their arguments often run like this: because in the sixth century BCE Babylon destroyed Jerusalem, and in 70 CE it was Rome that destroyed Jerusalem, therefore Rome is symbolically Babylon.[55] However, we believe that this argument fails to explain the use of harlot imagery for Rome in a satisfactory manner.[56] There is, at least, a possibility that if John had OT prophetic development in mind, for a city to be called a "harlot" would require her to have had an earlier covenant relationship with God. This was surely not the case with Rome,[57] but it certainly was the case with Jerusalem. In the OT, only two other cities are ever referred to as "harlots": Tyre (Isa 23:15–17) and Nineveh (Nah 3:4), and that most likely

---

Gottes Land. Festschrift W. Hertzberg, edited by H. G. Reventlow, 67–77. Göttingen: Vandenhoeck und Ruprecht, 1965.

53. See Vos, *Synoptic Traditions in the Apocalypse*, 162. Although Vos acknowledges a close link between Rev 18:24 and Luke 11:50, he argues that John had changed the reference of the symbolic desolation of the great city to Rome.

54. Bauckham, *Climax of Prophecy*, 172, has to work hard to deny the most obvious reference to Jerusalem at 11:8 in order to uphold his point concerning Rome. In his opinion, Rome took upon itself the role of a harlot city by persecuting Jesus' witnesses. He does not explain, however, which persecutions he has in mind. Likewise, Beale, *Revelation*, 25, reads 11:8 as referring to Rome only because the verse itself encourages a figurative reading. This he does even in spite of the fact that some lines later he acknowledges that Israel was called or compared to Sodom and Egypt by the prophets (Isa 1:10; 3:9; Jer 23:14; Ezek 16:44–58).

55. So Beale, *Revelation*, 19.

56. Bauckham, *Climax of Prophecy*, 346, has argued that Rome was being compared to OT Tyre. He suggests that Tyre's commercial enterprise was regarded as prostitution. Thus, it is valid to describe Rome's commerce as prostitution. We suggest that this proposal ignores Tyre's previous covenant relationship with Israel's God as well as the OT context of the national-prostitution symbolism. See the argument below.

57. Cf. Terry, *Biblical Apocalyptics*, 435.

in the context of their previous covenant relationship with Yahweh.[58] In addition, a more natural contrast between Rev 21–22 and 17–18, which many scholars tend to overlook, would be between the *new* Jerusalem and the *old* Jerusalem, not between the *new* Jerusalem and the *old* Rome. This suggestion will be supported further by our case study below.

There is also a possible solution to the problematic verse 18 in Rev 17. Before pointing to it, however, we need to notice that verse 15 could be equally difficult because of the meaning of the term "waters." The picture in v. 15 suggests that the woman has some kind of dominance over many ethnic groups. Therefore, it is not surprising that many see Rome in this vision as one with great authority in the first century CE. But this does not have to be the precise meaning of the text. The 'sitting' in v. 15 may point to the inter-dependence of the Harlot and the nations concerning trade, not to political control over them.[59] It is therefore possible that the verse has commercial overtones, which John elaborates on in chapter 18. It is, of course, a widely recognized fact that Rome's trade was on an enormous scale.[60] The word "exploitation" would perhaps be more appropriate in this case, as the flow of goods was virtually a one-way traffic: all the best merchandise of the provinces was brought into the city.[61] In exchange, the provinces gained the militarily secured *Pax Romana*, but this often through the bloodshed of pacification rather than by the creation of a political solution.[62] Yet, only a small number of exegetes have recognized the importance of Judea, with its capital, in the commerce system of the first century CE. Nevertheless, evidence presented may well support the "Jerusalem" interpretation of Rev 17:15. Judea was in charge of Oriental and African trade by the late second century BCE.[63] By the late first century BCE, Asia Minor had to rely on this trade and transit-trade for their luxury and more ordinary wares.[64]

---

58. Cf. Chilton, *Days of Vengeance*, 424 n2. It seems that Tyre was brought into the covenant with Israel and God during the Golden Age of David and Solomon (2 Sam 5:11; 1 Kgs 5:1–12; 2 Chr 2:11–12; cf. Amos 1:9; Ezek 28:12–19). Nineveh came to a relationship with Yahweh under Jonah's ministry (Jonah 3:3–10).

59. See Terry, *Biblical Apocalyptics*, 427.

60. See esp. Wengst, "Babylon the Great," 193. Cf. Bauckham, *Climax of Prophecy*, 350–71, for a detailed list of allegedly Rome's cargoes.

61. Cf. Wengst, *Pax Romana*, 36.

62. Ibid., 13.

63. Safrai and Stern, *Jewish People in the First Century*, II: 668.

64. Ibid.

Even Rome depended on Jerusalem's commerce for such products as dates, opobalsam, and certain varieties of vegetable.⁶⁵ In addition, Jews of the Diaspora were also significant contributors to Jerusalem's wealth.⁶⁶ It was only the destruction of the Temple in 70 CE that changed Judea's economic situation,

> Undoubtedly the destruction of Jerusalem dealt a shattering blow to the Jewish economy, eliminating the principal hub of Jewish commerce and crafts and the community's largest source of internal and external income.⁶⁷

It is noticeable that the OT itself praised Jerusalem some centuries earlier for its fame among the nations due to its riches (Lam 1:1; Ezek 16:14; cf. Deut 15:6). It seems that the city gathered considerable wealth in times preceding its final Temple's fall (e.g., Luke 21:1; Mark 13:1; cf. Mark 12:41; cf. Josephus *Ant* xv.11).⁶⁸ It also attracted Jews and proselytes from "every nation under heaven" as the centre of religious worship (Acts 2:5, 9–11). Therefore it would not be strange to view Jerusalem as of prominent position among the nations of its contemporary world.

However, the main obstacle to the "Jerusalem view" seems to be 17:18 with its claim that the city reigns over τῶν βασιλέων τῆς γῆς. But we would propose that the Greek phrase does not need to be read in a universal sense as implying the whole world. Bauckham has suggested that a similar phrase at 18:9 does not have to refer literally to the kings of the world, but can signify the local ruling class (cf. Ps 2:2).⁶⁹ In fact, the use of the phrase οἱ βασιλεῖς τῆς γῆς in Ps 2:2 and Acts 4:26–27 would imply that it can designate the leaders of the Jewish land.⁷⁰ In this sense, the phrase can refer to the group of people mentioned in the

---

65. Ibid., II: 675–76.

66. By paying the temple tax. Ibid., II: 677–78.

67. Ibid., II: 698.

68. Ibid., II: 683. The Antiquities of the Jews xv.11 in Whiston, *Works of Josephus*, 977–84.

69. *Climax of Prophecy*, 372.

70. See Russell, *Parousia*, 494. In fact the Greek γῆ in the LXX (standing for ארץ, in the MT) often refers to the country of Israel/land of Canaan (e.g., Neh 9:15; Jer 6:12; 10:18; Hos 4:1; Joel 1:2, 14; 2:1; cf. Rev 3:10). Cf. Beagley, *Church's Enemies*, 35. Acts 4:25–27 does not exclude the participation of pagans (Pilate and the Gentiles) in the plot against Jesus. However, even Pontius Pilate was a ruler residing in the land of Palestine (cf. v. 26). Thus, one can assume that the leaders of the Jewish land are meant in the phrase: Jews in collaboration with the Roman authorities.

first part of Rev 6:15. Therefore it is possible that Rev 17:18 has in view Jerusalem ruling over the leaders of the land. Or else, Rev 17:18 can be viewed "in terms of contemporary Jewish or Roman opinion concerning it [Jerusalem], its presumed status in the eyes of Yahweh, its anticipated future political situation, or even a combination of all these."[71] This option gains even more support in light of the biblical conviction that the fate of the whole world depended on Israel's faithfulness to her God (1 Kgs 10:24; Isa 2:10–22; cf. Rom 2:17–24).[72] Whichever of the two options is regarded as the more plausible, it seems that internal evidence does not necessarily favor the view that Rev 17:18 refers to Rome as the great harlotrous city.

In the light of the above discussion, Wright's observation regarding Jerusalem as Babylon in the Gospels[73] may well be valid for Revelation's symbol of the great harlotrous city. In this case, the *Sitz im Leben* of the Apocalypse could reflect the events leading to God's judgment upon Jerusalem, with all that it represented. The old Jerusalem had become an enemy of God's people: their new Pharaoh/Egypt (11:8).[74] This is evident from the Christian tradition preserved in the Acts of the Apostles (e.g., 2:14, 23; 3:1, 3:12—4:21; 5:17–18, 27–40; 6:7—7:1, 54–60; 12:1–4; 21:27–31; 23:12–15). Jerusalem had become guilty of the rejection and murder of the Messiah and thus deserved God's judgment.[75] She had violated the covenant with her God and so would be punished according to the covenant stipulations for disobedience (Lev 26:14–19; Deut 28:15–68), and harlotry (Rev 18:3). Chilton has indicated that Revelation resembles the sevenfold covenant judgment announced in Lev 26:18, 21, 24, 28, "by speaking of four sevenfold judgments in Leviticus 26, God is saying that a full, complete judgment will come upon the land of Israel for its sins."[76] John's Apocalypse seems to follow this pattern insofar as it

---

71. Beagley, *Church's Enemies*, 108.

72. So Chilton, *Days of Vengeance*, 443.

73. Wright, *JVG*, 323, 356 n.137. See also Goulder, "Annual Cycle of Prophecies," 342, who believes that Revelation follows the traditional order of the dominical 'Little Apocalypse' in the Synoptics.

74. Beagley, *Church's Enemies*, 28. According to Beagley, Rom 11:25 compared with 9:17–18 supports the claim that hardening of some Jews resembles that of Pharaoh, preceding the Exodus from Egypt. Cf. Wright, *Romans*, 688, who links Rom 11:25 via 11:7 with 9:14–25. The issue at stake is a Pharaoh-like hardening (cf. ibid., 639).

75. Chilton, *Days of Vengeance*, 40.

76. Ibid., 16.

presents four declarations of the sevenfold judgment coming upon the system represented by Jerusalem (viz., the letters to the seven churches, the opening of the seven seals, the sounding of the seven trumpets, and the outpouring of the seven bowls).[77] Even though this view still awaits a constructive scholarly critique,[78] it offers a plausible explanation of the relationship between Revelation and the covenant traditions. Chilton remarks,

> When the covenantal context of the prophecy is ignored, the message St. John sought to communicate is lost, and Revelation becomes nothing more than a vehicle for advancing the alleged expositor's eschatological theories.[79]

But Revelation is not only a story about the judgment on God's unfaithful people. It also seems to be an account of the ultimate vindication of God's Messiah and his people through God's salvific act, as predicted in the Gospels.[80] In our opinion, Wright's explanation of Mark 13:24–25, 27 sheds further light on Revelation's *Sitz im Leben*,

> The days of Jerusalem's destruction would be looked upon as days of cosmic catastrophe. The known world would go into convulsions: power struggles and *coups d'état* would be the order of the day; the *pax Romana*, the presupposition of "civilized" life throughout the then Mediterranean world, would collapse into chaos. In the midst of that chaos Jerusalem would fall. The "son of man" would thereby be vindicated.[81]

If one agrees with this suggestion, a further remark could be made concerning John's writing his Apocalypse to the churches in Asia Minor. An important factor is the scholarly consensus that the address to the Asian

---

77. Ibid., 17.

78. The observations of Bauckham, *Climax of Prophecy*, 31, and Beale, *Revelation*, 60, could support Chilton's conclusion.

79. *Days of Vengeance*, 11.

80. Cf. Wright, *NTPG*, 459–60, 462.

81. *JVG*, 362. Cf. *NTPG*, 278 n.140, where Wright seems to assume some kind of parallelism between Mark 13 and parts of Revelation. In *JVG*, 358 n.141, Wright notes that Mark 13 and Rev 17–18 are regarded by some scholars as parallels. In *Millennium Myth*, 29, he states that "some have argued cogently of late that the passage [Rev 18:2–3] really refers to the fall of Jerusalem in AD 70." We assume that only Wright himself could finally settle the question of how cogent this is to his mind.

churches extends to the church universal.[82] Seven is a number signifying fullness/completeness in Revelation.[83] Thus the seven churches of Asia may represent the whole church of that region or even the whole church in the contemporary world. However, it seems that there is a more particular explanation of the issue. If one agrees with Rowland's observation that apocalyptic is a demonstration of God's activity on the arena of human history seen as a whole,[84] the address to the Asian churches can anticipate their particular role in the new covenant established now in Christ. In the context of impending judgment on Jerusalem, the church in Asia Minor (once a pagan territory) would testify to the fact that the Christian Temple is not associated with the Jewish capital anymore (Mark 14:58; John 2:21; cf. Rev 21:22).[85] For Christians, even Jerusalem is not tied to this geographical location (Rev 21:2, 10). As Paul has remarked in Gal 4:26, the Jerusalem that the Christian belongs to is in God's realm "above" and, therefore, the Christian is free from the system of Jewish worship (cf. chapter 6 above). Thus, addressing Revelation to the Asian churches can be viewed as a next step in early Christianity's split from earthly Jerusalem toward the realm in Christ which spreads far beyond the boundaries of Israel.

However, there seems to be another, temporal reason for the Asian address. It has been widely recognized that the Asian churches experienced antagonism in their local communities at the time of John's ministry. Rev 2:9 and 3:9 suggest that the enmity emerged from the synagogues of those Jews who rejected Jesus as the Messiah.[86] But Rev 3:10 indicates that the Roman Empire was somehow involved in this harassment.

82. Thus Charles, *Revelation*, I: 24–25, considers that the location of seven churches would help spread the messages through the rest of the Province. Bauckham, *Theology of Revelation*, 2, believes that the seven letters, as well as the entire book, were circular and reached all seven churches. Cf. Aune, *Revelation 1–5*, 119. Schüssler-Fiorenza, *Vision of a Just World*, 53, has argued that the book was addressed to the whole church in Asia Minor.

83. Bauckham, *Theology of Revelation*, 26.

84. *Open Heaven*, 189.

85. Cf. Wright, *JVG*, 333–36, 493–94, 497–501, demonstrates that the Synoptics more than once refer to the establishment of a new temple by Jesus, which would follow the destruction of the corrupt temple in Jerusalem. John 2:21 further explains that Jesus' body would become the new Temple. It seems likely that Rev 21:22 can stand in the same tradition. See Mathewson, *New Heaven*, 115.

86. Cf. again Yarbro Collins, "Revelation," 1: 392, and Beagley, *Church's Enemies*, 31–36.

We are well aware that most NT scholars argue that the oppression came almost exclusively from the supporters of Rome, be it Roman authorities or local people supportive of the imperial system. If, however, the evidence in the seven letters is considered carefully, a somewhat different picture begins to emerge. Chilton explains,

> The Roman persecution came about through the Jews' instigation and connivance, as the Book of Acts constantly informs us. Jerusalem's whole history, in fact, was one of relentless persecution of the godly, and especially of the prophets (Matt. 21:33–44; 23:29–35; Acts 7:51–53).[87]

Thus, we believe, if the Apocalypse is compared with apostolic traditions recorded in the Gospels and Acts, the book's internal evidence can modify the majority opinion. Consequently, another purpose of writing Revelation to the churches in Asia would be to reassure them that faithfulness in the midst of persecution is still worthwhile, given the divine perspective on their history.[88]

In conclusion to this section, we do acknowledge that there are various approaches to interpreting the Apocalypse's content. For some scholars, it is important to start with economic, political or their peculiar ideological interests. We admit that such approaches have their appropriate place in the academic discipline of interpretation of ancient texts, as the reader's perspective is always important in this enterprise (cf. chapter 1 above). However, we would like to attempt to examine Revelation's visions with particular reference to the second exodus motif in the context of redemption history. The motif, associated with divine covenant, was present in and developed by other early Christian traditions, which were acknowledged as authoritative by the church in history. In this section, we have shown that taking the traditions into account, one may view Revelation's *Sitz im Leben* as concerned with Jerusalem's fall, even from a pre-70 CE perspective. Likewise, the main conflict presented in the book can be regarded as caused by the non-messianic Jews, who instigated the persecution of Christians among adherents of the Roman imperial system. However, at the same time, the Apocalypse seems to be concerned with a hope for early Christians: vindication alongside their Leader at the time when Jerusalem's system,

---

87. *Days of Vengeance*, 431–32.
88. This is still in line with general suggestion by Rowland, *Open Heaven*, 189.

regarded as corrupt, would be judged by God amidst the collapse of Roman order (cf. 1:7).[89] The book's internal evidence seems to indicate that the events were expected to happen within a short space of time of the visionary experience of John (1:1, 3; 2:16; 3:11; 22:6, 7, 10, 12, 20).[90] We believe that these considerations and our previous discoveries regarding the metaphor of divine marriage in biblical thought may help us in interpreting various visions in the book.

Structure

The last point to discuss, before we examine the text of Revelation for our metaphor, is the structure of John's work. Our aim is not to provide a detailed structure of the book, but rather to indicate the way the structure relates to the sequence of the events described by the Visionary. We would also like to suggest that the structure of the book supports its covenantal setting.

There have been tendencies in the past to try to divide the book according to particular marking phrases, such as "in the Spirit."[91] Thus scholars have usually arrived at structures that pointed to four major divisions of Revelation (1:10; 4:2; 17:3; 21:10). However, this approach has been criticized for failing to do justice to the way the book brings together its various units by the method of intercalation.[92] Consequently, scholars have preferred to elaborate a chiastic scheme of the Apocalypse. This, however, frequently reveals something of their ideological interests. Stefanovic's proposal is no exception,

---

89. See Chilton, *Days of Vengeance*, 43. Gentry, *Before Jerusalem Fell*, 121–23. The theme of 1:7 is repeated throughout the book (2:5, 16, 25; 3:3; 11, 20; 16:15; 22:7, 12, 20). OT background to the cloud coming is Pss 18:7–15; 104:3; Isa 19:1; cf. Joel 2:1; Nah 1:2ff.; and Zeph 1:14, 15, and in the NT Matt 24:30; 26:64. For such cosmic catastrophe in the Synoptics see Wright, *JVG*, 362. Cf. *NTPG*, 278 n. 140.

90. See Gentry, *Before Jerusalem Fell*, 134–42. Thus Revelation is not a 'telescopic' vision of history as Beasley-Murray suggested (*Revelation*, 52).

91. See, e.g., Wallis, "Coming of the Kingdom," 15. Also Smith, "Structure of Revelation," 392.

92. Schüssler-Fiorenza, "Structure of Revelation," 362. The method of intercalation has been simply explained by Payne, "Narrative in Revelation," 369. Payne explains that John narrates two formal units or episodes, A and A', that belong together and then places in between them another form or scene: B. Yet, he wants the reader to see the combined text as a whole.

A. Prologue (1:1–8)
  B. Promises to the overcomer (1:9—3:22)
    C. God's work for humanity's salvation (4:1—8:1)
      D. God's wrath mixed with mercy (8:2—9:21)
        E. Commissioning John to prophesy (10:1—11:18)
          F. Great controversy between Christ and Satan (11:19—13:18)
        E.' Church proclaims the end-time gospel (14:1–20)
      D.' God's final wrath unmixed with mercy (15:1—18:24)
    C.' God's work for humanity's salvation completed (19:1—21:4)
  B.' Fulfillment of the promises to the overcomer (21:5—22:5)
A.' Epilogue (22:6-21).[93]

One can quickly identify Stefanovic's agenda simply by reading the successive points of his chiasm. Thus, for example, Rev 4:1—8:1 has to be about the salvation of the whole of humanity, this being the interpreter's imposed conclusion. Nevertheless, the marks of chiastic structure suggest that the book is not a chronological description of historical events, but rather a theological-thematic construction.[94] Beale explains,

> All agree that the dominant themes from 6:1 to 20:15 are, in order of importance, judgment, persecution, and salvation/reward and that these themes are intensified as the book progresses. Many deduce that this progressive intensity is evidence that the book is in chronological order. But the numerous repeated parallelisms point to a structure of recapitulation.[95]

This implies that various visions in one part of Revelation find their parallels in another part of the book and that they both represent the same events.[96] Even though there exists no agreement between scholars as to the exact parallels, we will consider some of their suggestions in studying the text. The major problem with this approach, however, is the lack of agreement concerning the centre of the chiasm. Beale has pointed to

---

93. Stefanovic, *Revelation of Jesus Christ*, 26–27.

94. Schüssler-Fiorenza, "Structure of Revelation," 350, 366. See also McKelvey, "Millennium," 86.

95. *Revelation*, 144. Aune, *Revelation 1–5*, xciii, has objected to the theory of recapitulation. He prefers to view the narrative as chronological. Yet, he explains, "That does not mean, however, that many of the constituent visions and traditions used as sources by the author could not have referred to essentially the same eschatological events from different perspectives and used variegated imagery."

96. Cf. Russell, *Parousia*, 377.

the two wars of chapters 11–12, earthly and heavenly, as being close to the centre.[97] Payne has proposed the centre at 11:1—14:20,[98] Schüssler-Fiorenza at 10:1—15:4,[99] Stefanovic at 11:18—13:19, whereas Strand, while proposing a chiastic structure, appears not to be concerned with a centre.[100] It seems therefore that even arranging the text of Revelation into a chiastic structure is not the ultimate solution to interpreting its message.

This lack of agreement concerning the Apocalypse's structure has led others to abandon the chiastic model, though not the recapitulation theory itself. They have instead chosen outlines, which indicate parallelisms. Bauckham's plan is a good example:

1:1–8	Prologue
1:9—3:22	Inaugural Vision of Christ and the churches including seven messages to the churches
4:1—5:14	Inaugural vision of heaven leading to three series of sevens and two intercalations:
6:1—8:1; 8:3–5	Seven seals, numbered 4 + 1 + (1 + intercalation) + 1
8:2; 8:6—11:19	Seven trumpets, numbered 4 + 1 + (1 + intercalation) +1
12:1—14:20; 15:2–4	The story of God's people in conflict with evil
15:1; 15:5—16:21	Seven bowls, numbered (4 + 3) without intercalation
17:1—19:10	Babylon the harlot
19:11—21:8	Transition from Babylon to the New Jerusalem
21:9—22:9	The New Jerusalem the bride
22:6–21	Epilogue.[101]

---

97. *Revelation*, 143.

98. "Narrative in Revelation," 369. Although he prefers the pattern of menorah rather than chiasm: six branches linked together leaving the central on its own. This apparently is to signify God's presence through Christ.

99. *Vision of a Just World*, 35–36.

100. Strand, "Chiastic Structure of Revelation," 401.

101. *Climax of Prophecy*, 21–22. Cf. Yarbro Collins, *Combat Myth*, 19, for her outline. But see Bauckham, *Climax of Prophecy*, 1–21, for reasons to doubt Collins's overall proposal.

Some scholars have proposed a time movement from John's time to the eschatological future on the basis of their structures.[102] But this does not need to be the case. It seems that their structures, together with the recapitulation theory, may in fact encourage the opposite view. If different visions can represent the same events, then some at least of the visions claimed to be about the distant future (perhaps even the *Endzeit*) do not really have to refer to that distant future. Therefore it would seem right to follow the book's own time-references in attributing historical counterparts to the visions.

One final issue to discuss here concerns Revelations' resemblance to the covenant form. A few scholars have attempted to demonstrate a covenant structure in John's prophecy. Shea[103] has particularly focused on the letters to the seven churches. He has claimed that they resemble in form the Hittite suzerainty treaty: 1) they have the Preamble ("these are the words…"); 2) Historical Prologue ("I know your works…"); 3) Stipulations (instructions to rectify deficiencies or appeals to continued faithfulness); 4) Witnesses (the Spirit is the witness in this case: 2:7, 11, 17, 29; 3:6, 13, 22); 5) Sanctions: blessing or curse (the potential curse is absent in the letters to Smyrna and Philadelphia, but a promise of blessing is given to those who will overcome).[104] Thus each of the letters can be regarded as a renewal of the original covenant, in a similar way to the covenant renewals of the OT people of God under Joshua, Hezekiah or Josiah.[105] Likewise, Revelation as a whole might correspond to the five parts of the covenant treaty: 1) Preamble (Jesus is described as the Suzerain: 1:12–20; 19:16); 2) Historical Prologue (the redemption motif: 1:17–18; 5:9–10; 7:14–17; 12:7–11); 3) Stipulations (instructions to the church and commandments of God: 12:17; 14:12; 22:14); 4) Witnesses (testimony or witness: 1:2, 9: 6:9; 11:7; 12:1, 17; 15:5; and 19:10); 5) Stipulations (seven blessings: 1:3; 14:13; 16:15; 19:9; 20:6: 22:7; and 22:14; and seven woes: 8:13; 9:12; 11:14; 12:2; 18:10, 16, 18; 22:3).[106]

---

102. In the sense of the *Endzeit* of the space-time universe. Schüssler-Fiorenza, *Vision of a Just World*, 36; Stefanovic, *Revelation of Jesus Christ*, 37; Strand, "Chiastic Structure of Revelation," 401.

103. Shea, "Covenantal Form," 71–84.

104. Ibid., 74–75.

105. Ibid., 83.

106. Ibid., 72–74. Beale, *Revelation*, 227–28, seems to support Shea's proposal with a few modifications.

This last point seems even more valid if one accepts the claim of scholars that the whole apocalypse must be read in the terms defined in the letters to the seven churches.[107] In general, Revelation can stand in the covenant tradition of both Testaments.[108]

Chilton has presented another attempt to read Revelation as a covenantal document. He advocates Revelation's strong link with the OT covenantal form, especially as found in Lev 26.[109] He believes that the entire Apocalypse resembles the covenant treaty arrangement: 1) Preamble (Vision of the Son of Man in chapter 1); 2) Historical Prologue (the Seven Letters in chapters 2–3); 3) Stipulations (the Seven Seals in chapters 4–7); 4) Sanctions (the Seven Trumpets in chapters 8–14); and 5) Succession Arrangements (the Seven Chalices in chapters 15–22). However, his proposal seems to create some problems. Shea's study has shown that Chilton's Historical Prologue can, in fact, contain a number of treaties. Likewise, other parts specified by Chilton can contain elements from various parts of the suzerain treaty. Another problem is that Chilton's proposal does not recognize parallels, which are discernable when one allows the recapitulation theory to play its part. Hence, Shea's insights seem the more convincing. Nevertheless, both proposals show that Revelation shares forms with other biblical and extra-biblical covenant traditions. Thus, it should probably be approached as a covenant document.

In conclusion, Revelation's technique of recapitulation helps one to properly approach the issue of time sequence in the book. It is possible that its various visions may refer to the same point of history rather than being a strict chronological sequence. This technique also holds one back from making premature decisions concerning the eschatology of the book, especially with regard to the *Endzeit* claims of scholars. On the other hand, a study of structure reveals the importance of the covenant idea in Revelation. Consequently, one approaching the book should give due attention to its covenantal setting. It appears that this setting opens some interesting interpretive possibilities for the difficult issue of Babylon's meaning and role.

---

107. Cf. once more Knight, "Christ of Revelation 5:6," 44; and Beale, *Revelation*, 132–33.

108. Shea, "Covenantal Form," 83.

109. *Days of Vengeance*, 17.

Having discussed the most significant points of Revelation's genre, *Sitz im Leben* and structure, we can now focus on its use of the divine marriage metaphor. We will examine the use and scope of the metaphor in the book. We will also indicate the metaphor's associations with the exodus motif. We will examine the explicit instances of the metaphor first. Then, we will turn to places which are less obvious examples, before finally suggesting other possible instances, where the metaphor may play a role in John's argument.

EXPLICIT INSTANCES OF THE USE OF DIVINE MARRIAGE METAPHOR IN REVELATION

Revelation 19

Rev 19:7–9 has widely been recognized and discussed as explicit instance of the use of nuptial imagery.[110] We, therefore, do not intend to repeat all the earlier arguments. Nevertheless, we feel that the relationship between the divine marriage metaphor and covenant development in redemption history has yet to receive the degree of scholarly attention that it deserves. For this reason we would like to devote particular attention to this issue below.

The chapter begins with a heavenly hymn of praise to God for his judgment upon Babylon, which results in salvation (vv. 1–4).[111] Hence, it is a continuation of the preceding material of chapters 17–18.[112] Consequently, it would appear that the next vision does not have to refer to the remote future, but to John's situation contemporary with the fall of Babylon.[113]

Verse 5 can be viewed as a transition to the second part of worship in 19:1–10, which ultimately focuses on the wedding of the Lamb

---

110. Recently by Zimmermann, "Nuptial Imagery," 153, 163–69.

111. Cf. Fekkes, *Prophetic Traditions in Revelation*, 89; Metzger, *Breaking the Code*, 89; Miller, "Nuptial Eschatology," 303.

112. Going back at least to 17:1. Cf. Bauckham, *Climax of Prophecy*, 4. 17:1—19:10 and 21:9—22:9 are parallel sections, bringing the whole book to its climax: the destruction of Babylon and her replacement by the New Jerusalem. Chilton, *Days of Vengeance*, 468, has suggested that 19:1–5 resembles the worship of 11:15–18, which concluded with the vision of the ark of the covenant. Caird, *Revelation*, 233, has argued that Rev 19:5–10 is an attempt at a more detailed exposition of that which was said in 11:15–19.

113. Cf. Müller, "Analysis of Revelation 20," 227, who argues that Rev 19:1–10 presents the celestial celebration following the fall of Babylon.

(vv. 7–9).[114] Verse 6, thus, is a response to the call of the voice from the throne to praise God (cf. 11:17).[115] Some scholars have suggested that the resurrection of two witnesses in Rev 11 can be a picture of the church's vindication, which will lead to the judgment on her oppressors (cf. Rev 20:7–10; Ezek 38).[116] Thus it seems that Rev 19:5–10 continues the same theme of the eschatological vindication of Christ and his people, which results in the establishment of his and God's rule (cf. 11:15). However, it is God's rule that is emphasized in this context (19:6b). It is established at the time of the arrival of Christ's marriage (v. 7).[117]

Only a minority of scholars have denied the importance of the marriage imagery in 19:7–9. Rossing has argued that the only purpose of the imagery was to bring to mind the two women *topos* of Prov 1–9, which should have resulted in the audience's support for the inheritance of the good woman, the new Jerusalem.[118] It should only have encouraged the audience to desire the opposite of Babylon's unjust imperialism, i.e., Jerusalem's distribution of free gifts.[119] However, her dismissal of the divine marriage tradition is not sufficiently justified. A number of scholars have demonstrated that the Lamb's marriage elaborates on earlier prophetic as well as divine marriage Synoptic traditions.[120] Moreover, we

---

114. Cf. Miller, "Nuptial Eschatology," 303. Ruiz, "Praise and Politics," 77, argues that v. 5 is joined to v. 8 so that God's servants and the saints are the same group.

115. See Chilton, *Days of Vengeance*, 473. The sound of many waters is similar to that of the heavenly orchestra in 14:2. Cf. Lee, *New Jerusalem in Revelation*, 264. However, in 14:1–5 the focus is on the remnant represented by the 144,000 (cf. below on Rev 14). Here, it seems, the great multitude resembles those who have overcome the great tribulation from every nation (cf. 7:9–17).

116. Beale, *Revelation*, 597. See also Ford, *Revelation*, 180–81; Aune, *Revelation 6–16*, 623, who both see references to Ezek 37 and 38 in Rev 11: a picture of corporate restoration of God's people.

117. Miller, "Nuptial Eschatology," 302, 304, has argued that the wedding of the Lamb becomes the establishment of God's rule as well as its manifestation.

118. Rossing, *Two Cities*, 136, 141, 144. She insists that γυνή should be rendered woman, not bride. However, pressing this point too far could result in disregard for other words clearly expressing the marriage idea.

119. Ibid., 144. Rossing believes that the fact that the anticipated wedding never unfolds is a point in favor of her position. She believes that the motif of the city is prominent. But see McIlraith, "Works and Wife in Revelation 19:8," 524, who insists that the imagery of covenant and marriage is essential to interpreting Revelation.

120. It seems that one of the more prominent is Isa 62:1–5, which uses the marriage imagery in a positive manner. However, Isa 61:10 provides a background to the bride's attire in Rev 19:8b. See Fekkes, "Nuptial Imagery," 272–73. Fekkes suggests that other

have already indicated that the OT marriage metaphor is indispensable in identifying Babylon. Since the present section is linked with the previous account of the great whore, one would expect the divine marriage motif to be important here. And we believe that consideration of OT material regarding divine marriage could shed more light on the historical significance of the Lamb's marriage.[121]

In chapter 3, we have observed that Isa 62:3–5 refers to the restoration after exile of Israel's covenantal fidelity, and of her virginity/innocence. In chapter 5, we have argued that Jesus reinterpreted that tradition around himself. He acted on Yahweh's behalf to restore the broken covenant, which was expressed by the metaphor of permanent betrothal or new (or re-) marriage. Hence, if John relied on earlier prophetic traditions, a possibility emerges that he would have used the Lamb's marriage imagery to express the same idea of the new covenant. This seems convincing because the context itself points to the establishment of God's rule (Rev 19:6). Consequently, it would appear that the restoration of the marriage of God (through the Messiah) and his people has in view the inauguration of the new covenant. However, scholars have often argued that the inauguration is a betrothal, the consummation being the marriage proper in the future.[122] Yet, some of them have recognized the links

---

places concerned with the eschatological Jerusalem may be important. We would agree with this, as we have acknowledged in chapter 3 that Isaiah stood in the same tradition as Hosea and others. Bauckham, *Climax of Prophecy*, 94 n.10, sees a special dependence of Rev 19:9 on Matt 22:1–14. Beasley-Murray, *Revelation*, 274, acknowledges Matt 22:2–14 and 25:1–13 as background to Rev 19:7–9. These Gospel passages link the marriage and feast concepts of the OT (cf. chapter 5 of this book).

121. However, Batey, *Nuptial Imagery*, 57, insists that Revelation's view of marriage differs from that of deutero-Isaiah. The former is still future although the latter anticipated just a restoration of marriage. However, his conclusion is based on his particular understanding of the term parousia, as the second (physical) appearance of Christ (p. 67). We have, however, argued that another (biblical) understanding can view parousia as divine presence/visitation, which was to be marked out by the destruction of the Temple (cf. chapter 5 on Matt 24).

122. See Batey, *Nuptial Imagery*, 57; Bauckham, *Climax of Prophecy*, 167; Beasley-Murray, *Revelation*, 273–74. In this sense even Rossing, *Two Cities*, 144, realizes that the wedding never unfolds in Revelation. However, one needs to remember that originally the consummation of *hieros gamos* took place while Israel was still wandering in the desert, during the Exodus, on Mount Sinai. Cf. Levenson, *Sinai and Zion*, 77, 79. Perhaps one could argue for a kind of analogy here. The wedding takes place for the Christian community while still in her exodus.

between this account of John and the Synoptic parables.[123] This tendency helps our argument because we have proposed in chapter 5 that these parables refer to the restoration of covenant as a result of Christ's ministry. We have argued in chapters 5 and 6 that the futuristic view of Christ's marriage probably emerges from the error of assuming that the course of natural marriage in ancient Israel should govern one's thinking about covenant renewal. According to the view, a period of betrothal should precede the marriage of Christ. However, we have argued that the renewal of God's covenant equals the new marriage. One would have to notice that, at least, part of the early Christian tradition assumed that the marriage was already consummated and that this consummation resulted in the birth of new offspring. This happened at Christ's resurrection, not his future coming (see chapter 6 on Gal 4:28). Thus, we have argued, the restoration of the covenant and marriage was the main concern of Paul in Gal 4:21—5:1. He saw it as prerequisite to the salvation to liberty of the church's offspring. One would therefore need to reconsider the preliminary issues of methodology to decide whether or not John stood in the same realized tradition. According to our view, it is more likely that the restored (new) covenant relationship is the main motif behind the marriage metaphor in this instance, not a map of future eschatological events.[124]

Rev 19 links the γάμος of the Lamb with the destruction of Babylon and the vindication of Christ and his church, not with a remote future event.[125] Salvation from the oppression by the great harlot opens the marital festivities.[126] Then the marriage is fully revealed. We have pro-

---

123. Cf. esp. Beasley-Murray, *Revelation*, 274. He argues that the salvation feast (characteristic of the eschatological wedding) belongs to the future (cf. Isa 25:6; Matt 22:1–14; 25:1–13).

124. Cf. McIlraith, "Works and Wife in Revelation 19:8," 528.

125. Chilton, *Days of Vengeance*, 5, has indicated that the "seventy sevens" of Daniel's prophecy would end with the destruction of Jerusalem (9:24–27). Thus the exile of God's faithful would finish with that event.

126. Ibid. 473. He takes the judgment on the Harlot and the marriage of the Lamb as correlative events. But it may well be that the marriage was inaugurated earlier (cf. 1:5) with the wedding/salvation feast to follow on the destruction of the church's foes. It seems that the wedding is an ongoing reality reaching its fuller expression after the destruction of Jerusalem. We are here in agreement with Wright, *NTPG*, 460, that "one of the main early Christian meanings of the word 'salvation' had to do with historical liberation from the great city that had been persecuting those who transferred its claim, to be the place of YHWH's dwelling, on to their crucified Messiah-figure and thence on to themselves."

posed in chapter 5 that Jesus himself linked the marital/covenant restoration with the eschatological feast of salvation (see on Matt 22:1–14). Here, the persecution caused by the church's enemies ceases with the destruction of Babylon, the event leading to the salvation of the church. The bride is freed from the dangerous influence of the harlot who causes others to fornicate alongside her. The bride has properly responded to the covenant of her husband (Rev 2:19).[127] Her fine linen, works caused by her first love (cf. 2:4), testify to the faithfulness of the salvation community and perhaps to their restored virginity (19:8; cf. Isa 61:10; 49:18; 62:5; Ezek 16:10).[128] She is the one who has not succumbed to the deception to commit harlotry (cf. Rev 2:20; 3:4–5). Therefore, she is spared in judgment and receives the Exodus-like salvation. Her attire is that of the bride, not of the harlot (cf. 17:4). In this sense, she has prepared herself for the appearance of her bridegroom.[129] Her members are those of the churches of John's age who have overcome amidst the tribulation preceding the fall of the harlot (cf. Rev 7:14).[130] They become the kingdom

---

The joy of this salvation (19:7) can resemble the joy of the bridegroom's presence in Mark 2:18–20. Cf. Vos, *Synoptic Traditions in the Apocalypse*, 169.

127. McIlraith, "Works and Wife in Revelation 19:8," 514, 527. Miller, "Nuptial Eschatology," 304, 309, explains that, although the epithet 'bride' is not used in Rev 19, it becomes obvious that the invitees constitute her. This is, then, similar to Matt 22:1–14.

128. Cf. Fekkes, "Nuptial Imagery," 273, 287. He explains that δικαίωματα in Rev 19:8 may translate צדקה of Isa 61:10. The saints are the woman since their righteous deeds are her pure linen. So Miller, "Nuptial Eschatology," 304. Pace Rossing, *Two Cities*, 140.

Scholars have usually recognized the tension between the bestowing on the bride of fine linen and her "working" for it. Cf. the discussion in Beale, *Revelation*, 953. However, the tension can be explained by acknowledging that Rev 19:8 is based on Isa 61:10; 49:18. Cf. Fekkes, *Prophetic Traditions in Revelation*, 233. It seems that both God's gift of salvation and the bride's accepting it in her loving response are in view. Her attire may signify her spiritual faithfulness and her holy conduct. So Fekkes, "Nuptial Imagery," 287.

129. Cf. Fekkes, *Prophetic Traditions in Revelation*, 253.

130. Cf. Miller, "Nuptial Eschatology," 309, who has suggested a link with the overcomer of the letters in Rev 2–3. It also seems that some similarity with Matt 25:1–13 is possible here. There, the wise virgins were those who have chosen faithfulness to Christ. They constituted his bride at his appearance. In Rev, the overcomer proves to be the faithful bride at Christ's appearance. Cf. Ford, *Revelation*, 311.

of God and, at the same time, they replace the wicked that sank in the sea.[131] The new marriage leads the bride to her inheritance.[132]

We would also submit the thesis that the marriage theme is developed throughout the battle of Armageddon (19:11–21). The vision does not need to be viewed as some end time event because it is associated with Babylon's destruction in Rev 17–18.[133] It seems to be the epilogue of the judgment. The vision of the first horse-rider can resemble the messianic figure of Ps 45, who claims his bride after conquering his enemies.[134] Hence, it is possible that this messianic Psalm is a source behind the Armageddon scene. It should not create a problem that the sequence is here reversed: first the wedding, then the eschatological war. It may only be a stylistic matter to help juxtapose the two contrasting women in Rev 17–19, 21–22.[135] Moreover, scholars have argued that Rev 19:13, 15 depend on Isa 63:1–3.[136] The Isaiah text, in its wider context, also

---

131. Cf. Miller, "Nuptial Eschatology," 309. Miller argues that God's reign (kingdom) and the Lamb's nuptial union are simultaneous results of the same work of Christ as the Lamb of God (5:5–6, 9–10). Shea, "Revelation 5 and 19," 254, observes that in Rev 5 Christ comes to the Father as the redeeming Lamb, whereas in Rev 19 he goes from the Father to introduce his kingship as King of kings (cf. v. 16).

Ford, *Revelation*, 317, argues that 18:21 pictures Babylon as drowned in the sea, like the Egyptians during the original Exodus. Therefore, this new exodus leads to a new covenant.

132. Cf. Wallis, "Coming of the Kingdom," 55. This inheritance theme is developed in chapters 21–22.

133. See LaRondelle, "Armageddon," 23. He views Armageddon as future. But this is not necessary on our view of Rev 16–18 (cf. below). Briggs, *Temple Imagery*, 102 n. 187, has argued that Armageddon is the unfolding of the seventh bowl judgment starting at 16:17, and prepared during the sixth bowl in 16:16. Cf. Yarbro Collins, *Crisis and Catharsis*, 149.

134. Cf. Ford, *Revelation*, 318. She observes that Ps 45 and Wis Sol 18 both associate the marriage theme with war. Zimmermann, "Nuptial Imagery, 163, regards Ps 45 as an important contextual background for Rev 19. The sharp sword striking nations echoes Isa 49:2 and 11:4 (cf. Ps 2:9) See Beale, *Revelation*, 961.

135. This juxtaposition is clearly the intention of John. Cf. Bauckham, *Climax of Prophecy*, 133. See also Ortlund, *Whoredom*, 163 n. 62, who suggests that strict sequence is not required here. However, Fekkes, "Nuptial Imagery," 287, assumes this sequence as chronological and explains that the preparation of the bride was to take place before Christ's parousia. McIlraith, "Works and Wife in Revelation 19:8," 525, proposes that Rev 19:11–16 resembles a bridal procession inaugurating the wedding. However, the introduction of the wedding and the eschatological war of Armageddon can both be viewed as simultaneous events. Cf. Miller, "Nuptial Eschatology," 302, 315–16. The bride is the bride first in fighting alongside her bridegroom (19:14).

136. Beasley-Murray, *Revelation*, 280–81. But Metzger, *Breaking the Code*, 91, believes the message of Isa 63:1–3 was altered to point to Christ's own blood shed at redemption

links the themes of marriage and judgment on God's enemies. These two events belong to the same time of the eschatological restoration of God's people. Furthermore, some scholars have suggested that within the context of Revelation, the battle of Christ's army on the white horses also refers to their vindication (Rev 19:11, 14).[137] This would imply that the full appearance of the wedding of the Lamb correlates with the messianic vindication, which, according to some Synoptic traditions, was to take place at the destruction of Jerusalem's Temple (cf. chapter 5 on Matt 25:1–13).[138] It seems a possibility that Rev 19 is in agreement with these early traditions.

The reign of Christ over the nations will begin with the punishment of the beast and the false prophet in the lake burning with sulfur (19:19–20; cf. 14:10–11).[139] The agents of Satan will not endanger the church any more, but their commander is dealt with in a different way (20:1–3, 7–10). Nevertheless, the unfaithful of the earth are killed by Christ's sword and eaten by birds (vv. 19, 21).[140] The scene looks like a

---

(Rev 5:6, 9). However, the close affinity of 19:15b with 14:19 may suggest that the blood of his enemies is on his robe. Cf. Chilton, *Days of Vengeance*, 484. Others doubt that Christ's garment was dipped in blood prior to the battle, e.g., Caird, *Revelation*, 242–44. Caird claims that the blood belongs to the Christian martyrs whom their Lord is going now to avenge. This is based on his peculiar view of Rev 14:19–20. But the fact that the blood is on the garment prior to the battle can stress the certainty of the victory. Caird's view of the prophecy seems to be too mechanical. Isa 63:1–3 speaks in the past tense of the events, which will occur in the future. Cf. Beale, *Revelation*, 959.

Aune, *Revelation 17–22*, 1061–62, notes that Isa 63:1–3 was originally against Edom, although it became a cipher for the punishment of nations in *Midr.Ps.* 8.8.79. Yet, here the unfaithful Israel can be in view.

137. See esp. Beale, *Revelation*, 950, 960. He explains that the colour white throughout Revelation refers to vindication of those who have overcome tribulation (2:17; 3:4–5; 4:4; 6:11; 7:9, 13; 14:14).

138. Wright, *JVG*, 342, has argued that in Mark 13 the vindication of the Messiah was marked by the Temple's destruction. We have noted in chapter 5 on Matt 25:1–13 that the vindication of Christ was to be associated with an exodus-like judgment upon the unfaithful wife of God.

139. This punishment echoes that of Sodom and Gomorrah in Gen 19:24–26 (cf. Luke 17:29). Thus, the picture may be one of the destruction of the enemies of Christ's reign. Cf. Chilton, *Days of Vengeance*, 491. Chilton explains that the beast and the false prophet are evil personifications of pagan Rome and apostate Israel united to fight the church. Cf. our discussion on Rev 13–14 below.

Ford, *Revelation*, 315, suggests that the lake burning with sulfur resembles Gehenna (Targ. Isa 30:33).

140. Chilton, *Days of Vengeance*, 489, shows that being eaten by the birds of prey was a basic covenant curse (Deut 28:26, 49). He also proposes a link with Matt 24:28, which

parody of the messianic banquet of salvation.[141] If the alternative meaning of the βασιλεῖς τῆς γῆς in Revelation be accepted, then the picture can be of a group of Jews who expected God's eschatological meal of salvation, but became a meal for birds in rejecting Christ.[142]

Rev 19 appears to set an explicit contrast between two women: the bride of Christ and the harlot who rejects the Messiah. The former can rejoice at being delivered from the oppression of Babylon for the wedding festivities: covenant blessing. The latter will become food for the "festivities" of birds: covenant curse. However, it is clear that the chapter employs the marriage metaphor to make a point about salvation through Christ.

Revelation 21–22

Scholars have already examined the explicit instances of our metaphor in Rev 21–22. They have also pointed to the possible sources behind the visions in this section. However, there has not been unanimity concerning the metaphor's importance and its *Sitz im Leben*.[143] We are, therefore, compelled to discuss afresh the most important issues.

---

implies that Israel became a dead corpse for the eagles/vultures to eat (cf. Luke 17:37). Birds of prey, like eagles or vultures, were unclean (Lev 11:13–19; Deut 14:12–18) and could symbolically represent foreign nations in the OT (Ezek 17:3, 7). See Wenham, "Animal Rite in Genesis 15," 135. Although Rev 19:17, 21 do not specify the birds, they resemble those that Abraham had to drive off from his sacrifice in Gen 15:11 (the same Greek word for birds is used in the LXX). Wenham has proposed that the picture is symbolic of the foreign nations attacking the sacrifice representing Israel, the priestly nation. Wright, *JVG*, 360, has recognized the possibility of regarding the eagles/vultures in Matt 24:28//Luke 17:37 as symbolizing the armies of Rome. It seems that the symbolism could match history, when Roman armies 'devoured' Jerusalem.

141. Aune, *Revelation 17–22*, 1063–64. The invitation to the birds in Rev 19:17–18 may echo Ezek 39:17–18, where the flesh of God's enemies becomes a sacrificial meal for birds and other animals. But Aune (p. 1068) also recognizes that the curse of being eaten by birds was uttered against the impenitent Israel on a number of occasions (Jer 7:3; 15:3; 16:14; 19:7; 34:20).

142. See above the *Sitz im Leben* section. One should notice that the βασιλεῖς τῆς γῆς in Rev 19:19 do not have to be the same group as the βασιλεῖς τῆς οἰκουμένης in 16:14. We have suggested that the *earth* may have a particular reference to Israel's land, whereas *world* signifies the civilization of the Roman Empire. Therefore, it is possible that the enemies of Jesus in the land of Palestine may be in view in v. 21.

143. It seems that many scholars have still preferred to view our metaphor as only informing the new Jerusalem motif and that from the entirely futuristic perspective. See, e.g., C. Deutsch, "New Jerusalem," 112–15.

The scholarly opinion has generally been that, since the vision in 20:11–15 mentions the sea, the disappearance of the sea in 21:1 must absolutely point to a post-last judgment situation.[144] Such a view is especially favored among those who take the symbol of the sea to signify all the destructive forces of chaos and thus all evil in the world.[145] In this sense, the vision can signify the final exodus of God's people, after he will have 'dried up' all the causes of the affliction of his people.[146] For Mathewson, Jer 51:36 is particularly important in this context since the text predicts God's future judgment on Babylon, a theme developed in Revelation.[147] Schmidt's study introduces to the debate the claim that the sea symbolizes the rebellious humanity aligned with demonic forces of mythical chaos as seen in Rev 19:18 and 20:3, 10.[148] However, according to our argument above, neither judgment on Babylon nor the battle of Armageddon in Rev 19 need to refer to the *Endzeit* events leading to the salvation of God's people.

A number of scholars have argued that the vision of the new heaven and earth is strongly influenced by Isa 65:17–25.[149] If this Isaiah context is accepted as background to Rev 21–22, the picture can be one of a new world-order. To be sure, its total physical manifestation is still future, while also breaking through the present order.[150] Hence, there

144. Cf. Bauckham, *Climax of Prophecy*, 70. Also, Ortlund, *Whoredom*, 164, 166.

145. See Bauckham, *Theology of Revelation*, 53; cf. Deutsch, "New Jerusalem," 115. Bauckham explains that the destruction of the sea terminates the realm in which a reversion of creation to chaos is possible. However, Beale, *Revelation*, 142, suggests that the sea was not destroyed but rather transformed into the lake of fire in 21:8. For him, the point is the absence of any threat to God's people in the future (1041–42). Ortlund, *Whoredom*, 166, has pointed to Isa 57:20, where the sea symbolizes a 'restless mass of godless humanity.' But this may well support the less futuristic view, as presented below. However, Rossing, *Two Cities*, 145, claims that the absence of the sea suggests the cessation of a shipping economy. In another article, she shows that her conclusion is based on parallels with *Sib.Or.* 5.447–49. See Rossing, "River of Life," 495. But it seems that the OT context is more important here, as others have argued.

146. See Mathewson, "New Exodus," 245–55.

147. See ibid., 253. Cf. ibid. 246, where he suggests that the sea-symbolism is occurs first in Rev 13:1; 17:1, 15 and 20:13.

148. Schmidt, "Water as People, Not Place," 246–48.

149. Beale, *Revelation*, 1040–41; Beasley-Murray, *Revelation*, 306; Aune, *Revelation 17–22*, 1116.

150. Caird, *Revelation*, 263, explains that the visions of Rev 21:1–27 are about "a future, which interpenetrates and informs the present." Minear, "Ontology and Ecclesiology," 99, preferred the term "trans-historical reality" to describe the interrelatedness between the future and the ongoing history.

could also be a reference to a reality parallel with the millennial reign of Christ and his saints, with a fullness still to follow.[151] Yet, even this view does not completely solve the problem of the sea. It has been noticed that in the OT the sea sometimes symbolized the abode of sea monsters (Job 26:12–13; Ps 74:12–14; Isa 27:1; 51:9–10; Ezek 32:2) from which oppression came on God's people (cf. Rev 13:1, 7).[152] In this sense the sea corresponded to the abyss (cf. Rev 11:7),[153] which pointed also to the rebellious nations in OT times.[154] Consequently, another view of the sea is possible in Rev 21:1c. The disappearance of the sea could suggest a shift in thinking about the nations. They no longer are regarded as an extension of the abyss, because Christ's salvation includes also them (21:3; cf. 5:9–10).[155] They have been freed from the deception of Satan, who made them servants of chaos/rebellion against God in the past (20:3; cf. Eph 2:2, 13–14, 16!). According to Pauline tradition, Christians of pagan nations have experienced their exodus at the time of Israel's restoration in Christ (Cf. chapter 6 on Gal 4). Moreover, according to the Exodus pattern, this new exodus demanded another drying up of the sea (cf. Isa 44:27; 50:2).[156] Following the same pattern, the drying up of the sea leads to salvation—perceived as a new creation (Isa 51:9–10; cf. Wis 19:6)—a picture quite apparent in Rev 21.[157] Thus, we would suggest that following the helpful observations of such scholars as Schmidt and

---

151. See Terry, *Biblical Apocalyptics*, 460; Chilton, *Days of Vengeance*, 537–40. Chilton argues that there already exists a reality described under the symbols of new heaven and new earth. This is due to the fact that biblical language expresses God's salvation in terms of *recreation* (cf. Isa 65:17–25; 2 Pet 3:1–14). Thus the new creation describes the covenant restoration. Even the newness in 21:1 (καινός) is not chronological (as expressed by νέος), but qualitative. Pace Lee, *New Jerusalem in Revelation*, 268.

152. Stefanovic, *Revelation of Jesus Christ*, 402.

153. Mathewson, "New Exodus," 246 n. 15. Also Schmidt, "Water as People, Not Place," 246.

154. Ford, *Revelation*, 219.

155. Bauckham, *Climax of Prophecy*, 311, has argued that in Rev 21:3 all humanity (τῶν ἀνθρώπων) becomes God's covenant people. He suggests that there is to be observed here a dependence on the OT traditions of Isa 19:25; 25:6; 56:7; Amos 9:12; and Ps 47:8–9. Similarly, Wengst, "Babylon the Great," 200, explains that Rev 21:3 focuses on all peoples' belonging to God, instead of to the whore Babylon.

156. Mathewson, "New Exodus," 253, argues that the restoration of Jerusalem in Isa 44 and 50 implied "a repetition of the drying up of the sea in the future." He believes John used this exodus motif in Rev 21:1c.

157. Ibid.

Mathewson, one can still perceive a temporal aspect in the new creation vision described in Rev 21–22. Perhaps Minear's notion of "trans-historical reality" should be given more thought in considering this issue. And it may be true that only the post-*Endzeit* future will not encounter any threat from the chaotic powers symbolized by the sea, but, likewise, some early Christian traditions suggest a temporary change in the influence the sea can have on the nations.

However, the major objection to the more temporal view of Rev 21 is the content of v. 4, which speaks of the absence of death, pain and sorrow within the new order.[158] Yet, the advocates of this view have argued that the Christian already has eternal life through his union with Christ (cf. 7:15–17).[159] In general, it is difficult to decide between these two interpretive options. It seems that a relationship is assumed between the future to come and the present as wrought by Christ, as John's message had to be relevant to the original audience.[160] On the other hand, the vision encourages a radical-change view, one that will result in the new totally replacing the old. While unable to choose between the two above approaches, we propose to discuss the divine marriage metaphor keeping in mind possible tensions between the time references of the symbols involved.

Rev 21:2 explicitly associates the new Jerusalem "coming down out of heaven from God" with a "bride adorned for her husband." Scholars have tried to explain this descent in two slightly different ways. Some have focused on the future readiness of the church to be married on her descent to the new earth.[161] Others have attempted to explain the relation of the descending bride/new Jerusalem to the time of restoration

---

158. Cf. Beale, *Revelation*, 1041–43. In his opinion, the picture may be one of the final crossing through the "removed sea" at the consummation of the ages. Lee, *New Jerusalem in Revelation*, 269, also suggests that a more radical change is needed for a new creation to exist.

159. Terry, *Biblical Apocalyptics*, 461. Chilton, *Days of Vengeance*, 547, takes John 11:25–26 to support his approach here. The link with Rev 7:15–17 may suggest that the church experiences her freedom from death before the future consummation. Caird, *Revelation*, 265, argues that the new is already present in the old.

160. It appears that the whole vision gives support and a promise to the overcomer mentioned earlier in Rev 2–3 (21:7). Cf. Miller, "Nuptial Eschatology," 311.

161. Bauckham, *Theology of Revelation*, 130, suggests that the bride will be married on the city's arrival on the earth, a future event. Cf. Batey, *Nuptial Imagery*, 57, 67; Deutsch, "New Jerusalem," 118; Gundry, "New Jerusalem: People as Place," 259, 261; Miller, "Nuptial Eschatology," 310.

marked out by the destruction of Babylon.[162] The former replaces the latter.[163] But when the whore is destroyed, the new Jerusalem exists in heaven ultimately to descend to the new earth. It is plausible that an echo of a Pauline tradition from Gal 4:26 is present here.[164] In that passage, the heavenly city was a system opposed to the earthly Jerusalem, which consisted of Abraham's promised offspring (cf. chapter 6 on Gal 4:26-27). She was a restored Jerusalem/Zion, mother of many children (cf. Isa 54:2-3), and God's new creation in the same realm as the new heaven and earth (cf. Gal 6:15-16; Rev 3:12; 12:1). In that context, it would be difficult to admit that the marriage was regarded as future. Moreover, we have already observed in studying Rev 19:7-9 that the wedding of the Lamb equals the restoration of covenant, the time of salvation, as already inaugurated by Christ.[165] Hence, the wedding cannot be a future event. It is also quite striking that the descending-from-heaven bride in Rev 21:9-10 (a parallel to 21:2)[166] is also called the Lamb's γυνή, i.e., woman/wife.[167] This would sound strange if the wedding was still to follow the

---

162. Cf. Kik, *Eschatology of Victory*, 243; Kraybill, *Commerce in John's Apocalypse*, 206. McIlraith, "Works and Wife in Revelation 19:8," 527 n. 38, explains that in the present the new Jerusalem is constantly coming down from heaven. Possibly, to an extent, Yarbro Collins, "Feminine Symbolism," 24-25, who suggests that sacred marriage has in view the fertility of the time of salvation. In our overall argument, the marriage has already been realized with the outcome still unfolding.

163. See, e.g., parallels between Babylon and the new Jerusalem, as indicated by Fekkes, *Prophetic Traditions in Revelation*, 94. Also Giblin, "Theology of Revelation 16-22," 489; Lee, *New Jerusalem in Revelation*, 264.

164. Beagley, *Church's Enemies*, 177, has acknowledged that Gal 4:26 could have been in the same tradition as Revelation's heavenly city, the restored Zion.

165. This would be in line with the OT pattern of divine marriage: the consummation takes place still within the Exodus, not during the final indwelling of Israel's inheritance. Cf. Levenson, *Sinai and Zion*, 77.

166. Beale, *Revelation*, 1063, claims that Rev 21:9-10 recapitulates 21:2. Rev 21:9—22:5 forms the so-called "Jerusalem appendix" that develops the motif of the new Jerusalem from 21:1-8.

167. Although, Aune, *Revelation 17-22*, 1151, suggests that this word could have been added later to accommodate the contrast with the woman Babylon in 17:3, 4, 6, 7, 9, 18. However, evidence of a later alteration of the text is lacking. Moreover, John's usage of the word could have had two purposes: 1) literary: to remind of the contrast between the harlot city and the bride; and 2) to indicate that the bride is also a wife. It may well have been that the 'bride' had in view the restoration of innocence to God's people (cf. chapter 3 above), whereas the 'wife' could have emphasized the covenant union with Christ/God. We would suggest that our view helps to solve the otherwise vague statement of Rev 21:9b. The explanation of Beasley-Murray, *Revelation*, 318, that betrothal was regarded almost as marriage in the ANE is of no great help here.

descent. But we believe that there is a better explanation of Rev 21:2. We have already indicated (cf. above on Rev 19:7–9) that the wedding leads to the possession of the inheritance, which was guaranteed in Israel by the *mohar* payment of the bridegroom (cf. chapter 2 above). Thus the descent of the bride would not have to be for the wedding, but in order finally to possess her inheritance (cf. 21:7).[168] Consequently, the bride's adornment for the husband would not need to mean being prepared for the wedding.[169] It could signify both the splendid beauty of the bride (cf. Ezek 16:11) as well as her devotion in her beauty exclusively to her husband, a reversal of Ezek 16:15–16.[170] Such an explanation seems to be more consistent with the overall development of the marriage metaphor in John's thought and in other NT writings.[171]

It appears that the relationship between the bride and the new Jerusalem has not been fully appreciated. Some scholars have preferred to focus on the symbol of the city, only mentioning its association with the bride.[172] However, it should be acknowledged that the two motifs are coexistent and of equal importance for understanding the message of John. We have already indicated in chapter 3 that the two motifs of Yahweh being Zion's (Jerusalem's) builder as well as the husband of Jerusalem (people represented by the city) are connected (cf. our comments on Isa 54:5, 11–12; 65:5). The former refers to Yahweh dwelling with his people, while the latter signifies his intimate covenant union with them. This OT context instantly solves the problem of identifying

168. This taking possession of the inheritance could parallel the vision in 21:9–27. Wallis, "Coming of the Kingdom," 59, has argued that Rev 21:9–27 refers to the bride coming to the inheritance, although we would add that she is also a wedded wife. It is quite striking that now the whole new creation (world) becomes the inheritance, as opposed to the inheritance of one particular land. Cf. Wright, *NTPG*, 451.

169. Pace, Caird, *Revelation*, 263, and others holding to a similar position.

170. The fine linen was looked for at the time of the covenant renewal (cf. Matt 22:11–12; Rev 19:8). It is also noteworthy that the sequence of Ezek 16 was: the wedding first, and then the adornment with riches leading to fame among the nations.

171. Otherwise, one would have to agree with Rossing, *Two Cities*, 144, that the anticipated wedding never unfolds in Revelation. Scholars who have the tendency to place it in the distant future often assume it.

172. A somewhat extreme approach has been presented by Rossing, *Two Cities*, 144, who insists that the city motif overtakes that of the bride in Rev 21–22. She argues that such a transition was known from the story of Joseph and Aseneth 15.7–8 (p. 148 n. 43). Others have paid more attention to the description of the city in Rev 21 than to that of the bride. Cf. Casey, "Exodus Theme in Revelation," 40; Deutsch, "New Jerusalem," 111–13, 118.

the constituents of the city/bride: they are the people of God themselves.[173] Hence, in Rev 21, the association of the two symbols of the city and the bride may point to two aspects of God's relationship to the church: his living with them and the intimacy of his covenant relationship with his people. In fact, Rev 21:3 seems to confirm this conclusion. The first part of the verse implies that the new Jerusalem is the indwelling of God, his *tabernacling* presence among or rather within his people.[174] In addition, we would suggest that it may also echo the tradition of the people being God's inheritance, which he bought in an act of redemption, and which he finally possesses (cf. Deut 9:26, 29; 1 Kgs 8:51; Ps 94:5; cf. Rev 5:9–10). It would also imply their role as priests in God's dwelling (cf. 1:6; 5:10). Concerning the next part of Rev 21:3, scholars have noted that it echoes

---

173. The problem for some interpreters has been to identify the city/bride with the community of saints. See, e.g., Schüssler-Fiorenza, *Vision of a Just World*, 102, who does not identify the bride with the church, but with the renewed world. Others, however, have reached the opposite conclusion from the context of Revelation itself. Cf. Gundry, "New Jerusalem: People as Place," 256–57; Miller, "Nuptial Eschatology," 304.

174. Minear, "Ontology and Ecclesiology," 99. Cf. Ortlund, *Whoredom*, 166, who observes that this is an echo of Lev 26:11–12; Ezek 37:23, 26–28; and John 1:1, 14. In a covenantal context, these passages speak of God's tabernacling presence among his people in times of obedience and restoration. The last two refer to the post-exilic situation at the time of restoration. In addition, God's presence among his people implied the presence of his blessings and care. Rowland, "Apocalyptic and Targumic Tradition," 499, argues that John 1:14 and Rev 21:3 are different: the former refers to the realized presence of God in Christ at his first coming, but the latter refers to the future bliss of the "new age." Wright, *New Heavens, New Earth*, 11, indicates that Rev 21:3 is still future. Caird, *Revelation*, 264–65, seems to imply the realized aspect of the promise, which is the permanent guarantee of the privileges enjoyed by those who "have lived as citizens of the city whose builder and maker is God (Heb. xi.8–16; cf. Gal iv.26)." Thus, there seems to be some present reality to the still future hope. Gundry, "New Jerusalem: People as Place," 256, argues that God's dwelling is in the saints (the new Jerusalem), not among them on the new earth. Fekkes, *Prophetic Traditions in Revelation*, 96–97, observes that now the entire city, not only the temple, is the dwelling of God. In fact, the temple extends to the whole city and virtually becomes the city. Gundry (261), alongside similar lines, explains that the saints/city will be the inmost room of God's new creation. Chilton, *Days of Vengeance*, 546, observes that the access to God's presence has been provided to the greatest possible degree. However, something more than access is here in view: God's *Shekinah* presence in men. Cf. Jankowski, *Apokalipsa*, 274. However, Briggs, *Temple Imagery*, 109, seems to suggest that disappearance of the temple (its complete removal?) signifies the arrival of ultimate perfection. But this would imply the cessation of the priestly nature of the Lamb's community, something Revelation does not seem to sustain, but rather points to an opposite view (cf. 22:3). Cf. Casey, "Exodus Theme in Revelation," 41; Fekkes, *Prophetic Traditions in Revelation*, 276.

the covenant formula/promise (cf. Exod 6:7).[175] We have argued in chapter 6 that the formula could indicate the marital relationship of God (or Christ) and his people (see on Eph 5:26; cf. Ezek 16:8). By implication, the covenant formula could be regarded as a marital oath introducing that intimate relationship.[176] Thus the evidence of Rev 21:3 could support our earlier contention that the motifs of city and bride are equally important for John and should be taken together, if we are to appreciate the full impact of his theological symbolism. They both operate within the framework of God's covenant and supplement each other. Together they embrace the whole meaning and promise of the original Exodus, which is a way of God's dealing with his people.[177]

The two motifs appear equally central to what follows. Based to a large degree on Isa 65:19, Rev 21:4 has in view the time of God's renewal of Jerusalem the bride's fortunes.[178] Rev 21:6b also uses the two covenantal themes of city and bride. The imagery may be a reversal of Jer 2:13,[179] where the harlotries of the wife Jerusalem (v. 20) made her forsake her true source of life, which resulted in the land's death (3:3).[180]

---

175. E.g., Lee, *New Jerusalem in Revelation*, 272; Fekkes, "Nuptial Imagery," 283 n. 34. He explains that the promise "I will be their God, and they shall be my people" is often found in the OT in connection with marriage. Cf. chapter 3 above.

176. However, this does not need to imply that the marriage has still to come. The promise of Rev 21:3 may look to the consummate reality of that which is already present. The original formula in Exod 6:7 referred to the time of Exodus when God would espouse Israel. It may well be that the new marriage refers to the time of Christian exodus, which, according to some early Christian traditions, came to pass in Christ.

177. Cf. Casey, "Exodus Theme in Revelation," 41, who suggested earlier that the final visions of Revelation describe the final completion of all that was involved in the Exodus.

178. For sources behind Rev 21:4 see Beale, *Revelation*, 1049–50. We have already acknowledged in chapter 5 that Isa 65 was an important testimony, which Jesus and his followers used to describe the time of restoration of Zion/Yahweh's wife (cf. esp. on Matt 22:1–14).

179. Although Beale, *Revelation*, 1056, gives primary importance to Isa 49:10 in this context, the wording of the Jer 2:13 in the LXX (πηγὴν ὕδατος ζωῆς) is closer to John's (τῆς πηγῆς τοῦ ὕδατος τῆς ζωῆς). It is less probable that Prov 16:22 is the primary source here. Pace Rossing, *Two Cities*, 151.

180. Similarly in Hos 2:3, the drought kills the land. Cf. chapter 3 on Jer 2–3. See also Carroll, *Jeremiah*, 126–27, who explains that the sense of Jer 2:10–13 is similar to that found in Jer 18:13–17. God's people forsake the source of life and thus they die. The land becomes desolate (cf. Jer 15:8).

Caird, *Revelation*, 266, argues that the End at 21:6a is a person (*eschatos*), not a final event (*eschaton*). This End or Goal of history entered the temporal in the person of Jesus.

The Metaphor of Divine Marriage in the Book of Revelation 265

Yet, the new Jerusalem, the restored wife of God, is provided with life for anybody who thirsts (cf. Isa 55:1; John 7:37–38; Rev 7:17).[181] It is the overcomer who can participate in these promises of God (Rev 21:7). Perhaps this statement brings closer the idea that the visions had in view the contemporary situation of John's addressees.[182] Although still to be fully realized in the future, they provide a picture of the reality belonging to those of the churches who resist the temptation and persecution and remain faithful to their Husband. The community of the overcomer will inherit sonship, according to the promise of the Davidic covenant (2 Sam 7:14; cf. Ps 89:26–27; Isa 55:3).[183] This may again imply a similarity with the Pauline tradition (cf. Rom 8:17; Gal 3:29; 4:7).[184] In Paul's thought, becoming God's son and an heir to Abraham's promise was through union with Christ (cf. chapter 6 on Gal 4). This sonship meant belonging to the heavenly city, the restored Zion's offspring. Nations were given to the offspring as their inheritance, with a view towards the renewal of the whole of creation. A somewhat similar case seems to be found in Rev 21:7. We have noted earlier that the motif of inheritance in the Apocalypse recalls the OT motif of *mohar* payment. This would indicate that the bridal-gift becomes the portion of God's sons, who receive dominion over his creation as his royalty (that is again through their union with Christ, cf. Rev 5:5–6).[185] Thus, it is possible that this

---

181. Aune, *Revelation 17–22*, 1128, notes that the Christian tradition in John 7:37–38 (cf. 4:10, 14) developed the OT promise into a christological formulation, which is also echoed in Rev 21:6; 22:17. It can be suggested that this final reality breaks through the temporal in the believer's union with Christ.

182. Cf. Chilton, *Days of Vengeance*, 549, explaining that John's prophecy in 21:6 "has never lost sight of its character as a practical, ethical message to the churches (rather than a bare 'prediction' of coming events)."

183. Ford, *Revelation*, 368, recalls that not an individual but a community of the overcomer is meant (cf. 21:3). Cf. Casey, "Exodus Theme in Revelation," 40, who thinks that the sonship is a feature of a corporate inheritance of God's faithful ones. Beale, *Revelation*, 1057, has suggested a link between the promise of the thirst-quenching in Isa 55:1 and of the establishing of a permanent covenant, according to the Davidic promise in Isa 55:3.

184. This interconnection has been suggested by Jankowski, *Apokalipsa*, 276. He shows that sonship also has an ultimate aspect to itself (cf. Rom 8:23; 1 John 3:2; also Luke 20:36).

185. Cf. Deutsch, "New Jerusalem," 119–20, who has pointed out the link with the Davidic promise of dominion. The extent of the new inheritance is the whole world, not merely a land. Cf. Wright, *NTPG*, 451. We have noted in chapter 2 that the *mohar* was associated with the bride's inheritance, which she could claim for a potential heir. Here, we see that the heirs receive the inheritance of their mother.

reference to the Davidic promise enhances the divine marriage motif. It may also refer to the city motif, as the overcomer belongs to the new City of God (cf. 3:12).[186] Being part of the new Jerusalem implies the priestly function of the new community of God, because they are filled with God's special presence. Therefore, it may be concluded that the two motifs of city and bride come together to elaborate on the theme of royal priesthood indicated for the first time in Rev 1:6.

The same two motifs negatively express the situation of those who have not proved to be the overcomer (21:9).[187] It is possible to view them as whoring, i.e., being unfaithful and disloyal to Christ (cf. 2:14, 20–22; 9:21).[188] They are the antithesis of the bride. However, the motif of the city helps to explain their being cast outside the community: they do not participate in the new Jerusalem, but in the lake of fire.[189] The unfaithful have no access to God's holy presence in his tabernacle. They are ultimately cut off from God's blessings and equally deprived of security (cf. 21:10, 12, 14).[190]

It has been suggested that Rev 21:9—22:5 parallels 21:1–8.[191] One could, therefore, expect the two motifs of city and bride to be prominent in the material starting at 21:9. It is quite evident that the motif of the city gains John's particular attention in this new section, but it would be

---

186. Although Miller, "Nuptial Eschatology," 311, insists that the city is the overcomer's inheritance, it would be more appropriate to view the inheritance as all things made new by God. See Gundry, "New Jerusalem: People as Place," 261. The city represents rather the priestly function of the overcomer community, because the role of the temple is expanded into the whole city.

187. Gundry, "New Jerusalem: People as Place," 258, has argued that Rev 21:8 particularly focuses on those within John's churches who turned their backs on their previous Christian confession. Similarly, Beale, *Revelation*, 1059, argues that the list of vices in the verse describes the sins against which John was warning the churches.

188. Cf. Beale, *Revelation*, 1059 and Lee, *New Jerusalem in Revelation*, 275, who explain that the vice list describes those who failed to be faithful to Christ. Other vices characterized those whom Christ was displeased with earlier in Revelation (δειλός cf. 2:10; ψευδής cf. 2:2; 3:9; ἀπίστοις contrasts 2:13; 13:10; ἐβδελυγμένοις cf. 17:4–5; φονεῦσιν cf. 13:15; 16:6; 17:6; 18:24; εἰδωλολάτραις cf. 2:14, 20; 9:20; 13:4, 12–15).

189. Thompson, "Mythic Unity," 26, explains that burning in the lake of fire in 21:8 is apparently the same as dwelling outside the city gates of the new Jerusalem in 22:15 (the two vice lists are similar).

190. Concerning the city's security see Gundry, "New Jerusalem: People as Place," 260. Lee, *New Jerusalem in Revelation*, 278, insists that perfect security, not protection, is behind the symbol of the city's wall.

191. Cf. Deutsch, "New Jerusalem," 110; Beale, *Revelation*, 1063.

a mistake to conclude that the bride motif is dropped out or diminished. After all, a bowl angel shows John the bride, the Lamb's wife (v. 9). She comes down as a city to possess her inheritance.[192] However, just as the apparel of the harlot characterized Babylon's system, the new Jerusalem's characteristics point to the bride's nature.[193] She reflects God's glory, as the city is filled with God's presence (v. 11; cf. 4:3; 1:16; 12:1).[194] But it may be suggested here that the wife is the reflection of her husband's glory, an idea somewhat similar to that of Paul in 1 Cor 11:7 (cf. NJB).[195] As a city, she is surrounded by walls with twelve gates, having twelve foundations (Rev 21:12–14).[196] To translate this into the motif of bride, one would have to point to the undisturbed and inviolable nature of her

---

192. Wallis, "Coming of the Kingdom," 59.

193. For a comparison between Babylon and the new Jerusalem see Giblin, "Theology of Revelation 16–22," 489; Kramer, "Contrast as a Key," 109; and McIlraith, "Works and Wife in Revelation 19:8," 525.

194. Cf. Lee, *New Jerusalem in Revelation*, 286. He suggests that the bride's glorious apparel resembles Isa 61:10 (cf. Rev 19:8). We have, however, suggested that the wedding apparel in 19:8 should probably be distinguished from the later embroidery of the wife in 21:11–21 (cf. Ezek 16:8–14). Similarly, Fekkes, "Nuptial Imagery," 285. Muirhead, "Bride of Christ," 178, has proposed that this glory implies the restored image of God after he has finished "building" up the Christian community. Terry, *Biblical Apocalyptics*, 466, has argued that the verse also alludes to *Shekinah* (cloud of glory), which covered the tabernacle (Exod 40:34–38; cf. Isa 58:8; 60:1–2, 19; Zech 2:5). This idea reoccurs later in 21:23. Thus it is God's tabernacling glory presence that clothes (and illuminates) the bride. Cf. Beale, *Revelation*, 1066.

195. It needs to be remembered that, although the church is the wife of Christ, in another sense she is the wife of God, with Christ acting as an agent on God's behalf. Cf. chapter 5 above on this. Perhaps a similar idea of the wife being the reflection of her husband glory is expressed in Isa 60:19.

196. The picture may echo Ezek 40:5–6 and 48:31–34. The walls have on them the names of the twelve tribes of Israel and their twelve foundations have the names of the twelve apostles on them. This picture suggests the completeness of God's restored people. Cf. Beale, *Revelation*, 1068. Wallis, "Coming of the Kingdom," proposes that the imagery encompasses the saints of both Testaments. The foundations (with the names of the apostles) are adorned with precious stones, probably echoing the temple foundation stones (Rev 21:19–20; cf. 1 Kgs 5:17). See Chilton, *Days of Vengeance*, 557. Lee, *New Jerusalem in Revelation*, 286, has argued that the jewelry of Jerusalem points to the fulfillment of a new temple and new Eden expectations. However, it may also have in view the priesthood of those who constitute the city, as the twelve stones resemble those on the high-priest's breastplate (cf. Exod 28:17–20). Thus the city may corporately stand for a high priest and by implication have the same access before God as that one. Cf. Ford, *Revelation*, 342.

relationship with God, by his protection (cf. v. 27).[197] The cubical shape of the city probably signifies the perfection of God's dwelling place and thus also of his wife (vv. 15–17).[198] But it can also reflect the intimacy of God indwelling his wife, an intimacy only possible within wedlock (cf. Gen 2:24; 1 Cor 6:17).[199] The marital relationship is reciprocal and therefore God and the Lamb become the indwelling of the bride, her intimate partner (Rev 21:22).[200] Hence, it seems that both parties within the marriage have special access to each other's heart. Their relationship also has in view a multitude of offspring: those who enter the city (vv. 24–26; 22:2).[201] This suggests that the ultimate breaks through the tem-

---

197. Cf. Beale, *Revelation*, 1068; Lee, *New Jerusalem in Revelation*, 278. There are twelve angels protecting the gates of the city, a picture resembling the protection of Eden by a cherub (cf. Gen 3:24; Isa 62:6). See also Jankowski, *Apokalipsa*, 278.

198. See Metzger, *Breaking the Code*, 101: a cube shows harmony and symmetry of perfect proportions. Gundry, "New Jerusalem: People as Place," 260, thinks that the proportions of the city are reminiscent of the twelve thousand from each of the twelve tribes of Israel (cf. 7:1–8; 14:1–5). He explains (p. 261) that the cubical shape matches the shape of the inner sanctuary of the temple (1 Kgs 6:20), which implies that those who belong to the city are "God's most sacred dwelling place, the inmost room of his new creation." Cf. also Jankowski, *Apokalipsa*, 279.

199. The one flesh union expresses a special covenant bond between a husband and his wife. Cf. chapter 6 on Eph 5:29. Also Hugenberger, *Marriage as a Covenant*, 162–63.

200. Gundry, "New Jerusalem: People as Place," 262, has observed here a reciprocity similar to that of John 14–17 (reciprocal abiding of God and Christ's followers). However, he has failed to associate it with the covenant union. Ford, *Revelation*, 344, suggests that the lack of the temple is not a new idea for it was already found in Jer 3:15–17. However, Vogelgesang, "Ezekiel in Revelation," has argued that John was original in his abandoning the temple.

201. The open gates of the city welcome all who would enter. Rossing, *Two Cities*, 154, explains that the gates "underscore the invitational character of the New Jerusalem." In Ezek 48:30 the gates are exits, but here they are entrances. This would imply that a temporal perspective is implied here. It is possible that here only in Revelation the phrase οἱ βασιλεῖς τῆς γῆς should be taken in a universal sense (cf. Isa 60:5–6, 9, 11; 49:22–23). This is because the rule of God has now spread over the whole world in the messianic kingdom. Likewise, the inheritance of the new people of God has been transposed into the whole world. Cf. Wright, *NTPG*, 451. It is noteworthy that these kings/rulers are not in opposition to Christ and his people, but rather join the community of life (Rev 21:27; cf. 1:5–6). Cf. Chilton, *Days of Vengeance*, 562–63, who points to Isa 49 and 60 as sources. Our suggestion is plausible because the "kings" expand the meaning of Isa 60:3, 11. Cf. Beale, *Revelation*, 1097, who however assumes that the once-wicked world rulers of 17:2, 18, may now be converted. But it is possible that "new" kings replace those who did not want Christ's rule over them (cf. 1:5; 6:15; 17:2, etc.). Christ has made for himself new kings out of every nation (cf. 1:6; 5:10). In general, it can be said that Rev 21:24–26;

poral, as the nations accept God's rule.²⁰² Bearing in mind the Pauline tradition, one could propose that the Lamb's wife here is the mother of the multitude of many nations (cf. Gal 4:27). She is perfectly free of any defiling elements, anything that would direct her steps towards being a harlot (Rev 21:27; 22:3).²⁰³ She is sealed up for perfect loyalty to her one and only husband (22:4; cf. 3:12; 7:3–4). The wife and her offspring are going to reign as a royal priesthood alongside her husband for ever (22:5; cf. 1:6; 2:26–27; 3:21; 5:10; 20:6; Ps 45:16–17; also Dan 7:18; 27).²⁰⁴

Rev 22 contains a closing prophetic assurance concerning the unavoidability and nearness of the visions' fulfillment (Rev 22:6–7, 12, 20; cf. 1:1, 3; 2:16; 3:11).²⁰⁵ Hence, the time reference of this section probably looks backward to the point before Christ's vindication spoken of in 1:7. Now, John recalls that Christ's contemporary coming in judgment will result in dividing the unjust from the righteous (22:11–12; cf. 2:22–23).²⁰⁶

22:2 fulfill the OT motif of the nations' pilgrimage to the restored Zion (cf. Isa 2:2–4; 60:1–14; Zech 2:11; 14:16). Cf. Lee, *New Jerusalem in Revelation*, 287.

Rev 22:1–2 also echoes the promise of the restoration of Zion according to the patterns of Eden in Isa 51:3. Cf. Ford, *Revelation*, 345. It is the regaining of life lost in Eden (Gen 3:22, 24; Ezek 47:1–12; Rev 2:7). Cf. Casey, "Exodus Theme in Revelation," 41. However, now the single tree of life in Eden has emerged into many trees to provide for a multitude of the new Paradise's inhabitants. Cf. Gundry, "New Jerusalem: People as Place," 262. See also Wright, *RSG*, 476.

202. The city still waits for many to enter it, so that they may be cured (cf. 22:2). See Caird, *Revelation*, 280. God's rule becomes irresistible. Cf. Lee, *New Jerusalem in Revelation*, 291.

203. Jankowski, *Apokalipsa*, 284, has suggested that κατάθεμα in 22:3 is a synonym of ἀνάθεμα: a person or thing cursed, which should be cut off/destroyed (cf. Deut 2:34; 3:6; 7:2).

204. Thus it seems that their reign extends beyond the millennium probably throughout eternity. Cf. Aune, *Revelation 17–22*, 1181, who links Rev 22:5 with Dan 7:18, 27.

205. Chilton, *Days of Vengeance*, 574–75. On nearness compare the *Sitz im Leben* section above. Cf. also Gentry, *Before Jerusalem Fell*, 134–42. We are inclined to accept the wide scholarly consensus concerning 22:6–21 as constituting the book's conclusion. See Caird, *Revelation*, 281; Beale, *Revelation*, 1122. But see Aune, *Revelation 17–22*, 1181–82. However, he does not escape the conclusion that 22:6–9 refers to the rest of Revelation.

206. We cannot agree with Vos, *Synoptic Traditions in the Apocalypse*, 174, who has contended that 22:12 refers to the remote parousia of Christ. However, his proposal that the verse resembles Matt 16:27 seems convincing (178). It is quite telling that the immediate context in Matt 16:28 resembles the time references of Rev 1:3b, 7, etc. (79). Beale, *Revelation*, 1134, has noted here a connection with 2:22–23. Chilton, *Days of Vengeance*, 577, believes that the angel in v. 11 is calling for the differentiation of the righteous and the wicked.

Those of John's addressees who keep God's commandments will soon enter the new city of God's presence (22:14). By implication, they will have their share in the wife of the Lamb. Others will stay out because they have a share in the whore and therefore ultimately in the lake of fire (v. 15; cf. 21:8; 18:4).[207] Meanwhile, the bride is expecting her bridegroom's coming in judgment to bring her into the wedding feast of salvation, which should follow the destruction of the whore (22:17).[208] Thus, the time of the wedding for those of John's audience who prove obedient is near (v. 20). Their conflict with the whore (e.g., 11:8) will soon be ended. But they are also assured that the bridal reality, in which they will soon participate, endures for ever, even beyond their physical death (22:14; cf. 20:4).

Our study so far indicates that the metaphor of divine marriage plays an important part in the argument of the last few chapters of Revelation. We will now examine other passages in the book, tracing probable employments of the metaphor. Since some scholars have suggested that various parts of Revelation are interrelated (see the section above on Structure), one would expect some relationship between the metaphor in the last chapters and the content of the previous and early chapters. First, we will turn to those passages that naturally encourage the quest for the *hieros gamos* as they refer to women or a relationship

---

207. This group of people is probably the same as that in 21:8. Cf. Thompson, "Mythic Unity," 26. It is significant that "dogs" can signify male prostitutes (cf. Deut 23:18). See Jankowski, *Apokalipsa*, 288. Thus the term is linked with prostitution. However, Beale, *Revelation*, 1142, has suggested that the OT sometimes used the word also of Israelites who violated God's covenant (Ps. 59:6, 14; also 22:16, 20). We would suggest that the term could have had the specific meaning of spiritual adultery, πορνεία. It is striking that in the NT Paul uses the word for Jews in Phil 3:2. O'Brien, *Philippians*, 355, observes that Paul calls the Judaizers "the dogs": those who place themselves outside the covenant. They are God's people who violate the covenant.

208. Scholars have argued that Rev 22:17 is similar to the Pauline *maranatha* in 1 Cor 16:22. Cf. Jankowski, *Apokalipsa*, 289. Beasley-Murray, *Revelation*, 348, has argued also that whereas the reference in 1 Cor 16:22 is to a judgment, the one in Rev 22:17 is about grace to come. This, however, cannot be entirely right, since the context refers also to an imminent judgment. Yet, the verse is an invitation to people to join the bride after leaving the whore (18:4). Cf. Rossing, *Two Cities*, 161. The invitation is to receive life (21:6). Beale, *Revelation*, 1148, explains that the first two imperatives 'come' may be addressed to Jesus and the last two can be urging people to join the community of the faithful. Thus the two would be a response to v. 12 and in line with v. 20b. Cf. Aune, *Revelation 17–22*, 1227–28.

The Metaphor of Divine Marriage in the Book of Revelation 271

with women. Lastly, we will propose instances in which echoes of the divine marriage metaphor can be discerned.

LIKELY INSTANCES OF THE USE OF DIVINE MARRIAGE METAPHOR IN REVELATION

Revelation 17–18

We have noticed above that the visions in Rev 19 continue the themes described in Rev 17–18.[209] Therefore, we expect that these preceding chapters can constitute a background to the marriage imagery in Rev 19.

We have already discussed in the Introduction some of the interpretive issues regarding the identity of the great harlot in Rev 17–18. We have suggested that the comparison of Rome and Babylon does not necessarily have strong biblical support.[210] It fails to explain the identification of the city as a harlot.[211] Moreover, it can be shown that certain parallels with the OT and the thrust of the argument in these chapters may point to the Jewish capital.

Scholars have generally argued that the main sources for Rev 17–18 are Isa 23, 47, Jer 50–51, and Ezek 27–28: the prophecies against Tyre and Babylon.[212] The texts are often regarded as political and commercial critiques of the systems represented by those cities. This has led some scholars to conclude that the woman imagery is incidental and that the two-women *topos* is merely the rhetoric of choice for contrasting two opposing political systems represented by two cities/empires.[213] Thus,

---

209. Bauckham, *Climax of Prophecy*, 4, supports this observation.

210. It is based on the post-70 CE Jewish identification of Rome as Babylon: the OT Babylon destroyed the Temple in 587 BCE, so did Rome in 70 CE. Cf., e.g., Aune, *Revelation 1–5*, lxi; Beale, *Revelation*, 19.

211. Bauckham, *Climax of Prophecy*, 346, insists that the prophecy concerning Tyre's trading activity in Isa 23:15–18 best suited Rome's economic exploitation. He assumes that since Tyre was called harlot in the context of her commercial activity, Rome can also be. This, however, misses the point that Tyre was very likely in a covenant with God (2 Sam 5:11; 1 Kgs 5:1–12; 2 Chr 2:11–12; cf. Amos 1:9; Ezek 28:12–19). Cf. Chilton, *Days of Vengeance*, 424 n.2. Hence, also pace Rossing, *Two Cities*, 70.

212. See, e.g., Boxall, "Many Faces of Babylon," 53; Fekkes, *Prophetic Traditions in Revelation*, 211; Friesen, *Imperial Cultus and the Apocalypse*, 139; Kraybill, *Commerce in John's Apocalypse*, 149, 152.

213. See esp. Rossing, *Two Cities*, 82. The two-women *topos* is derived from the story of Heracles (pp. 18–20), probably via Prov 1–9 (pp. 41, 44, 53, 58). The rhetoric of Rev

the woman imagery is subject to the central imagery of the city.[214] This, however, contradicts the opinion of others who have recognized that the woman-city-whore imagery of Ezek 16 and 23 is the major source for the imagery in Rev 17, with a number of parallels between these visions.[215] This strongly implies that the woman-harlot motif is, at least, equal to that of the city, if not the leading one. Therefore, we suggest that the identification of the city is closely linked with the identity of the harlot and the nature of her harlotry. We have indicated in chapter 3 that the metaphor of harlotry stands either for the open idolatry of God's people or their alliances with foreign nations, and sometimes the two together. If a city/nation were to be called a harlot, she would first have to be in the covenant with God. Her prostitution was a violation of that basic relationship and did not refer primarily to an economic system based on alliances with foreign nations.[216] This suggests that the Babylon of Revelation was previously close to God, she was his wife.

Moreover, there are certain phrases and motifs in Rev 17–18, which resemble the Synoptic traditions concerning the disaster coming upon Judea and Jerusalem. The command to 'come out of her' is reminiscent of Matt 24:15–21, where Jesus warned his disciples to leave Judea, in the face of an approaching crisis.[217] Likewise, the statement about 'the blood of the prophets and saints' found in Babylon (Rev 18:24) resembles a charge brought by Jesus against Jerusalem in Luke 11:50 and Matt 23:35.[218]

17–18 attempts to persuade the audience to come out of Babylon and participate in the new Jerusalem (59). Hence, it transforms the two-women tradition from the realm of wisdom and morals to the realm of politics and economics. The *topos* helps to warn against Rome's seductive economic power (62).

214. Ibid., 82.

215. See, e.g., Moyise, *Old Testament in Revelation*, 72. Cf. Ford, *Revelation*, 283, 286–87, and Beagley, *Church's Enemies*, 93, 109.

216. Pace Bauckham, *Climax of Prophecy*, 346, Rossing, *Two Cities*, 70, Wengst, "Babylon the Great," 192–93, and others who have failed to demonstrate to whom Rome was unfaithful in her activities. While it is possible for an individual to be a prostitute while unmarried, the OT does not seem to presume the same when a city/nation is involved. It appears that every harlot city was first in covenant with God.

217. Cf. Vos, *Synoptic Traditions in the Apocalypse*, 161. Although the command in Rev 18:4 echoes Jer 51:6, the motifs of false prophets, tribulation and wickedness are common to both Rev 17–18 and Matt 24:1–28. However, Vos maintains that John changed the application of Jesus' traditions (163). But then, he is not certain why John alludes to Jesus' sayings in such cases. We suggest that this was because he wanted to deliver a similar message to Jesus' own.

218. Ibid., 162–63. Vos observed that these similarities are "not only in thought and wording, but are also in the word order." Yet, Vos thinks that the meaning of Rev 17–18

It could be argued that these Synoptic traditions provide appropriate models of expression for Revelation. But it may well be that this parallelism points to similar theological interest on the part of the author of Revelation (see above *Sitz im Leben*).

Finally, we need to turn to the subsequent symbols in order to examine whether or not they confirm our proposal.

The harlot to be judged "sits upon many waters" (v. 1; Jer 51:13). They are "peoples, multitudes, nations, and tongues" (v. 15). We have already suggested above that this may point to the commercial relations of Jerusalem with other nations.[219] Jewish leaders, especially those of priestly families, were apparently the ones who gained most wealth from Judean commerce associated with the Temple.[220] Jerusalem also had strong influence throughout the cities of the Roman Empire, where Jews had established synagogues. These, in turn, contributed to Jerusalem's wealth (cf. Acts 2:5).[221]

The characterizing of the woman as πόρνη probably echoes the whore Jerusalem in Ezek 16:15–16.[222] The βασιλεῖς τῆς γῆς have 'fornicated' with her (Rev 17:2). Scholars have usually assumed that the phrase means kings/rulers of the world: the lovers of the harlot, with whom she had metaphorical intercourse. Yet, it is likely that the phrase βασιλεῖς τῆς γῆς denotes the rulers of the land of Israel.[223] The picture would then be of the rulers of the land committing adultery *in company with, together with,* or *alongside* the harlot.[224] They belong to the harlot and they are as

---

is not dependent on these traditions because Revelation is not interested in the old Jerusalem system. However, others have recognized John's dependence on the Synoptics. E.g., Russell, *Parousia*, 497.

219. Cf. Safrai and Stern, *Jewish People in the First Century*, II: 668.

220. Ibid., II: 691. Safrai and Stern explain that, "The upper echelons of the priestly families enriched themselves from the Temple perquisites and exploited the poorer priests, in conformity with the opportunistic and egoistical character of those high-priestly families which were prepared to respond to the requirements of the Herodian rulers and the Roman government."

221. They were paying the temple tax. Ibid., II: 677–78. See also Chilton, *Days of Vengeance*, 438–39.

222. Cf. Moyise, *Old Testament in Revelation*, 72. He sees the parallel, but does not insist on the Jerusalem reading.

223. See our discussion in Introduction on 17:18.

224. μετά with the Genitive often denotes association . Cf. Danker, *Greek-English Lexicon*, 636–37. The same lexicon indicates that μετά with the Genitive in Rev 2:22 points to the influence that one party has upon the other or that one brings the other to

promiscuous as she is. Accordingly, the meaning of the phrase could be similar to 2:22, where those committing adultery with Jezebel are in fact those engaging in adultery *alongside* her. They are the children following their mother (cf. 2:23; 17:5).[225] Furthermore, the second part of Rev 17:2 mentions οἱ κατοικοῦντες τὴν γῆν, a phrase that could be more specific than usually admitted. Following our earlier suggestion, ἡ γῆ can refer to the land of Judea. This would imply Jerusalem as the harlot influencing and affecting all who dwelt in Judea with her fornication.

The next vision is of the woman sitting on a scarlet beast in the wilderness (17:3). Her destiny is desolation.[226] She relies on her association with the scarlet beast.[227] Her rich attire and ornaments may point to Jerusalem's splendor (v. 4).[228] Her golden cup full of abominations

---

adopt a corresponding attitude (p. 637). The latter is more likely since the verb πορνεύειν is normally intransitive. Cf. Aune, *Revelation 17–22*, 907.

This section of Revelation is more specific than the reference to Isa 23:17 would allow. Besides, the LXX uses the word οἰκουμένη. Pace, Beale, *Revelation*, 849–50.

225. Aune, *Revelation 1–5*, 205.

226. The name on her forehead in v. 5 suggests that she is the same as the great harlot in vv. 1–2. The wilderness here probably contrasts the "great and high mountain" in 21:10. Cf. Aune, *Revelation 17–22*, 933. Ford, *Revelation*, 287, shows that the wilderness in 12:6, 14 appears with the definite article, which makes a difference in reference. She suggests that the wilderness in 17:3 refers to a place forsaken by God (cf. 18:2). We have indicated in chapter 3 that Hosea 2:5, 16 (cf. Isa 6:11; 62:4; 64:9) presents God's unfaithful wife as a desolate place. This desolation was linked with Israel's exile, esp. in the Isaianic tradition. However, the vision of wilderness in Rev 17:3 could correspond to the oracle against Babylon in Isa 21. There the prophet receives a vision from the desert (vv. 1–2). Later, Babylon is declared fallen (v. 9). But before that, Isa 13:21 pronounced that she will become desolate as a desert. Cf. Beale, *Revelation*, 851–52.

227. The beast seems to be associated with both the dragon and the sea beast, i.e., with both Satan and his earthly servant, the Roman Empire. The sequence "seven heads, ten horns" resembles 12:3, but the blasphemies echo 13:1. See Chilton, *Days of Vengeance*, 428–29. The context may suggest that the focus is on the sea beast, the Roman Empire. Yet, the color scarlet may suggest the association with the red dragon. Cf. Beale, *Revelation*, 853. Some scholars have suggested that the color may evoke the picture of the Empire's luxury and magnificence. See Charles, *Revelation*, II: 64. But scarlet can also be the color of blood and oppression (cf. 2 Kgs 3:22–23; Rev 6:4), symbolic of the oppression that was found in the harlot Jerusalem, so that her hands were covered with blood (cf. Isa 1:15, 18, 21). Cf. Stefanovic, *Revelation of Jesus Christ*, 507.

228. Scholars often maintain that the purple clothes signify royalty (cf. Esth 8:15; Dan 5:7, 16, 29; John 19:2). Although scarlet can generally mean oppression, they recognize that the color could have been one of the characteristics of a prostitute. In Jer 4:30, the harlot Judah wears both scarlet and ornaments to attract her lovers. However, it could also point to wealth (2 Sam 1:24; Prov 31:21). Cf. Aune, *Revelation 17–22*, 935. Chilton, *Days of Vengeance*, 429, has argued that there is no need to look at the woman's

testifies to her guilt.²²⁹ She appears as though having learnt harlotry from her mother in order to become the mother of all harlots (cf. Ezek 16:43–45).²³⁰

This brief survey of the symbols in the opening verses of Rev 17 implies that the harlotrous tendencies of Jerusalem's authorities may be in view. Jerusalem rests on the ungodly power of Rome for her well-being and this makes her a harlot in God's eyes. With the help of Roman authorities, she constitutes a serious threat to Christians, of whose blood she is guilty (Rev 17:6; cf. 18:24).²³¹ Thus she becomes the enemy of God's people. Hence, to the Christian, she is a Babylon.

Scholars have extensively discussed the references of the beast's heads and horns. In fact, this part of Rev 17 belongs to one of the most difficult passages to interpret in the book. Therefore, we will limit ourselves to indicating briefly possible solutions to some interpretive tensions. First, Rev 17:8 seems to suggest that the beast in view is associated with the one in 11:7 coming out of the abyss, and is perhaps a demonic figure, very much like the dragon itself.²³² It causes marvel in the dwellers

---

apparel as an extravagant form of a prostitute dresses. The clothes and ornaments belonged to Yahweh's royal wife Israel (cf. Ezek 16:10–14). Ford, *Revelation*, 278, 287, has proposed that the woman's apparel echoes the materials used to build the Temple and make the priestly garments (cf. Exod 25:3–7; 26:1, 31, 36; 27:16; 28:5, 15, 23, 31–35). Thus, it is likely that the priestly and royal Israel is in view, although she plays a harlot. Beagley, *Church's Enemies*, 99, has remarked that purple clothes may echo Luke 16:19. Luke 16:19–31 can be regarded as attacking Jewish leaders, mainly the Sadducees. Pace, Wengst, "Babylon the Great," 193, who gives a less precise explanation of the luxurious fabrics and jewelry, as referring to the dominant class of Rome.

229. "Abomination" may point to apostasy and idolatry (Deut 29:17; Ezek 5:11). Cf. Chilton, *Days of Vengeance*, 430. The golden cup could resemble the sacred utensils of the Temple. See Ford, *Revelation*, 288.

230. Cf. Ford, *Revelation*, 288, who proposes Ezek 16:43–45 as the background to Rev 17:5. It is quite likely that Jerusalem could have become a prime example of all prostitution because she whored in a more "sublime" way than all the others (Ezek 16:31–34, 47–48). The name written on the forehead is the opposite of the saints' names (3:12; 7:3; 14:1) and a symbol of rebellion (cf. Isa 48:4; Jer 3:3; Ezek 3:9). Cf. Chilton, *Days of Vengeance*, 430–31. "Babylon the Great" refers to the great enemy of God's people (cf. Dan 4:30; Jer 50:23). Cf. Wright, *JVG*, 323, 356 n. 137, on Jerusalem as the enemy in the Synoptics.

231. Cf. Chilton, *Days of Vengeance*, 431–32, remarks that, "The Roman persecution came about through the Jews' instigation and connivance, as the Book of Acts constantly informs us." Cf. Ford, *Revelation*, 288.

232. Scholars recognize that the beast is here a parody of God: "the One who is and who was and who is coming" (1:4, 8; 4:8). The beast "was, and is not, and is about to

of the earth, perhaps by reviving the power of the materialized beast (cf. 13:3; 12).[233] Second, the heads are said to signify hills (17:9), which are also kings (v. 10).[234] If hills (mountains) and kings are taken to symbolize kingdoms, in accordance with the OT sources,[235] the problem of identifying the exact list of Roman emperors ceases to pertain.[236] The seven

---

ascend from the abyss and go to destruction." In both cases, the formula seems to imply the eschatological role of the subject. Cf. Aune, *Revelation 17-22*, 939-40. The coming of the beast should probably be viewed as contemporary with Christ's *parousia* (cf. 3:11; 16:15; 22:7, 12 , 20). Cf. Beale, *Revelation*, 864. The beast seems to be symbolic, by comparison with the Lamb in vv. 13-14. Cf. Chilton, *Days of Vengeance*, 433, who thinks that Satan himself comes to the fore here, as the power behind the actual beast of the sea, the Roman Empire.

233. Some scholars argue that 17:8 is about the subsequent revivals of the Roman Empire under successive emperors. Cf. Ford, *Revelation*, 288-89. Others take it as referring to the Nero *redivivus* myth. See Yarbro Collins, *Combat Myth*, 174-76; Aune, *Revelation 17-22*, 940. Still others take it to stand for the final outbreak of the dragon's enmity towards God. See Sefanovic, *Revelation of Jesus Christ*, 513-14. However, it is possible that an event within the context of Revelation's eschatological expectation, expressed in 1:7, is being referred to.

234. Terry, *Biblical Apocalyptics*, 431, rejects the link between the mountains (v. 9) and the kings (v. 10) as producing "confusion in the whole picture." Most commentators, however, choose the more difficult rendering.

235. Mountains as kingdoms: Isa 2:2; Jer 51:25; Ezek 35:3; Dan 2:35, 45; Zech 4:7. Kings can stand for kingdoms as in Dan 7:17, 23. Cf. Wallis, "Coming of the Kingdom," 38, and Beale, *Revelation*, 868, who indicates that Dan 7:4-7 takes heads for kingdoms, a passage often regarded as the source for the vision in Rev 13:1. Consequently, the interpretation does not have to depend on somewhat confusing geographical information: apparently both Rome and Jerusalem were located in the midst of seven hills. See Aune, *Revelation 17-22*, 944-45, Friesen, *Imperial Cultus and the Apocalypse*, 137 (supporting Rome), and Russell, *Parousia*, 492; 1 *Enoch* 24-25 (supporting Jerusalem).

For a number of scholars, proper identification of the heads/emperors in Rev 17:9-11 remains the crux of the problem concerning the dating of Revelation. Cf. Bell, "Date of John's Apocalypse," 97.

236. Scholars are not unanimous concerning the counting of the emperors. Bell, "Date of John's Apocalypse," 98, is not certain whether the list should start with Julius Caesar or Augustus. Yet, he chooses Augustus to make Nero the fifth and thus to accommodate the *redivivus* myth. Marshall, *Parables of War*, 91, suggests that the fifth, sixth, and seventh heads, were subsequently: Nero, Otho, and Galba. Otho would be the eighth. But this count omits Julius Caesar. Moberly, "When Was Revelation Conceived?," 385, argues that the count should concentrate only on the emperors who have fallen sensationally, either by assassination or suicide. He lists: Julius Caesar, Gaius, Nero, Galba, and Otho. This allows him to place the writing of Revelation soon after Otho's death (under Vittelius) in 69 CE. Vespasian would be the seventh, and Titus the eight. Wilson, "Problem of the Domitianic Date," 603, claims that one could follow Tacitus and start the count with Augustus. Nero, then, becomes the fifth and Galba the one who is.

The Metaphor of Divine Marriage in the Book of Revelation 277

kings may stand for kingdoms (centres of the beast's power), of which five have fallen, one is at the vision's present, and the other will come.[237] Then, it appears, the beast will rise as an eight power, which belongs with "the seven" (v. 11).[238] Third, if the kings of v. 10 are in fact kingdoms, the horns probably point to ten rulers, who receive authority along with the eighth beast, the "resurrected" Rome (v. 12, 16).[239] They will go against the Lamb who will fight, accompanied by his chosen ones (v. 14).

We find ourselves unable to point out the exact historical counterparts of these visions. However, there is, at least, a possibility that the

---

The rest are just imprecise prophecies. However, he says that following Seutonius is also legitimate: Nero is the sixth and Revelation was written during his reign. Gentry, *Before Jerusalem Fell*, 158, starts with Julius and identifies Nero as the sixth and Galba as the seventh. The eighth would be Otho. However in his other work (see *Beast of Revelation*, 76) he argued that the eighth should be read as *an* eighth: because the Empire was revived under Vespasian who was the tenth. Why would John concentrate on the list of Roman emperors to deliver his message concerning the beast? The question of criteria for including/excluding emperors are far from certain.

The *redivivus* myth itself is of dubious relevance to Revelation. Why would it be as important to John as it is to the modern scholar trying to make Nero the beast? Why would John be interested in employing this "fabulous and superstitious rumor"? Cf. Terry, *Biblical Apocalyptics*, 432. Rev 17:10 could rather point to the downfall and presence of certain kingdoms, probably parts of the Roman Empire. The turbulent year 69 CE could be a suitable context for such changes. Cf., e.g., Wright, *New Heavens, New Earth*, 9.

237. Scholars have tried to identify the historical counterparts of the subsequent seven kingdoms. Wallis, "Coming of the Kingdom," 52, has suggested that they were: Egypt, Assyria, Babylon, Medo-Persia, Greece, Rome, and the kingdom of the beast. Thus Rome is the sixth. The seventh is to follow. The problem with this view is similar to the one concerning the emperors: one would have to ask where to start calculating and which ones to include. Beale, *Revelation*, 865, suggests that the sequence of the beast corresponds to 20:1–10, where Satan is said to appear again in the future for "a little time." However, this overlooks the context of 17:10, because it appears that the beast-to-be is going to fight with the Lamb (cf. vv. 12–14), whereas in 20:1–10, the final defeat of Satan is by fire from heaven (v. 9). "Seven" may rather be symbolic of the total scope of the imperial power of Rome. Cf. Terry, *Biblical Apocalyptics*, 431. Since the beast is the Empire, its heads are probably connected to its existence. It seems that losing 5 weakened the Empire.

238. Chilton, *Days of Vengeance*, 436, recalls that eight is the symbolic number of resurrection, a parody of Christ's. But it refers here to the regaining of power by the beast, not by an individual. Cf. Gentry, *Beast of Revelation*, 76.

239. Bauckham, *Climax of Prophecy*, 429, has argued that the 10 horns are the kings from beyond Euphrates, i.e., Parthians. But this interpretation is driven by the Nero *redivivus* myth. Instead, the number ten may symbolize either ten imperial provinces of Rome or the totality of Rome's allies. Cf. Chilton, *Days of Vengeance*, 437, and Terry, *Biblical Apocalyptics*, 432–33.

references to the heads and horns may point to events within the scope of John's contemporary situation, not to trans-temporal or entirely futuristic occasions. After all, the woman Jerusalem sits on the seven heads of the beast, which probably means that she rests on the completeness of Roman power.[240] She plays a harlot with Rome. Only the rise of the eighth head will change her situation, turn her lover against her (cf. Ezek 16:37, 39).

It appears that the ten horns and the eighth beast will destroy the woman (17:16). The very power she relied on for her well-being, and for help in fighting Christians, will turn against her in hatred. The paramour will make her desolate, naked, eat her own flesh, and burn her with fire. We have indicated earlier in this work that the metaphor of desolation is the opposite of that of being married (cf. chapter 3 on Isa 62:4; 54:1–4; cf. Hos 2:5, 16). The land becomes desolate through the pollution caused by the harlotries of God's wife (cf. Jer 3:2–3). Within the same prophetic tradition of divine marriage, the punishment for entering into political alliances with foreign nations could have resulted in Jerusalem being stripped naked and burnt with fire by her lovers (Ezek 16:39, 41; cf. 23:25–27).[241] Only in this way could her harlotry have been exposed. Eating her flesh, however, could be reminiscent of the Jezebel story and the punishment for her idolatry (1 Kgs 21:23–24; 2 Kgs 9:22, 30–37).[242] This reference may link the two great harlots of Revelation: Jezebel and Babylon, both endangering Christ's bride. The splendor of the great whore Babylon will be taken away. She was the great city over Israel. Yet, only shame and death will be left to her as the marks of her exile.

---

240. It does not need to be the Roman civilization supported by the imperial military power. The evidence may well point to Jerusalem as Babylon. Pace Bauckham, *Climax of Prophecy*, 343. Even if the sitting means that the harlot is enthroned upon the beast, it need not automatically point to Rome. Pace Rossing, *Two Cities*, 68.

241. Some scholars argue that the attack against Babylon may refer to the return of Nero at the head of Parthians to destroy Rome. So Aune, *Revelation 17–22*, 957. This seems, however, to rely on an extra-biblical myth over against the well-established biblical tradition regarding the harlot-city punishment. For the question of the sources used to interpret John's symbolisms see our discussion in chapter 1. Aune also seems to be inconsistent in his proposal that Rome should be sentenced with the punishment of the unfaithful daughter of a Jewish priest (Lev 21:9). Why such a conclusion?

242. Chilton, *Days of Vengeance*, 439, supports this. Caird, *Revelation*, 39 has remarked that "nobody ever accused Ahab's wife of harlotry except in a metaphorical sense (2 Kings ix.22)."

The Metaphor of Divine Marriage in the Book of Revelation 279

Rev 18 opens with a vision of an angel announcing the fall of Babylon because of her harlotries. In addition to the accusation in chapter 17, 18:3 reproaches the merchants of the earth for getting their wealth through the corrupted system of 'Babylon.'[243] Scholars have argued that this merchandise motif echoes prophecies concerning Tyre, mainly in Ezek 27.[244] However, in accordance with our present argument, it seems that the meaning of the harlot should also qualify the trading motif.[245] Therefore, we suggest, a reference to Jerusalem's merchandise should be preferred over a reference to the merchandise of Rome. Moreover, if Revelation's reliance on covenant traditions is allowed, it seems that the critique is not of the commerce *per se* but rather of a trading system that leads to the oppression of God's poor people, which violates divine matrimony (Rev 18:6-7, 9).[246] Her sin is not so much wealth as unfaith-

243. Rome's highly developed trading system is clear beyond dispute. Thus, the majority of NT exegetes prefer to view Rome's commerce as fornication. Cf., e.g., Wengst, "Babylon the Great," 193. This, however, creates the problem of explaining the city/nation's harlotry in biblical terms. The phrase οἱ ἔμποροι τῆς γῆς may point to the link between the merchants and the land of Judea. It should also be remembered that Jews of that time had been involved in trading on quite a large scale. The Hasmonaeans developed Jewish seafaring. Herod built a fleet with a very successful harbor at Caesarea (cf. Rev 18:17). Much of the eastern Mediterranean basin was dependent on Jewish trade for many oriental luxurious and common goods. See Safrai and Stern, *Jewish People in the First Century*, II: 668, 679, 689. It also is likely that Jerusalem commerce was strongly linked with the Temple system (pp. 677-78). Cf. Chilton, *Days of Vengeance*, 448.

244. Fekkes, *Prophetic Traditions in Revelation*, 211. Cf. Moyise, *Old Testament in Revelation*, 72.

245. It seems that the chapter is not so much a critique of Rome's political economy as of the harlotrous system of Jerusalem. Pace Callahan, "Critique of Political Economy," 46.

246. We can agree with Rossing, *Two Cities*, 115-16, that Babylon becomes rich at the expense of people's suffering and also that John's critique focuses on the city's trade and alliances. However, we disagree with her application of these observations to Rome. For her, the critique becomes an attack on Rome's exploitative trade and dominion. Cf. Rossing, "River of Life," 491. But she does not recognize the importance of the harlotry motif and thus of the covenantal framework, in which it should be interpreted. For the exploitive policy of the upper priestly families, see Safrai and Stern, *Jewish People in the First Century*, II: 691. For the distribution of wealth during Jesus' time, see Hoehner, *Herod Antipas*, 70-73. It seems that the wealthy royal class in Judea oppressed the poor, not only by heavy taxes (pp. 75-77). Oppressing the poor was strongly condemned by God's law and the prophets: cf. Lev 19:13; Deut 24:14; Ezek 16:49; 18:12; Hos 12:7; Amos 4:1; 5:11-12; Zech 7:10. Thus we may agree with Wengst, "Babylon the Great," 196, that John's vision favors the lowest classes, because they are victims.

The double payment for sins in 18:6 was imposed in the OT on unfaithful Israel (cf. Isa 40:2; Jer 16:18; Zech 9:12) likely according to the law of restitution (Exod 22:4, 7). Cf. Chilton, *Days of Vengeance*, 450.

fulness to her Husband.[247] Therefore, she will be deprived of the wealth, which bedecked God's royal wife (18:14, 16). She was bestowed with gifts from different parts of the world (vv. 12–13),[248] but she will be left 'naked', i.e., with nothing (v. 14, 16). She will be burned with fire in the sight of the public (vv. 8–10).[249] No longer will she be a queen: she will indeed become a sorrowful widow.[250] She will realize that she is (still?) in exile.

The once great city will be lamented over by the Palestinian rulers, merchants and sea traders (vv. 9–11, 15–17a, 17b–19).[251] They will all lose their share in the riches of the corrupted system of Babylon because she will become desolate: her Husband will turn against her and she will be left unmarried.

The judgment of Babylon is a cause of joy (v. 20). In it, God will finally avenge the martyrdom of his apostles and prophets.[252] They will be vindicated in the judgment.[253] But the harlotrous city will be thrown

---

247. Pace Kramer, "Contrast as a Key," 112. Material goods were regarded in the OT as gifts from God the loving husband (cf. Hos 2:5, 8–9, 13; Ezek 16:10–13).

248. Beale, *Revelation*, 60, suggests that the 28 items listed in vv. 12–13 can be regarded as the totality (4x7) of products from the entire world. Safrai and Stern, *Jewish People in the First Century*, II: 670–79, list among Judean imports in the first century CE: metals, marble, incense (including frankincense, aloe wood, and cinnamon), precious stones, pearls, fine linens, cattle and sheep, grain and other foods. Oil and wine figured among Judea's exports. Safrai and Stern also observe that Josephus (*War* iv:3:508, 4:510) implies that slavery was present in Judea in the years preceding 70 CE. Cf. Heohner, *Herod Antipas*, 72. One should remember that kings in Israel were forbidden to multiply gold, horses, and wives (Deut 17:16–17). However, according to Rev 18:12–13, the kingdom was involved, at least, in multiplying the first two.

249. Ford, "Divorce Bill," 141. Ford argues that this resembles the punishment for the unfaithful priestly daughter in the Mosaic legislation (Lev 21:9).

250. We have indicated in chapter 3 that widowhood was a state of misfortune and misery. However, in the metaphorical sense, it could refer to Israel's exile. Rev 18:7 may be reminiscent of Isa 47:6–11, which condemns Babylon for oppressing God's people. Cf. Chilton, *Days of Vengeance*, 450.

251. Rossing, *Two Cities*, 103–6, suggests that Rev 18 resembles the genre of city laments, as can be found in, e.g., Amos 5:2; Lam 2:13; Ezek 27:32. Wengst, "Babylon the Great," 195, explains that it is a funeral lament. Ford, *Revelation*, 298, 304, observes here the resemblance to the three-fold woe uttered by an angel in 8:13.

252. Beale, *Revelation*, 916, argues that this echoes Jer 51:49. But Ford, *Revelation*, 299, argues that a closer parallel can be found in Deut 32:43, where Yahweh is avenging the blood of his servants. She suggests that there is also an affinity of thought with Matt 23:37. However, Beale's suggestion that the vengeance is a response to the prayers of martyrs in 6:9–11 seems plausible.

253. Cf. Chilton, *Days of Vengeance*, 459.

down as a millstone (v. 21).²⁵⁴ Her whole life is fading away (v. 22).²⁵⁵ Moreover, the condemned Babylon will not have the light of a lamp anymore (v. 23a; cf. Jer 25:10). This could simply refer to the cessation of daily life activities. But the light in Jer 25:10 could signify either the temple lamp (rnE cf. Exod 27:20; Lev 24:2), or the lamp of testimony (cf. Pss 119:105; 132:17; Prov 6:23; 20:27), or more particularly the lamp of Israel's witness (Isa 42:6–7; 49:6; 60:1–3; cf. Matt 5:15).²⁵⁶ Each of those options seems plausible. However, the occurrence of lampstands in the wider context of Revelation could suggest the presence of testimony in/among God's people. Therefore the picture can concern the withdrawal of God's testimony from Jerusalem. Similarly, the "voice of bridegroom and bride" may involve slightly more than just a description of the cessation of life activities. The source for this imagery can be Jer 25:10.²⁵⁷ There the lack of marital festivities in Jerusalem symbolized her exile and the absence of her Husband in her midst. This is confirmed by the wider context of Jeremiah's message, where the divine marriage theme

254. The imagery is probably based on Jer 51:63–64. Beale, *Revelation*, 918–19. Both Beale and Vos, *Synoptic Traditions in the Apocalypse*, 157–58, have acknowledged that the imagery of the millstone resembles the Synoptic tradition about those, who cause others to stumble concerning the Gospel (Luke 17:2; Matt 18:6; Mark 9:42). Yet, despite their final conclusions, it is possible to view the unfaithful Jerusalem as creating offences to others, i.e., influencing others to reject the Gospel (cf. Luke 17:2; Matt 18:7; Mark 9:42–48). Cf. Wright, *JVG*, 329. The notion of the judgment's permanency does not have to be interpreted in a literal geographical sense. We have already indicated rather that certain systems/people are being judged. Cf. Chilton, *Days of Vengeance*, 461–63.

255. The imagery could have been inspired by Isa 24:8 in its context of judgment upon the earth (i.e., the land of Israel—cf. vv. 2, 5, 21–22). Cf. Aune, *17–22*, 1008. Ford, *Revelation*, 306, remarks that both the flute and the trumpet were religious instruments in Israel. Chilton, *Days of Vengeance*, 464, notices that the Levitical orchestra also included harpists (cf. 1 Chr 25:1–6). However, religious orders of other nations included similar sets of musicians (cf. Dan 3:5). Nevertheless, this suggests that the picture may be more of a cultic one than is normally assumed (e.g., by Beale, *Revelation*, 920).

The disappearance of craftsmen could refer to the cessation of the land's productivity. Cf. Chilton, *Days of Vengeance*, 464. Chilton has also proposed that the symbol of the mill could signify the foundation of the cosmos in the ancient world. He follows the earlier study by G. deSantillana and H. von Dechend, *Hamlet's Mill: An Essay on Myth and the Frame of Time* (Ipswich: Gambit, 1969). However, we cannot find strong enough evidence for the millstone symbolism in the OT to happily accept this. Aune, *Revelation 17–22*, 1009, has noticed a more obvious link with Jer 25:10. He also shows that in the OT the millstone is one of the essentials of life (Deut 24:6). Thus the picture is similar to the one of approaching death in Eccl 12:3–6. Cf. Thompson, *Jeremiah*, 513.

256. Thompson, *Jeremiah*, 513.

257. Cf. Aune, *Revelation 17–22*, 1009. See also Jer 7:34; 16:9.

is linked to the main motif of exile (cf. Jer 2–25).[258] Thus, although Jer 25:10 is not a direct reference to the divine marriage theme, it points to it. Within this context, the harlot in Rev 18 appears to be Jerusalem, which is going to be divorced, since exile is divorce. Her exile marks an end to her deception of the nations, symbolized by sorcery.[259] She is punished for the righteous blood of God's martyrs (Rev 18:24; cf. Luke 11:50).

We have observed that OT traditions of the divine marriage metaphor may play a key interpretive role in Rev 17–18. Thus we submit that only by placing Babylon's harlotry in its right covenantal context is one able to explain the symbolism of the unfaithful city in these chapters. The context allows us to identify the great whore as God's unfaithful people. She plays the harlot but has also become a Babylon: the enemy of God's faithful and the messianic community. Corrupt Jerusalem places herself in exile, which is her divorce and God's abandonment. She is contrasted with the faithful city of God depicted in the following chapters. That one is the faithful wife clothed in God's righteousness (cf. 19:8). She also participates in the marriage supper of the Lamb (19:9). Thus, the contrast of the two women of Revelation becomes now more apparent.

The Letter to Thyatira (2:18–29)

We have indicated in the previous section that the harlotry of Babylon in Rev 17–18 resembles that of Jezebel from the letter to Thyatira (2:18–29).

---

258. Cf. Carroll, *Jeremiah*, 113.

259. The reference to Babylon's sorcery may be based on Isa 47:9. It could also echo Nah 3:4. Cf. Aune, *Revelation 17–22*, 1010. Although Aune suggests that the reference is generally to the magic of Babylon/Rome, we believe that another explanation is more plausible in biblical context. Beale, *Revelation*, 922, has suggested that the last phrase of Rev 18:23 does not imply so much magic, as deception of people into idolatry. He indicates that idolatry and sorcery are linked together in Rev 9:20–21 and Gal 5:20. Isa 57:3 seems to juxtapose sorcery and idolatry. Still, it should be noted that 2 Kgs 9:22 links together Jezebel's harlotries and sorceries. Cf. Caird, *Revelation*, 39. Thus, it is likely that the sorcery in 2 Kgs 9:22 refers to leading others into idolatry. If Jezebel in Rev 2 is a type of Babylon in Rev 17–18, Babylon's sorcery probably refers to her influencing others towards idolatry (cf. Isa 57:3). Furthermore, according to 1 Sam 15:23 rebellion against God is 'a sin of sorcery' (NJB). Babylon's idolatry could have consisted of her rejection of Jesus and her support to the Empire. Pace Duff, "Witchcraft Accusations," 131, who reads Babylon's sorceries against the background of New Guinean magical practices.

For this reason, it seems appropriate to consider briefly this passage in search for the divine marriage theme.

In this vision, the church is loyal in her devotion to Christ (v. 19).[260] But she tolerates the false prophetess Jezebel (v. 20), who is involved in harlotry (cf. 1 John 4:1–3).[261]

Scholars have debated the identity of this person. Although some have suggested an individual character,[262] it is plausible that a group of people was represented by that name.[263] Moreover, some interpreters have observed that the charge of πορνεία links Jezebel to the Great Whore Babylon (14:8; 17:2; 18:3; 19:2).[264] She, thus, fornicates herself and teaches others to do the same (2:22). Her followers/children become a spiritual harlot whom Christ will judge (v. 23).[265] The parallelism between Jezebel and the Great Harlot may prove helpful in establishing the identity of the former. Although based in Thyatira, she can resemble in her practices the corrupt system in Jerusalem, which rejects Jesus the Messiah. Hence, Christ's church is in danger of becoming a harlot and thus sharing the same fate as the harlot.

---

260. McIlraith, "Works and Wife in Revelation 19:8," 515, observes that the four works listed in 2:19 are the covenant response of God's people. Rev 19:8 reveals the works as the bride's response to her covenant Husband (ibid., 527).

261. See Beale, *Revelation*, 261. Cf. the figure of false prophet in 13:11; 16:13; 19:20. Caird, *Revelation*, 43–44, has indicated that the woman could have been accepted into the community because of her prophetic gift. But she may have been guilty of proto-Gnostic teaching. Although there is a connection between Jezebel and the woman of chapters 17–18, one cannot be sure if sorcery is also her crime (cf. 18:23). Pace Duff, "Witchcraft Accusations," 130–31, who reads back magic elements of contemporary cultures into this text.

262. Charles, *Revelation*, I: 70, has spoken of an influential woman, perhaps a false prophetess. Cf. Ford, *Revelation*, 405. Chilton, *Days of Vengeance*, 114, has proposed that she might have been the church's leader's wife because some manuscripts read γυναῖκα σου. But he also recognizes that the phrase "your wife/woman" can refer to the failure of the church to take care of their woman.

263. See Beale, *Revelation*, 260–61, who proposes that the reference to the woman and her children in 2:23 evokes the phrase from 2 John 1: "the elect lady and her children."

264. Aune, *Revelation 1–5*, 204–5.

265. Sickbed can stand for suffering. Cf. Beale, *Revelation*, 263. The "great tribulation" may be the same as the "hour of testing" in 3:10. V. 21 may imply that she has already been warned/exhorted, but did not repent. Cf. Stefanovic, *Revelation of Jesus Christ*, 131.

The vision closes with a promise to the overcomer, who will receive authority over the nations (vv. 26–27; cf. Deut 15:6?). This reference to Ps 2 supports the promise concerning the overcomer's share in rule with Christ in the messianic kingdom.[266] Ps 2 probably mentions the plot of Jewish leaders against the Lord's Messiah (v. 2), though in the end the Messiah will judge them if they anger him (vv. 10, 12; cf. above *Sitz im Leben*).[267] This can suggest that the Son of God is offering victory over the enemies of the Messiah, who emerged from among God's own people, to the overcomer. The overcomer's hardship will be ended. He will receive "the morning star" (v. 28; cf. 22:16; Num 24:14-20).[268] Thus, the Messiah and his victory will be the overcomer's reward. In a manner analogous to Rev 17–19, he who resists the harlotry of Jezebel will have a share in the wedding of the Lamb and also in the Lamb's victorious conquering (cf. above on Rev 19 and 17–18). It appears that the previous exegetical discoveries of scholars can support the view that the letter to Thyatira refers to the covenant marital relationship between Christ and the Christian community.

The Letters to the Churches Section

We have indicated above that, according to some scholars,[269] the whole of the Seven Letters section may be programmatic to the rest of Revelation. They may also reveal their covenant interest, as they resemble other covenant renewal documents of antiquity (see Structure above). Moreover,

---

266. Beale, *Revelation*, 266. Because John seems to be in agreement with Ps 2:9LXX (ποιμανεῖς) rather than the MT (תְּרֹעֵם), some scholars have accused him of poor knowledge of Greek and making the same mistake as the translators of the LXX. So Caird, *Revelation*, 45–46. However, it seems that the Greek word ποιμαίνω can also be rendered "judge" or "devastate" in Rev 19:15 (cf. 12:5). Cf. Charles, *Revelation*, I: 76. He explains that the Hebrew word רעה generally meant "to shepherd," but sometimes was rendered "to devastate/destroy" (Mic 5:5; Jer 6:3; 2:16; 22:22; Ps 80:14). Therefore John could have used its equivalent in Greek. Also Beale, *Revelation*, 267; Ford, *Revelation*, 404. It seems that the idea of shepherding in Hebrew thought included also that of judging by a king. Cf. also chapter 1 of this book on John's use of sources.

267. Bauckham, *Climax of Prophecy*, 372.

268. Beale, *Revelation*, 268–69, has observed that the prophecy of Balaam in Num 24:17 (cf. v. 14) assumed the rise of a star/scepter. It is interesting that in the previous letter to Pergamum the figure of Balaam was used. Hence, Beale proposes combining the traditions from Num 24 and Ps 2. Also Aune, *Revelation 1–5*, 212–13.

269. Such as Knight, "Christ of Revelation 5:6," 44; and Beale, *Revelation*, 132–33.

Stefanovic has suggested recently that the letters are arranged chiastically according to their themes. He explains,

> The first and the last messages, to Ephesus and Laodicea, are clearly parallel; both churches are in great danger of lovelessness and legalism. The second and sixth, to Smyrna and Philadelphia, commend the churches for faithfulness; they do not receive a rebuke, and both are opposed by those "who call themselves Jews" (2:9; 3:9). The third and fifth messages, to Pergamum and Sardis, are parallel in apostasy; there is little good to be said about them. The fourth message, to the middle church of the series, Thyatira, is clearly different. It is a divided church; and this message is the longest of all. In parallel structures such as this one, an understanding of one side of the parallel helps us to understand the other side.[270]

If the letter to Thyatira stands in the chiasm's centre, with its probable reference to the divine marriage metaphor, the question of whether or not other parts of the scheme reveal a similar interest in the divine marriage metaphor emerges. We will consider briefly some instances which appear to be significant.

Ephesus (2:1–7)

There is debate among scholars as to the identity of the false apostles in Ephesus. Some scholars believe that they are the same group as the Nicolaitans in 2:6.[271] Others, however, have expressed some doubt about the identification of the two groups.[272] Nevertheless, they have almost unanimously inferred that the teaching of the false apostles was probably similar to that of the Nicolaitans.[273] Scholars have also noted that there exists some resemblance here with the conflict recorded by Paul in 2 Cor 11 (cf. ψευδαπόστολοι in v. 13).[274] We have examined this passage in the previous chapter and have observed that the false apostles could have been either Judaizers connected to the Jerusalem church or Hellenistic

---

270. *Revelation of Jesus Christ*, 76–77. Moreover, the seven-churches passage may reflect the menorah arrangement.

271. Ibid., 111; Smith, *Redating the Revelation*, 34.

272. Aune, *Revelation 1–5*, 143, has argued that the group called "false apostles" refers to individuals who were behind the past struggles of the Ephesians (2:2). The Nicolaitans are their present problem (2:6).

273. Ibid., 145; Beale, *Revelation*, 229.

274. E.g., Beale, *Revelation*, 229.

Jewish missionaries of the diaspora. Paul was concerned that these Jews might deceive the Corinthians, as the serpent did Eve. The outcome of this could have been a weakening of their devotion to Christ, their Husband (2 Cor 11:3). But the Ephesians of Rev 2 have proved mature enough not to allow themselves to be deceived by "cunning craftiness and deceitful plotting" (cf. Eph 4:14).[275] It may well have been that their opponents were also of Jewish origin. They endangered the Ephesian community causing them to be threatened with, to use Paul's imagery, the possibility of losing their devotion to Christ. However, this single link does not automatically prove that the divine marriage metaphor was the background of John's thought.

Verse 4, however, does give possible support to the divine marriage theme being in the background of the passage. Some scholars have recognized that the Ephesians' "first love" echoes Jer 2:2.[276] There, Jerusalem/Israel's love of betrothal during the wilderness period was something Yahweh commended her for.[277] Yet there was only a short time when their marital relationship was at its best. At that time, the bride was characterized by three attributes: loyal devotion (חֶסֶד), love (אַהֲבָה) and discipleship (לֶכֶת אַחֲרֵי; cf. chapter 3 on Jer 2:2). Only later did it all go wrong. Israel chose unfaithfulness reflected in idolatry and sinful alliances with foreign nations. Only on the day of God's salvation could she now be restored to the status of a pure virgin (cf. 31:3–5). However, the Ephesians in Rev 2 are accused neither of idolatry nor of illicit alliances. They have rather ceased doing their first works (v. 5). The works, though, are not explicitly mentioned. Nevertheless, if the link with Jer 2:2 is accepted, the love may refer to covenant love closely linked to loyalty and discipleship. The loyalty and love of young Israel produced fruitfulness and the lack of the love seen later reversed her well-being. In the case

---

275. Our intention is not to show the dependence of Rev 2:2 on Eph 4, but rather to indicate some parallels between the problem within the church in Ephesus about the time Revelation was written and similar problems described in other accounts of early Christian tradition. It is worth observing that the theme of apostles occurs in Eph 4:11. The true apostles seem to be guardians of the churches, over against the cunning attacks of "false apostles."

276. Terry, *Biblical Apocalyptics*, 292; Stefanovic, *Revelation of Jesus Christ*, 114. Also more reluctantly Beale, *Revelation*, 230.

277. Given passages like Jer 7:25–27; 11:7–8; 32:30, one may wonder if Jeremiah regarded the whole period of wilderness wanderings of Israel as a "honeymoon." The reference could be perhaps to the shorter period of time following the Exodus from Egypt until the first act of disobedience (cf. Exod 32). Cf. chapter 3 on Jer 2:2–3.

of the Ephesians, the abandonment of the first love could lead them to forsaking God's commandments (cf. 1 John 5:2–3; Rom 13:8–10).[278] The church may still be good at recognizing false teaching, but she no longer keeps God's covenant. Consequently, her loyal devotion and discipleship are abandoned. This is why she is in danger of being rejected (v. 5). The promise to those who overcome[279] concerns their inheritance (cf. 21:3; 22:2, 14).[280] It is as if it were still to be proven which of the recipients constitute the true bride, who would inherit God's promises.

If the proposed OT background is accepted, one may conclude that Rev 2:4 is the first fairly explicit reference to the bride of Christ in the book. Although the congregation in Ephesus was but a part of Christ's church, we have already acknowledged that in Christian thought particular communities might be referred to as 'bride.'[281] Thus the picture may well be of the Bridegroom/Husband coming to his Bride/Wife in order to regain her love or to punish her if she does not repent.

Smyrna (2:8–11)

The community at Smyrna is exposed to tribulation and poverty (2:9).[282] It is possible that such a situation could have been created by the attitude

---

278. Chilton, *Days of Vengeance*, 96. Beale, *Revelation*, 230, has argued that the lack of the first love is the lack of zealous witness for Christ in the world (because of the mention of the lampstands and the connection with Matt 24:12–14). We would suggest that lack of love caused the witness to cease (cf. John 13:34–35; 1 John 5:2–3).

279. The parallel with the same phrase in the Gospels (Matt 11:15; 13:9//Mark 4:9; 8:18 and Matt 13:34; Mark 4:23; Luke 14:35; cf. Isa 6:9–10) suggests a mixed audience of which only part will respond positively. See Beale, *Revelation*, 234. Cf. Vos, *Synoptic Traditions in the Apocalypse*, 71. Yet, in every case the promise to the one who overcomes is the promise to all the churches: ". . . let him hear what the Spirit says to the church*es*." The νικάω word group in Rev 2–3 seems to point to the victorious perseverance of the churches in the face of crisis. See Beale, *Revelation*, 235. The word has the same root as Nicolaitan. Cf. Chilton, *Days of Vengeance*, 98. See below on 2:14–15. A helpful hint on the nature of Christian overcoming is offered in 1 John 5:1–5.

280. Aune, *Revelation 1–5*, 152, explains that the tree of life is "the *cosmic center of reality* where eternal life is present and available, and where God dwells." Thus the new earth will be a restored Garden of Eden (cf. Gen 2:9; 3:22; Isa 51:3). Cf. Stefanovic, *Revelation of Jesus Christ*, 116. God's promise through Ezekiel for the *eschaton* included trees of special proprieties (Ezek 47:12).

281. Cf. chapter 6 concerning 2 Cor 11:2–3. A particular church is partaking in the reality of the entire church of Christ. Thus, the universal can be expressed in the particular.

282. Smith, *Redating the Revelation*, 39, has suggested that the church could have been poor because of its small numbers at the time John wrote. However, others have

of certain Jews in the local synagogue, who did not recognize Jesus as the Messiah.[283] Their blasphemy could further support this suggestion (v. 10; cf. Acts 13:45).[284] It appears that for John those Jews who reject Christ are not real Jews: they are a synagogue of Satan.[285] In such a context, Christ exhorts Christians that they should not fear the approaching suffering (v. 10). The devil will throw some of their community into prison,[286] but this will be a test for them. The tribulation will last only ten days.[287] It is likely that the ones responsible for this period of persecution were some Jewish synagogue leaders who incited the local authorities, appointed by Rome, to act against the Christians.[288] However, the Christian at Smyrna is promised the crown of life if only he remains faithful.

---

proposed that the poverty could have been due to the antagonism of the place. See, e.g., Caird, *Revelation*, 35.

283. Charles, *Revelation*, I: 56–57. He has indicated that Jewish hostility towards Christians often turned into furious enmity. Some non-messianic Jews were even using the Roman authorities to fight against Christians. Cf. discussion in Beagley, *Church's Enemies*, 33.

284. Cf. Charles, *Revelation*, I: 57. The term "blasphemy" can also refer to the denunciation of Christians before Roman authorities. So Aune, *Revelation 1–5*, 162. However, Aune considers Acts 26:11 to be an instance of Saul forcing Jewish Christians to blaspheme the name of Christ (ibid., 163).

285. Yarbro Collins, "Revelation," I: 392. Jesus said that the unbelieving Jews had Satan as their father (John 8:39–44). We have suggested that Israel was redefined under the ministry of Jesus (cf. chapter 5 on Matt 25:1–13). Only the followers of Christ are the true Israel of God. Satan was the "accuser," the "adversary" of Christians, and certain Jews acting accordingly would have been easily identified with him (cf. Acts 6:9–15; 14:2–5; 17:5–8; 21:27–36). But to be a true Jew means to follow God in Christ (cf. Rom 3:28–29; Gal 3:7–9, 26–29). Cf. Chilton, *Days of Vengeance*, 102–3.

286. Prison was not itself the punishment. It was rather "a means of coercion to compel obedience to an order issued by a magistrate or else a place to temporarily restrain the prisoner before execution . . ." Aune, *Revelation 1–5*, 166. Thus the threat to life was real in that context, although Aune thinks that the ten days period refers to the coercion aspect of imprisonment. The period appears rather to be a time of tribulation for the church. Christ exhorts her to stay faithful even to death, so death is a real threat. So Beale, *Revelation*, 242.

287. This probably echoes the test of Daniel and his friends (Dan 1:12–15). They were tested to see if they would compromise their faith. See Beale, *Revelation*, 242. The number ten can be symbolic and refer to a short period of time. Cf. Charles, *Revelation*, I: 58.

288. Charles, *Revelation*, I: 58; Caird, *Revelation*, 35; Beagley, *Church's Enemies*, 33. Yet, we do acknowledge that there is a tendency among scholars to attribute all the responsibility to the Romans. Thus Aune, *Revelation 1–5*, 166.

The interpretation of the crown symbol has caused scholars some problems. Charles has proposed that the picture is taken from the games, which were popular in Smyrna.[289] Aune has taken the symbol to signify a wreath of immortality that could have been awarded posthumously.[290] Beale has suggested that the crown of life stands for eternal life itself.[291] While the last option appears to be quite a common interpretation among evangelical scholars, one might still expect to find a more exact meaning of the crown symbolism. Zimmermann has proposed that the crown symbolism depends on the OT Judaic traditions, which used the image of the bridal wreath occasionally worn by Zion/Jerusalem.[292] We have indicated that priority in interpreting Revelation should be given to its OT background.[293] Moreover, because the crown in our passage implies a crown worn by a corporate entity, it is worth pursuing the traces of this symbolism along the lines suggested by Zimmermann.

It is significant that the Greek word στέφανος often translates the Hebrew עֲטָרָה in the sense of a royal crown (cf. 2 Sam 12:30; 1 Chr 20:2; Ps 21:3; Song 3:11; see also Esth 8:15).[294] In one OT instance a crown was given to God's people as a whole (Ezek 16:12). Israel received a crown when Yahweh made her his royal spouse. He gave her life (v. 6) and took care of her so that she developed beauty and grace (v. 7). Then she became God's covenant wife (v. 8). Yet she despised her husband and went whoring with her many lovers (vv. 15–34). As a result, she had to be pun-

289. *Revelation*, I: 58.

290. *Revelation 1–5*, 167–68.

291. *Revelation*, 244. He has linked this with the reward for those who endure testing (Jas 1:12).

292. "Nuptial Imagery," 156. Cf. Lam 2:15LXX; Ezek 16:12; and on the metaphorical reading: Song 3:11 (cf. *Taan* 4,8).

293. The "crown of life" in Jas 1:12 appears to have an OT background. Martin, *James*, 33, has argued that the promise of blessing in Jas 1:12 is in line with the Jewish pronouncing of blessing for faithfulness to Yahweh (cf. Prov 8:32; Isa 56:1–2; Dan 12:12), which was carried forward in the teaching of Jesus (Matt 5:3–11//Luke 6:20–26). According to Martin, the "crown that offers life" was an eschatological reward in Jewish thought. Although Prov 1:9; 4:9; 12:4; 16:31; 17:6, link the promise with the bestowal of wisdom, Wis Sol 5:15–23 combines those ideas with the reward of a glorious kingdom (or crown: NJB) and a beautiful diadem for the righteous. "Life," therefore, refers to the "eschatological joy of the new age that God will bring in."

294. Pace Stefanovic, *Revelation of Jesus Christ*, 118–19, who denies such royal overtones. Yet Revelation itself reveals the link between the crown and a royal warrior theme (cf. 4:4, 10; 14:14). στέφανος occurs also in Matt 27:29 (Mark 15:17//John 19:2, 5) to describe Jesus' crown of thorns: a mockery of the royalty claimed by him.

ished. She was to be killed with stones and swords (v. 40), and taken into captivity (v. 53).[295] It is possible that the return from captivity in the same tradition was regarded as a return to life, Israel's resurrection.[296] Other similar traditions also record the punishment (exile) of Jerusalem as a loss of her crown (Jer 13:18-19; Lam 5:16). Yet other places elaborating on the crown imagery present the picture of Israel becoming a crown of glory at the time of her restoration, the new exodus (Isa 62:3). It is noteworthy that Isa 62:3 is placed in the context of the divine marriage motif (vv. 4-5). Nevertheless, it seems that Ezek 16, together with its wider context (cf. 37:1-14), could be a thematic background to the "crown of life" imagery in Rev 2:10. The Smyrnean church will be vindicated if she remains faithful. They will receive a crown of life, i.e., resurrection/restoration itself.[297] They will be Christ's royal wife, even though their present lives may be endangered. They will gain their life from the one who has already been raised and therefore has the power to raise others, by bringing them out of their present captivity (cf. v. 8).[298] This is why those who are faithful in all churches do not need to be afraid of the second death, which is another punishment and exile for the unfaithful, those who are not vindicated by Christ (v. 11; cf. 20:6, 14; 21:8).[299] The faithful will inherit God's promises (cf. 21:7).

295. It is a paradox that capital punishment is not the end of the story. We have also noted in chapter 3 that turning the land into a wilderness in Hos 2:3 was also regarded as the death of the land. Death of the land is a similar punishment to the capital punishment for adultery.

296. Caird, *Language and Imagery*, 246, has demonstrated that the language of resurrection was used for return from exile (Ezek 37:1-14; cf. Hos 6:1-2). Cf. Wright, *NTPG*, 200, cf. 322. Exile was seen as a 'death' (e.g., 276).

297. Zimmermann, "Nuptial Imagery," 156, observes that the crown of life is linked with OT statements about faithfulness, fortitude and life.

298. Cf. Wright, *NTPG*, 460-61 for this idea in other parts of early Christian tradition.

299. See Ford, *Revelation*, 393-94, who points out that in Targum Isa 65:6 the unfaithful of God's people are punished in Gehenna (constant fire) with a second death. The closest parallel with the second punishment within the Hebrew canonical writings comes from Jer 51:39, 57, where "perpetual sleep" is indicated. The Targum on these verses speaks of a second death that the Babylonians would experience. They will not have a share in the new world. Cf. Matt 12:38-39, 41; 23:32-36//Luke 11:45-52. In the Gospels, Gehenna is a place of fiery punishment for the unbelieving generation of the Jews contemporary with Jesus. Jerusalem becomes an extension of her own rubbish-dump because of her unbelief. Cf. Wright, *JVG*, 331, 336. It is noteworthy that the unfaithful Jews who put their hope in the Temple but disregarded Yahweh's word

Yet, this picture does not have to assume that the marriage between Christ and the church at Smyrna is non-existent at the present. It seems that the Son of Man is already in a covenant relationship with her. If the letter can be interpreted as a covenant renewal document, one may assume that the marriage envisaged is an ongoing relationship. However, as in the case of Ezek 16, the divine marriage metaphor may function as an exhortation to God's people to be faithful. There is still a future reward. Only those who are faithful as the bride now will continue being the bride in the future, and obtain the inheritance from God.

Philadelphia (3:7–13)

Christ is pictured here as holding the key of David (cf. Isa 22:22). This implies that he is the royal figure with authority over God's kingdom who replaces a false steward over God's people (v. 19).[300] Apparently, he decides on who will enter the realm of life.[301] He has also set an open door before the Philadelphian Christians. This probably signifies their admittance to the eschatological messianic kingdom regardless of the fact that their enemies have attempted to hold them back from this eventuality.[302] Other parts of early Christian tradition use the picture of a shut door to symbolize the withdrawal of the possibility of entering the realm of God's salvation. In chapter 5, we have examined the Parable of the Ten Maidens, which presented such a prospect. There were 'foolish' people who disregarded Jesus' teaching and, as a consequence, could not share the blessings of the renewed covenant. They were excluded from God's eschatological community and remained in exile. The message to the church in Philadelphia may have similar implications. Those within the community have remained faithful and loyal to Christ's word, yet the local Jews rejecting the Messiah have proven unworthy: they followed Satan's rather than the bridegroom's voice (v. 9; cf. 2:9). As a consequence they will not find the door to the feast of salvation open. Furthermore,

---

were warned that they would be exiled and the valley of Hinnom (="Gehenna") would become a mass grave (cf. Jer 7:15, 31–32; *JVG*, 419 n. 186).

300. Chilton, *Days of Vengeance*, 126–27. Beale, *Revelation*, 283–84, has suggested that the picture resembles that in 1:18: Christ holding the key of Death and Hades. Hence, Jesus has power over salvation and judgment.

301. Cf. Beale, *Revelation*, 285.

302. Chilton, *Days of Vengeance*, 127, argues in favor of this view rather than the one suggesting an "open door" for evangelism. Pace Ford, *Revelation*, 416, Metzger, *Breaking the Code*, 41, and Stefanovic, *Revelation of Jesus Christ*, 141.

they will have to bow down before the faithful disciples of Jesus (3:9; cf. Isa 60:14)[303] and acknowledge his love for those who belong to him. Perhaps this love resembles the divine love of God's covenant (Isa 62:4–5; cf. 63:9).

Those who keep Christ's commands faithfully will be preserved during the time of trial (Rev 3:10; cf. Dan 12:1, 10; Rev 7:14).[304] We have already acknowledged that the 'hour of trial' was to come upon the whole Roman empire (οἰκουμένη) but the test was to be focused on the inhabitants of the land of Israel (οἱ κατοικοῦντες ἐπὶ τῆς γῆς).[305] This will be Christ's response to the enemies of his church, including those of God's people who reject him.[306] However, 3:10 also suggests that the churches themselves may be exposed to trials, yet with a hope for salvation.

Verse 11 assumes that the announced testing is imminent.[307] The Philadelphian church is called to continue in faithfulness or else she will lose her crown.[308] Zimmermann has argued that the mention of crown

---

303. Cf. Chilton, *Days of Vengeance*, 128, who remarks that the Jews rejecting the Messiah put themselves in the position of the heathen persecuting God's people of the renewed Zion.

304. Terry, *Biblical Apocalyptics*, 309, has argued that the "hour of trial" in Rev 3:10 is the same as the "great tribulation" in Matt 24:21, 29//Mark 13:19. See also Beale, *Revelation*, 292 on the links with Dan 12, although we do not agree with him on the notion of Christ's final coming.

305. Cf. Beagley, *Church's Enemies*, 35–36. He also observes that the same group of people in 6:10 were responsible for the bloodshed of the martyrs (cf. 8:13; 11:10; 17:2, 8). Charles, *Revelation*, I: 289–90, has argued that the same phrase at Rev 11:10 refers to the inhabitants of the land of Palestine (cf. Hos 4:1; Joel 1:2, 14; 2:1; Jer 6:12; 10:18). See also Gentry, *Before Jerusalem Fell*, 142–43, and Chilton, *Days of Vengeance*, 129–30. Russell, *Parousia*, 373, believes that the trial refers to the Neronic persecutions of Christians since 64 CE. But here the shaking of the whole οἰκουμένη is in view. This perhaps refers to the events of 69 CE. Cf. Bell, "Date of John's Apocalypse," 102; Wright, *JVG*, 362; also Wright, *New Heavens, New Earth*, 9, who explains that the "earth-shattering" events included the turbulent year of four emperors (69 CE) and the capture of Jerusalem in 70 CE. Yet, the time of trial could refer to the whole period of Jewish War in 66–70 CE. However, many NT scholars take the phrase to be a general reference to the pagan world in hostility to God. E.g., Stefanovic, *Revelation of Jesus Christ*, 141.

306. Josephus, *Wars*, ii.18ff, indicates that the disaster coming on the Jews extended beyond the land of Palestine in the years preceding the destruction of Jerusalem.

307. Gentry, *Before Jerusalem Fell*, 141–42.

308. This parallel confirms Stefanovic's earlier observation that the letters are arranged according to the chiastic pattern or menorah-like parallelism. Cf. *Revelation of Jesus Christ*, 76.

in this verse parallels the crown in 2:10 (cf. discussion above).³⁰⁹ By implication, the letter to Philadelphia can be another likely instance of the marriage metaphor. It finishes with a promise to the overcomer. He will become a pillar of the eschatological temple of God (v. 12a).³¹⁰ The name of God and the name of the new Jerusalem will be written on him together with the name of Christ (vv.12b–13; cf. 2:17).³¹¹ This suggests the connection with Rev 21:2: a picture of the bride, who is also the new Jerusalem (cf. Isa 65:17–24; cf. chapter 6 on Gal 4:26). It is perhaps this parallelism with the last chapters of Revelation that sustains the likelihood of the occurrence of divine marriage metaphor in this section.

Laodicea (3:14–22)

Christ finds this community without zeal (v. 19) and lukewarm (v. 16): self-satisfied and indifferent (v. 17).³¹² This echoes the half-hearted love of the Ephesians in 2:4, the fading love of the covenant. This parallelism may indicate that the nuptial theme is also important in this letter. However, the situation here may also echo the words of Lev 18:24–28, where the land spews out its inhabitants for not keeping God's commandments and thus defiling it.³¹³ The idea would be, then, one of expulsion, perhaps rejection and exile as a consequence of disobedience and disloyalty.

309. "Nuptial Imagery," 153–54, 156.

310. Aune, *Revelation 1–5*, 241.

311. Beale, *Revelation*, 293, explains that the identification with Christ's name is the same as identification with God's name and the name of the new Jerusalem (cf. 14:1–4; 22:3–4; see also Isa 62:2; 65:15; Ezek 48:35). It refers to the establishment of the restored people of God. See also Gundry, "New Jerusalem: People as Place," 256, says that 3:15 gives the earliest hint that the new Jerusalem consists of persons, i.e., it is not a material city. The theme is developed in 21:1—22:5.

312. Ford, *Revelation*, 422. Most scholars draw attention to the geographical situation of Laodicea: the city needed a supply of water from the hot springs of Hierapolis often used for healing baths. The water by the end of its journey was tepid and caused nausea. Ibid., 419. However, cold drinking and refreshing water was found in Colossae. Thus the contrast between the two kinds of water may suggest the uselessness of lukewarm water (neither for healing nor for drinking). Cf. Chilton, *Days of Vengeance*, 134. Aune, *Revelation 1–5*, 258, explains that being neither hot nor cold could refer to indecisive way of living. This, of course, creates an immediate problem of whether Christ would commend complete disloyalty (cold). But see 2 Pet 2:21, which evokes the theme of false teachers who follow the way of Balaam.

313. Chilton, *Days of Vengeance*, 135. The Hebrew verb קיא in Lev 18:25, 28 signifies the land vomiting those who defile it.

In contrast to the church in Smyrna, Christians in Laodicea appear to be rich, the condition causing their self-satisfaction and pride.[314] Scholars have suggested that this picture resembles Hos 12:8.[315] There Ephraim's (i.e., Israel's) wealth depended on his sinful ways of oppression (v. 7). His sin was greed and dishonesty related to religious apostasy (v. 11; cf. 2:5, 8).[316] Thus, this reference to Ephraim evokes the divine marriage theme of the first chapters of Hosea. Laodicea is close to the point where, in her wealth, she does not remember her loving husband any more, a picture resembling the situation of Israel from Hos 2:8. Beale has argued that the Laodicean church has become like the merchants who enriched themselves through the ungodly system of Babylon (Rev 18:3, 15, 19).[317] Yet, despite her riches, her condition is miserable: she is poor, blind and naked (3:17b). Blindness in the OT could refer to man's injustice resulting in separation from God (cf. Deut 16:19; 28:29; Isa 6:10). But the overall picture may well resemble the condition of total helplessness described in Ezek 16:4–8. Apart from God, Israel was like a defiled naked child without the resources to live. Later, in her rebellion, she suffered exile: she returned to her original state of shame and lack of resources (Ezek 16:37, 39; cf. chapter 3 on Hos 2:3). Likewise, Laodicean nakedness can testify to their disobedience and abandoning of God's ways.[318] The Laodiceans need to repent and purify themselves by leaving behind sinful ways ("refined gold": cf. Job 23:10; Mal 3:2–3).[319] They have to obtain white garments, which are required for participation in the Lamb's wedding banquet of salvation (cf. Rev 19:8). The robes probably point to the righteous deeds of love, service, faith and endurance (cf. Isa 61:10).[320] The Laodiceans need an ointment for their eyes so that they may return to a place of fellowship with Christ and God (cf. Isa 42:7;

---

314. Although Aune, *Revelation 1–5*, 259, argues that it should be taken figuratively as in 1 Cor 4:8, the contrast with v. 18 seems to require a more literal sense (cf. Luke 12:19, 15b; Matt 6:19). Cf. Vos, *Synoptic Traditions in the Apocalypse*, 193 n. 391.

315. Beale, *Revelation*, 304.

316. Andersen and Freedman, *Hosea*, 616. It is noteworthy that Col 3:5 describes greed/covetousness of money in terms of idolatry.

317. *Revelation*, 305. Beale explains that the πλοῦτος word group describes ungodly Israelites in the OT.

318. Stripping the woman naked was a partial punishment for an adulterous wife. Cf. chapter 3 on Ezek 16:37–39.

319. Cf. Beale, *Revelation*, 305.

320. McIlraith, "Works and Wife in Revelation 19:8," 515.

The Metaphor of Divine Marriage in the Book of Revelation 295

Matt 13:15; John 9:6, 11, 15; 1 John 2:11). It seems that only Christ the Bridegroom can provide them with these things.

Verse 20 may be a call to the fellowship renewal that would allow the church in Laodicea to participate in the eschatological meal of salvation.[321] If the proposed link with Luke 12:35–37 is allowed, then the picture emerging is one not only of salvation, but also of judgment. The Lukan passage is part of a longer pericope consisting of a number of short parables about Yahweh's return to Zion executed in the coming of the Son of Man (Luke 12:35—13:9).[322] The point is clear: the faithful who are watchful will be rewarded and the unfaithful punished on the day of the Son's coming. If the Lukan context is accepted, the picture becomes more compelling. Then, the point of Rev 3:20 is not a mere encouragement to the church to open itself up for Christ, but a warning against the imminent judgment coming on those who prove unfaithful and corrupt servants (cf. Matt 24:36–51; 25:1–13; Mark 13:33–37; Luke 13:35).[323] The point would resemble those Gospel passages that stand close to the tradition describing faithfulness and unfaithfulness by employing the *hieros gamos* symbolism as seen in the OT prophets. We therefore submit that the above considerations suggest that the letter to Laodicea is another likely instance of the metaphor of divine marriage in Revelation.

Revelation 12

We have suggested above that the mention of women or a relationship with women can be an important indicator pointing to the likely in-

---

321. Beale, *Revelation*, 307–8. He has recognized a similar scene in the account of Song 5:2, although the focus of Rev 3:20 seems to be on the meal. Vos, *Synoptic Traditions in the Apocalypse*, 97–100, has recognized the link with Luke 12:35–37, the Parable of the Returning Master. Aune, *Revelation 1–5*, 261, is more reluctant because Rev 3:20 does not imply that Jesus is the returning host. However, the similarities are striking.

322. Wright, *JVG*, 640–42. Dan 7:13–14 explains this link: the Son of Man comes to the Ancient of Days when the latter himself comes to establish his kingdom. This is on the day of judgment and salvation. There is a note of judgment on those who will be unprepared, lacking fruit for God (cf. 13:6–9).

323. We suggest that this view corresponds with the context of Revelation. It does not seem that Stefanovic, *Revelation of Jesus Christ*, 150, presents a fair explanation in saying that Jesus is standing at the door of the human heart asking permission to enter. The context cannot support this suggestion. Jesus is rather about to come in judgment and the "lukewarm" have one last chance to repent before they are cut off. He stands at the door of the church rather than of the individual.

stances of the divine marriage theme. Therefore, the two other passages to examine here are Rev 12 and 14.

Scholars have paid particular attention to Rev 12, probably because it evokes some major OT traditions concerning the "woman," her "child," the "dragon," and the angelic being "Michael." They have, however, varied in their interpretation of the references of these symbols and, consequently, the *Sitz im Leben* of the passage.

Metzger may be regarded as representative of one end of the interpretive spectrum. He believes that Rev 12 is a "flashback" to the time of Christ's birth and the subsequent attempt by Herod to kill the child (cf. Matt 2:16–18).[324] The dragon's efforts to devour the child could also refer to the violent opposition that Jesus encountered during his earthly ministry.[325] The woman, he claims, is a personification of the ideal community of God's people in both its Jewish and its Christian forms.[326]

At the other end of the interpretive spectrum are those who have claimed that the figure of the child should be read in exclusively corporate terms.[327] The child may be regarded as the first fruits consisting of the apostles and martyrs (cf. Rev 11:3–12; 6:11; 20:4).[328] Consequently, the child resembles the overcomer of Rev 2:26–27 (cf. 12:11).

Having noted these two opposite approaches, one needs to examine the context of the passage's symbols in order to verify which of the two is the more likely explanation.

The symbol of a woman clothed with the sun, standing on the moon, and being crowned with twelve stars echoes various OT traditions (12:1).[329] Some exegetes have seen here a reference to Gen 37:9, the

324. *Breaking the Code*, 72.

325. Ibid., 73.

326. Ibid., 74. Some still try to suggest that a secondary reference to Mary, Jesus' mother, is possible (cf. John 19:26–27). So Bruns, "Contrasted Women," 360. However, Fuller, "The Woman in Revelation 12," 237, observes that only by comparing Rev 12 with the Fourth Gospel, are scholars able to argue for the presence of Mary in Revelation.

327. Terry, *Biblical Apocalyptics*, 384.

328. Ibid., 391. See also pp. 368–69 concerning the two witnesses in Rev 11 as the apostles. Wallis, "Coming of the Kingdom," 35, claims that the child is the entire body of Jews and Gentiles gathered to Christ at the first resurrection.

329. However, some scholars have preferred to read the symbols against the background of pagan religions. Thus, they compare the woman to the Greek Leto, the Syrian Atargatis, or the Egyptian Isis. See esp. Yarbro Collins, "Feminine Symbolism," 20–24. Consequently, such a history-of-religions approach claims the influence of the sacred marriage of the ancient religions on the formation of the bride symbol in Revelation.

origin of the tribes of Israel.[330] Others have also seen additional support in Isa 60:1–2, where the restored Zion appears as though she is clothed in God's glory, bright as the sun.[331] We would suggest yet another possibility at this point: one that comes close to the meaning of Isa 60:1–2 and which can be deduced from the meaning enclosed in Ps 45. We have not discussed this Psalm in chapter 3 because there we limited ourselves to the more explicit instances of the divine marriage metaphor.

It is, of course, a widely recognized fact that the Psalm is peculiar in the OT.[332] In fact, OT scholars have struggled to make even an approximate guess as to its original *Sitz im Leben*, and as yet no final agreement has been reached. Nevertheless, there is an academic consensus that the Psalm was interpreted messianically in both post-exilic Jewish and early Christian traditions.[333]

Ps 45 mentions the royal messianic wife clothed in gold, which could provide additional background to the symbol of woman in Rev 12 (Ps 45:9, 13 [44:10, 14LXX]).[334] It is possible that the radiance of gold can be compared to the radiance of the sun, both signifying the brightness of glory.[335] Thus in the Apocalypse, the woman could be wearing the

---

Whilst, it may be true that the origin of the marriage metaphor in the Bible is related to Hosea's polemic with the Canaanite *cultus*, the proposal of these scholars is an unnecessary deduction. We have previously argued that attention should primarily be given to the OT as the source of Revelation's symbolism. Cf. chapter 1 of this book.

330. See Fuller, "The Woman in Revelation 12," 230. He explains that the sun is Jacob, the moon Rachel, and the twelve stars imply Jacob's children, Joseph included. Cf. Wallis, "Coming of the Kingdom," 35. However, it may well be that the twelve stars refer to the church built on the foundation of the twelve apostles (Eph 2:20). Cf. Terry, *Biblical Apocalyptics*, 382.

331. Cf. Chilton, *Days of Vengeance*, 297.

332. Kraus, *Psalms 1–59*, 453. His assessment well summarizes the opinion of scholarship on this matter: "There is no parallel to Psalm 45 in the OT – not even anything approaching it." Cf. Craigie, *Psalms 1–50*, 337, has noted the result of this uniqueness "little internal evidence can be used in the interpretation of the psalm."

333. Craigie, *Psalms 1–50*, 340; Delitzsch, *Psalms*, II: 73–74. He has suggested that Isa 9:5 probably refers back to Ps 45. Christian tradition is even clearer in Heb 1:8–9. Hengstenberg, *Psalms*, II: 124, thinks that the parallels between Ps 45:2–3 and Ps 72 and Isa 11 as well as those between Ps 45:6–7 and Isa 9:5; Ps 110; Mic 5:1; Dan 7:13, 14; Zech 12:10, 13:7, reveal the messianic character of Ps 45. See also Weiser, *Psalms*, 365.

334. It is noteworthy that both the LXX of Ps 45:9 and Rev 12:1 use the same form of περιβάλλω for the clothing of the radiant women.

335. In Song 6:4, Solomon's queen resembles Jerusalem and in v. 10 she is resplendent as the sun. Russell, *Parousia*, 450, has suggested that the symbolism in v. 10 (the sun, moon and stars) well applies to Christ's bride full of dignity and glory.

Messiah's glory (cf. Rev 1:16).[336] The fact that in Rev 12 she is in heaven does not need to diminish the link with Ps 45. We have seen above that Christ's wife is in heaven (cf. 21:2), which may parallel the Pauline picture of a heavenly city, the mother of all believers, in Gal 4:26–27.[337] In Gal 4, the new Jerusalem belongs to the same realm as the new heaven and earth (cf. Isa 65:17–25). She has more children than the old Jerusalem has ever had (cf. Isa 54:2–3). She is, in fact, the new creation of God (cf. Gal 6:15–16). Thus the symbol of the woman, against these backgrounds, may point to the eschatological remarried people of God.

The fact that the woman is in birth pains has directed scholarly attention to the context of Isa 66:7–8.[338] Moreover, the 'sign' in Rev 12:1 seems to echo the σημεῖον of Isa 7:14LXX.[339] The reference to Ps 2:9 at Rev 12:5 adds to the overall picture. Thus, most exegetes have tended to interpret Rev 12 as referring to Jesus' birth, the emergence of the Messiah. However, we have already indicated in chapter 5 that one of the leading motifs of Isaiah is the restoration of Zion through the faithful remnant. In fact, both Isa 66:7–8 and 7:14 may be regarded as referring to the appearance of the faithful remnant.[340] Hence, a corporate rendering of the child in Rev 12:5 is plausible here (cf. 2:26–27). The cry of the mother

---

336. Cf. Stefanovic, *Revelation of Jesus Christ*, 380. A link with 2 Cor 4:6 is possible here. Another link may be with Isa 61:10, the passage referring to the restoration of Zion's marriage to Yahweh and her priesthood (v. 6).

337. Cf. Terry, *Biblical Apocalyptics*, 382. It is noteworthy that Gal 4:27 is probably related to the expectation expressed in Isa 66:7–11. Once barren (Isa 54:1), the restored Zion was to be full of offspring. Cf. chapter 6 on Gal 4:27.

338. For close verbal links between the passages see Aus, "Relevance of Isaiah 66:7," 254–56.

339. Ibid., 255. Aus has also argued that Midrash Rabbah Genesis 85, Leviticus Rabbah 14/9, and Targum Jonathan on Isa 66:7, all support the messianic interpretation of Isa 66:7.

340. See Webb, "Zion in Transformation," 81–82. Webb explains that Isa 66:7 is a riddle to which an answer is provided in v. 8b. Thus, not so much a son is in view as a community of servants (v. 14), the remnant nucleus of the new Zion. The theme of remnant is linked with the kingly messianic figure in Isaiah 9:6 and 11:1 (p. 83).

Concerning Isa 7:14 see Rice, "Immanuel Prophecy," 222, who explains that under the Immanuel symbol there are the disciples who heed the prophetic word: they are the remnant. Their mother is Zion personified. It is noteworthy that Immanuel is the only child in the OT whose name is formed with the first person plural pronoun. This can be resolved on the corporate reading (223).

Additional support for the corporate reading may be found in Isa 26:16–19. Cf. Beasley-Murray, *Revelation*, 194.

resembles apparently the cry of the martyrs to God in 6:10.[341] It may, therefore, be that the cry of the faithful of God leads to the birth of a new community and, by implication, of a new creation. The only problem then would be to explain her being "caught up to God and his throne." Even more so, since the action still takes place in heaven.[342] On the corporate reading, the remnant nucleus of the restored Zion has been transported to God's presence, a place of security and authority. They are the faithful overcomers who have gained victory over the dragon (v. 11).[343] They are indebted to Christ for this victory, the one who ascended in power to heaven after his resurrection.[344] However, because of the lack of any mention of physical death and placing the scene in heaven, the corporate reading for the 'child' is probably the main emphasis here.[345] Therefore, the passage does not need to be a flashback to Jesus' birth, but merely a reference to the birth of the restored Zion through the Messiah's blood (cf. 5:9–10). Consequently, Christ could be regarded here as the husband in union with the new Jerusalem bringing forth her offspring.

The symbol of the "dragon" relates to the "serpent" that was a figure of evil in the OT (cf. Gen 3:14–15; Isa 27:1).[346] It often personified the enemies of God's people: Egypt (Ps 74:14; cf. Isa 51:9–10), Pharaoh (Ezek 32:2ff), Syria and Babylon (Isa 27:1).[347] However, when this "sign" is introduced in Rev 12:3, the location is still heaven. Nevertheless, some correspondence with earthly events is also assumed. The seven heads and ten horns of the dragon may represent his authority and power,

---

341. Ford, *Revelation*, 198. Isa 26:17 pictures a woman crying in her birth pangs. God's blessing and a promise of resurrection follow this. The subsequent chapter of Isaiah presents the defeat of the serpent (Leviathan) by the Lord. See also Mic 4:9.

342. Cf. Fuller, "The Woman in Revelation 12," 227.

343. Cf. Terry, *Biblical Apocalyptics*, 385. This could resemble the early Christian principle expressed in 2 Tim 2:12.

344. This reflects the traditional Christian understanding of the passage. Cf. Aune, *Revelation 6–16*, 689.

345. Cf. Terry, *Biblical Apocalyptics*, 385. Yet, even on such a reading it can be remarked that the messianic community/the restored Zion could only have emerged because of the Messiah. The idea of representation can play its role here, as in the case of, e.g., Matt 1:23. After all, the Messiah is the precursor of the messianic community. He is the firstborn from the dead (cf. Rev 1:5).

346. Cf. Bauckham, *Theology of Revelation*, 19. Some interpreters suggest that the dragon corresponds to Apollyon in 9:11. See, e.g., Terry, *Biblical Apocalyptics*, 381.

347. Schüssler-Fiorenza, *Vision of a Just World*, 81.

which extends throughout the Roman Empire (v.9; cf. 3:10).[348] He tries to attack first the faithful remnant, presumably the faithful of the Jews (v. 5), but after failing in this he turns to fight the church in general (v. 17). The picture reflects an ongoing conflict with the woman and her seed that began in Eden.[349]

The scene shifts, in turn, to earth when the woman flees into the wilderness for protection (vv. 6, 13-14).[350] In the meantime the dragon has been defeated in heaven and his access before God barred (vv. 7-10).[351] He and his angels have been cast down to the earth (v. 9), which will result in him giving vent to his wrath on the earth and the sea (v. 12).[352] Also, part of the woman's offspring will be endangered (v. 17). It appears that the final solution to this struggle only comes in Rev 20, which pic-

---

348. Cf. Beale, *Revelation*, 633-34. The fourth beast of Daniel's vision had ten horns (7:3, 7). But although the beast in Daniel stands for a political power, the dragon/Satan of Rev 12 seems to be a figure behind that and other beasts. The dragon figure corresponds to the beast of the sea in chapter 13. Cf. Chilton, *Days of Vengeance*, 303. However, the throwing down of a third of the stars does not need to refer to the fall of angels (as in 1 Enoch 6-19), but rather to a defeat of part of Israel (Rev 8:12). Cf. Beale, *Revelation*, 635-36 and Terry, *Biblical Apocalyptics*, 384, for the link with Rev 8:12. Pace Fuller, "The Woman in Revelation 12," 228.

349. Cf. Bauckham, *Climax of Prophecy*, 15, 284.

350. The historical referent may be the escape of the Judean Christians from the destruction of Jerusalem. See Chilton, *Days of Vengeance*, 309. However, scholars recognize here an echo of the Exodus from Egypt (cf. Exod 19:4; Deut 32:11-12). See Fuller, "The Woman in Revelation 12," 231, and Schüssler-Fiorenza, *Vision of a Just World*, 81. The wilderness here seems to be a place of security, though in 17:3 it is a wasteland. Cf. Rossing, *Two Cities*, 71-72.

351. Michael may be viewed as a heavenly patron of God's people (Dan 10:13, 21; 12:1). See Metzger, *Breaking the Code*, 74. It is not necessary to view Michael as another manifestation of Jesus. Pace Terry, *Biblical Apocalyptics*, 386; and Stefanovic, *Revelation of Jesus Christ*, 42. The expulsion of the dragon from heaven seems to be the outcome of Christ's work and the arrival of his kingdom (cf. John 12:27-31; Luke 10:18; Col 2:15). Cf. Fuller, "The Woman in Revelation 12," 234; Beale, *Revelation*, 666. This is the reason for the joy in heaven (Rev 12:12).

352. According to Aune, *Revelation 6-16*, 704, this verse creates some problems because it is not at all clear why the author includes the sea in his woe. Possible help comes from the rendering of the Textus Receptus and a few Majority Text versions, which read "woe to those inhabiting the earth and the sea." Cf. Ford, *Revelation*, 194. Understood in this way, the woe could refer to the inhabitants of Palestine and of other (pagan) nation(s). According to Rev 17:1, 15, the waters are nations. In the OT, Gentile nations were often compared to seas (cf. Ps 65:7; Isa 17:12-13; 57:20; Jer 6:23; 51:42). Cf. Ryken et al., *Dictionary of Biblical Imagery*, 765. Therefore it is possible that a satanic force behind the conflict of two peoples is in view here.

tures the final defeat of the devil.³⁵³ Yet the time of Satan's activity is short and his end imminent (v. 12).

Rev 12, read against the background of OT divine marriage prophecies, presents the restored Zion's conflict with Satan, the spiritual force behind her enemies. She finds protection from heaven, presumably her husband. However, her seed is endangered, as though the offspring was to be bruised on his heel (cf. Gen 3:15).

Revelation 14

Rev 14 is important for our survey because of its reference to the relationship with women in v. 4. Yet, the passage has created its own interpretive difficulties. Scholars have not agreed on the significance of the male παρθένοι and their "abstinence" from women. They have not even reached consensus concerning the identity of the 144,000 in this passage. There have been those who have taken the number as a universal reference to the whole church.³⁵⁴ There have also been those who have tried to limit its significance to a particular group within the church.³⁵⁵ However, if the 144,000 are the same as in Rev 7:4 and the phrase οἱ ἠγορασμένοι ἀπὸ τῆς γῆς (v. 3) is given its due weight, one could conclude that the faithful remnant of ethnic Israel are in view (cf. Ezek 9:4).³⁵⁶ We have earlier proposed that the remnant could be the nucleus of the restored Zion of Isaiah's prophecy (cf. Isa 65:8–10).

Bearing this in mind, one can approach the uneasy task of explaining their identity as παρθένοι. Scholars have often suggested that the term refers to soldiers' abstinence from women before engaging in the

---

353. Cf. Shea, "Revelation 12 and 20," 46.

354. Casey, "Exodus Theme in Revelation," 38; Ortlund, *Whoredom*, 159; Vos, *Synoptic Traditions in the Apocalypse*, 138.

355. Yarbro Collins, "Women's History," 85. She thinks that they refer to martyrs, not to all believers.

356. Zimmermann, "Nuptial Imagery," 157, has argued that they are the same group as the 144,000 in 7:4. However, some scholars claim that they are the whole people of God of the end time. So Schüssler-Fiorenza, *Vision of a Just World*, 67, and possibly Metzger, *Breaking the Code*, 61. Caird, *Revelation*, 95, thinks it improbable that the 144,000 should be limited only to the ethnic Jews (cf. 14:1). The twelve tribes did not exist in the first century CE. But see Russell, *Parousia*, 405, Chilton, *Days of Vengeance*, 206–12, and an extended discussion in Beale, *Revelation*, 416–23. The number could perhaps be all-inclusive, but with a particular reference to the remnant of ethnic Israel. Thus, it could signify not only the vast complete number of God's people, but also the army of the Lamb (cf. Num 31:4–6). So Bauckham, *Climax of Prophecy*, 36, 216, 218.

holy war.³⁵⁷ Some have also pointed out that abstinence from women was demanded of an active priest.³⁵⁸ However, explaining "virgins" along the lines of the OT sexual purity laws does not seem to give a satisfactory solution to the problem of the virgins. Olson explains:

> The greatest difficulty with this interpretation ... is that the cited strictures for holy war and regulations for cultic purity do not call for anything like *virginity* from troops (or priests); they call merely for temporary abstinence. No clear instance can be found where παρθένια refers to a short-term foregoing of sexual relations, and so the main issue—John's choice of words—remains unresolved.³⁵⁹

He prefers to explain the vague term as referring to total celibacy of the redeemed who were to replace the fallen angels.³⁶⁰ He finds here a parallel with 1 Enoch 15:2–7, where angels were never intended to have sexual relationships with women, but they have trespassed that boundary.³⁶¹ The only problem is that 1 Enoch 15 never uses the term παρθένος.³⁶² Thus even suggesting that it could perfectly describe the state of angels before the fall is not ultimately convincing. We simply do not know if angels were ever thought of in early Judaism as παρθένοι. Also, his comparison to Jesus' teaching on men's state after death being like that of angels seems to strain the interpretation of the word παρθένοι.³⁶³ It is indeed

---

357. This could have special significance if the number 144,000 echoes Num 31:4–6. Bauckham, *Climax of Prophecy*, 232, believes that a military group is in view. See also his *Theology of Revelation*, 78, where he implies that the purity of the army is demanded in the face of holy war (Deut 23:9–14; 1 Sam 21:5; 2 Sam 11:9–13). Yarbro Collins, "Women's History," 86–87, explains that because God and his angels were fighting alongside men, the men had to be pure.

358. Yarbro Collins, "Women's History," 88. The priest had to be pure because of his closeness to God.

359. Olson, "Revelation 14:4 and the Book of Enoch," 495.

360. Ibid., 505.

361. Ibid., 497. He suggests that the use of μιαίνω in 1 Enoch 15:2–7 and μολύνω in Rev 14:4, both referring to defilement, creates a verbal link between the two texts.

362. A fact recognized by Olson himself. Ibid., 500.

363. See ibid., 503. His main reference is to Luke 20:34–36. The focus of the passage, however, does not seem to be on purity of sexual life but on marital relationships for procreation (cf. vv. 28–31). The point of comparison between men and angels seems to be immortality in which state "divine Fatherhood replaces human parentage." So Marshall, *Luke*, 741–42.

surprising that men should ever be called virgins in biblical literature: the word is normally reserved for young unmarried women.[364]

We would like to suggest that a metaphorical use of the word may offer a possible solution to the παρθένοι problem. We have already indicated in chapter 5 that the plural of παρθένος can, in fact, relate to the people of Israel (see on Matt 25:1–13; cf. Isa 37:22; Jer 18:13; 31:4, 21; Lam 2:13).[365] In the Parable of the Ten Maidens, Israel was divided into two groups of παρθένοι facing two divergent destinies on the day of Christ's vindication: admittance to the new covenant or exclusion from it, i.e., salvation or judgment. Consequently, the 144,000 may be those φρόνιμοι παρθένοι, who heed Jesus' words: "they follow the Lamb wherever he goes" (Rev 14:4).[366] The other problem then is to explain their chastity regarding "women." Identification of these women is perhaps the most difficult. However, we would suggest that the context helps in this task. Beale has argued that the group of words derived from the verb μολύνω was used in the LXX when speaking of Israel's idolatry, which was also regarded as adultery (cf. Isa 65:4; Jer 23:15; 44[51]:4).[367] This could, at least, imply that the women in Rev 14:4 should be interpreted figuratively.[368] This suggestion could avoid the tensions that emerge when one insists on a more literal reading. It seems that the women can signify all those nations/systems that cause the church to commit adultery, if she associates with them.[369] Such association could result in the

364. Aune, *Revelation 6–16*, 811. He notes that the other fairly early instance where a man is called παρθένος is found in *Jos.As.* 4:9, where Joseph is called a virgin like Aseneth.

365. Beale, *Revelation*, 739, has noticed interesting parallels between Rev 14:1–4 and Jer 31. In the time of restoration Israel was to: 1) sing aloud about her salvation (Jer 31:7; Rev 14:3); 2) "shout for joy on the height of Zion" (Jer 31:12), in the presence of God (v. 6); 3) be recognized as the "remnant" of Israel (v. 7); 4) be identified as God's "firstborn" (v. 9; cf. Rev 14:4).

366. Zimmermann, "Nuptial Imagery," 159, has argued that their following the Lamb resembles Israel's following YHWH as described in Jer 2:2.

367. *Revelation*, 740.

368. It is noteworthy that the OT used "women" as symbolic of nations in the context of the divine marriage metaphor. See, e.g., Ezek 16:4; 23:2.

369. Cf. Kramer, "Contrast as a Key," 113, who argues that spiritual adultery, or rather lack of it, is in view. See also Metzger, *Breaking the Code*, 78, who thinks that pagan worship is behind the women symbol. Schüssler-Fiorenza, *Vision of a Just World*, 88, suggests that imperial cult worship was that which endangered the church. But in the light of what we have said before, it appears that associating with women would rather point to becoming supportive of the political system represented by the sea-beast (or any

loosening of her loyalty to Christ. Yet, the remnant has proven undefiled by the pagan political systems. They have become the first fruits of God's harvest for his kingdom.[370] They do not have any defect (14:5). Scholars have usually acknowledged the sacrificial connotations of ἄμωμοί.[371] However, Pauline tradition has already associated the term with the perfection of Christ's bride for whom he has laid down his life (Eph 5:27). Through Christ's death, she has become unblemished, with the emphasis being on the ceremonial and the ethical (cf. Lev 21:17–23; Eph 1:4). By his death, she has become ceremonially clean, a prerequisite necessary for the marriage between the divine and human (cf. Ezek 16:9).[372] She has become a royal wife full of glory (cf. Ezek 16:10–14). Therefore, it seems a better option that the perfection of the royal and priestly wife of Christ is in view in the context of our passage, rather than a sacrifice by the remnant's death.[373] Christ's bride is indebted to her husband for

---

other anti-God system), not necessarily the emperor cult as such. It seems unlikely that Jews were involved in open worship of the emperor. They have rather acknowledged Caesar as their king (John 19:15). Cf. Chilton, *Days of Vengeance*, 341.

370. Zimmermann, "Nuptial Imagery," 159, has noted the link with the first fruit of Jer 2:3. Cf. Beale, *Revelation*, 742. The first fruits point to the prospect of many more to follow. Yet, according to our argument, they are the first believers from among Jews. They constitute the nucleus of the restored Zion, the first fruits of the restored Israel (cf. Jer 2:3). Ford, *Revelation*, 235, remarks that the first fruit relates to the first-born. Thus, this could point to their union with Christ, the first-born, in his resurrection (cf. Rev 1:5).

371. So Bauckham, *Climax of Prophecy*, 232: the sacrificial animals were to be without blemish (Exod 29:38; Lev 1:3; 1 Pet 1:19). Thus Bauckham concludes that the remnant win their victory through sacrificial death. He also shows (p. 292) that the first fruits were to be accompanied by the offering of a lamb without blemish, presumably Christ in this context (cf. Lev 23:12). But Rev 14:4b clearly implies that they are first fruits not only to God but also to the Lamb. Therefore, the sacrificial context does not solve all problems. However, it could help us to understand that the offering of first fruits to God set free the rest of the crop for general use and thus the harvest could begin. Cf. Caird, *Revelation*, 191. But Casey, "Exodus Theme in Revelation," 39, has suggested that the lack of blemish was required of priests (Lev 21:17, 18, 21, 23). The priests were the first born (first fruits) of Israel (cf. Num 8:14–18; Exod 4:22; 13:15). Cf. Ulfgard, *Feast and Future*, 39 n.169. This explanation is plausible because the purchased in Revelation have become a priestly nation (5:9–10; 1:5–6). Aune, *Revelation 6–16*, 822–23, remarks that ἄμωμοι interprets the word παρθένοι.

372. A somewhat similar argument has been made by Zimmermann, "Nuptial Imagery," 159.

373. Stefanovic, *Revelation of Jesus Christ*, 437, suggests that ψεῦδος refers not so much to general lying but in particular to the lying of the antichrist powers (cf. 1 John 1:5–10; 2:21–22). Hence, the remnant are not deceitful (cf. Zeph 3:13; this is also a mes-

The Metaphor of Divine Marriage in the Book of Revelation 305

everything she is and has. She stands in contrast to the harlot in Rev 17, who despised her husband.[374] The above considerations make it likely that the marriage metaphor is important to understanding Rev 14:1–4. Also, it seems that the metaphor can shed light on the meaning of the rest of the chapter.

The vision of an angel proclaiming judgment on the καθημένους ἐπὶ τῆς γῆς (probably Judeans) and other nations[375] precedes the announcement of the fall of Babylon (v. 8). The symbol of Babylon is significant for our subject because it introduces the woman who is the opposite of Christ's bride. She appears to be the same great city Jerusalem (cf. 11:8),[376] which committed sexual immorality with "all nations" (14:8).[377] It seems that, in contrast to the bride, she deceived nations to practice immorality with her, i.e., to enter into alliances with her, as it is doubtful whether Jews would encourage any open idolatry at that time.[378] We have already indicated in chapter 3 that alliances with foreign nations were regarded

---

sianic quality in Isa 53:9). Cf. Aune, *Revelation 6-16*, 823, who claims that the late second temple worldview associated Satan with lying (1QS 4:9; 10:22; Titus 1:22; John 8:41–47; Rom 3:4). Beale, *Revelation*, 745, thinks that the 144,000 are the opposite of the lying Jews from the synagogue of Satan (cf. Rev 2:9; 3:9). They appear to be similar to the false prophets in Jer 23:14. However, in this case they can deny Christ (cf. 1 John 2:22).

374. Cf. Casey, "Exodus Typology in Revelation," 188.

375. Cf. Ford, *Revelation*, 236. Beale, *Revelation*, 748–53, thinks that the message (gospel) is not of grace only but also of judgment, anticipating dire consequences for those who reject it. Thus the angel can be a messenger of judgment summoning people to acknowledge God's sovereignty (cf. 11:13). Otherwise, 14:8 would have to be a final decree for genuine conversion. Pace Caird, *Revelation*, 183–84, who thinks that the notion of judgment in this context refers to the death of martyrs, which liberates them from the influence of Satan (cf. John 12:31–32). The proclamation involves martyrdom and it corresponds to the flight of the angel. However, the proclamation is clearly to the dwellers of the land (implying the rulers of Palestine) and other nations. It demands a prompt response from them in the face of an impending judgment, so that they might be spared. Cf. Chilton, *Days of Vengeance*, 361–62.

376. Cf. Beagley, *Church's Enemies*, 81; Chilton, *Days of Vengeance*, 362–63, against the others. The exclamation: "Fallen, fallen is Babylon" may be reminiscent of Isa 21:9, which finishes on the notion of the destruction of gods' images. Cf. Ford, *Revelation*, 248. Another source for the image of Babylon as a great city may be Dan 4:30. Cf. Moyise, *Old Testament in Revelation*, 50.

377. This seems to be the meaning of the phrase "who gave all nations to drink of the wine of the passion of her fornication." Θυμός can mean "intense desire" (heat) but also "fury/intense anger" in v. 10. Cf. Aune, *Revelation 6-16*, 831. While it is possible that the phrase echoes Jer 28:7LXX (51:7MT), drinking can, in general, signify involvement in something, being under someone else's influence (cf. Isa 29:10).

378. On the last point see Chilton, *Days of Vengeance*, 341.

as Israel's harlotry. Here, it can perhaps be deduced that her immorality found its ultimate expression in her relationship with Rome. She chose Caesar as her king, over Jesus the Messiah (cf. John 19:15). Thus the old Jerusalem system, disloyal to God in rejecting Christ, plays the whore, and is in direct opposition to the loyal wife of Christ. Her end is short; she is "fallen."

The third angel's message clearly announces judgment on everybody who is in alliance with the beast Rome (Rev 14:9-10). It can be deduced that since the unfaithful Jerusalem has intoxicated other nations with the wine of her harlotry, she will now be intoxicated with the wine of God's wrath (cf. Ps 75:8; Isa 51:17, 21-23; Jer 25:15-18; Ezek 23:31-34).[379] The supporters of Rome will experience permanent judgment with fire and sulfur (Rev 14:10-11).[380] However, the same judgment is a test for the faithful: they are called to persevere in their loyalty to Christ (v. 12). The faithful are called 'blessed' (happy) because even their death is not a threat to them: it rather translates them into the realm of rest (14:13).[381]

---

379. This drinking is probably a prelude to death. See Chilton, *Days of Vengeance*, 364–65; Beale, *Revelation*, 759. The mark of the beast (Rev 14:11), as contrasted with the seal of the elect (7:1–8), destines its bearers for judgment (16:2). Cf. Yarbro Collins, *Crisis and Catharsis*, 125.

380. Beale, *Revelation*, 760, argues that the torment may be psychological as indicated by the use of the cognates of βασανισμός in Rev 9:5 (cf. 11:10; 18:7). But it is more difficult to explain "psychologically" the instances in 18:10, 15 and 20:10. However, some sort of torture(s) is implied. Yet, the punishment echoes that of Sodom and Gomorrah in Gen 19:24–26 (cf. Luke 17:29). Cf. Ford, *Revelation*, 249. The picture of judgment upon those two cities has been enlarged and intensified in the prophecy against Edom in Isa 34:9–10. See Terry, *Biblical Apocalyptics*, 408. Caird, *Revelation*, 186, has argued that the notion of permanency of judgment leaves no room for restoration. The duration of judgment points to its unlimited nature. It seems that the system of the old Jerusalem is permanently judged. Stefanovic, *Revelation of Jesus Christ*, 450–51, explains that the phrase "for ever and ever" designates completeness of judgment. Although the NT acknowledges the punishment on Sodom and Gomorrah with "eternal fire" (Jude 7), it would be unimaginable to claim that those places are literally burning in modern Jordan. However, they remain places of God's judgment "forever."

381. This is the second of the seven beatitudes of Revelation (the first occurs in 1:3). Cf. Ford, *Revelation*, 249. Their works (cf. v. 12) bring them rest as reward, after the time of exhausting labor. See Stefanovic, *Revelation of Jesus Christ*, 455. This rest probably stands in contrast to the eternal torment of the beast's worshippers. Cf. Beale, *Revelation*, 767. Russell, *Parousia*, 471, has argued that their blessedness consists of their immediate transportation to the rest prepared for God's people (cf. Heb 4:1–11; 11:9, 10, 13, 39, 40).

The following vision of the Son of Man introduces the theme of harvest (14:14–20). His appearance may resemble the vindication-of-the-Messiah theme from 1:7, although here he appears as one who has already assumed his kingship (golden crown).[382] The harvest of grain and vintage in the OT both represented God's judgment on his people or on their enemies.[383] However, the wider context of our passage may suggest that the unfaithful part of Israel has become the enemy of God's people, so that the variegated harvest traditions may culminate in this one passage, presenting the ultimate judgment on Israel's unfaithfulness. Some scholars have also argued that the harvest echoes the Synoptic traditions concerning the gathering of the elect (Mark 13:26–27//Matt 24:29–31//Luke 21:25–28) and perhaps also those regarding retribution for the "seed of Satan" (Matt 13:24–30).[384] This would suggest that the harvest is a separation of the faithful from the unfaithful: a picture of salvation and judgment. However, the vision of vintage seems to focus on judgment only.[385] Ford has argued that the figure of the vine symbolizes Israel (Isa 5; Ps 80).[386] The fact that the pressing of the winepress takes place outside the city and that blood spreads over a distance similar to the area of Palestine offers additional support to that argument.[387] It is,

---

382. Cf. Ford, *Revelation*, 238. She remarks that sitting recalls the One sitting on the throne and may symbolize sitting in judgment (p. 250). This is supported by the fact that both Rev 1:7 and 14:14 are reminiscent of Dan 7:13 (cf. Mark 14:62; 9:1; 13:26).

383. Caird, *Revelation*, 189. The clearest examples are those of Hos 6:11 and Lam 1:15—both referring to judgment on the unfaithful people of God. However, the picture of vintage also echoes Jer 51:33. This last passage could still have in view the unfaithfulness of Jerusalem, since she has become Babylon. Harvest and vintage can also picture judgment on other nations, enemies of God's people (cf. Isa 63:1–6; Joel 3:12–13). But Caird believes that, although reminiscent of the two last passages, Rev 14 has in view judgment upon Babylon and her inhabitants (cf. vv. 9–11). Pace Bauckham, *Climax of Prophecy*, 296, 309, who believes that the harvest and vintage mainly focus on the conversion of the nations.

384. Vos, *Synoptic Traditions in the Apocalypse*, 147. The Gospel traditions suggest that some Jewish leaders became the dupes of Satan. Satan has sown his bad seed in Israel (cf. Luke 11:29–31; 13:16; 16:14–15). See Wright, *JVG*, 460–62.

385. We cannot agree with the approach of Caird, *Revelation*, 191, who assumes that since in the harvest there is a notion of the gathering of the elect, the same must be the case in the vintage.

386. *Revelation*, 250. See also Ezek 15:6. However cf. Joel 3:13.

387. Ibid. "Outside the city" could refer to Gehenna, the waste disposal site of Jerusalem (cf. 19:20). See Beagley, *Church's Enemies*, 83. Pace Caird, *Revelation*, 192, who thinks that "outside the city" echoes Christ's death and therefore the subsequent death

therefore, likely that this closing vision of Rev 14 develops the motif of God's wrath and judgment from vv. 9–11. However, the implied parallels, indicated in the footnotes to this section, may also suggest that the harvest/vintage motif is closely linked with the judgment upon the unfaithfulness of God's people otherwise expressed by the metaphor of harlotry (Hos 6:11; cf. Ezek 15:6).[388] Thus the picture can be of the Son of Man punishing the whore, but vindicating his elect, his bride (cf. Rev 14:4). In our opinion, Rev 14 can be regarded as a likely example of the use of divine marriage metaphor, which describes the fate of two opposite groups within God's people.

ECHOES OF DIVINE MARRIAGE METAPHOR IN REVELATION

If our above proposals concerning the importance of the divine marriage metaphor to the interpretation of some visions gain some acceptance, it should be asked whether or not the metaphor's biblical contexts can shed more light on the argument of other passages in Revelation. We believe that the book's structure, which reveals various parallels between sections (see Structure above), encourages the quest for other possible instances or echoes of the metaphor in the visions. According to Mathewson, even an echo (understood as a less obvious allusion) can evoke previous contexts, which may add to the overall thrust of a passage.[389] Therefore we would like to consider below a number of passages

---

of his martyrs (Heb 13:12–13). It seems improbable that God exposes his martyrs to be trampled in the winepress of his wrath (14:19) in order to fill the cup of his wrath. The two visions of cup and winepress, although aiming at the same point, are still separate. The "vine of the earth" seems to stand for more than the martyrs, i.e., Israel.

1,600 furlongs approximates two hundred miles, the distance from the north to the south of Palestine (cf. Isa 63:6). See Terry, *Biblical Apocalyptics*, 413, and Bauckham, *Climax of Prophecy*, 47–48. Yet, perhaps a more symbolic meaning of the land is implied: four (earth/land) squared, times ten squared (completeness/largeness). See Chilton, *Days of Vengeance*, 376. Thus the measure may be more concrete than the symbol for the whole creation proposed by Ellul, *Apocalypse*, 177.

388. We have indicated in chapter 3 that some scholars regard the marriage metaphor in Hosea as the most important and therefore perhaps the leading one. Thus Hos 6:11 can be subject to that major metaphor. On the other hand, the mention of the judgment upon the vine Israel in Ezek 15:6 comes shortly before the extended example of the broken marriage motif in Ezek 16. Cf. also Ezek 17:6–10.

389. Mathewson, *New Heaven*, 22. According to him, even a "word or a phrase" which points to prior contexts is worth considering, because the previous contexts may

The Metaphor of Divine Marriage in the Book of Revelation   309

in different parts of Revelation, which may echo previous traditions using the divine marriage metaphor.

Revelation 1

In general, scholars have not recognized traces of the OT divine marriage metaphor in Rev 1.[390] In fact, on its face value, the chapter does not seem to mention it at all. However, we believe that there exists a premise, which, if properly considered, could change the way in which scholars study the first chapter of the Apocalypse.

Revelation 1:5

We propose to focus first on the somewhat problematic fifth verse of this chapter. The reading of the verse is complicated because the manuscripts give two major variants in its last part: "released/freed" or "washed." According to modern standards of textual criticism, the former is commonly preferred because it is supported by the oldest available documents containing the text of Revelation.[391] Thus the majority of scholars claim the superiority of these manuscripts.[392] Some of them, however, have recognized that the alternative reading at 1:5 also has the support of early versions.[393] Nevertheless, they argue that the evidence of the first group of manuscripts outweighs the latter option. However, they need also to consider arguments from the context of Rev 1:5, as it seems unwise to draw firm conclusions from the manuscript evidence alone. Thus, for instance, Westcott and Hort have argued that the reading λούσαντι is

---

add to our understanding of Revelation as though rich ornaments to a symphony's harmony. Cf. ibid., 234.

390. Some, e.g., Fekkes, "Nuptial Imagery," 287, have wondered if Christ's adornment in Rev 1:12–20 can be that of a bridegroom. However, he himself doubts this proposal (p. 287 n.50). He concludes that John reserved the nuptial imagery for the latter stage only to indicate the eschatological transition of the church. However, we have already observed some traces of the imagery in early chapters of the Apocalypse.

391. 𝔓[18] ℵ A C , which come from third-fifth centuries; plus the good fam 1611. Cf. critical apparatus of UBS3 or NA27. For explanation of the manuscript abbreviations see introductory sections of these Greek New Testaments and/or Aune, *Revelation 1–5*, cxxxvi.

392. See esp. Metzger, *Textual Commentary*, 662. Cf. Aune, *Revelation 1–5*, 42, cxxxiv–clx; Beale, *Revelation*,70–75.

393. As did, e.g., Metzger, *Textual Commentary*, 662. The fairly strong evidence for this reading comes from vg cop[bo] eth, ranging from III through VI century, plus the good fam 1006.

a corruption in the text "due to failure to understand the Hebraic use of *evn* to denote a price" as in the case of Rev 5:9 or LXX of 1 Chr 21:24.[394] In consequence, the copyist misapplied Rev 7:14 to 1:5. Metzger has followed this reasoning, adding that the idea expressed by λύσαντι is in accord with Isa 40:2LXX and also that it better suits the following clause in Rev 1:6a.[395] Moreover, the pronunciation of λύσαντι would sound like λούσαντι to the copyist's ear.[396] Others have generally followed these arguments only adding that the λύσαντι reading conforms better to the exodus imagery, which they have found in Rev 1:6.[397] Finally, they have taken it as a better reading because it seems to be the *lectio difficilior*, i.e., the more difficult reading.[398] But these arguments do not banish all doubt. Is it really right to claim that the big textual families simply misread the word in this case? Can it be shown that "υ" was pronounced in the same way as "ου" in the Koine Greek of that time? Could not such an argument be turned around to undermine the λύσαντι option? Could the λούσαντι reading be an outcome of theological reflection on an earlier misread verse and thus a return to John's original intention? Could this reading preserve the original version apart from other textual evidence? We propose that only by considering the usage of the verb λούειν in its various contexts will we be able to conclude with a modicum of confidence the answers to these questions. However, to limit our examination we intend to consider only those passages where the verb occurs together with other ideas important to the latter part of Rev 1:5: love, sin and blood. But before we do that, we need to consider Isa 40:2LXX as a possible background to our verse.

The closest parallel NT exegetes can find for their reading of 1:5 is in Isa 40:2LXX. There, the verb λύειν refers, they claim, to the 'removal' of Jerusalem's sin, her particular iniquity. But the word must be taken in its context. The passage speaks words of comfort to Jerusalem in exile (40:1). She has undergone (lit. 'accepted') double punishment for her

---

394. Westcott and Hort, *Introduction to the New Testament*, 136.
395. *Textual Commentary*, 662.
396. Ibid.
397. Beale, *Revelation*, 192, 194; Beasley-Murray, *Revelation*, 57. Also Aune, *Revelation 1–5*, 42.
398. Aune, *Revelation 1–5*, 42. Cf. Ford, *Revelation*, 378, who does not decide on the reading option.

sin. The sentence for her iniquity is now full.³⁹⁹ Thus the translation "is undone/annulled," in the sense of "brought to an end," seems to be a good rendering for both the Hebrew רָצָה in the Niphal perfect and the Greek λύειν in the perfect passive, in the context of Israel's enduring (lit. 'accepting') the punishment of sin (cf. Lev. 26:41, 43).⁴⁰⁰ It seems that the verb λύειν synonymously parallels the previous aorist of πίμπλημι, both designating an end of something. Thus, although Isa 40:2LXX uses the same verb as Rev 1:5, the imagery seems somewhat different: in Isaiah, Israel's sin is terminated/annulled, whereas the alleged meaning in Revelation assumes the act of "freeing/releasing" as pointing to the work of Christ.

We can now consider a few instances of the use of the verb λούειν, which seem particularly important to our case. In the Septuagint, the verb sometimes appears in connection with blood. 1 Kgs 21[20LXX]:19 is part of Elijah's prophecy against king Ahab. The prophet announces that in the place where Nabuthai (Naboth) was murdered for his vineyard, "the dogs will lick" the king's blood and "the prostitutes will wash/bathe themselves" in his blood (καὶ αἱ πόρναι λούσονται ἐν τῷ αἵματί σου). The fulfillment of this prophecy came about, as related in 1 Kgs 22:38. The verse repeats the verb λούειν in connection with blood, "the prostitutes washed/bathed themselves in the blood."⁴⁰¹ Thus, in this sense, λούειν stands close in meaning to the verb πλύνειν (cf. Gen 49:11LXX: Judah "shall wash his garment in the blood of the grapes").⁴⁰² However, in those instances, the washing in blood has overtones of contempt and violence. The former example could also bring to mind defilement with blood (cf. Lam 4:14; Ezek 16:6). Yet the verb λούειν in other contexts stands close to the idea of cleansing: in 2 Kgs 5:13: λοῦσαι καὶ καθαρίσθητι ("wash and be cleansed!"); or in Isa 1:16: λούσασθε καθαροί ("wash yourselves clean!"); both have an ethical reference. Nevertheless, the OT contexts do not help much in determining a parallel reading to Rev 1:5.

399. Brueggemann, *Isaiah 40–66*, 16–17.

400. Cf. Delitzsch, *Isaiah*, II: 140.

401. The scene is probably one of "ignominious contempt." So Keil, *Kings*, 281. We cannot be sure if a rite of magic for fertility was involved as suggested by Gray, *I and II Kings*, 455.

402. The picture may be of the violent victory of Judah's descendant over his enemies (cf. Isa 63:2–3). See Waltke, *Genesis*, 609. Another option would be to read this as referring to the abundance of wine in the golden age (cf. Isa 25:6; Joel 2:24). See Wenham, *Genesis 16–50*, 479.

However, the way the NT uses the cognates of λούειν is interesting. In two places the word is connected to Christ's ἀγάπη. The first instance comes from the Gospel of John. In the first verse of chapter ten, it is said that Christ "loved his disciples to the end" (John 13:1). Then, verse 10 presents Jesus, who says to Peter that the one who is bathed (ὁ λελουμένος) does not need to be washed (οὐκ ἔχει χρείαν νίψασθαι). This verse has caused a number of disagreements among NT interpreters. Some of them have preferred to omit the longer reading including the phrase εἰ μὴ τοὺς πόδας.[403] Accordingly, they have concluded that the perfect passive participle of λούειν and the infinitive aorist middle of νίπτειν are synonyms. Thus, they have concluded that Jesus' feet-washing points to cleansing by his atonement and also to baptism.[404] Others have objected to this deduction, arguing for the legitimacy of the longer reading.[405] Ridderbos, in particular, has separated the feet-washing from the complete bath signified by λούειν.[406] He has acknowledged that the feet-washing referred to Jesus' servanthood rather than the disciples' impurity.[407] This meaning is supported by v. 14 where Jesus calls his disciples to follow his attitude. Ridderbos believes that "according to Jesus' explanation . . . , the footwashing that the disciples must render to each other is not washing but self-denial."[408] However, he concludes that ὁ λελουμένος points not to the purification that the disciples will have to undergo in the event of the cross, but rather to the purity they have already received as Jesus' disciples ("and you are clean, but not all of you . . .").[409] They are clean because

---

403. E.g., Lindars, *John*, 451.

404. Ibid. Cf. Bernard, *John*, II: 463; Barrett, *John*, 368, but he is against a sacramental interpretation. See also Beasley-Murray, *John*, 235.

405. See esp. Ridderbos, *John*, 461–62, who also remarks that λούειν cannot refer to the feet-washing because it normally refers to a complete bath. Cf. Carson, *John*, 466.

406. *John*, 462.

407. Ibid.; Carson, *John*, 466, seems to suggest that the feet-washing of the disciples refers to their spiritual existence: although they are already cleansed once and for all, they need a "minor" washing as they still remain people who sin. But Ridderbos's earlier remark about the significance of feet washing seems more convincing. He said that Jesus' act confronted the disciples with the attitude that was in their Leader. Additional help on this has been offered by Smalley, *John*, 200, who takes the feet-washing as an "acted parable." Its significance is Jesus' obedience to God and his humiliation unto death.

408. *John*, 462

409. Ibid.

Jesus accepted them into the fellowship of his love (cf. John 10:27ff.; 15:1ff., 9, 16–17; 17:6; Luke 22:28f.).[410] Yet, it seems that the mention of Jesus' love to the end (εἰς τέλος) in John 13:1 bears some climactic overtones, as the following scene is on the eve of Jesus' trial and death. Moreover, Jesus himself explained that the greatness of his love for his disciples was still to be revealed: expressed in his death (John 15:13). Thus Carson's observation that the complete bath of the disciples was in the context of Christ's death seems justified.[411] Therefore the picture evolving in John 13 concerns cleansing through Jesus' death, because he loved his disciples to the end.

The second instance where a cognate of λούειν is connected with Christ's ἀγάπη is in Eph 5:25–26, a passage we have examined in chapter 6. There the self-sacrificial love of Christ was expressed in his death, which was probably intended as an atoning offering to God (Eph 5:2, 25). As a result of his sacrifice, the church has become fit for her relationship with God. Christ the Bridegroom has bathed her in a similar manner to Israel, who was washed clean of the blood that defiled her (cf. Ezek 16:9).[412] She has become not only ceremonially, but also ethically pure (cf. Lev 21:17–23; Eph 1:4). Thus the restoration of God's marriage to his people took place at Christ's death. The purification of the church by the application of God's Spirit resulted in Christ's pronouncement of the new covenant over his people (Eph 5:25).

Our study of the divine marriage metaphor in the OT has acknowledged that Yahweh's love is a prerequisite of the covenant with his people (cf. conclusions to chapter 3 above). Such covenantal love was well expressed in terms of the most intimate relationship known to mankind: marriage. Furthermore, we have observed in Paul's letters that the love of Christ has to do with the promise of a new betrothal, which is demonstrated in the restoration of God's covenant. Thus, it is quite likely that the love language found in both Jewish and Christian traditions was associated not only with the covenant but also with the metaphor of divine marriage, which expresses this covenant in the best possible way.

---

410. Ibid., 461. Scripture references his.

411. *John*, 466.

412. This was probably the blood of Israel's natural and ritual depravity (cf. chapter 3 on Ezek 16:9). The bath was covenantal. She has become, in consequence, a kingdom of priests (cf. Exod 19:6).

We would, therefore, propose that the reference to Christ's love in Rev 1:5 may be an indication that the statement should be read as an allusion to the divine marriage metaphor. We have observed above that the cognates of λούειν are sometimes associated with cleansing in the OT. On two occasions, the Septuagint refers to bathing in blood not so much in the context of purification, but of defilement. Moreover, Christian tradition links λούειν with the sacrificial death of Christ that cleansed his people, thus making them fit for the new covenant/marriage relationship with God. However, it remains to be examined if the use of λούειν can easily be assimilated to the context of Rev 1:5, the church as a kingdom of priests to God the Father.

Commentators have usually accepted that Rev 1:6a echoes a similar usage in Exod 19:6. There, Yahweh commanded Moses to tell the Israelites that if they would keep God's covenant they would be to him "a kingdom of priests." Yet, as we have already observed, Israel failed to keep the covenant. She had to be punished in exile. Only after her exile was over, would she be called "the priests of the Lord" (Isa 61:6).[413] Thus only her new exodus, the renewed covenant (v. 8), would bring her into true priesthood. It seems that it is exactly at this point that the theme of the priesthood is linked with the divine marriage metaphor (v. 10; cf. chapter 3 on Isaiah 61). Even though Isa 61 itself reveals this link, we think it can additionally be demonstrated by consideration of priesthood in the OT. The priest had to be purified with blood (Exod 19:22; 29:1, 19–21, cf. vv. 26–27: "the ram of consecration"; also Lev 8:22–30). The blood was sprinkled on him. Thus if the λούσαντι reading is accepted in Rev 1:5, the picture emerging is one of Christ who has bathed the church's sins in his blood. As a result, she can be a kingdom of priests. At the same time, the bath could intensify the imagery of the sprinkling of blood in order to signify, presumably, the superior quality of the act. Thus the meaning of bathing in blood would be the complete opposite of prostitutes defiling themselves by bathing in Ahab's blood. Christ's application of the bath in blood brings purification and consecration for the priesthood of the new covenant. He is the ram of consecration (cf. 5:6).[414] In this

---

413. Aune, *Revelation 1–5*, 48, has acknowledged this echo.

414. Ford, *Revelation*, 86, where she explains that although ἀρνίον linguistically means "lamb," the references to wrath, horns and the similarity to Dan 8:3 suggest a ram. Our link can add to the debate concerning the meaning of the word in Revelation. However, the significance of the ram imagery in the context of the purchase by his blood (5:9) will be considered below.

sense λούσαντι would be a word well suited to Rev 1:5. Even if λύσαντι resembles God's deliverance from the bondage of Egypt, λούσαντι seems more appropriate in the context of the restoration of the priesthood to God's people. Likewise, the imagery would not point to baptism or to a baptismal formula, but to Christ's work of consecrating a people.[415]

If this less popular reading is accepted at this point, we may suggest a further link with the OT divine marriage metaphor. Some scholars have recognized the use of λούειν for the prenuptial bath (cf. Ruth 3:3).[416] However, in Ruth 3:3 it is the woman who bathes herself, and the bath is not in blood. Nevertheless, we have acknowledged that the bath metaphor was applied to Israel when Yahweh made her his nation (Ezek 16:9). We have remarked in chapter 3 that the bath signified the newborn state of Israel, the cleansing of her depravities (cf. v. 4).[417] Moreover, the bath was a prerequisite for Israel's becoming a kingdom of priests. Yet again, the bath was to cleanse people of blood, in water, and not in blood. Eph 5:25–26 presents a similar picture, although here the issue at stake is purification by the Spirit, and the ceremonial purity demanded of priests is referred to (v. 27; cf. Lev 21:17–23). We would suggest that the author of Revelation has possibly mingled different traditions to reach his goal, a method common to OT prophets who employ the divine marriage metaphor, as well as to some NT authors who use it in the context of interpreting the Christ event. Hence, it seems, John could deliberately be contrasting the washing from blood of Ezek 16, with the washing in blood performed by Christ. The effect in both cases would be similar: purification of iniquities, bringing the cleanness required to approach the holy God (cf. Exod 19:22). However, it seems that in John's case the elaboration of the priestly motif suggested the use of the consecration ram theme: thus "washing in blood." Nevertheless, the two pictures are close to each other, because the reception into God's covenant together with the divine act of cleansing makes a nation a kingdom of priests. The additional advantage of reading Rev 1:5 as a reference to the divine marriage metaphor, instead of reading it as a direct reference to the original Exodus, would be the note of covenant renewal. The new marriage had special significance for Jewish Christians, for whom the

---

415. Contra Casey, "Exodus Theme in Revelation," 34.
416. Block, *Ezekiel Chapters 1–24*, 484.
417. So Allen, *Ezekiel 1–19*, 238.

fulfillment of OT promises came in Christ.[418] Christ was presented to them as the Messianic king of David's line, the "faithful witness" (cf. Isa 43:10–13; 55:4).[419] He was also the "firstborn," the inaugurator of the new creation (Ps 89:27; cf. Rev 3:14).[420] In addition to all of this, he was the "ruler over the kings of the earth," a phrase that might well signify his kingship over the rulers of Israel as in Ps 2:2 and Acts 4:26–27 (cf. above on Rev 17:18).[421] Now, he also appears as their bridegroom, effecting their restoration. He loved them and ended their exile by dealing with their sin through his sacrifice. He made them a new priestly kingdom restoring the covenant they violated (cf. Isa 61:6). Presently, he sends a message to his beloved bride[422] about the imminence of his vindication following his rejection by the unfaithful Jews (Rev 1:7).[423] This imminent appearance of the bridegroom becomes one of the major themes of the whole book.[424]

REVELATION 1:13–16

Another passage worth considering for traces of the divine marriage metaphor in Rev 1 is verse 13 and its surrounding context. The major-

418. Beagley, *Church's Enemies*, 32, argues that the churches of Revelation consisted of both Jewish and Gentile converts but also that John could have regarded as a true Jew everyone who acknowledged Jesus as the Messiah. Cf. Yarbro Collins, "Revelation," I:392.

419. Beale, *Revelation*, 191; Ford, *Revelation*, 380.

420. Beale, *Revelation*, 191.

421. Pace Beale, *Revelation*, 191

422. Ford, "Divorce Bill," 137, has observed that the Lamb in 1:6 appears as espoused to a priestly community. However, she has not grounded this observation in the text.

423. We agree with the primary observation of Aune, *Revelation 1–5*, 56, that γῆ in Rev 1:7 could mean the land of Israel when compared with Zech 12:12. But we cannot agree with his further suggestion that Rev 1:7 universalizes the Zechariah passage. Matt 24:30 does not support this suggestion, as it can refer to the Jews. Cf. chapter 5 on this. It is equally likely that the original context of Zech 12 is important: Israel being guilty of the piercing of the Messiah (v. 10). But pace Beale, *Revelation*, 26, 196–97: we cannot be sure if πᾶσαι αἱ φυλαὶ τῆς γῆς was a fixed phrase referring always to all the nations of the world. In Zech 12:11–14, it is the families (perhaps in the sense of tribes) of Israel that mourn over the sufferer they have pierced. See Mitchell et al., *Haggai, Zechariah, Malachi and Jonah*. Cf. Smith, *Micah-Malachi*, 277–78. See also Russell, *Parousia*, 371. It also seems that the phrase in Rev 1:7 is closer to Zech 12:10 than to John 19:35, 37. Thus pace Vos, *Synoptic Traditions in the Apocalypse*, 69.

424. Cf. Gentry, *Before Jerusalem Fell*, 121; and Russell, *Parousia*, 380. Even those who do not agree with our time reference view Rev 1:7 as stating the theme for the whole book. See, e.g., Stefanovic, *Revelation of Jesus Christ*, 67–68.

The Metaphor of Divine Marriage in the Book of Revelation   317

ity of NT interpreters have regarded the image of the Son of Man as representing one wearing the garments of the high priest in Israel.[425] This is a possibility, because the word ποδήρης referred in the LXX to the long priestly garment (Exod 25:7; 28:4, 31; 29:5; 35:9; Sirach 45:8). Furthermore, the figure appears amidst the seven menorahs, which may suggest a temple setting.[426] Additionally, this attire of the Son of Man parallels that of the seven angels coming out of the heavenly temple with golden belts around their chests (Rev 15:6). It is therefore likely that the priestly motif is involved here. We would, however, suggest that the contextual evidence points also to another motif.[427] A number of considerations challenge the exclusively priestly interpretation.[428] Ποδήρης translates five different Hebrew words (חֹשֶׁן: "breastplate" in Exod 25:7; 35:9 ; מְעִיל: "robe" in Exod 28:4; 29:5; אֵפוֹד: "ephod" in Exod 28:31; בַּד: "white linen" in Ezek 9:2, 3, 11; and מַחֲלָצוֹת: "robe" in Zech 3:4) so it can hardly be regarded as a technical term.[429] Aune explains,

> Actually, the most common Hebrew term for the robes of the high priests and priests in the OT is כתנת *kĕtōnet*, which is usually translated χιτών (e.g., Exod 28:4, 39, 40; 29:5, 8; 35:19; 39:27; 40:14; Lev 6:3).[430]

So, without a further qualification ποδήρης does not necessarily describe the high priest's garment. If John meant the Hebrew מְעִיל here, it could simply be referring to a vestment of a man of high rank (cf. 1 Sam 18:4; 24:5, 12; Ezek 26:16).[431] If he meant בַּד, the picture emerging would be that of an angelic being as in Dan 10:5. This instance is even more appealing as the angel is girded with gold around his waist. In the case of מַחֲלָצוֹת the rendering of "festal robe" (NASB), "party dress" (NJB), "fine robe" (NIV), or 'festal apparel' (NKJV), as seen in Isa 3:22, is possible. Thus the claim that the attire of the figure in Rev 1:13 is exclusively priestly cannot be

---

425. Caird, *Revelation*, 25; Chilton, *Days of Vengeance*, 73–74; Schüssler-Fiorenza, *Vision of a Just World*, 52.

426. So Beale, *Revelation*, 209.

427. Even if Josephus's evidence for the priestly belt is considered. See his *Antiquities* iii.7.2. Reference in Charles, *Revelation*, I:28.

428. See, e.g., a challenge from Aune, *Revelation 1–5*, 93–94. He suggests that a long robe and a golden sash are not enough to conclude in favor of the priestly vestments.

429. Ibid. 93.

430. Ibid.

431. Charles, *Revelation*, I: 27.

sustained. Furthermore, it seems that the priestly belt was of linen, never of gold (Exod 39:29; Lev 16:4).[432] The only argument for the priestly context is the picture of the seven λυχνίας. Some exegetes have linked them with the seven heavenly λαμπάδες of Rev 4:5;[433] however, these are the seven spirits of God. Furthermore, the vision of the lampstands in Rev 1:13 is explained in 1:20: they represent the seven churches, which presumably are on earth. Although the menorahs themselves may bring to mind their OT temple counterpart, it seems that John's emphasis was on the lampstands/churches as God's witnesses on earth (cf. Zech 4:2).[434] If they do not repent, their Lord will remove them from their place (Rev 2:5). In the light of all the above considerations, it seems that the closest parallel to the appearance of somebody like a Son of Man in Rev 1:13 is the heavenly angelic being in Dan 10:5 (girded around the waist with gold),[435] or the angels in Rev 15:6. In both passages, the figures are militant, as the first was fighting with a hostile angelic being of Persia (Dan 10:13), and the other seven were responsible for bringing disasters upon the earth (Rev 16:1ff.). Perhaps for similar reasons, some scholars have concluded that Rev 1:13 presents a vision of a divine warrior.[436] This would be in accord with the vision of Jesus the Messiah coming on the clouds in Rev 1:7 (cf. Dan 7:13).

432. Even as described by Josephus, *Ant.* iii.7.2. The girdle of the priest was a loosely woven scarf. Cf. Charles, *Revelation*, I: 28.

433. E.g., Beale, *Revelation*, 206–7. Is there any significance in the fact that Rev 1:12, 13, 20 uses the word λυχνία and 4:5 λαμπάς? It appears that the 'lampstand' refers to light-bearing activity whereas the 'lamp' signifies the act of light-giving.

434. Charles, *Revelation*, I: 25. Stefanovic, *Revelation of Jesus Christ*, 95, explains,

> In Jewish tradition, the image of the lampstand symbolized "the obedience of Israel to God." In the Old Testament, Israel was appointed to be God's light-bearing witness (Isa 42:6–7; 49:6; 60:1–3). In the New Testament, this role is transferred to the church. According to Matthew 5:14–16, the church is like a lamp that gives light to the world (cf. Phil 2:15). The lamp is to be put on a "lampstand" to shine (Mark 4:21; Luke 8:16). In Revelation 11:4, God's two witnesses in their prophetic role are identified as the "two lampstands standing before the Lord of the earth" (cf. Zech 4:2–6, 14). The foregoing references suggest that the lampstand emblem defines the essential role of the church as God's witness in the world.

It is noteworthy that part of the early Christian tradition regarded the church as a bearer of light, i.e., the prophetic word (2 Pet 1:19). Thus the church could have been regarded as the lampstand for this light.

435. Cf. Caird, *Revelation*, 25.

436. Longman and Reid, *God Is a Warrior*, 181.

The verses following Rev 1:13 further explain the appearance of the Son of Man. NT exegetes have generally agreed that verse 14 resembles the vision of the Ancient of Days in Dan 7:9 and the warrior angel of Dan 10:6.[437] Consequently, Rev 1:15 is similar to Dan 10:6, although others have also tried to link this to the image of bronze feet in Ezek 1:7 and that of the voice in Ezek 43:2: the voice of God's returning glory.[438] These descriptions suggest that the appearance of the Son of Man is astonishing, transcending that of the angels. His characteristics come close to those of Israel's God.

Rev 1:16 pictures the Man as a king, ruler over the churches, holding a scepter of seven stars.[439] He has the power to judge by means of the sword that comes out of his mouth (Isa 49:2; cf. Isa 11:4; Heb 4:12; 2 Thess 2:8; Rev 19:15; 2:16).[440] The "face shining like the sun" again resembles Dan 10:6, although scholars have recognized a link with Matthew's account of Jesus' transfiguration, which comes close to a theophany or, at least, to an angelophany (Matt 17:2).[441] Therefore, it is not surprising

---

437. Caird, *Revelation*, 25; Aune, *Revelation 1–5*, 94–95: Apparently in 1 Enoch 106:5–6, the newborn son of Lamech has "eyes like the rays of the sun," which characterizes angels. See also Duff, "Witchcraft Accusations," 116–33. While recognizing his claim that the fiery-eyes can signify somebody's supernatural strength or even a deity's avenging judgment, we do not agree with his method of reading back the magical elements of ancient and contemporary cultures into Revelation. His conclusions cannot be supported from Jewish or early Christian traditions. A relevant point, however, concerns Sir 23:19, which states that the eyes of the Lord "are ten thousand times brighter than the sun." The passage's context points to God's penetrating gaze at the secret wrongdoings of men with a prospect for judgment.

438. Caird, *Revelation*, 25. Also Beale, *Revelation*, 210. Pace Metzger, *Breaking the Code*, 27 who compares the feet to Dan 2:33, 41.

439. Cf. Ford, *Revelation*, 385. Cf. Rev 1:20. Stars correspond to the angels of the seven churches and can be their heavenly counterparts (Charles, *Revelation*, I: 34), or perhaps the leaders/governments of the churches (Stefanovic, *Revelation of Jesus Christ*, 97). In the context of chapters 2–3, Christ communicates his messages to them (humans can be called angels: Mal 2:7; 3:1; cf. Dan 12:3). Terry, *Biblical Apocalyptics*, 290, has argued that the angels of the churches must represent the churches as organisms, for they are praised or found guilty. In this sense the churches can be messengers of Christ in the world. This option is particularly significant, because we do not find references to the heavenly reality in this context. Although the letters may have reached the churches through their elders, the messages were addressed to whole communities.

440. It is noteworthy that the LXX of Isa 11:4 renders the Hebrew שֵׁבֶט "rod" as λόγος "word" coming out of his mouth. Aune, *Revelation 1–5*, 99, suggests that Rev 1:16 may be a combination of the two Isaianic passages.

441. Aune, *Revelation 1–5*, 99. Beale, *Revelation*, 212, has noted that the image of the sun shining in its full strength follows the wording of Judg 5:31LXX, as typological of the ideal messianic warrior.

that John falls at the feet of that incredible heavenly warrior figure (Rev 1:17) who walks in the midst of the seven churches (2:1).

Although we have identified key references in this section to OT sources, we would like to suggest that there is yet more background to the vision of the Son of Man. We need to bear in mind that the picture in Rev 1:12–17 concerns an awesome figure, somebody exceeding human and angelic appearance. He is a king and a warrior. Another such extraordinary person is pictured in Ps 45. We would like therefore to propose that there are some similarities between the two characters. We have already suggested that the Psalm was peculiar (see on Rev 12), but perhaps best understood as describing the great Messiah to come. This indicates that there may exist a number of contact points between Ps 45 and the appearance of the Son of Man in Rev 1:12–16. We will now consider each of these similarities in turn.

The king described in the psalm is the most beautiful of the 'sons of men' (45:2[44:3LXX]; cf. Ps 50:2).[442] Yet his beauty transcends the merely physical.[443] His splendor and majesty resemble God's beauty (v. 4; cf. Ps 96:6, but also Ps 21:5): a picture too idealized for any human king.[444] He is called אֱלֹהִים (vv. 6–7), a term never used for a human king in the OT except in the case of the messianic figure in Isa 9:6.[445] The beauty of the messianic king is likely to apply only to somebody like the Son of Man in Rev 1:12–16, who not only outshines every human being and angel, but even resembles the Ancient of Days (Dan 7:9–10).

Furthermore, the king of Ps 45 appears as a great hero, a renowned brilliant warrior carrying a sword at his side (vv. 3–5).[446] He probably rides a horse or a chariot (רְכַב) fighting "for the cause of truth and meekness and righteousness" (NASB). This has led some OT scholars to compare this with the picture of the conquering Christ in Rev 19:11.[447] His enemies are the enemies of those virtues.[448] Delitzsch explains,

---

442. For convenience, from now on, we will follow the numeration of the English translation.

443. E.g., Craigie, *Psalms 1–50*, 339; Delitzsch, *Psalms*, II: 79.

444. Cf. Craigie, *Psalms 1–50*, 339.

445. Kraus, *Psalms 1–59*, 455. But see Weiser, *Psalms*, 363. He tries to avoid the deification of the king.

446. Cf. Briggs and Briggs, *Psalms*, I: 386. Kraus, *Psalms 1–59*, 455.

447. E.g., Delitzsch, *Psalms*, II: 80.

448. Craigie, *Psalms 1–50*, 339.

> The poet desires that the king whom he celebrates may rule and triumph after the manner of the Messiah; that he may succour truth and that which is truly good, and overcome the enmity of the world, or, as Ps. ii expresses it, that the God-anointed King of Zion may shatter everything that rises up in opposition with an iron sceptre.[449]

Moreover, the king is to take his throne after he has conquered the enemies of righteousness (vv. 6–7) in a similar manner to God, who has taken his throne after the conquest of mythical forces of chaos.[450] Thus the king's throne can be seen as a counterpart to God's throne. Again, we have observed that the Son of Man in Rev 1:13–16 appears as a warrior, presumably a royal warrior, as his attire may testify.[451] He is using his two-edged sword (v. 16). The blaze of his eyes may refer to his penetrating gaze at the wrongdoings of the unrighteous (v. 14; cf. Sir 23:19).

Another point of contact, closely connected to the previous one, is the picture of a royal judge. The king of Ps 45 is just (vv. 6–7). His scepter symbolizes the judge's arbitrating power (v. 6a).[452] He is the helper of all the disfranchised and the protector of uprightness in his community (cf. Isa 11:2–5; Ps 72:2–4).[453] His delight is in righteousness, but he hates wickedness: the picture of a perfect judge (v. 7). We have noticed that it is possible to view Christ in Rev 1:16 as holding in his hand a scepter of seven stars symbolizing perhaps his power of judgment over the churches and the ability to punish with the sword.

Finally, we need to acknowledge that commentators take Ps 45 to be about a royal messianic wedding.[454] Craigie has even claimed that the psalm resembles the parable of the royal wedding in Ezek 16.[455] Although this suggestion is possible, one wonders if the Psalm is not simply describing the proper relationship between the Messiah-king and his bride (or spouse: 'He is your Lord' v. 11). She seems to be called to be

---

449. *Psalms*, 82.

450. Craigie, *Psalms 1–50*, 339. He refers to Gray, J. *The Legacy of Canaan*, 287. Leiden: E. J. Brill, 1965, for evidence concerning God's conquest of chaos.

451. Besides warfare is one of the functions of a king. See Longman and Reid, *God Is a Warrior*, 181.

452. Kraus, *Psalms 1–59*, 455.

453. Ibid.

454. Ibid., 453; Craigie, *Psalms 1–50*, 339; Delitzsch, *Psalms*, II: 85.

455. *Psalms 1–50*, 341.

loyal to her husband (v. 10). Whichever option one decides to choose, we would like to indicate the possibility of linking the royal bridegroom theme of Ps 45 with the figure of Christ in Rev 1:13–16. If our arguments concerning Rev 1:5 are accepted, the possibility of the divine marriage metaphor as background to Rev 1 becomes even more likely. The link is, admittedly, not very explicit, but the symbolic language in Revelation probably has more roots in Jewish traditions perhaps than anywhere else. We have suggested some similarities between the royal messianic bridegroom of Ps 45 and the appearance of the Messiah in Rev 1:13–16. Yet the final conclusion depends on the way one handles the material in both passages and whether one allows some less forceful echoes/allusions to be recognized in this case.[456]

In addition, however, we want to suggest another link with OT marriage imagery in Rev 1. We propose that due attention should be paid to Jer 25:10 in its context. Jer 25 is situated in the context of the year 605 BCE (v. 1).[457] OT scholars have suggested that verses 1–14 may be a conclusion or a prefatory speech to the scroll, which Baruch read to Jehoiakim in the same year.[458] The message of the passage is one of judgment for Judah's disobedience and her evildoings (vv. 4–7). The just punishment for her sins is exile in Babylon for seventy years (v. 11). As a result of God's judgment, Judah will be deprived of the "voice of joy and gladness, the voice of the bridegroom and the bride, the sound of millstones, and the light of the lamp" (v. 10, NASB; cf. 7:34; 16:9). The imagery in this last verse resembles that of approaching death (cf. Eccl

---

456. Cf. Hays, *Echoes of Scripture*, 30: his criteria for the volume of a scriptural echo. We believe that our proposal can pass a number of Hays's seven tests: 1) the source, i.e., Ps 45, was available; 2) it is possible that some of the ideas from the Psalm recur later in Revelation (esp. chapter 19); 3) the ideas from the psalm do not seem to disturb the thematic coherence of Rev 1; and 4) it is possible that John could have intended the allusion and that his readers could have understood it, as long as they had knowledge of Jewish traditions; 5) concerning the history-of-interpretation test, we can remark that Chilton, *Days of Vengeance*, 45, Fekkes, "Nuptial Imagery," 287, and Ford, "Divorce Bill," 137, have recognized a possibility of occurrence of the bridegroom theme in Rev 1. Finally, the issues of volume and satisfaction can be met by acknowledging the importance of the metaphor in other parts of the book as indicated above. For discussion concerning the legitimacy of the method of intertextual echo in Revelation see Moyise, *Old Testament*, 18–19, 109, and Mathewson, *New Heaven*, 22–23.

457. Cf. Craigie et al., *Jeremiah 1–25*, 364.

458. Thompson, *Jeremiah*, 511.

The Metaphor of Divine Marriage in the Book of Revelation 323

12:3–6).[459] There will be no more experiencing the joys of life in Judah, or the joy of marriage, harvest, or even the continual light of the lamp (either the temple lamp נֵר cf. Exod 27:20; Lev 24:2; or the lamp of testimony: cf. Pss 119:105; 132:17; Prov 6:23; 20:27; or more particularly the lamp of Israel's witness: Isa 42:6–7; 49:6; 60:1–3; cf. Matt 5:15). God will punish Judah according to the covenant treaty.[460] Although the passage does not speak clearly about the divine marriage metaphor, we have indicated in chapter 3 that the theme is important in the book of Jeremiah (cf. Jer 2–3; 13:20–27; 31:3–5). The motif is closely linked with the threat of exile, a major theme of Jer 2–25.[461] It is used again in Jer 31 concerning the restoration and total rehabilitation of Judah, which will result in the renewal of her status as a virgin (vv. 2–5). The time of restoration will bring a new joy to the people of Judah (31:13). It will be the time of the new covenant (31:31ff). The voice of the bridegroom and the voice of the bride will again be heard in Judah (33:11). Jer 25:10 (and 33:11) gains a new significance when we bear in mind the context of Israel's/Judah's exile. We have noted in chapter 1 that it was hardly over after the seventy years. In fact, it was going to last for seventy 'weeks of years' (Dan 9:24–27).[462] We have also indicated above that some commentators compared the voice of Jesus Christ in Rev 1:15 to the voice of Yahweh's returning glory of Ezek 43:2, which marked the time of restoration, the end of exile. Moreover, the presence of the lampstands at Rev 1:12–13 could signify the restored testimony of God's people. Therefore, we suggest that these factors may point to a thematic connection between the marriage imagery of Jer 25:10 and the appearance of the Son of Man in Rev 1:13–16. The sound of marital festivities in Israel marks the time of the Husband's presence among his people.

Finally, we would also like to propose that Dan 9:24–27 may be the text that binds together the variegated prophetic traditions that we have

---

459. Ibid., 513.

460. Cf. Carroll, *Jeremiah*, 496. Carroll seems to regard the covenant as a suzerain-vassal treaty. He argues that a malediction similar to Jer 25:10 can be found in the vassal treaties of Esarhaddon. He refers to Weinfeld, M. *Deuteronomy and the Deuteronomic School*, 141–42. Oxford: Clarendon Press, 1972, and Wisemann, D. J. "The Vassal-Treaties of Esarhaddon." *Iraq* 20 (1959) 62 line 444.

461. Cf. Carroll, *Jeremiah*, 113.

462. Wright, "In Grateful Dialogue," 258. Wright shows that Jer 25:11–12 has been reinterpreted in Daniel, a text that was vital for Jews of Jesus' day. The point was that the Babylonian exile had been extended to seventy *sevens*, beyond the initial seventy years.

mentioned, which lie behind both Rev 1:5 and 1:13–16. Israel's hope was for a new exodus (Dan 9:15–19), which would "finish her transgression, make an end to sin, and atone for iniquity" (v. 24).[463] This was accomplished in every respect through Jesus' sacrificial death. The Messiah-Bridegroom has 'bathed' away the sins of his people after the manner of Yahweh (Rev 1:5; Ezek 16:9). He has prepared a pure bride for himself and she has succeeded to royalty (Rev 1:6; Ezek 16:13). After the seventy *sevens* (Dan 9:24–27), the royal messianic bridegroom (Rev 1:13–16; Ps 45:2-9) has announced the return of God's glory (Rev 1:15; Ezek 43:2) and his rule over his people (Rev 1:16). This return would mark the end of exile, the restoration of joy and the light/witness of God's people. Accordingly, we suggest that the echoes of the divine marriage metaphor in Rev 1 can shed new light on the understanding of the exodus motif in this section of the book.

Revelation 2-3

We have suggested above the possibility that five letters to the churches contain references to the divine marriage metaphor. However, given the parallel structure of all the seven letters section, one may expect also to hear some echoes of the metaphor in the letters to Pergamum and Sardis.

PERGAMUM (2:12–17)

The church in Pergamum had held fast to their confession, even though this could have endangered their lives. Yet, Christ stands against her because she tolerates the "doctrine of Balaam" and those who follow the teaching of the Nicolaitans (vv. 14–15; cf. Num 22:5—25:3; 31:8,16). It seems that there were some influences within the church that could distract the loyalty of Christians from their Lord through εἰδωλόθυτα and πορνεία. Scholars have argued that, whereas some sort of involvement in eating idolatrous food might have been the case in Pargamum, πορνεία should rather be understood in a metaphorical sense (cf. 14:8; 17:2, 4; 18:3, 9; 19:2).[464] Moreover, other pieces of early Christian tradi-

---

463. Cf. ibid.

464. Beale, *Revelation*, 250. Thus the issue at stake is faithfulness to the Lord (cf. Num 31:16). It is noteworthy that the church in Pergamum is not accused of eating sacrificial meat. It is possible that the idol food here could be symbolic. It could be in contrast with the heavenly manna in v. 17, which signifies a life-giving identification

tion indicate that those who teach falsely for profit are following the bad example of Balaam (cf. Jude 11; 2 Pet 2:15–16).[465] Through this teaching, the church is exposed to the possibility of being disloyal to their Lord. Thus, given the likely references to the marriage metaphors in the surrounding letters, one may suspect that the matter at stake is covenant faithfulness as opposed to promiscuity.

Exegetes have usually recognized the parallel between vv. 14 and 15. The οὕτως in v. 15 coordinates the immediately preceding phrase in v. 14 and should be rendered "thus" or "in this way."[466] This implies that the teaching of the Nicolaitans and that of the Balaamites are the same: they dilute the church's faithfulness to her Lord and husband. From the parallels in 2:6 (and perhaps 2:2), it can be deduced that the Nicolaitans could have been some Jewish converts to Christianity, who, however, went against the apostolic doctrine.[467] It has been suggested also that the woman Jezebel in Thyatira is guilty of spreading similar teachings (2:20–24).[468] She and her followers have learned the deep things of Satan (v. 24),[469] which may represent anti-Christian doctrine. One might also

---

with Christ (cf. John 6:31–35). The meaning of manna and the contrast with v. 14 have been recognized by Beale, *Revelation*, 252. Aune, *Revelation 1–5*, 189, also recognizes the contrast between vv. 14 and 17, but takes "manna" to mean "eternal life." These observations would imply, by contrast, that the idol food is a life-taking identification with the false teachers. However, outside Revelation εἰδωλόθυτος refers to food offered to foreign gods (cf. Acts 15:29; 21:25; 1 Cor 8:1, 4, 7, 10; 10:19).

465. Cf. Aune, *Revelation 1–5*, 185–86.

466. Ibid. Cf. Beale, *Revelation*, 251. This parallel is further supported by the meaning of both names: Nicolaos (Gr. νικάω + λαός 'conqueror of the people') and Balaam (Hebr. עַם + בָּלַע "destroyer of the people"). See Chilton, *Days of Vengeance*, 98. Cf. Stefanovic, *Revelation of Jesus Christ*, 111. These names may correspond to Abaddon and Apollyon in 9:11. See Terry, *Biblical Apocalyptics*, 294.

467. The parallel with 2 Cor 11 can also in part support this point. Smith, *Redating the Revelation*, 31, argues that they were Hellenistic Jews trying to syncretize the philosophies of Hellenistic dualism with Christian beliefs. Thus they were proto-Gnostics. One may also wonder why John was concerned to describe the problem within the church by deliberately using Jewish imagery. A possible solution would be that he wanted those who were causing the problem to repent, after they had understood his allusions (v. 16).

468. Aune, *Revelation 1–5*, 148. Caird, *Revelation*, 39, has remarked that "nobody ever accused Ahab's wife of harlotry except in a metaphorical sense (2 Kings ix.22)."

469. Although they may have claimed that they know the "deep things of God," John sarcastically labeled them the "deep things of Satan." Cf. Aune, *Revelation 1–5*, 149; also Beale, *Revelation*, 265; Ford, *Revelation*, 404. Who would be claiming to be in possession of a deep knowledge of God in the early church if not Jewish teachers? Scholars

acknowledge a parallelism between the "deep things of Satan" and the "synagogue of Satan" in 2:9. Both descriptions seem to point to a similar attitude. Therefore, it is plausible that the sect of Nicolaitans emerged among unorthodox Jews who collaborated with the Roman political and religious system.[470] They infiltrated the Asian churches spreading their false teachings, probably persuading Christians to relax their devotion to Christ. We may also suspect that they gained high status in some of the churches because of their Jewish origin; a more open pagan influence would perhaps have been detected and dealt with earlier (cf. 2:13-14).

The church has to repent or otherwise her Lord will come in judgment upon the troublemakers, who make his bride unfaithful. But the faithful in the churches are promised manna, i.e., life from Christ, and a white stone, probably a token of admittance to the marriage feast (cf. 19:7-9).[471] The stone has a new name (of God? cf. 3:12) written on it. Scholars have recognized here parallels with Isa 62:2.[472] We have

---

have sometimes argued that the teachers in the early church (e.g., in Pauline congregations) were Jews (cf. Rom 2:17-20). Cf. esp. Holland, "Paschal-New Exodus Motif," 61-62. Holland has argued that the evangelistic principle "to the Jew first, then to the Gentile" also characterized teaching in the primitive church. Jewish converts were more prepared to be teachers, as they possessed scriptural knowledge that had now been reshaped around the Jesus event. See also Campbell, *Rhetoric of Righteousness*, 132-33, 133 n.1. Wright, *NTPG*, 453-54, has argued that even the so-called Gentile Christianity derived all its beliefs and practices from Jewish Christianity.

470. Cf. Beagley, *Church's Enemies*, 12-17. He has argued that during the time of Hellenization apostate Jews were often keen to use the pagan authorities against their pious brothers to gain control. Cf. Wright, *NTPG*, 160: There were some Jews who compromised their faith by rendering unto Caesar what was due to him. Smith, *Redating the Revelation*, 193-240, has offered a more comprehensive treatment of the Nicolaitan sect. He has reconstructed information about them from various NT writings showing that the same group of people could have created some of the problems in the congregations addressed in those documents. Although his proposal still awaits a constructive scholarly critique, it seems plausible that the Nicolaitans could have been Hellenistic Jews with proto-Gnostic views. See also Chilton, *Days of Vengeance*, 101, who suggests that the Nicolaitans, Balaamites and the Jezebel group are some Jews who reject Christ.

471. On "manna" see Beale, *Revelation*, 252. On the last point see Stefanovic, *Revelation of Jesus Christ*, 123, although one cannot be sure if the 'white stone' was a reward for the victor in the games. As Charles, *Revelation*, I: 66, has observed, it is difficult to find in ancient writings a white stone with an inscription on it. Chilton, *Days of Vengeance*, 110, has proposed that the white stone is *bdellium* (Exod 16:31 with Num 11:7), which points to the restored Paradise (cf. Gen 2:12). It may resemble the onyx stone of the high priest in Exod 28:9-12. The context does not seem to support Aune, *Revelation 1-5*, 191, who has inferred that the white stone could have been an amulet.

472. See esp. Beale, *Revelation*, 255-58.

observed in chapter 3 that the Isaiah text pointed to the end of exile and Israel's restoration, which would be marked by covenant renewal and a new fertility of the land.[473] God's wife would then be reloved and remarried (62:4–5). This link would perhaps suggest that the church's contemporary experiences are a sort of exile; she is awaiting her exodus, which will culminate in a wedding feast with the Lamb.

Sardis (3:1–6)

The church in Sardis is not commended for its works. It is rather called to repentance (vv. 2–3a).[474] As the church in Pergamum held fast to Christ's name, so the church in Sardis, in contrast, holds dearly its name of being "alive," yet ironically the church is described as "dead," with only a few things remaining alive.[475] It is possible that this contrast between life and death signifies the real parallelism between faithfulness and unfaithfulness to Christ.[476] It seems that the loyalty of the church to her Lord, with the exception of some members, has lapsed. The church seems to be on the edge of exile from the realm of union with Christ. There is no explicit mention of the way in which the apostasy took place. However, it is possible that the parallel with the situation in Pergamum sheds light on this conflict. Ford has observed that Sardis had a wealthy and influential Jewish community in the years preceding 70 CE.[477] There is a possibility that some Jews of the community infiltrated and endangered the new messianic movement, as it was the case in other places (e.g., 2:14). Alternatively, the church in Sardis could simply have relaxed the standard of their Christian living. Whatever the reason for the present situation, the issue at stake is the church's disobedience to God's commands. She must return to the teaching, which she previously received or else she may be unprepared at her Lord's coming and thus suffer punishment (v. 3b).[478]

---

473. The idea could be close to that of resurrection.

474. Although Beale, *Revelation*, 272, suggests that the situation here is similar to that in Ephesus (2:1), it seems that there are parallels with the church in Pergamum. A few positive things can be said about both. Cf. Stefanovic, *Revelation of Jesus Christ*, 76.

475. This description can refer to the church's lethargy regarding her faith. Beale, *Revelation*, 273.

476. Cf. Charles, *Revelation*, I: 79: the church has still a nucleus of faithful members. See also Aune, *Revelation 1–5*, 219, who regards life and death as metaphors.

477. *Revelation*, 410–12. Cf. Josephus *Ant* 16.6.6 (171); 14.10.24 (259–61).

478. Scholars have recognized parallels with the Synoptic exhortations to be watchful in the context of the approaching day of the Lord (cf. Matt 24:42; 25:13). See Vos,

Verse 4 explains that there is still a group of Christians in Sardis who are worthy. They wear white garments and will walk with Christ. Scholars have proposed various OT backgrounds to 'clean robes.'[479] But we would suggest that the contrast between defiled and pure garments may be an echo of the Matthean Parable of the Wedding Banquet (Matt 22:12–14).[480] We have observed in chapter 5 that in this parable the issue at stake was probably the clean garments, which designate works of righteousness. Only clean garments could guarantee admittance to the wedding feast of salvation. They are secured only by accepting the message of Jesus. The same symbolism can be found later in Rev 19:8 (cf. 7:14).[481] We also have indicated in chapter 5 that, although clean robes are the righteous acts of the saints (Rev 19:8), the parallel with Isa 61:10 suggests that the clothing is a gift from God (cf. Rev 3:5a). It signifies participation in his salvation. By implication, those who reject the teaching of Jesus are unable to participate in the feast, but the overcomer will take part in the wedding/salvation feast of the Lord (v. 5). He will not be excluded from the community of the righteous who will inherit God's new earth (cf. 21:27; see also Exod 32:32–33; Ps 69:28).[482] He will be acknowledged before God (cf. Matt 10:32–33; Luke 12:8–9).[483] These few considerations suggest that the letter to Sardis may contain an echo of the divine marriage metaphor.

Revelation 5

Beasley-Murray regards Rev 4 and 5 as the fulcrum of the whole book.[484] The chapters contain heavenly visions of God and the Lamb. They pic-

---

Synoptic Traditions in the Apocalypse, 76–77: who proposed that Rev 3:3b refers to the Parable of the Thief (Matt 24:42–44). We have argued that the Matthean announcement of a coming crisis was linked with judgment on the impenitent Israel (cf. chapter 5 on Matt 25:1–13). The coming may refer to a historical visitation of Christ. So Beale, *Revelation*, 275.

479. Metzger, *Breaking the Code*, 39, mentions Zech 3:3–5 (purity), Dan 7:9 (symbol of heaven) and Eccl 9:8 (festivity).

480. In Matt 22:8, those originally invited were not worthy (cf. chapter 5 on this). The few in Sardis who have white garments are worthy.

481. Cf. Miller, "Nuptial Eschatology," 311.

482. Cf. Stefanovic, *Revelation of Jesus Christ*, 137.

483. Ibid.

484. Beasley-Murray, *Revelation*, 108, has argued that the chapters link Rev 1–3 with the rest of the book. At the same time, they provide a fuller understanding of the

The Metaphor of Divine Marriage in the Book of Revelation   329

ture God as the sovereign creator (4:11), who occupies the throne of judgment.[485] The vision of his majesty evokes the former theophanies of the Exodus tradition and those of Ezekiel, Isaiah 6 and Daniel 7:9–10.[486] It seems that, at least, those from Exodus and Ezekiel were associated with covenant: in Exodus with establishing the covenant and in Ezekiel with covenant sanctions for Israel's disobedience. Like Ezek 2:1ff, Rev 4 seems to be a preparation for the judgments to come. However, it is the vision of chapter 5 that is of greater interest to our study.

Scholars have debated the three symbols of Rev 5: those of the scroll (5:1), of the seven-horned Lamb that was slain (5:6), and of his blood-purchase (5:9). We shall discuss the three symbols in turn because they can help us to determine whether or not the divine marriage is in view here. An examination of the blood-purchase image can also explain its relation to our proposal concerning Rev 1:5.

The seven-sealed scroll in the right hand of God is a somewhat problematic image. This is probably due to the lack of evidence for any other seven-sealed document in the ANE. Nevertheless, scholars have attempted to give possible meanings to this symbolism. Chilton has argued that the wider context suggests a testament containing covenant stipulations.[487] The document written on the front and on the back evokes the two tablets of Sinaitic covenant (Exod 32:15). However, this view fails to explain the meaning of the seals, as Chilton is unable to offer a biblical parallel to the sealed testament.[488] The proposal of Bauckham

---

figure that dominates the letters to the churches and, indeed, the whole book. Similarly, Vogelgesang has viewed Rev 5 as the central passage of the entire book. See "Ezekiel in Revelation," 11.

485. Cf. Rev 8:5; 11:19; 16:18–21, which reflect the theophany of 4:5. It thus appears that the context of this theophany is the coming series of judgments. Cf. Bauckham, *Theology of Revelation*, 42; *Climax of Prophecy*, 249.

486. Scholars have often referred to Exod 19:16–18 as the source for 4:5. Cf., e.g., Beasley-Murray, *Revelation.*, 115. However, some traces of Ezekiel's symbolism have been recognized (Ezek 1:26, 28; 9:2LXX; 10:1LXX; 28:13; at Rev 4:3). Cf. Beale, *Revelation*, 320. Vogelgesang has acknowledged the presence of parallels with Ezekiel, Isaiah and Daniel. Caird, *Revelation*, 65, has suggested that the sea of glass like crystal in 4:6a refers to the reservoir of evil out of which arises the sea monster in 13:1. It could also point to the ante-type of the Red Sea as in 15:2. However, the closest parallel in this context seems to be the floor in heaven in Ezek 1:22 (cf. Exod 24:9–10). See Ulfgard, *Feast and Future*, 35 n.150.

487. *Days of Vengeance*, 141, 166–67.

488. He tries to argue from modern reconstructions of the manner of testament-making in antiquity. Ibid. 166.

that the scroll resembles the one of Ezek 2:9–10 seems more appropriate in the context of the approaching judgment.[489] Yet, he also understands the scroll of Rev 5 to be the last will of the Lamb, the testament.[490] Once more, this conclusion concerning the testament does not seem to find strong support in the text of Revelation. However, the link with Ezek 2:9–10 may be valid, as God's word contained in that scroll concerns judgment for disobedience and salvation for obedience, a theme familiar to John's Apocalypse (cf. Ezek 3:4; 17–21). A disadvantage of this view is that the scroll in Ezek 2 is not sealed, although a sealed document with a similar purpose appears in Isa 29:11–12. Nobody is able to open it. The context reveals that God's salvation would follow after a period of judgment and that his people would then understand his counsel (29:13—30:26).[491] Presumably, the words of the scroll relate to God's counsel. Consequently, scholars have concluded that the scrolls of Ezek 2 and Isa 29 contain the prophetic interpretation of the Law.[492] However, there still is another possible source for the sealed scroll in Rev 5. A similar document appears in the vision of Dan 12:4, 8–9: there the content of the scroll will be revealed only at the end time, in the context of judgment followed by the salvation of God's people and their possessing of an inheritance (12:1–3, 10–13).[493] The Danielic context also helps us to acknowledge that the opening of the book takes place when the Ancient of Days entrusts the dominion over his kingdom to the One like a Son of Man (cf. Dan 7:9–14; Rev 5:6–7).[494] The document could therefore relate to Christ's enthronement as the eschatological Lord and to the way his kingdom is introduced.[495]

Ford has presented a different, somewhat peculiar, view. She has suggested that the sealed document in Rev 5:1 could be a priestly divorce bill.[496] In ancient Israel, she argues, the divorce bill was usually sealed,

489. *Climax of Prophecy*, 246.

490. Ibid., 248.

491. Cf. Beagley, *Church's Enemies*, 37.

492. Ibid.

493. Beale, *Revelation*, 339. This parallel was observed earlier by Vogelgesang, "Ezekiel in Revelation," 313.

494. Cf. Beale, *Revelation*, 347–48. Cf. also Wright, *JVG*, 640.

495. Concerning the two points, see subsequently Schüssler-Fiorenza, *Vision of a Just World*, 57–58, and Bauckham, *Climax of Prophecy*, 249. We do not agree with their eschatological time references.

496. Ford, "Divorce Bill," 136–37. Ford's argument rests entirely on comparing the scroll of Rev 5:1 with the rabbinic material of *BabaBathra* 10:1–2 and Babylonian

giving the husband more time to change his mind. She has concluded that Rev 5 is a prelude to the divorce of Jerusalem and the wedding of the new Jerusalem.[497] Although attractive to the theme of our study, this view raises problems. The OT does not explicitly mention a sealed divorce document: the divorce certificate given to Israel (cf. Isa 50:1) is of unknown form.[498] Even Ford's examples from *Baba Bathra* 10:1, 2 and Babylonian Talmud 160a refer to folded documents and do not explicitly mention seals.[499] And since there are other more convincing references to the sealed scroll in the OT, we have reservations, together with Vogelgesang, concerning the validity of her proposal.[500]

One final observation concerns a sealed document in Jer 32:6–15.[501] The scroll is signed and sealed as a deed for Jeremiah, which confirms that he has taken upon himself the right of redemption of Hanamel's field (32:10, 7). Jeremiah's purchase guarantees his inheritance in the land, which will be repossessed by God's people after the time of calamity and exile (vv. 14–15, 24, 36–44). It is noteworthy that Rev 5:9 speaks of another purchase made by the Lamb with his blood. He has paid the price of his blood to purchase people of all tribes to God.[502] Interestingly enough, in the OT the people of God were referred to as God's inheritance as a result of his ransoming them from Egypt (Deut 9:26, 29; 1 Kgs 8:51;cf. Ps 94:5). This might suggest a parallel with Christ's work of paying for his people in order that they could become his inheritance. This new priestly kingdom will be vindicated and will possess the new

---

Talmud *B.B.* 160a. However, one may question the relevance of these sources to the study of Revelation (cf. our argument in chapter 4 above).

497. Ibid., 137.

498. Ibid.

499. Ford has noted that only a few rabbis regarded the folding as seals. See ibid.

500. See Vogelgesang, "Ezekiel in Revelation," 59.

501. Aune, *Revelation 1–5*, 341–42, mentions this passage when discussing Rev 5:1, yet, he does not study its relevance to Rev 5. However, he indicates that the original deed and its copy, mentioned in the text, could have been a model for the document written inside and on the back in Rev 5.

502. A number of manuscripts read that Christ has purchased "us," i.e., the crowd around the throne in heaven, including the twenty-four elders. However, the problem with such a rendering is that in the very next verse a group of the same manuscripts reads "them." Cf. Metzger, *Textual Commentary*, 666. However, a few Old Latin, Vulgate, and early Coptic, read "us." Cf. UBS3 critical apparatus. Such rendering, however, complicates the identity of the worshipping elders and drastically limits the scope of redemption, unless the twenty-four elders represent the entire church.

earth as their inheritance (Rev 5:10; cf. 3:12, 21:7; 22:5b, cf. also Dan 7:18, 22, 27).[503] Hence, it is possible that the scroll of the Lamb resembles Jeremiah's deed of redemption and inheritance. This background should therefore be kept in mind in studying Rev 5.

The vision of the Lamb in Rev 5:6 is another problematic description. The word ἀρνίον is a diminutive of ἀρήν, signifying a little sheep or lamb. The word occurs only a few times in the LXX (Pss 114[113]:4, 6; Jer 11:19; 50[27]:45; cf. Ps Sol 8:23). In the NT, it appears only once outside Revelation in John 21:15. In the OT, the word translates either the Hebrew צאן or כֶּבֶשׂ. The former may evoke the lamb of the Exodus (cf. Exod 12:21) and the latter any sacrificial lamb of the Levitical system. Yet, one may ask why John has used this peculiar rare word ἀρνίον instead of the most common word used for all sorts of offerings πρόβατον? Scholars have argued that the lamb in Rev 5 is the Passover lamb (cf. 1 Cor 5:7; 1 Pet 1:18).[504] This is a valid point, bearing in mind the purchase of the royal priesthood with blood.[505] However, this still does not address the problem of John using such a rare word. We would suggest that a possible solution comes from Jer 11:19, the only place in the LXX where the word is used to denote a suffering little lamb. There, Judah the beloved of Yahweh has gone astray and will be punished.[506] She is unrepentant and even plots against the life of the prophet, who delivers to her the message of warning and judgment. The willingness to destroy the innocent lamb turns against the plotters themselves (vv. 21–23). It appears that the early church has employed this vision, together with a similar one in Isa 53, to describe the betrayal of Christ to his death (cf. Acts 8:32).[507] Yet, the Jeremiah context clearly suggests that the slaughter of the innocent lamb will be followed by God's vengeance upon the enemies of the lamb. This, we suggest, would fit the wider context of Rev 5. Here the Lamb will be vindicated over his enemies.

---

503. Both Aune, *Revelation 1–5*, 362, and Beale, *Revelation*, 360–61, have noted the reference to the prophecy of Dan 7. On vindication and representation in Dan 7, see Wright, *NTPG*, 294. Concerning reigning in the new earth see Beale, *Revelation*, 363.

504. Beasley-Murray, *Revelation*, 125; Fekkes, *Prophetic Traditions in Revelation*, 156; Schüssler-Fiorenza, *Vision of a Just World*, 61.

505. Casey, "Exodus Theme in Revelation," 34, argues that because 5:10 "quotes" Exod 19:6, the imagery is based on the paschal lamb tradition. He doubts whether Isa 53 could have been in the author's mind.

506. Carroll, *Jeremiah*, 273–75.

507. Thompson, *Jeremiah*, 350.

The Metaphor of Divine Marriage in the Book of Revelation   333

Additionally, it needs to be noted that the Lamb in Rev 5:6 has seven horns: a picture of the fullness of strength (cf. Deut 33:17; 1 Kgs 22:11; Ps 89:17; Dan 7:7).[508] This figure resembles the strong warrior ram, the leader of the Israelite flock (cf. 1 Enoch 85–90).[509] This could, then, synonymously parallel the image of the lion of the tribe of Judah and the root of David who has overcome and won the victory (Rev 5:5; cf. Gen 49:9; Isa 11:1–5).[510]

The last element of the vision in Rev 5 that we need to consider concerns the blood purchase of the Lamb in v. 9. Scholars have generally recognized the link between Rev 5:9–10 and Exod 19:5–6.[511] Christ has constituted a people as the priestly kingdom. We have argued above that Rev 1:6 may refer to the restoration of Israel's priesthood at the end of her exile (cf. Isa 61:6). We have also observed that the priest had to be consecrated with the blood of the consecration ram (Exod 19:22; 29:1, 19–21, cf. vv. 26–27: 'the ram of consecration'; also Lev 8:22–30). Thus, within that context, the ram was quite appropriate to the ceremony of consecration. In Rev 5:9, however, the problematic verb is ἀγοράζω, which predominantly refers to money transactions resulting in purchase (e.g., Gen 42:7; 47:14 ; Matt 13:46; Mark 15:46; Luke 14:18, but Isa 55:1 speaks of buying without money). The NT uses the verb a few times to describe the idea of Christians having been bought (1 Cor 6:20; 7:23; 2 Pet 2:1). But more difficult to explain is the purchase terminology in the context of Christian redemption theology. Some scholars have suggested that the purchase is the same as ransoming from slavery (cf. Deut 7:8; Isa 35:10; 51:11).[512] However, the verb which usually describes redemption is λυτρόω (cf. also 1 Pet 1:18). Hence, others have gone even further and suggested that the image of buying is borrowed from the market place with reference to the manumission of slaves.[513] In fact, 1 Cor 7:23 could encourage such an interpretation because the context assumes a kind of slavery. Yet, it would be virtually impossible to explain the relationship between the seller and the buyer in the case of this particular transac-

---

508. Beasley-Murray, *Revelation*, 124. Beale, *Revelation*, 351.

509. Longman and Reid, *God Is a Warrior*, 181–82. Cf. Ford, *Revelation*, 89.

510. Cf. Beale, *Revelation*, 349–52. On the tension between the symbols of lion and lamb in Rev 5 see, e.g., Moyise, "Does the Lion Lie down with the Lamb?" 181–94.

511. E.g., Bauckham, *Theology of Revelation*, 70.

512. Ibid., 71.

513. Casey, "Exodus Theme in Revelation," 34.

tion. Hence, we would like to propose another option. The point may be similar to that in 1 Chr 21:24LXX, which also uses ἀγοράζω. There the purchase of Ornan's (or Araunah's) field has to cost David something since it was "for the Lord." Thus in a purchase transaction the emphasis may be entirely on the personal cost of somebody offering something to God. Accordingly, Christ's purchase cost him his own blood, i.e., life (cf. Gen 9:4; Lev 17:11, 14).[514] This self-giving of Christ has guaranteed God a people (Rev 5:9–10), which can be understood as his inheritance (cf. Deut 9:26, 29). In this sense, it was a sacrificial, costly gift. The priestly tradition claimed that only life atones for and can give others life (cf. Lev 17:11). In this sense, the death of Christ would evoke the theme of the suffering servant in Isa 53, where he is made a sacrifice for the sin of the exiled nation (v. 10).[515] This sacrifice was necessary for the messianic community because of their sin (cf. Rev 1:5). Furthermore, we would suggest that this act of self-giving is comparable in the Christian tradition only to the self-giving love of the Husband/Christ in Eph 5:25. This finds support in the fact that the revival of the priestly kingdom in Israel was closely linked with the restoration of the marital union of God and his people (Isa 61:6, 10; cf. Ezek 16:12). Therefore, Christ has given his life in order that God's people might gain theirs, that the exiled wife might be resurrected (cf. Ezek 37:1–14). His act is similar to that of Yahweh in Ezek 16, that of giving life and royalty and priesthood to

514. The word σφάζω is frequently used in a sacrificial context (cf. LXX: Lev 4:24, 29; 6:25; 7:2; 14:13; Deut 28:31; Ezek 40:39), where various animals were killed as burnt, sin or guilt offerings. The verb could also describe a violent killing of a person (cf. LXX: 2 Kgs 10:7; Jer 52:10).

515. Those who argue that the slaughter of the Lamb refers exclusively to his martyrdom seem to overlook the fact that, according to some pre-Christian sources, martyrdom was linked with atonement. Cf. Wright, *JVG*, 579–84. See, e.g., 1QS 8.1–4 (cf. 5.6; 9.4). This may perhaps outweigh Ford's insistence on the martyrdom of the Lamb. See *Revelation*, 90–91. Ford follows an earlier suggestion of Dodd that during the Day of Atonement the atoning blood was that of a bull (cf. Lev 16). However, this overlooks the fact that a ram was offered on that occasion also (cf. Lev 16:3, 5). The ram was associated with a burnt offering: sacrifice atoning for sin (Lev 1:3–4, 10–13), or the trespass offering: sacrifice for an unintentional sin (5:15–18). Moreover, the ram's blood was for the consecration of priests (8:22). It has also been noted that the burnt offerings of rams were sacrificed during the inauguration of the Tabernacle/Temple (Exod 40; 1 Kgs 8). See Paulien, "Plot and Structure of Revelation," 251. This point may be particularly valid in the context of anticipation of the erection of a Temple consisting of the overcomer (cf. 3:12). It seems that all those sacrificial functions could have been contained in Christ's offering.

a helpless people. Christ's life-giving was perfect because he is now ὁ πρωτότοκος τῶν νεκρῶν (Rev 1:5), the beginning of God's new creation in the power of resurrection (cf. 2:8). It may also be noted that his people are temporarily awaiting inheritance (3:12; 21:7). In this sense, therefore, Christ's gift can be compared to the *mohar* price guaranteeing the wife and her offspring an inheritance.

It seems that an additional supporting factor for the marriage theme in this context is the structural parallelism between Rev 5 and 19:1–16.[516] It is widely agreed that Rev 19 presents Christ as the bridegroom. We would, therefore, suggest that the parallelism implies that the bridegroom/marriage theme has been interwoven into the plot of Rev 5. Though not explicit, the theme could have been introduced to inform the theology of John. Its use in this place would allow John later to disclose and develop the motif later in chapter 19.

It seems that the main advantage of our interpretation is that it helps in relieving the tension between the purchase by blood in Rev 5:9 and the washing with blood in 1:5. Both phrases may refer to the same act of Christ in which he has atoned for and consecrated his people, making them a priestly kingdom. Yet, it is the metaphor of divine marriage standing for God's eschatological salvation, which provides in the background a strong link between these two motifs. They also seem to be connected with the expectation of a new exodus accomplished in Christ.

Revelation 6

The events described in chapter 6 are generally recognized to be the result of Christ's subsequent breaking of the scroll's seals mentioned in chapter 5. Thus, it may be worth examining whether or not this chapter continues to sound echoes of the nuptial imagery.

Breaking the first four seals (6:1–8) results in the sending forth of four horse riders who deliver all sorts of calamities on the enemies of God's people (cf. vv. 12–17). Although it has been argued that the first rider on the white horse could be Christ himself,[517] this seems unlikely

---

516. This point has been made by Shea, "Revelation 5 and 19," 249–57.

517. So, e.g., Chilton, *Days of Vengeance*, 186. Those who claim that Rome is the main troublemaker for God's people have proposed that the bow of the first rider resembles the Parthian archers who invaded the Empire's capital. See Metzger, *Breaking the Code*, 58; Schüssler-Fiorenza, *Vision of a Just World*, 63. However, as Terry, *Biblical*

because he is consistently presented as the Lamb/ram in the surrounding chapters (5:1–14; 6:1; 7:17). He is the one who breaks the seals. Therefore, it may suffice here to say that the riders are God's agents bringing judgment.[518] It appears that the disasters brought about by them resemble similar ones in Ezek 5–7 (cf. Ezek 14:21).[519] The threats in that context may be directed against the rebellious people of God because they resemble the covenant stipulations from Deut 32:23–25.[520]

Breaking the fifth seal introduces a vision of the martyrs killed because of the testimony of God, who receive white robes (6:9–11). The robes guarantee their participation in the eschatological wedding of the Lamb, i.e., their share in God's promised salvation.[521] They cry in God's heavenly temple for judgment to come upon the "dwellers of the earth." There will be other martyrs joining them soon and, then, God will judge their persecutors.[522] We have already noted in the Introduction that the phrase "earth-dwellers" in 6:10 may refer to the inhabitants of the land of Israel. This would accord with the already identified background of Ezek 5–7, where the covenant judgment comes on the inhabitants of the land of Israel (cf. יוֹשֵׁב הָאָרֶץ at Ezek 7:7; also Matt 23:35).[523] Accordingly, the seven groups of people mentioned in v. 15 do not need to have a universal scope. They can be limited to a complete number of the inhabitants of the land mentioned in v. 10.[524] Their desire to hide themselves in caves and their desire to be covered by the mountains, away from God's wrath, echo the trembling of idolatrous and corrupted Israel in Isa 2:10, 19, 21;

Apocalyptics, 327, has noted, the symbol could refer to the outbreak of the Roman war against Jerusalem. Thus, the rider could denote both strength and victory.

518. On their characteristics and the link with Zech 1:7–11; 6:1–8, see Beale, *Revelation*, 372–74, 375–78; Aune, *Revelation 6–16*, 390, 393–401. See also Ford, *Revelation*, 104.

519. See Beagley, *Church's Enemies*, 41; cf. Ford, *Revelation*, 102.

520. Beagley, *Church's Enemies*, 41–42. If one agrees with Beasley-Murray, *Revelation*, 129, that Rev 6 has its closest parallels in the Synoptic "eschatological" discourses (Mark 13//Matt 24//Luke 21), this, then, further supports the proposal that the enemies of God's people are the anti-Messiah Jews represented by Jerusalem. Wallis, "Coming of the Kingdom," 22, favors the parallel.

521. Cf. Schüssler-Fiorenza, *Vision of a Just World*, 64.

522. Cf. Beale, *Revelation*, 394.

523. Beagley, *Church's Enemies*, 41.

524. Cf. Ford, *Revelation*, 112, who thinks that the seven groups are the Israelites. We have discussed above the possibility of taking the phrase οἱ βασιλεῖς τῆς γῆς as referring to the rulers of Israelite land (cf. Ps 2:2; Acts 4:26).

Hos 10:8, and Jer 4:29.[525] Thus, our argument concerning God's enemies and the overall purpose of John's Revelation may be reflected in this passage. V. 11 indicates that those who have suffered for the righteous cause will participate in the eschatological messianic wedding banquet, having obtained the white attire (cf. Rev 2:10; 3:5). Thus this seal vision can facilitate the identification of the constituents of Christ's bride and therefore echo the nuptial imagery of final chapters of Revelation.

Revelation 7

Rev 7 depicts an interlude in the opening-of-the-seals visions. It presents the sealing of the 144,000 (7:2–4). Since, it is likely that they are the same as the 144,000 in Rev 14:2–4,[526] it is worth examining this passage in search of echoes of the marriage metaphor.

It appears that the sealing of the 144,000 in Rev 7 echoes Ezek 9:4, where the faithful Jews of Jerusalem are sealed for protection.[527] Others are destroyed because of their guilt (9:6). This OT background may indicate that a similar calamity is now coming again on the unfaithful people of God. Commentators have proposed that the 144,000 could refer to those spared of the ethnic Israel.[528] They seem to be a different group from the Gentile multitude in verse 9. The picture can, thus, imply that there is a special group of Jews who will be protected against the coming disaster. They may echo OT traditions concerning the remnant of Israel.[529]

---

525. Beagley, *Church's Enemies*, 44. Pace Beale, *Revelation*, 400, who universalizes v. 15 and refers it to the time of the final judgment. Caird, *Revelation*, 88–89, shows the difficulties if v. 15 is universalized.

526. So, e.g., Zimmermann, "Nuptial Imagery," 157.

527. Bauckham, *Climax of Prophecy*, 216; Beagley, *Church's Enemies*, 47. Cf. Casey, "Exodus Theme in Revelation," 37, indicates a further reference to the Exodus tradition (Exod 8:22–23; 9:4; 10:23; 12) of God's protection of his people during the calamities in Egypt. He argues that in Rev 7 the mark of protection is against the end time disasters in 20:4–6. We would, however, suggest that Ezekiel's context is more appropriate because both there and in Rev 6 the disasters come upon the unfaithfulness of God's people.

528. See Russell, *Parousia*, 405, Chilton, *Days of Vengeance*, 206–12, and Beale, *Revelation*, 416–23. Optionally, the number could perhaps be all-inclusive, but with a particular reference to the remnant of ethnic Israel.

529. We have observed in chapter 5 that the key to Zion's transformation in Isaiah is a purifying judgment that spares only the remnant of Israel. They become the nucleus of the restored Zion. God clearly makes a distinction between his "servants" (65:13–14; cf. 65:8–10) and the "rebels" (66:24; cf. 65:2–15). See Webb, "Zion in Transformation," 72–84.

Thus they would be the servants of God (Rev 7:3; cf. Isa 65:8–10; 13–14), who constitute the nucleus of the restored Jerusalem/Zion (cf. Rev 14:1–5). We have already indicated that some early Christian traditions linked the two Isaianic 'restoration hopes' of the remnant and of the wife into one picture of the remnant, the wife's children partaking in God's eschatological wedding feast of salvation (cf. chapter 5 on Matt 22:1–4 and 25:1–13).[530] It is possible that this early Christian tradition can shed light on the interpretation of Rev 7. Accordingly, the bride mentioned later in Revelation could be identified at this early stage with the faithful remnant of ethnic Israel.

However, John's picture of the Messiah's wife seems more developed. The following vision in Rev 7:9 suggests that she is also constituted of a countless multitude of people gathered from different ethnic groups.[531] They wear white robes, a symbol of admittance to the messianic wedding, i.e., into salvation itself (cf. 3:5; 19:8). This can echo the Isaianic prophecy of the remnant/new Zion being joined by the Gentile nations (66:18–21; cf. 60:1–22).[532] They together with the remnant of Israel constitute the bride of Christ, the true Israel of God.[533] However, this multitude seems to be located in heaven before the Lamb's throne (Rev 7:9, 15). They come out of the great tribulation (7:14; cf. 2:9–10; 22; 3:10; Dan 12:1).[534] However, it is not necessary to view them as murdered martyrs of various congregations across the Roman Empire.[535] They may

---

530. It is also noteworthy that this remnant community is collectively the Immanuel of Isa 7:14 (cf. 8:16–18). In Matthew's Gospel, they are the followers of the Messiah/Immanuel. See Rice, "Immanuel Prophecy," 222–26. Cf. Webb, "Zion in Transformation," 82.

531. Ford, *Revelation*, 126, has suggested that this may refer to the diaspora Jews (cf. Isa 49). But the multitude may rather be a fulfillment of the Abrahamic promise. See Beale, *Revelation*, 426–30.

532. See Webb, "Zion in Transformation," 71.

533. Although this may be in accord with the claim regarding the all-inclusiveness of the symbol 144,000, it still cannot answer the problem of why the sealed are dying as martyrs. Perhaps, the sealing only protects from judgment coming directly from heaven, and thus saves from the second death.

534. It has been argued that they are still coming out of the tribulation (ἐρχόμενοι). Cf. Charles, *Revelation*, I: 213. But Aune, *Revelation 6–16*, 473, has explained that it is proper to translate οἱ ἐρχόμενοι by the past tense because the phrase represents the action parallel to the main verbs ἔπλυναν and ἐλεύκαναν. It points to the reality of those who overcome the tribulation.

535. Beale, *Revelation*, 433. Beale favors a continuous-historical view of the multitude (435). His major objection to the contemporary tribulation view is its inability to

The Metaphor of Divine Marriage in the Book of Revelation 339

rather represent the faithful of the new covenant who have access before God's throne to serve him in the heavenly temple (cf. 1:6; 5:10).⁵³⁶ The overcomers have washed their garments white in the Lamb's blood.⁵³⁷ So, it seems that their works qualify them to be the bride of Christ (cf. Exod 19:10, 14 and Ezek 16:8–14). Their faithfulness guarantees them access to the new Jerusalem (7:17; cf. 21:4; Isa 25:8).

Verse 15 confirms the priestly character of the faithful (1:6; 5:10; cf. Exod 19:6). Their service in the temple can be symbolic of a special close relationship with their God and the Lamb (cf. 21:3, 22; 3:12).⁵³⁸ Thus, it appears that the overcomers have somehow been translated into the reality of the eschatological priesthood and to a new earth and heaven. They have been incorporated into the eschatological bride of Christ who is also God's temple (cf. on Rev 21 above).

Revelation 8

Chapter 8 continues the seal visions from chapter 6. Yet, instead of introducing more calamities, the seventh seal initiates the vision of seven trumpets (8:2).⁵³⁹ The prelude to this series of judgments is another manifestation of God's holiness (8:5; cf. 4:5).⁵⁴⁰

---

explain how the churches in Asia Minor would be affected by the tribulation limited to Jerusalem and/or the land of Palestine. But we have already indicated that the churches in Asia Minor also undergo trials because of Christ's enemies, which are linked with the corrupt system of the unfaithful Jerusalem.

536. Cf. ibid., 439–41. Beale argues that 7:15 is a clear echo of the prophecy of Israel's restoration in Ezek 37:26–28LXX: the tabernacling of God with his people. The temple, thus, is his presence among his people (cf. Rev 21:22).

537. We have acknowledged that in the parable of the wedding feast in Matt 22:1–14, the clean garments were a token of admittance to the eschatological salvation feast of God. Throughout Revelation, the white garments belonging to humans seem to serve a similar purpose (see on 3:5). Here, the cleansing of the garments is possible through Christ's blood (Isa 1:18?; cf. Rev 1:5). However, the emphasis seems to be on Christian responsibility for being faithful to their Lord: only he who overcomes will have his garments clean (cf. 3:5). Cf. Caird, *Revelation*, 102, concerning the human responsibility point. See Aune, *Revelation 6–16*, 475, regarding the atonement of Christ's blood.

538. See Beale, *Revelation*, 441, who claims that the temple 'consists' in the presence of the Lamb. The verb σκηνόω occurs here and in 21:3 denoting God's dwelling with his faithful people. See also Ezek 37:26–28 and Lev 26:11.

539. See Bauckham's structure concerning this intercalation in our Introduction. It is possible that the trumpets announce the Day of the Lord (cf. Zeph 1:14–18). Cf. Schüssler-Fiorenza, *Vision of a Just World*, 70.

540. Bauckham, *Theology of Revelation*, 40. Also *Climax of Prophecy*, 199, 202.

Some scholars have argued that the trumpet disasters resemble the Egyptian plague narratives.[541] But even in the best case, they are able to show only some resemblance between four trumpets and plagues of Egypt.[542] It may be proposed that some trumpet plagues have their origin in particular prophetic oracles against the corruption of Israel, an example of which can be the third-trumpet judgment.

Sounding the third trumpet introduces the plague of wormwood.[543] It is noteworthy that in the OT wormwood was given to the promiscuous Israel and the false prophets in Jer 9:15 and 23:15 (cf. Lam 3:15, 19). Such bitter herbs were believed to be poisonous (Deut 29:18; Amos 5:7; 6:12). Hence, wormwood became a symbol of God's punishment for apostasy. In our passage, it made a third of the waters bitter. It is possible that the test for adultery is implied in the symbol of bitter water (cf. Num 5:11–31).[544] In this case, however, the guilt is immediately proven:

---

541. The advocates of this view are Casey, "Exodus Theme in Revelation," 36, and Jenkins, *Old Testament in Revelation*, 68. See also Metzger, *Breaking the Code*, 64, who believes that God's judgment on Rome is comparable to the plagues of Egypt.

542. Casey, "Exodus Theme in Revelation," 36, claims that the first trumpet resembles Exod 9:23–26; the second Exod 7:20–21; the third reverses the pattern of Exod 15:23 and the bitter water of Marah; and the fourth is reminiscent of the limited darkness over Egypt in Exod 10:21–23. Jenkins, *Old Testament in Revelation*, 68 has made similar suggestions concerning the first, second and fourth trumpets. But he drops any comparison with the third trumpet and proposes instead that the fifth trumpet causing the plague of locusts echoes Exod 10:1–20. Thus, these two scholars can suggest a background for only four disasters. However, they are hardly close parallels. Hence it may be helpful to look also for other backgrounds to the trumpet visions.

543. Scholars are unanimous that the star in this context symbolizes an evil angelic being (cf. Isa 14:12–15). Cf. Beale, *Revelation*, 497. Cf. Stefanovic, *Revelation of Jesus Christ*, 292. He explains that 'wormwood' (Gr. *apsinthos*) is the name for the group of bitter herbs in the Near East known as *artemesia absinthium*.

544. Although there is no clear linguistic correspondence between Rev 8:11 and Num 5, the concepts mentioned in these texts are similar. Douglas, *Defilement in Numbers*, 160–69, suggests that the "laws-for-women" sections in Num 5 and 30 may well be regarded as instances of constitutional law referring to the woman Israel (Isa 54:5). She also indicates that Ezek 23:32–34 is a good example of the application of the "rite of wayward wife" of Num 5 to Jerusalem: she will drink the same cup as Samaria. It is noteworthy that the bitter water in this rite washed the ink of the scroll containing curses on the unfaithful wife (Num 5:23). The woman had to drink it for a curse (v. 24). Douglas has observed that a similar curse on Israel occurs in Jer 24:9, which, we could add, is in fairly close proximity to Jer 23:15, where wormwood and bitter water are applied to the false prophets and the promiscuous people of Judah. The only element missing in the immediate context is writing down the curse on a scroll, so that the ink may be mixed with the bitter water. However, Jeremiah is later told to write all

"many men died." The overall picture may suggest that God's apostate people are in view. They are adulterous like Judah in Jeremiah's times (cf. Rev 17–18). Therefore we suggest that the third trumpet may contain an echo of the punishment for breaking God's marriage.

Revelation 11

Chapters 10 and 11 break the sequence of the trumpet judgments. Rev 10 presents a picture of a mighty angel, who gives John a small scroll.[545] It has been argued that the small scroll is the same as the seven-sealed scroll in chapter 5.[546] However, the two seem to be somewhat different.[547] The majority of exegetes have concluded that eating the scroll resembles Ezek 2:8—3:3, where the prophet was commissioned to preach God's message of doom to the unfaithful Israel.[548] Therefore the scene in Rev 10 may be viewed as the commissioning of the prophet to announce God's message concerning many "peoples, nations, tongues, and kings" (v 11), which can refer particularly to the post-trumpet events in chap-

---

words against Israel on a scroll (36:2). Despite this, the conceptual correspondences are striking.

545. Wallis, "Coming of the Kingdom," 25, believes that the angel is the same as Christ (cf. 1:15–16), but it is more likely that an angelic being having Christ's authority is in view here. Cf. Stefanovic, *Revelation of Jesus Christ*, 318. Yet, Caird, *Revelation*, 125–26, sees a close resemblance to the angel leading God's people in Exodus (pillars of fire evoke the *Shekinah* presence during the Exodus from Egypt).

546. So Bauckham, *Climax of Prophecy*, 242, 250. He suggests that the last seal is broken in 8:2 and the scroll is presented open in 10:2. Also Ford, "Divorce Bill," 139. Beagley, *Church's Enemies*, 58, seems to be right in rejecting Ford's view because the adulterous woman was never commanded to eat a scroll, but only to drink bitter water. Also, it is the prophet who eats scroll, not the woman.

547. The use of the diminutive has not been explained in a comprehensive manner. Some have suggested that it connotes part of a larger scroll (Stefanovic, *Revelation of Jesus Christ*, 319). It certainly points to a distinction between the two scrolls. Schüssler-Fiorenza, *Vision of a Just World*, 73–74, suggests that the difference between the scrolls is that the first introduced the visions of eschatological cataclysms from a heavenly perspective, whereas the second directs one's attention to the earthly reality behind them. The bitterness of the scroll may imply its deadly contents (cf. 8:11; p. 76).

548. See Beale, *Revelation*, 547; Beagley, *Church's Enemies*, 57–59. Vogelgesang, "Ezekiel in Revelation," 357–58, explains that the small scroll signifies the commission of the prophet based on the revelation of the now-opened scroll of Rev 5.

ters 13 and 17.[549] The same commission extends to 11:1-2, where the prophet is asked to perform a sign-action.[550]

The symbols of Rev 11 have been problematic for NT exegetes. The meaning of the sanctuary measured by John has been explained in terms of either the literal temple in Jerusalem[551] or as a metaphorical use, speaking of the people of God.[552] One of the strongest reasons for preferring the latter view seems to be John's use of the construction ἐκβάλλω ἔξωθεν in v 2. Applied to the literal temple, this phrase would create the difficulty of "throwing out outside" the outer court, which is already outside the inner sanctuary.[553] Moreover, similar constructions appear elsewhere in the NT to express the idea of excommunication or exclusion.[554] Consequently, some scholars have argued that Rev 11:2 describes the separation of the faithful from the apostate among God's people.[555] The unfaithful will be delivered into the hands of the nations to be destroyed (cf. Luke 21:24; Isa 63:18-19). Hence, the 'holy city' could refer to Jerusalem, not the new city of God.[556] Thus the dichotomy in-

549. Yarbro Collins, *Combat Myth*, 27. Also Beagley, *Church's Enemies*, 58-59. Stefanovic, *Revelation of Jesus Christ*, 319, assumes that the prophecy given to John refers to Rev 12—22:5. Rev 10:7 (cf. Dan 12:7) may imply that the prophecy of Dan 11:29—12:13 will be fulfilled after the sounding of the seventh trumpet. So Beale, *Revelation*, 540. Cf. Schüssler-Fiorenza, *Vision of a Just World*, 75.

550. Schüssler-Fiorenza, *Vision of a Just World*, 76. Bauckham, *Climax of Prophecy*, 266, believes that 11:1-3 gives the essential message of the scroll.

551. E.g., Beagley, *Church's Enemies*, 62; Gentry, *Before Jerusalem Fell*, 165.

552. E.g., Beale, *Revelation*, 21; Kik, *Eschatology of Victory*, 243.

553. Cf. Ford, *Revelation*, 176. Also, one could add the observation that Jerusalem's temple was entirely destroyed together with its inner part in 70 CE.

554. Ibid. See Luke 4:29; 20:15; Acts 7:58; esp. John 9:34-35; 12:31; 15:6; Rev 22:14-15.

555. Ibid., 177. Ford suggests that this separation is similar to that in Rev 7, where the remnant received God's seal of protection against the coming judgment. Cf. Chilton, *Days of Vengeance*, 272-73. Early Christian traditions regarded the church as God's temple. See John 2:19; 1 Cor 3:16; Eph 2:19-22; 1 Tim 3:15; Heb 3:6; 1 Pet 2:5; Rev 3:12.

556. Beagley, *Church's Enemies*, 62-63, explains that although the phrase would naturally signify the new Jerusalem, here it may be used to challenge Jewish thinking concerning their city. The period of trampling may resemble Dan 7:25, where the three and a half years refer to the period of the persecution of God's people. But Luke 21:24 modifies Daniel's prophecy. Interestingly, the siege of Jerusalem under Vespasian and Titus lasted three and a half years, from 67 to 70. See Chilton, *Days of Vengeance*, 275 n. 5. Pace Beale, *Revelation*, 568-70. However, he notices that the καὶ in v. 2 links the "holy city" with the "outer court."

dicated earlier by the two contrasting women is here expressed by the metaphor of the temple.

The two witnesses of Rev 11 may signify God's messengers delivering the message of doom to Jerusalem (vv 8, 13).[557] Some scholars have linked these two figures with the requirement of the Mosaic Law that, at least, two witnesses are necessary to bring a case against a guilty party (Num 35:30; Deut 17:6; 19:15).[558] Yet, it seems to be an often overlooked fact that two witnesses were especially required if an adulteress was to be put to death (Deut 22:22–27; Lev 20:10).[559] Since the two witnesses of Rev 11 appear to be bringing the message of judgment to some unfaithful Jews and their "holy city," it is possible that the charge may be spiritual adultery. They, however, die after they are attacked by the "beast from the abyss."[560] This beast may represent the enemies of the church, especially in the land of Judea. This last point is additionally supported by the fact that the death of the two witnesses causes joy among the inhabitants of the earth (v 10). It is noteworthy that the location of the witnesses' death appears to be Jerusalem, the city compared to Sodom and Egypt (v. 8). The corrupted system of Jerusalem has previously been compared to Sodom in Isa 1:10 (cf. Jer 23:14). However, the suggestion that Jerusalem is called Egypt finds its closest possible parallel within

---

557. The exact historical counterpart of the two figures is difficult to determine. Their identification as the two "olive trees" and "lampstands" suggests churches. See an extended discussion in Beale, *Revelation*, 572–75. Beasley-Murray, *Revelation*, 177, has argued that verses 8 and 13 point to Jerusalem. However, because he took v 2 to refer to the church (p. 182) he was unable to demonstrate the connection between Rev 11:1–2 and vv. 3–13 (p. 177). Pace Bauckham, *Climax of Prophecy*, 172. Even with the best intentions, one would find it difficult to argue that the city of Jesus' crucifixion was Rome. The leaders of Jerusalem were compared to Sodom in Isa 1:10 and the city was accused of bringing her harlotry from Egypt (cf. Ezek 23:27). Cf. Beagley, *Church's Enemies*, 67. "Sackcloth" can point to the attire of the prophets mourning over national apostasy (2 Kgs 1:8; Isa 20:2; Jonah 3:6; Zech 13:4; Matt 3:4; Mark 1:6). So Chilton, *Days of Vengeance*, 276.

558. So Chilton, *Days of Vengeance*, 276; Stefanovic, *Revelation of Jesus Christ*, 344.

559. But see Budd, *Numbers*, 64.

560. The definite article in front of θηρίον may suggest that the figure was well-known to the addressees of Revelation, although not previously mentioned in the book. Cf. Beagley, *Church's Enemies*, 69. Stefanovic, *Revelation of Jesus Christ*, 345, has argued that since Satan is represented in Revelation as the dragon, the beast should be regarded as a political power, similar to those within the prophecy of Daniel. Minear, "Ontology and Ecclesiology," 97, has acknowledged that the context here suggests the necessity of a prophet's (witness's?) death in Jerusalem.

the framework of the OT divine marriage motif, as developed in Ezek 23:3, 8.[561] There, Israel is regarded as a promiscuous wife who had learnt her harlotries in Egypt. Thus, it may well be that the conflict between the church and the harlot underlies the theme of the passage.

Despite their death, God resurrects the witnesses (v. 11) before the eyes of their enemies, thus causing fear.[562] Scholars have argued that this picture is heavily influenced by Ezek 37:5, 10, which refer to the national restoration of Israel.[563] Hence, resurrection does not need to refer to the literal rising from the dead, but may describe the vindication of the church and judgment on her oppressors (cf. Rev 20:7–10; Ezek 38).[564] The ascension in a cloud to heaven may then symbolize the vindication (Rev 11:12).[565] It is very likely that Ezek 37:1–14 was regarded as signifying the restoration after exile, which was like death.[566] In the context of the prophecy, it also referred to God renewing the royal status of and the marriage to his people, a new exodus that was their salvation. Consequently, it is possible to view the previous killing by the beast as the oppression and bondage of God's people.

The third woe brings about the vision of the seventh trumpet sounding the arrival of the Messiah's kingdom (Rev 11:14–15). This completes the revelation of God's mystery (10:7). The kingdom of God is established amidst the judgment on the unfaithful city (11:13).[567] It is

---

561. Beagley, *Church's Enemies*, 67; Terry, *Biblical Apocalyptics*, 371. Cf. Amos 4:10–11, which links both Sodom and Egypt with Israel. Ezek 16:45–56 also links Jerusalem's harlotry with that of Sodom. Otherwise, scholars try to universalize the reference. See Beale, *Revelation*, 591–92.

562. Cf. Beale, *Revelation*, 596. But we do not agree with his time references.

563. Ibid., 597; Ford, *Revelation*, 180–81; Aune, *Revelation 6–16*, 623.

564. Beale, *Revelation*, 597.

565. Perhaps a Jesus-like vindication (Mark 13:26). Cf. Wright, *Millennium Myth*, 42; also *JVG*, 361.

566. Caird, *Language and Imagery*, 246, has acknowledged the link between resurrection and the return from exile (Ezek 37:1–14; cf. Hos 6:1–2). Cf. Wright, *NTPG*, 200, cf. 322. Wright has argued that exile was seen as a "death" (e.g., 276).

567. Terry, *Biblical Apocalyptics*, 379, has observed that "the time of the dead to be judged" in v. 18 refers to God's vengeance for the blood of his servants. Chilton, *Days of Vengeance*, 287, believes that the arrival of the messianic kingdom, which spreads across the world, is parallel to the arrival of the fifth kingdom in Dan 2. There is no need to make it future (as Beale, *Revelation*, 609), because it may be associated with the judgment coming upon Jerusalem. The reference to Ps 2 in the verse seems to support the temporal introduction of the kingdom. The "destroyers of the land" may refer to those who act against the land given by God to his people (cf. Lev 18:24–30). So Chilton, *Days of Vengeance*, 291.

possible that this trumpet still sounds through the following visions of the book until the "great harlot" is finally destroyed in 17:1—19:8.[568] This would further link Rev 11 with the metaphor of divine marriage found in these later chapters.

Revelation 13

It has widely been recognized that the sea monster in Rev 13 has characteristics similar to those of the dragon in chapter 12 (13:1; cf. 12:3). It is his servant. However, this time the monster clearly stands for the political power of imperial Rome.[569] The fact that it arises from the sea supports the interpretation that the monster refers to a pagan nation invading God's people (cf. 12:12).[570] The ten horns may symbolize the mighty power derived from Satan, the ten-horned dragon.[571] Yet, less certainty exists concerning the mortal wound to one of the heads in 13:3, 14. A considerable number of exegetes have favored the reading that claims that these texts have the suicide of Nero Caesar in view.[572]

---

568. Cf. Aune, *Revelation 6–16*, 524.

569. Bauckham, *Theology of Revelation*, 34–35; *Climax of Prophecy*, 343; Moyise, *Old Testament in Revelation*, 52. Scholars have usually argued that the sea-beast is composed of the four beasts of Dan 7:2–7 (Rev 13:2), although it particularly resembles the fourth beast of Dan 7:7. E.g., Beagley, *Church's Enemies*, 73; esp. Gentry, *Beast of Revelation*, 41.

570. Stefanovic, *Revelation of Jesus Christ*, 402, explains that, "In the Old Testament, the sea often symbolizes the abode of the sea monsters (Job 26:12–13; Ps. 74:12–14; Isa. 27:1; 51:9–10; Ezek. 32:2), from which the evil enemy powers come that oppressed Israel . . ." The sea corresponds to the abyss: it can be a symbol of unregenerate humanity. Cf. Ford, *Revelation*, 219. Beale, *Revelation*, 682, explains that people in Asia Minor might have thought of that which came from the sea as foreign and that from the land as native. However, we would suggest that the land of Palestine is in view here, rather than Asia Minor.

571. However, Ford, *Revelation*, 210, observes that the meaning of the horns is explained in 17:12. They stand for ten rulers supporting Roman power (cf. Dan 7:24). The note that the horns, not heads, wear diadems/crowns also supports this.

572. Bauckham, *Climax of Prophecy*, 433; Beagley, *Church's Enemies*, 75; Beasley-Murray, *Revelation*, 210, all view the wounded head as the emperor. Gentry, *Beast of Revelation*, 14, argues that the beast specifically refers to Nero, although its generic identity is Roman power. Similarly, Schüssler-Fiorenza, "Reading Theologically," 10. The main support of this view comes from Hebrew gematria: the number 666 in Rev 13:18 is the sum of numeric equivalents of נרון קסר. This view gains attraction as some early manuscripts read 616 in this verse by spelling Nero's name differently (נרו קסר). Cf. Wilson, "Problem of the Domitianic Date," 598; Gentry, *Beast of Revelation*, 35. Beale, *Revelation*, 24, doubts whether the Hebrew gematria should be used to interpret the

But this view seems to ignore the fact that 'head', when read against the background of Daniel's vision, stands for a kingdom or the extent of an empire's power, rather than for an individual ruler (cf. 17:9).[573] In this sense, the seven heads could represent the complete scope of the Roman Empire: the centers of the imperial power.[574] Consequently, the deadly and yet healing wound may refer to a temporary weakening of part of the Empire, but also its quick recovery.[575]

The beast gains many followers in all the earth[576] because of its power (13:3b). By supporting the Roman order, they worship Satan and the beast itself.[577] Some scholars have seen a reference to the alleged emperor worship in the Roman provinces at this point (13:4, 13–15).[578] However, it is worth noting that the word for worship could simply refer to admiration and parallel the marvel in v. 3b.[579] Thus, the point of

---

number. Yet, scholars still conclude that the healing of the head refers to the myth of Nero's return, made popular in Rome after his death. E.g., Friesen, *Imperial Cultus and the Apocalypse*, 137. See Gentry, *Before Jerusalem Fell*, 300–317, for a full-length discussion of this. Wilson, "Problem of the Domitianic Date," 600, thinks that the assassination of Julius Caesar is in view, after which the Empire recovered quickly. This, however, fails to explain why Revelation would be interested in looking back several decades at Rome's history.

573. Cf. Wallis, "Coming of the Kingdom," 39. Mountains (17:9) usually signify kingdoms in the Bible. Kings can also stand for kingdoms (cf. Dan 7:17, 23 with Rev 17:10). On the meaning of the heads in Dan 7 see, e.g., Lucas, *Daniel*, 180.

574. Cf. Terry, *Biblical Apocalyptics*, 393.

575. Beale, *Revelation*, 687–88, suggests that the unnamed cause of the wound was God, since πληγή usually refers in Revelation to a punishment inflicted by God. The wound on the head seems to echo Gen 3:15. Gentry, *Beast of Revelation*, 75, remarks that the mortal wound may refer to the chaotic late 60s CE.

576. The majority opinion is that an all-encompassing universal reference is in view here. But Charles, *Revelation*, I: 334, notes that elsewhere in Revelation the idea of the whole world is expressed by the phrase ἡ οἰκουμένη ὅλη (3:10; 12:9; 16:14), yet without explaining the change of reference in this case. However, we have indicated that ἡ γῆ may refer to the land of Palestine. Jerusalem had a good record of making friends with Rome. King Agrippa II, Herod, and Antipas all supported Roman policy and were therefore given a share in Roman rule. See Wengst, *Pax Romana*, 25. Cf. Joseph *War* i:14:2; i:20:1, 3; iii:9:7.

577. Yarbro Collins, *Crisis and Catharsis*, 114, explains that the followers of the beast are supporters of the Roman order.

578. Gentry, *Beast of Revelation*, 57; Metzger, *Breaking the Code*, 75.

579. Beale, *Revelation*, 693. θαυμάζω can be synonymous with προσκυνέω and in the context of vv 7–17 can have the nuance of "rendering admiration for one's own advantage" since those who do not do that suffer economically and politically.

13:4 may be the idea of making oneself deferential in the face of Roman military power.

The blasphemies[580] of the beast are directed against God, his name, his dwelling place and the dwellers in heaven. It is likely that God's dwelling place (σκηνή) implies a community of the faithful who live in particular intimacy with God rather than signifying a building.[581] It appears that this intimacy is explained later in terms of God having a special union with those who constitute the new Jerusalem, 'prepared as a bride' (21:3, 2).[582] We have indicated above that Rev 7:15 combines the two motifs of eschatological temple/tabernacle and eschatological bride into one picture of eschatological existence before God. Thus it is possible that the picture reappears here.

The beast is given authority to fight against and overcome the saints (13:7; cf. Dan 7:8LXX). He also receives authority over all the ethnic groups. The inhabitants of the land, whose names are not written in the book of life, become supportive of Roman power.[583] The exhortation will be of no use to them (Rev 13:9).[584] They will be repaid according to

---

580. The beast's speaking of great things probably echoes Dan 7:6, 8LXX. In this context, a boastful speech as well as deception of God's people may be in view (cf. Dan 7:25; 11:32, 36). Cf. Beale, *Revelation*, 695–96. 42 months may signify a time of trouble (a broken seven). See Chilton, *Days of Vengeance*, 333.

581. Briggs, *Temple Imagery*, 99. It seems that the phrase 'those dwelling in heaven' immediately qualifies the previous one. Cf. Beale, *Revelation*, 697. It is possible that John had in mind the faithful on the earth in referring to those in heaven (cf. Dan 8:10–11). Similarly, Pauline traditions view the church as seated in heaven (cf. Eph 2:6; Col 3:1).

582. Beale, *Revelation*, 697, pays attention to the fact that the noun σκηνή and the verb σκηνόω occur together only at 13:6 and 21:3.

583. The book of life probably resembles Ps 69:28 and possibly echoes Dan 7:10. Rev 21:27 indicates that only those written in the book have access to the heavenly city. Cf. Beale, *Revelation*, 701–2. It appears that the book determines one's destiny. The syntax of the verse is somewhat vague and it cannot be established with total certainty whether ἀπὸ καταβολῆς κόσμου should be connected with ἐσφαγμένου or γέγραπται. The latter is supported by the parallel in 17:8. See Aune, *Revelation 6–16*, 746–47.

584. The exhortation "if anyone has an ear, let him hear" resembles Mark 4:23. Vos, *Synoptic Traditions in the Apocalypse*, 73. We have suggested in chapter 5 that, in that context, only disciples of Jesus could understand his parables. Those who do not understand the words of prophecy have their hearts hardened.

their deeds (v. 10).[585] Yet the faithful will also be tested in this context (v. 10b).[586]

The other beast of Rev 13 has been a matter of controversy among NT exegetes. Some do not distinguish between the two at all, seeing them as different aspects of the same Roman power.[587] Others make a slight distinction usually by universalizing the second beast.[588] However, such an approach fails to assess critically the fact that the beast comes from the land, as opposed to the sea, and also fails to place it in Revelation's *Sitz im Leben*. A group of interpreters, however, have noticed the distinction between the origin of the first and second beasts: the sea and the earth. They have consequently tried to find a satisfactory explanation for the association of the second beast with the land of Israel.[589] A helpful hint has been provided by the text itself, suggesting that the beast stands for false prophets (13:11; cf. 16:13).[590] Consequently, it would appear that the beast stands for those among God's covenant people who started leading the people astray, i.e., the leaders opposed to Christ. We have noted above that some non-messianic Jews were eager to collaborate with the Roman authorities to their own advantage. They could exercise

---

585. It seems that the passage combines the words of Jer 15:2 and Matt 26:52. Vos, *Synoptic Traditions in the Apocalypse*, 104–5. Both passages announce judgment upon Israel. However, the link with Matt 26:52 may suggest that the judgment is on that part of Israel (esp. its guardians) who did not accept God's way and his kingdom as revealed in Jesus. Cf. Wright, *JVG*, 327. Now, they will receive their deserts.

586. Beale, *Revelation*, 705. However, we think that both the punishment of the unfaithful and the suffering of the faithful are implied in v. 10.

587. Chavasse, *Bride of Christ*, 92.

588. Kik, *Eschatology of Victory*, 224–25, has offered a peculiar view that while the first beast is the ancient Roman Empire, the second beast is papal Rome. Metzger, *Breaking the Code*, 75, takes the second beast to be paganism. Vos, *Synoptic Traditions in the Apocalypse*, 133, thinks it represents all "pseudo-religions and philosophies of the world."

589. Beagley, *Church's Enemies*, 78–79, has acknowledged the possibility of referring the beast to a Jewish figure or institution. Yet, he preferred to refer it to Roman officials in Asia Minor. Russell, *Parousia*, 467, has proposed that the beast could refer to Gessius Florus, a Roman procurator in Judea during Nero's reign.

590. Vos, *Synoptic Traditions in the Apocalypse*, 131, has indicated that Rev 13:11, 13 echoes Matt 7:15, although he fails to recognize any specific reference of the beast. The figure of the beast resembling the Lamb reminds us of the false prophets disguising themselves and acting as sheep. Chilton, *Days of Vengeance*, 336, has pointed to Deut 13:1–5 as a possible background for the false prophet figures. In that context, the false prophets were a test to God's people. Deut 13 also suggests that they arose from among the covenant people (see also Matt 24:5, 11).

the first beast's authority in its presence so that all following their teaching may become devotees of the Roman system (v. 12). The "great signs" performed by the false prophet may simply refer to his exercising of his authority in order to deceive people (v. 13).[591] This leads the inhabitants of the earth into idolatry: "worship" of the political power (vv. 14–15).[592] We have observed in chapter 3 that political alliances with the foreign powers were regarded as religious apostasy and, metaphorically, as marital promiscuity. It is, therefore, possible that the vision in Rev 13 is an early criticism of the harlotry described later in Rev 17. The vision may be regarded as a criticism of the Jewish alliance with the Roman Empire (cf. John 19:12, 15; Luke 23:2; 20:25).[593] The Israelites who rejected Jesus as the Christ have become bearers of the mark of apostasy: 666 (Rev 13:18).[594] But those who accepted him could not have normal access to basic and essential economic activity.[595]

---

591. Wall, *Revelation*, 173. The picture is similar to that of the false prophet in Deut 13:2–3. It is possible that "making fire come down" refers to the beast exercising its judgmental role, maybe even in persecuting the church. See Chilton, *Days of Vengeance*, 339.

592. The worship of the beast's image can be understood in this way. So Chilton, *Days of Vengeance*, 339.

593. For a similar problem described in the gospels cf. Wright, *JVG*, 502–7. Jesus' saying about paying to Caesar and to God that which belongs to them (Luke 20:25) is probably a protest against "Jewish compromise with paganism" (506). It is also a call to true devotion and total obedience to God (507).

594. 666 does not have to be a reference to Nero Caesar. In a Jewish context, it could rather refer to the remarkable instance of Israel's apostasy during her Golden Age. King Solomon has broken God's threefold command (Deut 17:16–17) starting to multiply gold: he received 666 talents of gold annually (1 Kgs 10:14; 2 Chr 9:13). The multiplying of horses followed (1 Kgs 10:26–29). After that, the multiplying of wives (11:1–6). See Chilton, *Days of Vengeance*, 350. Soon after that, the country fell into religious promiscuity (11:7–8), which resulted in God's wrath and tearing away the whole kingdom, except for the tribe of Judah (vv. 11–13; 12:20). The Davidic promise was thus jeopardized (2 Sam 7:8–16). DeVries, *1 Kings*, 144, explains that Solomon's acts "at the very best, . . . expressed a faulty religious imperialism aiming at the advance of Yahwism through power and wealth." Yet, the reality behind Solomon's act was complete disobedience to the kingly command of the Deuteronomist. The result was to change totally the future of God's people and deprive most of them of the privileges of the Davidic line (but see Isa 55:3). Thus 666 may symbolize the apostasy of Israel.

595. Cf. Aune, *Revelation 6–16*, 768, although not necessarily agreeing with his notion of the Christian exclusion from trade guilds. The restriction in buying and selling could possibly refer to the context of famine in 6:5–6. Cf. also Beale, *Revelation*, 715.

It seems that the conflict between two women—the faithful and the apostate—undergirds the thrust of Rev 13. Both ideas are implied under the concepts of God's tabernacle and the beast worship. Nevertheless, the wider context of the chapter seems to support our interpretation.

Revelation 15–16

Rev 15 begins with the announcement of the seven last plagues, which bring God's wrath to an end (v. 1).[596] The plagues may be based on the sevenfold punishment announced in Lev 26 (vv. 18, 21, 23–24, 28) for idolatry (vv. 1–2; cf. Rev 13–14).[597] Thus from the outset, it becomes apparent that the plagues are for spiritual adultery. However, before the plagues are poured down on the earth, John describes a vision of the overcomers of the beast standing firmly on/by the sea of glass mingled with fire (cf. 4:6).[598] They worship God, not the beast (15:3–4; cf. 13:3–15). The majority of scholars have claimed that their singing of the song of Moses and of the Lamb echoes the triumph of God's faithful in the Exodus from Egypt (cf. Exod 15:1–18).[599] This common view, however, has been modified by Chilton, who has demonstrated that the song of Moses and of the Lamb corresponds to the Song of Witness in Deut 32, which was also probably called the Song of Moses and of Joshua

---

596. Beale, *Revelation*, 786–88, explains that the 'last' does not need to have a futurist application. It can point to the order in which John saw the vision. The bowls complement the seal and trumpet visions.

597. Beagley, *Church's Enemies*, 84 and Ford, *Revelation*, 255.

598. Ford, *Revelation*, 257, believes that they may be the same as the remnant portrayed in 14:1–5. Perhaps their possession of harps on both occasions may support such a position. Cf. Beale, *Revelation*, 791.

Ulfgard, *Feast and Future*, 35 n. 150, explains that, although it is tempting to view the sea of glass as an antitype of the Red Sea (cf. Exod 15), the image can be an echo of the floor in heaven in Ezekiel's throne vision (Ezek 1:22; cf. Exod 24:9–10). This last proposal is particularly telling because the vision was associated with God's fire (cf. Ezek 1:4; 27). Charles, *Revelation*, II: 33, thinks that the fire symbolizes God's wrath and, therefore, that the vision is different from that in 4:6, where the sea is peaceful. Others have tried to combine various traditions and concluded that the sea could resemble the Red Sea full of blood, which covered the whole land of Palestine (Rev 14). Fire, then, refers to the great tribulation. Cf. Chilton, *Days of Vengeance*, 384. But Caird, *Revelation*, 197, prefers to view the sea as representing the mythical chaos (the abode of the dragon) over which God has established his authority at creation.

599. Cf. Caird, *Revelation*, 198; Bauckham, *Climax of Prophecy*, 306, 309, who claims that the song has in view the conversion of the nations. See also Casey, "Exodus Theme in Revelation," 39.

(cf. v. 44).⁶⁰⁰ Chilton's suggestion is particularly convincing because the context of the Song in Rev 15 is the punishment of Jerusalem's harlotry, a theme continued in chapters 17–18 (cf. Deut 31:16).⁶⁰¹ We have already indicated that Israel's unfaithfulness is also one of the major points in early chapters of Revelation. She has become the enemy of God's faithful people who follow Christ. Therefore, she will be punished as the adversary of God, just as the Song of Witness pronounced (Deut 32:43). However, the Song may correspond to Exod 15 in the way that the judgment upon the unfaithful becomes salvation to the faithful.⁶⁰² Thus the last judgments give way to the marriage of the Lamb and his bride (19:7–9) followed by the appearance of the bride and with her the new creation (21:1ff).⁶⁰³ This could perhaps recall the events following the deliverance from Egypt, leading to Yahweh's original marriage at Sinai, as reflected in some prophetic traditions (cf. chapter 3 above), as well as the ensuing occupation of the promised land by Israel as her inheritance (Exod 15:17; Deut 31:7; Josh 11:23; Jer 2:7; 3:18–19).

In general terms, the advantage of the modified view on the Song is that it does not require viewing 15:2–4 as interrupting the flow of the judgment theme in chapters 15–16.⁶⁰⁴ Thus, the worship of the faithful, in the face of judgment upon Israel's unfaithfulness, is immediately followed by the revelation of the last plagues (15:5). They are going to be delivered by seven angels with seven bowls from God's heavenly temple

---

600. *Days of Vengeance*, 380–81. It may well be that the audience knew that the Lamb was Jesus, the greater Joshua.

601. Ibid., 381. This finds further support in the fact that the seventh bowl reveals that all seven plagues culminate in judgment upon Babylon. See Schüssler-Fiorenza, *Vision of a Just World*, 95. Cf. Metzger, *Breaking the Code*, 85, and Yarbro Collins, "Feminine Symbolism," 25, who both claim that the seventh plague extends into the judgment upon Babylon.

602. Cf. Chilton, *Days of Vengeance*, 386–87. The song itself is composed of various allusions to the OT. However, its main theme is the "great and marvelous" final acts of judgment. Beale, *Revelation*, 794, has noticed that "great and marvelous works" resemble the prediction of Israel's future judgment in Deut 28:59–60. There, Israel is warned that "the Lord will magnify your plagues . . . *great and marvelous* (μεγάλας καὶ θαυμαστάς) plagues . . . And he will bring on you all the evil pains of Egypt of which you were afraid . . ." Thus the song is not only about salvation, as Bauckham, *Climax of Prophecy*, 299, implies.

603. Cf. Giblin, "Theology of Revelation 16–22," 503.

604. This is a better solution than that of Beale, *Revelation*, 784–85, who seems to emphasize the interruption.

(vv. 6–7).⁶⁰⁵ But the Temple is temporarily filled with the smoke of the glory of God, which points to another turn in the history of his people.⁶⁰⁶ It seems to anticipate the fall of the harlot city and the establishment of the new city of God's dwelling, which is also Christ's bride (cf. 21:2–3).⁶⁰⁷

Rev 16 describes the seven angels delivering the bowl judgments on the earth (v. 1). The fact that the plagues are poured out on the earth may indicate that the final judgments are on the land of Israel, although particular bowls affect various parts of creation or the beast's throne.⁶⁰⁸ Scholars have usually maintained that the plagues resemble those preceding the Exodus from Egypt.⁶⁰⁹ This is, of course, a plausible suggestion in the light of such warnings as Deut 28:60. However, the same Deuteronomic tradition announces that the plagues, which God would bring on his unfaithful people, may differ from those of Exodus (v. 61). Like the calamities of the trumpets in Rev 8–9,⁶¹⁰ the plagues of the bowls may resemble some of the Exodus plagues, but may also refer to prophetic announcements of curses upon Israel's unfaithfulness. Could the bowl plagues, then, be connected to the punishment of the harlot?

---

605. Beale, *Revelation*, 806, suggests that the bowls of judgment are linked with those filled with prayers in 5:8. Thus the prayers of the saints for retribution are now answered in plagues. He also suggests that the symbol of bowls is derived from Isa 51:17, 22, where Israel drank of the chalice of God's wrath.

606. Ford, *Revelation*, 258. She lists Exod 40:35; 1 Kgs 8:10–14; 2 Chr 7:2–3l; Isa 6:4; Ezek 10:3–4, as evidence that the filling of the temple with the smoke of/or God's glory always signified strategic points in Israel's history. Similarly, Paulien, "Plot and Structure of Revelation," 253, argues that 15:5–8 points to a cultic inauguration.

607. Ford, *Revelation*, 258.

608. The meaning of ἡ γῆ would, thus, be consistent with the previous instances. Rev 16 should be read in the context of what was said concerning the plagues in chapter 15. The plagues are coming because of Israel's unfaithfulness (cf. Lev 26:1–2, 18, 21, 23–24, 28; 51:17, 22). Cf. Beagley, *Church's Enemies*, 84. Beale, *Revelation*, 812, observes that the LXX uses "pour out God's wrath" (ἐκχέω + θυμός) as an indication of judgment upon covenant-breakers (Ezek 14:19) or oppressors of God's people (Jer 10:25). In Revelation, the unfaithful Israelites who rejected the Messiah become both.

609. So Beasley-Murray, *Revelation*, 232; Casey, "Exodus Theme in Revelation," 36; Ford, "Revelation 16," 327–31, who argues that all the disasters resemble or reverse the Exodus event. But Ulfgard, *Feast and Future*, 38, claims that the 4th and 6th plagues do not relate to the Exodus tradition.

610. For correspondences between the bowls and the trumpets see Beale, *Revelation*, 808–12.

The first three plagues clearly correspond to the Exodus calamities. The first plague of "bad and painful sores" echoes the sixth affliction of Egypt (16:2; Exod 9:10–11), but also one of the calamities for the disobedience of Israel (Deut 28:27, 35).[611]

The second plague brings death to all marine life (16:3; cf. 8:8–9), but the sea itself turns to blood as if of a dead man. Although a correspondence to the first Egyptian plague may be valid here (cf. Exod 7:17–21), it seems that the completion of judgment against Babylon's maritime commerce can be in view here (cf. Rev 18:17–19).[612]

The third bowl's judgment turns rivers and springs of water into blood (16:4). Ford has argued that this resembles the first plague of Egypt (Exod 7:17–21; cf. Wis 11:5–8; Ps 78:44).[613] However, there appears also to be some correspondence to the calamity of the third trumpet, which would suggest another judgment on the harlot Babylon (8:10–11).[614] The point of this plague is clear: those who shed the blood of the saints will be given (their own?) blood to drink (v. 6). The voice from the altar in v. 7 may suggest that the retribution for the death of the martyrs from 6:9–10 is in view.[615] Hence, the "inhabitants of the earth" finally meet God's justice.

The fourth plague of the scorching of the sun does not have a direct correspondence to the Egyptian plagues (16:8). However, some scholars have suggested that it is a reversal of God's protective cloud found in

---

611. Stefanovic, *Revelation of Jesus Christ*, 481, argues that this kind of plague was often a punishment for sin (cf. 2 Kgs 5:25–27; 2 Chr 26:16–21).

612. Beale, *Revelation*, 815. Beale indicates that the last part of Rev 16:3 may suggest the death of those whose lives were sustained from sea trading and may point to a famine.

613. Structure, 328.

614. Beale, *Revelation*, 816–17. He suggests that this plague may also be against the maritime commerce of Babylon, all resulting in famine. This can be supported by verbal parallels between 16:6 and 18:24. She is drunk with the blood of saints and martyrs (17:6; cf. Matt 23:34–37). The drinking of blood may echo Isa 49:26, although now it can be reversed against the unfaithful Israel, as indicated by Chilton, *Days of Vengeance*, 401–2. Thus the enemies of God's people will drink their own blood and perhaps eat their own flesh, a pronouncement of cannibalism fulfilled during the final siege of Jerusalem (cf. Deut 28:53–57; Josephus *War* VI:3:3–4). However, we have already indicated that the wormwood plague of the third trumpet had particular significance in the context of Israel's adultery. See above on 8:10–11.

615. Beagley, *Church's Enemies*, 85. Cf. Beale, *Revelation*, 818, 820.

Exodus (see Exod 13:21–22; cf. Ps 91:1–6).[616] But the plague may also be a reversal of various Jewish traditions concerning God's protection of his people (cf. Ps 121:5–7; Isa 49:10; Jer 17:7–8) as well as of John's prophecy concerning the future of the redeemed bride (Rev 7:16).[617] However, Beale has proposed that this plague also echoes the curse in Deut 32:24MT, which is closely linked with famine (cf. Rev 18:8).[618] This may suggest that the plague could be another curse upon impenitent Israel, as she still does not repent (16:9).

The fifth plague is poured out over the beast's throne so that his kingdom becomes "full of darkness" (v. 10; cf. 13:2). This may recall the ninth Egyptian plague (Exod 10:21–23), but it may also echo the darkness associated with the day of the Lord (Amos 5:20).[619] It may point to political turmoil in the beast's kingdom (cf. Isa 13:9–10; Amos 8:9; Ezek 32:7–8).[620] However, it should be acknowledged that the land of Palestine was part of the beast's kingdom in the first century CE.[621] It is probably this land that experiences to some degree all the plagues (Rev 16:1). Moreover, because it is difficult to establish why darkness should cause pain to people within the beast's kingdom (v. 10b), scholars have suggested that their pain is the outcome of previous plagues, especially that of sores (v. 11; cf. v. 2).[622] It would, therefore, seem that the fifth plague

---

616. Ford, "Revelation 16," 328; Chilton, *Days of Vengeance*, 402.

617. Cf. Chilton, *Days of Vengeance*, 402–3.

618. *Revelation*, 822. Beale has also suggested that the fourth bowl plague is similar to the sixth trumpet (9:20–21) because both are followed by a refusal to repent. Hence, he proposes that the scorching of the sun with fire is similar to the suffering of the "three plagues of fire and smoke and brimstone" in 9:18. Thus, he takes the scorching to be synonymous with "fire" and suggests that the fourth bowl anticipates the burning with fire of the harlot Babylon (cf. 17:16; 18:8). This may give a possible solution to the apparent contradiction that the angels were to pour bowls on the earth (v. 10), whereas the fourth angel pours his on the sun. See also Ford, *Revelation*, 272.

619. Cf. Ford, *Revelation*, 272, 262. She also thinks that this plague is a reversal of the pillar of fire in the night. See also Ford, "Revelation 16," 328.

620. Cf. Chilton, *Days of Vengeance*, 405; Beale, *Revelation*, 823. Also Aune, *Revelation 6–16*, 890. We have already noted that the Empire experienced particular turmoil in the year 69 CE, the so-called "year of the four emperors."

621. So Chilton, *Days of Vengeance*, 405. One needs to recognize that during the time that the Empire was politically unstable, it was still pursuing the military campaign against Jewish rebels.

622. Aune, *Revelation 6–16*, 890, posing the problem, and Chilton, *Days of Vengeance*, 407, and Beale, *Revelation*, 826, giving this possible solution to it.

also has the unfaithful part of God's people in view. They turn against God (cf. v. 9), while not recognizing his hand behind the plagues.[623]

The sixth bowl's judgment causes the Euphrates to dry up in order to prepare the way for the kings from the east (v. 12; cf. above on 9:14).[624] The OT context of the drying up of the river suggests that the destruction of the oppressive power of Babylon, followed by the exodus of God's people, is in view.[625] Meanwhile, the unclean spirits of Satan and the two beasts gather the rulers of the empire to the battle of Armageddon on the day of the Lord (16:13–14, 16).[626] Geographical identification of the place has been one of the most difficult interpretive tasks for students of Revelation.[627] However, if a figurative approach is allowed here, the etymology of the name may suggest Jerusalem.[628] Even if the city Megiddo is the preferred reading, the place has a clear eschatological link with Jerusalem (cf. Zech 12:10–11).[629] The inhabitants of Jerusalem were to

---

623. Beale, *Revelation*, 825, remarks that this hardness resembles that of Pharaoh during the original Exodus.

624. Ibid., 827. Beale explains that from "Israel's vantage point the Euphrates was to the north as well as the east." The vision may also evoke the picture of Cyrus conquering Babylon, which was oppressing God's people (cf. Isa 41:2, 25; 44:27–28). Jer 50:41; 51:11, 28 mentions "kings," whom God was preparing to bring against Babylon. This should result in the restoration of God's people in a new exodus.

625. Cf. ibid., 828.

626. The day of the Lord brings punishment for the apostate Israel (Amos 5:18–27; Zech 14:1–4), but it is also a day of salvation for its faithful remnant (cf. Joel 2:32; Hab 2:4; Zeph 3:8–13; Zech 12:10–12; Dan 12:1–2). Cf. LaRondelle, "Armageddon," 26.

627. There is no record of such a geographical place. The attempt to find a geographical location has usually pointed to a mountain (Heb. *har*) in the surroundings of Megiddo (e.g., Mt. Carmel), or to the city (Heb. *ar*) of Megiddo, an important OT battle-site. Cf. Charles, *Revelation*, II: 50–51; Aune, *Revelation 6–16*, 898–99. However, Megiddo itself was a plain. Cf. Fekkes, *Prophetic Traditions in Revelation*, 203. As an important battle site it could signify both the end of Exodus (Judg 5:19) and the reversal of Exodus, i.e., the defeat of Israel (2 Kgs 23:29–30; 2 Chr 35:20–24). Cf. Beagley, *Church's Enemies*, 89.

628. Some scholars have suggested that the name means Mount of Assembly (*har môʻēd*) referring to Mount Zion (Rev 14:1; cf. Isa 14:13). Cf. Aune, *Revelation 6–16*, 899; Ford, *Revelation*, 274, among those who recognize such a possibility. LaRondelle, "Armageddon," 23 n. 4, argues that the Jewish translators of LXX regarded the verb *gādad* as the root of Megiddo (cf. Zech 12:11). Therefore the meaning should be "Mountain of Destruction."

629. Chilton, *Days of Vengeance*, 412. Zech 13 announces that Yahweh will remove from Israel idols, false prophets and evil spirits. Thus, it could be seen as purification from idolatry, i.e., spiritual adultery. Then, Zech 14 announces the gathering of the nations against Jerusalem.

mourn over him, whom they have pierced. This could refer to Christ's death and his subsequent vindication in the sight of his oppressors (cf. above on Rev 1:7). The actual battle of Armageddon is described later in 17:14 and 19:11–21 as a clash between Christ and the armies of Satan.[630]

The repeated theme of coming as a thief, which resembles the Synoptic traditions—where it is linked with the impending judgment upon Jerusalem (cf. Matt 24:42–44, above on 3:3; and chapter 5 on Matt 25:1–13)—could further support our interpretation. However, of particular interest here is the motif of shame associated with nakedness. This single motif may evoke the OT traditions describing the punishment of an adulterous wife Israel (cf. above on Rev 3:18; also chapter 3 on Ezek 16:36; 23:29). This may also lend support to the proposal that Rev 16 echoes the divine marriage metaphor.

The final bowl's plague, poured out into the air, brings hail from heaven (Rev 16:17, 21; cf. 11:19). The great city Babylon is affected by it (v. 19; cf. 11:8; 14:8).[631] The cities of Gentile nations fell at the same time. This last plague is elaborated on in Rev 17–18.[632] Then again, it is likely that all seven bowl plagues work together towards the vision of the ultimate punishment of Babylon in Rev 17:1—19:3.

Our brief study of Rev 15–16 suggests that the Exodus tradition may work in these chapters alongside the metaphor of divine marriage to indicate the subjects of God's punishments. The punishments probably find their climax in the destruction of the great harlot Babylon, which is unfaithful Jerusalem. At the same time, Rev 15 offers a picture

---

630. Cf. LaRondelle, "Armageddon," 24; Briggs, *Temple Imagery*, 102 n.187. Another reference to this battle is suggested at Rev 20:7–10. Cf. Beale, *Revelation*, 838 and Aune, *Revelation 6–16*, 898. However, that battle seems different because of the thousand years' gap during which Satan is bound in the pit. Moreover, if a kind of parallelism is assumed between Cyrus and Christ the vision of 19:11–21 better suits the *topos* of the eschatological battle of Armageddon, with a similar set of characters depicted. 20:7–10 does not picture a battle *per se*, but a disaster (fire) falling from God on Satan's armies.

631. Beagley, *Church's Enemies*, 91, has noted that Ezek 13:8–16 may be the background for the great hailstones, which came on the false prophets. It is particularly noteworthy because the second beast can refer to the false prophets of Israel. Although suggestions have been made that the hailstones found their historical counterpart in the stones thrown by Romans on Jerusalem from catapults (cf. Joseph *War* V:3:270–73), the symbolism of the hailstones is more important. It could resemble the seventh plague of Egypt (Exod 9:22–33; cf. Deut 28:60). Cf. Aune, *Revelation 6–16*, 901. Now, it seems to be turned against impenitent Israel.

632. Schüssler-Fiorenza, *Vision of a Just World*, 95; Yarbro Collins, "Feminine Symbolism," 25.

of the triumph of God's faithful who should expect a Sinai-like marriage to follow these calamities.

Revelation 20 and Its Relationship to the Marriage Metaphor

Rev 20 has been a source and encouragement to millennial debates within Christian circles. Scholars have often argued about the time references in the chapter and also concerning its relation to the preceding and subsequent visions. We will limit our discussion to the central issues of the chapter.

Some scholars have argued that Rev 19:11–21 describes Christ's second coming to earth and chronologically precedes the events of chapter 20.[633] However, we have argued in this book that the usual scholarly understanding of Christ's *parousia* is not necessarily consistently biblical. We have also proposed that Rev 19:11–21 is about a messianic eschatological battle, which takes place during the same time-span as the messianic wedding following the destruction of Jerusalem.

Other scholars have maintained that Rev 19:11–21 and 20:7–10 describe one and the same eschatological battle at the end of the space-time universe.[634] But again the strength of their argument rests on a futuristic and universal understanding of the events in 19:11–21.[635] This is, however, unlikely in the light of our earlier argument. Hence, we would suggest that there exists a better explanation of the events presented in Rev 20.

---

633. See, e.g., Müller, "Analysis of Revelation 20," 249; Wallis, "Coming of the Kingdom," 60.

634. See esp. McKelvey, "Millennium," 95. Cf. Steinmann, "Tripartite Structure," 77 n. 18. Steinmann insists, on a linguistic basis only, that 20:10 is a recapitulation of 19:20. He explains that the omission of a verb governing "beast" and "false prophet" in 20:10 requires the translator to supply one in English. Most translators chose one of the verbs that place 20:10 chronologically after 19:20. Steinmann, however, argues that it would be more natural to provide a verb in the aorist that would agree with the tense of the main verb concerning the beast and the false prophet. Yet, he recognizes that the ellipsis of a third-person-plural of *einai* is rarely possible. Thus, we suggest, one needs to decide the sequence on the basis of the context, rather than on the basis of linguistics.

635. McKelvey, "Millennium," 86, argues that the chronological view creates tension between 19:18, 21 and 20:7–10, because all the opponents of Christ in the *world* are killed in 19:21. Then, no one would be left to attack again in 20:8. But the tension is only created because McKelvey reads 19:11–21 in a universal sense. Our explanation, however, does not run into such difficulties.

Rev 20 opens with the vision of the incarceration of Satan for a period of a thousand years.[636] It seems to occur after or at the defeat of the beast and the false prophet.[637] The same period is a time of the reign of Christ and his saints (vv. 1–6). It is called the "first resurrection" of those who have been beheaded because of the testimony of Christ, and of those who have not worshipped the beast and his image (v. 4).[638] This resurrection has sometimes been viewed as referring to the raising of the redeemed at Christ's second coming in the future.[639] However, the context of Rev 19 would suggest a more temporal view. The resurrection appears to be linked with the vindication of Christ and his church in Rev 19. It appears to be linked with salvation from bondage under the whore Babylon. Hence, it could refer to the national restoration of God's faithful after the time of captivity/exile (cf. Ezek 37:1–14; Hos 6:1–2).[640] It is

---

636. Terry, *Biblical Apocalyptics*, 449, draws attention to the fact that nothing is said here concerning the angels cast down to earth with Satan (cf. 12:9). Does that imply that they are left on earth? If so, this could help in explaining the existence of evil during the millennial era. Cf. Kik, *Eschatology of Victory*, 194. Beasley-Murray, *Revelation*, 286, suggests a possible link with Isa 24:21–22 here.

637. A chronological continuity with chapter 19 is assumed here, because otherwise the picture of the eschatological battle is incomplete (19:11–21). One would still expect a kind of dealing with the main opponent behind the forces of the two beasts. Cf. Ford, *Revelation*, 330. She suggests that the defeat works towards the establishment of the faithful woman in the place of the destroyed whore.

638. The millennium reign is not limited to the martyrs who have borne testimony to Jesus (cf. 6:9); it probably also includes the OT witnesses (cf. Luke 24:25–27; John 5:45–46; Acts 10:43; Rom 1:1–3; 3:21–22). Cf. Chilton, *Days of Vengeance*, 512–13. Pace McKelvey, "Millennium," 97, Aune, *Revelation 17–22*, 1088, and Wright, *RSG*, 472. The millennium reign also has in view another group of Christ's followers: those who have not worshipped the beast. Beale, *Revelation*, 999, 1001, suggests that this is equally possible as the view that this second description refers to the previous martyrs. The construction καὶ ὅστις introduces a group different from the first one (cf. Matt 5:41; 23:12). Moreover, "if οἵτινες were dependent on "souls," it should also be accusative as a second object of the implied εἶδον ("I saw"), but the case may be changed in order to indicate a different group. Therefore, unless there is a multiple grammatical solecism, ὅστις functions not as an adjective modifying "those beheaded" but functions nominally to refer to another group. As such, it functions as the subject of the verbal phrase οὐ προσεκύνησαν ("they did not worship"), yet it is still conceptually an object of the implied εἶδον ("I saw")." We would suggest that taking 20:4 as describing two variegated groups of people helps to explain the significance of the first resurrection. Yet, Ford, *Revelation*, 349, prefers to view the latter phrase as an interpolation.

639. E.g., Stefanovic, *Revelation of Jesus Christ*, 565.

640. It should not create a problem that the resurrection is of both the beheaded martyrs and of the faithful people. The reign of Christ can be regarded as taking place both

a resurrection to reign in the messianic kingdom.[641] Those partaking in it will not experience the second death of Gehenna (Rev 20:6; cf. 2:11).[642] The lake of fire is prepared for those who do not share in the first resurrection (20:5).[643] Consequently, the millennium may be the period of Christ and his church following their vindication, which is signified by the destruction of the temple.[644] In this sense, the new priesthood would

---

in heaven and in the world. Such an idea was not foreign to early Christian thought. The Pauline tradition spoke of the thrones of saints in heaven (cf. Eph 2:6), and Revelation itself assumes a reign on earth (cf. 2:26–27; 5:10; 11:15). See Chilton, *Days of Vengeance*, 514. It is noteworthy that, if our proposal concerning the resurrection is accepted, the pattern would resemble that of Ezekiel: first, there is a national restoration/resurrection in chapter 37 followed by the attack of Gog of the land of Magog (chapter 38) and his defeat through heavenly fire (39:6). Cf. also Chilton, *Days of Vengeance*, 536.

641. Cf. Caird, *Revelation*, 255, while not agreeing fully with his notion of martyrs. Some scholars have suggested that this "first resurrection" is similar to the raising of the believer at baptism (cf. Rom 6:4; Col 2:12; 3:1; Eph 2:6). See Shepherd, "Resurrections of Revelation 20," 36. Cf. Wright, *RSG*, 275. But the first resurrection seems to be corporate in the context of the messianic reign. This seems plausible if John is now using Ps 2, as applied to the Messiah (Rev 19:15) and the saints in heaven and on earth (2:27). Hence, the "first resurrection" could refer to the passage from the exile to exodus/salvation. Terry, *Biblical Apocalyptics*, 452, has argued that the first resurrection should be read symbolically as referring to living and reigning with Christ. Pace Wallis, "Coming of the Kingdom," 65, who thinks that bodily resurrection is necessary for a man to exercise rule over God's creation. On his view, the man is still endangered by evil after his bodily resurrection (Rev 20:7–9).

642. Concerning the second death, see above on Rev 2:11.

643. The unfaithful people of God are probably the special focus of the phrase "the rest of the dead." However, exegetes have also preferred to extend it to all the ungodly awaiting the last judgment (20:11–15). Cf. Chilton, *Days of Vengeance*, 515. In general, the sense is of the wicked remaining in exile and death. Cf. Terry, *Biblical Apocalyptics*, 453. One can only wonder if John was particularly concerned with the theme of the bodily resurrection (1 Cor 15:20–54). However, some scholars suggest that the postmillennial judgment of the dead implies bodily resurrection (20:12, 15). Cf. Wright, *RSG*, 474–75.

644. Some scholars view 1,000 years figuratively to signify a long-time of the church era. See, e.g., Beale, *Revelation*, 150, 995. He shows that 1,000 (the third power of 10) is a long period of time in comparison to the short-ten days period of trial (cf. Rev 2:10). Kik, *Eschatology of Victory*, 205, explains that a thousand symbolizes vastness in biblical literature (cf. Deut 1:11). For a brief overview of the millennial views in the church throughout history, see Ford, *Revelation*, 350–51. She also notes that Jubilees 23:26–31 describes a messianic era, when man would live reaching a thousand years. Beale (*Revelation*, 1019) explains, "The thousand-year period in *Jub.* 23:27–30 is clearly figurative for the complete perfection of the eternal time of blessing for God's people..." *Jub* 4:29–30, giving a context to that idea, suggests that Adam fell short of living up to 1,000 years. Thus the future messianic reign has to reverse the shortcomings of Adam

be replacing the old (20:6).[645] Moreover, as we have indicated above, the bride of Christ consists of the martyrs in heaven (6:11) as well as of the faithful ones on earth (7:9–17). Hence, it would appear that the millennial reign described in Rev 20 is one of Christ and his bride both in heaven and on earth.[646] The simultaneous freedom from Satan's deception allows the nations to come under the reign of Christ.[647]

Yet, at the end of the millennial reign, Satan is released and he resumes his role of deceiving nations (vv. 7–8, cf. v. 3b).[648] By his influence, the nations assault the camp of the saints and are instantly destroyed by God's fire (v. 9).[649] The picture would be one of an attack on Christ's

---

(cf. Isa 65:22LXX). Chilton, *Days of Vengeance*, 514, has proposed that 1,000 years is the complete reign-period ("forever"), which the Davidic kingdom failed to achieve (cf. 2 Sam 7:8–29; 1 Chr 17:7–27; 2 Chr 13:5; 21:7; Ps 89:19–37; Ezek 34:23–24; Luke 1:32–33). We are unable to provide a better explanation of the millennial reign here. Yet, we would agree with Beale that the millennium focuses more on the reign following the vindication of Christians, than on a time-period.

645. It is worth remembering that which was said above concerning the priesthood of saints in Rev 1:5–6. To mention the most significant point, one needs to acknowledge that Israel had not fulfilled the words of Exod 19:6 so she went into exile. However, there was a prophetic promise for the restoration/renewal of God's people's priesthood (Isa 61:6) at the time of the covenant/marriage renewal (Isa 61:10).

646. Kik, *Eschatology of Victory*, 214, has argued that "throne" must translate somehow into the earthly reign. McKelvey, "Millennium," 98, has argued that the role of the saints as priests during the millennium needs to assume their earthly function (20:6, 9; cf. 1:6). However, the martyred saints also reign with Christ. This probably implies that their "spiritual"/heavenly existence participates somehow in Christ's reign on earth. Cf. Terry, *Biblical Apocalyptics*, 451. See also Chilton, *Days of Vengeance*, 514. We would also suggest that a reference to Ps 45 is possible here, especially to v. 16, which speaks of the offspring of the Messiah and his bride ruling over the nations of the earth (cf. Ps 2:9; Rev 2:26–27).

647. Satan no longer controls pagan nations as he did before Christ's victory over him. Cf. Kik, *Eschatology of Victory*, 204. Thompson, "End of Satan," 265, observes that the binding of Satan ironically reverses his previous career of binding others (cf. Luke 13:10–17). People of all nations can now be drawn to Jesus (cf. John 12:31–32). See Beale, *Revelation*, 985. Ellul, *Apocalypse*, 208, explains: "It is the time of the work of man outside of the control of Satan; it can then possibly, hypothetically, virtually be characterized by *love* and *reconciliation*."

648. Cf. Kik, *Eschatology of Victory*, 237; Metzger, *Breaking the Code*, 93. Although this vision looks forward far beyond the time of John's audience, yet it provides an additional encouragement to the afflicted church of the ultimate destruction of forces opposing her. Cf. Terry, *Biblical Apocalyptics*, 455.

649. The names Gog and Magog may designate here the new enemies of God's people under old (well-known) names (cf. Ezek 38–39). Cf. Kik, *Eschatology of Victory*, 237. We suggest that there is no need to argue that they must be the same as in Rev

bride and her Husband's protection.⁶⁵⁰ Finally, Satan is cast into the lake of fire and sulfur for permanent affliction (v. 10).⁶⁵¹ This scene pictures the last attempt of God's enemies to attack his people and their ultimate defeat.⁶⁵²

Next comes a vision of judgment at the great white throne (v. 11). Scholars have generally agreed that this refers to the distant future, subsequent to the millennium, when God will ultimately judge people's deeds (v. 12).⁶⁵³ Rev 20:5 seems to assume another (second?) resurrec-

---

19:18–21, although both this passage and 20:8 echo Ezek 38–39. It is possible that every new enemy of God's people, to an extent, resembles the old one in symbolical language. The description "like the sand of the sea" (cf. Ezek 38:15) in Rev 20:8 may resemble the multitude of the Canaanite nations conquered by Joshua (Josh 11:4) and/or the number of the Midianites defeated by Gideon (Judg 7:12). See Chilton, *Days of Vengeance*, 524. Thus, the vast number of enemies should not create panic among God's people, but rather encourage a great victory. It may also imply that the complete number of enemies is gathered for destruction. Similarly, gathering them from the four corners of the earth may imply drawing them out into the open from everywhere. There are no enemies left anymore. Cf. Beale, *Revelation*, 1023–24. Otherwise such a vast number was associated with Israel (Gen 22:17; 2 Sam 17:11).

The beloved city is probably the same as the new Jerusalem in 3:12, 21:2, 3, 10 (cf. Jer 11:15; 12:7; Ps 78:68). See Terry, *Biblical Apocalyptics*, 455. He also suggests that the fire from God echoes the Elijah story in 2 Kgs 1:10, 12. Yet, it may also resemble the punishment of Gog and his armies in Ezek 38:22

650. Cf. Deutsch, "New Jerusalem," 255, who indicates that the description "beloved city" in 20:9 may recall the marital relationship between the Lamb (and God) and his redeemed. It would be strange if the "beloved city" referred to the old earthly Jerusalem, since that had previously been called "Sodom and Egypt" in 11:8. Cf. Charles, *Revelation*, II: 150.

651. Satan's punishment resembles that of the beast and false prophet in 19:20. Thus, it is again a picture of Gehenna, or of the complete judgment upon Sodom in Gen 19:24–25, 28. However, a new element is added in this place, a continuous torment. It appears to echo the tortures of 9:5 (cf. 14:10), which were, however, temporary (five months). Here, the torture seems never-ending. Cf. Beale, *Revelation*, 1028–30.

652. Satan's activity after the release is very short, in comparison with the millennial reign of the saints, and only provokes the Last Judgment. Cf. Beale, *Revelation*, 1021; Ellul, *Apocalypse*, 209.

653. The only exception here being Russell, *Parousia*, 525, who insists that the judgment refers to the termination of the Jewish dispensation in the first century CE. He argues that Rev 20:11–15 describes the same events as Matt 25:31–46. However, whereas Matt 25:31–46 may indeed refer to the imminent judgment upon God's people (cf. Wright, *JVG*, 182–86, 533), it seems that John the Seer had another judgment in view, in the context of Rev 20:5. See also Wright, *RSG*, 442 n. 126, 473–76. Likewise, the reference to the ultimate abolition of Death and Hades suggests a future event (cf. 1 Cor 15:26, 54). See Kik, *Eschatology of Victory*, 264; Terry, *Biblical Apocalyptics*, 458. Jankowski, *Apokalipsa*, 272, noted that according to Wis 2:24 death was linked with

tion before the judgment takes place (v. 13).[654] The vision finishes with Death and Hades being cast into the lake of fire (v. 14).[655] Those whose names are not written in the Book of Life follow Death and Hades into that permanent perdition (v. 15).

In general, Rev 20 presents a picture of the messianic reign, which follows the destruction of Babylon, the enemy of God's people. The bride of the Messiah partakes in the millennial age of ruling and judging the nations, possibly an echo of Ps 45. She is assured of her security with God. Finally, she is assured that history will lead to the final defeat of evil and the vindication of God's justice.

Satan. Thus, the destruction of Satan may assume that of the other. Ford, *Revelation*, 359, notes that in 14:14-20 and 19:11-21 it was Christ who was judging the living, but here it is God who judges the dead.

The books may echo Dan 7:10, where the books might have referred to the Jewish tradition of the two books recording the deeds of the righteous and of the wicked (cf. Ps 56:8; Isa 65:6; Jer 22:30; Mal 3:16). See Aune, *17-22*, 1102. The Book of Life may resemble the register of Israelite citizens in the OT (cf. Exod 32:32; Ps 69:28; Isa 4:3, etc.). So Ford, *Revelation*, 359.

654. It appears that this resurrection concerns mainly the previously unfaithful people of God. Cf. Chilton, *Days of Vengeance*, 515. However, scholars also suggest that all the ungodly are in view here: meanwhile they are a property of Death and Hades. Cf. Wright, *RSG*, 473. Wright also thinks that before the judgment, there is a general (bodily?) resurrection of all people, of which many are found to have their names written in the book of Life (474). However, Terry, *Biblical Apocalyptics*, 457, has remarked that, "It is noticeable that in this entire passage (verses 11-15) there is no word indicative of blessedness to accrue to these dead, as in the case of those 'that have part in the first resurrection' (verse 6)." They do not seem to have been written in the Book of Life since they are soon judged "according to their works." The text is not explicit concerning the bodily resurrection. Understandably, scholars are usually dependent on 1 Cor 15 when speaking of the bodily resurrection in Rev 20:11-15.

655. Some scholars have suggested that sea is another place, besides Hades, that imprisons dead souls. Caird, *Revelation*, 260, argues that the sea held the souls of those who died while travelling in it. Hence, the sea is hostile in the same way as Death and Hades. But then, the text is silent concerning the destruction of this enemy. It is not punished in the lake of fire, but simply disappears in 21:1. Bauckham, *Climax of Prophecy*, 70, argues that the destruction of Death and Hades marks the destruction of the sea. But perhaps this symbol is open to other ways of interpretation. We have earlier indicated that 'sea' sometimes symbolized the pagan nations in the OT. Could it be that the realm of the pagan world gives up its dead? Beale, *Revelation*, 1034, suggested that it may signify the realm, in which satanic forces imprisoned people (cf. Rev 4:6; 13:1; 15:2). But, concerning 13:1, we have concluded that the sea referred to the pagan world.

This casting into the lake of fire is the "second death," i.e., exclusion from the new world, which is another exile. Cf. above on Rev 2:11.

CONCLUSIONS

We have argued in this chapter that the book of Revelation may be regarded as a covenant document, standing in the same tradition as OT prophecy. There is evidence that in his work John elaborated on the theme of the new exodus, as envisioned and expected by God's people before Jesus' appearance. As in other NT writings, the exodus theme here is also placed in the context of the acts of God's Messiah. He, who once suffered at the hands of the unfaithful, is now to be vindicated in the defeat of his enemies. His people will be vindicated together with him from the oppression of the new Pharaoh, the disloyal part of Israel. This will be to them a salvation, an exodus, and a wedding feast.

We have indicated at various places that Revelation could have applied the divine marriage metaphor in its covenantal context. The messages to the seven Asian churches suggest that the covenant marital union between God (and the Lamb) and his people was already a reality. However, part of that people remained unfaithful to God, regardless of Christ's work. They rejected their Husband by killing the Messiah and persecuting his church, his beloved bride. They also threatened the bride's purity through their various harlotries, i.e., acts of covenant unfaithfulness. But the bride was going to be rescued and would enjoy a marriage feast at the defeat of the new Babylon. This, we have argued, was to involve the full establishment of the new covenant and the removal of the old, together with its temple. The bride was to appear pure and innocent after the temporary period of tribulation, due to the work of her Husband and her marital loyalty. We have indicated that the termination of the old covenant order was expressed by various judgment motifs underlined by the motif of divine marriage and that of divorce. We have also acknowledged that the new covenant order would have its new priesthood. Its relationship with God could be compared with that of the marital intimacy. However, the divine marriage motif in Revelation also has the very important role of depicting a conflict between two contrasting women in relationship to God: the bride and the whore. Accordingly, we have argued that Revelation was mainly interested in its original audience's contemporary situation, rather than in a set of timeless principles. The book focused on the audience's real crisis, created by the adherents of the disloyal Jerusalem, and presented its coming resolution as reaching throughout eternity. The marriage and its feast are contemporary events in the Apocalypse, to be sure, but possession of the inheritance by the bride and her offspring is an ongoing event, ultimately fulfilled by the replacement of the old physical world with a new one. Thus the marriage metaphor offers a hope beyond the immediate present. Yet, most of Revelation's material has in view the situation leading up to the destruction of Jerusalem's temple in 70 CE, together with the aftermath of that incident for the bride of the Lamb, on the one hand, and for the members of the whore, on the other.

We have also suggested that there is a possibility that the divine marriage metaphor appears very early in Revelation, first depicting the glory of Christ the Bridegroom in chapter 1. It is even possible that the metaphor is echoed throughout John's work, with a number of likely allusions and some explicit references. Thus, it appears that the metaphor is more central to the book than has been acknowledged previously. Its purpose seems to be the presentation of God's covenantal dealings with his people, following the death and resurrection of his Messiah. In this sense, Revelation may be a continuation of the Gospel accounts. Here the once tortured and killed, but now triumphant Warrior-Messiah will act on God's behalf in the soon approaching day of judgment and defeat of his enemies. He will join his royal wife, after having destroyed the King's enemies (cf. Ps 45). They will reign together over the nations of the world in the realm of the church, the new Zion that belongs in the heaven of God's presence. They are also to reign together beyond the millennial reign, which takes place within the unfulfilled new creation.

It appears that OT background of the divine marriage metaphor is indispensable for understanding the Apocalypse. It facilitates the interpretation of the major conflict created by Babylon, a symbol that has caused many scholarly debates. We have proposed that only disciplined thinking along covenant lines can make possible the interpretation of the otherwise obscure message of Revelation.

Our approach can also shed some light on the debate concerning Revelation's relationship with the material of both the Old and the New Testaments. It indicates that the OT context may be crucial to examining the referents of John's visions. It suggests also that Revelation can be similar to other early Christian understandings of the work of the Messiah acting on God's behalf. This in turn can be significant to the debate concerning John's 'Christian' understanding of covenant renewal through the agency of Jesus the Christ. It appears that John associated the restoration of divine marriage with this divine figure, as had previously been the case with the Evangelists and Paul (e.g., Matt 22:1–14; 25:1–13; Gal 4:26–28). Therefore, it appears that John was familiar with the early Christian traditions and the method of their interpretation as taught by the founder of the movement himself, and followed by those who regarded themselves as his disciples. Hence, it is plausible to claim that there was a degree of continuity and progress in biblical thought in relation to the metaphor of divine marriage. This can be seen in the subsequent, although perhaps independent at times, uses of the motif by various authors in the Old and the NT, who often betray a common knowledge of the same traditions. On the basis of all of this, we propose to extract and to discuss briefly a biblical theology of divine marriage in the concluding section of this work.

Conclusions

Covenant and the Metaphor of Divine Marriage in Biblical Thought

IN THE COURSE OF our studies, we have acknowledged that the divine marriage metaphor originated in the prophetic reflection upon the covenant traditions of the Pentateuch. To Hosea, pre-exilic and exilic prophets, the events at Sinai, which accompanied the Exodus, came to be regarded as a wedding, sealing with a mutual oath the inaugurated relationship of Yahweh and his people Israel (Ex 19:5-6, 8). In the Exodus and later in the land of Canaan, Yahweh acted as a loving and caring Husband of his once miserable and helpless Wife; as a most prominent lover, he provided her with every good thing (Ezek 16:4-14; cf. Ex 21:10; Hos 2:9). By his acts, she was granted the status of royalty and received her priesthood. Moreover, as her lawful Husband, Yahweh provided his beloved with an inheritance, i.e., Canaan: a wedding gift belonging to her and their offspring. Certainly, no other *hieros gamos* of the ancient Semitic nations known to us had such repercussions: a god of might bestowing his constant loving and tender care on a people. This divine marriage testified to the most intimate union existing between Yahweh and Israel, a union which demanded of both parties exclusive faithfulness. However, the people violated this bond, engaging in heathen religions and alliances with foreign powers. Their prostitution left their good Husband angry and broken-hearted, wanting to punish his Wife according to the covenant, yet not willing to give up wholly on the relationship. We have seen that God, although wronged, strove to win back his unfaithful spouse. He sought to change her heart's attitude through the experience of judgments and eventually exile. But exile was not Yahweh's last word to unfaithful Israel; his covenant faithfulness and love still went out to her. Thus the main prophetic traditions give a hope of marriage restoration or of a new betrothal and of a miraculous restoration of Israel's chastity. This hope was to be realized thought a great salvific act of Yahweh, similar to that of old: it was to be a new exodus.

∙ ∙ ∙

Examining the way the NT uses OT material, we discovered a great degree of dependence on the scriptural traditions on the part of the NT authors. We have learnt that these authors often demonstrate respect for the OT contexts of the verses they quote. We have also seen that the OT expectation of the new exodus could have been their guiding principle in describing the Christ event together with its effects. Consequently, they needed to assume the covenantal framework organically connected to the exodus tradition. The validity of hypothesis seems to be proven in the light of our discoveries concerning variegated NT traditions. Therefore it would not be a mistake to claim that the NT writers based their theologies on OT concepts. They deliberately used the Hebrew Scriptures and read them within their redemptive historical context. This new context enabled them to see new meanings in those Scriptures, meanings, however, that did not necessarily violate the thrust of the original contexts. Their scriptural perspective was reshaped by the Christ event and it relied on his hermeneutical approach. For this reason, one can expect clear continuity with the OT concept of divine marriage in the NT.

∙ ∙ ∙

Studying the parables of the synoptic Gospels, we discovered that Jesus regarded himself as the Messiah, the one acting on behalf of Yahweh to bring the eschatological exodus of God's people, with all of the attendant promises, to fulfillment. He claimed to be the Bridegroom introducing the festivities associated with the arrival of God's salvation (see Mark 2:19), thus announcing the time of covenant/marriage restoration. His disciples were witnesses to this event, being close companions of the Bridegroom. Yet, he met with strong opposition from Jewish leaders and some of the people, who did not want to recognize God acting in him. By their unfaithfulness, they placed themselves outside the realm of the faithful remnant, who were to taste the blessings of the restored covenant through intimate union with God (Matt 22:1–14). Only the remnant who received Jesus, i.e., his disciples, would constitute the nucleus of the restored Zion, the chaste virgin Israel. They would also be joined by others who were not initially invited, presumably Gentiles. Thus the eschatological Bride was being redefined in Jesus' ministry. Consequently, the unfaithful Jews became a main obstacle in the way of God's kingdom. Their plot against the Messiah and ultimately their murder of him was to cause sorrow among the companions of the Bridegroom, breaking into the wedding festivities (Mark 2:20). But even more, it was to precipitate the expression of God's wrath on those who rejected the wedding (Matt 22:7). The outpouring of this wrath would avenge the Son's death and establish eschatological salvation by destroying the corrupt system. Faithful Israel would experience the true freedom of the new exodus at the vindication of her Messiah, which was to be marked by the destruction of Herod's temple (cf. 24:2, 3, 30). Therefore the eschatological wedding in the synoptic gospels began to be associated with the eschatological judgment on the unfaithful (cf. Matt 25:1–13). The Jews who chose the way of wisdom over the way of folly would experience God's salvation, not judgment. The foolish would be punished. Thus it seems that the violent removal of the Bridegroom in Mark ends the joys of the wedding festivities and leads in Matthew to the Messiah's vindication and the establishment of God's salvation in the subsequent covenant renewal. This happens amidst the Exodus-like judgments upon the Jewish capital representing the corrupted system.

The testimony of John the Baptist in the fourth Gospel confirms that the time of joy of salvation had arrived with Jesus the Bridegroom (Jn 3:29; cf. Mark 2:19). The Baptizer's words testify to the covenant renewal as he, the best man, witnessed the restoration of the marriage. Immediately, the Baptist withdrew from the scene to emphasize the superior role of the Bridegroom.

Our examination of the Gospels' material has led us to the conclusion that the transition within the marriage metaphor from Yahweh being the Husband of Israel to Christ being the Bridegroom of his people occurred in a manner consistent with the beliefs of second temple Judaism. Using the theology of eschatological fulfillment, Jesus the self-attested Messiah, acting on behalf of Yahweh, refocused OT prophecies regarding the divine marriage onto himself. This provided a hermeneutical method for his followers, which was rather consistently used by the NT writers. Thus the divine marriage traditions of the OT were embedded in the teaching of the Christian movement. Consequently, we have argued that the continuity of the covenant should be a guiding principle for interpreting the new messianic marriage, in contrast to those scholars who assume a scheme of ancient marriage customs in order to interpret the divine marriage in the NT. Such scholars deny any existence of marriage proper (or marriage restored) in the messianic age, looking forward to its establishment only at the *Endzeit*. For them, this age is one of betrothal. We have suggested that such an approach cannot be reconciled with Jesus' theology of fulfillment and the OT concept of divine marriage in the eschaton. Consistency demands rejection of such claims.

• • •

Our study of the Pauline literature has indicated that the apostle shared a perspective similar to other NT authors, viewing his churches as having been betrothed anew to God in Christ, necessitating their chastity (2 Cor 11:2) and ensuring the blessings of the covenant renewal (Rom 9:25–26). He based his theology on the OT traditions available to him. Thus one would expect him to present various concepts against the background of their OT counterparts.

To the Corinthians, Paul was like a father who makes sure that his daughter is not seduced from her single-minded devotion to her Husband. He is concerned that she does not follow teaching contrary to that of Christ. As the one who joined them to their Husband, as a father with authority and full of care, the apostle wanted to protect them from the mistake made by Eve in Eden, the error of listening to the voice of an intruder (2 Cor 11:3). The Bride of Christ should be faithful and persevere in the way of purity for her Husband.

Christians in Galatia are presented as part of the immense offspring of a heavenly Jerusalem, the restored Zion that is free as Sarah (Gal 4:26). Their exile has ended through Christ's death and resurrection, which accomplished a new exodus (5:1; 3:11–14). Those baptized into Christ, both Jews and Gentiles, now inherit the promises of Abraham for they are the restored Israel of God (3:26–29; 6:15–16; cf. Is 54:3). However, the old Jerusalem remains in the exile and bondage caused by her disobedience to the Torah; she is like Hagar (4:24–25). The supporters of this system cannot partake in the covenant restoration. They can only experience shame, which stands in sharp contrast to the great joy of the restored and fertile Zion.

Similarly, Christians in Rome were regarded as the children of the Abrahamic promise (Rom 9:7), called by God from both Jews and Gentiles (9:24). They constituted part of God's beloved Wife in the renewed covenant (9:25–26). The Gentiles joined the restored remnant of Israel, while a number of Jews remained in exile under God's judgment due to their unfaithfulness (9:27). Thus the letters to the Galatians and the Romans clearly redefine the Israel of God in the context of Christ's work, a concept reflected earlier in some of the dominical parables.

A continuation of Pauline thought in Ephesians presents the church as living in a loving relationship with Christ their Husband (5:25b–27). Christ's death was a sacrifice to God that completely purified his Bride, made up of both Jew and Gentile, for covenant renewal (5:2; 2:11–12). This death secured the betrothal gift, the kingdom of Christ and God (5:5), which is her inheritance, the Holy Spirit being given as a guarantee of this inheritance (1:14). Christ's self-sacrificial love made the church beautiful and full of splendor, like a royal Wife (5:26–27; cf. Ezek 16:10–14). Ceremonially pure, she entered a new marital bond, an intimate covenant union with Christ (5:32).

As in the case of the Gospels, we have argued against a non-covenantal view of divine marriage in the writings of Paul. For many scholars, the guiding interpretative principle is again based on ancient marriage customs. Thus they have not paid enough attention to the covenantal continuity of the marriage, influenced perhaps by their eschatological views. We have insisted, over against such positions, on the historical continuity between the OT and the NT, maintaining that the expectations of OT prophets regarding the marriage came to fulfillment in the act of Jesus the Messiah.

• • •

The main focus of our study of the metaphor of divine marriage was the book of Revelation. We have suggested that the apocalyptic in the NT shares much in common with OT prophecy. This led us to approach the material of Revelation as revealing a similar covenantal interest to that of the OT and probably other NT books. Consequently, we have dismissed various contemporary ways of reading Revelation as an economic, political, astrological, or even merely rhetorical treatise. We have rather proposed that the covenantal perspective, together with its expectation of a new exodus, is an indispensable tool to a more consistent interpretation of Revelation's concepts. Our study has provided some evidence to support such claim.

We have discovered that the corrupted system of Jerusalem became a new enemy of God's people, a new Pharaoh and Egypt (Rev 11:8). Such a conclusion is certainly not very remote from ideas emerging of Paul's conflict with the Judaizers in Galatia or Jesus' earlier struggle with Jewish leaders in the Gospels. The Jews were in covenant with God, and therefore those who were unfaithful deserved the punishment prescribed in the covenant stipulations (cf. Lev 26:14–19; Deut 28:15–68), a punishment for becoming a harlot (Rev 18:3). Their guilt was even graver as they were guilty of the blood of God's Messiah (cf. Matt 27:25). Having killed God's Son (Acts 4:26–27), they started oppressing his people (cf. 2:14, 23; 3:1, 12—4:21; 5:17–18, 27–40; 6:7—7:1, 54–60; 12:1–4; 21:27–31; 23:12–15). But the Messiah proved to be a warrior king and judge who would be vindicated together with his followers when God would take vengeance on the unfaithful and hostile city, as predicted in the Gospels (Rev 1:7; cf. Matt 24:2–34).

We have suggested that echoes of the metaphor of divine marriage can be heard very early in the book, in chapter 1. It is also possible that its echoes can be detected throughout, with a number of fairly explicit instances in a few chapters. The metaphor describes a covenant relationship between Christ and his Bride, the church, in the context of OT expectations. But it also challenges the Bride in the face of an approaching crisis: judgment that would purify her. The Husband expected love, faithfulness and loyal devotion of his Bride. Not finding such, he would judge her alongside the unfaithful at his appearance (Rev 2–3). The defiling elements diminishing her devotion would certainly have to be removed, as they may lead the Bride into harlotry, i.e., breaking of the covenant bond. It seems that the main threat to the Bride came from the unfaithful Jews and Judaizers, a woman leading others to sin (Rev 2:20–23; cf. 2 Cor 11:2). Therefore, we have concluded that the main conflict of Revelation concerns two juxtaposed women: the Bride of Christ and the harlot, representing the corrupted Jerusalem system. The former needs a new exodus—salvation—from the power and influence of the latter. Proving faithful, she will be vindicated as a royal priesthood of God, to gain her inheritance and establishment in the new creation of Christ (21:7). This inheritance is guaranteed in Revelation by Christ's payment of his life, the *mohar* price. His self-giving act atoned for and consecrated his people, preparing them for this inheritance and reign with Christ on the earth (5:9–10; 20:4).

We have indicated that Revelation also elaborates on the OT concept of the remnant, associating their salvation with the inclusion of the Gentiles. This theme was previously linked to the divine marriage in Matthew and some Pauline writings. This remnant of Jews, together with a countless multitude of every ethnic group and family, constitutes in Revelation the Bride of Christ, a restored Zion of God (7:4–8, 9). The remnant is sealed against the disasters coming on the unfaithful Jerusalem, which for the former will be an Exodus-like salvation and for the latter a reversal of the original Exodus accomplished by God.

Revelation appears to offer a more detailed description of the Bridegroom and the two conflicting women. His beauty and splendor outshines that of human beings (1:13–16). He possesses the attributes of a warrior, king and judge. In this, he possibly resembles the messianic figure of Ps 45. Even more, he appears as one similar to the Ancient of Days of the Danielic vision, full of majesty (cf. Dan 7:9–10). The royal Wife of the Messiah appears as clothed in her Husband's glory (Rev 12:1; Ps 45:9, 13). God himself protects her against satanic attacks so that she can freely deliver her offspring. Her attire is white as she is a pure virgin adorned with splendid beauty (Rev 19:8; 19:2). The other woman, although clothed in noble attire, resembles a prostitute defiled by her unchastity, drunk with the blood of God's servants (17:4, 6). On her forehead, she bears the marks of her whoredom (17:5), similarly to the unfaithful Judah of Jeremiah's time (cf. Jer 3:3). She will be left naked, be burned with fire and become a sorrowful widow: all punishments for the unfaithful wife (18:8–10, 14, 16; cf. Lev 21:9; Is 54:4). Thus in reality she will be left in exile, i.e., divorced, which may lead to the final eternal separation from God (20:5–6, 11–15).

The judgment of the Harlot Babylon and the marriage of the Lamb appear to be correlative events in Revelation (chapters 17–19). The marriage, however, was inaugurated earlier at Christ's washing of his Bride (1:5). Therefore we have suggested that the wedding/salvation feast, although fully experienced only at the time of deliverance from the power of the foes, is an ongoing reality for the churches in Revelation, reaching its climax at the destruction of Jerusalem. Consequently, we have again disagreed with the scholars who place the messianic wedding at the *Endzeit*. We have rather proposed that Christ's Bride/Wife has her heavenly existence until the appropriate time for her finally to descend to her inheritance, the new earth (21:2, 7). We have, however, implied that the wedding and the descent to possess the inheritance are two different events, characteristic of different times. Nevertheless, we have also indicated that even the reality of this ultimate inheritance penetrates the time of the church's wedding in many ways, as she experiences many of God's promised blessings in history (chapters 21–22).

Furthermore, we have also indicated that the motif of the city in the final two chapters of Revelation informs the metaphor of divine marriage. Both concepts work together to describe in more detail the special relationship of God and his people in Christ. The New Jerusalem is the restored Wife of God, resurrected and full of life. Being in the city points to the priestly nature of its indwellers, whereas being part of the Bride signifies the royal status. However, central to both concepts is the closeness and intimacy of this relationship, which is presented as mutual indwelling and which symbolizes the intimacy of partners in this marriage union (21:22). Both parties have a special access to each other's heart. Moreover, it is a relationship with a view to producing a multitude of offspring (21:24–26; 22:2; cf. Gal 4:27). Lastly, this relationship fulfils itself in the reign of the Husband and his Wife, together with their children, in eternity (Rev 22:5).

• • •

Therefore, in conclusion, we propose that the metaphor of divine marriage should be given more attention in scholarly studies of the covenant in the Bible. We propose that no other starting point is able to reach to the heart of covenant union as presented in the church's Holy Scriptures. Thus, we suggest that earlier comparative studies of ancient suzerain-vassal treaties, valid as they are, ought to be supplemented with the marital perspective when discussing the biblical covenant. Likewise, all previous attempts to describe God's covenant in purely legal terms should take our considerations into account. Furthermore, we believe that our argument throughout this work can perhaps clarify some issues regarding covenant continuity as well as those touching directly on ecclesiology and eschatology in particular. Finally, above all, we hope that our discoveries regarding the metaphor of divine marriage in Revelation can be an aid in further attempts to uncover the riches of John's theological reflection.

Bibliography

Aageson, James W. "Scripture and Structure in the Development of the Argument in Romans 9-11." *CBQ* 48 (1986) 265-89.
Alexander, Philip "3 (Hebrew Apocalypse of) Enoch." In *The Old Testament Pseudepigrapha: Apocalyptic Literature & Testaments*, edited by J. H. Charlesworth, vol. I: 223-315. New York: Doubleday, 1983.
Allen, Leslie C. *Ezekiel 1-19*. Word Biblical Commentary 28. Dallas: Word Books, 1994.
Allison Jr., Dale C. "Jesus & the Victory of Apocalyptic." In *Jesus & the Restoration of Israel: A Critical Assessment of N. T. Wright's 'Jesus and the Victory of God'*, edited by C. C. Newman, 126-41. Carlisle: Paternoster, 1999.
Andersen, Francis I., and David N. Freedman. *Hosea*. Anchor Bible 24. New York: Doubleday, 1980.
Arndt, William F., and F. Wilbur Gingrich. *A Greek-English Lexicon of the New Testament and Other Early Christian Literature*. Chicago: UCP, 1959.
Aune, David E. *Revelation 1-5*. Word Biblical Commentary 52A. Dallas: Word Books, 1997.
———. *Revelation 6-16*. Word Biblical Commentary 52B. Nashville: Thomas Nelson, 1998.
———. *Revelation 17-22*. Word Biblical Commentary 52C. Nashville: Thomas Nelson, 1998.
Aus, Roger D. "The Relevance of Isaiah 66 7 to Revelation 12 and 2 Thessalonians 1." *ZNW* 67 (1976) 252-68.
Bailey, Kenneth E. *Poet & Peasant*, combined edition. Grand Rapids: Eerdmans, 1994.
———. *Through Peasant Eyes*, combined edition. Grand Rapids: Eerdmans, 1994.
Barrett, C. K. *Essays on Paul*. London: SPCK, 1982.
———. *The Gospel According to St John: An Introduction with Commentary and Notes on the Greek Text*. London: SPCK, 1972.
———. "Paul's Opponents in II Corinthians." *NTS* 17 (1970-71) 233-54.
Barth, Markus. *Ephesians: Translation and Commentary on Chapters 1-3*. Anchor Bible 34. Garden City: Doubleday, 1974.
———. *Ephesians: Translation and Commentary on Chapters 4-6*. Anchor Bible 34. Garden City: Doubleday, 1974.
Bartsch, Hans~Werner. "Early Christian Eschatology in the Synoptic Gospels." *NTS* 11 (1964-65) 387-97.
Batey, Richard A. "Jewish Gnosticism and the 'Hieros Gamos' of Eph. V:21-33." *NTS* 10 (1963-64) 121-27.
———. "The MIA SARX Union of Christ and the Church." *NTS* 13 (1966-67) 270-81.
———. *New Testament Nuptial Imagery*. Leiden: E. J. Brill, 1971.
Batten, Loring W. "Hosea's Message and Marriage." *JBL* 48 (1929) 257-73.

Bauckham, Richard. *The Climax of the Prophecy: Studies in the Book of Revelation*. Edinburgh: T&T Clark, 2000.

———. "The Economic Critique of Rome in Revelation 18." In *Images of Empire*, edited by L. Alexander, JSOT Sup 122, 47–90. Sheffield: JSOT Press, 1991.

———. "The Eschatological Earthquake in the Apocalypse of John." *NovT* 19 (1977) 224–33.

———. *The Theology of the Book of Revelation*. Cambridge: CUP 1999.

Beagley, Alan J. *The 'Sitz im Leben' of the Apocalypse with Particular Reference to the Role of the Church's Enemies*. Beiheft zur ZNW 50. Berlin/New York: de Gruyter, 1987.

Beale, Greg K. *The Book of Revelation*. Grand Rapids: Eerdmans, 1999.

———. "Did Jesus and His Followers Preach the Right Doctrine from the Wrong Texts? An Examination of the Presuppositions of Jesus' and the Apostles' Exegetical Method." *Themelios* 14/3 (1989) 89–96.

———. "The Eschatological Conception of the New Testament Theology." In *'The reader must understand': Eschatology in Bible and Theology*, edited by K. E. Brower and M. W. Elliott, 11–52. Leicester: Apollos, 1997.

———. *John's Use of the Old Testament in Revelation*. JSNT Sup 166. Sheffield: Sheffield Academic Press, 1998.

———. "Questions of Authorial Intent, Epistemology, and Presuppositions and Their Bearing on the Study of the Old Testament in the New: a Rejoinder to Steve Moyise." *IBS* 21 (1999) 152–80.

———. "A Response to Jon Paulien on the Use of the Old Testament in Revelation." *AUSS* 39/1 (2001) 23–33.

———. "The Use of the Old Testament in Revelation." In *The Right Doctrine from the Wrong Texts? Essays on the Use of the Old Testament in the New*, edited by G. K. Beale, 257–76. Grand Rapids: Baker, 1994.

Beasley–Murray, George R. *The Book of Revelation*. London: Oliphants 1978.

———. *John*. Word Biblical Commentary 36. Milton Keynes: Word Publishing, 1991.

Beckwith, Roger. *The Old Testament Canon of the New Testament Church*. London: SPCK, 1985.

Bedale, Stephen F. B. "The Meaning of kefalh, in the Pauline Epistles." *JTS* N.S. 5 (1954) 211–15.

———. "The Theology of the Church." In *Studies in Ephesians*, edited by F. L. Cross, 64–75. London: A. R. Mowbray and Co. Ltd., 1956.

Bell Jr., Albert A. "The Date of John's Apocalypse. The Evidence of Some Roman Historians Reconsidered." *NTS* 25 (1978–79) 93–102.

Bernard, John H. *A Critical and Exegetical Commentary on the Gospel According to St. John*. Edinburgh: T & T Clark, 1963.

Bertram, Georg. "μωρός κτλ." In *Theological Dictionary of the New Testament*, edited by G. Kittel and G. Friedrich, vol. IV: 832–47. Grand Rapids: Eerdmans, 1964–76.

Best, Ernest. *Essays on Ephesians*. Edinburgh: T&T Clark, 1997.

———. *Mark: The Gospel as Story*. Edinburgh: T&T Clark, 1994.

———. *One Body in Christ: A Study in the Relationship of the Church to Christ in the Epistles of the Apostle Paul*. London: SPCK, 1955.

Betz, Hans D. *Galatians*. Philadelphia: Fortress, 1979.

Black, Matthew. *The Book of Enoch or I Enoch*. Leiden: E. J. Brill, 1985.

Block, Daniel I. *The Book of Ezekiel Chapters 1–24*. Grand Rapids: Eerdmans, 1997.

Blomberg, Craig L. *Interpreting the Parables*. Leicester: Apollos, 1990.

———. *Matthew*. Nashville: Broadman, 1992.
Boxall, Ian. "The Many Faces of Babylon the Great: *Wirkungsgeschichte* and the Interpretation of Revelation 17." In *Studies in the Book of Revelation*, edited by S. Moyise, 51–68. Edinburgh: T & T Clark, 2001.
Bratsiotis, Nikolaus P. "אִישׁ אִשָּׁה." In *Theological Dictionary of the Old Testament*, edited by G. J. Botterweck and H. Ringgren, vol. I: 222–35. Grand Rapids: Eerdmans, 1990.
Brenner, Athalya. "Pornoprophetics Revisited: Some Additional Reflections." *JSOT* 70 (1996) 63–86.
Brewer, David I. "Three Weddings as a Divorce: God's Covenant with Israel, Judah, and the Church." *TynBul* 47.1 (1996) 1–25.
Briggs, Charles A., and Emilie G. Briggs. *A Critical and Exegetical Commentary on the Book of Psalms*. Edinburgh: T & T Clark, 1906.
Briggs, Robert A. *Jewish Temple Imagery in the Book of Revelation*. Studies in Biblical Literature 10. New York: Peter Lang, 1999.
Brinsmead, Birger H. *Galatians—Dialogical Response to Opponents*. SBL Dissertation Series 65. Chicago: Scholars Press, 1982.
Bruce, Frederick F. *The Epistle to the Galatians*. Grand Rapids: Eerdmans, 1998.
———. "The New Testament and Classical Studies." *NTS* 22 (1975–76) 229–42.
Brueggemann, Walter. *Isaiah 40–66*. Louisville: Westminster John Knox, 1998.
———. *Theology of the Old Testament*. Minneapolis: Fortress, 1997.
Bruns, J. Edgar. "The Contrasted Women of Apocalypse 12 and 17." *CBQ* 26 (1964) 459–63.
Budd, Philip J. *Numbers*. Word Biblical Commentary 5. Waco: Word Books, 1984.
Bultmann, Rudolf. *History of the Synoptic Tradition*. Peabody: Hendrickson, 1963.
———. *Primitive Christianity in Its Contemporary Setting*. London: Thames & Hudson, 1983.
Burchard, Christoph. "Joseph and Aseneth: A New Translation and Introduction." In *The Old Testament Pseudepigrapha: Apocalyptic Literature & Testaments*, edited by J. H. Charlesworth, vol. II: 177–247. New York: Doubleday, 1983.
Burkitt, Francis C. "The Parable of the Ten Virgins." *JTS* 30 (1929) 267–70.
Burrows, Millar. "The Social Institutions of Israel." In *Peake's Commentary on the Bible*, edited by M. Black, 134–41. London: Nelson, 1967.
Caird, George B. *The Language and Imagery of the Bible*. London: Duckworth, 1980.
———. *The Revelation of Saint John*. Peabody: Hendrickson, 1999.
Caird, George B., and Lincoln D. Hurst. *New Testament Theology*. Oxford: Clarendon, 1995.
Callahan, Allen D. "Apocalypse as Critique of Political Economy: Some Notes on Revelation 18." *Horizons in Biblical Theology* 21 (1999) 46–65.
Campbell, Douglas A. *The Rhetoric of Righteousness in Romans 3.21–26*. JSNT Sup 65. Sheffield: JSOT Press, 1992.
Carmichael, Calum M. "Marriage and the Samaritan Woman." *NTS* 26 (1980) 332–46.
Carroll, Robert P. *Jeremiah*. London: SCM, 1996.
Carson, Donald A. *The Gospel According to John*. Grand Rapids: Eerdmans, 1991.
Casey, Jay S. "The Exodus Theme in the Book of Revelation Against the Background of the New Testament." *Concilium* 189 (1987) 34–43.
———. "Exodus Typology in the Book of Revelation." PhD diss., Southern Baptist Theological Seminary, 1981.
Casey, Maurice. "Where Wright Is Wrong," *JSNT* 69 (1998) 95–103.

Charles, Robert H. *A Critical and Exegetical Commentary on the Book of Revelation of St. John*. Edinburgh: T & T Clark, 1920.
Charlesworth, James H. (ed.). *The Old Testament Pseudepigrapha: Apocalyptic Literature & Testaments*. New York: Doubleday, 1983.
Chavasse, Claude. *The Bride of Christ: An Inquiry into the Nuptial Element in Early Christianity*. London: Faber and Faber Ltd., 1940.
Childs, Brevard S. *Isaiah*. Louisville, Kentucky: Westminster John Knox, 2001.
Chilton, David. *The Days of Vengeance: An Exposition of the Book of Revelation*. Tyler: Dominion Press, 1990.
Clements, Ronald E. "Apocalyptic, Literacy, and the Canonical Tradition." In *Eschatology and the New Testament: Essays in Honor of George Raymond Beasley-Murray*, edited by W. Hulitt Gloer, 15–27. Peabody: Hendrickson, 1988.
Clines, David J. A. "Hosea 2: Structure and Interpretation." In *Studia Biblica*, edited by E. A. Livingstone, vol. I: 83–103. Sheffield: 1979.
Cook, Stanley A. *The Laws of Moses and the Code of Hammurabi*. London: A & C Black, 1903.
Cosgrove, Charles H. "The Law Has Given Sarah No Children (Gal. 4:21–30)." *NovT* 29 (1987) 219–35.
Cothenet, Edouard. *Exégèse et Liturgie*. Latour-Maubourg: Les Éditions du Cerf, 1988.
Craigie, Peter C. *Psalms 1–50*. Word Biblical Commentary 19. Dallas: Word Publishing, 1986.
Craigie, Peter C., et al. *Jeremiah 1–25*. Word Biblical Commentary 26. Waco: Word Books, 1991.
Cranfield, Charles E. B. *A Critical and Exegetical Commentary on the Epistle to the Romans*. Edinburgh: T & T Clark, 1990.
———. *The Gospel According to St Mark*. Cambridge: CUP, 1963.
Crossan, John Dominic. *In Parables: The Challenge of the Historical Jesus*. New York: Harper & Row, 1973.
Culliton, Joseph T. "Lucien Cerfaux's Contribution concerning 'The Body of Christ.'" *CBQ* 29 (1967) 41–59.
Cullmann, Oscar. *The Christology of the New Testament*. London: SCM, 1959.
Danker, Frederick W. (ed.). *A Greek-English Lexicon of the New Testament and other Early Christian Literature*. Chicago/London: University of Chicago Press, 2000.
Davidson, Benjamin. *The Analytical Hebrew and Chaldee Lexicon*. Peabody, MA: Hendrickson, 1995.
Davies, Graham I. *Hosea*. Sheffield: JSOT Press, 1993.
Davies, William D. "Paul and the Law: Reflections on Pitfalls in Interpretation." In *Paul and Paulinism: Essays in honour of C.K. Barrett*, edited by M. D. Hooker and S. G. Wilson 4–16. London: SPCK, 1982.
———. "Reflections on Aspects of the Jewish Background of the Gospel of John." In *Exploring the Gospel of John: In Honor of D. Moody Smith*, edited by R. A. Culpepper and C. C. Black, 43–64. Louisville: Westminster John Knox, 1996.
Dąbrowski, Eugeniusz. *Listy do Koryntian*. KUL 7. Poznan: Pallottinum, 1965.
Decock, Paul B. "The Scriptures in the Book of Revelation." *Neotestamentica* 33,2 (1999) 373–410.
Delitzsch, Franz. *Biblical Commentary on the Prophecies of Isaiah*. Grand Rapids: Eerdmans, 1967.
———. *Biblical Commentary on Psalms*. Grand Rapids: Eerdmans, 1968.

Delling, Gerhard. "παρθένος." In *Theological Dictionary of the New Testament*, edited by G. Kittel and G. Friedrich, vol. V: 826-37. Grand Rapids: Eerdmans, 1964-76.

———. "Zum Gottesdienstlischen Stil der Johannes-Apokalypse." *NovT* 3 (1959) 107-37.

DeRoche, Michael. "Israel's 'Two Evils' in Jeremiah II 13." *VT* 31 (1981) 369-72.

Deutsch, Celia. "Transformation of Symbols: The New Jerusalem in Rv 21.1—22.5." *ZNW* 78/1 (1987) 106-26.

DeVaux, Roland. *Ancient Israel, Its Life and Institutions*. London: Darton, Longman & Todd, 1990.

DeVries, Simon J. *1 Kings*. Waco: Word Books, 1985).

Dewey, Joanna. "The Literary Structure of the Controversy Stories in Mark 2:1—3:6." In *The Interpretation of Mark*, edited by W. R. Telford, 141-51. Edinburgh: T & T Clark, 1995.

Dodd, Clement H. *According to the Scriptures. The Substructure of New Testament Theology*. London: Nisbet & Co., 1953.

———. *The Interpretation of the Fourth Gospel*. Cambridge: CUP, 1953.

———. *The Parables of the Kingdom*. London: The Religious Book Club, 1942.

Donahue, John R. *The Gospel in Parable*. Philadelphia: Fortress, 1990.

Donfried, Karl P. "The Allegory of the Ten Virgins (Matt. 25:1-13) as a Summary of Matthean Theology." *JBL* 93 (1974) 415-28.

Douglas, Mary. *In the Wilderness: The Doctrine of Defilement in the Book of Numbers*. Oxford: OUP, 2001.

Driver, Godfrey R. *Canaanite Myths and Legends*. Edinburgh: T & T Clark, 1956.

Driver, Godfrey R., and John C. Miles, *The Assyrian Laws*. Oxford: Clarendon, 1935.

———. *The Babylonian Laws*, vol. I: *Legal Commentary*. Oxford: Clarendon, 1956.

Drury, John. *The Parables in the Gospels: History and Allegory*. London: SPCK, 1985.

Duff, Paul B. "'I Will Give to Each of You as Your Works Deserve': Witchcraft Accusations and the Fiery-Eyed Son of God in Rev 2.18-23." *NTS* 43/1 (1997) 116-33.

Dunn, James D. G. *The Epistle to the Galatians*. London: A & C Black, 1993.

———. "John and the Synoptics as a Theological Question." In *Exploring the Gospel of John: In Honor of D. Moody Smith*, edited by R. A. Culpepper and C. C. Black, 301-13. Louisville: Westminster John Knox, 1996.

———. *Romans 1-8*. Word Biblical Commentary 38A. Dallas: Word Books, 1988.

———. *Romans 9-16*. Word Biblical Commentary 38B. Dallas: Word Books, 1988.

Earnshaw, John D. "Reconsidering Paul's Marriage Analogy in Romans 7.1-4." *NTS* 40 (1994) 68-88.

Edersheim, Alfred. *The Life and Times of Jesus the Messiah*. Grand Rapids: Eerdmans, 1962.

Ehrlich, Carl S. "The Text of Hosea 1:9." *JBL* 104/1 (1985) 13-19.

Eichrodt, Walter. *Ezekiel*. London: SCM, 1970.

———. *Old Testament Theology*. London: SCM, 1969.

Elliott, J. Keith. *The Apocryphal New Testament: A Collection of Apocryphal Christian Literature in an English Translation*. Oxford: Clarendon, 1993.

Ellis, E. Earle. *Prophecy and Hermeneutic in Early Church*. Grand Rapids: Eerdmans, 1978.

Ellul, Jacques. *Apocalypse: The Book of Revelation*. New York: The Seabury Press, 1977.

Emmerson, Grace I. *Hosea: An Israelite Prophet in Judean Perspective*. JSOT Sup 28. Sheffield: JSOT Press, 1984.

———. "Women in Ancient Israel." In *The World of Ancient Israel*, edited by R. E. Clements, 371-94. Cambridge: CUP, 1993.

Eslinger, Lyle. "The Wooing of the Woman at the Well: Jesus, the Reader and Reader-Response Criticism." In *The Gospel of John as Literature: An Anthology of Twentieth-Century Perspectives*, edited by M. W. G. Stibbe, 165-82. Leiden: Brill, 1993.

Evans, Craig A. "Jesus & the Continuing Exile of Israel." In *Jesus & the Restoration of Israel: A Critical Assessment of N. T. Wright's 'Jesus and the Victory of God'*, edited by C. C. Newman, 77-100. Carlisle: Paternoster, 1999.

———. "Parables in Early Judaism." In *The Challenge of Jesus' Parables*, edited by R. N. Longenecker, 51-75. Grand Rapids: Eerdmans, 2000.

Farla, Piet J. "'The two shall become one flesh': Gen. 1.28 and 2.24 in the New Testament Marriage Texts." In *Intertextuality in Biblical Writings: Essays in honour of Bas van Iersel*, edited by S. Draisma, 67-82. Kampen: J. H. Kok, 1989.

Fee, Gordon D. "'Another Gospel Which You Did Not Embrace': 2 Corinthians 11.4 and the Theology of 1 and 2 Corinthians." In *Gospel in Paul: Studies on Corinthians, Galatians and Romans for Richard N. Longenecker*, edited by L. A. Jervis and P. Richardson, 111-33. Sheffield: Sheffield Academic Press, 1994.

Fekkes, Jan. "'His Bride Has Prepared Herself:' Revelation 19-21 and Isaian Nuptial Imagery." *JBL* 109/2 (1990) 269-87.

———. *Isaiah and Prophetic Traditions in the Book of Revelation. Visionary Antecedents and Their Development.* JSNT Sup 93. Sheffield: JSOT Press, 1994.

Fennema, David. "Unity in Marriage: Ephesians 5:21-33." *Reformed Review* 25 (1971) 62-71.

Fensham, Frank C. "The Marriage Metaphor in Hosea for the Covenant Relationship Between the Lord and His People." *JNSL* 12 (1984). 71-78.

Fitzmyer, Joseph A. *The Gospel According to Luke X-XXIV.* Anchor Bible 28A. New York: Doubleday, 1985.

———. "The Use of Explicit Old Testament Quotations in Qumran Literature and in the New Testament." *NTS* 7 (1960-61) 297-333.

Ford, Desmond. *The Abomination of Desolation in Biblical Eschatology.* Washington: University Press of America, 1979.

Ford, J. Massingberd. "The Divorce Bill of the Lamb and the Scroll of the Suspected Adulteress. A Note on Apoc. 5,1 and 10, 8-11." *JSJ* 2 (1971) 136-43.

———. "The Parable of the Foolish Scholars." *NovT* 9 (1967) 107-23.

———. *Revelation.* Anchor Bible 38. New York: Doubleday, 1975.

———. "The Structure and Meaning of Revelation 16." *ExpTim* 98 (1987) 327-31.

Fox, Michael V. "Jeremiah 2:2 and the 'Desert Ideal.'" *CBQ* 35 (1973) 441-50.

France, Richard T. *Jesus and the Old Testament. His Application of Old Testament Passages to Himself and His Mission.* Grand Rapids: Baker, 1982.

———. *Matthew.* Leicester: IVP, 1985.

———. "On Being Ready (Matthew 25:1-46)." In *The Challenge of Jesus' Parables*, edited by R. N. Longenecker, 177-95. Grand Rapids: Eerdmans, 2000.

Fredriksen, Paula. *Jesus of Nazareth, King of the Jews: A Jewish Life and the Emergence of Christianity.* London: Macmillan, 2000.

Freedman, H., and Maurice Simon (eds.), *Midrash Rabbah. Vol. III: Exodus.* London: Soncino Press, 1939.

———. *Midrash Rabbah. Vol. VII: Deuteronomy.* London: Soncino Press, 1939.

———. *Midrash Rabbah*. Vol. IX: *Esther and Song of Songs*. London: Soncino Press, 1939.

Fridrichsen, Anton. "Jesus, St John and St Paul." In *The Root of the Vine*, edited by A. Fridrichsen, 37–62. London: A & C Black, 1953.

Friedman, Mordechai A. "Israel's Response in Hosea 2:17b: 'You Are My Husband.'" *JBL* 99/2 (1980) 199–204.

Friesen, Steven J. *Imperial Cultus and the Apocalypse of John: Reading Revelation in the Ruins*. Oxford: OUP, 2001.

Fuller, Reginald H. "The Woman in Revelation 12." In *Mary in the New Testament: A Collaborative Assessment by Protestant and Roman Catholic Scholars*, edited by R. E. Brown et al., 219–39. Philadelphia/New York/Ramsey/Toronto: Fortress/Paulist Press, 1978.

Fung, Ronald Y. K. *The Epistle to the Galatians*. Grand Rapids: Eerdmans, 1988.

Funk, Robert W., et al. *The Parables of Jesus: Red Letter Edition: A Report of the Jesus Seminar*. Sonoma: Polebridge Press, 1988.

Gentry Jr., Kenneth L. *The Beast of Revelation*. Tyler: Institute for Christian Economics, 1994.

———. *Before Jerusalem Fell: Dating the Book of Revelation. An Exegetical and Historical Argument for a Pre-A.D. 70 Composition*. Tyler: Institute for Christian Economics, 1989.

Georgi, Dieter. *The Opponents of Paul in Second Corinthians*. Edinburgh: T & T Clark, 1987.

Giblin, Charles H. "Structural and Thematic Correlations in Theology of Revelation 16–22." *Bib* 55 (1974) 487–504.

Gibson, John C. L. *Canaanite Myths and Legends*. Edinburgh: T & T Clark, 1978.

Ginsberg, Harold L. "Aramaic Papyri from Elephantine." In *Ancient Near Eastern Texts Relating to the Old Testament*, edited by J. B. Pritchard, 222–23, 548–49. Princeton: Princeton University Press, 1969.

Ginzberg, Louis. *The Legends of the Jews*. Philadelphia: The Jewish Publication Society of America, 1968.

Gould, Ezra P. *A Critical and Exegetical Commentary on the Gospel According to St. Mark*. Edinburgh: T & T Clark, 1896.

Goulder, Michael D. "The Apocalypse as an Annual Cycle of Prophecies." *NTS* 27 (1980–81) 342–67.

Gray, John. *I and II Kings*. London: SCM, 1977.

Grech, Prosper. "The 'Testimonia' and Modern Hermeneutics." *NTS* 19 (1972–73) 318–24.

Green, Joel B. *The Gospel of Luke*. Grand Rapids: Eerdmans, 1997.

Guelich, Robert A. *Mark 1—8:26*. Word Biblical Commentary 34A. Dallas: Word Books, 1989.

Gundry, Robert H. *Matthew: A Commentary on His Handbook for a Mixed Church under Persecution*. Grand Rapids: Eerdmans, 1994.

———. "The New Jerusalem: People as Place, Not Place for People." *NovT* 29/3 (1987), 254–64.

Günter, W. "γαμέω." In *The New International Dictionary of New Testament Theology*, edited by C. Brown, vol. II: 575–77. Exeter: Paternoster, 1976.

Habel, Norman C. *Yahweh versus Baal: A Conflict of Religious Cultures*. New York: Bookman Associates, 1964.

Hafemann, Scott J. "Paul and the Exile of Israel in Galatians 3–4." In *Exile: Old Testament, Jewish, and Christian Conceptions*, edited by J. M. Scott, 329–71. Leiden: E. J. Brill, 1997.

Hagner, Donald A. *Matthew 14–28*. Word Biblical Commentary 33B. Dallas: Word Books, 1995.

Hall, Gary. "Origin of the Marriage Metaphor." *Hebrew Studies* 23 (1982) 169–71.

Hamilton, Victor P. "Marriage: Old Testament and Ancient Near East." In *Anchor Bible Dictionary*, edited by D. N. Freedman, vol. IV: 561. New York: Doubleday, 1992.

Hanson, Anthony T. *Studies in Pastoral Epistles*. London: SPCK, 1968.

———. *Studies in Paul's Technique and Theology* (London: SPCK, 1974).

Hanson, Paul D. *Isaiah 40–66*. Louisville: John Knox, 1995.

Haupt, Paul. "Hosea's Erring Spouse." *JBL* 34 (1915) 41–53.

Hay, David M. "The Shaping of Theology in 2 Corinthians: Convictions, Doubts, and Warrants." In *Pauline Theology: Volume II: 1 and 2 Corinthians*, edited by D. M. Hay, 135–55. Minneapolis: Fortress, 1993.

Hays, Richard B. *Echoes of Scripture in the Letters of Paul*. New Haven & London: Yale University Press, 1989.

———. "On the Rebound: A Response to Critiques of *Echoes of Scripture in the Letters of Paul*." *Paul and the Scriptures of Israel*, edited by In C. A. Evans and J. A. Sanders, 70–96. JSNT Sup 83. Sheffield: JSOT Press, 1993.

Hendriksen, William. *More Than Conquerors. An Interpretation of the Book of Revelation*. London: Tyndale, 1969.

Hengel, Martin. "The Interpretation of the Wine Miracle at Cana: John 2:1–11." In *The Glory of Christ in the New Testament: Studies in Christology in Memory of George Bradford Caird*, edited by L. D. Hurst and N. T. Wright, 83–112. Oxford: Clarendon, 1987.

Hengstenberg, Ernst W. *Commentary on the Psalms*. Edinburgh: T & T Clark, 1846.

Hieke, Thomas. "A Review: *A New Heaven and a New Earth: The Meaning and Function of the Old Testament in Revelation* by David Mathewson, JSNT Sup 238, Sheffield Academic Press, 2003." *RBL* 07/2004. No pages. Online: http://www.bookreviews.org.

Hill, David. *New Testament Prophecy*. London: Marshall, Morgan & Scott, 1979.

Hoehner, Harold W. *Herod Antipas*. SNTS Monograph 17. Cambridge: CUP, 1972.

Holland, Thomas S. "The Paschal–New Exodus Motif in Paul's Letter to the Romans with Special Reference to its Christological Setting." PhD diss., University of Wales, 1996.

Homerski, Józef. *Ewangelia Według Św. Mateusza*. KUL III/1. Poznan–Warsaw, Pallottinum, 1979.

Hooker, Morna D. "Beyond the Things That Are Written? Saint Paul's Use of Scripture." In *The Right Doctrine from the Wrong Texts? Essays on the Use of the Old Testament in the New*, edited by G. K. Beale, 279–94. Grand Rapids: Baker, 1994.

———. "Paul and 'Covenantal Nomism.'" In *Paul and Paulinism: Essays in honour of C. K. Barrett*, edited by M. D. Hooker and S. G. Wilson, 47–56. London: SPCK, 1982.

Hornsby, Teresa J. "'Israel Has Become a Worthless Thing': Re-reading Gomer in Hosea 1–3." *JSOT* 82 (1999) 115–28.

Horsley, G. H. R. *New Documents Illustrating Early Christianity*. North Ryde: Maquarie University, 1981.

Hubbard, David A. "Hope in the Old Testament." *TynBul* 34 (1983) 33–59.

Hugenberger, Gordon P. *Marriage as a Covenant: A Study of Biblical Law and Ethics Governing Marriage Developed from the Perspective of Malachi.* VT Sup 52. Leiden, 1994.
Hultgren, Arland J. *The Parables of Jesus: A Commentary.* Grand Rapids: Eerdmans, 2000.
Isaac, E. "1 (Ethiopic Apocalypse of) Enoch." In *The Old Testament Pseudepigrapha: Apocalyptic Literature & Testaments,* edited by J. H. Charlesworth, vol. I: 5–89. New York: Doubleday, 1983.
Jankowski, Augustyn. *Apokalipsa Świętego Jana.* KUL XII. Poznan: Pallottinum, 1959.
Jenkins, Ferrell. *The Old Testament in the Book of* Revelation. Grand Rapids: Baker, 1976.
Jeremias, Joachim. "νύμφη νυμφίος." In *Theological Dictionary of the New Testament,* edited by G. Kittel and G. Friedrich, vol. IV: 1099–1106. Grand Rapids: Eerdmans, 1964–76.
———. *The Parables of Jesus* (London: SCM, revised edition, [1954] 1972).
Jobes, Karen H. "Jerusalem, Our Mother: Metalepsis and Intertextuality in Galatians 4:21–31." *WTJ* 55/2 (1993) 299–320.
Johnson, M. D. "Life of Adam and Eve." In *The Old Testament Pseudepigrapha,* edited by J. H. Charlesworth, vol. II: 249–95. New York: Doubleday, 1985.
Jones, Ivor H. *The Matthean Parables: A Literary and Historical Commentary.* NovT Sup 80. Leiden: E. J. Brill, 1995.
Kaiser Jr., Walter C. *Hard Sayings of the Old Testament.* London: Hodder & Stoughton, 1991.
———. *Toward an Old Testament Theology.* Grand Rapids: Zondervan, 1991.
Kautzsch, Emil (ed.), *Gesenius' Hebrew Grammar.* Oxford: Clarendon, 1898.
Käsemann, Ernst. *Commentary on Romans.* Grand Rapids: 1994.
Keener, Craig S. *A Commentary on the Gospel of Matthew.* Grand Rapids: Eerdmans, 1999.
Keesmaat, Sylvia C. "Strange Neighbours and Risky Care (Matt 18:21–35; Luke 14:7–14; Luke 10:25–37)." In *The Challenge of Jesus' Parables,* edited by R. N. Longenecker, 263–85. Grand Rapids: Eerdmans, 2000.
Keil, C. F. *Biblical Commentary on the Prophecies of Ezekiel.* Grand Rapids: Eerdmans, 1968.
———. *The Books of the Kings.* Grand Rapids: Eerdmans, 1950.
Kik, J. Marcellus. *The Eschatology of Victory.* No place. Presbyterian and Reformed, 1971.
Kio, Stephen Hre "The Exodus Symbol of Liberation in the Apocalypse and Its Relevance for Some Aspects of Translation." *The Bible Translator* 40/1 (1989) 120–35.
Klijn, Albertus F. J. "The Study of Jewish Christianity." *NTS* 20 (1973–74) 419–31.
Knight, Jonathan. "The Enthroned Christ of Revelation 5:6 and the Development of Christian Theology." In *Studies in the Book of Revelation,* edited by S. Moyise, 43–50. Edinburgh: T & T Clark, 2001.
Kostenberger, Andreas J. "The Mystery of Christ and the Church: Head and Body, 'One Flesh.'" *TrinJ* 12NS (1991) 79–94.
Kramer, Howard W. "Contrast as a Key to Understanding the Revelation of St. John." *Concordia Journal* 23 (1997) 108–17.
Kraus, Hans~Joachim. *Psalms 1–59.* Minneapolis: Fortress, 1993.

Kraybill, J. Nelson. *Imperial Cult and Commerce in John's Apocalypse.* JSNT Sup 132. Sheffield: Sheffield Academic Press, 1996.

Kruger, Paul A. "The Hem of the Garment in Marriage. The Meaning if the Symbolic Gesture in Ruth 3:9 and Ezek 16:8." *JNSL* 12 (1984) 79–86.

———. "Israel, the Harlot (Hos. 2:4–9)." *JNSL* 11 (1983) 107–16.

Kümmel, Werner G. *Introduction to the New Testament.* London: SCM, 1984.

Lane, William L. *The Gospel of Mark.* Grand Rapids: Eerdmans, 1974.

Langkammer, Hugolin (ed.). *Ewangelia Według Św. Marka.* KUL III/2. Poznan–Warsaw: Pallottinum, 1977.

LaRondelle, Hans K. "The Biblical Concept of Armageddon." *JETS* 28/1 (1985) 21–31.

LaSor, William S. "Prophecy, Inspiration, and Sensus Plenior." *TynBul* 29 (1978) 49–60.

Lee, Dorothy A. *The Symbolic Narratives of the Fourth Gospel: The Interplay of Form and Meaning.* JSNT Sup 95. Sheffield: JSOT Press, 1994.

Lee, Pilchan. *The New Jerusalem in the Book of Revelation: A Study of Revelation 21-22 in the Light of its Background in Jewish Tradition.* Wissenschaftliche Untersuchungen zum Neuen Testament II/129. Tübingen: Mohr Siebeck, 2001.

Levenson, Jon D. *Sinai and Zion: An Entry into the Jewish Bible.* Minneapolis: Winston Press, 1985.

Lincoln, Andrew T. *Ephesians.* Word Biblical Commentary 42. Dallas: Word Books, 1990.

———. *Paradise Now and Not Yet: Studies in the Role of the Heavenly Dimension in Paul's Thought with Special Reference to His Eschatology.* Grand Rapids: Baker, 1991.

———. "The Use of the OT in Ephesians." *JSNT* 14 (1982) 16–57.

Lindars, Barnabas. *The Gospel of John.* Grand Rapids/London: Eerdmans/Marshall, Morgan and Scott, 1981.

———. *John.* Sheffield: JSOT Press, 1994.

———. *New Testament Apologetic. The Doctrinal Significance of the Old Testament Quotations.* London: SCM, 1961.

———. "The Place of the Old Testament in the Formation of New Testament Theology." In *The Right Doctrine from the Wrong Texts? Essays on the Use of the Old Testament in the New,* edited by G. K. Beale, 137–45. Grand Rapids: Baker, 1994.

Linnemann, Eta. *Parables of Jesus: Introduction and Exposition.* London: SPCK, 1966.

Little, Joyce A. "Paul's Use of Analogy: A Structural Analysis of Romans 7:1–6." *CBQ* 46 (1984) 82–90.

Longenecker, Richard N. *Biblical Exegesis in the Apostolic Period.* Grand Rapids: Eerdmans, 1999.

———. "Can We Reproduce the Exegesis of the New Testament?." *TynBul* 21 (1970) 3–38.

———. *Galatians.* Word Biblical Commentary 41. Dallas: Word Books, 1990.

———. "'Who is the prophet talking about?' Some Reflections on the New Testament's Use of the Old." *Themelios* 13/1 (1987) 4–8.

Longman, III, Tremper, and Daniel G. Reid. *God Is A Warrior.* Carlisle: Paternoster, 1995.

Lucas, Ernest. *Daniel.* Leicester: Apollos, 2002.

Mace, David R. *Hebrew Marriage. A Sociological Study.* London: Epworth, 1953.

MacIntosh, Andrew A. *Hosea.* Edinburgh: T & T Clark, 1997.

Malina, Bruce J. "How a Cosmic Lamb Marries: The Image of the Wedding of the Lamb (Rev 19:7ff.)." *BTB* 28/2 (1998) 75–83.

———. *On the Genre and Message of Revelation: Star Visions and Sky Journeys.* Peabody: Hendrickson, 1995.
Manson, Thomas W. *The Sayings of Jesus.* London: SCM, 1971.
———. *The Teaching of Jesus: Studies of Its Form and Content.* Cambridge: CUP, 1931.
Marshall, I. Howard. "An Assessment of Recent Developments." In *It Is Written: Scripture Citing Scripture. Essays in Honour of Barnabas Lindars*, edited by D. A. Carson and H. G. M. Williamson, 1–21. Cambridge: CUP, 1992.
———. *The Gospel of Luke.* Exeter: Paternoster, 1998.
Marshall, John W. *Parables of War: Reading John's Jewish Apocalypse.* Studies in Christianity and Judaism 10. Waterloo: Wilfrid Laurier University Press, 2001.
Martens, Allan W. "'Produce Fruit Worthy of Repentance:' Parables of Judgment against the Jewish Leaders and Nation (Matt 21:28—22:14, par; Luke 13:6-9)." In *The Challenge of Jesus' Parables*, edited by R. N. Longenecker, 151–76. Grand Rapids: Eerdmans, 2000.
Martin, Ralph P. "An Epistle in Search of a Life-Setting." *ExpTim* 79 (1967–68) 296–301.
———. *James.* Word Biblical Commentary 48. Waco: Word Books, 1988.
———. *Mark – Evangelist & Theologian.* Exeter: Paternoster, 1972.
———. *2 Corinthians.* Word Biblical Commentary 40. Waco: Word Books, 1986.
Martyn, J. Louis. *Galatians.* Anchor Bible 33A. New York: Doubleday, 1997.
Matera, Frank J. "The Prologue as the Interpretive Key to Mark's Gospel." In *The Interpretation of Mark*, edited by W. R. Telford, 289–306. Edinburgh: T & T Clark, 1995.
Mathewson, David. "New Exodus as a Background for 'The Sea Was No More' in Revelation 21:1c." *TrinJ* 24NS (2003) 243–58.
———. *A New Heaven and a New Earth: The Meaning and Function of the Old Testament in Revelation 21.1—22.5.* JSNT Sup 238. Sheffield: Sheffield Academic Press, 2003.
Mays, James L. *Hosea.* London: SCM, 1969.
McDonald, J. R. B. "The Marriage of Hosea." *Theology* 67 (1964) 149–56.
McIlraith, Donal A. " 'For the fine linen is the righteous deeds of the Saints': Works and Wife in Revelation 19:8." *CBQ* 61 (1991) 512–29.
McKeating, Henry. *Ezekiel.* Sheffield: Sheffield Academic Press, 1993.
———. "Sanctions Against Adultery in Ancient Israelite Society, With Some Reflections on Methodology in the Study of Old Testament Ethics." *JSOT* 11 (1979) 57–72.
McKelvey, R. Jack. "The Millennium and the Second Coming." In *Studies in the Book of Revelation*, edited by S. Moyise, 85–100. Edinburgh: T & T Clark, 2001.
Merz, Annette. "Why Did the Pure Bride of Christ (2 Cor. 11.2) Become a Wedded Wife (Eph. 5.22-33)? Thesis about the Intertextual Transformation of an Ecclesiological Metaphor." *JSNT* 79 (2000) 131–47.
Metzger, Bruce M. *Breaking the Code: Understanding the Book of Revelation.* Nashville: Abingdon, 1993.
———. *A Textual Commentary on the Greek New Testament.* Stuttgart: Deutsche Bibelgesellschaft/United Bible Societies, second edition, 2000.
Michaels, J. Ramsey. "Old Testament in Revelation." In *Dictionary of the Later New Testament and Its Developments*, edited by R. P. Martin and P. H. Davids, 850–55. Downers Grove: IVP, 1997.
Miller, Kevin E. "The Nuptial Eschatology of Revelation 19–22." *CBQ* 60/2 (1998) 301–18.
Minear, Paul S. "Ontology and Ecclesiology in the Apocalypse." *NTS* 13 (1966) 89–105.

Mitchell, Hinckley G. T., et al. *A Critical and Exegetical Commentary on Haggai, Zechariah, Malachi and Jonah*. Edinburgh: T & T Clark, 1912.

Moberly, Robert B. "When Was Revelation Conceived?." *Bib* 73 (1992) 376-93.

Moo, Douglas. *Romans 1-8*. Chicago: Moody Press, 1991.

———. "The Theology of Romans 9-11: A Response to E. Elizabeth Johnson." In *Pauline Theology, Volume III: Romans*, edited by D. M. Hay and E. E. Johnson, 240-58. Minneapolis: Fortress, 1995.

Moody Smith, Dwight. "The Pauline Literature." In *It Is Written: Scripture Citing Scripture. Essays in Honour of Barnabas Lindars*, edited by D. A. Carson and H. G. M. Williamson, 265-91. Cambridge: CUP, 1992.

———. *The Theology of the Gospel of John*. Cambridge: CUP, 1995.

Moore, George F. *Judges*. Edinburgh: T & T Clark, 1895.

Motyer, J. Alec. *The Prophecy of Isaiah*. Leicester: IVP, 1993.

Moule, Charles F. D. *The Birth of the New Testament*. London: A & C Black, 1981.

———. *Essays in New Testament Interpretation*. Cambridge: CUP, 1982.

Mounce, William D. *Analytical Lexicon to the Greek New Testament*. Grand Rapids: Zondervan, 1993.

Moyise, Steve. "Authorial Intention and the Book of Revelation." *AUSS* 39/1 (2001) 35-40.

———. "Does the Author of Revelation Misappropriate the Scriptures?." *AUSS* 40/1 (2002) 3-21.

———. "Does the Lion Lie down with the Lamb?." In *Studies in the Book of Revelation*, edited by S. Moyise, 181-94. Edinburgh: T & T Clark, 2001.

———. "Intertextuality and the Book of Revelation." *ExpTim* 104 (1993) 295-98.

———. "Intertextuality and the Study of the Old Testament in the New." In *The Old Testament in the New: Essays in Honour of J. L. North*, edited by S. Moyise, 14-41. JSNT Sup 189. Sheffield: Sheffield Academic Press, 2000.

———. "The Language of the Old Testament in the Apocalypse." *JSNT* 76 (1999) 97-113.

———. "The Language of the Psalms in the Book of Revelation." *Neotestamentica* 37, 1 (2003) 68-83.

———. *The Old Testament in the Book of Revelation*. JSNT Sup 115. Sheffield: Sheffield Academic Press, 1995.

———. "The Old Testament in the New: A Reply to Greg Beale." *IBS* 21 (1999) 54-58.

———. "Seeing the Old Testament through a Lens." *IBS* 23 (2001) 36-41.

Muirhead, I. A. "The Bride of Christ." *SJT* 5 (1952) 175-87.

Munck, Johannes. *Paul and the Salvation of Mankind*. London: SCM, 1959.

Murphy-O'Connor, Jerome. "Another Jesus (2 Cor 11:4)." *RB* 97-2 (1990) 238-51.

Müller, Ekkehardt. "Microstructural Analysis of Revelation 20." *AUSS* 37/2 (1999) 227-55.

Neufeld, Ephraim. *Ancient Hebrew Marriage Laws With Special References to General Semitic Laws and Customs*. London: Longman, Green and Co., 1945.

Neusner, Jacob. *Rabbinic Literature and the New Testament: What We Cannot Show We Do Not Know*. Valley Forge: Trinity Press International, 1994.

Neusner, Jacob, and William S. Green (eds.). *Dictionary of Judaism in the Biblical Period*. Peabody: Hendrickson, 1999.

Newman, Barclay. "The Fallacy of the Domitian Hypothesis: Critique of the Irenaeus Source as a Witness for the Contemporary–Historical Approach to the interpretation of the Apocalypse." *NTS* 10 (1963–64) 133–39.

Newman, Carey C. (ed.). *Jesus and the Restoration of Israel: A Critical Assessment of N.T. Wright's Jesus and the Victory of God.* Downers Grove/Carlisle: IVP/Paternoster, 1999.

Noack, Bent. "A Jewish Gospel in a Hellenistic World." *Studia Theologica* 32 (1978) 45–55.

North, Christopher R. *Isaiah 40–55: The Suffering Servant of God.* London: SCM, 1966.

North, Francis S. "Solution of Hosea's Marital Problems by Critical Analysis." *JNES* 16 (1957) 128–30.

Nygren, Anders. *Commentary on Romans.* Philadelphia: Fortress, 1980.

O'Brien, Peter T. *The Epistle to the Philippians: A Commentary on the Greek Text.* Grand Rapids: Eerdmans, 1991.

Oepke, Albrecht. "παρουσία, πάρειμι." In *Theological Dictionary of the New Testament*, edited by G. Kittel and G. Friedrich, vol. V: 858–71. Grand Rapids: Eerdmans, 1964–76.

Oesterley, W. O. E., and Theodore H. Robinson. *Hebrew Religion—Its Origin and Development.* London: SPCK, 1952.

Olson, Daniel C. " 'Those Who Have Not Defiled Themselves with Women:' Revelation 14:4 and the Book of Enoch." *CBQ* 59 (1997) 492–510.

Ortlund Jr., Raymond C. *Whoredom: God's Unfaithful Wife in Biblical Theology.* New Studies in Biblical Theology 2. Leicester: Apollos, 1996.

Oswalt, John N. *The Book of Isaiah: Chapters 40–66.* Grand Rapids: Eerdmans, 1998.

Paterson, W. P. "Marriage." In *A Dictionary of the Bible*, edited by J. Hastings, vol. III: 262–77. Edinburgh: T & T Clark, 1898.

Paul, Ian. "The Book of Revelation: Image, Symbol, and Metaphor." In *Studies in the Book of Revelation*, edited by S. Moyise, 131–47. Edinburgh: T & T Clark, 2001.

Paulien, Jon. *Decoding Revelation's Trumpets: Literary Allusions and Interpretation of Revelation 8:7–12.* Andrews University Seminary Doctoral Dissertation Series Vol. XI. Berrien Springs: Andrews University Press, 1988.

———. "Dreading the Whirlwind: Intertextuality and the Use of the Old Testament in Revelation." *AUSS* 39/1 (2001) 5–22.

———. "The Role of the Hebrew Cultus, Sanctuary, and the Temple in the Plot and Structure of the Book of Revelation." *AUSS* 33/2 (1995) 245–64.

Payne, Michael. "Voice, Metaphor, and Narrative in the Book of Revelation." In *Mappings of the Biblical Terrain: The Bible as Text*, edited by V. L. Tollers and J. Maier, 364–72. London/Toronto: Associated University Press, 1990.

Perriman, Andrew C. "The Rhetorical Strategy of Galatians 4:21—5:1." *EvQ* 65:1 (1993) 27–42.

Philips, Anthony. "Another Look at Adultery." *JSOT* 20 (1981) 3–25.

Pippin, Tina. "Eros and the End: Reading for Gender in the Apocalypse of John." *Semeia* 59 (1992) 193–210.

———. "The Heroine and the Whore: Fantasy and the Female in the Apocalypse of John." *Semeia* 60 (1992) 67–82.

Plummer, Alfred. "Bride." In *A Dictionary of the Bible*, edited by J. A. Hastings, vol. I: 326–27. Edinburgh: T & T Clark, 1898.

———. *A Critical and Exegetical Commentary on the Second Epistle of St Paul to the Corinthians*. Edinburgh: T & T Clark, 1915.
Pope, Marvin H. "Mixed Marriage Metaphor in Ezekiel 16." In *Fortunate the Eyes that See: Essays in Honor of David Noel Freedman in Celebration of His Seventieth Birthday*, edited by A. B. Beck, et al., 384–99. Grand Rapids: Eerdmans, 1995.
Porter, Stanley E. "Did Jesus Ever Teach in Greek?." *TynBul* 44.2 (1993) 199–235.
Pritchard, James B. (ed.). *Ancient Near Eastern Texts Relating to the Old Testament*. Princeton: Princeton University Press, 1969.
Rabinowitz, Jacob J. "The 'Great Sin' in Ancient Egyptian Marriage Contracts." *JNES* XVIII (1959) 73.
———. "Marriage Contracts in Ancient Egypt in the Light of Jewish Sources," *HTR* XLVI/2 (1953) 91–98.
Räisänen, Heikki. *Paul and the Law*. Wissenschaftliche Untersuchungen zum Neuen Testament 29. Tübingen: J. C. B. Mohr, 1983.
———. "Paul's Difficulties with the Law." In *Studia Biblica 1978. Vol. 3. Papers on Paul and Other New Testament Authors*, edited by E. A. Livingstone, 301–20. Sheffield: JSOT Press, 1980.
Reddish, Mitchell G. "Martyr Christology in the Apocalypse." In *The Johannine Writings. A Sheffield Reader*, edited by S. E. Porter and C. A. Evans, 212–22. The Biblical Seminar 32. Sheffield: Sheffield Academic Press, 1995.
Rendall, R. "Quotation in Scripture as an Index of Wider Reference." *EvQ* XXXVI/4 (1964) 214–21.
Rice, Gene. "A Neglected Interpretation of the Immanuel Prophecy." *ZAW* 90 (1978) 220–27.
Ricoeur, Paul. *Interpretation Theory: Discourse and the Surplus of Meaning*. Forth Worth: Texas Christian University Press, 1976.
———. *Język, tekst, interpretacja*, 63–187. Warsaw: Państwowy Instytut Wydawniczy, 1989.
Ridderbos, Herman. *The Gospel of John: A Theological Commentary*. Grand Rapids: Eerdmans, 1997.
Ringgren, Helmer. "The Marriage Motif in Israelite Religion." In *Ancient Israelite Religion: Essays in Honor of Frank Moore Cross*, edited by P. D. Miller Jr., et al., 421–28. Philadelphia: Fortress, 1987.
Roberts Gaventa, Beverly. "Apostle and Church in 2 Corinthians: A Response to David M. Hay and Steven J. Kraftchick." In *Pauline Theology: Volume II: 1 and 2 Corinthians*, edited by D. M. Hay, 182–99. Minneapolis: Fortress, 1993.
Robinson, John A. T. *Redating the New Testament*. London: SCM, 1978.
———. *Wrestling with Romans*. London: SCM, 1979.
Rodgers, Peter R. "The Allusion to Genesis 2:23 at Ephesians 5:30." *JTS* 41 (1990) 92–94.
Rosner, Brian S. *Paul, Scripture and Ethics: A Study of 1 Corinthians 5–7*. Leiden: E. J. Brill, 1994.
Rossing, Barbara R. *The Choice Between Two Cities: Whore, Bride, and Empire in the Apocalypse*. Harvard Theological Studies 48. Harrisburg: Trinity Press International, 1999.
———. "River of Life in God's New Jerusalem: An Ecological Vision for Earth's Future." *Currents in Theology and Mission* 24 (1998) 487–99.
Rowland, Christopher. "John 1.51, Jewish Apocalyptic and Targumic Tradition." *NTS* 30/4 (1984) 498–507.

———. *The Open Heaven. A Study of Apocalyptic in Judaism and Early Christianity*. Eugene: Wipf and Stock, 2002.

Rowley, Harold H. *Men of God: Studies in Old Testament History and Prophecy*. London: Nelson and Sons, 1963.

Ruiz, Jean-Pierre. "Praise and Politics in Revelation 19:1-10." In *Studies in the Book of Revelation*, edited by S. Moyise, 69-84. Edinburgh: T & T Clark, 2001.

Russell, James S. *The Parousia: A Critical Inquiry into the New Testament Doctrine of our Lord's Second Coming*. Grand Rapids: Baker, 1985.

Ryken, Leland, et al. (eds.). *Dictionary of Biblical Imagery*. Downers Grove/Leicester: IVP, 1998.

Safrai, Shemuel, and M. Stern (eds.). *The Jewish People in the First Century; Historical Geography, Political History, Social, Cultural and Religious Institutions*. Philadelphia: Fortress, 1976.

Sampley, J. Paul. *'And the Two Shall Become One Flesh': A Study of Traditions in Ephesians 5:21-33*. Cambridge: CUP, 1971.

Sanders, Ed P. *Jesus and Judaism*. Philadelphia: Fortress, 1985.

———. *Paul*. Past Masters. Oxford: OUP, 1996.

———. *Paul, the Law, and the Jewish People*. Minneapolis: Fortress, 1985.

———. *Paul and Palestinian Judaism* (London: SCM, 1989).

Sanders, James A. "Paul and Theological History," In *Paul and the Scriptures of Israel*, edited by C. A. Evans and J. A. Sanders, 52-57. JSNT Sup 83. Sheffield: JOST Press, 1993.

Sanders, J. N. "The Case for the Pauline Authorship." In *Studies in Ephesians*, edited by F. L. Cross, 9-20. London: A. R. Mowbray and Co. Ltd., 1956.

Schillebeeckx, Edward. *Marriage: Human Reality and Saving Mystery*. London: Sheed and Ward, 1980.

Schmidt, Thomas E. "'And the Sea Was No More': Water as People, Not Place." In *Essays on New Testament Eschatology in Honour of R. H. Gundry*, edited by T. E. Schmidt and M. Silva, 233-49. JSNT Sup 100. Sheffield: Sheffield Academic Press, 1994.

Schnackenburg, Rudolf. *The Gospel according to St John*. Tunbridge Wells: Burns & Oates, 1990.

Schnelle, Udo. *The History and Theology of the New Testament Writings*. London: SCM, 1998.

Schrenk, Gottlob. "ἐκλεκτός." In *Theological Dictionary of the New Testament*, edited by G. Kittel and G. Friedrich, vol. IV: 186-87. Grand Rapids: Eerdmans, 1964-76.

Schüssler-Fiorenza, Elisabeth. "Composition and Structure of the Book of Revelation." *CBQ* 39 (1977) 344-66.

———. *Revelation: Vision of a Just World*. Edinburgh: T & T Clark, 1993.

———. "The Words of Prophecy: Reading the Apocalypse Theologically." In *Studies in the Book of Revelation*, edited by S. Moyise, 1-19. Edinburgh: T & T Clark, 2001.

Scott, Bernard B. *Hear Then the Parable*. Minneapolis: Fortress, 1990.

Scott, James M. "'For As Many As Are of Works of the Law Are Under a Curse' (Galatians 3.10)." In *Paul and the Scriptures of Israel*, edited by C. A. Evans and J. A. Sanders, 187-221. JSNT Sup 83. Sheffield: JSOT Press, 1993.

Seifrid, Mark A. *Christ, Our Righteousness*. New Studies in Biblical Theology 9. Leicester: Apollos, 2000.

Shea, William H. "The Covenantal Form of the Letters to the Seven Churches." *AUSS* 21/1 (1983) 71-84.

———. "The Parallel Literary Structure of Revelation 12 and 20," *AUSS* 23/1 (1985) 37–54.

———. "Revelation 5 and 19 as Literary Reciprocals." *AUSS* 22/2 (1984) 249–57.

Shepherd, Norman. "The Resurrections of Revelation 20." *WTJ* 37/1 (1974) 34–43.

Shillington, V. George. "Engaging with the Parables." In *Jesus and His Parables: Interpreting the Parables of Jesus Today*, edited by V. G. Shillington, 1–20. Edinburgh: T & T Clark, 1997.

Silberman, Lou H. "Once Again: The Use of Rabbinic Material." *NTS* 42/1 (1996) 153–55.

Sim, David C. "The Man without the Wedding Garment (Matthew 22:11–13)." *HeyJ* 31 (1990) 165–78.

Slater, Thomas B. "On the Social Setting of the Revelation to John." *NTS* 44/2 (1998) 232–56.

Smalley, Stephen S. *John: Evangelist and Interpreter*. Exeter: Paternoster, 1978.

Smith, Christopher R. "The Structure of the Book of Revelation in the Light of Apocalyptic Literary Conventions." *NovT* 36/4 (1994) 373–93.

Smith, Kym. *Redating the Revelation and Reconstruction of the Sixties of the First Century, Giving the Context and Completion of the New Testament*. Blackwood: Sherwood Publications, 2001.

Smith, Ralph L. *Micah–Malachi*. Word Biblical Commentary 32. Waco: Word Books, 1984.

Snodgrass, Klyne R. "From Allegorizing to Allegorizing: A History of the Interpretation of the Parables of Jesus." In *The Challenge of Jesus' Parables*, edited by R. N. Longenecker, 3–29. Grand Rapids: Eerdmans, 2000.

———. "Reading & Overreading the Parables of Jesus in *Jesus and the Victory of God*." In *Jesus & the Restoration of Israel: A Critical Assessment of N.T. Wright's 'Jesus and the Victory of God'*, edited by C. C. Newman, 61–76. Downers Grove: IVP, 1999.

Stauffer, E. "γαμέω γάμος." In *Theological Dictionary of the New Testament*, edited by G. Kittel and G. Friedrich, vol. I: 648–57. Grand Rapids: Eerdmans, 1964–76.

Stefanovic, Ranko. *Revelation of Jesus Christ: Commentary on the Book of Revelation*. Berrien Springs: Andrews University Press, 2002.

Stegner, William R. "Romans 9.6–29. A Midrash." *JSNT* 22 (1984) 37–52.

Stein, Robert H. "The Genre of the Parables." In *The Challenge of Jesus' Parables*, edited by R. N. Longenecker, 30–50. Grand Rapids: Eerdmans, 2000.

Steinmann, Andrew E. "The Tripartite Structure of the Sixth Seal, the Sixth Trumpet, and the Sixth Bowl of John's Apocalypse (Rev 6:12—7:17; 9:13—11:14; 16:12–16)." *JETS* 35/1 (1992) 69–79.

Stemberger, Günter. *Introduction to the Talmud and Midrash*. Edinburgh: T & T Clark, 1996.

Stibbe, Mark W. G. *John*. Sheffield: JSOT Press, 1993.

Stienstra, Nelly. *YHWH is the Husband of His People: Analysis of a Biblical Metaphor with Special Reference to Translation*. Kampen: Pharos, 1996.

Strack, Hermann L., and Paul Billerbeck, *Kommentar zum Neuen Testament aus Talmud und Midrash*. München: Beck, 1922–1961.

Strand, Kenneth A. "Chiastic Structure and Some Motifs in the Book of Revelation." *AUSS* 16 (1978) 401–8.

Stuart, Douglas. *Hosea–Jonah*. Word Biblical Commentary 31. Waco: Word Books, 1987.

Stuhlmacher, Peter. *Paul's Letter to the Romans: A Commentary*. Edinburgh: T & T Clark, 1994.
Suski, Andrzej. "Pieśń o miłości Chrystusa do Kościoła." *Studia Theologica Varsaviensia* 17/2 (1979) 3–42.
Swartley, Willard M. "Unexpected Banquet People (Luke 14:16–24): The Parable of the Great Feast." In *Jesus and His Parables: Interpreting the Parables of Jesus Today*, edited by V. G. Shillington, 177–90. Edinburgh: T & T Clark, 1997.
Swete, Henry B. *The Apocalypse of St. John*. London: Macmillan and Co., 1906.
Terry, Milton S. *Biblical Apocalyptics: A Study of the Most Notable Revelations of God and of Christ*. Grand Rapids: Baker, 1988.
Thielman, Frank. *Paul and the Law: A Contextual Approach*. Downers Grove: IVP, 1994.
———. "The Story of Israel and the Theology of Romans 5–8." In *Pauline Theology, Volume III: Romans*, edited by D. M. Hay and E. E. Johnson, 169–95. Minneapolis: Fortress. 1995.
Thiselton, Anthony C. "Communicative Action and Promise in Interdisciplinary, Biblical, and Theological Hermeneutics." In *The Promise of Hermeneutics*, R. Lundin, et al., 133–240. Grand Rapids: Eerdmans, 1999.
———. *New Horizons in Hermeneutics: The Theory and Practice of Transforming Biblical Reading*. Grand Rapids: Zondervan, 1992.
Thomas, D. Winton. *Documents from Old Testament Times*. New York: Harper & Brothers, 1961.
Thompson, John A. *The Book of Jeremiah*. Grand Rapids: Eerdmans, 1987.
———. "Israel's Lovers." *VT* XXVII (1977) 475–81.
Thompson, Leonard J. "The Mythic Unity of the Apocalypse." *SBL 1985 Seminar Papers*, 13–28. Atlanta: Scholars Press, 1985.
Thompson, Steven. "The End of Satan," *AUSS* 37/2 (1999) 257–68.
Thrall, Margaret E. *II Corinthians*. Edinburgh: T & T Clark, 2000.
Trudinger, L. Paul. "Some Observations Concerning the Text of the Old Testament in the Book of Revelation." *JTS* 17 (1966) 82–88.
Tushingham, A. Douglas. "A Reconsideration of Hosea, Chapters 1–3." *JNES* 12 (1953) 150–59.
Ulfgard, Håkan. *Feast and Future: Revelation 7:9–17 and the Feast of the Tabernacles*. Coniectanea Biblica New Testament Series 22. Lund: Almqvist & Wiksell International, 1989.
van Dijk-Hemmes, Fokkelien. "The Imagination of Power and the Power of Imagination: An Intertextual Analysis of Two Biblical Love Songs: The Song of Songs and Hosea 2." *JSOT* 44 (1989) 75–88.
Vanhoozer, Kevin J. *'Is there a meaning in this text?' The Bible, the reader and the morality of literary knowledge*. Leicester: Apollos, 1998.
van Selms, Adrianus. "The Best Man and Bride—from Sumer to St. John with a New Interpretation of Judges, Chapters 14 and 15." *JNES* IX (1950) 65–75.
———. *Marriage and Family Life in Ugaritic Literature*. London: Luzac & Co., 1954.
Vermes, Geza. *The Dead Sea Scrolls In English*. Sheffield: JSOT Press, third edition, 1987.
Via, Dan O. *The Parables*. Philadelphia: Fortress, 1977.
Vogelgesang, Jeffrey M. "The Interpretation of Ezekiel in the Book of Revelation." PhD diss., Harvard University, 1985.
Vos, Louis A. *The Synoptic Traditions in the Apocalypse*. Kampen: Kok, 1965.

Walhout, Clarence. "Narrative Hermeneutics." In *The Promise of Hermeneutics*, R. Lundin, et al., 65–132. Grand Rapids: Eerdmans, 1999.

Wall, Robert W. *Revelation*. Peabody: Hendrickson, 1999.

Wallis, Wilber B. "The Coming of the Kingdom." *Presbyterion* 8/1 (1982) 13–70.

Waltke, Bruce K. *Genesis*. Grand Rapids: Zondervan, 2001.

Waterman, Leroy. "Hosea, Chapters 1–3, In Retrospect and Prospect." *JNES* 14 (1955) 100–109.

Watts, John D. W. *Isaiah 34–66*. Word Biblical Commentary 25. Waco: Word Books, 1987.

Watts, Rikki E. "Consolation or Confrontation?: Isaiah 40–55 and the Delay of the New Exodus." *TynBul* 41.1 (1990) 31–59.

———. *Isaiah's New Exodus in Mark*. Grand Rapids: Baker Academic, revised and updated edition, 2000.

Webb, Barry G. *The Message of Isaiah*. Leicester: IVP, 1996.

———. "Zion in Transformation: A Literary Approach to Isaiah." In *The Bible in Three Dimensions: Essays in celebration of forty years of Biblical Studies in the University of Sheffield*, edited by D. J. A. Clines, et al., 65–84. JSOT Sup 87. Sheffield: JSOT Press, 1990.

Weiser, Artur. *The Psalms: A Commentary*. London: SCM, 1962.

Weiss, David H. "The Use of קנה in Connection with Marriage." *HTR* 57/3 (1964) 244–48.

Wengst, Klaus. "Babylon the Great and the New Jerusalem: The Visionary View of Political Reality in the Revelation of John." In *Politics and Theopolitics in the Bible and Postbiblical Literature*, edited by H.G. Reventlow, et al., 189–202. JSOT Sup 171. Sheffield: Sheffield Academic Press, 1994.

Wengst, Klaus. *Pax Romana and the Peace of Jesus Christ*. London: SCM, 1987.

Wenham, Gordon J. *Genesis 16–50*. Word Biblical Commentary 2. Waco: Word Books, 1994.

———. "The Symbolism of the Animal Rite in Genesis 15: A Response to G. F. Hasel, *JSOT* 19 (1981) 61–78." *JSOT* 22 (1982) 134–37.

Wenham, John. *Redating Matthew, Mark & Luke: A Fresh Assault on the Synoptic Problem*. London: Hodder & Stoughton, 1991.

Westcott, Brooke F., and Fenton J. A. Hort, *Introduction to the New Testament in the Original Greek – With Notes on Selected Readings*. Peabody: Hendrickson, 1988.

Westermann, Claus. *Isaiah 40–66*. London: SCM, 1969.

———. *The Parables of Jesus in the Light of the Old Testament*. Edinburgh: T & T Clark, 1990.

Whiston, William (tr.). *The Works of Josephus–Complete and Unabridged*. Peabody: Hendrickson, updated edition, 1998.

Whiteley, D. E. H. "Christology." In *Studies in Ephesians*, edited by F. L. Cross, 51–63. London: A. R. Mowbray and Co. Ltd., 1956.

Wilckens, Ulrich. "Statements on the Development of Paul's View of the Law." In *Paul and Paulinism: Essays in honour of C. K. Barrett*, edited by M. D. Hooker and S. G. Wilson, 17–26. London: SPCK, 1982.

Wilson, J. Christian. "The Problem of the Domitianic Date of Revelation." *NTS* 39/4 (1993) 587–605.

Wise, Michael O., et al. (eds.), *The Dead Sea Scrolls: A New Translation*. London: Harper Collins, 1996.

Witherington III, Ben. *Conflict and Community in Corinth: A Socio-Rhetorical Commentary on 1 and 2 Corinthians*. Grand Rapids: Eerdmans, 1995.

———. *Grace in Galatia: A Commentary on St Paul's Letter to the Galatians*. Edinburgh: T & T Clark, 1998.

———. *Women in the Earliest Churches*. Cambridge: CUP, 1989.

Wolff, Hans W. *Hosea*. Translated by Gary Stansell. Hermeneia. Philadelphia: Fortress, 1989.

Wright, N. T. *The Challenge of Jesus*. London: SPCK, 2000.

———. *The Climax of the Covenant*. Edinburgh: T & T Clark, 1998.

———. "In Grateful Dialogue: A Response." In *Jesus & the Restoration of Israel: A Critical Assessment of N. T. Wright's 'Jesus and the Victory of God'*, edited by C. C. Newman, 244–80. Carlisle: Paternoster, 1999.

———. *Jesus and the Victory of God*. London: SPCK, 1996.

———. *The Letter to the Romans* The New Interpreter's Bible X. Nashville: Abingdon, 2002.

———. *The Messiah and the People of God*. PhD diss., Oxford University, 1980.

———. *The Millennium Myth: Hope for a Postmodern World*. Louisville: Westminster John Knox, 1999.

———. "New Exodus, New Inheritance: The Narrative Structure of Romans 3–8." In *Romans and the People of God: Essays in Honor of Gordon D. Fee on the Occasion of His 65th Birthday*, edited by S. K. Soderlund and N. T. Wight, 26–35. Grand Rapids: Eerdmans, 1999.

———. *New Heavens, New Earth: The Biblical Picture of Christian Hope*. Grove Biblical Series 11. Cambridge: Grove Books, 1999.

———. *The New Testament and the People of God*. London: SPCK, 1997.

———. *The Resurrection of the Son of God*. London: SPCK, 2003.

———. "Romans and the Theology of Paul." In *Pauline Theology, Volume III: Romans*, edited by D. M. Hay and E. E. Johnson, 30–67. Minneapolis: Fortress, 1995.

———. "Theology, History and Jesus: A Response to Maurice Casey and Clive Marsh." *JSNT* 69 (1998) 105–12.

———. *What Saint Paul Really Said?*. Oxford: Lion Publishing, 1997.

———. *Who Was Jesus?*. London: SPCK, 1994.

Yarbro Collins, Adela. "The Book of Revelation." In *The Encyclopedia of Apocalypticism. Volume 1: The Origins of Apocalypticism in Judaism and Christianity*, edited by J. J. Collins, 384–414. New York/London: Continuum, 2002.

———. *The Combat Myth in the Book of Revelation*. Harvard Dissertations in Religion 9. Missoula: Scholars Press, 1976.

———. *Crisis and Catharsis: The Power of the Apocalypse*. Philadelphia: Westminster, 1984.

———. "Feminine Symbolism in the Book of Revelation." *Biblical Interpretation* 1,1 (1993) 20–33.

———. "Women's History and the Book of Revelation." *SBL Seminar Papers* 26 (1987) 80–91.

Zimmerli, Walther. *Ezekiel*. Hermeneia. Philadelphia: Fortress, 1979.

Zimmermann, Ruben. "Nuptial Imagery in the Revelation of John." *Biblica* 84 (2003) 153–83.

Zipor, Moshe A. "'Scenes from a Marriage' – According to Jeremiah." *JSOT* 65 (1995) 83–91.

www.ingramcontent.com/pod-product-compliance
Lightning Source LLC
Chambersburg PA
CBHW071238300426
44116CB00008B/1081